x v i
17
30
33
35
36
38
44
46
47
66
79
81
100
108 ✓
111 ✓

women
31 - 35

Evangelicals and Politics
in Antebellum America

Evangelicals and Politics in Antebellum America

Richard J. Carwardine

Yale University Press
New Haven & London 1993

For Linda

Set in Meridien by Best-set Typesetter Ltd., Hong Kong
Printed and bound in Great Britain by Biddles Ltd., Guildford and Kings Lynn

Library of Congress Cataloging-in-Publication Data

Carwardine, Richard.
     Evangelicals and politics in antebellum America/Richard J. Carwardine
        p. cm.
     Includes bibliographical references.
     ISBN 0–300–05413–0 (alk. paper)
        1. Evangelicalism—United States—History—19th century.
   2. United States—Politics and government—1841–1845. 3. United
     States—Politics and government—1845–1861. 4. Christianity and
     politics—Protestant churches—History—19th century. 5. United
     States—Church history—19th century. I. Title.
     BR1642.U5C378 1993
     261.7—dc20
                                                              92–38540
                                                                CIP

A catalogue record for this book is available from the British
Library.

Contents

In a popular government, politics are an indispensable part of religion. No one can possibly be benevolent or religious without concerning himself to a greater or lesser extent with the affairs of human government.

Charles G. Finney, *The Necessity of Human Government*
(Lecture delivered 14 May 1841)

No sound is so doleful to corrupt politicians, as the conscience of a Bible-reading people speaking through the ballot-box. It falls upon their ears like the clods upon the coffin-lid of the dead.

James S. Smart, *The Political Duties of Christian Men and Ministers: A Sermon for the Times Delivered at Jackson, July 28, 1854*

God prosper the right! And in our humble judgment, the way is so clear which conducts to the path of duty, that he who runs may read:

Ohio State Journal, 6 November 1848

Mr. A.B., Bookseller —

Sir: Please send by the bearer
   1 dozen Village Hymns
   6 Bibles
   1 dozen Church Psalmodies
   2 dozen Clay Minstrels
   Your affectionate Christian brother,

Rev. N.B.C.

P.S. Send the Clay Minstrels by all means — the others I can wait for till after the election.

John Wentworth, *Speech of Mr. Wentworth of Illinois* (n.p., 1844).

Preface

This book argues that evangelical Protestants were amongst the principal shapers of American political culture in the middle years of the nineteenth century. It presents them as deeply engaged in the processes which tore political consensus apart and which opened the door to armed conflict. Its ambition is to secure for evangelicalism a more salient place in the historiography of the 1840s and 1850s, and of the coming of the American Civil War.

The book has been some years in the making. I began work on it before the full-blooded emergence of the New Christian Right, but political developments over the last decade or so have given my theme a pronounced topicality. Evangelical Protestants, to a degree unrivaled since the Civil War, have thrust themselves into the political mainstream, moving away from the political fringes that they inhabited for much of the first two-thirds of this century. The ideological divisiveness and bitter political conflicts of the 1970s and 1980s, like those of the antebellum years, were rooted in divergent religious and ethical understandings. Perhaps at no time since the era of the Civil War were Americans so divided over what it meant to be a true American citizen. Historically minded Americans who have experienced political eruptions over abortion, school prayer, and other moral and symbolic issues may be receptive to the claim that moral and religious questions played a central part in the process of national breakdown in the 1840s and 1850s. When Republicans in the 1992 presidential contest castigated their opponents for omitting God from their platform, they were adopting a strategy entirely familiar to antebellum party propagandists. However, this is not a book about contemporary evangelicals, nor is it concerned with the roots of their political engagement, at least not directly. Rather it is about a world long gone, and about Protestant Christians who sought to prosper not the Right, but their own (profoundly divergent) understandings of what was right.

My intellectual debts are principally to those successive generations of historians of antebellum culture and politics who have kept this field of study so remarkably fertile. None has sought quite so single-mindedly as I have here to present the political experience of that era through the lens of its evangelical Protestants; but I could not have written the book as it stands without the writings of several other historians who in recent years have given pointers to the importance of religion to antebellum political culture. The range of those debts will become clear to the persisting reader, but it is a pleasure to indicate the most personal ones here. The project might have remained but a gleam in the eye had it not been for the friendship, encouragement, and generous practical help of William E. Gienapp, who not only reassured me that the subject was important and viable, but lent me many of his own transcripts of manuscript sources. Clyde Binfield, Michael Heale, Patrick Renshaw, and Barton Shaw constructively commented on portions of the manuscript at various stages of its incarnation. William Brock, Gary Freeze, George Marsden, David Moltke-Hansen, Grant Wacker, and Harry Watson gave advice and boosted my morale at critical moments; Patrick Collinson, Kenneth Haley, Daniel Howe, David Luscombe, Howard Temperley, and John Walsh also extended timely support. Louis Billington, Richard Dupuis, and Aubrey Ellis made a number of valuable bibliographical and related suggestions. Robert Baldock and Rosemary Amos of Yale University Press have been patiently encouraging editors. Three friends in particular won long-distance medals for reading and commenting on the whole manuscript: Michael Paul, who brought a sharp literary eye to bear; my colleague Robert Cook, who proffered wise advice on matters of both substance and style; and Donald Mathews, who gave generously of his time and companionship, and without whose shrewd insights into southern religion in particular this book would be much the poorer. To all of these, most of whom know that justification does not come by works, and to the anonymous readers of Yale University Press, who made a number of constructive suggestions, I offer my sincere thanks.

Some portions of this book incorporate in revised form material which first appeared as essays or articles: "The Know-Nothing Party, the Protestant Evangelical Community and American National Identity", in *Studies in Church History*, vol. 18: *Religion and National Identity*, ed. S. Mews (Basil Blackwell: Oxford, 1982); "Evangelicals, Whigs and the Election of William Henry Harrison", *Journal of American Studies*, 17 (1983); "Methodist Ministers and the Second Party System", in Russell E. Richey and Kenneth E. Rowe, eds, *Rethinking Methodist History: A*

Bicentennial Historical Consultation (Kingswood; Nashville, 1985) and reprinted in Russell E. Richey *et al.* (eds) *Perspectives on American Methodism: Interpretive Essays* (Kingswood, Nashville, 1993); "The Reformed Churches and Secular Authority in the United States, 1776–1860", *Journal of the United Reformed Church History Society*, 3 (1987). I am grateful to the editors of these publications for granting permission to make use of part of that material here.

It is worth stating the obvious: that research into American history from the English provinces is fraught with difficulty, and that without cooperative librarians, financial assistance, and American hospitality I would have found it impossible. I have been particularly fortunate in the caliber and generosity of the librarians and archivists who have smiled on my work. First and foremost, I am pleased to thank all the staff of the Inter-Library Loans department of the University Library in Sheffield, and especially Julia Dagg, for their tenacity and good humor in processing mountains of what must have seemed ever more arcane requests. I also owe a special debt of gratitude to the staff of the Methodist Center at Drew University, and particularly to the energies of Kenneth E. Rowe, for feeding my (apparently insatiable) appetite for religious newspapers on microfilm. In addition I have been well served by the staffs of the following: the British Library; the Library of Congress; Davis Library, the Rare Book Room, the North Carolina Collection, and the Southern Historical Collection at the University of North Carolina at Chapel Hill; Buswell Memorial Library, and the Archives of the Billy Graham Center, Wheaton College; Dickinson College Library; Perkins Library, Duke University; Garrett-Evangelical Theological Seminary Library, Evanston; the Presbyterian Historical Society, Philadelphia; the Graduate Theological Union Library, Berkeley; the New England Conference Archives, Boston University; Oberlin College Library; Bird Library, Syracuse University; and Union Theological Seminary Library, New York.

I am pleased to have an opportunity to thank the following bodies for financial support: the University of Sheffield Research Fund; the British Academy; the Institute for the Study of American Evangelicals at Wheaton College (and in particular the good offices of Mark Noll); and the American Council of Learned Societies, which awarded me an ACLS-Fulbright fellowship at the University of North Carolina at Chapel Hill in 1989.

I have been blessed with a number of unstintingly generous American friends who have opened their homes to me during my periods of research in the United States: Patricia and John Chisholm, Erica and Bill Gienapp, Lynne and Bob Hayward, Julia and Ralph Ketcham, Phyllis and Roger Lotchin, Constance Rajala, and Bette Welch Schlezinger. I am grateful, too, to Fr Peter Sanders and his colleagues at the Dominican

House of Studies in Washington, DC, for making me such a welcome guest for several weeks when this project was in its early stages in 1981.

My parents, Beryl and John Carwardine, have been wonderfully supportive, and particularly so during the frenetic later stages of my Chapel Hill fellowship, when they uncomplainingly interrupted their American holiday to sort notes and scan fading microfilm. My greatest debt is to my wife, Linda Kirk, who has read successive drafts from beginning to end, and who has maintained my spirits when they threatened to flag. She shares many of the best qualities of some of the principal actors of this book, especially their steely veracity and eye for flabby argument. If her criticisms have not always been comfortable, they have always been loving, pertinent and constructive. She must take much of the credit for whatever merits the book possesses. It is dedicated to her, with love.

Sheffield
August 1992

Note on the Text

When quoting from manuscript sources I have occasionally made small adjustments in capitalization and have substituted modern punctuation for many of the ubiquitous dashes. The emphases in all quoted material are to be found in the original text.

Introduction

One of the striking developments in American historical writing over the last three decades has been a revival of attention to the place of religion in American culture, broadly understood. This interest surfaced well before the mid-1970s, but since then the flow of writings, especially on the intersection of American religion and politics, has swelled to a torrent as observers have watched the emergence of the New Christian Right, reflected on the power of moral questions like abortion and prayer in schools to disturb conventional political management, and noted the evident concern of candidates for public office to burnish their religious credentials. Collectively this literature maintains that evangelical Christian piety has exercised a continuing, though not necessarily steady, influence over American culture and public life from the Puritan era to the present day. Garry Wills is only the most recent scholar to have reminded us that in America the separation of church and state has not meant the separation of religion and politics.[1]

Yet, curiously, one of the great lacunae in American historical writing is a detailed study of evangelical piety and political life in mid-nineteenth-century America, on the eve of the republic's greatest trial. As both John Murrin and Daniel Howe have remarked, historians have devoted far more attention to unraveling the connections between the eighteenth-century Great Awakening and the coming of the Revolution than to a relationship at least as significant: that between the surging evangelicalism of the Second Great Awakening and the onset of civil war.[2] This is not to denigrate or to ignore work of high quality on the public guises of evangelical Christianity in antebellum America. Recent scholarship has told us much about northern evangelicals' manifold relationships with abolitionism, antislavery, and other reform causes;

and about southern Protestants and their entanglements with slavery and other social issues. Historians of Jacksonian and antebellum politics have increasingly reflected on the denominational orientations of voters and on the extent to which their religious preoccupations affected the course of public events. Two impressive works, Daniel Howe's examination of Whiggery and William Gienapp's meticulous investigation of the origins of the Republican party, have underscored the evangelical elements in those parties' pedigrees.[3] Yet, for all that, we have only a partial sense of how effectively evangelical Protestants in the quarter-century before the war engaged in politics *as evangelicals*, how far they may have shaped American political culture and party development, and how instrumental they were in fashioning or blurring the lines of sectional antagonism.

This book approaches evangelical Protestantism as the principal subculture in antebellum America. The sheer number of evangelical Christians and their relative status in society gave them considerable political significance, whether they wished it or not, and for that reason alone their world deserves to be taken as seriously by the political historian as by the denominational apologist. In a literal sense that world is easily accessible, for there is no lack of historical documentation. In their private correspondence and diaries, and in their sermons, tracts, quarterly periodicals, weekly newspapers and other contributions to public debate, evangelicals set out their perceptions of their civic responsibilities, their rules of conduct for political engagement, their political aspirations and their entreaties to others. Yet the task of entering their culture is also daunting, not simply because of the sheer mountain of evidence, but because there was of course no single evangelical community, but a series of overlapping circles or "connexions" of believers which did not conform in any straightforward way to denominational labels.

It is as well to state at the outset that I have attempted to take the public and private discourse of these evangelical men and women seriously: that is, I have proceeded on the understanding that what they said in and about the political sphere was what they meant. Thus, while at times they may have deliberately used exaggerated, formulaic language for rhetorical effect, I have taken their lamentations and warnings to represent real fears, and their postmillennialist expectancy to mark real aspirations. Similarly I have not sought to interpret their religious beliefs and theologies as mere epiphenomena, or secondary symptoms of more "real," if subconscious, materialist ambitions and concerns – though of course evangelicals did have economic interests and needs which they might also seek to advance by political means.

What follows deals in part with the effects of religious loyalties, beliefs, and groupings on everyday political behavior, particularly on the voting habits and partisanship of evangelicals. As such the book naturally complements the work of those "ethnocultural" historians, or practitioners of the "new political history," who over the last three decades have argued that religious loyalties were a major, and often the main, determinant of party attachment amongst nineteenth-century voters.[4] Controversial as their work has been, and open as it remains to methodological questioning, it has richly enhanced our understanding of – and raised important questions about – antebellum political life. Their approach, based principally on the analysis of aggregate voting data, is very different from that which I have adopted here: the building up of a picture of evangelical political mentalities and behavior through the study of memoirs, autobiography, and other forms of personal testimony. But the conclusion that emerges, that evangelicals' party preferences reflected a world view conditioned by their religious beliefs and church associations, is very largely consistent with the ethno-culturalists' argument, even if it cannot amount to a complete vindication of their position.

During the mature phase of the "second party system" in the later 1830s and the 1840s evangelicals' responses to the two major parties, Whigs and Democrats, were neither random nor unrelated to their religious orientations, even though pious Protestants resided in both parties. The particular chemistry of interdenominational rivalry and antagonism, and evangelicals' views of the proper relationship between church and state, of the appropriate role for government in regulating a moral society, and of what constituted a Christian republic: these profoundly shaped party affiliation. Even in the South, where religious culture on the surface appeared much more homogeneous than in the North, denominational conflicts within Protestantism, reflecting antagonistic perspectives on the world, helped bind voters to particular parties. But those ties, often strong, were by no means immutable. They would snap if party leaders proved unresponsive to the moral and religious imperatives that spurred evangelicals on. This is what underlay the political disruption in the early and mid-1850s. The break-up of the second party system derived very largely from Whig and Democratic politicians' perceived lack of Protestant fiber in defending the republic against Catholics, infidels, drunkards and (as many northerners saw it) ambitious slaveholders. Out of the ruins of that political order and the subsequent turmoil emerged a new alignment built around the polarities of a continuing Democratic party and a northern Republican party which many evangelicals believed came closer than any previous political grouping to being "the Christian party in politics."

This study, however, is concerned with more than establishing the party loyalties of different groups of pious Protestants at election time. Its broader theme is the contribution of evangelicals – their values, public discourse, and moral agendas – to the shaping of American political culture at a time when that culture, and American society itself, were in flux. The mass democracy that had emerged by the 1830s demanded political socialization: that is, it required the induction of a population only partially literate in politics into new forms of citizenship. The instruments available for that process included party, school, family and, of course, church.[5] Churches provided a model of how to organize people in the mass behind a principled program of public action. Through their benevolent and moral reform societies at local and national level, evangelicals offered an example of how the world might be changed through systematic public agitation. Despite their early "antipartyism" and distaste for many features of the second party system, they exercised their enormous cultural influence to pull citizens into political activity. Though Donald Scott describes New England churches in 1850 as "protected and withdrawn islands of piety," and Robert Wiebe contends that "[r]eligious territory turned back toward the house rather than out toward the lanes of opportunity," these conclusions, if they hold at all, do so only as tendencies, not absolutes.[6] Evangelicals encouraged voting, and responsible and dutiful citizenship. They provided the professional organizers of parties with operational models for mobilizing public opinion. Their Manichean perspectives reinforced the institutional pressures towards polarized two-party, adversarial politics.

As part of their preparation of citizens for electoral participation in a mass democracy, evangelicals helped establish a discourse of politics which offered a way of interpreting events and public issues not just at election time but continuously. Their pursuit of individual salvation and reformation raised an expectation of moral integrity amongst public men. Their stress on individual moral discipline and self-control had implications for social regulation and order. Their emphasis on duty and conscience ensured that they treated political issues less according to the measure of social utility than to that of moral propriety and scriptural injunction. They brought their ethical perspectives to bear on banking and other aspects of government economic policy. With even more energy they variously ensured that the questions of education, Indian removal, war, drink and, above all, slavery were placed firmly at the center of the political agenda and were judged in relation to the Christian's obligation conscientiously to advance a moral republic. Without political parties and professional political leadership, of course, popular sentiments would have tended to remain unchanneled and unfocused. But party leaders by no means had a free hand in setting the limits and terms of political debate.

Evangelical experience shaped antebellum politics in another way. Tension between northern and southern Christians, particularly within the same denominational families, created perspectives which significantly influenced the way in which evangelicals aligned themselves in the wider battle between North and South. Clarence Goen has usefully identified many of the wider implications of the Presbyterian, Baptist, and Methodist church schisms of the 1830s and 1840s, and properly stressed the ultimately damaging effect of this institutional fracturing on the political Union.[7] What his work does not do is to locate or contextualize that damage more precisely in the political chronology of antebellum America. Nor does he recognize the full extent of the bloody frictions that marked the border areas where once institutionally joined churches failed to live in peace and harmony after formal separation. The civil wars, litigation, intimidation, and violence that scarred the border region not only foreshadowed the later, larger conflict but, in establishing "slave power" and "abolitionist" stereotypes, did much to create the casts of mind without which fatal sectional alienation could not have occurred. Just as evangelicals' partisan loyalties developed out of a world view nourished by their religion, so their sectional chauvinism derived not simply from remote political developments, but from ecclesiastical antagonisms much closer to home.[8]

Thus, when we pursue the roots of the conflict that broke out in April 1861 we are obliged to pursue them into the religious as well as the secular sphere, and while doing so to recognize that though these might be analytically helpful categories they were not discrete areas of human existence. The certainties that southern evangelicals may have felt over the rightness of slavery and their other social arrangements, and about the moral bankruptcy of northern Republicans, derived in large part from their experiences as members of churches in contention with erstwhile fellow communicants in the free states, but linked by connexionalism and church-fellowship to like-minded souls at home. The equally firm certainties of northern evangelicals, that their social arrangements enjoyed the blessing of the Almighty, or that an expansionist slave power was bent on national dominion, also derived in part from ecclesiastical experience.

Evangelical religion, then, was an integral part of antebellum politics and a much more pervasive influence than is apparent if we simply limit our attention to religious issues addressed in election campaigns or the legislative chamber. It is the contention of this book that hundreds of thousands of American citizens felt a commitment to a particular party (and, increasingly, to a section) because they understood that party (and their section) to be most in tune with their religious concerns and with the material ambitions which their religion fostered or sanctioned.[9] It is important not to claim too much, of course: the electorate, as one Presbyterian put it in 1840, was "a motley and mixed assemblage –

virtuous, religious, profane, impious, intemperate."[10] Large numbers of voters were not evangelicals, many not even churchgoers. Yet even these – the lapsed believer, the religiously devout anti-evangelical, the "nothingarian" – might settle more comfortably into one party rather than another because it better served their understanding of the proper relationship of the state to moral questions. What follows thus encourages us to regard the differences between political parties as profound and meaningful. It also invites the conclusion that the gathering conflict between the sections was based on seriously divergent ethical perceptions. By 1861 the depth of alienation between northern and southern churches suggests that the two halves of the Union no longer shared the same religion, or at least that evangelicals in the two sections offered two very different solutions to the question of how to be part of the world.[11] The political experience of evangelicals through the antebellum period reinforces the view of the American Civil War as much more than a conflict over material issues and vested interests.

To impose some limits on the study, I have focused attention on the major denominational families, which together provide a broad representation of the variegated social, doctrinal, and institutional expressions of evangelicalism. In theology and church organization Methodists, Baptists, Presbyterians, and Congregationalists ran the gamut from Old School Calvinism to Arminianism, and from congregational independence to more centralized, hierarchical polities. Together they drew their members from across the social spectrum, with Methodists and Baptists in particular recruiting amongst those of modest means and endowments. All but the Congregationalists (essentially New Englanders) were genuinely national churches.

Though what follows has to rely disproportionately on the written and spoken words of an articulate leadership, there is good reason to believe that the people I have cited were representative of many more in the wider constituency of their churches. Lewis O. Saum's study of the mentality of the common folk of the era concludes that their "vestigial Puritanism" and faith in God's ordering of the cosmos gave a religious orientation to much of the country's popular culture before the Civil War.[12] If the ministers and laity on whom I depend represented an elite then it was less a social than a devotional one: that is, those within the churches, from all social classes, who took their religion most seriously, not those only loosely and nominally attached.

The United States as a country was made up of a number of distinctive cultural areas whose characters were shaped by the religious orientation of their populations as much as by a region's ethnicity, economy, and physical landscape. The religious culture of New England, and of areas settled predominantly by New Englanders, to take the most obvious example, was discernibly different from that of the South and of parts of the free states where Yankees lacked influence. Within the South the religious orientation of Appalachia was by no means the same as that of, say, tidewater Virginia or low-country South Carolina. Context mattered. Much of the best recent work on the social history of religion in America (as indeed in other societies) has profitably adopted a narrow regional or even local focus, so allowing for a microscopic exploration of detail and texture, and providing opportunities for the fruitful testing of general hypotheses. In this context, it might seem perverse and foolish to attempt to write about the experience of evangelicals across the nation as a whole. In fact, I do not seek to homogenize the experiences and outlooks of antebellum evangelicals. It is their very variety and the significance of local context that explains the richness of the interplay of politics and religion, and the complexity of partisan support. But this need not preclude attempts to generalize about evangelicals' political engagement. Indeed, their role in the sectional polarization of politics cannot be completely treated at local level: rather the story is one of evangelicals' church and denominational structures acting as agencies by which national developments took on local significance. Citizens' experiences as evangelical churchgoers helped make sense of the wider world.

The book begins with a discussion of evangelicals' varying perceptions of their political duties and opportunities from the later stages of the Second Great Awakening onwards; this first chapter also examines the pressures within and outside evangelicalism which tended to make the pious more rather than less deeply engaged in politics, and considers the level of political influence exerted by leading evangelicals, ministerial and lay. Thereafter I have sought to develop a number of themes within a broadly chronological, developmental framework. Chapters 2 and 3, by focusing on the presidential campaigns of the 1840s, consider the place of religion in electoral politics in the era of the mature second party system. Chapter 4 explores evangelicals' party political loyalties through the same years and the considerations that lay behind those attachments. Evangelicals' varying responses to war, territorial expansion, and the issue of slavery in church and state are considered in Chapters 5 and 6, which also assess their contributions to the intensification of sectionalism and the debate over the future of the Union. Chapter 7 focuses on evangelicals' role in pushing the questions of anti-Catholicism, temperance, and education so firmly onto the political agenda that the second party system, already strained by the slavery issue, blew apart. The party realignment from 1854 to 1856, and the central role of evangelicals in that development, forms the subject of Chapter 8. The final chapter examines the interweaving of religious and secular influences in the process of sectional alienation, which reached its climax in Lincoln's election and the secession of the lower South.

Chapter 1

Protestant Evangelicals in an Age of Mass Political Parties

Successive tremors of religious revival rearranged the contours of the social and ecclesiastical landscape of the United States in the early decades of the nineteenth century. Evangelical Protestant churches, on the defensive against deism and rational religion through the Revolutionary era, recovered their confidence during what is known as the Second Great Awakening, and established themselves as the primary religious force in the country. Unable to depend on formal state support in fashioning a Christian society, evangelicals turned with formidable energy to the tasks of church-building and soul-saving, reshaping their theology and methods in the process. "New measure" revivalists emphasized sinners' free will and ability actively to seek their own salvation, and sought to introduce God's kingdom through the systematic application of the laws of religious psychology. During the urgent later stages of the Second Great Awakening, in the 1830s and 1840s, hundreds of thousands of new converts became full members of the Protestant churches. By mid-century evangelical Protestantism was the principal subculture in American society.[1]

This burgeoning, self-confident evangelicalism was only one element in the fundamental changes occurring in the country between the Revolution and the Jacksonian period. The accelerating development of a national market economy and the geographical mobility of a rapidly growing population, both aided by a revolution in transport networks and technology, inevitably eroded traditional social relationships. Families broke up, servants ceased to live within the households of their masters, systems of patronage were eroded, and established routes of social progress were closed as new ones opened up. True equality may have been as remote as ever, but a revolutionary spirit of egalitarianism challenged old social distinctions, eroded eighteenth-century patterns of deference, and fashioned new democratic and republican codes of manners and behavior. New certainties, new communities, new social networks, and new patterns of living were needed in this world of flux and disintegration. For thousands of Americans evangelical religion provided an answer, but only in so far as that religion neutralized "the repulsive force of the Calvinist doctrines of election and reprobation," the symbols – in this culture – of an elitist, aristocratic society. The democratic Arminianism of the Methodists, the most potent and pervasive doctrinal force of the Awakening, proffered a theology of human equality and opportunity, a "system that seemed to harmonise with itself, with the Scriptures, with common sense, and with experience."[2] It is possible to see, as have Donald Mathews, Gordon Wood, and Nathan Hatch, surging evangelicalism as an early nineteenth-century counter-culture through which ordinary farmers, artisans, laborers, and their families expressed their independence of the world of the gentry and the well-to-do commercial and professional classes, though by the later years of the Awakening it had so successfully challenged the established culture that it was no longer a movement of the fringes, and had itself become influential, respectable, and middle-class.[3]

Protestant evangelicalism at mid-century

By the mid-nineteenth century American religious life was dominated by an expansive, revival-focused evangelicalism which enjoyed considerable congruence of belief across denominational lines. The Presbyterian Robert Baird, anxious to rebut adverse European comment on American religious pluralism, argued that the evangelical communions in the United States "ought to be viewed as branches of one great body," for evangelical Christians "exhibit a most remarkable coincidence of views on all important points." Their creed comprehended a Trinitarian God; the depravity, guilt and condemnation of all mankind; an atonement by the Son of God sufficient to procure man's salvation; regeneration by the Holy Ghost producing repentance and faith; and the final judgment of all men, resulting in everlasting misery for the wicked and blessedness for the righteous. Mere intellectual adherence to these tenets was insufficient to admit a person to full church communion. A moral life and a personal experience of salvation were essential. "Nineteen twentieths of all the evangelical churches in this country believe that there is such a thing as being 'born again'," Baird claimed. "And very few, indeed, admit the doctrine that a man who is not 'converted' . . . may come without sin to [the Lord's Supper]."[4]

To these nearly universal elements in evangelical belief must be added two further ingredients: perfectionism and millennialism. The Wesleyan perfectionist doctrine of entire sanctification, or holiness, had a long pedigree. Through the preaching of Charles G. Finney and other "new measure" Calvinists it reached an audience well beyond Methodism. It was anathema to some, because it seemed to imply that absolute sinless perfection was attainable before the grave, but many found appealing its emphasis on continued growth in grace after conversion. As a doctrine it encouraged a similar optimism to that which lay at the heart of most evangelicals' understanding of the millennium. Their exegesis of the books of Daniel and Revelation led a small minority of evangelicals to conclude despairingly that no material progress would occur before Christ's imminent second coming inaugurated the thousand-year reign. The vast majority, however, articulated an energetic, nationalist post-millennialism that had provided the dominant expression of eschato-logical thinking since the turn of the century. They regarded America's recent experience of spectacular revivals and the impressive achieve-ments of the interdenominational empire of benevolent and missionary societies as indications of continuing and upward progress that would eventually bring about the millennium before the second coming; they enjoined active evangelical effort for the spread of the Gospel in preference to unproductive speculation about the date of Christ's return.[5]

Evangelical likemindedness on these theological fundamentals did not necessarily spell harmony between evangelical denominations nor even within denominational families. Organizational, doctrinal, and social differences sustained traditional lines of division and engendered new ones. Methodists had adopted a hierarchical, episcopal polity; Presbyterians, Reformed, and Lutherans maintained a presbyterian system; Congregationalists and Baptists adhered to congregational independence. Arguments over infant immersion separated the various Baptist bodies from the remainder of Protestantism. The stress on liturgy and traditionalism in the conservative "confessional" wings of the Lutheran, German Reformed, and Episcopalian churches found little sympathy in more revival-centered denominations. Strict Calvinism was still strong enough to contribute to a major schism in Presbyterianism in 1837. The revivalist, "Arminianized" Calvinism of New School Presbyterians, Congregationalists and New Lutherans may not have differed significantly from the Arminianism of the Methodists, Freewill Baptists, and Cumberland Presbyterians, the division being essentially, in Timothy Smith's words, "a matter of custom rather than creed." Yet social and ecclesiastical custom was in many cases the most powerful cement in denominational allegiance.[6] The social advance achieved by so many poorer Baptists and Methodists, for example, had not secured the full acceptance of those churches by the wealthier elements in, say, refined Presbyterianism. American evangelical Protestantism was certainly more homogeneous than the multiplicity of denominations suggested, but for many church members their attachment to denomination meant more to them than being part of a wider evangelical community – a fact of some significance to American political life, as will become clear.

The numerical strength of evangelical religion in these years is more open to approximate calculation than to precise measurement. The principal source for any assessment must be, not the religious censuses, which listed only church sittings, but the membership statistics returned by the churches themselves. These are far from reliable, though the compilers' sins were mostly those of omission and error, not of deliberate deceit. The complaint of a Wisconsin Baptist over "the loose manner in which the minutes of the various associations are prepared" was more common and justified than the lament from Georgia that ambitious Methodist preachers made exaggerated returns "to swell [their] ranks and outnumber [their] Baptist friends."[7] The statistics do, however, offer a broad indication of relative denominational standing, patterns of growth, and the proportionate strength of evangelical churches to the population as a whole. They demonstrate that Protestant church membership grew at twice the rate of the population during the course of the Second Great Awakening, some 15 percent of Americans in 1840 standing in full membership as compared with under 7 percent forty years earlier. Much of this expansion resulted from the work of Baptists, particularly in rural areas and in the southern states, and of Methodists, who penetrated into every quarter of the country, including hostile, Calvinist New England, to become the largest denomination in the United States. From 1840 to the Civil War the relative strength of the Protestant churches remained fairly steady. Robert Baird's figures, based on a combination of denominational returns and rough estimates, suggest a barely significant upward shift in membership, from 14.6 percent of the total population in the early 1840s to 15.3 percent in the mid-1850s; the returns of the five major churches in 1840 and 1860 present a similar picture of a very slight strengthening of their relative standing [see Table 1]. This stability was achieved by above-average growth in rural and small-town America as a compensation for relative decline in the larger cities with their rapidly growing Catholic immigrant populations.[8]

Membership returns also make it evident that American Protestantism's strength lay overwhelmingly in its evangelical churches. Most of the eighteen denominations that in 1855 boasted a membership of over 50,000 each and represented well over 90 percent of all Protestants were unequivocally evangelical [see Table 2]. The remainder embraced a strong evangelical presence. Low-church Episcopalian, Lutheran, and Reformed theologians battled with conservative "confessionalists"

Table 1: Membership of the major evangelical churches as a percentage of the population of the United States in 1840 and 1860

	1840		1860	
	Members	Percentage of population	Members	Percentage of population
Methodist Episcopal Church Methodist Episcopal Church, South	817,513	4.78	1,738,868	5.55
Regular Baptist	572,122	3.34	1,025,135	3.25
Old School Presbyterian	126,583	0.74	292,927	0.93
New School Presbyterian	102,060	0.60	134,933	0.43
	1,618,278	9.46	3,191,863	10.16

Sources: Minutes of the Annual Conferences of the Methodist Episcopal Church . . . (New York, 1840, 1860); Minutes of the Annual Conferences of the Methodist Episcopal Church, South . . . (Nashville, Tenn., 1860); Baptist Home Missions in North America (New York, 1883), 554–5; Minutes of the General Assembly of the Presbyterian Church in the United States of America . . . [Old School] (Philadelphia, 1840, 1860); Minutes of the General Assembly of the Presbyterian Church in the United States of America . . . [New School] (New York, 1840, 1860).

for the souls of their denominations; Universalists were, as Sydney Ahlstrom has argued, "far more evangelical then is generally realised"; even Quakers paid increased attention to the theology of the cross.[9] Nearly 70 percent of all Protestants in 1855, or about 10 percent of the country's population, were to be found in Old and New School Presbyterianism, in Congregationalism, and in the northern and southern branches of Methodist and Regular Baptist Churches. These representatives of mainstream evangelicalism, supported by smaller churches within the same denominational families, set the pace and tone of American religious life.

The second party system and mass politics: evangelical critiques

Those democratic changes in American society that gave such impetus to evangelical revivalism during the Second Great Awakening were also

Table 2:   Membership of the largest Protestant denominations in the
United States, 1855

	Members
Methodist Episcopal	799,431
Methodist Episcopal, South	625,763
Regular Baptist (South)	537,907
Regular Baptist (North)	331,555
Old School Presbyterian	231,404
Congregationalist	207,608
Evangelical Lutheran	200,000
Disciples of Christ	170,000
New School Presbyterian	143,029
Protestant Episcopal	105,350
Universalist	100,000
Cumberland Presbyterian	90,000
German Reformed	75,000
Methodist Protestant	70,015
United Brethren	67,000
Antimission Baptist	66,507
Friends	64,000
Freewill Baptist	51,775
	3,936,344

Sources: Timothy L. Smith, *Revivalism and Social Reform: American
Protestantism on the Eve of the Civil War* (New York, 1965), 20–1; *Minutes
of the Annual Conferences of the Methodist Episcopal Church* ... (New York,
1855); P.A. Peterson, *Handbook of Southern Methodism* (Richmond, Va.,
1830), 115; *Minutes of the General Assembly of the Presbyterian Church in the
United States of America* ... [Old School] (Philadelphia, 1855); *Minutes of
the General Assembly of the Presbyterian Church of the United States of America*
... [New School] (New York, 1855); *American Congregational Year Book
for the Year 1855* (New York, 1855), 67; *The American Baptist Almanac*
(Philadelphia, 1857), 47.

responsible for a simultaneous transformation of American politics
and the emergence of a recognizably modern two-party system. Two
changes in particular in the constitutional and legal framework had the
effect of extending popular political participation: the broadening of the
franchise to the point that by 1826 all but three of the twenty-four states
had something approaching adult white manhood suffrage, and a shift

away from the system whereby state legislatures nominated presidential electors and towards popular elections. The consequent incessant electoral contests at every level of government called up a new breed of professional politician, the most effective of whom recognized that the eighteenth-century politics of deference and gentlemanly pretension had to give way to an active courting of the mass electorate by candidates who used dramatic techniques of electioneering. When Federalists and Republicans had done battle in the early Republic it had been common ground that there was no place for parties in a healthy polity. The new school of leaders, represented particularly by the New York Albany Regency and the Virginia Richmond Junto, championed a more positive view, seeing parties as essential and moral elements of the political system. They believed parties would offer a means of controlling the conflicts inevitable within a pluralistic society; they would help restrain the centrifugal thrusts within the body politic; they would provide a restraining channel for the democratic will, since the party delegate conventions that appeared to open up decision-making to the rank and file had, by enhancing party discipline, strengthened the leaders' power; not least, parties would present politicians with opportunities for permanent careers in their service.[10]

Between 1824 and 1840 the "second American party system" grew to fruition, shaped and defined, as Richard P. McCormick has argued, principally by the quadrennial contests for the presidency. By the 1840 election two evenly balanced, elaborately organized parties competed in all states of the Union, with the exception of South Carolina. At the same time, revolutionary changes in transport and communications helped shrink the nation and enlarge the political community. As party competition intensified, as the activities of party managers, organizers, and editors mushroomed and as campaigning grew more feverish, so levels of turnout rose: nearly 2.5 million voters, or four out of five of those eligible, cast a ballot in the Harrison–Van Buren contest of 1840. Although proportionate turnout in later presidential elections never quite reached those heights again, the mature second party system kept its vitality until the early 1850s. Moreover, most of its distinctive features – constant elections, a mass electorate, exuberant electioneering, image-building, political management and manipulation, and general acceptance of the permanence and necessity of parties – survived into the new party alignments that immediately succeeded it.[11]

Opposition to these developments was widespread, far more so than the high levels of electoral participation might seem to imply, since many voters cast their ballots for critics of the new political arrangements, principally found within the Antimasonic, Whig, and Liberty parties. "Antipartyism," as this resistance movement has been called, drew on various elements, ranging from social and political conserva-

7

tives who had a stake in the superseded order to those hostile to all concentrations of power, new or old.[12] It derived much of its force from the thrust of evangelical religion, which brought its own particular set of perspectives to bear on the political innovations of the Jacksonian era. Evangelicals were understandably sensitive to the evils of "party spirit" in view of their own "formidable divisions" during the 1830s and 1840s, when Presbyterian and Methodist churches in particular suffered major schisms and when each aggrieved grouping regarded its critics as "partisan" deviants from purity and community.[13] They saw in what they considered to be the new guiding maxims of public life – "party is the despot"; "all is fair in politics" – a fundamental threat to American liberty, democratic self-government, and the moral order on which the republic's health depended.[14] Their arguments were in essence threefold: that party conflict militated against the social harmony essential to millennial progress; that moral standards in public life had sunk as politicians had put the claims of party before those of country and conscience; and that the new style of electioneering tended to corrupt the morals of the population at large.

Drawing on the same vision of social unanimity that had informed much eighteenth-century political thinking, secular and Puritan, evangelicals commonly invoked the warnings of George Washington's Farewell Address and attacked the "foul spirit of party" for artificially dividing a naturally harmonious community and for unpatriotically putting the interests of a mere section before those of the nation as a whole.[15] Cornelius C. Cuyler, pastor of the Second Presbyterian church in Philadelphia, complained that "invidious distinctions are made, and the parties excited against each other" for selfish advantage, not because of any "natural and irreconcilable" enmity between them. Many thought that Americans' common attachment to republicanism, to free institutions, to the Union, and to Christian principles indicated an essential unity, a "pulse of social feeling," which was most evident at times of national crisis or tragedy. In Jacksonville, Illinois, Chauncey Hobart told those mourning Andrew Jackson's death that the country's response to his passing was proof "that the nation was really *one at heart*; that although party strife was now and then fierce and bitter, yet below this, there was a unity of sentiment which only needed a proper occasion to call it forth." When William Henry Harrison died shortly after the Log-Cabin campaign of 1840 evangelicals in unison told a stunned nation that his removal had been designed by God to demonstrate the folly of party strife and the essential brotherhood of Americans. After the tumultuous presidential contest of 1856 the Dutch Reformed minister, George W. Bethune, reminded his New York audience that they and their political enemies were all God's family: they should "banish from human hearts all envy and hate and quarrel, making the world we live in one wide and happy home."[16] Discord invited God's punishment and sabotaged millennial advance. For, as an Illinois Methodist put it, that progress depended on a nation of intelligent, virtuous, religious freemen "united in common support of a government established by common consent, and administered by the will of the majority," who would through united effort spread "knowledge and true holiness in their own happy land, and abroad over the face of the whole earth."[17]

Evangelicals shared the widespread belief that standards of morality in public life had degenerated under the pressures of the new political system. Candidates for civil office, objected the Congregational minister, Leonard Bacon, were selected by their parties on the evidence not of their ability but their "availability" or electoral potential. A Cincinnati Methodist denounced "the plan by which party becomes the qualification for office, in the place of moral, intellectual, and official qualifications"; one of his southern colleagues fretted that partisans chose their representatives "not because they are honest, God fearing, capable men, but because they are whole-hog whigs or democrats."[18] These "bagatelle politicians," as the Indianapolis Methodist Calvin Fletcher called them, were seen to have entered public life not to serve the national interest but to scramble for personal gain and the spoils of office in a period of expanding executive patronage. Alfred Brunson, a member of the Wisconsin territorial legislature and retired Methodist itinerant, watched aghast as fellow representatives stole federal government stationery. Fraud and embezzlement were rife.[19]

Public morals seemed particularly at risk from the tippling, heavy drinking and "bacchanalian orgies" evident at various levels of state and federal government. "Our public men," lamented an Illinois editor, "do more to perpetuate intemperance and to make it fashionable and respectable than any other class in the community." The sober young man entering a political career in Washington, and leaving the protection of his family, faced the lure of a community where bachelor habits prevailed. Drinking lit the fuse that "set . . . on fire the worst passions of a mortal nature." "Maddened, wine-heated politicians" quarreled, swore, spat, threatened and stabbed one another, and "in defiance of the laws of God and man, challenge[d] each other to deadly combat." Drinking, gambling, and profanity were a trinity of vices commonly attributed to steamboat-traveling politicians. Drink, too, the pious maintained, lay behind public Sabbath-breaking. Sunday sittings of Congress, insisted the Washington correspondent of the *Oberlin Evangelist*, resulted not from the pressure of business but from the indiscipline of the "phrenzied and half intoxicated multitude of the nation's counsellors."[20]

This lack of public virtue seemed closely related to an insidious and developing godlessness in civic life. By evangelical standards the

Christianity of many public men was, as Davis W. Clark argued, "a mere matter of form, a garb."[21] Even those with an apparently serious claim to religious character rarely professed an experience of conversion – a shortcoming which set a "dangerous and deadly example to the youth of the nation." William Seward, after the death of his baby girl in 1837, was baptized into the Protestant Episcopal church, but he told Thurlow Weed: "I may as well be explicit with you – I do not profess to have experienced any miraculous change of heart or to have in any way gone through that ordeal of despair so commonly supposed to be the entrance and the only entrance upon Christian life." When Henry Clay joined the same denomination he confessed to a New Orleans clergyman: "I believe in the truth of Christianity, though I am not certain of having experienced that change of heart, which divines call the new birth. But I trust in God and Jesus and hope for immortality." Like James K. Polk, who believed in the Christian religion, had a staunch Presbyterian wife, and joined the Methodist church close to his death, he made no profession of faith until the end of his political career. William Marcy regularly attended Baptist worship but never became a church member. Evangelicals regretted that Franklin Pierce and James Buchanan stood respectively in a similar relationship to their New and Old School Presbyterian churches.[22] Even William H. Harrison, despite sitting under an evangelical ministry in Episcopal and Presbyterian churches, was not a church member by public profession. John Quincy Adams, too, widely regarded as one of the most devout politicians of his day, a "Bible Christian" and a regular attender at congressional services, was suspect for his unorthodox views on the Trinity. Indeed, Adams was the most active proponent of that Unitarianism so prevalent within Congress and so frustrating for those evangelical Christians who did hold public office.[23]

In their darkest jeremiads evangelicals nostalgically invoked an idealized model of an earlier generation of political leaders who had publicly recognized their responsibilities to a Christian God – in particular the exemplary Washington, who had maintained a "deep and home felt piety" in his public dealings. But the first president had so plainly been succeeded by "infidel, swearing, drunken blacklegs" that good, decent Christian men now refused to stand for election. In their unprincipled determination to please all men, a Harrisburg Presbyterian acidly complained, politicians were inclined "to laugh with the Infidel, and pray with the Christian." Calvin Fletcher thought that the "good pretensions to the moral and religious" of James Whitcomb, governor of Indiana, were typical of the duplicity that marked his profession. "The holding of office under the present system of politics," reflected William McCollom at Oberlin in 1852, "is considered prima facie evidence against a man's Christianity."[24]

The corrupting influence of the new party system seemed most evident during the "political phrensy," "volcanic and subterranean thunderings," and "reckless agitation" of election campaigns. Demagogues and conniving newspaper editors traded in "falsehood, slanders, bribes"; shunned solemn discussions of political principle in favor of the "scalping and roasting alive" of opponents; resorted to forgery and other forms of trickery; aroused "low passions" and "wild, blind reckless partisanship" in the "fickle multitude." In consequence men sank their reason and individual judgement – the very essence of both Protestantism and democratic republicanism – in servility to a party's success at the polls. "Men are always irresponsible, when they act in masses," Horace Bushnell reflected. "Conscience belongs to the individual, and when all individuality is lost, conscience is lost too." He and others considered political parties to be "the worst form of papacy ever invented."[25]

No-holds-barred electioneering threatened to destroy "the morals and the conscience of the community." The hickory poles, log cabins, cider barrels, and other partisan symbols were "a reckless waste in useless trappings . . . of that which might have supplied many perishing heathen with the bread of life," a mockery of serious republicanism. "Our city is all alive for some time with politics," the itinerating Thomas M. Eddy wrote to his wife-to-be from Madison, Indiana, during the Clay–Polk campaign. "*Polls* [sic] – coons – polkstalks – cabins &c are all the go. Well all the *fools* are not dead yet." More serious was the profanity and blasphemy that laced political dispute, and the encouragement to gamblers. Tobacco consumption reached distressing levels. Robert Emory reported from Baltimore at the climax of the 1844 election: "As the tidings grew more and more unfavourable to the whigs, the ladies say that they spit tobacco in such quantities, that Market St for several days, could not be promenaded with any safety to their dresses – the pavement was so flooded."[26] Most threatening of all was the general increase in the consumption of alcohol. Why, asked a South Carolina Methodist, did "civilization" retreat more in one month before an election than it advanced in the six months afterwards? "Is it not the practice of treating, and the vitiating influence that follows upon the artificial heat . . . gotten up during the canvass?"[27] A general election was a national calamity no less dangerous than war in its effect on community morals.[28]

Particularly upsetting was the apparent effect of election campaigns on the religious sensibilities of evangelicals themselves. Writing in 1852, Charles Elliott took it as axiomatic "that vital piety declines in the Churches very nearly in proportion to the increase of political excitement"; his fellow Methodist editor Abel Stevens declared after Abraham Lincoln's election in 1860 that all preachers agreed "that political clubs are no help to prayer-meetings, that torchlight processions do not make men grow in grace, and that presidential campaigns are no direct help to the general progress of God's church." Politics diverted time and energy from religious activity. "The mind will have one object prominently before it. Its unity forbids more than one." Evangelicals sucked into the maelstrom of the canvass developed irregular habits, neglected their home, including family prayer, and raised more money "for political *fandangoes* than for all the charitable purposes put together by three to one." An Indiana Methodist complained bitterly about such distorted priorities: "we have a good many souls who are horror stricken almost if some good sister or brother gets happy in the class-room and shouts a little, who can almost split their throats hurraing for Fremont or Buchanan." Even ministers' piety might suffer. James E. Welch, an itinerant agent of the American Sunday School Union working in upstate New York during the Log-Cabin campaign of 1840, privately confided: "For several months past I have not enjoyed the sweet inter-course of soul with my Saviour that I ought.... This I believe to be owing very much to my wandering manner of life ... and also to the fact, that I have allowed myself to feel too much interest in the political excitement which has surrounded me ever [*sic*] where I go for the last twelve months past."[29]

Elections destroyed the individual Christian's "calm and peaceful assurance of Divine favor" by encouraging "a wrong spirit." The strife that tore apart the wider community snaked its way into "the peaceful bosom of the church." The Illinois Methodist, Peter Cartwright, taking up his new appointment in Jacksonville district in 1840, grieved to discover "preachers and people ... filled with a *proscriptive* disposition." Another evangelist, the itinerant Baptist Thomas S. Sheardown, offered an especially graphic example of the "fearful alienations" of the same year. On the last evening of a largely unsuccessful protracted meeting in Lake County, New York, the revivalist overheard one member of the church offering thanks to God for answering his daily prayer "that little or nothing [be] effected." Incensed by the pastor's readiness to let the church be used for political meetings by one party but not the other, the man had vindictively tried to choke off the revival effort.[30]

Evangelicals in all sections of the country complained of revivals interrupted or thwarted by the "wild, reckless and destructive sirocco" of electioneering, particularly during presidential campaigns. The winter of 1839–40, for example, appeared to evangelicals of all persuasions to be a time of accelerating revival throughout the United States, promising much, but overtaken the following summer and fall by the Log-Cabin excitement. G.R. Jones, the Methodist minister in New Richmond, Ohio, set off for the annual conference in good heart, cheered by a successful camp meeting, by his church's financial well-being and by an addition over the year of 400 new members. "On my return ... I found a sad change. The political campaign had so engrossed the minds of many even of the members of the Church that a death chill was very evident." Four years later, following the Clay–Polk election, a Methodist minister in Charles City, Virginia, reported that there had been "a reviving spirit of grace abroad . . . in the early part of the year." Agitation within the Methodist Episcopal church (MEC) was succeeded "by a still greater prostration from political excitement. These are calamitous times to religion and to the Church of Christ."[31]

Devout evangelicals' understanding of parties and mass elections as political elements inimical to religion and good social order appeared to be confirmed by God's dealings with the nation. Why, for example, should he have seen fit to remove from presidential office William Henry Harrison and Zachary Taylor, if not to rebuke the gladiatorial warfare that surrounded them?[32] Yet from the earlier years of the second party system there were those who recognized that, as Tryon Edwards argued, "parties must ever exist in our land." "Honest party differences," he acknowledged, "we must expect will exist; and thorough and frequent scrutiny of opposing principles, we must expect will ever be made; and both are deeply to be respected and desired, for they are the pledge of our safety." Henry A. Boardman later took up the same theme. "A despotism may flourish without parties; for the dead are always still; but no free government has ever got on without them"; political conflict was inevitable in view of America's vast extent, increasing population, diversity of climate and economic activity, conflicting state and sectional interests, and fundamental heterogeneity.[33]

Through the years of the second party system the inherited, Puritan vision of a consensual, organic society grew dimmer as evangelicals increasingly accepted political parties as irremovable elements in free democratic life, a necessary evil whose worst excesses might perhaps be eliminated but whose presence had to be stoically endured. Many indeed went further, acknowledging parties' potential as agents of moral and religious progress. In fact from the outset of the new partisanship there had been calls for a "Christian party in politics." The pastor of the Seventh Presbyterian Church in Philadelphia, Ezra Stiles Ely, was one of the earliest to see the merits of a combination of evangelical voters cooperating to secure the election of "sincere friend[s] of Christianity" who would "act in conformity with its precepts." His rallying cry to "the truly Christian sects" in 1828 brought down a heap of abuse from within and without the evangelical churches: was this not the re-creation of a Calvinist establishment by other means? Yet the concept of evangelical Protestants acting positively in concert, whether through a newly created, separate party or through existing ones, refused to die. More and more in the antebellum period evangelicals can be seen seeking to advance their moral objectives by political means. As they combined politically under temperance, antislavery, and anti-Catholic banners, so their antipartyism melted even further. "There is no valid objection to the institution of parties for the fair and honest defense of great principles," wrote Jonathan T. Crane on the eve of the election of 1860. "The rise of new parties, and the occurrence of schisms and disintegration in the old ones, have aided in setting men free from party slavery, and making them independent in the bestowment of their votes."[34]

"Pietist" withdrawal

In nineteenth-century America evangelicals' reflections on political action incorporated elements drawn from one of two polarities of political thought. At one extreme stood the Calvinist, Puritan vision of politics as a means of introducing God's kingdom; postmillennialist and progressive, it characteristically emphasized God's law, the Old Testament covenant and the public, social responsibilities of Christians. In contrast, "pietist" evangelicals viewed politics from a New Testament, Pentecostal perspective which magnified the role of the Holy Spirit, stressed freedom from law, and tended towards holiness and pre-millennial revivalism; it drew on Christ's passive endurance of Roman oppression; it led to a more private Christianity and to an essentially negative view of government.[35] "As the 'millennium' approaches," the Baptist evangelist Emerson Andrews rejoiced, "there will be no need of preaching, much less of litigation, legislation, or penal inflictions. . . . 'Moses' law' is a school-master, a rule and a sword, while the gospel is a balm and physician. The law cries, 'Cut the barren fig tree down,' but mercy cries, 'Spare and save it.' Thanks be to God that grace has triumphed!"[36]

Conservative pietists were to be found in all denominational families in the antebellum period, most strikingly in Mennonite and some Quaker churches. They were also common amongst Methodists, Baptists, and the Disciples of Christ, especially in the South. Their primary concern was with personal devotion and piety, with the individual's direct experience of Christ; their intensely atomistic religion entertained no corporate, abstract view of the world or even their own church. They included laymen convinced, in the words of an Iowa Congregationalist, that "the standard of holiness is to be raised by preaching the pure, unadulterated doctrines of the cross" and not by "harangues on national policy." They applauded ministers like Thomas B. Miller, Scotch-Irish Methodist and ex-Presbyterian elder, who "had but little to say about politics [and] . . . always said they were a bad tick to bite," and the New York itinerant Heman Bangs, who boasted in 1860, "From pure motives

I have ignored politics. . . . Since I became a minister of Christ, my only business has been to save souls." They adopted the perspective of the North Carolina Methodist John Davis that political life "spreads out a vast vortex in which thousands, that might have been agents of great good in other pursuits, have been engulfed with all their interests and hopes."[37]

Pietists took comfort in the thought that the language and themes of political discourse were more appropriately employed in a higher cause. During the great Log-Cabin rallies of 1840 in Baltimore, a Methodist protested that he gave politics scarcely a thought: "I am myself a candidate, but it is for *eternal life.* I aspire to a throne, but I must have one which will not perish." There could be only one successful presidential candidate, a Pittsburgh editor reflected, "but we may all be successful aspirants after the honor that comes from God[;] we may all be elected, and all make our election sure. . . . Our souls are at stake." Thus a small, heterogeneous minority of pietists, temperamentally close to the Anabaptist tradition of avoiding all political activity, refused even to vote. "I have not exchanged a word with . . . anyone here on the subject of politicks," Enoch Mudge confided from Massachusetts in 1844. "I am not a voter." He erected his political thinking on the providentialist premise that ultimately only God could rescue American society from its ills, that faith in the political process represented an over-reliance on human instrumentality. "I . . . abide the decision of Providence reposing on the arm that overrules & directs the storms in church & state, as in our physical world."[38]

The most unequivocally dismissive statements emanated from the band of pre-millennialist evangelicals in antebellum America. For them American institutions were not only beyond remedy but supremely irrelevant during "the last days" preceding Christ's return "to cleanse his sanctuary." What, wondered Millerite Adventists, did the result of a presidential election matter, or the enlargement of the Erie Canal, or the adjustment of the north-eastern boundary, when the universe itself was on the eve of destruction? A heated discussion between a Kentuckian canvassing in a presidential election and "a believer in the near approach of the final termination of all sublunary affairs" reached a crescendo as the millenarian protested: "I tell you my friend, you are going to be defeated: Christ is coming to take the reins of government before the next inauguration." (There is no record of his reaction to the politician's reply: "I will bet one hundred dollars he can't carry Kentucky.")[39]

It is important to emphasize, however, that non-voters were not *ipso facto* full-blooded pietists: many abstainers had a social vision and recognized the public obligations of Christians, but believed that the corruption of the existing political system put it out of bounds. Non-voting in the case of the Reformed Presbyterians, or "Covenanters," for example, was one of the principles fundamental to the organization of the church. Their refusal to profess allegiance to an immoral government could be traced back to the tangled origins of dissenting Presbyterianism in Scotland and to fiery conflicts over the union of church and state. Convinced of the morally deficient character of American government – the Federal Constitution failed to acknowledge the existence of God, the authority of Scripture, or the mediatorial reign of Christ over the nations – Reformed Presbyterians refused to "incorporate . . . with the political body." A schism in 1833 created a New Light church which allowed members to vote and to hold political office, but conservative, rural Old Lights maintained their view of the Constitution as a godless document. Here was no apolitical temperament. Rather the Reformed Presbyterians' sense of the importance of politics and political structures was so strong that they would have nothing to do with a polity built on non-Christian foundations.[40]

A similar caveat needs to be entered in the case of radical, non-voting, largely Garrisonian, abolitionists – many of whom, in fact, commended the electoral abstinence of Covenanters. These reformers drew together various strands of conventional Protestant belief into a theory of Christian anarchism and non-resistance. Lewis Perry has brilliantly shown how, from the millennialist and perfectionist determination to do away with all institutions obstructing the inauguration of Christ's kingdom, and from the doctrine of the individual's accountability to the moral government of a sovereign God, there developed the conviction that all human governments were sinful manifestations of force and, as Henry C. Wright argued, *"usurpations of God's power over Man."* This antinomian determination that there should be no intermediaries between man and the Supreme Ruler resulted in a form of political "come-outerism," the severing of connections with political authority. For a few non-resistants this implied not paying taxes or fines, or not petitioning the government; for most it meant not holding governmental office or voting. There was some ambivalence on this latter point – some "no-human-government" advocates did take an interest in election results and tried to exert political influence – but most shared the view that "genuine government does not come from ballot-boxes," and adopted Bronson Alcott's perspective: *"Vox populi, vox diaboli."*[41] Yet their rejection of conventional politics did not, of course, mean that they had no social vision or political agenda. They do not qualify as pietists.

Nor do those erstwhile Federalist clergy who turned away in disgust from political action in the early years of the century to establish and direct the national moral reform and benevolent societies of the 1820s and 1830s. These men did have a social vision as well as a concern for individual souls, but their ambitions were to be realized through their own voluntary institutions rather than through untrustworthy political parties. Their essentially "Calvinist" rather than "pietist" outlook on social duty necessarily drew them and their successors back into party politics through the 1830s and 1840s as the "evangelical united front" lost its coherence and the opportunities for renewed political mobilization and new political initiatives became apparent. Their standing aloof from voting did not imply any unconcern about civil issues. In 1842, after twenty-six years of non-voting, the Reverend Mark Tucker explained that he did not expect to deposit a ballot in his life; but at the same time he took a firm stance on social and political issues in his pulpit and believed "every layman ought to make himself acquainted with civil concerns, and avail himself of all the privileges of freemen."[42]

After the Civil War the pietistic mode gained ground, evangelical interest in political action waned and in due course fundamentalist Protestantism evacuated the territory of social concern, in a so-called "Great Reversal."[43] In the antebellum period, however, the vast majority of evangelicals, instead of opting out of political life, sought to fashion their own code of proper political activity, convinced, as Charles Finney argued, that "[p]olitics are a part of the religion in such a country as this." Those who said "we take no interest in politics" were, it seemed to Thomas Eddy, really saying "we take no interest in human progress"; they also indulged in a "criminal neglect" of the political and religious freedoms secured by the blood of the Pilgrim Fathers and revolutionary patriots. The non-political temper seemed "unchristian" to Charles Elliott, and unpatriotic to Augustus B. Longstreet, two of many Methodists to concur with James V. Watson's castigating of "the piety that is too etherial [*sic*] for the duties of citizenship" and with his celebration of the true religion that "sanctifies the citizen and sends him to the ballot-box to glorify God and bless his fellow man." It was broadly understood that "Christians must do their duty to the country as part of their duty to God": their alienation from politics played directly into the hands of "the Devil and all other despots."[44]

"Calvinist" involvement: sustaining a Christian republic

Essentially two sorts of pressure drove evangelicals towards political engagement, one from outside, the other from within. First, total withdrawal from politics would have set evangelicals swimming against the tide of American popular culture in an era when in so many other ways they found themselves swimming with it. Evangelical Protestants, ministers as well as laymen, found it difficult not to be carried along by the unprecedented popular enthusiasm for electioneering. H.H. Green recalled at the end of his life that in the 1840s and 1850s "politics was the very breath of life, every man was a politician. They talked politics in the morning, they thought politics through the day, and they drank politics and fought politics around the corner grocery at night.... The preacher was systematically scolded by one party because he preached politics and by the other party because he did not preach politics." Samuel Patton, a Methodist presiding elder in the upper counties of eastern Tennessee during the early 1840s, described the transforming power of partisan politics on the life of the community:

> The hotels, the stores, and even the shops, were regarded as Whig or Democratic, and thus patronized by the parties. There was scarcely any such thing as neutrality. Almost every one – high or low, rich or poor, black or white – was arranged on one side or the other; and if any one, though a minister of the Gospel, refused to allow himself to be classed with either party, he was very apt to be denounced by both.

Under the pressure of high partisanship some religious groups retreated from an earlier "no politics" position. The Reformed Presbyterian schism followed directly on dissident members' voting in the 1832 election; the followers of Jacob Osgood in New Hampshire, who had seen the federal government under the Virginia Dynasty as "the beast," had professed Christ as the only ruler and had been "Redeemed from town meetings/ And voting for men," were drawn from these earlier loyalties into the Jacksonian coalition of the 1830s and 1840s.[45]

Secondly, most antebellum evangelicals – especially, but by no means exclusively, Calvinists of the Reformed tradition, and many of them southerners – remained profoundly influenced by the Puritan conception of the state as a moral being and by its corollary, that Christians had a political duty to develop and maintain virtue and the highest standards in the conduct of civil affairs.[46] They recognized their responsibility not just as citizens but as Christians to protect their country's precious but vulnerable experiment in republicanism and representative democracy, widely thought to be "the purest and best of all human governments," one which, as Alfred B. Ely observed, came closer to the ideal standard of excellence than any other that man had devised. Evangelicals' faith in democratic republicanism ran far deeper than their defensive, conservative reaction to the social changes of the first half of the nineteenth century might suggest. What caused concern were the excrescences and perversions of the political system, not its basic principles. A chorus of voices that included Thomas H. Skinner, influential east-coast Presbyterian, and Leonidas L. Hamline, Methodist editor and bishop, extolled the American democratic experiment and attributed the nation's prosperity to the placing of supreme power in the hands of a popular majority. It seemed to a Michigan Methodist that the world was entering a climactic era in which patriarchalism, monarchy, despotism, and demagoguery would give way to the "grand experiment" of popular self-government. Such men saw the positive side of elections: the "sublime moral spectacle" of millions of freemen scattered across the country peaceably choosing their next ruler; the essential "self-control" of the electorate; the "self-recovering energy" of the United States Constitution; the orderly transfer of power from one administration to another.[47]

What gave American civil institutions their particular charm and significance was not their efficacy or novelty but the fact that they were, in William T. Dwight's words, "consonant with the genius of Christianity." There was some argument over the scriptural justification for democracy. Rezin Sapp described the Bible as a "purely demo-cratical" handbook, while Horace Bushnell demanded to be told where precisely Christ had sanctioned democracy and warned sternly against "Gospel jacobinism," but there was general agreement that American republicanism enjoyed biblical sanction and that, as Theodore Freling-huysen argued, "Republic is a word of Christian meaning." Benjamin F. Tefft discerned the "republican tendency in Christianity" in the "absolute justice and the most consummate equality of [God's] moral government" and in "the main principle of practical Christianity," the instruction "to love our neighbours as ourselves[,] ... the first maxim of all free institutions." Then, too, there was the emphasis on individual judgement and personal responsibility in both Protestant faith and republican practice. A French commentator, Michel Chevalier, saw clearly this evangelical sense of "harmony between ... political and religious schemes" in America: "Protestantism is republican; puritanism is absolute self-government in religion, and begets it in politics."[48]

American republicanism appeared not just scriptural but God-given. It was part of the Lord's "grand and glorious destiny" for the country, a step towards "the introduction of [the] Political and Civil Millennium," evidence that Americans were "repositories of an important trust." A divine Providence had protected the nation's civil and religious liberties through the Revolution, superintended their codification in the Federal Constitution and ensured their survival through the trials of the war of 1812: what better evidence was there that the United States was God's new Israel? It was clear to the New York Presbyterian, John M. Krebs, that "*God ... has made us to differ.*" Nathaniel Bouton elaborated on the same theme: the free inhabitants and institutions of the United States contrasted starkly with "the benighted ... subjects of despotic power in Asia and Africa," "the serfs of Russia," "the unenlightened ... tenants of Ireland," "the vassals of Spanish and Turkish domination," "the ... convulsive and unintelligent liberty of France," and "the mixed freedom and oppression of England." It was a common refrain that America's function was to provide "a monument and pattern of liberty" that would "spread joy over the whole earth," secure "the world's enfranchisement," lead the nations to peace, prosperity, and civil and religious freedom, and thwart the ambitions of despots who prayed the American experiment would fail. These evangelicals offered a new variation on an established theme, encapsulated in Bela B. Edwards's invocation of John Winthrop: "our invaluable civil polity . . . is like a city set on a hill."[49]

Republicanism was a beautiful but tender plant, a form of government "which has never yet succeeded since the world stood" and which would perish without the protection of public virtue and religion. As Benjamin Tefft put it, "A republic is the body, Christianity is the soul." This conviction had in part originated in the blend of Common Sense philosophy and Reformed theology found in the teachings of John Witherspoon and Samuel Stanhope Smith at the College of New Jersey. It was a belief that found its way into Washington's Farewell Address and was deeply to affect political and religious thinking. It had sought a public and influential place for religion even while the framers of the Federal Constitution were formally separating church and state, ruling that "Congress shall make no law respecting an establishment of religion." Its mid-nineteenth-century proponents made reflex disclaimers. Cornelius Cuyler stressed that he was "not a believer in the absurdity of making men religious by law," and a Methodist chorus attacked the impropriety of encouraging the "sway [of] the sceptre over conscience," of "trammelling" the churches by state connection. Yet these same voices were quick to explain the distinction between what a Cincinnati Congregationalist called "a government under the control of a usurping church" and "one which is pervaded by the religious sentiment holding itself responsible not to a church, but to God, wielding a power derived, not from hierarchy, but from Jehovah's throne." As Thomas Skinner explained, "Between legislative interference [in religion] and absolute unconcern, there lies a wide field of favorable and most genial influences." The moral code of Christianity had a clear part to play, not just in keeping individual citizens up to the mark but in ensuring that the political body in its different manifestations should be "an image of the great king." Though not all would have taken the position of an Ohio Methodist that "Christian people should be governed by Christian rulers," there was widespread agreement that government should be "honestly administered *on christian principles*, and with christian ends in view." It was not just a social compact of human creation, but an instrument of God.[50]

In practical terms this meant, first, that rulers were expected to follow Washington's and Harrison's commended example in publicly recognizing God's providential government, something on which the Constitution was sadly silent. One means was through a wider adoption of the Puritan annual thanksgiving for national blessings, a biblical duty, explained Samuel D. Burchard, "consonant with the purest feelings of Christian patriotism." By no means a universal practice, despite the example of the first Congress in urging the President to recommend a day of thanksgiving, and prayer, it achieved wider currency during the antebellum period. Alfred Brunson recalled that in Wisconsin Territory in 1840 the governor called for a thanksgiving day to satisfy the Christians of eastern origin, but it was such a novelty that westerners "knew not how to begin or end the service." Iowa Congregationalists set up their own organization in 1841 to press the state governor into adopting what had been for them a familiar custom in New England. There were hopes, too, that chief executives would appoint days for fasting, humiliation, and prayer similar to those called during the Revolutionary struggle. John Tyler's recommendation of a national fast at the time of Harrison's death was warmly applauded, as was Zachary Taylor's suspending public business in August 1849 to implore God's mercy in the face of advancing cholera. Evangelicals rejoiced when Daniel Haines of New Jersey, George N. Briggs of Massachusetts and other state governors addressed their fellow citizens in unequivocally evangelical terms, stepping beyond the early Republic's conventional Hebraic rather than Christian language of civil religion, which invoked an austere, guiding, "Unitarian" God, not a saving Christ.[51]

Many believed that the best way for the nation's rulers to acknowledge their dependence on God was to provide Christian chaplains for Congress and the army and navy. Government chaplains had, after all, predated the Constitution and the first Congress. There was a certain resistance to their appointment, not least because the government's paying of clergymen seemed a direct violation of the separation of church and state, and evangelicals complained bitterly when state legislatures defeated proposals to appoint chaplains for daily prayer, as in Georgia in 1853. At Washington, however, both the Senate and House of Representatives had their own chaplains to pray at the opening of the day's business, to attend and officiate at the funerals of members, to preach on the Sabbath, and generally to provide for the spiritual interests of those in the government's employ. As in the case of the annual election sermons in Massachusetts, ministers of religion welcomed this chance to present the Gospel "to minds that need [it] . . . and . . . have been slow to profit." By 1857 there were in all 58 chaplains, including 30 employed in the army and 24 in the navy, at an annual expense to the federal government of about $100,000.[52]

Secondly, rulers had a duty to ensure that their civil laws reflected "the Divine law," that legislation was consistent with "the book of liberty" and "great statute book," the Bible; they should seek to promote their subjects" spiritual interests by honoring the institutions of Christianity and safeguarding religious liberties. Evangelicals supported state laws against blasphemy, for example, and those that protected them in their right to undisturbed worship. Many sought to uphold "the Sabbath and its sanctions" against erosion by state and federal laws. It was understood that church attendance was not a matter for state enforcement; but it was equally clear that the government, in blessing Sunday travel by railroad, canal, and turnpike, and in opening post offices and moving federal mails on the Sabbath, trampled on the religious liberties of pious citizens. A contributor to the *Philadelphia Repository* complained of the widespread and damaging impression "that the violation of the Sabbath by a state is not a crime of the same magnitude as its violation by an individual."[53]

A nation had the same duty as any individual to behave in a moral, Christian fashion. It had a collective personality and, as John P. Durbin explained, could "fill up the measure of its iniquity" as well as any one of its inhabitants. "Nations in their embodied capacities as nations," concluded Rezin Sapp, "have the power of denying the existence of God, violating... the fundamental precepts of God's moral adminis- tration, trampling... upon the institutions of religion." Commonly taking as their text Proverbs 14. 34, "Righteousness exalteth a nation, but sin is a reproach to any people," evangelical preachers pursued through the pages of the Bible and their history books the evidence that "destruction awaits a wicked nation," that God's superintending providence meant the chastising of delinquents "with a rod of iron." "Where," asked a Cincinnati Presbyterian, "is Nineveh and Babylon, and old Tyre? Where is the throne of Alexander, the seat of the Caesars, ... the dukedoms of Edom and the mighty republics of Greece?" More recently, Revolutionary France had been "drenched in blood" for abolishing the Sabbath and pronouncing all religion a delusion. Most persuasive of all was the destruction of Jerusalem, the scattering of the Jews and the other sufferings that the sins of God's chosen people called down upon them.[54] The lesson for America was clear: if her rulers, ignoring the voice of God, lapsed from the highest standards of public virtue, she would forfeit her status as most favored nation and exemplar to the world; "the destroying angel," as Joseph Abbott warned, would "number the days of our prosperity"; the dawn of the millennium would be postponed.[55]

"Calvinist" involvement: duties of the Christian citizen

Most evangelicals believed they had a duty to promote and sustain a moral nation in two ways: through aggressive soul-saving and through active citizenship.[56] Since free government rested on the moral power of an educated, self-disciplined, and religious citizenry, the principal civic responsibility of American Christians was to introduce their fellow citizens to the means of salvation, to encourage Christian education through Sunday Schools and the distribution of tracts and bibles, and to sustain the manifold activities of the interdenominational benevolent societies. A southern Methodist put it bluntly: "give the mongrel multitudes the pure Gospel, lead them to Christ, get them converted, give them the regenerating grace of God, and they will become good neighbours and honest citizens." Stephen Colwell, an active Presbyterian layman, recognized that Christ enjoined "no interference with political institutions" but stressed that the evangelical's *raison d'être* of converting sinners had inevitable political consequences: "Christianity ... regenerates the man and leaves the man to regenerate the State; it works from the heart to the life." The new man, "radically upright," "thoroughly under the sway of [God's] word and his will," exercising strenuous inner discipline and self-control, would carry his purified conscience into the political arena.[57]

There he ought to cultivate an energetic, participatory citizenship, whose staple ingredient should be "frequent and earnest prayer" for the country's rulers. The Scriptures enjoined intercessions for magistrates and those in authority. "As without prayer for ourselves, we cannot hope for the blessings of heaven," a New Orleans Presbyterian observed, "so without prayer for our rulers, we have no right to look for public blessings." Even good men needed heavenly assistance when confronting the arduous duties of office; wicked rulers naturally needed God's grace. The Almighty would surely reward those who diligently implored his help for He was, as a Virginia Methodist explained, "intimately concerned with the passing events of time." He had intervened actively in response to the prayers of the Jews, the Pilgrim Fathers, and the leaders of the colonists' Revolution. He would continue to respond to Christian pleading.[58]

Prayer alone was insufficient. Just as evangelicals developed an "instrumentalist" theology of revivals that encouraged means extending well beyond prayer so they advocated various active measures to achieve Christian political ends, the most essential being "a regular and conscientious exercise of the elective franchise." Voting was more than a banal mechanism of democratic politics. For many it was a priceless trust with a near-mystical significance. "Heaven has provided the ballot box," Samuel Lewis asserted, and another Methodist, Granville Moody, explained: "That folded vote becomes a tongue of justice, a voice of order, a force of imperial law, securing rights, abolishing abuses, and erecting her institutions of truth and love." Francis Wayland insisted that Christian citizens were morally obliged to vote in every election. They should not be bullied out of their democratic rights by those who raised the specter of a return to Puritan restrictions on the franchise, and who wished to encourage a "public sentiment" that it was improper for ministers to vote.[59]

In practice most ministers as well as laymen were active, often determined, voters. Ashbel Green, after many years' absence from the polls, reconsidered his position when party competition intensified during the 1830s and concluded that "as I live under a republican government ... [voting] is a duty which I dare not neglect." George Bethune, the Dutch Reformed minister, "would stand at the poll ... for hours to deposit his vote." A fellow New Yorker, the equally persevering George Coles, described a closely fought city election in 1844: "I tried three or four times to get a chance to put in my vote but the press was so great that I could not get to the door between 3 & 4 p.m." Henry Ward Beecher recalled that his father interrupted preparations for his heresy trial to "drag ... me away six miles, in an excess of patriotism, to deposit his *vote*." Methodist itinerants complained that their travels tended in practice to disfranchise them; bishops in particular, as Joshua Soule noted sadly, were particularly affected. Yet they made strenuous efforts, sometimes riding long distances to reach the polls and barely arriving before they closed. David Lewis recalled how the business of the Ohio Annual Conference of 1840 was hurried to a premature conclusion to allow members to return home to vote.[60]

Evangelicals stressed the need to prepare painstakingly for voting by scrutinizing the moral character of the candidates and addressing the divisive issues of the day. James Gilruth, when presiding elder in the Detroit district, dutifully chewed over a mixed diet of Whig circulars and a biography of Andrew Jackson. Prayer, too, was essential: "Go ... before you vote to your closet," Erwin House advised, "and ask God to give you light and direction." Special election prayer meetings, as in Boston on the Sunday before the presidential vote in 1848, were a logical development. When he cast his ballot, the Christian's aim should be to glorify God and promote the general good of the community, not to advance his selfish individual or partisan purposes. Far too many evangelicals, complained an Old School Presbyterian, were Christians only in church, praying on the morning of election days for "just men, ruling in the fear of God" and then perversely stepping out to commit the sin of "bad voting." The devout churchgoer should vote for honest men of sound moral principles, regardless of political labels. Some believed this meant voting only for the openly Christian, but most shared Horace Bushnell's conviction: "There are many [candidates for office] who do not pass by that name, who are governed by the fear of God, as truly as many who do." The evangelical's duty was to keep from public office those "stained with *drunkenness, Sabbath-breaking, profaneness, gambling, or murder*." Each voter should choose as solemnly as if his vote would alone decide the election; he was accountable for the public actions of those he elected. "I as much expect to give an account to God for the manner in which I vote as for the manner in which I pray," explained Thomas Eddy, sharing Samuel Lewis's view that at the day of judgment men would not be able to hide behind the skirts of party but would have to answer personally for their political actions.[61]

In a world where lay evangelicals often participated actively and significantly in the political life of the community, many argued that the evangelical's duties properly extended no further than "silent voting" and a "pious resignation in face of the result."[62] The true Christian would avoid party caucuses or "gabbling about party questions." He would not succumb to poisonous abuse and personal denigration, staples of electioneering wholly at odds with his obligation to avoid "speaking evil of magistrates." Equally ruinous was the "idolatrous homage" and "fanatical praise" political supporters tendered their leaders.[63] Their faith in human instrumentality superseded a proper trust in God. President Harrison's death was widely regarded as a rebuke to the "man worship" of the preceding campaign.[64] Even then, complained a Cincinnati Methodist, the lesson was not wholly learnt, for at the Ninth Street church on the day of mourning, "we had three hymns composed and sung to the praise and glory of W.H.Harrison.... [S]uch is my ultraism I would not rise while the praise of man was sung instead of the praise of God.... The sermon was much better adapted to a fourth of July than a National fast."[65]

If these limits on political activity were appropriate for lay evangelicals then they were *a fortiori* proper for ministers. The American reported by Harriet Martineau to have said that clergymen were "a sort of people between men and women" nicely represented their position, which fell short of the adult white male's unquestioned freedom to air his political opinions and engage energetically in party politics, but which exceeded that of the unfranchised woman.[66] Both evangelical and a wider public opinion tended to the view that as far as possible ministers should in public remain politically neutral. Of course, at a time when the ballot was far from secret, the determined citizen could with little difficulty discover the political affiliation of his pastor. Wilson L. Spottswood was just one preacher who had to overcome his "cowardly" fear of partisan exposure before he would cast his first vote.[67] But silent ministerial voting was a qualitatively different act from active canvassing for a political party or candidate: "petty popes" should not use their pulpits or other public platforms for partisan purposes. Thomas Cleland, a Presbyterian, lifelong Democrat, and friend of Andrew Jackson, was presented as an exemplary model of how even the most politically committed minister could keep partisanship out of his pulpit. Ichabod S. Spencer of Brooklyn was clear that "[if] a minister of God would do his duty he must be independent of both sides." Otherwise he would lose the confidence of his congregation and as a corollary his ministerial "usefulness" in matters spiritual. Thus William Capers, who had a reputation for staying "fixedly aloof from all parties and politics," carefully declined John C. Calhoun's invitations to stay with him in Washington in 1844 to discuss the upheavals in Methodism. At Indiana Asbury University, where during the 1844 presidential election campaign it was alleged that William C. Larrabee "spends at least half of his hour in the recitation room in teaching Locofocoism [the tenets of Jacksonianism]," Lucien W. Berry was terrified that the charge would weaken the institution's standing at a critical juncture in its history.[68]

"There seems to be something repulsive in the exclusion of ministers of the Gospel from offices of government, to a people who are taught from their very infancy, that all men are 'born free and equal'," reflected one commentator on the policy of North Carolina, Virginia, and of some other (mainly southern) states in barring from civil office clergymen actively engaged in the pastoral ministry. Yet there was considerable sympathy for such a restriction. Where, since neither Christ nor the apostles had interfered with civil matters, was the scriptural justification? How could devout men keep their reputation for piety in the face of political conflict, duplicity, and the "dirty work of detraction"? Would they not degrade the ministerial office, lose their influence and divide their churches? Were not the worst and most religiously intolerant governments those composed of ecclesiastics? Andrew Jackson's advice to a pious supplicant for office seemed particularly pertinent: "Go home, young man, and preach the gospel. God Almighty has conferred a higher office upon you than it is in my power to give you." Invariably, respected and popular ministers who resisted entreaties to accept nomination for political office – Elijah H. Pilcher in Michigan, Simeon Waters in Iowa, William S. Plumer in Virginia – attracted praise for not "descending in grade." More satisfactory still as cautionary models were those who, having experienced political office, beat an anguished retreat: William W. Crane, elected supervisor and school inspector of Eaton, Michigan, and the target of rough partisan attack, quickly lost his appetite for public office and vowed never again to stand as a candidate.[69]

Similar considerations encouraged the editors of evangelical newspapers, most of them ministers, to remain politically neutral. Election campaigns slipped by barely noticed as nervous editors, determined not to lose readers, avoided comment on candidates or platforms "for fear," mourned the *Presbyterian*, "that the most innocent expression might be perverted to a political leaning." Even the digests of local, state, and national political affairs, a regular feature of the religious press, could be a source of embarrassment for editors in view of the "morbid sensitiveness of parties." Thomas E. Bond, editor of the New York *Christian Advocate and Journal*, was driven to exclude all political matter for a period in the 1840s. The political self-denial of the press, in many cases the official organs of their church, was symptomatic of the determined institutional neutrality of the ecclesiastical bodies in party political affairs. Such neutrality was both prudential, since a clear partisan alignment would alienate many members, and principled: it was the only course consistent with the separation of church and state. For, as a senior Methodist argued in 1856, if the Methodist Episcopal church (MEC) attempted to control Methodist political action it would represent a major step towards turning it into the established church of the United States. "All political parties would pay court to our ministers, and from a spiritual Church we should be degraded to a mere government machine."[70]

This emphasis on restraint and self-denial represented only one, though a significant, element within politically engaged evangelicalism. Many evangelicals, who occupied a variety of points at the "Calvinist" end of the "pietist"–"Calvinist" continuum, aspired to and indeed often achieved a more active political involvement, arguing that since they willed "good and righteous measures" they should logically will the means, which would go well beyond prayer and "silent voting." Additionally there were those whose attitudes were not so easily classifiable, incorporating as they did the ambivalent convictions that active political involvement corrupted the true Christian, but that the moral citizen should nevertheless seek the triumph of Protestant values by encouraging legislative enactment and benevolent government by all means open to him. In Detroit Elizabeth S. Stuart, Presbyterian and mother of a United States congressman, was determined to see her son reorientate his life: "Why David, the child of so much & fervent prayer . . . should run such a career, I cannot understand – Now I ask but one thing, that God in his power would arrest him in his career & set him clothed and in his right mind at the feet of Jesus." Yet on other occasions she was in no doubt of the value of political action and urged that "[e]very Christian . . . buckle on his Armour" to secure the electoral triumph of Protestantism and the defeat of "his Satanic Majesty's Standard Bearers."[71]

A variety of political opportunities beckoned those ready to buckle their armor on. It was open to all evangelicals to write to their senators and representatives or even, less discreetly, to lobby Washington and state capitals; many denominational causes, especially educational ones, were advanced in this way. More publicly still, they could sign and circulate petitions for government assistance, for instance in protecting outdoor religious gatherings from hooligan interruption, in sustaining a decent observance of the Sabbath, or in the cause of temperance.[72] Nor was open identification with a political party necessarily undesirable. A Baptist editor urged "the *Christianizing* of an organized party" through believers' carrying their religion with them into party meetings. Benjamin Northcott, a Methodist local preacher in Kentucky, thought it his duty to be present whenever election candidates locked horns in public debate, "and was neither afraid nor ashamed to speak out in favor of one class, or in opposition to another."[73]

There was inevitably much argument over the extent to which political issues should be discussed in the pulpit. It was not only in New England, although there the tradition was most firmly rooted, that ministers believed, as did Eden Burroughs Foster, "that the pulpit should be used as much as the press in shaping public opinion in all great questions of the day." Some went so far as to advocate the claims of particular candidates or parties, but much more prevalent was Leonard Bacon's view that "the minister . . . may urge temperance, but not the claims of the Prohibition party, . . . liberty, but not the claims of the Republican party." European visitors commonly alluded to this "political meddling," noting that in America the pulpit had a "license for political discussion" which it happily lacked in the Old World. They were aware that on some estimates canvassing, parading with candidates, taking the stump, and even editing political newspapers were legitimate activities for both laymen and ministers provided the aims were righteous and the means honest. Preachers of this partisan stripe naturally attracted the fire of their less assertive colleagues. Many could not easily forgive John Chambers, Philadelphia Democrat and Presbyterian, for parading publicly with the Keystone Club and working so explicitly for the nomination of James Buchanan in 1856. Equally unseemly was William Gannaway Brownlow's vituperative, fearless, even reckless journalistic mode as a Whig editor in eastern Tennessee, but as a Methodist local preacher with considerable influence over his quarterly conference he (unlike a Democratic rival) survived his trial for unministerial and unchristian conduct.[74]

The doctrine of political activism reached its logical conclusion in evangelicals standing for and serving in public office. That there were disreputable men in political service did not fundamentally challenge the view that the life of a statesman was "a high and holy calling." Immediately following his conversion in 1852 Ruliff S. Lawrence, a New Jersey Methodist, felt impelled to run for the state legislature as the most telling way of serving his God; only in defeat did he experience the call to enter the ministry. The disciplined evangelical would not, of course, employ the doubtful election practices of careerist politicians. When in 1849 William Winans stood for Congress in Mississippi, a combination of evangelical propriety and a chronic throat condition inhibited his campaign: he refused to be drawn directly into public debate (though a number of influential Whigs, including three Methodist preachers, read his addresses for him) or into maligning his opponent. Some years later Erastus O. Haven accepted the nomination for the Republican ticket for the Massachusetts Senate on condition that he would not have to electioneer. As these instances suggest, although most evangelical candidates were laymen, preachers too stood before the electorate. Disproportionate attention in historical writing to ministers' involvement in the Know Nothing movement in the early and mid-1850s has tended to obscure the persistence of their political ambitions in local, state, and national arenas throughout the antebellum period. "I do not know that I have ever seen a legislative body in session," a southern Methodist complained in 1849, "which did not contain more than one Preacher."[75] Many others found satisfaction in minor offices: clerks to circuit or county courts, sheriffs, tax-collectors, postmasters. Probably the most sought-after of positions was that of state superintendent of schools, often, though not inevitably, regarded as a non-party post, but one which – as with so many public offices – it was thought might advance the cause and status of the successful candidate's denomination. There was considerable denominational pressure on Methodist preachers in many states in the 1840s and 1850s to participate in elections for public school officers and to serve if elected; one election in Kentucky in 1851 saw three clergymen in competition for the state superintendency.[76]

Many of these "ministers" were in fact local or licensed preachers, men like Samuel Lewis, popular stump orator, and Liberty and Free Soil candidate for state and national office. With no pastoral commitments, nor any financial support from the church, they depended on secular employment for their living. Some, too, had retired from the full-time ministry, often for reasons of health, as in the cases of Alfred Brunson, member of the Wisconsin territorial legislature, and Samuel Brenton, United States congressman from Indiana. Yet in a significant number of instances ministers with full-time pastoral commitments sought public office. Daniel C. Eddy, a Baptist pastor and the Speaker of the Massachusetts House after the Know Nothing revolution of November 1854, missed only one day of the four-month legislative session, yet continued to write and deliver new sermons, attended all evening meetings of his church, visited the sick, officiated at weddings and funerals, gave pastoral advice, and delivered a course of evening lectures on Bunyan's *Pilgrim's Progress*. His record was reminiscent of the Georgia judge, United States senator, and Methodist minister, Walter T. Colquitt, of whom it was said that he could make a stump speech, try a court case and plead another at the bar, christen a child, preach a sermon, and marry a couple "all before dinner."[77]

Through the antebellum period this ever-present strain of political activism within Protestant churches grew inceasingly pronounced as issues with more manifest religious and moral contours came to dominate party politics. When in the 1830s and 1840s the political questions of principal significance to many evangelicals (the regulation of the Sabbath; the elimination of dueling, gambling, and horse-racing; and so on) assumed a relatively marginal importance in state and national political debate, and for as long as that debate focused primarily on issues whose moral or religious dimensions were not immediately evident – currency, banking, and economic development – then some found it relatively easy to resist full-scale partisan embroilment. For these evangelicals party differences seemed irrelevant, factitious, and insignificant. Yet the existence of a rationale for political activism meant that when the focus of American political argument shifted through the 1840s and 1850s to embrace the issues of temperance, Roman Catholicism, war, the extension or restriction of slavery, and the future of the Union itself, more and more evangelicals adopted a highly visible political, often partisan, posture. Editors of religious newspapers fired political salvoes, ministers thundered from their pulpits on secular themes, assertive laymen rallied openly to party standards. Political quietists increasingly denounced the "meddling" political pulpit, urging Christians to render unquestioningly unto Caesar what belonged to him. But those who shared John S. Inskip's presupposition that "all political questions have a connection, more or less direct, with both morality and religion" could not avoid being drawn by events into a determined political stand. Even in the South, where many church leaders used the doctrine of the spirituality of the church to encourage its political silence, theocratic Presbyterians and other socially concerned evangelicals could not disguise their concern over a wide range of public issues and were to act forcefully in the climactic events of 1860 and 1861. Few of them would have considered the antislavery Methodist minister, Calvin Kingsley, a kindred spirit, but they would not have demurred from his dictum that evangelicals had a duty to "approve what is clearly right, and condemn what is clearly wrong, God's word being the standard, even though the thing condemned or approved may happen to have its political aspects." "Politics" and "religion" were for these men and women not separate categories but part of an organic, seamless whole.[78]

''The most decided politicians'': evangelicals' political influence

Most evangelical Protestants, then, possessed a highly cultivated sense of their political responsibilities. This need not of course mean that they wielded a determinative political influence, though this is the case that will be developed in subsequent chapters. Here it is worth reflecting on four arguments that seem to call into question or minimize evangelicals' political importance: that a majority of them, namely women and apolitical pietists, were unable or temperamentally ill equipped to carry their religion into politics; that evangelicalism was a disparate entity whose confused voices could achieve no coherent political effect; that ministers, instead of enhancing their authority in society, lost status and influence in the years after church disestablishment; and that since evangelicals were only ever a minority in the population at large there is a *prima facie* case against their having exercised a shaping influence on antebellum politics.

It is indeed true, as we have seen, that evangelical churches included pietists who entertained neither wish nor obligation to translate their religious profession into active citizenship. Even more telling was the numerical predominance in the churches of those who lacked the vote and an assured public political role – women and children. Evidence yielding precise gender ratios does not exist for most churches but there is little reason to believe that the figures for New England Congregational churches, where in the early and mid-nineteenth century there were commonly two female members to every male, were unique to that section and denomination.[79] Men were supposedly more likely to be alienated by the "effeminacy" of Christian experience and "the feminine softness of ordinary exhibitions of Christian character" – tears, "tenderness of soul," and self-abasement.[80] When, as occasionally happened, more men than women were converted in revivals, it was a matter of note; there is some evidence, too, that men backslid from religious profession more frequently than women.[81]

Most evangelical ministers, magazines, and handbooks of advice encouraged the exclusion of women from the tainted, corrupt, masculine world of politics and commerce. Endowed with "a deeper and more immovable knowledge in those holier feelings which are peculiar to womanhood," and idealized as the most effective instructors of children and channels of divine grace, women were encouraged to avoid becoming what Horace Bushnell called "mere female men," and instead to "grace the fireside by their retiring softness, whispering in the ears of their husbands their pious cautions, or nice religious scruples." Through the sentimentalizing influence of mid-century evangelicals, the home, as William G. McLoughlin has remarked, "became a model of heaven and the mother the image of Christ."[82]

Yet in practice these evangelical groups did have an impact on political discourse and configurations. The pietist's Christianity could not remain wholly private in its implications; apolitical stances necessarily had political repercussions in a democratic and polarizing society. As will be seen, many southern Methodists and Baptists in particular worked hard to keep their personal religious enjoyment thoroughly separate from any political discussion of slavery and related issues during an era when northern evangelicals were more and more persuaded of the individual's political duty to work to sustain a moral society. Yet pietism, despite itself, took on a political meaning.

Equally, it is erroneous to infer from the language of separate spheres and from women's exclusion from the franchise that pious church-women had no instrumental role to play in the wider world of politics beyond the polling place. Though the public sphere was generally regarded as a masculine arena in the Jacksonian and antebellum years, many women were ready to challenge this male prerogative. The most radical of these females were rarely orthodox evangelicals; rather they were freethinkers like Fanny Wright, or Spiritualists who had consciously shed their Calvinist orthodoxy in favor of a highly individualistic, scientific faith which rejected male headship over women in religion and politics, and offered a radical social program.[83] But even amongst more conservative evangelical churchwomen, disdainful of "ultra" reformers and the corruptions of the new party politics, concern for the moral welfare of society pulled them towards a more public role and discourse. Barbara Berg and Lori Ginzberg have established that from early in the century, well before the advent of the women's suffrage issue, and continuing into the antebellum years, conservative women called for legislation to regulate asylums, and energetically (and successfully) sought public funds for a variety of female charitable organizations, including the Orphan Asylum Society in New York, the Society for the Promotion of Industry Among the Poor, and the American Female Guardian Society. Often socially prominent, these benevolent women had some access to legislative bodies, which were more likely to listen to the approaches of essentially traditional and ameliorative relief organizations than to abolitionists and other radical reformers.[84]

Benevolent women were also deeply involved in writing, circulating, and presenting petitions, bearing hundreds of thousands of disfranchised names, to local, state, and national governments, and sometimes addressing legislators directly on the issues so raised. Often employing the language of religious supplication, a torrent of petitions and memorials called for laws criminalizing seduction, regulating asylums and prisons, changing property laws, opposing Indian removal, restricting slavery, and prohibiting the sale of liquor. For many, petitioning represented a means of operating in an era of mass politics without being compromised by the corruptions of the new partisanship. But as the full reality of the era's compulsive engagement in electoral politics asserted itself, disfranchised women concerned to act for their country's moral well-being had to face up to the issue of their electoral power-lessness. Increasingly through the 1840s and 1850s churchgoing women came to look more kindly on the possibilities offered by the new political order.[85]

Tens of thousands of women – not all, but many of them, evangelical in orientation – were caught up in the excitement of political campaigns. They attended election rallies, clambakes, barbecues, and pole-raisings, joined in processions, waved their handkerchiefs, made flags, carried banners and generally acted as political support groups. As Mary Ryan has explained, male political managers set out deliberately to decorate the border of the public sphere with a few symbols of femininity. Party leaders toasted women at political dinners; campaign speakers delivered paeans to wives, daughters, sisters, and mothers. From 1840 organizers encouraged them to attend their rallies by setting aside seats for them, though women took no part in the public de-liberations. They exploited their enthusiasm and extolled them in song: "Calhoun, Tecumseh, Cass or Van,/ With the LADIES' aid we'll beat the whole clan," Whigs chanted in 1844. Whigs, in fact, with a domestic ideology rooted in femininity, forced the pace in the construction of this political pageantry, but Democrats were no laggards in incorporating women into their own political theater. Then, as the political temper-ance and nativist movements gathered strength, they too exploited similar language and iconography. Ryan tells of United Americans and Know Nothings in New York recruiting women and whole families to their meetings, and wrapping themselves in "the mantle of domestic propriety."[86]

Women's increasing visibility in political campaigns also testified to their own growing appreciation of electoral power. Once incorporated into election managers' theatricals, women would not necessarily remain satisfied with a symbolic or merely decorative role. Many of those drafted as electoral support troops caught "the fever of political frenzy," exulted and despaired as unrestrainedly as the men, and were to develop into "the most decided politicians." Evangelical women moved by concern for benevolent reform and the protection of middle-class, Yankee values, rallied energetically and in disproportionate numbers to the Whig party. Some sought an instrumental role within the anti-Catholic crusade: Catholics in Philadelphia complained during the fiery summer of 1844 that "Political Nativism is stirring up the women to forget their fire-side duties . . . by preparing flags for the upholders of Lynch rule," and by raising subscriptions through the spattering of houses with mud and through other forms of intimidation. Church-women, often openly encouraged by their clergy, were particularly active in the temperance cause. As well as petitioning, they organized temperance leagues and conventions that adopted partisan postures, pressed their husbands to vote for particular candidates, and even, as in New York City in 1854, handed out voting tickets at the polls. Antislavery politics similarly impelled women into action – attending Liberty, Free Soil, and Republican party meetings and publicizing their support for antislavery candidates. "The Clergy and old women get the Church members to go" for John C. Frémont, a New Hampshire Democrat moaned in 1856.[87]

Party managers themselves recognized the instrumental role that women could play in the molding of public sentiment, particularly through their powers of persuasion over their menfolk. Whigs in 1852 sang: "The Ladies fair, with grateful art/ Will lead their beaux to take a part;/ They'll pledge them first in whispers tender,/ 'Vote for SCOTT and I'll surrender!'"; and in 1860 the *Ohio State Journal* expressed the hope "that every wife of every married Republican who fails to vote today, will pout for a month to come." As these examples suggest, some male politicians patronizingly assumed that the principal female weapon was emotional manipulation, not energetic discussion between political equals; but in reality women could be as assertively argumentative as men. Wilson Spottswood recalled two particular cases of female independent-mindedness: a wife and mother in a Pennsylvania Methodist family who as a dyed-in-the-wool Democrat openly ribbed her Methodist minister for his misplaced confidence in Henry Clay in 1844; and – more uncomfortably – his own wife, who shamed him out of his covert flirtation with Know Nothingism.[88]

Women, then, were not restricted to an exclusively private, domestic, family-bound code of behavior. Even though they lacked the vote, some of them became central actors in politics. Determining their proper relationship to the public sphere set up enormous stresses amongst women, not only between freethinkers and the religiously heterodox on one side, and Protestant evangelicals on the other, but within the ranks of orthodox evangelicalism. Most evangelicals were conservatives who subscribed to the ideology of "the woman's sphere" and whose initial reaction to the new politics of the second party system was to dismiss them as a dirty business. Yet many of them, driven by a doctrine of benevolence and a vision of a morally purified society, sought to influence public life, albeit by non-partisan means. With the passage of time, the possibilities of the ballot box beckoned more invitingly and pressed both radical and conservative women to reappraise their positions on political action. Abolitionists split bitterly into the camps of Christian anarchist non-resisters and politically oriented reformers. Ambiguous responses marked those holding less radical views. We have already noted Elizabeth Stuart's uncertain reactions to the antebellum political order. The wife of a prominent California Republican, confiding to her diary that "I find myself deeply interested in politics this season, though Sister Mattie Cole thinks it sinful of me," nicely captured the female evangelical's predicament, full of ambivalence and conflict.[89]

What of the possibility that evangelical Protestants were such a disparate body, so variegated in theological perspective, institutional allegiance, and social location, that they could exert no uniform, and thus no effective, political influence? If, as Horace Bushnell claimed, religious believers "more or less equally divided between the parties," did that not neutralize their political impact?[90] The premise is correct but the conclusion does not follow. Later chapters will confirm that the partisan loyalties of evangelicals were divided and that no party could justly claim the exclusive title of the "Christian party in politics." But this did not prevent evangelicals exerting their influence by shaping and giving definition to political parties, and by charging the whole political atmosphere.

Under the second party system both Whigs and Democrats annexed the support of evangelical Protestantism, but each party stood in a somewhat different relationship to it, and the particular character of that support contributed to the distinctiveness of each party's tone and image. Whig evangelicals, for example, tended to look towards an active, benevolent government that would regulate social behavior and maintain moral standards; Democrats leant in the direction of a neutral state in which regenerate individuals regulated their own behavior voluntarily. When the second party system collapsed in the early 1850s it did so under the pressure of two destructive forces: hostility to immigrants, particularly Catholics, and sectional venom over slavery and expansion. These were issues whose potency owed much to evangelicalism, many of whose adherents had grown increasingly uncomfortable within the constraints of the second party system. Under the new arrangements that took shape in the mid-1850s northern evangelicals, showing more political cohesion than before, gravitated towards the Republican party, while those in the South encouraged and sanctioned what they regarded as the necessary defensive actions of politicians, Democrats in particular, in their own section. Protestant evangelicalism, then, may have been a splintered, diverse entity with a variety of political loyalties, but it played a continuing role in the shaping, eroding, and reshaping of those loyalties throughout the period.

Evangelicals, irrespective of their partisan coloring, exerted a further, even more pervasive, influence through their contributions to the language, tone, and mood of politics. They often showed a contempt for the pragmatic routine of politics, for the bargaining and necessary compromising of principles that was the essence of day-to-day government and policy-making. Their temper was less yielding, more visionary,

35

even utopian, than that of the practical politician. This influence was felt even during the years of Jackson's and Martin Van Buren's administrations, for although the major issues of political debate were more explicitly economic and material than moral, the gulf between the administration and its critics was widened by a rhetoric that invoked fundamental moral principles. Once explicitly moral questions entered national, state, and local arenas in the 1840s and 1850s the evangelical temper – crusading, unyielding, principally responsive to appeals to conscience – gave politics a new and distinctive character. William Brock has pointed to the contrast between the prevailing political virtues of the post-Revolutionary era, utility and expediency, and the mid-nineteenth century's romantic and religious stress on the moral character of government: "The imperatives of individual morality were transmitted to the wider stage of national affairs, and the new disruptive force that emerged can best be described as 'political conscience'."[91] Much of this study is concerned with the way that the evangelical conscience helped shape antebellum conflict and charged it with a passion and moral intensity that made pragmatic compromise and backing away from absolute positions all the more difficult, if not impossible.

A number of historians have argued that the experience of church disestablishment during and after the Revolution was accompanied by a decline in the status and economic standing of Protestant clergy and, correspondingly, in their political authority and influence.[92] Levels of stipend varied considerably at mid-century, but average clerical salaries appear relatively to have declined since the late colonial era. Stars in the Presbyterian, Congregationalist, and Episcopalian firmaments might command an annual salary of $3–5,000 (and even higher) in an urban pulpit, but the far greater numbers of poor Baptist and Methodist preachers laboring for a pittance brought the average annual remuneration for an evangelical minister nearer to a lean $500–600. In rural areas it was even lower. These sums were well below those paid to certain other professional groups, to doctors and lawyers in particular, and were reckoned by some to "subject ministers to social suffering and lessen their respectability in the eyes of the world." Congregations tended to supplement inadequate salaries with gifts, often large, but these did no more than mitigate the minister's "pecuniary dependence" while at the same time serving to underline his moral thraldom to his flock. Harriet Martineau considered this to be at the bottom of "the disinclination of the clergy to bring what may be disturbing questions before the people."[93]

Another feature of nineteenth-century ecclesiastical life, the geographic mobility of ministers and the more frequent breaking of their congregational ties, may have further eroded the pastor's authority in the community. Lyman Abbott, though certain that the minister had a duty in principle to offer a lead on political questions, refrained from immediately pressing the claims of antislavery when he took up his pastorate in Terre Haute, Indiana, in 1860; he recognized that it was unlikely that "in the first few months of my ministry, a stranger among strangers, I could exert much influence on the moral issues involved. I must secure the confidence of the community before I could even get a hearing." In New England, as Donald Scott has demonstrated, during the nineteenth century it became less and less common to serve one congregation for life. By mid-century the New England clergy offered no more than "a private service to a specific clientele."[94]

Even when ministers were ready to speak out on public issues the question of course remains as to how far they were able to shape their hearers' thinking. How typical, for instance, was the Reverend Henry P. Scholte, leader of the Pella colony of Netherlanders in Iowa, who successfully shepherded these new settlers into the Whig party in the 1840s and then, after 1854, to escape nativist predators, into the Democratic fold? Language barriers and cultural confusion encouraged these settlers to defer to a knowledgeable and strong-willed leader. Yet the pattern was to break down in the late 1850s as Scholte, failing to carry an increasingly independent-minded community with him, defected alone to the Republicans. Some historians question whether, in an age of declining habits of social deference, even recognized political leaders managed to mold the perceptions of the mass of voters. Why should religious leaders, often regarded as remote from the world and unfitted for politics, have been any more successful?[95]

While some of the clergy of previously established churches may indeed have suffered a crisis of confidence and a sense of declining influence in the early Republic, they were hardly typical of the mood of evangelicalism at mid-century and of its sense of power. Most responded positively to the challenge of sustaining their moral authority within a voluntarist system, and some successfully built up large, sophisticated, and loyal congregations. Lyman Beecher's conversion to the merits of disestablishment is legendary; his son Henry Ward emerged as one of the most effective agents of the new system. The vast majority of American ministers, of course, belonged to denominations that had never known the privilege of state support, many belonging to churches – Methodist and Baptist in particular – that enjoyed increased social standing and influence in these years. Even preachers who lacked education and wealth could by force of personality and an earthy, demotic appeal attract popular attention and respect. Amongst the candidates in the Illinois gubernatorial election of 1830 was "one of the old sort of Baptist preachers, who went forth electioneering with a

Bible in one hand and a bottle of whiskey in the other" and won the confidence of all.[96]

Alexis de Tocqueville was not alone amongst foreign commentators in recognizing the immense power of the American clergy, and among native-born Americans Robert Baird asserted "that in no country in the world [were] ministers of the Gospel more respected by the people" than in the United States. True, much of that influence derived from their not being closely associated with the civil power and not "meddling" continuously in political affairs, but the natural authority of the clergy in their own sphere could carry over into the political arena when the issues at stake were moral ones or had a direct bearing on religion. James Russell Lowell reflected privately to Charles Sumner during the crisis over the Kansas–Nebraska bill that it was prudent to cultivate the New England clergy: "Three thousand men who have the ear of the people once a week are formidable. Probably five hundred of them will preach sermons about [the bill] & a hundred or so may get printed. I fancy I see, '*I will spew thee out of my mouth*, a sermon by Rev. Eldad Hicks,' & '*Ichabod, or his glory is departed*, a discourse delivered on Fast Day by Revd. Silas Hopkins.'"[97]

Lowell's reflection is an instructive reminder of the power of the press in an era of revolutionary changes in printing technology. Evangelical authors and editors were among the most effective exploiters of the potential of the steam press, turning out an unceasing stream of theological treatises, handbooks of practical religion, popular biographies, sermons, and evangelical tracts. The most dramatic and influential innovation in these years was the mass circulation weekly religious newspaper. As in so many other areas of popular evangelical activity Methodists led the way, first with their *New York Christian Advocate and Journal* and later with its various regional offspring. The New York issue and its counterpart, the *Western Christian Advocate*, together reached 55,000 subscribers in 1856, making them the two most widely circulated religious newspapers in the world. The Old School Presbyterian *New York Observer* and the Congregationalist New York *Independent*, each of which sold over 12,000 copies weekly, were in almost the same league. Circulation figures in the South were less spectacular, but the section's most read evangelical newspaper, the *Nashville Christian Advocate*, reached a weekly sale of 13,000 copies by the mid-1850s. Subscription lists indicated the respect in which certain of these papers were held. The *Western Christian Advocate*, for example, found its way into evangelical circles outside Methodism and into the homes of the unchurched, while the *Independent* enjoyed a circulation well beyond the boundaries of New York and New England. For many readers, whether by choice or force of circumstance, the evangelical weekly was the only source of news. Many of the South Carolinian readers of the *Southern Christian*

Advocate took no other newspaper. William I. Fee told of the only literate inhabitant of a remote mountain settlement in western Virginia, a retired army officer, who regularly made a twenty-seven-mile trip to the nearest post office to collect the *Western Christian Advocate*.[98] Responding to the power of the religious press, even strictly secular newspapers began during the 1840s and 1850s to devote far more space to religious topics.[99]

The frequency, persistence, and success with which congregations pressed their ministers to publish their sermons suggests that both parties recognized the power of the written word. When Matthew Simpson became editor of the *Western Christian Advocate* Thomas A. Morris encouraged him to remember that his newspaper could "accomplish more than the entire episcopal board. Suppose the five Bishops to preach weekly to 1,000 souls each, and Dr. Simpson to converse familiarly through his weekly paper with 50,000 and you have the proof to sustain my position."[100] These editorships of denominational papers were enthusiastically sought after, as the sometimes highly competitive elections for them made clear. Editors treasured their papers both as weapons in the general armory of evangelism and as platforms for the discussions of topical issues, by no means all of them strictly ecclesiastical. They generally avoided party political postures, but they were determined to flourish their pens in the cause of morality, correct behavior, and social justice, and they could scarcely avoid discussing issues – especially temperance, Sabbath observance, Roman Catholicism, and slavery – with a clear political significance. When Simpson himself, for instance, wrote a series of articles in 1850 attacking the new Fugitive Slave Law, his stand "created quite a fluttering among the 'smaller fry' politicians" and drew sharp rejoinders from Democratic editors who feared the Methodist paper's "controlling interest" over its readers. The *Western Christian Advocate* circulated as freely as any political sheet: "You would be amused to see [it] ... about the Hotels of Indianapolis – and passing from room to room," William M. Daily told the editor. Simpson's four-year term of office helped double the paper's subscribers and advance his standing both inside and outside the church.[101]

If ministers maintained their influence in church and society by grasping the opportunities of the printing revolution, they and their lay brethren were similarly determined to preserve and broaden their access to the terrain of high politics after disestablishment. Evangelical leaders, as congressional chaplains, preachers, office-holders, and personal friends of politicians, sought to keep close to the levers of government. Congressional chaplains were not well paid, they ministered to a changing and not particularly devotional constituency, and they might be sucked unwillingly into political argument. Nor were they held consistently in high regard. Nonetheless, candidates were ready to risk ignominy in competitive election and to suffer the rebuffs of politicians they approached for support. Through the first half of the century evangelicals tightened their grip on congressional chaplaincies and the prevalent tepid Unitarianism of Congress found little echo in the appointments made. Episcopalians, too, lost the influence they had exerted in the early decades of the republic (though they maintained their near-monopoly of army and navy chaplaincies) while Methodists relished their own increasing authority: *"the Episcopalians* made a hard struggle to hold on, but failed in both Houses," exulted Henry Slicer after the elections in 1853 had returned him for a unique third term and put the ambitious Presbyterian James Gallaher into the House chaplaincy. Slicer and a number of other popular ministers of his church – the urbane John Durbin; the plain, unassuming but compelling revivalist George C. Cookman; the blind and forthright William H. Milburn – clearly enjoyed the respect and confidence of the bodies that elected them.[102]

We have already seen that a number of evangelical ministers sought and even won political office. Less immediately remarkable but probably more influential in the political world was a larger body of committed evangelical laymen. Some of these carried with them a reputation as leaders in church, missionary, and benevolent work. John McLean, considered "a truly religious lawyer & Judge," worked for tract and Bible causes; Daniel Haines, governor of New Jersey, was similarly prominent among lay Presbyterians. The most active layman of his time and the holder of an impeccable Reformed pedigree, Theodore Frelinghuysen, earned the title of "the Christian Statesman" by combining his ardent championing of evangelical causes as a United States senator and, later, vice-presidential candidate with an impressive list of responsibilities in national benevolent societies. From a similar mold was George N. Briggs, urbane Whig congressman from Massachusetts, later to become state governor, whose Baptist upbringing and early conversion established the basis for lifelong prominence in revivals, overseas missions, and moral reform, particularly as president of the Baptist Missionary Union and the American Temperance Union.[103] Others enjoyed a more humble status in church affairs but carried the essentials of their religion into the murk of politics. The Methodist teacher James Harlan entered the United States Senate convinced of "the *particular* superintendence of the *Divine* mind over the affairs of men"; Salmon P. Chase, at home in the overlapping circles of Ohio Episcopalianism and evangelicalism, professed to approach his political duties with "some proper sense of my responsibility to God."[104]

Always a minority amongst office-holders, there were still enough committed evangelicals to contribute a unique flavor to American politics. This they did principally through the vocabulary and the substance of the agenda they set for political action. But they also sought through their personal behavior to encourage higher standards of morality and respect for religion in the public arena, and to challenge the supposition "that religion could not be enjoyed by one engaged in active political life."[105] This underlay the strict sabbatarianism of men like the Methodist Trusten Polk, governor of Missouri, who not only refused to receive or send letters on the Lord's Day but never bought or read a Sunday newspaper, and of Lewis Cass, who was known to leave the Senate if debates threatened to run over into the Sabbath.[106] It encouraged Briggs ("the strong tower," as John Marsh called him), Cass, McLean, Felix Grundy, and others to press the claims of the Congressional Temperance Society in Washington and of similar societies in state capitals.[107] The pledges these groups secured from prominent politicians may often have been only nominal, but reinforced by the example of committed cold-water men they served to set a tone. President Tyler's teetotal wedding levée for his daughter, Governor William Seward's lemonade and cold-water New Year reception in 1842, and Zachary Taylor's strict teetotalism as President-elect suggested that the excess of Andrew Jackson's infamous inauguration was not the only model for political celebrations.[108]

The evangelical elite generally pushed at an open door when they sought access to politicians, with whom they often established close friendships. George Foster Pierce, bishop of the Methodist Episcopal church, South, was on excellent terms with Robert Toombs, Alexander H. Stephens, and Richard M. Johnson, even if politically they did not see eye to eye. Edward Norris Kirk's lifelong friendship with William Seward dated back to their days as student lawyers. John Chambers spent several summers with President James Buchanan at Bedford Springs. John Mason Peck's friendship with Governor Thomas Carlin of Illinois, and Augustus B. Longstreet's with John C. Calhoun, were equally close. In many cases a politician's family connections drew him into the evangelical orbit. Franklin Pierce's attention to family prayer and regular churchgoing, and his sabbatarian distaste for conducting presidential business on a Sunday, were undoubtedly encouraged by the strict New England Congregationalism of his wife and her family, and underscored by the deep sense of guilt produced by the tragic death of a son. The friendship that the Tennessee preacher John B. McFerrin struck up with James K. Polk as state governor and president derived in part from his role in converting two of Young Hickory's sisters at a Methodist revival in the early 1830s; Polk's Sabbath observance and general respect for religion were more immediately encouraged by a devout Presbyterian wife who banned liquor and dancing from the White House.[109]

The attention and respect the non-evangelical majority of politicians afforded the evangelicals in their midst was part of a broader pattern of support for religious authority. There were few dissenters from Lewis Cass's dictum that "the fate of republican government is indissolubly bound up with the faith of Christian religion." Politicians did not dare attack religion in general. The imprisonment of the freethinking heretic Abner Kneeland in Massachusetts in the 1830s offered an eloquent if extreme warning to those so tempted. "In the United States," observed Tocqueville, "if a politician attacks a sect, that is no reason why the supporters of that very sect should not support him; but if he attacks all sects together, every one shuns him, and he remains alone."[110]

Politicians and party managers recognized that under a democratic political system all constituencies and minorities had to be cultivated. The extremes of solicitous regard and bitter criticism that evangelical groups attracted from seasoned campaigners was an index of their perceived importance. It seemed to Thomas Bond, for instance, that as the Methodist churches grew in strength and social influence, particularly in the western states, they became increasingly vulnerable to courting by political aspirants who lacked "proper spiritual qualifications." Francis Hodgson complained that "when the [Methodist] Church was weak, politicians cared but little for her; but now she has grown strong each is eager to make her his tool."[111]

Many politicians wished to be seen in church, patronizing good causes, and even contributing financially to the well-being of religion: Lewis Cass gave land and money to Methodist church-building projects, and the candidates for local political office in Oak Hill, New York, vied with one another in their pledges of financial support for a much-needed new church. Some sought more ruthlessly to harness the power of the pulpit. Andrew Jackson encouraged Martin Van Buren, smarting from electoral defeat in 1840, to appoint a highly esteemed Methodist preacher to a Tennessee postmastership on the grounds that if President-elect William H. Harrison were to dismiss him the county would swing to the Democrats. Another influential minister, Elijah H. Pilcher of Michigan, who some thought "the ablest statesman in the west," found himself simultaneously nominated for office by state Democratic, Republican, and Abolition conventions in 1856; although he declined, the Democrats still put his name on their ticket, and he won.[112]

When clergy addressed secular issues politicians paid attention, ready to extol wisdom or mock folly. Aggrieved politicians, thought G.W. Ames, "take it upon themselves to exercise a censorship over clergymen and religious journals altogether unwarrantable." Conversely, the words of sympathetic clergy were quickly exploited. Political propagandists sought access to the religious newspaper press by sending speeches and other documents to sympathetic editors and, less scrupulously, by surreptitiously enveloping partisan materials in evangelical journals.

Hundreds of Van Burenite handbills circulated in New York in 1840 with the front page of the Presbyterian *New York Observer* printed on one side and an advertisement for a Democratic meeting on the other. Conniving Democrats were happier about the implied endorsement than were the newspaper's editor and, naturally enough, the Whigs.[113]

Evangelical leaders, then, had not so lost social status that they lacked leverage over their elected political representatives. But did politicians overestimate the power of the evangelical constituency that they cultivated? After all, if we take church membership statistics as a measure, the formal hold of evangelical religion on the antebellum population was relatively weak. As we have seen, Robert Baird's contemporary figures indicate that in the 1850s only some 15 percent of Americans were formally members of Protestant denominations, of whom about two-thirds belonged to the major Methodist, Baptist, and Presbyterian churches. How could this minority have exercised such disproportionate influence that they helped shape the politics of the majority?

First, this minority was by no means as small as the raw membership figures suggest: taken alone these do not provide an accurate or complete indication of evangelical strength. To be admitted as a full, communicating member of a church the individual had to give evidence of personal conversion or make a public testimony of Christian discipleship. Most churchgoers even in evangelical denominations were not members but unconverted "hearers": regular and irregular attenders who had yet to experience what one described as a "cyclonic mental disturbance," who professed at least a nominal belief in Christianity and the Bible, who provided the principal pool of potential converts in times of revival, and who in many cases were children or young people. The ratio of hearers to members in the overall "population" of the church was a matter of some debate and varied considerably both between and within denominations. The editor of the *Methodist Quarterly Review* conceded that "a greater number of non-professors attend the ministry of [Presbyterians, Congregationalists, and Baptists] . . . in proportion to their membership than . . . the Methodist ministry"; this may have reflected the more intensive trawling of the pool of hearers in the most revivalist of denominations. Baird's estimate of church populations in the early 1840s suggests a ratio of 7:1 in the Protestant Episcopal church, 5.6:1 in Presbyterian churches, over 4.5:1 in Baptist and Congregational churches, and 3.2:1 in the family of Methodist churches. But where detailed evidence does exist, as in the case of the Dutch Reformed church, the ratio of hearers to members could be much lower, a little over 2:1. Indeed, amongst Rhode Island Baptists in 1853 it was as low as 1.2:1.[114]

If these were the real proportions, it is wise to approach with caution contemporary estimates of aggregate evangelical strength which, building on Baird, claimed that in the mid-1850s nearly two-thirds of the country's population – 17 million out of 27 million – were either members in full communion or under the direct influence of evangelical churches.[115] Such figures resulted from treating all 4 million Protestant church members as evangelical and supposing a ratio of hearers to members of over 3 : 1. Yet even by a more stringent and realistic measurement – calculating an evangelical church membership of about 3.5 million, and only twice that number of hearers – over 10 million Americans, or about 40 percent of the total population, appear at that time to have been in close sympathy with evangelical Christianity. This was the largest, and most formidable, subculture in American society.

Secondly, we should take as much care to avoid too sharp a disjunction between the categories of evangelical and non-evangelical as between church member and non-communicating adherent. Many Americans who did not attend evangelical churches regularly, or even at all, were the products of a Protestant upbringing, or children of an evangelical culture. If they had shed, or perhaps never wholly absorbed, formal evangelical doctrine, their ethical understanding and their perception of the forces at work in the world were deeply indebted to the Protestant evangelical tradition, with its Manichean dualism, its sense of direct Providential intervention, its respect for Scripture, and its faith in the particular destiny of the United States. Lewis Saum's study of the largely unheard, obscured common people of antebellum America points to the strength and persistence even amongst non-churchgoers of popular religious belief – of residual Puritan, Calvinist, or more attenuated evangelical convictions.[116]

Loosely attached "adherents" and those with even more tenuous church connections naturally earned the rebuke and scorn of the devout, who regarded them as – at best – Laodiceans: nominal or lukewarm Christians of superficial piety whose evangelicalism was certainly not the organizing principle of their secular lives. These were the people who could manifest "much religion, but little godliness," those whom the Baptist Nathaniel Colver had in mind when he explained sardonically, "We've got no sinners in Detroit." They left "religion behind when they plunge[d] into . . . the politics of the world."[117] In that political arena they were represented, all too appropriately, by men like Van Buren, who might attend church, but who confessed wryly to a friend that "I am accustomed when men are preaching, to occupy my mind with my political thoughts." A Methodist visitor to Washington found particularly objectionable the demeanor of some members of Congress during prayers: "listless, uneasy, moving about, and . . . reading newspapers or some other papers." Matthew

Simpson sighed at certain contemporary politicians' incomplete grasp of scriptural Christianity: Governor Peter Hansborough Bell of Texas, in his proclamation of thanksgiving for the Compromise measures of 1850, gave himself away by invoking "the beautiful and expressive language of the Bible" to rejoice that "the Winter of our discontent is gone," as did the Ohio politician who announced that the course of the opposition party reminded him of the passage of Holy Writ, *"Whom God intends to destroy he first makes mad."*[118]

But what intensely pious critics of these low-wattage Christians underestimated was the extent to which even they were at ease using evangelical currency in political trade. As voters they might not actively solicit appeals to religious conscience but neither were they immune to the tug of Protestant loyalties: their denominational allegiance and congregational ties, however loose or historically remote, provided reference points and tribal totems for themselves and for others, whether the enemy was the Catholic church, other Protestant denominations, or aggressive churchmen in another section. As political leaders, they may have failed, as Caleb Cushing confessed, to make "an acceptance of the world's Redeemer" and become "a professor of piety in the technical sense of those words," but they were shrewd enough to know the importance of proceeding publicly in ways that showed their "deepest respect and observance of the articles of our religion."[119]

The antebellum political landscape is strewn with striking examples of political figures who were scarcely evangelicals, but whose political course, language, and moral posture derived from their Protestant – and often more narrowly evangelical – roots. They shared many values with evangelicals. They also respected their electoral potential. They knew that evangelicals were technically a minority but they knew, too, that this did not make them a marginal constituency, either by the measure of social class (though relatively weak amongst the highest strata, they were strongly represented amongst the articulate middle classes and aspiring, "respectable" working people), or in terms of their cultural pedigree and values as heirs of the Puritans and more recent evangelical groups. James W. Grimes, a Whig-Republican, the governor of Iowa in the mid-1850s and United States senator from 1859, offers an example. Grimes grew up in a New England Congregationalist home. As a student at Hampton Academy during the religious revival of 1831 he "found joy, and peace, and comfort to my soul." He later lost his Calvinist faith and told his friend the Reverend Jonathan Blanchard that he held "no settled religious convictions." Nonetheless he remained a regular attender of the Congregational church in Iowa, "fully assured," as his biographer tells us, "of the ethical, the practical, and the humane parts of Christianity." The legacy of Grimes's evangelicalism was his belief "that men should judge in themselves what is right, and that the preparation necessary for another world is to do our duty in this." It was this that philosophically underpinned his advocacy of temperance and antislavery causes, and that made him so receptive to the reform crusade of the Reverend Asa Turner and the band of transplanted Yankee Congregationalists in Iowa. Though not strictly an evangelical, Grimes acted to enhance and extend, not subvert, the social and political authority of postmillennialist Protestants.[120]

The quintessential exemplar of this political type was, of course, Abraham Lincoln. Born to Separate Baptist parents in Kentucky, exposed as a youth to predestinarian, hard-shell Baptists in Indiana, and made familiar with Methodist and kindred forms of frontier revivalism during his young manhood in Salem, Illinois, Lincoln developed an antipathy to sectarian divisiveness and religious emotionalism which was to keep him aloof from church membership throughout his life. It was during these years that he also acquired that profound knowledge of Scripture which underpinned his rejection of what he considered narrow religious dogma. Never an "infidel," despite the claims of political opponents, Lincoln affirmed his faith, as William J. Wolf has persuasively explained, in "man's need of salvation in terms of Adam's fall, God's loving purpose behind the infliction of punishment, and Christ's atoning work through his sacrificial death." Espousing a doctrine of predestined universal salvation through Christ, he challenged both the popular Calvinism and Arminianism of the day. Though he regularly attended his wife's Presbyterian church following his marriage in 1842 and never denied the biblical realities on which Protestant creeds were based, Lincoln could not accurately have been described as an orthodox evangelical Protestant.[121]

But Lincoln knew only too well the electoral disadvantages of being tarred with the brush of atheism or heterodox belief. In 1843 the charge cost him the Whig nomination for the US congressional elections: "it was every where contended that no ch[r]istian ought to go for me, because I belonged to no church, was suspected of being a deist, and had talked about fighting a duel." In 1846 he secured the nomination but was once more subject to the charge of infidelity, this time from his Democratic opponent, the Methodist revivalist, Peter Cartwright. To limit the damage that he knew the accusation could inflict, Lincoln issued a handbill insisting that he had never denied the truth of the Scriptures, and secured his election to Congress. There was no artifice behind Lincoln's claims, nor did he wear his religion on his sleeve. But when necessary he had no qualms about injecting into politics a moral element which drew essentially on his religious faith. His return to political life in 1854 has to be seen in the context of his moral anger at what he considered a reprehensible indifference towards slavery by

Stephen A. Douglas and the other supporters of the Nebraska bill. Through the rest of the antebellum years Lincoln drew from his evangelical inheritance a strong sense that right and wrong were in mortal combat, that God's will underlay what was right, that what was right was only perceptible through scriptural revelation, and that (borrowing from Leonard Bacon) if slavery was not wrong, then nothing was wrong. From Genesis Lincoln extracted the scriptural basis for the Declaration of Independence, which stood at the heart of his philosophical critique of slavery: if mankind were created in the divine image, then all men were necessarily equal in the sight of God. We do not impugn the sincerity of Lincoln's moral responses to the threat of slavery's expansion if we also note that the emphasis in his speeches and writings on right and wrong, on the moral enormity of slavery, and on the implications of a house divided against itself, implicitly and pragmatically recognized what his own electoral experience had taught him: that evangelicalism was a powerful force which might be harnessed for political advantage.[122]

This was certainly the lesson drawn by the authors of possibly the most effective public political document of the antebellum period, the Appeal of the Independent Democrats, issued in January 1854. It is significant that its six signatories, who included Joshua R. Giddings and Salmon P. Chase (its principal author), protested against the Nebraska bill less as a misguided proposal than as a moral enormity, and berated its supporters as diabolical traitors rather than mistaken policy-makers. Seeking to galvanize and maximize opposition, they "implore[d] Christians and Christian ministers to interpose" against a "gross violation of a sacred pledge," which would set back "the advancement and regeneration of the human race" and "the cause of human freedom[,] . . . the cause of God." The Appeal was brilliantly successful in focusing moral outrage and in nucleating political opposition. Its authors understood that in addressing the issue of slavery's expansion in the moral absolutes and language of evangelical Protestantism they would tap deep into America's cultural wellsprings.[123]

It was not only the slavery question that gave evangelicals an opportunity to translate their substantial minority position into majoritarian influence. By no means all anti-Catholic sentiment was restricted to evangelical ranks, but it was evangelicalism that provided the philosophical legitimacy for political restrictions on Catholics and foreigners, for restrictions on the availability of alcoholic liquor, and for defense of the common school system. In each case the local and state laws which resulted were an indication that at least some of the dualistic, Manichean patterns of thought within evangelicalism extended to a wider constituency beyond. Similarly, the threats that Freemasonry and Mormonism presented to traditional values and sexual mores generated

47

anti-Masonic and anti-Mormon agitations through which evangelicals successfully exerted moral and political leverage over philosophical allies outside their churches.

Evangelicals' influence beyond the walls of their homes and churches was a matter of frequent comment by foreign visitors. Evangelicals so influenced the tone of American life that European travelers, stirred by the widespread respect for the Sabbath, the vigor of the temperance and various charitable movements, the dominant presence of evangelicals in higher education and in much of public life, were ready to conclude that the United States was a profoundly religious society. "Christianity pervades the United States in vigorous action...[It] touches and influences the entire social and political state," explained the English Methodist, James Dixon. "It is not meant by that that every individual is a pious Christian, but that the spirit of the evangelical system is in sufficient power to give to religious opinion and sentiment the complete ascendant in society."[124]

Dixon's judgment seemed to many Americans to ignore the reality of vice and ungodliness in their society. But what he and a host of other visitors noticed more clearly than those who lived closer to the surface of their culture was that the impact of evangelical Christianity might be assessed not just statistically – by the numbers of conversions, temperance pledges, and charitable donations, or by the degree of church absenteeism, crime, and drunkenness – but by its more intangible effects on the mental attitudes, social relationships, and public discourse of the American people. Evangelicalism helped to shape thinking about national mission and purpose; about entrepreneurialism and economic individualism; about the relationships between men and women, parents and children, blacks and whites, immigrants and native Americans, rich and poor; about public and private morality; and, most important of all for the present study, about the political responsibilities of the moral individual in a democracy and a republic.[125]

* * *

Democratic politics and mass political parties appeared in the United States at the very time that the evangelicalism of the Second Great Awakening was suffusing American culture. The way was open for the dominant religious culture to leave an indelible mark on American political life. Mass democracy meant that politicians in the 1820s and 1830s had to devise new organizing strategies, while the electorate they addressed were obliged to learn a new political grammar. As American citizens sought to give meaning to politics, evangelicalism offered them a perspective and critical apparatus for the task. The spokesmen for evangelical religion – pastoral clergy, revivalist ministers, and denominational editors – were men of considerable social influence: they spoke not only as local leaders but as representatives of churches that locked into wider religious communities bridging locality and nation. They generally advocated political engagement, delineated the Christian republican's duties in the political sphere and, though usually avoiding open endorsement of any one party, encouraged a conscientious and discriminating use of the franchise.

These two worlds, of evangelicalism and secular politics, were implicitly in conflict, of course. Evangelicals were concerned with moral absolutes, with straining after standards usually beyond the achievement of fallen humankind. Their fundamental concern was with behavior, with the maintenance of certain moral rules in personal life, both in the public eye and the private sphere. Evangelical Manicheanism and unforgiving, uncomplicated moralism worked against the thoughtful discussion of complex political issues. By contrast, politicians' broad visions generally yielded to the harsh demands of worldly reality – to the contingent, to the unexpected, and to the countervailing force. The most effective politician was by temperament a realist, a compromiser who ultimately accepted any working solution even if it fell short of his original ambitions. The temper of the compromise-seeking political trimmer had little in common with that of the conscience-driven, crusading evangelical, who believed partisanship, electioneering, and legislative bargaining undermined Christian virtue and spiritual growth, and encouraged dishonesty and hatred.

Yet cultures and tempers that appeared mutually exclusive did have certain sectors or points where the two worlds interpenetrated. Evangelicals did not turn their back on the new politics: the "Calvinist" temper was much more prevalent than the "pietist." Most saw the political arena as an appropriate forum for discussing the regulation of public behavior and community morals. This did much to shape politicians' agendas. At the same time "Calvinist" evangelicals insisted on measuring public policy by the standards of private – and purified – evangelical conscience. This was to shape antebellum politics every bit as much as appeals to natural law and natural rights had molded the politics of the Revolutionary era.

Chapter 2

Presidential Electioneering and the Appeal to Evangelicals: 1840

The interpenetration of the worlds of the evangelical and of the professional politician became most apparent at election time. It was then that the politician came closest to sharing evangelicals' romantic temper and speaking their language. Elections encouraged him to proffer a vision of a new political order and to exchange the quotidian vocabulary of the legislative chamber, the language of compromise and narrow horizons, for a more utopian script. Campaigning politicians held out the promise of a transforming, regenerative, and cleansing solution to present ills, a promise remarkably similar to that held out to his unregenerate audience by the postmillennialist gospel minister. Evangelicals' concern with electing "good men" to office, commonly articulated throughout the era, invited politicians to focus on personality as much if not more than issues at election time. To the detriment of thoughtful analysis of programs and policy, canvassers regularly flung accusations of personal immorality at an opposition they portrayed as flouting all established moral rules. This was of course not the only reason why electoral politics descended into name-calling (not least there was a structural encouragement to polarization in the shape of a first-past-the-post electoral system which encouraged two-party conflict), but the Manichean perspectives of popular politics and the hurling of moral abuse owed much to the temper of evangelicalism.

It may not be profitable to reflect on what the character of the second party system might have been had there been no interpenetration of the worlds of evangelicalism and politics. But it is doubtful if the extraordinary popular interest in politics, the huge electoral turnouts, and the impressive mobilization of the electorate in that era could have occurred without the engagement of evangelicals, and their organizational structures, in the new order. Paul Goodman has shown how in New England the mass social movement of Antimasonry, tapping deep roots of religious faith, was transformed into an active third party in the later 1820s and early 1830s: endorsed and even led by clergy, and pioneering the use of the party convention, it succeeded in mobilizing masses of New Englanders unmoved by the appeals of Andrew Jackson and John Quincy Adams in 1828. Sabbatarians, too, similarly harnessed the religious enthusiasm of the Second Great Awakening for political purposes.[1] In the unprecedentedly professional election campaigns of the 1840s, as the second party system moved into its mature phase and as party competition extended into almost every corner of the republic, evangelical Protestants shaped discourse, voting blocs, and outcomes. There is some irony in the fact that revivalist Protestants could be heard speaking out vociferously against many aspects of the new political order at a time when their own community was contributing so significantly to its style, language, and characteristic forms. Examination of campaigns for the presidency, where excitement and turnouts tended to be highest of all, confirms that evangelicals possessed a realistic sense of their political authority as voters and as molders of political agendas. It also suggests that of all the elements which the organizers of the new party system borrowed from evangelical culture none exerted so profound an influence as the religious revival, the most conspicuous element in the American religious reformation of the early nineteenth century.[2]

''How long halt ye between two opinions?'': the campaign as revival

It was a French observer, Michel Chevalier, who saw more clearly than most the parallels in style and social function between American election festivities and revivalist camp meetings, which he regarded as the country's only truly popular festivals, comparable to the popular religious pageantry of Catholic Europe. There is no doubt that American political campaigners drew both deliberately and less consciously on the revivalist and his milieu. Determined to establish their parties' godly moral purposes, they saw to it that ministers customarily offered prayer at the opening of national, state, and county nominating and ratifying conventions, which were often accommodated in churches. Some regarded their party as a political church and its activists as a hierarchy of quasi-evangelists. A buoyant Tennessee Whig reported at the opening of the presidential campaign in 1840: "The [presidential] electors are to be the presiding elders, under the superintendence of Bishop [Hugh Lawson] White and Bishop [Ephraim H.] Foster [the Whig senators]. In each county we will have a sufficient number of local preachers, to make war upon the heathern [*sic*], & carry the glad tidings of our political salvation to every corner. . . . And when a sufficient number of local preachers cannot be procured, we will send missionaries." Political "sermons," triumphalist and doom laden, redolent with biblical imagery and theological terminology, were a feature of the age. Democrats who in 1844 expressed contempt for "Whig preacher[s] of panics, uttering *jeremiads* for the fate of [the] 'Credit System'" chose not to see the beam in the eye of their own party, but it was there.[3]

Party organizers learnt much from revival preachers about reaching a mass audience through printing press and indoor and outdoor pulpit, about the efficacy of persevering, continuous, and dramatic effort, and about consolidating loyalties. The multiplication of political gatherings and the rotation of speakers to maintain and deepen interest found a direct parallel in the revivalists' "protracted meeting." Some managers organized political camp meetings spread over two, three, or four days. During August and September in particular, the season of Methodist camp meetings, huge outdoor gatherings met in great excitement and expectancy on sites normally reserved for more spiritual assemblies. Introductory prayer preceded sustained "political preaching." The singing of political hymns – "Come, cheer up, ye Whigs! for most holy's your cause" – manifested a fervor and gusto, not to mention a familiarity in tune, that reminded those listening of Methodist revivals and the catchy melodies of religious folk music. At times real revival meetings even served as an adjunct to a political campaign, as in Peter Cartwright's contest with Lincoln in Illinois in 1846, though they did not necessarily heighten spirituality. On one occasion the seasoned Methodist revivalist called first on those who were going to heaven to stand, then on those who were going to hell; when he asked Lincoln, present but seated throughout, where he was going, the lawyer replied, "To Congress, Mr. Cartwright," and convulsed the congregation.[4]

There was a more profound connection between revivals and electioneering. Both encouraged and exploited a cast of mind which saw the world as a battleground for conflict between irreconcilable powers. The revivalist cultivated in his audiences a sharp-focused millennialism that interpreted the whole of history as a continuous conflict between the opposing forces of God and Satan. His sermons, with their polarized language of heaven and hell, good and evil, salvation and damnation, sin and grace, Christ and Antichrist, reinforced this dualistic framework of thought. He stressed the individual's miserable inclination to prevaricate, his need to make a firm commitment. "How long halt ye between two opinions?" was a favorite text.

The Jacksonian party system and its successor equally depended on the existence and exploitation of antitheses, ideological and political. The choice, moreover, lay not between two sets of morally neutral policies to be judged on the basis of cool pragmatism, but between two moral orders. Candidates and platforms took on an ethical, even religious, significance. Parties offered voters a choice between political salvation and political ruin: "Come aid in your country's salvation,/ And vote for the patriot Clay." On the one hand stood the stewards of righteousness: Whigs characterized Harrison as "Heaven's agent" and Clay, who was "in form a man... [but] LOOKED A GOD," as "the *redeemer* of the country"; Free Soilers presented Van Buren in 1848 "as a sort of political divinity, whose political resurrection has been vouchsafed as a providential boon to rescue the country from peril." They faced, on the other hand, the forces of darkness, "false Christs," "political sinners" groaning in the "anxious seat," those "second only, in the violations of trust, to him who sold his Lord and Master for thirty pieces of silver." A Free Soiler in 1848 bluntly asserted "that God Almighty was the leader of the free soil party, and that the Devil was the leader of the two opposing parties," while the Democratic candidate for the governorship of New Jersey in 1850, George F. Fort, believed the "powers of hell" had been let loose against him and that "the *devil* himself" had an interest in his defeat. Apocalyptic language of this kind, as Michael Heale has recognized, was common to antebellum electioneering: far more than simple hyperbole, it reflected serious division over moral imperatives.[5]

The aim of the political campaign was, as with the revival, to turn the community into the ways of righteousness. Revivalists and party activists sought to rally the faithful and stiffen their resolve, to increase the commitment of lukewarm Laodiceans, to draw in the undecided, and to reclaim lapsed members and Devil-worshipers. The joy in heaven over the repenting sinner was as nothing to the ecstasy in party head-quarters when a "reclaiming committee" secured the return of a backslider or defector. Whigs in 1844 sang lustily of an apostate now returned to the fold "like a prodigal son." Political "conversions" might be accompanied by mock baptisms (high-spirited Democrats allegedly baptized a new member "in the name of Andrew JACKSON, the Father! James K. POLK, the Son!! and TEXAS, the Holy Ghost!!!") and by mock communion services, involving the distribution of whiskey or cider and corn bread as "sacraments."[6]

Political organizers raised emotional excitement to levels commonly associated with religious enthusiasm. At the huge Southwestern Convention in August 1840, when 30,000 turned out to hear Henry Clay, "[m]en acted as if possessed, some of them embracing each other in transports of rapture, others with tears in their eyes choking with emotion... [W]omen... were as ungovernable in emotions as the sterner sex, and several fainted, overcome by an excess of zeal and enthusiasm." When the Methodist local preacher William G. Brownlow waved coon-skins and water gourds, and "s[a]ng louder, jumped higher, and fell flatter and harder than any body else in the whole state of Tennessee" he was doing no more than making a public demonstration of strong feelings wholly of a piece with the emotional atmosphere of western revivalism. The emotional intensity of both revival and election campaigns provided opportunities (more regular and predictable in the case of the latter) for cathartic release, for personal and community purification. In the climax of revival and of electoral victory came exuberant escape from psychological tension together with the conviction.that new birth would bring a new order. "Thank God!" exclaimed the editor of the *Memphis Enquirer* on hearing of Harrison's victory, "THE MORNING COMETH!" and in a similar vein an Ohio Whig exulted in 1848: "Old Zach Has Come!! Let the Patriotic Shout Go Forth! A Nation is Redeemed!" Electoral defeat and political disappointment induced similar extremes of reaction, including tears and numbing mental depression, as a prelude to soul-searching and critical self-analysis. "It is impossible to describe the disappointment & mortification of the whigs of this city," Robert Emory reported from Baltimore soon after Clay's defeat in 1844: "when, at length, the astounding & overwhelming truth forced itself upon them that they were defeated, numbers went home & went to bed. The ladies appear to have suffered as much in their feeling as many. One told me she had had several hearty cries."[7]

Both William Brock and Richard P. McCormick see the 1840s as the decade when the presidential election, having incorporated much of the enthusiasm previously associated with revivalism, came to supersede religion as the principal source of popular excitement.[8] There is some truth in this: the revival fervor of the Second Great Awakening subsided significantly in the mid-1840s, and rates of church growth dramatically fell back, following the schisms in the Methodist and Baptist churches, and the contemporaneous collapse of the Millerite Adventist excitement. At the same time the level of voter turnout at elections was one of the most impressive in the whole of American history. In presidential elections between 1840 and 1860 average turnout in the North as a whole never dropped below 72 percent, and even the less passionately fought non-presidential contests regularly achieved participation levels of over 60 percent; figures in the South were lower, but still impressive.[9] Yet there was no simple switch from religious to political excitement. Religious enthusiasm continued to simmer – indeed, to bubble up furiously in the wave of revivals of the later 1850s – and to exert a potent influence over political practice and discourse. In each of the presidential elections of the 1840s political strategists sought to tap the energy of evangelicalism. Like all energy, however, it was not easy to channel and contain, and the political experience of the next two decades prompts the question: was it the party manager or the conscientious evangelical who exerted the greater control over the nation's political destiny?

"Redeeming the nation": the Log-Cabin campaign

Few American presidential elections have engaged the passions of contemporaries or exercised the imaginations of later generations more than the "Log-Cabin" campaign of 1840. By their parades, slogans, symbols, and songs party managers deliberately played down questions of public policy likely to divide their ranks, reasoned discussion was overwhelmed by an organized torrent of feeling, and the carefully cultivated images of the candidates obscured the reality of their outlooks. Unscrupulous propagandists undoubtedly manipulated the emotions of the electorate. William Henry Harrison was indeed, as Philip Hone put it, "sung into the presidency."[10]

Yet style alone did not create the passion. The economic distress consequent upon the Panic of 1837 allowed the Whigs to act as a focus for those who blamed the Democrats for the hard times and who looked for a more vigorous stimulus to capitalist development than Martin Van Buren was likely to provide. In the South, as William J. Cooper has argued, the intensity of the 1840 conflict grew out of the exploitation of the politics of slavery, as each party presented itself as the surer guardian of the peculiar institution, and not out of party differences in financial matters, though these had dominated state politics in the preceding few years. Again, the disparate groups opposed to the Jacksonians had found a sufficient sense of identity to rally behind a single candidate, and for the first time to threaten the Democrats in almost every state of the Union.[11]

What is perhaps less well understood is that much of the passion of the campaign was religious in origin, as an analysis of campaign propaganda, especially of the Whigs, and of the state of mind of the evangelical community will make clear. For pious evangelicals the election of 1840 was not a campaign devoid of issues, nor was the economic collapse their main preoccupation; the contest between Whig and Democrat had a profound religious significance, Whig propagandists encouraged evangelicals to turn Harrison into a spiritual and religious symbol, and the campaign was thereby invested with a strong moral dimension.[12] Indeed, the death of Harrison, the first "martyr president," was widely interpreted in that community as an indictment of the nation's public and practical Christianity.

The Methodists, Presbyterians, Congregationalists, and Baptists who formed the backbone of American Protestant evangelicalism found themselves in the late 1830s faced with the task of interpreting mixed signals from on high. Believing profoundly in an interventionist God who revealed Himself in every daily event, however minor, they recognized that they were obliged to learn from "his Providence as well as . . . his Word," "to observe, study, and improve 'the signs of the times'," particularly as the latter days approached. The clusters of revivals and hundreds of thousands of conversions that had accompanied a new and more urgent phase of the Second Great Awakening in the earlier part of the decade seemed to confirm both the imminence of the millennium and the special place which the United States, the new Israel, held in God's plan. A slight statistical lull in evangelical progress in the middle of the decade was soon overtaken in many parts of the community by a renewed burst of religious activity. But this cheering advance was clouded by signs of God's displeasure directed against the nation as a whole. In 1832 the Asiatic cholera struck, leaving thousands of deaths in its wake; the New York City fire of 1835 destroyed over 600 dwellings and stores and over $17 million worth of property; the decade's newspapers were studded with reports of lives lost at sea and on inland waterways through shipwreck and steamboat explosions; war with Britain threatened, war with the Seminole Indians became a reality. Most devastating of all was the collapse of the economy after 1837: bankruptcies, business failures, and unemployment were thrown into stark relief when measured against the country's natural wealth, the resources that God Himself had provided. In sermon after sermon during the later 1830s evangelicals analyzed the events of the decade to show "that God has a controversy with us."[13]

That controversy sprang from two principal sources: the public sins of private citizens and the increasing disrespect for Protestant Christianity in the activities of government and politicians. Foremost in the litany of the former were the frenzied pursuit of wealth in Jacksonian America and the increasingly lax observance of the Sabbath. The honest labor, steady industry, and frugality of Americans of an earlier era had given way to "visions of sudden wealth"; a "spirit of adventurous cupidity," declared George Duffield, "eager after large and rapid accumulation of property, has prompted . . . abuse of the whole system of credit, dishonest attempts to evade obligation, and avaricious and usurious efforts to take advantage of the necessities of others." Such attitudes, allied to the rapid improvements in transport, served to undermine the customary New England Sabbath: ministers complained that stagecoaches, canalboats, railroads, and steamboats were swollen with merchants and their goods on the Lord's Day. The noise of the boatman's horn was matched only by that of military parades and bands or the crowds assembling at the horse races. Everywhere, but especially in cities, Protestant clergy feared the effects on social order and the Christian religion of a challenge to their Sabbath from the spirit of commercialism and the very different attitudes to Sunday amusements encouraged by the Roman Catholic church. Similar threats to the fabric of a pious society derived from "licentiousness" – swearing, drinking, gambling, whoring, theater-going – and a disrespect for the law which at its most extreme resulted in the violent rampaging of mobs. The only major crack in the evangelical consensus appeared in the debates over whether God was more troubled by American slaveholding than by the "fanaticism" and "ultraism" of those who opposed it.[14]

Few doubted that the decline of religion in the public life of the nation since the early republic had been accelerated by the activities and outlook of state and federal governments. "There is scarcely another government on earth," Edward Stearns complained, "in which there is so little recognition of God as our own"; John C. Lord acidly remarked that there was little in public references to God that would offend deists, Mahommedans, or pagans. No president had instituted a national fast since James Madison had succumbed to evangelical pressure during the war of 1812; Andrew Jackson remained unmoved by calls for a day of fasting and prayer during the cholera epidemic of 1832. Efforts in both state and federal arenas to remove congressional chaplains during the 1830s caused further evangelical hand-wringing, though less than did the failure of the campaign to repeal the federal law by which mails were carried on Sundays.[15]

Indian "removal," and the reversal of earlier adminstrations' benevolent policies to the "red man," seemed further evidence of the hold of "political irreligion." But what other than a "wanton disregard of human life" and of law could be expected of legislators who in their "pride, malevolence [and] vainglory" continued to abide by a code of honor that sanctioned "anti-social, barbarous, unjust, cruel, revengeful" dueling? If one congressman could kill another, as did William Graves the unfortunate Jonathan Cilley in 1838, what congressional sympathy could be expected for defenseless Indians? If elected representatives could legalize intemperance by licensing the retail of intoxicating liquors, if they could tolerate "the sot in ... our legislative halls, our chairs of state, the judge's seat," what hope was there of protecting the Indians from the whiskey bottle and other forms of exploitation countenanced by the government? Few would have quarreled with the verdict of Otis Hutchins of New Hampshire, that a "reckless and unprecedented mode of Legislation & of administering the government has, of late years, prevailed to an alarming degree."[16]

On the eve of the 1840 election, then, there was a heightened sense of concern in devout evangelical circles that the dwindling influence of Protestantism on the public and political life of the nation, a corollary of the new party system, was offensive to God, would inevitably postpone the coming of the millennium and, unremedied, would invite retribution and disaster. Jacksonians had applied the doctrine of the separation of church and state too rigidly: disestablishment was one thing, the elimination of Christian influence on laws and lawmakers quite another. Without religion, liberty would spiral into the abyss of licentiousness, as it had done in France. Was this where the "bar-room politicians" of the Jacksonian era were leading the country? Evangelical leaders exhorted their congregations to turn the young republic back to the paths of righteousness by voting only for "honest, well-known men of sound morals." They went into the election of 1840 publicly denying any partisan preference, but anxious to behave as "Christian patriots" determined to translate the sentiments of what they considered to be the Christian majority of the population into active piety in government. What America needed in her hour of moral peril was a "class of men scarcely known in the political world, who, like Cincinnatus of Rome, and the father of this republic, would come from the plough to stand in the breach . . . for God and their country."[17]

Whigs found their Cincinnatus in retirement at North Bend, Ohio. At the party's national convention in December 1839 William Henry Harrison's supporters secured the nomination for a man whose "availability" comprised his residence in the fourth largest state of the Union, his promising electoral victories in 1836, his military record against the Indians and in the war of 1812, and his image as a man of the people. Historians of the Log-Cabin campaign and of image-making in presidential elections have properly stressed the democratic, patriotic, military emphases of Whig propaganda and its efforts to cast the Democrats and Van Buren in the role of effete aristocrats remote from the common man. They have made much less of the explicitly religious appeal in the Whig party's campaign literature. Yet Whigs had chosen a candidate who they believed would run well in areas where the evangelically oriented Antimasonic party had established itself – particularly in Massachusetts, western New York, and western Pennsylvania; they recognized, as did the Democrats, the enormous social and potential political influence that the evangelical community possessed; and as the campaign developed they continued to emphasize Harrison's religious outlook, humanity, and moral probity, by which they could lay claim to being the "Christian Party."[18]

The Whigs' stress on the personal integrity of their candidates should not be regarded as an election ploy somehow less real or significant than the party's stand on substantive issues. As Daniel Howe has shown in his sensitive study of Whig political culture, moral issues were as fundamental to the definition of the party as its economic program. Whigs derived from Scottish moral philosophy and from the Second Great

Awakening an "ethical absolutism," a stress on duties before rights and a concern for self-control and self-restraint. Their evangelical outlook was closely related to their distinctive, conservative views on the social order, and their conception of the organic unity of society; they believed Jacksonian policies worked to aggravate social conflict and inflame popular passions. Their evangelicalism was also congruent with the American System, their economic program of centralized banking, protective tariffs, and government-sponsored internal improvements; for economic progress, like moral improvement, was to be realized by the prudent intervention of government and by the sobriety, thrift, and sense of responsibility of the individual. By contrast, a more humanistic and reason-based morality permeated their rivals' political thought: Democrats denounced exclusive privilege and partial legislation, extolled *laissez-faire* principles, and demanded a limited government that protected person and property but left the people "free to act, and untaxed, untrammelled, and uncontrolled." Lacking the party discipline of the Democrats, the Whigs instead resorted to moral appeals in elections as their means of rallying support. Their campaigns, in Howe's words, "formed part of a cultural struggle to impose on the United States the standards of morality we usually term Victorian." Ronald Formisano, too, describes Whig electioneering in Michigan as "a form of political revivalism." It was no accident that Whigs made far more of their candidates' probity and Puritan moral code than the Democrats did of theirs.[19]

Harrison's sympathy for Protestant Christianity was an undoubted fact. As he was a regular attender at the Episcopal church in Cincinnati that he had helped to found, it was probably legitimate for Whig publicists to portray him as a "sincere Christian," "*a good Sunday school . . . church going man*," "one who highly respects religion." But to establish a more than perfunctory church attachment for their candidate less prosaic pens were needed. Isaac R. Jackson reported, in his campaign biography, how "more than once, on entering at day break the chamber of General Harrison," he had "found him on his knees at his bedside absorbed in his devotions to his Maker, when he could not have supposed that any other eye save that of his God was resting on him." It was said that when his political advisers urged him to woo Philadelphian Christians of the various sects by attending the services of each, Harrison had replied: "Gentlemen . . . I thank you for your kindness, and regret only that I cannot take advantage of it – but I have already promised to attend divine service tomorrow, and when I go to church I go to worship my God and not court popularity." The frequent visits of preachers from the status of the Beechers down to more humble Methodist itinerants to his North Bend home, where they might well have heard Mrs Harrison exploding angrily at Andrew Jackson for "taking off people's minds from religious subjects," presented Whigs with equally hopeful material for sentimental tales of Harrisonian do-goodery. Such incidents as his donating a saddle and a horse to an itinerant preacher whose own exhausted creature had died in the North Bend stable were aimed to exploit a reputation he had acquired over the years as the friend of Christian ministers – the defender of James B. Finley and his family from Indian attack, the lone supporter of the young William Winans in early unpromising days in Indiana Territory, the admirer of the urbane John Price Durbin.[20]

Harrison himself was aware of the political capital that derived from a well-timed identification with the evangelical community. Soon after his nomination for the presidency, in January 1840, during a major religious revival in Cincinnati's Protestant churches, the candidate attended for over a week meetings in its Methodist "center of motion," Wesley Chapel. Here the major attraction was the flamboyant revivalist, the silver-tongued, morally ambiguous John Newland Maffitt. Each night Harrison joined the penitents at the altar. The stationed minister, Maxwell P. Gaddis, described as "electrical" the effect on a moist-eyed congregation of the General's walking to the foot of the pulpit steps to seize Maffitt's outstretched hand as the revivalist sang: "Old soldier, travel on;/ I'll meet you in bright glory,/To die on the field of battle/ With glory in my soul."[21] The experience confirmed the view of those who argued that Harrison was "a friend of *new measures*," a non-sectarian Protestant who would, so the Boston *Atlas* argued, take on as had no president since Washington the mantle of "a Christian President – one who fears God and is a terror to evil doers." The Democratic party's publicists denied that Harrison made "any pretension to vital piety" and cited instances of his blasphemous language, but as Thomas Nichols, an active Van Burenite, reflected some years later, Old Tip continued to sustain his image of "an honest, worthy man, capable of making a respectable vestryman."[22]

Whigs were quick to emphasize the practical consequences of Harrison's Christianity, of his yielding, as the Whig songsters chanted, "to no dictates but conscience and God." His campaign biographers stressed that as an officer in the army of the Northwest he had taken a firm stand against the widespread practice of dueling. In Ohio at least it was reckoned that this posture helped him seize the nomination from the morally spotted Henry Clay.[23] Harrison's sabbatarianism helped him even more. Much was made of his refusal to discuss politics with Sunday visitors on the grounds that he had "too much respect for the religion of [his] wife to encourage the violation of the Sabbath." There were some fears that Harrison was not strict enough: John Wheelwright of New York, an evangelical Whig, told him that the religious community had "noticed with deep regret that you have been inclined to travel on that sacred day" and warned him that "[t]he *Globe, Argus* and *Post* with other opposition papers will publish in italics any violation of the Lord's Day by our candidate, and tho' we understand the motive, we cannot but join in the condemnation & some good men may be alienated without considering who must be the President, if you are not." Van Burenites did indeed attempt to exploit the issue, though with more reference to Whig Sabbath-breaking in general (log-cabin building on Sundays and the holding of political meetings) than to Harrison's foibles in particular. But the Democrats were much more vulnerable to the issue than their opponents. In some state legislatures in the 1830s they had largely obstructed, while Whigs encouraged, sabbatarian legislation. Their most likely vice-presidential nominee, Richard M. Johnson, was branded an infidel for his Senate Report of 1829, on the Sabbath mails, which had torpedoed the efforts of the "theocratic" lobby. To the delight of Whig editors nosing out an issue and to the indignation of their evangelical readers, the "political caravan" of Johnson, Governor Wilson Shannon, and Senator William Allen paid no heed to the day of the week as they traveled through Ohio in September.[24]

Bizarre and implausible as it may seem in an election remembered as the hard-cider campaign, Whig image-makers, fully aware of the temperance enthusiasm within a section of Whiggery, set about turning Harrison into a model of sobriety. Richard Hildreth, representing the wing of the temperance movement that sought progress through political action, legal coercion, and the election of men who were "inflexible friends to prohibition," celebrated Harrison's "habitual activity . . . temperance . . . [and] bodily vigor." As a general he had disapproved of drinking amongst his men. As an Ohio farmer he had followed the common practice of converting his surplus corn into whiskey, a more durable, transportable, and profitable commodity, but "soon, however, perceived the injurious effects resulting from such manufactories, and *abolished his distillery*" despite the financial loss involved, announcing to the local agricultural society: "I shall sin no more."[25]

Democrats were scathing about this Janus-like stance. They reminded voters that Whig election campaign log cabins were spirit-selling "groggeries" in all but name, that the great central cabin in New York City's Broadway had a bar some thirty feet long, that Whigs were better named "swigs" and their candidate "Old Tip-ler." By stressing, as did Stephen A. Douglas, Whig "scenes of dissipation" that nourished "moral degradation" and "blunted the moral sense of the community," the Van Burenites sought to exploit a concern in the temperance ranks that the election would set back the cause. Whigs were understandably skeptical about their opponents' "holy horror" of hard cider, labeling them the whiskey party, purveyors of "double distilled destructive loco-focoism" and their candidate a drinker with an effete plutocratic taste for wine and champagne.[26]

There is clear evidence of evangelicals' unhappiness about the stimulus the campaign gave to intemperance: the New Haven Congregationalist Leonard Bacon considered "the hard cider humbug [would] prove more disastrous to this country" than the "hard money humbug"; the Methodist Henry Slicer gave "beer, wine, and even *hard cider*, a well deserved drubbing" before a mass audience in Baltimore. Some were explicitly critical of the Whigs. The *New York Evangelist* criticized their "base compliance with the coarsest appetites" when they offered cider freely at one of Daniel Webster's meetings and the evangelical New York lawyer of the Tappan circle, E.W. Chester, hoped the electorate would "give a proper rebuke to Harrison's subserviency . . . to the 'hard cider' cry. . . . I will not give my sanction . . . to the Demon of Intemperance." For the wife of a Presbyterian missionary, watching the election from remote Iowa, distance failed to lend enchantment: "I think the friends of temperance have dishonored themselves & the cause by following the train of 'Hard Cider' even though it was but an empty barrel."[27]

Yet, remarkably, Whigs held onto significant temperance support. This was, first, because they were already more closely identified with the cause than the Democrats, particularly in areas where the party had subsumed Antimasonry. Where pressure for legal coercion did exist it was more likely to originate from them than from the Democrats.[28] Secondly, Harrison was seen personally to rise above the campaign his supporters were conducting on his behalf. His image-makers confirmed many evangelicals in their view that the old General had maintained "a vestal's purity" during a public career in which he had been assailed from every side by "fashionable dissipation and sin." Many evangelicals were led to believe that the president-elect would lend his moral authority to the cause.[29]

The image-makers' triumph in turning the candidate of the hard-cider party into a paragon of temperance was matched only by their transformation of the victor of Tippecanoe and the Thames into the Indians' most determined protector and friend. The point of departure for this assessment was the celebration of Harrison's Christian kindness and benevolence. Campaign literature cast him not only as "The Hero – the Patriot – the Farmer – the Statesman," but also as the Philanthropist blessed with "a diffusive humanity"; this is what lay behind a Nantucket Whig's earnestly telling a gathering of the party faithful that "the only reason why General Harrison had not been regarded great was that he was so good."[30] As governor of Indiana in the first decade of the century Harrison had been given the impossible brief of protecting the Indians against unfair dealings from white settlers while securing for the federal government the cession of as much Indian land as possible. His biographers made much less of his successful acquisitions of millions of acres of Indian territory than of his sensitivity to the wrongs suffered by these "children of nature" – the killings, seizure of land, destruction of game, and fraud carried out by white Americans. In particular they reminded the electorate of Harrison's express concern, "consistent with the spirit of Christianity," to protect the tribes against the liquor sales and intemperance that threatened to corrode Indian culture. By these accounts, when war with the Indian came it was the direct responsibility neither of an even-handed, peace-loving Old Tip, nor of the noble Indians, who had been driven to misguided armed resistance by a combination of white exploitation and the connivance of British agents. As for Harrison's military victories, they reflected his valor, skill, and daring, not cruelty or inhumanity: "like a true hero, he tempered his victories with mercy, and when the smoke of battle was over, was the first to perform acts of kindness to the vanquished."[31]

In his own *Discourse on the Aborigines*, delivered in 1838 but published in 1840 as a campaign tract, Harrison aimed to point the contrast between his Indian policies, endorsed by Thomas Jefferson and James Madison, and the cynical breaches of faith shown by the Jacksonians. The Seminole War, during the course of whose fighting Cuban bloodhounds had been used, seemed graphically and bloodily to exemplify his thesis, and Whigs unforgivingly chastised the Democratic administration for "hunting men in our *CHRISTIAN* country"; Harrison had fought Indians "in the old-fashioned style, but it was reserved for General Van Buren to introduce the *quadruped* mode of warfare." One of the *Harrison Melodies*, "The Blood Hounds Have Come," added poetic to electoral license: "And a deep-mouthed bay is ascending to Heaven,/ Great God! can the nation's dark sin be forgiven?" The appeal to the religious community on this issue was clear enough and was perhaps most explicit in the frequent reprinting in Whig newspapers of Michael H. Barton's "Address to the Society of Friends throughout the United States." Though aimed at Quakers in the first instance, Whigs hoped it would reach all religious groups. Barton argued that since American Christians held the balance of power between Whigs and Democrats, they should vote for the man most likely to implement Christian principles: the Van Buren administration, in relation to Seminole and Seneca Indians, had displayed a "criminality[,] ... treachery, and wickedness" which in disposition and outlook Harrison was all set to repudiate. Democrats could do little against Whig exploitation of the Indian issue – though they rather desperately manufactured tales of Harrison's fathering three children by a Winnebago squaw – and by the time of the election Harrison was widely identified in evangelical quarters as the best hope for arresting the process of Indian extirpation and for aiding the elevation of "the degraded red man to the blessings of civilization and Christianity."[32]

Whigs exploited Harrison's image as a man of moral integrity most effectively when they played upon popular fears that the Democrats were endangering the republican experiment. Under the Jacksonian order, Jacob B. Moore asserted, "PROBITY and HONOR have been expelled from the highest offices, and government is in the hands of weak and selfish, or wicked and designing men."[33] Jackson himself, William Seward had declared a few years earlier, had "proscribed public virtue . . . and introduced high handed corruption into public affairs"; thanks to the spoils system public duty had given way to dishonesty, patriotism to a love of money and office. The progress in "corruption, hypocrisy and wickedness" reached its climax under Van Buren, whose appointees, Millard Fillmore alleged, were "mere brawling adherents," engaged in booty-hunting and "the most flagitious and culpable devices." What else could be expected, Whigs asked, from a President whose name was a byword for "bad faith, double dealing, and dis-ingenuousness," who operated on the premise that every man had his price, and who would, according to Wheelock S. Upton, be the first example of an American President who had grown rich in office? The message was clear: "there is no republicanism in Van Burenism."[34]

Harrison was a tailor-made antithesis, "a sterling, uncorrupted republican," the defender of his country on the field of battle, the patriot in whose veins coursed the blood of a seventeenth-century regicide and a signer of the Declaration of Independence. Whigs turned him into the epitome of the faithful, disinterested public servant who as governor of Indiana had resisted abundant opportunities to collude with land speculators in self-enrichment. Carrying no spoils of office into retirement, Harrison lived at North Bend the simple, frugal life of the unostentatious republican; morally opposed to gambling and specula-tion he sustained his family by "the fruits of his daily industry." This "modern Cincinnatus" was just the man to sweep away the poisonous influence of the Swartwouts and Van Burens and restore the govern-ment "to [the] original purity and republican simplicity" of Washington's era; like Washington he was determined to refuse the offer of an addi-tional presidential term, if elected.[35]

Whigs also sought to exploit what they took to be Harrison's strongest republican credential in an area of some concern to evangelicals, his condemnation of party spirit. The antiparty appeal of the early Whigs is well established and needs little elaboration here.[36] Harrison's commit-ment to the Antimasons in 1838, that he would never use the presidency to advance party interests, and his extensively published criticisms of party at the Dayton convention in September 1840 were carefully deployed to call to mind Washington's Farewell Address. Like the Father of his Country, Harrison could be portrayed as the servant of the general welfare. Van Buren, the mere head of a political party and a stranger to selfless military sacrifice, could never be an impartial chief magistrate. Only Harrison could honestly administer the government "for the best interests of the WHOLE PEOPLE." Whereas Democrats sought "to divide and embitter one part of the people against the other," to array class against class, rich against poor, section against section, Harrison and the Whigs presented themselves as the harbingers of union and harmony.[37]

Harrison's candidacy consequently reinforced the image of the Whigs as the party of moral rectitude and Christian influence in politics, an image which helped give to the "discordant combination of the odds and ends of all parties," as Thomas Ritchie described the Whig coalition, some cementing coherence. Thanks to Harrison in particular, they were able to turn the campaign into something akin to a religious crusade, a fight for righteousness and good in the face of Locofoco sin and evil. From the moment that the proceedings of the Whig nomination convention in the Harrisburg Lutheran church opened with and were punctuated by the prayers of Lutheran and Methodist ministers, the tone was established. Whigs frequently held their packed meetings in church buildings; Lyman Beecher, the Methodist Arthur W. Elliott, and the veteran Indian missionary, temperance advocate, and sabbatarian Joseph Badger were amongst the ministerial luminaries who exerted their moral authority over the vast crowds that gathered during Harrison's Ohio tour. Massachusetts Whigs were encouraged to demand a Democratic surrender of the presidency "in the name of the Great Jehovah." The moral fervor of the campaign was captured in the slogan "Harrison and Reform," which as Formisano has rightly argued held religious and not simply secular connotations. For evangelicals like Charles White, "righteousness and reform" were closely related concepts. Old Tip was to be the country's salvation, whose victory would "redeem the nation," secure the triumph of morality and provide every reason for thanksgiving to God.[38]

Whigs reinforced this vision of their own righteousness by sustaining a counter-image of their opponents as atheists and religious perverts. In this they were aided by the Jacksonians' adherence to a strict interpretation of the separation of church and state.[39] The refusal of many Democrats to provide any special treatment for the informal Protestant establishment – as for example over Sabbath mails or in the case of the Methodists' call for the legal protection of camp meetings – made the party the natural home for freethinkers, the anticlerical lobby and such minority religious groups as the Mormons and Roman Catholics. Whigs pitched enthusiastically into their opponents for their suspect Christian morality and what George Templeton Strong called their "indecent heathenism." Van Buren himself was held to possess a "wild, visionary mind, undisciplined in ethics, morality and religion," but the most prominent landmark in the terrain of lax Democratic morals was Richard M. Johnson. The vice-president's Baptist pedigree might have offered him some protection against the charge that he was an enemy of the Sabbath; it was no defense against his living openly with a mulatto common-law wife by whom he had fathered two daughters. Andrew Jackson expressed his fears to Francis P. Blair that Johnson's "family connection . . . [would] prevent the whole religious portion" of Tennessee and Kentucky from voting for him, and it was in part for this reason that Johnson was not formally given the vice-presidential nomination in 1840.[40]

Most damaging to the Democrats, however, was their identification with freethought and "infidelity." Whigs located the "real substratum" of Democracy in the revolutionary and apparently atheistic tenets of Tom Paine, Robert Dale Owen, and particularly Frances Wright, enemies of "Marriage, Morality and Social Order." The ultimate aim of the party, Whigs baldly insisted, was to "expunge the whole decalogue from our morals," and to secure "the OVERTHROW OF THE CHURCH IN ALL ITS FORMS AND SECTS and the *destruction of the ministers of religion.*" They embroidered the charge with tales of mock communion services celebrated with bread and whiskey by blasphemous Democrats. Calvin Colton asked Christians if they were "willing to give up their religious ordinances, their holy temples to the desolating sweep of an infidel, savage dynasty . . . of lust, and fire, and blood." The echoes of the French Revolution in his apocalyptic warnings were pronounced and deliberate. Convinced that the "thousands of honest and sincere Christians in the ranks of the Locofoco party" remained there in ignorance of the principles of the *"Fanny Wright Agrarians,"* Whigs set out to frighten them by fixing the stigma of infidelity on the entire party.[41]

For many evangelicals in the 1830s the most disturbing threat to the true faith, millennial advance, the progress of republicanism, and the preservation of sound social habits emanated from Roman Catholicism. The broad shape of anti-Popery and nativism in that decade is reasonably well established.[42] So too are the political consequences of the increased Catholic strength. Though native-born Catholics showed some attachment to the Whig party, the pattern of clear Irish Catholic alignment with the Jacksonians was set, at least in New York, by 1832.[43] In that state and wherever else Catholics developed electoral muscle, Whigs gradually, though not consistently, annexed political nativism and came to be identified as a party sympathetic to calls for controls on the foreign, principally Catholic, vote. Indeed, during the 1840 campaign Democrats set about tracing their opponents' descent from the party of the dread Alien and Sedition Laws of 1798, circulating the former amongst Ohio Germans, for example, to make them believe it would be enforced if Harrison were elected. Everywhere they tapped the considerable wellsprings of anti-British feeling in Jacksonian society, especially amongst the Catholic Irish, by labeling their adversaries "British Whigs" and exposing what were in reality profound Whig sympathies for England and Anglo-Saxon Protestantism.[44]

The Whigs' counter-offensive celebrated Harrison's victories over the British and his "warmest sympathies for the victims of tyranny and oppression in the old world" who had taken refuge in the new, especially the United Irishmen. Believing that the General was capable of attracting what Abraham Lincoln called "the grocery sort of Van Buren man," Whigs set up German Tippecanoe Clubs and produced Harrison songs for the "warmhearted sons of Erin": "Whether fighting her battles, or guarding her pelf,/ Sure it's little he cared for *his own darlin self* – / For such is the man/ They call Tappacanoe." At the same time they disputed the Democratic party's claim to a natural alliance with Roman Catholicism by drawing attention, for example, to an article of Bishop John England which some years earlier had – mistakenly – accused Van Buren of refusing a seat in the New York legislature to a Catholic who had objected to a test oath. The most celebrated example of Whig overtures to the Roman Catholic community came in New York, where Governor Seward sought to dampen enthusiasm for a registry law that would check illegal voting, and to respond sympathetically to Catholic demands for a reform of the system of school funding.[45]

Harrison and the Whigs wore these Catholic garments on special occasions only; their most comfortable everyday clothes had a more nativist cut. In the previous presidential election nativists had gladly attended Whig celebrations for Harrison; once again they warmed to his occasional unguarded expressions of concern at the growing Catholic presence in the West. Whigs presented him as a secure Protestant sheet anchor when compared with "Patrick O'Buren," alleged member of the Catholic church, the instrument of the "Jesuitical" Roger B. Taney's elevation to the Supreme Court, flatterer of the Pope, and leader of a political party demanding, like the papacy, an unqualified obedience to its arbitrary will. Van Buren's particular crime was his "fulsom" letter to Rome, written when he was Jackson's secretary of state, expressing the administration's high esteem for the Pope and the Catholic church. By such stratagems the ingratiating Van Buren hoped to secure the political loyalty of the church hierarchy and its lesser priests, whose access to the confessional gave them direct influence over the actions of the "ordinary Irish." Duff Green and other Whig editors professed their horror at the letter of Bishop England, the "Inquisitor-General of the United States," to the Democratic Committee of Columbus, Georgia, in which he explicitly absolved the Van Buren administration from responsibility for the country's economic distress: here was devastating evidence of the Catholic priesthood's anti-republican, despotic influence. The

Democrats' control by proxy of an often illegally employed Catholic vote had defrauded the Whigs of rightful victory in 1836.[46] Would they repeat the crime in 1840?

Finally, it should be understood that the Whigs' use of Harrison as a moral talisman was not their only assertion of ethical superiority. Rival economic programs, too, were judged as much by moral as by utilitarian criteria. For both Whigs and Democrats banks symbolized something much more than financial institutions, and the conflict between "hard money" men, who favored specie or government-issued currency, and upholders of the credit system, under which banks issued currency, took on the character of moral warfare. Hard-money Democrats like William Leggett and William Gouge, whose views became party orthodoxy in the late 1830s and who, in William Brock's words, "echoed the moral precepts of rural society," were convinced that central banking, paper money, and speculation fostered privilege, rewarded the undeserving, and undermined virtue, industry, and public morality. Whig ripostes adopted a similar tone. Taking up the fight in his "Junius" tracts, Calvin Colton, once a Presbyterian revivalist and now an Episcopalian gladiator for Clay, explained how Jackson's veto of the Bank recharter bill, the removal of federal deposits, the Specie Circular, the "despotic" Independent Treasury scheme and *"the abolition of credit"* represented *"the abolition of morality"*:

> Define credit as we will, we cannot disjoin it from public morality. It is always the exact measure of the soundness of the social state. What could be more preposterous, . . . more shocking, than for a Christian Government . . . to undertake [its] abolition . . . ? Is it possible there should be too much, 'a redundancy,' of public morality, or that it should be too influential? . . . Yet [the Democrats] seem to have set themselves to eject it from the body politic, as if it were a foul demon!

A vote for the Whigs was a vote not just for economic progress and financial well-being, but for national redemption through the Christian party.[47]

Harrison's death a month after he took office stunned the nation. Those evangelicals like John Wheelwright who before the election had considered "the finger of Providence . . . to point to [Harrison] as [the] country's deliverer" were *a fortiori* impelled to see God's hand in his death. Harrison's age and the debility induced by his exhausting official engagements were only secondary causes, subordinate to an all-wise and all-merciful First Cause. Both at the time of the funeral and on 14 May, the day called by the new President for national fasting and prayer, ministers in sermon after sermon explored the meaning of this "public calamity," sure that through the very first death of a President in office God was speaking directly to the nation.[48]

Logically one of two explanations had to apply. Only mischievous Democrats argued the first: displeased with the nation's choice of Harrison, the Almighty had struck the old man down and set Whigs against one another. Instinctively it was to the second that most evangelicals were drawn: a godly man had been removed because the nation was unworthy of his services. Simultaneously, and with remarkable consistency, ministers across the nation confirmed from their pulpits and their religious newspapers the appearance of the first presidential martyr. Through an inaugural address which invoked religion for the first time since Washington, through his introduction of Bible-reading into the White House, through his preparing to enter into Episcopal church membership shortly before his fatal illness, Harrison had appeared to be on the brink of inaugurating that godly era in public life for which the devout had yearned. They saw his removal as nothing less than God's punishment for those public sins they had so frequently lamented: Sabbath-breaking, intemperance, abuse of racial minorities, the worship of money and, in the recent election, the "volcanic and subterranean thunderings of party strife." Having ignored the warning fires, floods, threats of war, and economic disasters of the previous decade, the American people deserved to pay the ultimate price, the death of their president – ironically a man better equipped than most of his predecessors to set the nation to moral rights. "His sudden death," Nathaniel Hewit declared, "may well be regarded . . . a martyrdom."[49]

Most marked of all, evangelicals were unanimous in believing that through Harrison's death God was reproving the nation's over-dependence on human instrumentality, for expecting too much of political parties and mortal politicians. "Had we," asked Heman Humphrey, "placed less dependence upon our new President and more upon the wisdom and care of our fathers' God . . . is there not reason to think he might have been spared?" Prayer and religious revivals, not political propaganda and rallies, were the agencies through which the millennium would be inaugurated. Yet for this very reason, Harrison's martyrdom had not been in vain. Underlying the manifest disappointment in the fast-day sermons is an optimism bred of the mood of national unity on 14 May, the common gathering "before the throne of heaven, . . . cheering evidence that there is still much leaven in the country. . . . Bad as we are there is yet Christianity enough on board of our National ship to insure her against wrecking." In the spring of 1841 the pace of religious revivals quickened again as political partisanship waned and the President's death allowed ministers to remind their hearers of the mortality of man. David H. Riddle captured the mood when he assured his Pittsburgh congregation that "prosperous times may be expected . . . till that day cometh, when . . . the nights of earthly calamity lose themselves in the day of unclouded, uninterrupted, universal millennial glory."[50] Even more in death than in life was Harrison the herald of a new dawn.

Chapter 3

Presidential Electioneering and the Appeal to Evangelicals: 1844 and 1848

The Log-Cabin campaign taught party managers and propagandists many lessons about electioneering in a mass democracy, not least the persisting importance of tapping the political support of the churches and their members. Through the years of the mature second party system Whigs and Democrats continued in their efforts to woo the devout either by addressing issues known to preoccupy them or by treating prosaic political matters in lofty moral terms. In the presidential elections of both 1844 and 1848 the pattern of 1840 was repeated as the two major parties engaged not just in political argument but in moral and religious one-upmanship.

"The wicked walk on every side": the campaign of 1844

The country was again engulfed by high political excitement in 1844.[1] The Whigs, who soon after Old Tip's election had seen the cup of victory snatched from their lips by Harrison's death and John Tyler's subsequent apostasy, rallied enthusiastically behind their pre-eminent leader, the gifted and magnetic Henry Clay. That Clay's Democratic opponent, the dark-horse candidate James K. Polk of Tennessee, had secured his party's nomination largely by his unqualified enthusiasm for territorial expansion gave notice that this would become a hinge of the campaign. Certainly the annexation of Texas and its implications for slavery and the Union generated intense and furious debate, as did the tariff question. Yet, as in 1840, the extraordinary enthusiasm of the campaign derived not simply from the discussion of issues of public policy but from a sense that the election offered an opportunity for moral and religious engagement.

Some propagandists sought to transform Clay into a moral replica of the much-mourned Harrison: an upright, God-fearing, and benevolent citizen. Henry B. Bascom, one of his staunchest ministerial supporters, conceded that "Mr. Clay . . . offers no claim to Christian piety" in the sense, as another Methodist acolyte was later to explain, of experiencing "indisputable evidence of his acceptance with God and of the pardon of his sins," but much was made of his father's having been a Baptist preacher "of piety and zeal," and of his own pew-holding and regular attendance at the Protestant Episcopal church in Lexington. A bevy of local ministers and elders were paraded to give credibility to the claim that "[h]e has the highest respect and greatest deference for religion and its ministers." Such claims received seemingly objective corroboration from the new science of phrenology, whose practitioners, studying Clay's gratifyingly large head, concluded that his "veneration" was "large," that he "love[d] to adore and worship God, especially through his works."[2]

Whigs argued that the firm religious context of Clay's thought led him when advocating new laws to invoke "solemnly . . . the aid of the MOST HIGH." It explained his Senate resolution of 1832 calling on a resistant Jackson to appoint a day of national fasting, prayer, and humiliation in the face of Asiatic cholera. It underpinned his "probity" and his "honesty of heart," making him "one of the purest public men the country has known since the days of Washington." It helped explain his private confession to William Patton that he "would rather be right, than be President." It underlay his much celebrated "benevolence" and the phrenologist's claim that "he scatters blessings wherever he goes [and] is one of the kindest-hearted of persons." Little wonder that in 1839 some had argued that Clay was "too good a man to be President."[3]

As a rule, in elections Whigs tended to dwell much more than did Democrats on the personal qualities of their opponents, but on this occasion the strategy that had worked so well in 1840 was flawed. Whatever his many qualities, Clay was no moral paragon. "Of all their public men, the Whigs could scarcely have selected one more assailable than Mr. Clay," exulted the editor of the *Albany Argus*. Democratic presses solemnly presented "The Answer of Twenty Eight Methodists to the Rev. Dr. Bascom's Certificate of Mr. Clay's Morality," which presented the statesman's life as "one continued scene of vice and immorality from his earliest manhood to decayed old age." Particularly encouraging were the public renunciations of their Whiggery by erstwhile supporters who could not swallow what the Vermont minister Aaron Kinsman considered "an insult to the intelligence and moral sense of the community," the nomination of a candidate of "the most abandoned and vicious practices."[4]

A variety of elements conspired to make Clay electorally vulnerable in the eyes of the high-minded. In part he continued to be dogged by the cry of "corrupt bargain" that dated from the electoral deadlock of 1825. However unfair the charge that he had been wrong to deliver his support to John Quincy Adams and to accept the post of secretary of state, he was unable to eliminate the suspicion that he had been underhand and improperly ambitious. Springing to his defense, his supporters in 1844 attacked the "mock morality and religion" of Pharisaical and hypocritical Democrats, and reminded voters that John Quincy Adams had recently declared that when the time shortly came for him to appear before his Maker, *"should those charges have found their way to the Throne of Eternal Justice,* I WILL, IN THE PRESENCE OF OMNIPOTENCE, PRONOUNCE THEM FALSE." But the doubts remained.[5]

Even more damaging was Clay's history of dueling and gambling. A passionate and impetuous man, particularly in his earlier years, he took the claims of the honor code seriously and twice had even exchanged shots, with Humphrey Marshall in 1808 and John Randolph seventeen years later. Democrats made sure that no detail was forgotten as they appealed to "the keen moral sense of the American people." They printed 50,000 of Amos Kendall's pamphlet on Clay's duels. These flooded the North, especially New England, but were kept broadly clear of the South, where the honor code retained greater popular respect. Whigs like Thomas L. Clingman found it hard to stomach the "barefaced hypocrisy" of supporters of Andrew Jackson – who had himself once killed an antagonist in a duel – teaching "virtue and religion," especially when the moral authorities they invoked were Whiggish preachers. Lyman Beecher in particular was discomfited to find his sermon against dueling, first delivered in 1806 and then directed against Jackson in 1828, now reissued in an edition of 40,000 to thwart the very party whose cause he publicly supported. Clay's supporters stressed that in each of his duels his antagonist had been the guilty party, and that theirs was a man of honor and courage now firmly opposed to dueling. Clay himself, rattled by the Democrats' offensive, resorted to issuing public letters in which he condemned the practice as "pernicious," reminded voters of his support for political measures to suppress it, and stressed the need to "regenerate" public opinion "by reason, religion and humanity."[6]

For all the Whigs' protestations, their opponents maintained the advantage. Not only did Clay decline in his public letters to make a categorical commitment never to duel again ("paltry non-committalism" was the verdict of one New York newspaper) but his actions in more recent years could be taken to show he had not outgrown the indiscretions of his youth. By his own account his involvement in the bloody duel in 1838 between congressmen Jonathan Cilley of Maine and William Graves of Kentucky, with whom he shared lodgings, was restricted to his having helped Graves draft a challenge intended to settle the dispute amicably. But the Maine representative had lost his life, and Democrats were eager to present Clay as Graves's "chief adviser," who had "excited and promoted the duel"; he was a murderer who had driven Cilley's young widow to mental breakdown and early (if electorally opportune) death. Further evidence that Clay was far too respectful of the honor code followed in 1841, when a duel with William R. King of Alabama was only narrowly averted, and the Kentuckian was put under bond to keep the peace. Such wickedness was wholly consistent with the "propensity for blood" of his knife-wielding, cock-fighting sons and nephews. "Can . . . any man who pretends to respect and obey the mandate of high Heaven," asked the editor of the *Coon Dissector*, "support Henry Clay[,] . . . whose hands are [red] . . . with the blood of his fellow man?"[7]

Clay's gambling – his great passion for card games of betting and bluff, particularly poker, brag, and whist – was a constant point of vulnerability. Randolph caught him on the raw in 1825 with his taunt of "blackleg," or card-sharp, and almost paid for it with his life, and Democrats now bustled to exploit the hostility in evangelical circles towards an activity that was seen at best as a distraction from more serious pursuits and more severely as an enticement to duplicity, financial recklessness, violence, and crime. According to a Lexington church elder, Clay had habitually played cards for money in private houses, taverns, and steamboats, and at the race track; he had won at a gaming table the portrait of a beautiful Welsh woman now hanging on the wall of his Ashland home; once he had even put up a stake against a picture of the Virgin Mary. Banners at Democratic rallies conspicuously bore the legend "No Duelist or Gambler" and portrayed Clay with a pack of cards in one hand and a pistol in the other, aimed at a distant representation of Marshall or Randolph.[8]

Instead of trying to deny the undeniable, Whigs argued that what might be immoral in others was not blameworthy in this instance: Clay's card-playing was a modest social diversion; he did not keep cards in the home; he had never associated with professional gamblers; he had staked money only "to enliven the interest of the game, . . . not for the purpose of gain"; he had forfeited substantial winnings to avoid ruining his debtors. But Whig explanations could hardly repair the damage to Clay's reputation. Democrats could be confident that not all would be as forgiving as his wife, who, when asked if she was not pained by her husband's gambling, replied: "Oh no, he almost always wins."[9]

Gambling and dueling were not Clay's only sins. He had violated the whole decalogue. His God was Mammon. He idolized monied corporations. His political "malignity" drove him to "IMPIOUS APPEALS TO HEAVEN," most pertinently his blasphemous attack on Polk as Speaker of the House of Representatives: *"Go home! God damn you! where you belong!"* His triumphalist Sabbath campaigning in southern cities was accompanied by military parades, music, and carnival processions which "drown[ed] with their noise the *trumpet of the Gospel,* and compell[ed] worshiping congregations to break and disperse"; "men, coons, buffaloes and white virgin heifers mingle[d] . . . to honor the modern Robespierre in his hellish purpose of corrupting the morals, perverting the tastes, and dissipating the minds of the people." Clay was a trimmer and a liar, a "high royal arch mason" who pretended never to have relished the mysteries of the order. His "debaucheries and midnight revelries" were "too disgusting to report."[10]

By contrast, Democrats presented Polk as a model of moral strictness and discreet respect for religion, celebrating his family's pedigree of Revolutionary patriotism and doughty Scotch-Irish Presbyterianism. Although the candidate himself was not a church member nor even yet baptized (his father had quarreled bitterly with the local Presbyterian minister), the piety of his mother and of her father James Knox shaped his upbringing, as the religious orthodoxy of his university education did his young manhood. Polk's sympathies in reality lay rather with Tennessee Methodism than North Carolinian Calvinism, and before his death he was to follow these inclinations. But for most of his married life he took his cue from his lively, strong-minded Presbyterian wife, Sarah Childress, attending her church and respecting the restraints that their piety imposed on their Washington social life. On these sound foundations had Polk's "unambitious honesty, purity and patriotism" been erected. His private life, explained a visitor to his home in Columbia, was without "spot or blemish": he treated his slaves well; he was "strictly a temperance man in every thing – in liquor, tobacco, in eating, and in all respects"; he never gambled and was "an anti-duellist on Christian principles". His supporters were convinced that his "incorruptible integrity" – coupled with the "unsullied" private life of his running mate, George M. Dallas – were vote winners: *"His character wins as it wears."* Whigs attacked Polk for "cold-heartedness" (some even connived in the crudely fabricated story that his slaves carried the marks of a branding iron) but they were largely forced to concede the "respectability" of his private character.[11]

The Whigs, sneered John Wentworth, "are for religion, but they want Clay first." It was to resolve this tension that their national convention had selected as the party's vice-presidential candidate Theodore Frelinghuysen. It reveals much about the natural instincts of Whiggery that when its champions were given a free vote to choose Clay's partner they opted for probably the most illustrious lay evangelical in the country. As attorney-general of New Jersey, as United States senator between 1829 and 1835, and then as mayor of Newark, Frelinghuysen established at both state and national level a reputation as "the Christian Statesman," for he carried into political life the values of the Reformed church tradition and of the benevolent and religious organizations in which he played such an active part. In the mid-1830s he had seriously considered entering the full-time ministry, but his ordained friends, particularly Gardiner Spring, shrewdly and successfully pressed him to stay at the bar and in the political arena, where he could do more good than in a conventional pastorate. He retired from political life in 1839 to become chancellor of the University of the City of New York, but when the Whigs' unexpected invitation arrived in 1844 he was more than ready to run alongside the man he much admired. When in his letter of acceptance he spoke of putting his trust in Divine Providence, and when he privately told Clay that he would pray for both their souls, these were no empty formulae: their winning of high political office would bring a Christian republic several steps nearer.[12]

For the party's propagandists Frelinghuysen was quite literally a godsend, "a gift," as a southern Whig exulted, "of God to man." Cortlandt Parker's paean on his life and public service rooted his "stern adherence to right" and "scorn for petty artifice and chicanery" in the Calvinism of his eighteenth-century Dutch forebears. This same theology, warmed by the doctrine of disinterested benevolence, under-lay his commitment to good works, his defense of the "friendless and penniless" – including blacks and Indians – and his generosity to charitable causes. "The key of his character," Parker explained, "lies in one principle, the determination to do good to his fellow men, and honor his Creator."[13]

Frelinghuysen played a largely inactive part in the canvass itself, but this was unimportant in view of the powerful images that his name conjured up. Whig editors took enormous pleasure in reporting Thomas H. Stockton's challenge delivered, amidst great cheering, at the May meeting of the New York Sunday School Union: "If any [Democrat] find fault with us for . . . alluding to [Frelinghuysen's nomination], I say to them, give us a better man! . . . [U]ntil you do, we *shall testify at the ballot box the feeling with which we regard the homage thus paid to the Christian religion.*" If Frelinghuysen was seen in public it was not on the hustings but on the religious platform, taking the chair and speaking at the anniversary meetings of the American Bible Society and the American Tract Society. When he told the September gathering of the American Board of Commissioners for Foreign Missions that the "Puritan element is at this day the solid foundation of our prosperity; the conservative influence mixed with our institutions, which, under God, shall fulfil the best hopes of the Christian," the line that divided political candidate from evangelical reformer was barely distinguishable.[14]

Democrats were naturally scornful of the two-facedness of the Whig ticket. Their party banners in Yates County, New York, included one on which a distant Frelinghuysen could be seen turning towards the foreground figure of Clay, who carried a pack of cards in his hand. "Free, will you take a hand?" asks Clay, to which the stern evangelical replies, "I am no gambler nor duellist." Amos Kendall proposed to exploit the dichotomy in a lurid juxtaposition of portraits: Clay at the gambling table as Frelinghuysen receives the sacrament at communion; the duelist shooting his adversary or kissing a prostitute while his running mate prays amidst a pious sisterhood; the Kentuckian watching his overseer whipping his slaves while Frelinghuysen walks arm in arm with a black dandy. The sequence should conclude, Kendall suggested, with "a grand procession of Whig *clergymen* who support the ticket, escorting their JUGGERNAUT, Henry Clay, *in the shape of Old Nick*, to the temple of the Civil Power; while Frelinghuysen, *with angel's wings on*, sits beside him on the same car, with this motto: 'OUR HEAVEN IS POWER THOUGH THE DEVIL BE ITS GOD.'"[15]

With Frelinghuysen "sanctifying" the ticket, Whigs could again pose as the guardians of a Christian polity before an evangelical constituency acutely sensitive to the fragility of republicanism and convinced that America was "ceasing as a nation to have any conscience about public matters." A Whig administration, "[r]eliant on JUSTICE and GOD," would revive public morality after nearly sixteen years of plundering Democratic rule. Under John Tyler, "the Tory-King," the poisons in the body politic had continued their malign work. Congress had become a "mere executive tool" cowed by "ONE MAN POWER" and restrained by the straitjacket of party. Polk was a logical nominee: "a high party man" and the grandchild of a Tory in the Revolution. Frelinghuysen, however, was an ideal representative of those who sang: "We for the country firmly stand,/ As a patriotic band;/ From party men, of party-brand,/ We of course, withdraw." Clay's "attachment to purely republican principles" was equally evident: in championing "freedom's sacred cause" in the struggling republics of South America, in "downtrodden Poland," and in "*Christian* Greece" against the brutal excesses of the infidel; in advocating a single presidential term and restrictions on the presidential veto; in trusting in the American people and respecting the stirrings of the conscience of the moral individual, for "[t]here never was a more intelligent, or a more moral people, than the people of this country." Whigs were "the true DEMOCRATS," representatives of the Jeffersonian tradition, whereas "Jackson 'Democracy' was the ascendant star of ONE MAN" sustained by "black-cockaded Federalists."[16]

Whigs offered Frelinghuysen as a prophylactic against the particular diseases to which evangelicals believed the republic was especially vulnerable. For those preoccupied with the corrosive effects of alcohol, and who believed "virtue and intelligence" had seriously suffered from the Log-Cabin campaign, here was an officer of the American Temperance Society. For those troubled by the slaughter of the Indians and the violation both of their rights and of the nation's honor, here was the articulate if unsuccessful opponent of the forced removal of the Cherokees from Georgia and the Southwest. For those scandalized by the ever-increasing violations of the Sabbath, here was the most earnest political sabbatarian of the age, the leader of the political drive against the opening of post offices and the transporting of mails on Sundays.[17]

The two major policy questions of the campaign – the protective tariff and Texas – have to be seen in this context. Both touched on material interests and raised practical questions, but seemed equally to bear on the moral direction of the republic. In the South, with the exception of Louisiana, and in parts of the West the Whigs soft-pedaled the tariff question, but in Pennsylvania and those parts of the Northeast where American manufacturing interests demanded a defense against foreign competition they made much of the tariff of 1842 and of Clay's – and Frelinghuysen's – identification with the protectionist cause. Their arguments for "discriminatory" tariffs, as opposed to those which merely raised revenue, were part of a cluster of propositions which bore on both the economic and the moral well-being of the country. The economic depression in the years since 1837, they argued, had resulted from "wild and visionary" locofoco policies. Democrats had wrought havoc on a soundly based credit system, attacking the Bank of the United States, removing the government deposits, and setting up pet banks that acted as an enticement to general extravagance and wild speculation; in the ensuing economic collapse some Democratic state legislatures had repudiated their debts. Here was a catalogue of both inexpediency and immorality. Bank-burners were of the same ethical stripe as infidels and Bible-burners; the advocates of repudiation, "this *MONSTER* of American public morals," had "endorsed the ethics of the pickpocket and the swindler."[18]

"Credit is morality," Calvin Colton asserted. "To think of living without it, is turning the eye and footsteps back to the state of barbarism. Credit is the moral peculiarity of civilization." A protective tariff was an essential element in the return to soundly based prosperity. It would contribute to a secure currency by keeping essential specie in the country. It would provide the basis for fair trading arrangements. It would advance the well-being of those who were "honored of God," the laboring classes (whose interests were wholly at one with those of capital), by keeping their wages high. For their part, Democrats sought to benefit from a widespread popular perception of the protective tariff, and indeed other elements of the Whig economic program, as partial in intent and effects, unethically advantaging one section of the community at the expense of others. A tariff for revenue only, setting a uniform rate on all imported articles, was the only moral basis for action. There was considerable sympathy for the Tennessee Democrat who believed "no man's soul was fit to be saved who favored the present black Tariff." Whigs were confident, however, that Clay's economic program, morally secure, would win the support of "the Philanthropist, the Patriot, and the Christian."[19]

Both Clay and Polk were border-state slaveholders representing parties that contained many layers of pro and antislavery opinion. Their respective stands on the issue of Texas annexation, with its implications for the spread of slavery and the integrity of the Union, were to be critical to the outcome of the election. Polk's position was the less vulnerable, for expansionist sentiment ran much deeper in his party, and northern Democracy's enthusiasm for new territory smothered worries that slavery might thereby be strengthened. Clay, thwarted in his efforts to keep the potentially divisive issue out of the campaign, led a party far less territorially ambitious – southern Whigs tended to be at best cautious and many were as hostile to annexation as their northern colleagues – but much more threatened by the advancing forces of political abolition in electorally strategic areas of the North. It was in their overtures to this antislavery opinion, religious and Whiggish, while attempting not to alienate southern support, that the parties' spokesmen were most inclined to speak the language of religion and morality.

Whigs sought to commend Clay and Frelinghuysen to the broad body of voters by stressing their moderation, sagacity, and statesmanship on the slavery issue. They regarded the institution as "a great evil," but for the benefit of their southern audience strenuously rejected the contention that "all Christian feeling, principle and duty [was] ranged on the North of the Delaware." Convinced that immediate abolitionists preached an unconstitutional, revolutionary doctrine that would engender "anarchy, commotion and civil war," they aimed to reassure moderate antislavery sentiment that they hungered for peaceful and effective change, especially through the agency of the American Colonization Society, and that they were firm champions of the reformer's "sacred right of petition." Here were two Christian statesmen acting judiciously to protect the Union.[20]

This strategy foundered as Clay came under pressure from the South to shift from the stand he had taken in April opposing annexation. In July he issued his "Alabama letters," in which he expressed his support for annexation so long as it was achieved "without dishonor, without war, with the common consent of the union, and upon just and fair terms." Aghast, Clay's northern managers immediately felt a hemorrhaging of their antislavery support. Democrats had already embarked on a strategy of driving abolitionist Whigs into the arms of the Liberty party by presenting Clay to the "moral and religious portion of our countrymen" as a harsh, hypocritical slaveowner and asking whether "any Christian parent wishes his sons to follow Mr. Clay's example in *gambling, duelling and slave holding*." Clay's stand on Texas seemed to prove them correct. Whigs responded by repeating the arguments they had developed since the start of the campaign: defections by Christian voters to James G. Birney's Liberty standard could only result in the "triumph of slave-breeding annexationists," representatives of "the Fanny Wright school," Calhounite bigots "who defend Slavery as a *Divine Institution*"; only through Whiggery would annexation be frustrated, for even southern Whigs were agreed that it would involve the nation "in an unjust war, and in an unholy cause." Desperate to prevent further losses, Whigs took to brazen forgery in "Mr. Roorback's" account of a western tour in 1836 during which he had encountered forty slaves on their way to market with Polk's initials branded on their shoulders. Can "a Nation boasting of its intelligence, civilization and Christianity," asked an Ohio newspaper, "elevate to the Presidency a man who sells human beings ... WITH HIS NAME BRANDED" into their flesh? Thanks to the very Liberty party intervention that Whigs feared, the answer in November was yes.[21]

If slavery assumed greater electoral prominence in 1844 than it had done four years earlier, then so too did the issue of Roman Catholic intrusions, but whereas only a portion of evangelical voters saw slavery as an unmitigated evil, almost all were clear that Romanism was, and many believed it to be the greatest curse of all, "the mother of abominations." The millennial context of most Protestant thinking had over generations encouraged unremitting hostility to the Catholic church, the institutional embodiment of the Antichrist. In the cosmic battle between the forces of righteousness, religious liberty, and virtuous republicanism on the one side and those of the Devil, sin, and tyranny on the other, American Protestants well understood their role as God's agents in strangling "the first-born of Satan." They had stood firm to defeat popish tyranny during the era of American and French Revolutions. Now, in the early 1840s, it seemed clear from the "sly and serpentine encroachments" of the church of Rome that a new phase in this conflict was under way. "Have you studied the Roman Catholic question?" Robert Emory inquired of fellow Methodist, John McClintock. "A great battle is soon to be fought on it. The forces on both sides are gathering in formidable array both in Europe and America."[22] Emory himself was uncertain whether it was "best to oppose this dreadful error by direct attacks, or to trust in the simple preaching of Christ crucified," but surer front-line evangelicals organized themselves into a number of interdenominational defense and propaganda organizations to meet the challenge.[23]

In part the threat emanated from the ritualist, "popish" thrusts within high-church Protestantism, particularly the Oxford movement, whose impact in America began to be significantly felt after 1840. More visibly, there was the alarming surge in the numbers of foreign immigrants, over 100,000 of whom arrived in 1842, the majority Catholic, and nearly half of them Irish. Many remained at their point of disembarkation, in the major east-coast cities, but others reinforced existing immigrant communities in Cincinnati, St. Louis, and other bridgeheads from which Protestants feared they would overrun "The Great West." Poor, often disorderly, unsympathetic to the teetotal, sabbatarian code of Puritanism, unversed in democratic politics, Catholic immigrants seemed a pestilential threat to the evolution of a healthy, virtuous, and Christian republic.[24]

It is only too easy to understress the religious dimension of the conflict between Protestant evangelical and Catholic, and to explain those tensions in terms of xenophobic, ethnic rivalries and concerns about status. Certainly these were potent ingredients which often co-existed alongside more strictly religious antipathies in evangelical responses to the Catholic newcomers. James Welch, an itinerating agent of the American Sunday School Union, confided in his diary his distaste for the "unblushing iniquity" on the streets of New York of foreigners from the very lowest ranks of society; at the same time the ambiguity of his response and his concern for religious reclamation is clear in his punning prayer: "May divine grace purify the Mass!!!!" The power of evangelicals' anti-Catholicism is misunderstood if it is seen principally as a vehicle or a cover for more "real" economic or social concerns. Moreover, those who have interpreted it as an expression of the insecurity and paranoia which the social and economic flux of Jacksonian America generated amongst many native traditionalists, tend to lose sight of the reality of the religious confrontation. The Roman Catholic church under Gregory XVI and Pius IX was no imaginary or empty threat dreamt up by anxious evangelical Protestants. It was in fact powerful, exclusive, and aggressively expansionary (just like its evangelical opponents), suspicious of free, republican institutions and it identified itself with political conservatism.[25]

What gave these generalized fears of resurgent Popery particular focus was the dramatic battle over religion in the common schools. In 1839 the American Bible Society had committed itself to a policy of securing the reading of the King James, or Authorized, version of the Scriptures in all the country's public classrooms. An intense and spectacular conflict developed in New York City. Here the Public School Society, a private,

Protestant body, exercised almost total control over the funding of common schools, in which the King James version and anti-Catholic textbooks were in daily use. Bishop John Hughes's efforts to secure for Catholics a share of the state's school fund introduced the issue into the state and national elections of 1840, and the bitterness and conflict were to become even more intense in succeeding years. Through electoral and other pressures, Catholics successfully challenged the power of the Public School Society and by 1844 had managed to eliminate Bible-reading from thirty-one of the city's schools.

Protestants everywhere watched events in New York with much anxiety, for it was widely understood that the outcome there would have a strategic significance for other cities. The scene of the most consequential debate was Philadelphia. Here Bishop Francis Kenrick, responsible for a smaller Catholic population but facing a similar situation to Hughes, pressed the district school board to allow Catholic children to read the annotated Douay Bible instead of the King James version. Mounting antagonism in 1843 and 1844 between the two religious communities reached combustion point when a Catholic school director was falsely reported to have forced a Protestant schoolteacher to abandon Bible-reading in her class. Anti-Catholic zealots, stirred by apoplectic cries of "the Pope reigns in Philadelphia!" and encouraged by more opportunistic political nativists, set out in the spring and early summer of 1844 down the short road of sectarian assertiveness that would lead to church-burning.[26]

The roots of the Philadelphia riots were tangled. A long depression had eroded the economic position of the skilled native artisan class and had generated intense hostility to immigrant groups. That there were tensions that ran beyond or across sectarian animus seems implicit in the immunity of the German Catholic churches from the destruction that nativists meted out to the Irish citadels of St Michael's and St Augustine's.[27] Yet both religious communities, Catholic and Protestant, regarded the conflict essentially, even exclusively, as an expression of sectarianism. For a variety of Catholic commentators it was "a pestiferous exhalation from the hot-bed of rampant, lying Presbyterianism," the bitter fruit of the recently established American Protestant Association, the inevitable consequence of "the fell spirit of Orangeism"; transplanted Ulster animosities between Protestant and Catholic had given rise to the city's Gideonite riot of 1831 and there was more than a sinister echo of this when fife and drum played the Orange tune "Boyne Water" as the flames licked around St Michael's church.[28] For their part, many evangelical Protestants were embarrassed by this resurgence of the very "mob spirit" that their jeremiad literature had lamented over the previous decade; a few, in their "deep humiliation," were prepared to follow John Bayless and Calvin Fletcher in condemning from afar what they regarded as lawless, disgraceful, and tragic persecution; most agreed that the only proper weapons for Protestants "clad in the armor of light" were kindness and the Gospel. Yet the spirit of apology was less evident than the conviction that the principal responsibility for the violence lay with the provocations of the Catholic Irish, who had sought "to gain by force what they [could] not secure by stratagem and fraud." Events in Philadelphia demonstrated all too evidently the determination of "Babylon" to secure "the entering wedge," to use any means to hand, and never to yield ground.[29]

It is clear from the fury and urgency with which evangelicals entered these public school controversies that for them the issues had more than local significance. In the first place, to attack the Authorized Version was to strike at the heart of America's religious values and civic order. The rights of private religious judgement and the spirit of free investigation at the heart of Protestantism depended on the lay Christian's guaranteed access to a vernacular Bible untainted by priestly notes. At the same time the Scriptures formed "the grand basis of our free institutions," a handbook of republicanism on which American civil as well as religious liberties were founded. Its principles, reflected the *New York Observer*, "are so interwoven with the institutions of our land, that we must ... amend our constitution, revise our statutes, and *destroy our memories* before we can abolish ... teaching the religion of the Bible" in public schools. Those schools were, after all, *common* schools designed to inculcate common values throughout the population; their role was that of "a great moral police, to preserve a decent, orderly, and respectable population," and to secure the political fabric. The Bible was thus "the sheet-anchor of *American* as well as *Christian* hopes."[30]

Secondly, the common school agitation left evangelicals aghast at what they regarded as Catholics' blatant and unprincipled manipulation of the political process. Few questioned that the mass of the immigrant poor, naturalized, as John M. Duncan reflected, with "amazing promptness," were the violence-prone puppets of priests and political managers: "Intoxicated by a few inspirations of the air of liberty, ... they gather around our ballot boxes, the inflammatory materials for tumult, or the inviting dupes of the designing." Events in New York in particular seemed to indicate Catholics' readiness to use their concentrated influence to secure favorable legislation, either by exploiting the political balance of power and throwing their influence to the highest bidder (usually the Democrats); or, when that failed, to create their own ticket, as occurred in the fall of 1841. On this occasion both Whigs and Democrats, fearful of mounting evangelical anger, either stood firm by the existing school system or tried to sidestep the issue. Four days before the election, at a public meeting in Carroll Hall, Bishop Hughes ("after the true O'Connell fashion") announced the creation of an independent ticket in an unsuccessful effort to make the parties move. The upshot was victory for the Whigs, a lesson to Democrats not to take the Catholic vote for granted, and a legacy of evangelical bitterness over the Catholics' *imperium in imperio* and Hughes's "formal and decided movement toward a union of Church and State."[31] The repercussions were to resound electorally for several years.

Both the Catholics' offensive against the King James Bible and their political strategy seemed to confirm the essential authoritarianism of the Roman church and the "servile obedience" of priests and people to a foreign despot. The papal decree of May 1844 prohibiting Catholics from countenancing unauthorized, corrupt versions of the Scriptures was not just an attack on the Sacred Word but an assertion that when the church spoke there could be "no appeal, no individual opinion." Partisan allegiance, too, was determined in the Vatican. "It is well known," a New York editor complained, "that the Romanists, as a body, with few exceptions, take one side in politics; ... their political preference is decided at Rome, and comes from the eternal city through the bishops, priests and other officers of the papal See, to the members of their church in this country." Hughes took his orders from Rome and put them into effect via the confessional.[32]

So throughout the election year evangelical Protestants were in a state of high agitation over the challenge from Rome. From the humblest pulpit to the highest church councils there issued calls for a vigorous defense of the Protestant cause in a war of profound, eschatological significance. Managers of both major parties had to control these politically fissile energies, seeking to alienate as little as possible the foreign-born, while at the same time striving to keep nativists loyal. Protestants throughout the common school controversy had made clear their determination to use their political muscle, letting it be known that the party which sacrificed the schools' interests "to purchase the support of Bishop Hughes, and the vote that he controls, will find they have paid too dear for the whistle." During 1843 and 1844 many of them made good their threat. Confronting in the east-coast cities Democratic governments that rewarded Catholics with minor offices in return for their electoral support and facing at least some Whig leaders who actively cultivated the Catholic hierarchy, a substantial number of evangelicals succumbed to the lure of new nativist political organizations. In New York City the American Republican party sprang up in 1843 committed to introducing stricter naturalization laws, resisting papal power, sustaining the Bible in public schools, and upholding "an entire separation of religion and politics." In the city elections of spring 1844 its candidates, including its nominee for mayor, the Methodist, Whiggish publisher James Harper, carried the day. A similar Native American movement unsettled Philadelphia's politics, and during 1844 further local parties took root in Boston, Charleston and other cities in the East and South. It is not clear how far ministers and evangelicals were directly involved, but even the Philadelphian organization, which was perhaps the most secular in orientation and which took up the Bible question relatively late on, appeared to contemporaries to have been "organized on the broad basis of the Protestant faith."[33]

These new local political forces drew support from both major parties, but it was the Whigs who proved particularly vulnerable. Some Whig spokesmen, such as Horace Greeley, were anxious not to yield to a movement that collaborated in promoting a flawed view of the public role of religion: "this whole broad assertion of a *'predominant* National Religion,' and that Religion not the Christian but the Protestant, and not the Protestant, but such Protestant sects as the majority pronounce 'Orthodox' or 'Evangelical' is fatally at variance with the fundamental principles of our Constitution." Either (and preferably) there should be no religious teaching at all in public schools, he insisted, or that teaching had to respect the convictions of a majority of the parents associated with each individual institution. But to take a measured and seemingly pro-Catholic view of the Bible issue in what Thurlow Weed recognized was such a highly charged political atmosphere appeared to many Whigs to court electoral disaster. For them political survival entailed exploiting to the full the party's evangelical credentials and, eventually, engineering electoral coalitions with the outspokenly anti-Catholic Native American parties in Philadelphia and New York. Near to the election Clay himself sent to Philadelphia nativists a letter for private circulation favoring stricter naturalization procedures.[34]

From this perspective Frelinghuysen was the ideal vice-presidential candidate. His mere nomination was a clear signal to anti-Catholics of Whig intent, and when shortly afterwards, at the time of the first Philadelphia riots, he spoke at the annual meeting of the American Bible Society, the political as well as religious implications of his message were clear. Denouncing efforts to eliminate the use of the Bible in common school, he reminded his audience that "our free institutions are based on the oracles of the Living God." Later he was to deny that he had said anything "in disrespect or prejudice of the Catholics," but a New York Catholic editor reflected sorely that "while people in a neighboring city were committing murders and burning churches in the name of the Bible, and some others were ready here in New York to begin the same horrors, it was no time to be making speeches in crowded meetings about our resolve, 'Mr. Chairman,' 'to live by the Bible and TO DIE FOR THE BIBLE.'"[35]

A more explicit anti-Catholicism entered the campaign as part of Whig efforts to identify the Democrats, as in 1840, with satanic and infidel forces. William Brownlow was not the only editor to explain the "foul blot" on Philadelphia as the work of Democratic Irish Catholics encouraged by priests and locofoco journals, though few drew his extreme conclusion that "we can have no peace in this country until the CATHOLICS . . . ARE EXTERMINATED." Democrats, "to the disgrace of Protestant America," had elevated the Catholic Roger B. Taney to a cabinet post and elected a papist, Charles Pise, to a congressional chaplaincy. Whigs encouraged fears that furtive members of the Roman church included Polk's running mate George M. Dallas (and even the Liberty candidate James G. Birney, whose son was at a Catholic school).[36] They sneered at "Loco Jacobins" for allying themselves with rabble who shouted "Three groans for the President of the damned Bible Society!"[37] Whigs also exploited the Illinois anti-Mormon excitement that culminated in June with the murders of Joseph and Hyrum Smith and the calling out of the state militia. A Methodist later recalled that in the emotion of the canvass "it was affirmed and believed by many that leading democrats" (including Stephen A. Douglas, whose energetic defense of Mormon rights had earned him the Freedom of the City of Nauvoo) "were in league with the Mormons" and were in some instances covert members of that church.[38] Democrats' support for Catholicism was but a part of their wider collaboration with the forces of infidelity, blasphemy, and religious desecration.

Polk himself remained silent on the issue of nativism, for fear of alienating nativist sentiment in his own party, but his Democratic supporters worked hard to recruit the foreign-born and to remind them of the Whigs' Federalist ancestry and of their approval of the Native American demand for tougher naturalization rules. Seward and others who courted Catholics and foreigners were bamboozling them. The *Coon Dissector* told of a Clay Club Room in Dayton, Ohio, where there hung a picture of the Pope astride a huge bull with Daniel O'Connell kneeling and sucking the pontiff's toe, while a crowd of native Americans looked on and sneered at "those d——d ragged Dutch and Irish." Here in crude portraiture was the "unholy alliance of Religion and Politics" that had spawned the Philadelphia riots. "The federal koon party have . . . waged a bloody and revengeful war against Irishmen, Germans and Welchmen; they have drenched the eastern cities in blood, and they have fired . . . the dwellings and churches of our adopted citizens; and they have . . . converted the pulpit into a rostrum from which their hired bigots excite rebellion."[39] The alleged congruity between Whigs and Native Americans became all the more plausible once the August charter elections in New York City and the Pennsylvania elections in October had demonstrated the concrete alliance between them.[40]

Most of the Democratic press refrained from direct personal attack on Frelinghuysen, "whose moral character," the *Albany Argus* agreed, "is above reproach," though there were those who denounced the hypocrisy of a "psalm-singing professor, with a hymn book in his hand and a bible under his arm" (Amos Kendall's description), letting himself be used to deodorize "the stench of Clay's debaucheries." His sectarianism, however, variously assessed as "prejudiced if not illiberal," proscriptive, bigoted, and nativist, presented a legitimate target. Frelinghuysen's *Inquiry into the Moral and Religious Character of the American People*, published in 1838, had complained of the growing "cant among us" that citizens should be indifferent to their rulers' religious sentiments and that in politics *"Papists and Protestants are all one."* Contemptuously quoting from the work, a Democratic editor concluded that Frelinghuysen's meaning "is not difficult to divine. It is 'Native Americanism' and 'evangelicalism'." Such indictments helped shape Catholic opinion. On the eve of the election the *Boston Pilot* stepped into the fray. "We ... condemn no candidate but one, and he is – Theodore Frelinghuysen. We have nothing to say to him as a Whig ... but to the President of the American Board of Foreign Missions, the friend and patron of the Kirks and the Cones, we have much to say. We hate his intolerance ... and shudder at the blackness and bitterness of the school of sectarians to which he belongs." At a more vulgar level of hostility, the muddy streets of Buffalo saw a jeering, ribald crowd rolling along a large ball bearing the words "Church and State" and decorated with a portrait of Frelinghuysen in clerical robes, with one hand on the Bible and the other raised towards heaven.[41]

Democrats attacked Clay's sectarianism by a different route: as the embodiment of "British Whiggery" he was by definition the enemy of adopted citizens and more specifically Irish Catholics. He favored a national bank along British lines; he opposed Texas annexation, as did British abolitionists; he looked to co-partnership with Britain in the occupation of Oregon; his "British" preference for "our own race" had led him to support restrictions on alien suffrage and the limitations on foreigners' access to public lands. There could be little doubt, then, of his position on the pre-eminent Irish issue of the day, Daniel O'Connell's campaign for the repeal of the Act of Union of 1801 that had abolished the Irish Parliament. Thousands of Irish Catholics in American cities joined Repeal associations during 1843 and 1844 in support of a movement they believed would remove Catholic civil disabilities and even achieve Irish independence. The more enthusiastically the American hierarchy and newspapers backed the cause, the more evangelical Protestants declared their misgivings. Relations between Irish Catholics and Orangemen remained tense throughout the summer and fall of 1844 in both the United States and Canada. Democrats sought to link Clay with Orangeism by reminding the Irish of his earlier attack on O'Connell and asserting his antipathy to Patrick Collins and the other Irish-American Repealers. On the anniversary of the Boyne, Pittsburgh

Orangemen "startled the citizens with loud huzzas for 'KING WILLIAM and CLAY'" and Democrats made prompt and patriotic capital. "In this country," reflected the *Post*, "the Orange oath is not sustained by British bayonets, and although those who hold its principles may connect it with the name of Henry Clay, the American people will never tolerate its infamous doctrines, or countenance its supporters."[42]

Whigs were determined not to yield the foreign, Catholic vote without a struggle and indignantly reminded Irish and Germans that Democrats ("loco-natives") had contributed substantially to Native American success in Philadelphia, New York, and other cities. Indeed, was not Polk himself tainted with having opposed a congressional bill designed to aid the financially pressed Catholics of St Louis?[43] More positively, Whig spokesmen claimed to understand the needs of adopted citizens and celebrated their patriotic contributions. The Irish-born George Collins reminded voters of Clay's opposition to the Alien and Sedition Laws ("unjust, tyrannical, inexpedient, and unconstitutional") and his tribute in a Senate speech to what the Germans, French, and especially Irish had contributed to American life. No lackey of the British, Clay had urged war in 1812 to punish "British arrogance and oppression." The true allies of Britain were not Whig protectionists, who had the interests of American native and foreign-born working men at heart, but Polkite free-traders, "the adjuncts of British agents and capitalists, in war against American manufactures." Clay respected the Catholic religion and its adherents ("They worship the same God with us"). He had defended the South American republics and paid tribute to the prosperity of Catholic France, Switzerland, and Germany.[44] He found no difficulty in supporting a "free and untrammelled" Ireland, in voting for the Catholic nominee to the Senate chaplaincy in 1842, and, at a more personal level, in reconciling himself to his daughter's marriage to a Roman Catholic.[45] Determined to reclaim at least part of the Irish vote, Whigs at times resorted to transparent Irish blarney. The singing of political doggerel to Irish melodies was a well established practice: "The Song of the Whig," for example, was set to "Remember the day when Erin's proud glory." Less subtle was the Whigs' parading at their convention an old Irish woman to commend their choice of Frelinghuysen: "You have indeed done a good act . . . : he has been 'eyes to the blind, and feet to the lame!'"[46]

Such stratagems ultimately failed. Having tasted the wormwood of Harrison's death, Whigs had now to digest the gall of Clay's unexpected defeat in the November election. Across the country they gave vent to their "inexpressible agony," "pain and mortification." The Whigs' "holy cause," as Philip Hone saw it, had been foully defeated; "the 'scepter has departed from Israel.'" A Baltimorean, reflecting on the humiliating defeat of "enlightened intelligence, virtue, and patriotism," called to mind the text, "The wicked walk on every side, when the vilest men are exalted." There was widespread agreement that Polk owed his victory to two elements in particular, the abolitionists and the foreign vote. The 15,000 ballots for Birney in New York, drawn principally from abolitionist Whiggery, gave the state (and, by that margin alone, the presidency) to Young Hickory. But it was the role of foreign Catholic voters that attracted the greatest criticism, partly because of the alleged fraud and corruption involved in the Democrats' issuing last-minute naturaliza-tion papers to thousands of immigrants, and partly on account of the "ingratitude" of the Irish and the Germans towards the Whig ticket. Clay, Frelinghuysen, Millard Fillmore, and other leading Whigs explained the defeat in these terms, with profound consequences for the party's future electoral strategy. For the time being, however, Frelinghuysen took comfort in looking "to brighter and better prospects and surer hopes in the promises and consolations of the Gospel of our Saviour." He, and indeed others of an evangelical orientation, urged Clay to "seek this blessed refuge, stable as the everlasting hills." As in the hour of trial after Old Tip's death, the faithful should repair to the Lord, not leaning on an arm of flesh but trusting in a dependable Savior.[47]

"Some old fashioned notions about right and wrong": *the free-soil campaign of 1848*

The United States' war with Mexico almost immediately propelled the issue of slavery to the forefront of domestic politics. The Pennsylvania Democrat, David Wilmot, sought by law to exclude slavery from any new territories that the conflict might yield, and thus opened the door to a four-year-long crisis. The question of the spread of slavery west-ward stood at the heart of the 1848 election campaign, affecting the choice of candidates, pattern of debate, and eventual outcome.[48]

Whigs at their nominating convention returned to the strategy of 1840. To the chagrin of Clay's supporters, delegates once again chose a "drum and fife" candidate, General Zachary Taylor, the popular hero of Buena Vista, in the hope that he would repeat Old Tip's achievement. Having never cast a vote in his life and encumbered by no party political past, he could be presented variously as a respecter of free-soil and proslavery positions. Lewis Cass of Michigan, the Democrats' nominee and a political opportunist, was a more orthodox choice, but his public record as Jackson's secretary of war, as minister to France, and as United States senator left him vulnerable to criticism. He had at first seemed to favor Wilmot's proviso, but in his published letter to A.O.P. Nicholson he pressed the doctrine of popular sovereignty, which called for the issue of slavery to be settled locally. After three months of the campaign a third force intervened, in the shape of the Free Soil party, a coalition of ex-Liberty men and disaffected antislavery Whigs and Democrats. The evangelical orientation of the creed, membership, and style of the Free Soilers will be considered later. What presently demands attention is the major parties' continuing determination to tap the political support of evangelicals by asserting their moral superiority over their opponents, particularly over slavery.

Once again it proved especially important for the Whigs to establish the personal integrity of their candidate. Not only did the party's having no formal policy platform throw all the more attention on the figure of "Old Rough and Ready," but it was essential that the man himself be trusted if the electorate were to believe his pledges on slavery. Thus many of the qualities successfully attributed to the soldier-plowman of 1840, and rather less plausibly to Clay in 1844, were claimed for this new Cincinnatus. The candidate himself remained silent (but periodically issued confusing public letters), while his supporters offered a catalogue of tributes to his Washingtonian decency. A Methodist visitor to his Louisiana plantation extolled his "good sense, unaffected kindness . . . and moral integrity"; one of his army chaplains, addressing an assembly of New Hampshire Congregationalists and Presbyterians, praised his regular church attendance. In fact, Taylor was not a church member, nor had he made any profession of faith. It was his wife, a devout Episcopalian, who was the moving spirit behind the religious services in the military stations where they resided. But this did not prevent his being presented (along with his running mate Millard Fillmore, married to a clergyman's daughter) as "the decided friend of Christianity and Christian institutions."[49]

According to Whig pamphleteers, all the chilling allegations of Taylor's political enemies about his traveling and theater-going on the Sabbath, his profanity, his taste in "choice *Jamaica*," his gambling, and his cruel use of bloodhounds in the Indian wars melted before the truth of his moral probity. At Fort Jesup he was the only commander never to drill his troops on a Sunday, Sabbath observance being "essential to the good order and regularity of society." He never swore, even when provoked. He avoided all liquor and successfully extended his beneficial cold-water habits to some 600 of his men. At his camp at Corpus Christi, concerned as ever for the moral well-being of his soldiers, he broke up "the faro-banks and groggeries" set up by a gang of "rowdy camp followers." He was a benevolent father not only to his own troops, but to his enemies, whether Comanche Indians or Mexicans. The bloodhounds he had used only to track down the perpetrators of "unchristian cruelties," not to injure them. The charge (amplified by Democrats to discredit him especially amongst Whiggish Quakers) that he was "a man of blood" who in Mexico had fought "a war against God" defied the abundant evidence of his "old-fashioned kindheartedness," fairness, and humanity. Old Zach's good-humoredly yielding up his bed to a wounded common soldier offered a happy picture "to the eye of the Christian and Philanthropist." Well aware that Taylor's nomination seemed scarcely consistent with their criticisms of Polk's Mexican adventures, Whigs reminded voters of one of the General's recent statements: "I AM A PEACE MAN, and . . . I deem a state of peace to be absolutely necessary to the proper and healthful action of our republican institutions."[50]

Whigs mocked Free Soilers for their hypocritical choice of Van Buren as presidential candidate; this "Judas Iscariot," an infidel and atheist, echoing Milton's Satan, "would rather rule in hell than serve in heaven"; his followers were Jesuits, "penitents with stained hands." Similarly they attacked Lewis Cass's personal credentials even though his commitment to evangelical religion was well known in the Northwest. He had helped bring a settled minister to Detroit in 1816, became president of a newly organized Bible society in the following year and continued to promote the educational and religious interests of the section over the following decades. He paid more than lip-service to sabbatarianism, and the piety of his Presbyterian wife was undoubted. Political admirers lauded his "high-mindedness" and lack of "moral blemish."[51]

But Cass's political opportunism left him open to the accusation of "corruption of heart." "[W]hat a dishonest, immoral *old rogue of a demagogue* Lewis Cass is," mused one Ohio editor. He was, Whigs explained, a land speculator and a violator of the rights of the Cherokees. As governor of Michigan territory, he had grown fat on the spoils of office and had approved "God-dishonoring" laws whose cruel punishments included horse-whipping and the selling of whites into temporary slavery. His supposed lifelong cold-water principles and the Democrats' claim that as secretary of war he had abolished the whiskey ration did not square with his building and owning the first distillery in Michigan, nor with his making "pretty free use of the ardent" when, as commissioner of Indian affairs, he had negotiated with the Saginaws ("How the General compromised with his conscience in the matter . . . the Indians were too drunk to remember.") Not even Cass's sabbatarianism counted for much, given that his southern running mate, General William O. Butler, went to Sunday horse races. The contrast with Old Zack could not be clearer.[52]

Taylor's religious and moral credentials provided the bedrock for subsequent Whig claims. In the slaveholding states Whigs simply projected Old Zack as the cotton planter with a hundred slaves, the southerner of "stern integrity," who would honestly defend his section's interests. He was "a God-send" to the South, wholly different in moral caliber from Cass, the Janus candidate who adopted one position south of the Mason-Dixon line and another to the north. Northern Whigs had a more complicated task. They insisted that Taylor's slaveowning need be no obstacle to those who considered the peculiar institution unchristian and sinful. Whigs had a "sacred obligation" to vote for the only candidate who could realistically hold slavery in bounds. For Taylor had promised not to veto congressional legislation that incorporated the Wilmot Proviso. Here was no ultra southerner or annexationist, but a man with a "decided preference for the institutions and customs of the North" who would "do more for *peace* and *emancipation* than any Northern man would be allowed to do." Old Rough and Ready could be trusted to keep his word. Not so the chameleon Cass, whose Nicholson letter demonstrated his "sycophancy" and "submission to southern dictation"; nor General Butler, a slaveowner who could produce no title deeds for his slaves (he "probably stole" them) and who had enthusiastically supported congressional gag laws; and certainly not the hypocrite Van Buren, who might have bamboozled gullible Free Soilers, but whose "specious deviltry" could not dim Whig memories of his servility as President to southern interests. Only through the Whig party would the moral force of the northern people end slavery.[53]

Southern Democrats countered by circulating documents that purported to expose the Whig nominees as covert abolitionists in league with northern fanatics. Such charges against Old Zack were hardly persuasive, though the criticism that he had not publicly opposed the Wilmot Proviso cut more ice. Fillmore was more vulnerable, for his opponents produced a letter he had written ten years earlier to an antislavery society in Erie County, New York, in which he had made clear his opposition to the annexation of Texas, the internal slave trade, and slavery in the District of Columbia. For their part, northern Democrats attacked Whig inconsistency. They emphasized the "shocking morality" and "base betrayal of truth and honesty" in the Whigs' pretending "to be horror-stricken at slavery" yet "supporting for president a man . . . who has been . . . purchasing slaves nearly all his life" and whose throat-cutting victories in Mexico opened the door to slavery's advance. A writer in the *Cleveland Plain Dealer* protested that "Hell itself" and "every hater of God's humanity" were in Taylor's camp. "Are there no honest men in the Whig ranks to be disgusted by such arrant knavery in politics?" asked the *Albany Argus*. "Let the religious men of the Whig party be guilty of such conduct, and reconcile it to their conscience if they can." Voters would not find the New-England-born Cass suppressing his horror of slavery.[54]

Free soil dominated the campaign, but this was by no means the only matter on which the parties consciously addressed the religious constituency. Once again nativism served as a focus for passionate argument, especially in northern areas with a large mix of Catholics and foreign-born. The circumstances of Whig defeat in 1844 had made the party wary of formally liaising with nativist groups, and the strategy of trying to outbid the nativists in their appeal to anti-Catholic and anti-immigrant sentiment had by 1846 been abandoned as counterproductive by many leading Whigs. Thurlow Weed, William Seward, and Horace Greeley were firmly opposed to merging with nativists or changing the naturalization laws. This climate partly explains why John McLean failed in his bid for the Whig nomination, since his sympathy for nativist restrictions on alien voting, and his "Methodistical cant," rather called up memories of Frelinghuysen's "sectarianism." Winfield Scott's claims were similarly weakened in the spring of 1848 when Greeley exposed him as the author of a pseudonymous nativist tract of 1844. It was true that Taylor himself had received the Native American presidential nomination in September 1847, but he had not solicited it, and retained support amongst anti-nativist Whigs, who sought to woo the foreign-born.[55]

Events in Ireland formed a backdrop to their efforts. Failing potato harvests and famine since 1845 brought social catastrophe and, in the summer of 1848, encouraged a futile and quickly suppressed revolt against British rule by a group that called itself Young Ireland. Greeley and other Whig editors made much of Cass's supposed failure early in 1847 to vote in the Senate in favor of the Irish Relief Bill introduced by the Kentucky Whig John J. Crittenden, and they contrasted his inaction with Henry Clay's efforts for the victims of starvation. In some cases they associated themselves closely with the Appeal to the Friends of Ireland in the United States. They also maintained that Cass had encouraged the robbery of Catholic churches in Mexico during the recent war. The true benefactor of "the honest naturalized citizens" was Zachary Taylor, who had opposed the plundering of Mexican churches, had entered "minutely into the private affairs of the German and Irish soldiers under his command," and had been described by one of the Catholic chaplains to his forces as *truly a great and good man.*"[56]

It was not, however, quite so simple for Whigs to shed their nativist reputation. Democrats reminded the foreign-born and Catholics that in Boston, New York, Philadelphia, St Louis, Baltimore, Richmond, and elsewhere Taylor had received the support of "church-burning partizans." The London *Times* had declared its clear preference for Taylor: how, then, could "any true-hearted Irishman" vote for him? German voters, too, were taught (in their native language) that Old Zach was determined to deprive them of all political rights for twenty-one years. The Catholic *New York Freeman's Journal* lamented that the General had allowed his name to be associated with the Native Americans. As one Irish American explained, it was not Taylor personally that Irish Democrats attacked, but those who supported him: "If St Paul was the candidate for President, and St Patrick headed the electoral ticket, he would not receive the support of the Catholics and naturalized citizens under such an organization."[57]

Despite Van Buren's Democratic pedigree, Cass's supporters fashioned a similar attack on the Free Soilers' nativist posture. If their indictment of the Little Magician (for his lukewarm commitment to the Repeal agitation) carried little conviction, they were on more fruitful ground in trying to link his vice-presidential running mate, Charles Francis Adams, with the hated Alien and Sedition Acts of his grandfather: who could believe the commitment to "Free Speech" of this latter-day Federalist? Ultimately, Democratic propagandists explained, Irish-Americans would best protect their liberties and Catholicism by trusting in Cass, who *had* voted in the Senate for Irish relief measures, who was as thoroughly hated by John Bull as had been Andrew Jackson, who had broad-mindedly attributed the current movement for liberty throughout so much of Europe to the "moral courage" of the new Pope, and whose running mate boasted Irish ancestry. His party was the friend of "civil and religious liberty throughout the world."[58]

Where Whigs had the advantage in appealing to evangelicals was in Taylor's political virginity. Never having voted or held political office, he was even more of an antiparty figure than Harrison had been. Much of the early enthusiasm for a Taylor candidacy, in fact, came from political independents outside Whig and Democratic parties who wanted to see him run as a non-party man; and his determination to sit rather loosely to Whiggery caused him some problems with party regulars both before and after his nomination. In his two letters to Captain J.S. Allison, however, he made enough of his loyalty to Whig principles to calm much of their disquiet, while also making it plain that he "would not be the mere President of a party," but would serve "the whole people." One of the "Rough and Ready Songs" presented Taylor as "The People's Candidate": "The country's tired of party striving,/ Which so retards our Nation's thriving,/ And hence she calls on *Zachary Taylor,*/ Since nothing else can now avail her."[59]

At the core of Taylor's appeal, as it had been with Harrison's, was the simple, uncomplicated republicanism of the "rough and ready" citizen. His plain, Christian integrity would restore *"the government to the REPUBLICAN PLATFORM provided by the fathers of the Republic."* Old Zack was "upon the track": "Get out of the way for Zachariar,/ He's the White House purifier." For the last twenty years Democrats had mounted a sustained attack on the nation's unique and vulnerable polity. As neo-Federalists they had expanded executive power and patronage; as neo-Jacobins they had fanned popular passions and prejudices, most recently encouraging rebellion in Rhode Island. Taylor, as a good Whig, would limit executive power; he could be trusted never to veto congressional legislation "except in cases of clear violation of the Constitution or manifest haste." Democrats' motto was "*power – plunder –* and extended rule." Amongst Whigs, mercifully, there was "a proneness . . . to entertain some old fashioned notions about *right and wrong* – and to be prying into matters to see whether they conform to those notions." With "the blessing of Heaven, upon the truth, the right" Taylor would triumph and proper standards of morality would return to government.[60]

Whigs, then, stressed in this campaign, as they had done in those of 1840 and 1844, their mission as the party which would restore traditional morality and purity to public life. Throughout the decade they addressed evangelical fears, nostalgia, and aspirations by contrasting their own moral probity with their opponents' poisonous amalgam of slack Christianity and Painite infidelity. John McLean wrote as both a disquieted evangelical and an aspiring Whig that to get and keep political power his party had to "reach and voice the moral tone of purity" of the country "and bring it to bear upon the whole action of Government." Whigs elevated the purpose (if not the practices) of the presidential campaign to one of moral cleansing; they turned voting into an act not just of good citizenship but of sound religion. At election time, voters were told, "[t]he truth . . . is within your reach – and the issue is between you and your country – your conscience and your God." And, of course, the *true* Christian's conscience would lead him to vote for Harrison, Clay, and Taylor.[61]

By contrast the Democrats, as the party holding the presidency for most of the two decades before 1848, were in no position to present themselves as the purifiers of government. As defenders of religious and freethinking minorities, and philosophically opposed in many cases to making private religious belief a public issue, they were in a weaker position than the Whigs assertively to sustain evangelical Protestant values. They, of course, trumpeted the private virtues of their candidates when, as with Polk's and Cass's temperance habits, it seemed advantageous to do so. But they were less likely than the Whigs to be comfortable in this area of debate. Much of their time was spent fending off attacks on locofoco "Fanny Wrightism" and "blasphemy," and in denouncing the hypocrisy of the "all the decency" party which, wearing its religion on its sleeve, made claims for its representatives which their private behavior did not justify.

In reality the distinction between Whig and Democrat was much less sharp than the propagandists asserted. John Wentworth, speaking in the House of Representatives in 1844 against the proposal of his fellow Democrat and Illinoisian, John Pettit, to abolish army chaplains, groaned in anticipation of what he knew would be a Whig effort to turn Pettit's views into "infidel principles," and those principles into the philosophy of all Democrats. "[P]erhaps, while I speak, letters are on the wing to operate on distant elections, bearing the wilfully false intelligence that . . . Fanny Wright principles . . . have been openly avowed on the floor of Congress, and from appearances, the whole party is likely to back them." Yet who, Wentworth asked, was Fanny Wright? "I never saw her. I never saw a person who said he had seen her, nor did I ever read a line of her writings or even see a person who said he ever had read them. . . . [E]ven now her spectre haunts the imagination of politicians in want of capital." The fact was, he continued, that there were "Christians in all parties"; many Whigs were devout believers, yet each "belong[ed] to a church that ha[d] democrats for members."[62]

Wentworth's complaint, uttered though it was in a partisan context, was a real one, and his argument had substance. Neither Whigs nor Democrats enjoyed a monopoly of Protestant churchgoers' political loyalties, not even amongst evangelicals. Whigs' rhetoric suggested they wanted to be seen as the Christian party; it undoubtedly indicated a reservoir of sympathy within the party for evangelical goals. And they certainly commanded much support from evangelical men and women. Yet it is clear that, despite the Whigs' best efforts to tar their opponents with a brush of infidelity, large numbers of devout evangelicals persisted in their political affection for Jacksonian Democracy. It is to the variety and sources of these partisan loyalties of evangelical Protestants that we must now turn.

Chapter 4

Patterns of Electoral Response:
Evangelicals and Partisan Allegiance
During the Second Party System

For whom did evangelical church members vote and why did they vote as they did? What ambitions, prejudices, anxieties, and legacies of custom exercised them at the polls? What role did their religious beliefs and ecclesiastical attachments play in shaping their political faiths and perspectives? The questions are simple, but lead immediately into a thicket of historiography and a continuing debate over the sources of partisan loyalty during the second party system.

In essence that debate is between those who consider party political differences to have been rooted principally in ethnic, religious, and broader cultural antagonisms, and those who propound an essentially economic interpretation of political behavior. "Ethnoculturalists" draw their particular inspiration from Lee Benson's study of Jacksonian New York, which located the origins of the second party system (and its demise in the 1850s) in the conflict of religious and ethnic groups. A number of local and state studies of other northern and western areas have sought to confirm the view that party differences had much less to do with wealth, occupation, or class than with a complex pattern of cultural antagonisms that not only ranged Protestant against Catholic, native against immigrant, but produced internal divisions within those four categories.[1] This ethnocultural, or ethnoreligious, perspective has by common consent enriched our understanding of nineteenth-century political history. But it fails to satisfy those who contrast the national scope of the second party system with the more limited incidence of ethnocultural politics, which was most evident in areas of ethnic diversity experiencing large-scale immigration. For these historians – some of them, significantly, historians of the South, a section relatively homogeneous in religious outlook and ethnic composition – the party

97

alignments of the second quarter of the nineteenth century were essentially based on conflicting responses to rapid and qualitative economic change, which affected the whole nation. In the main they see political conflict growing rather less out of class antagonism than out of disagreements over whether, and how enthusiastically, communities should embrace the opportunities for economic development offered by the revolution in transportation and the broadening of the national market economy. On this interpretation political conflict over banking or government-sponsored development of canals and harbors, for instance, was far more than disagreement over cultural symbols; it tackled the fundamental question of what kind of republic the country should become. Ethnic and religious conflict, according to this view, should be seen as secondary, a channel through which more basic economic disagreement was expressed.[2]

The methods and assumptions of ethnocultural historians have also raised doubts.[3] Given the absence of substantial and systematic evidence relating to individual voting, they have been driven to looking for correlations between a community's voting habits and its demographic profile.[4] But positive correlations, even when they exist, do not in themselves prove a causal connection. Moreover, the means of establishing the religious contours of a community are flawed; historians have measured relative church strength principally by reference to census listing of churches' seating capacity, or "accommodations", rather than to the more precise (but less accessible, and by no means wholly reliable) denominational membership returns. Further, membership rolls give little idea of the differing levels of commitment and piety within the church body; but if religion was a primary determinant of voting then the degree of intensity of a person's faith would surely have been electorally significant. Put another way: the ethnoculturalists' dependence on aggregate data forces them to make inferences about the relationship between religion and voting which may be correct, but which are not proven.

The subject can be profitably approached from another perspective: that of the devout churchgoer himself and of those who ministered to him. Evangelicals spoke and wrote, privately and publicly, about their political hopes and attachments. Their letters, diaries, memoirs, and autobiographies constitute a huge corpus of material which, though scattered, unsystematic, and often anecdotal and impressionistic, provides a much more persuasive and reliable explanation of individual motivation than do aggregated data. Of course, evangelicals' tongues did not wag in harmony and their pens tell a variety of stories. Nor can evidence relating to the restricted community of committed evangelicals reveal whether the electorate in the nation as whole was moved principally by religiocultural or socioeconomic concerns. But the writings of politically involved evangelicals encourage a number of important conclusions. Many churchgoers did indeed see politics refracted through a religious lens, even though ethnicity, status, and class were often constituent elements of the churchmanship that informed their voting. At the conscious level evangelicals moved towards a given partisanship for a variety of reasons, which could include supporting a party's stand on particular moral issues or its broader posture, voting with or against members of a sympathetic or hostile religious group, sustaining the political loyalties of their fathers, and endorsing a particular candidate for his personal qualities. Patterns of evangelical voting do suggest some congruence between church membership and theological perspective on one side, and party choice on the other; but these varied considerably according to demographic, denominational, and other contexts, were not wholly consistent even within local churches, and suggest that many evangelicals felt only a loose attachment to party. Loyalties shifted during the course of the second party system, but those changes did not extend to achieving what some at least desired, the creation of a Christian party in politics.

Evangelical motives behind party choice

The sheer complexity of political motivation cautions against viewing religion as the only, or even the primary, influence on the voting behavior of evangelicals, even in the case of those who determinedly organized their lives on the basis of their Protestant piety. We should remember that the churches to which such committed evangelicals belonged provided them with not only a religious perspective on political life. They additionally offered an institutional and social context for cementing those secular ties of ethnicity, status, and class which also helped shape political belief and action.[5] As evangelicals pursued their political goals and responded to party postures and candidates, a blend of secular and religious considerations operated, in ratios that varied from case to case.

Religious concern was most unequivocally evident when churchgoers sought to secure laws that would defend religious observance against public abuse, and especially protect open-air worship and Sabbath observance. When the Democrats in the Ohio Senate worked to block a bill designed to prevent the disruption of camp meetings, Charles Elliott and other leading Methodists left their members in no doubt that the obstructionists should pay the political price; Illinois Methodists took a similar stand.[6] Worries over Sunday travel and the movement of federal mails were even more likely to encourage partisanship. The sabbatarianism of north-eastern Presbyterians, Congregationalists, and other radical revivalists in the later 1820s had helped define the political divisions of the emergent second party system: those who wanted to stop Sabbath mails were often Antimasons and certainly hostile to the Jacksonian administration once Richard M. Johnson's report, rejecting their petitions, had been adopted. Whigs inherited much of the Antimasons' sabbatarian support, not least owing to Theodore Frelinghuysen's championing of the cause in Washington. The anti-Jacksonian sentiments of so many evangelicals on this issue in the 1830s and 1840s were particularly evident in their sermon literature. Their mildly Whiggish public statements often obscured more earnest private attachment. John Wheelwright and Harmon Kingsbury told William H. Harrison in 1840 that he had "the support of a large portion of the people who regard the oracles of God as of paramount obligation" and who looked to him as the Lord's "instrument . . . for the removal of this great national sin from our beloved country" by repealing the obnoxious sections of the Post Office Law of 1825 and by appointing a man of sound evangelical views, perhaps John McLean, to the position of postmaster-general.[7]

The call for a political defense of the Sabbath sharpened partisanship, but did so by dividing the evangelical world, not by uniting it behind the anti-Jacksonians. Not only freethinkers paled at the prospect of a revival of Puritan blue laws. Those churches that had suffered historically at the hands of a religious establishment were disposed to see the Sabbath mails campaign as just one thrust of a developing momentum towards a new evangelical – principally Presbyterian and Congregationalist – domination. A state-supported Sabbath was the "opening-wedge" that would "cleave asunder" America's delicate structure of civil liberty and replace it with religious tests and ecclesiastical despotism. Significantly, the presenter of the Senate Report of 1829 was the son of active Kentucky Baptists and had many Baptist friends, one of the closest of whom, the Reverend Obadiah B. Brown, was a staunch Jacksonian and the Report's actual author. Baptists were foremost, though far from alone, in resisting this supposed "church and state" movement. Their worst suspicions receded with time, and during the 1830s and 1840s yielded to quite different concerns. But even so the conviction that the Democratic party was the best guarantor of religious freedom kept many evangelicals clinging to her skirts, as the examples of the Jacksonians Thomas Morris and George Bethune, who was convinced that "religion is not to be advanced by civil power," clearly indicate.[8]

Matters of social policy which affected the country's religious or moral well-being, especially public education and the control of alcohol, also bore on evangelicals' choice of party. State provision of free schools did not necessarily divide Whigs and Democrats: the Ohio School Law of 1838, for instance, was not a partisan measure. Thus evangelicals who wished to promote the spread of common schools were to be found in both parties. But, as Daniel Howe perceptively remarks, the parties' positions were not identical. Whigs supported free public education as a means of securing the literate and disciplined population that the new social order needed, whereas the less forceful commitment of the Democrats (with their anti-intellectual, low-taxation tendencies, especially in the South) rather grew out of their attachment to equal opportunity. There is evidence that when evangelicals were particularly exercised about what Nathan Beman regarded as "popular ignorance" and the need for the moral improvement of the poor, they tended to favor Whiggery. Samuel Lewis, a Methodist local preacher and firm believer in Whiggish, active government, regarded universal common school education as one means of combatting the tendencies towards mob rule in Jacksonian America. Calvin H. Wiley, Whig superintendent of common schools in North Carolina and a Presbyterian fearful of class conflict, believed common schools would make Americans "homogeneous ... intelligent, eminently republican, sober, calculating, moral and conservative." Other reformers in the field – Atticus G. Haygood in Georgia, Colin Dew James in Illinois, David R. McAnally in Tennessee, Robert J. Breckinridge in Kentucky, Benjamin Mosby Smith in Virginia, James Henley Thornwell in South Carolina, and Horace Eaton in Vermont – looked to Whiggery for the more dependable support. When James Harlan ran for the post of superintendent of public instruction in Iowa in 1847 it was on the Whig ticket, and it was as a Whig that Lewis himself served as Ohio's first superintendent of common schools.[9]

The politicizing of the temperance crusade caused sharper divisions within evangelicalism. To some extent these followed the fault lines exposed by the contemporaneous campaign for teetotalism. Most churchgoers came to accept the evils of hard drinking, but there was considerable suspicion of the "ultra" position of total abstinence from all alcohol in all circumstances. In part that division was geographically based. The strongest support for strict temperance pledges was in the Northeast; according to John Marsh 1,900, or over 80 percent, of the clergy in New York state were total abstainers by 1839. In the South, however, where drinking was deeply rooted in the culture, conservative Old School Presbyterians and "hard-shell," Antimission Baptists stiffened the resistance of evangelicals to the encroachments of temperance radicals. At the Methodist General Conference in the summer of 1840 Lovick Pierce, William A. Smith and others, afraid that what they conceded to teetotalers one day would be demanded by abolitionists the next, fought successfully to prevent those they called "ultraists" (in practice the overwhelming majority of northern and western ministers, and a substantial minority in the South) from reviving the strict Wesleyan rule prohibiting the drinking and sale of liquor. But in the North, too, there was conflict over the issue, especially over the propriety of using unfermented wine at communion.[10]

Through the 1830s teetotalers called more and more insistently for the withdrawal of liquor-selling licenses and legal prohibition of the sale of drink. A conviction that moral suasion alone could not work in the face of legally protected and economically entrenched liquor interests took root in all parts of the country. But sobriety, piety, and benevolence enforced on a citizenry by law was too much for many evangelicals to swallow. Once again, as with sabbatarianism, the concept revived fears of clerical dictation amongst churchgoers who recalled discrimination at the hands of a religious establishment. The mere hint of political support for the cause in New York state in 1829 had provoked cries of "Priestcraft! Church and State!" and similar fears persisted in Massachusetts amongst Baptists and Methodists suspicious of Congregational sponsorship of prohibition measures.[11]

These evangelical divisions, sometimes reinforced by those over teetotalism, seem to have followed partisan lines more often than not. The firmest advocates of political teetotalism, men like Edmund Broadus in Virginia, William Salter in Iowa, and George Duffield in Michigan, found their natural political home in Whiggery, despite some occasional ambiguity in its position on legal enforcement of moral behavior and despite, as we have seen, evangelical criticisms of its hard-cider campaign in 1840. Democrats had their temperance men, too: Peter Cartwright pushed for restrictions on saloons; as governor of Ohio (and later of Iowa) Robert Lucas sponsored laws to regulate the liquor traffic. But the party's stand on drink was often seen as merely tactical by the sternest reformers. Its more typical Protestant supporters included not only rural anti-mission, anti-reforming elements but representatives of more sophisticated churches who had not yielded to the stricter forms of abstinence. George Bethune castigated "ardent spirits" but remained as partial to wine as to Jacksonian Democracy. William Anderson Scott, southern Presbyterian, Democrat and "no teetotaler or blue-stocking Puritan," relished strong coffee, cigars, wine "and sometimes imbibed a stronger drink." But reason as well as thirst drew these evangelicals towards a party that doubted the wisdom of legislation in matters of private morality. William G. Baker, a pious young lawyer of Maryland and a strong supporter of temperance and other moral reforms, adamantly refused to forsake his Democratic loyalties to stand as a temperance candidate. Baker feared that hypocrites and adventurers would exploit the "fever of excitement" that attended moral crusades in politics, and that the "shortsightedness and fallibility" of human legislation would invite reaction and resistance. Instead he looked to "the superiority of Divine legislation, so omnipotent in its simplicity of design and operation – that of making each man a law unto himself, by writing His law upon the heart, the mind, and the conscience."[12]

The Hopkinsian theology of disinterested benevolence that guided the thinking of temperance activists equally encouraged many, largely northern, evangelicals to take a stand on two further public issues of the era: Indian removal and the future of slavery. Here again matters which held for churchgoers a religious and humanitarian significance helped determine their choice of party. The Indian question, especially the removal of the Cherokee nation from Georgia, was a major element in the political polarization of the 1830s. Jackson's and Van Buren's policies were bitterly criticized for breaking with the "Christian" approach of earlier administrations. The expropriation of land, forced Indian migration, and bloodshed widely shocked an evangelical constituency that considered existing treaties inviolable and believed in the positive protection of "the red man of the forest." The loudest denunciations emanated from the New England pulpit, supported by those in the Northwest, like Alfred Brunson and William Crane, whose sympathetic concern for the Indian was a clear element in their Whiggery. There were many, of course, who welcomed the Jacksonians' delivery of whites "from the scalping-knife and torture of wily and ferocious savages," and who believed that the settling of Indians in western colonies was a more realistic solution than assimilation; by no means all of these were southerners, though most were. Southern evangelicals seem generally to have considered the issue to be outside the jurisdiction of the churches and many vehemently attacked the northern pulpit for its interference. Yet even in the South there were those like William Winans, whose anxiety about the plight of Creeks, Choctaws, and Cherokees and despair over Jackson's "crooked and disgraceful policy" cemented his attachment to the Whig party.[13]

The place of slavery in evangelicals' political thought and action will receive a fuller treatment in the next chapter. But already in the 1840s, the stands of the two major parties helped determine the political allegiance of the growing number of evangelicals for whom the issue was of paramount importance. Although in the South the differences between the two parties on the issue often lacked substance, with the result that evangelicals with a determined commitment to sustaining the peculiar institution could feel comfortable in either, the situation in the free states was clearer cut.[14] Here abolitionist and anti-extensionist church members tended, for most of the life of the second party system, to look to Whiggery as the best hope for achieving antislavery ends. The pattern is particularly evident in the national campaigns of the 1840s.

It was not that antislavery evangelicals suffered any serious delusions about Whigs' commitment to the cause; rather they saw the party as the only viable alternative to the dangerous, proslavery Democracy of Van

Buren. In 1840 John Rankin, Samuel Lewis, and others judged that Harrison would do less harm as president than his opponent, and to vote for the abolitionist third party would only reduce Old Tip's chances. Third-party men railed against a "dastardly Whig plot," but antislavery evangelical voters generally remained loyal to Harrison.[15] Much the same line of argument won the day in 1844, when anti-annexationists saw a vote for Clay, with all his faults, as the best security against Polk's avowed expansionism. Calvin Fletcher believed Texas the only serious issue and "suffered himself to become a little violent" for Whiggery, despite his qualms; in New England Nathaniel W. Taylor asked rhetorically, "If two devils are candidates for office, and the election of one [or other] is inevitable, is it not one's duty to vote for the least, in order to secure the greater good?" Four bitter years later, after the trauma of war with Mexico, the same antislavery constituency proved markedly more responsive to the appeal of a third party, but numbers still held firm to Whiggery. James W. Alexander looked to Taylor's election as a vote for peace; George R. Crooks was clear that in "the present tug and strain of the war [against slavery], I shall hate, with all my objections to Taylor, to throw away my vote" on the Free Soil candidate; William Salter and others in Iowa hostile to slavery rejoiced at the Whig victory. There were of course many northern evangelicals of a Democratic bent who did not regard slavery as inherently sinful and who found no difficulty in sustaining that allegiance. But through the decade, as the Michigan antislavery editor Theodore Foster explained, the salience of the issue and the limited political options available ensured that "tens of thousands of *religious* men" would continue to vote with the Whigs.[16]

Sabbatarianism, education, temperance, and policy towards Indians and slaves all manifestly touched on the religious sensibilities of evangelicals, but what of the economic issues around which so much public political debate revolved during the second party system? Did the community of the pious develop any clear perspectives on banking, currency, and other economic policies, did their religion contribute at all to the shaping of their attitudes, and how far did their views influence their choice of party? Concentration on soul-saving, revivals, and growth in piety undoubtedly bred a certain otherworldliness in some evangelical leaders, and even amongst those who did take an interest in the things of this world there were many who found economic questions impenetrable, secondary, and even peripheral. Edward R. Ames, visiting Congress in 1841, was largely bewildered by the discussions relating to bank, tariff, and distribution; at the same time a Methodist editor refrained from commenting on the expediency of a national bank "because we are not competent and, happily, not called on to decide." Many shared Davis Clark's view that the so-called "immutable principles" associated with these issues were "in many instances but little more than the watch-words of party." Even those who did take a firm stand on economic questions might give greater electoral priority to more directly religious matters: William Brownlow saw the bank question as the critical issue in 1844, but in the following year fought Andrew Johnson for a congressional seat over the defense of evangelical orthodoxy against Catholics and infidels. The secondary significance of economic policy in evangelical thought was particularly evident during the depression of the late 1830s and early 1840s, when ministers commonly identified the acute distress as more a judgment of heaven on the moral shortcomings of Americans than as the result of deficiencies in economic strategy. Lyman H. Atwater regarded economic suffering as a punishment for spiritual decline; Jonathan Brown for the persistent violation of the Sabbath. "Prosperity is God's gift," Charles Elliott explained, "adversity is his correction."[17]

Most evangelical churchgoers, however, men and women with livelihoods to protect and families to feed, were much too directly vulnerable to changes in the economic climate to yield up all interest in these matters. The merchants, manufacturers, bankers, and professionals who largely made up the lay leadership of the churches, together with the aspiring artisans, tradesmen, and farmers who supplied the bulk of the membership, were not without their convictions about the nature and extent of government action and its direct bearing on the country's prosperity. Their views, of course, could have been generated by their economic circumstances alone, independent of religious context: Methodist merchants in Ohio who pressed for the construction of a canal, or Presbyterian manufacturers in Philadelphia who sought a protective tariff, or Baptist farmers in Kentucky who loathed the Bank of the United States, might have done so as merchants, manufacturers, and farmers with specific needs shaped by their immediate economic context, and not as members of particular churches. In practice, however, it is clear that their economic attitudes were not freestanding: they were sustained by a moral vision whose sharp focus derived from religious belief.

This can be seen most clearly in the conflict over banking and currency. Robert Kelley and others have plausibly argued that the radical Democratic platform calling for sound money, immediately convertible to gold, offered more than a technical proposal for controlling wild price fluctuations; it represented the common man's moral protest against the dark forces of speculators and other grasping capitalists operating through the Bank of the United States.[18] Many of Jackson's early western supporters seem to have been unsophisticated, egalitarian Methodists and Baptists hostile to the Bank for its supposed encouragement to "extravagant speculations"; related attitudes appear to have moved rural sects like the New Hampshire followers of Jacob Osgood to rally to a party which, they said, "gives to all an equal share." But the conviction that the Bank was a "dangerous power" in the hands of a corrupt few, that the removal of the federal deposits was a statesmanlike act and that the later wreck of the bank was not chargeable to Jackson himself, was held well beyond these circles and well after Old Hickory's death. George Fort, a staunch Methodist of a pious New Jersey family and a Democrat whose political drive emanated from an unrelenting antagonism to "special privileges and monopolies," interpreted his election as state governor in 1850 as a triumph for those principles; in office he tried to equalize taxation, vetoed various bank bills and took a firm, hard-money line on the matter of banknote redemption, hoping to hasten the day when the country would enjoy a currency based on specie alone.[19]

Theological outlook and Jacksonian attitudes to banks show no clear congruence. Anti-bank energies emanated from churches holding disparate theological perspectives, from Arminian Methodists to Arminianized Calvinists of the New School to strict Old School Calvinists. There may, however, have been some correlation between critics of Whiggish banking arrangements and evangelicals who saw themselves as social outsiders. Here the case of James B. Walker, New School Presbyterian and Congregationalist of the Western Reserve, is instructive: though he shared the antislavery opinions of his Whig co-religionists, his Scottish Covenanter and Pennsylvania origins set him apart and may explain his earnest support for the Democrats in their early years, when they were "opposed to monopolies – to class legislation, and class education . . . to the money power and the lobby power in legislation." However, the only safe generalization is that Jacksonian banking precepts had their defenders within all major denominations, that these evangelicals brought an additional urgency to the cause, and that they lent credibility to the Democrats' image as (in Walker's perception) "the party of morals and progress."[20]

Whig cosmology also linked moral and material progress, but in a different way. Drawing succor from the optimistic millennialism of the Second Great Awakening, it stressed not class conflict but the socially transforming power of wealth for an essentially organic society. When Lucien Berry, president of Indiana Asbury University and staunch Whig, spoke of humankind's facing a "boundless future and illimitable fields" and of America's "destiny . . . to be the great leader and abettor of social progress throughout the world" his confidence derived from the wealth-creating potential of his country's commerce. Wealth (properly exploited and never "abused") was a social and moral good; so, consequently, were all government policies that encouraged the development of the commerce by which that good would be promoted. It is in this context that evangelical support for "sound banking" has to be gauged.[21]

It would be facile to ignore the elements of material self-interest that generated that commitment. Charles Hodge, for example, feared the "revolution of property" that would result when Van Buren's administration withdrew bank charters and threatened dividends; the banking interests of Calvin Fletcher, Gurdon Trumbull, and others clearly pushed them towards Whiggery; the livelihood of the editors and owners of religious presses depended on banking and currency policies that would prevent any deterioration in the quality of money; Abraham Hagaman of Jackson, Louisiana, a Presbyterian minister and stockholder in railroads and banks, watched aghast through the later 1830s as others faced ruin, the consequence, as he saw it, of Democratic "political quacks tampering with their country's currency"; the silk-producing interests of the Virginia Presbyterian minister, Robert Hall Morrison, made him all the more anxious to see a Whig victory in 1840 that would overturn Van Buren's "mad & astounding" policies. But it would be equally facile to deny the moral concern that infused Whig evangelicals' faith in a national bank and a stable currency. Many saw the controlled expansion of credit as an essential protection against the speculative fever that grew out of unregulated banking: it was not only Democrats who lamented the corrosion of "honest industry" and thrift. Whiggish sermons during the years of greatest depression regularly denounced the growth of a "gambling" spirit, and many privately criticized Jacksonian actions for paving the way to panic and collapse. "Any action producing financial distress in time of peace, equal to that experienced in time of war must be wrong, and no political logic under heaven can justify it in the court of sound morality," concluded the Protestant Methodist George Brown as Pittsburgh and Alleghany factory hands were thrown out of work in 1837. William Crane and Alfred Brunson took a similarly jaundiced view of Jackson's specie circular and wildcat banking. None, however, quite matched Lorenzo Dow's earlier dramatic protest against the injury done to the Bank of the United States; rising from his deathbed, the eccentric revivalist made his way to the White House to remonstrate with his old acquaintance and, leaning feebly on his staff and refusing Jackson's hospitality, "like the prophet Elijah before Ahab . . . reproved him, in the name of the Lord, for the injury he had done to his country."[22]

Probably the most concerted evangelical attack on the perceived immorality as well as the incompetence of Jacksonian policy followed the Panic of 1837 when several Democratic legislatures repudiated their states' public debts. This was quite simply "public swindling," a reneging on "the just and righteous obligations of public contracts," prompted by "an avarice and selfishness which stop at no bounds marked out by heaven or earth." Across the Union, and in all denominations, evangelicals fretted at the "horrid disgrace," ashamed at the stain on the

American character caused by this particular swell in "the dark tide of *Locofocoism.*" "Oh how it grieves me to say it, but I feel it a disgrace to be an American Citizen," protested William Winans in the face of Mississippi's failure to repay state bonds (a policy supported in some high ministerial circles), while Moses Stuart concluded that without some act of public redemption "we shall surely become a hissing and a by-word among all nations." A lower order of outrage marked evangelicals' criticisms of Democrats who opposed protective tariffs and internal improvements, though here too questions of policy could take on a moral dimension. When Stephen Colwell advocated protection for domestic industry his concern was generated as much by the theory of benevolent action for one's fellow man (a doctrine especially dear to New School Calvinists) as by current economic theory. Samuel Lewis called as earnestly for state funding to develop canals and other elements of an economic infrastructure as he did for state provision of education; all were means of humanitarian and moral progress.[23]

So by their own admission, evangelicals in many cases allowed matters of policy to influence their choice of party. More important, however, were parties' broader political postures and controlling attitudes. Especially significant for the devout Christian was the credibility of each party's claim to be the nation's best hope for moral progress and social order. It was in the light of this that many evangelicals chose their party. To take an example, William Crane was a devoted free-trader, convinced that protectionism could not be squared with "Christian benevolence and universal brotherhood"; an internationalist, he "felt no sympathy with starving foreign operatives to enrich our American manufacturers." On this logic he should have been a Jacksonian. Yet through the 1830s he occasionally voted Whig, despite "their cardinal doctrine" of protective tariff, for he believed the party offered the country a more secure morality than their free-trade opponents. Democrats were flawed, for "they despised no man for his sins." They embraced "most of the moral dregs, and scurf, and pollution of the land. Atheists, blasphemers, Sabbath-breakers, drunkards and brothel-haunters flocked to this party, because here in all political circles, and political movements they were treated as nobility."[24]

What worried Crane and many other evangelicals was the houseroom that the Democratic party offered freethinkers and secularists. Whatever the justification in theory for political tolerance towards those who dissented from orthodox religious belief, numbers of devout Protestants of all camps froze at the mention of the names of Fanny Wright, Abner Kneeland, Robert Dale Owen, and other latter-day Painites. Jacksonians' welcoming of dissenting religious and freethinking groups into the fold on equal terms undoubtedly tainted the party in the eyes of the informal

Protestant establishment, which was shocked that "clergymen could walk arm in arm with the most debauched men." It gave rise to a widely held view that "the moral & religious part" of the community would, and did, find a more natural and sustaining habitat within Whiggery. Significantly Crane had earlier been sympathetic to Antimasonry, which had played potently on fears of a spreading conspiracy of paganism, rationalism, and degraded theology, and many others like him seem to have responded positively to the Whigs' posing as guardians of religious orthodoxy.[25]

Closely related was the churchgoer's perception, commonly held, that it was "the ascendancy of Locofocoism" that had sent "moral pestilence ... abroad through the community." The dominance of the Democrats in national politics for so much of the second party system (together with their strength in those areas, especially the eastern cities, where socially concerned evangelicals had most to do) meant that they were much more likely to be blamed for "wicked mismanagement" and for the catalogue of national sins and corruption that formed the target of evangelical jeremiads in the 1830s and 1840s. Posing as the "outs," Whigs could more plausibly be taken as the party of social activism, moral cleansing, and political regeneration. Gabriel Crane, eccentric and visionary, wrote excitedly to Harrison during the 1840 campaign to report a divine revelation that God's purpose was "to restore the Government entire to the Whig party." Many evangelicals approved of Whiggery's antiparty posture and its attack on manipulative, corrupt politicians. It was helped by its antecedents in Antimasonry, which had convinced thousands of revivalistic Protestants that a tainted republic could be purified and re-Christianized by political action.[26]

When critics sarcastically described the Whigs as the "all the decency" party, their sneers captured not just Whiggery's posture as the guardian of morality but its purporting to beckon to "intelligence," "respectability," and "character." William Brownlow characterized Democrats' principles as tending "to array the poor against the rich – the ignorant against the intelligent – the wicked against the pious – the vulgar against the decent – the worthless against the worthy – and thieves against honest men." This is not to say that Whiggery appealed only, or indeed with complete success, to the rich and the well-to-do (though it seems that in many areas the more prosperous and the "better sort" tended that way), but rather that it presented itself as the natural haven for the hard-working, self-improving, sober, and thrifty of all classes. Philip Hone believed that nine out of ten of New York City's "respectable citizens" were Whig: "the merchants, the professional men, the mechanics and working men, all such as live by their skill and the labor of their honest hands, who have wives whom they cherish and children whom they strive to educate and make good citizens, men who go to church on

Sundays, respect the laws and love their country." It seems that especially in the expanding communities of the Northeast and the advancing Yankee belt of settlement, in particular among New School churches, such people did indeed respond to that appeal, with rather more enthusiasm than they appear to have done a few years earlier to Antimasonry.[27]

But Whig evangelical "improvers" proliferated well beyond Yankeedom. In the southern Appalachian highlands, to take possibly the most striking example, they proved particularly vocal and industrious. The *New York Observer* might have regarded the area's inhabitants as *"backwoodsmen . . . entirely shut out from the world,"* but many evangelical leaders there, especially Methodists and New School Presbyterians, regarded the mountain region as "the garden spot of the Union, and the El Dorado of America," which needed only capital investment and internal improvements to realize its enormous economic potential. David Rice McAnally, Samuel Patton, and William Brownlow were all clerical Whig boosters who believed that religious, social, and economic improvement were inextricably intertwined. As one of their circle put it, "The interests of Education, Agriculture, and Commerce, are more nearly allied to the prosperity of Christ's Kingdom than most men, perhaps, are willing to admit."[28] McAnally established his *Highland Messenger* in Asheville, North Carolina, to propagate Whig economic and moral doctrine, promote the railroads and credit facilities essential to the growth of this strategically well-placed mountain town, and secure a well-behaved Christian population through temperance societies and publicly funded education.[29] Brownlow threw his support behind similar causes in eastern Tennessee and outlined his philosophy for improving Jonesborough in his own inimitable Methodist-Whig prospectus: "We want less *idleness* and more *industry*; . . . less *extravagance* and more *economy*; . . . more *honest* men and fewer *rogues*; . . . more *capital* and less *credit*; . . . more *shirts* and fewer *ruffles*; . . . more *Christian morality*, and fewer *grog shops*; . . . more *laboring men* and fewer *loafers*; . . . more *mechanics* and fewer *dandies*; . . . less *ignorance* and more *education*; . . . less *aristocracy* and more *democracy*."[30]

For enterprising evangelicals Whiggery offered not just a progressive economic stance but a conservative approach to social order. The anti-abolitionist, anti-Catholic, and anti-bank mobs of Jacksonian America, together with the crisis over nullification and other seismic shocks to the status quo, horrified those who believed that legal order and public discipline were "the Palladium of our liberty" and the basis of American republicanism. Many thought the contempt for authority sprang from the Jacksonians' disrespect for law at the highest level. More fundamentally they blamed what they considered to be contemporary America's perversion of the principle of equality. "The child is equal with his parents; the student with his teachers. And any deference to them, as implying they have authority to govern, is the concession, not of duty, but of courtesy," a Maine pastor reflected with some bitterness. "This principle of equality, possessing an omnipotence it never before dreamed of, sweeps over the face of society, and all its distinctions are levelled." Gardiner Spring, too, lamented that "[t]he bonds of authority hang loosely around the rising generation," and that Americans' celebrated love of liberty had degenerated into a spirit of insubordination and aversion to all legal restraint. He was writing in the aftermath of the Dorr Rebellion of 1842 in Rhode Island, where a movement for constitutional reform had culminated in the setting up of a rival government and its crushing by the authorities. From many an evangelical pulpit, both outside and within that state, ministers denounced the insurrection, spoke of the inviolability of the social compact, and invoked the apostolic command to submit to the powers that be. Social conflict of this kind represented a loss not just of public discipline but of that personal self-control that religion aimed to foster. It also challenged the evangelical's conviction that society's natural condition was harmonious, that citizens had "one common interest, and are traveling to one common home" and that politics should be based on the "mediatorial principles" of the Christian Gospels.[31]

Whig precepts spoke to this cast of mind. They were built on a residue of Federalism, with its mistrust of people in the mass, its attachment to elite rule and deferential politics, and its perception of evangelical religion as a means of regulating social behavior, and comprehended an organic society whose members' real interests did not conflict but harmonized. Evangelicals like Charles Hodge, Mark Tucker, and Francis Wayland, who feared "the ascendancy of the rabble," "the filth and offscouring of all things," and who desired to sustain the social primacy of "the mass of intelligence and property of the country," found their natural refuge in Whiggery. These attitudes clearly lay behind George Coles's political outlook. "When I first came to this country some called me a 'tory'," he explained to a friend in England. "Now, in politics at least, I am neither hot nor cold; not a proud aristocrat, nor a fierce democrat, and so they call me 'Whig'."[32]

The Democrats' broad posture was designed to attract a different breed of evangelical, one for whom the state's only proper role was to protect men and women from religious tyranny. The party's *laissez-faire* philosophy and distrust of government activism appealed strongly to those afraid that Whigs were reincarnated "church and state" Antimasons ambitious to advance the Yankee benevolent empire by statute.[33] Its anti-commercial stance also won sympathy from many of the same constituency: lower-class rural folk, particularly but not exclusively in the rural South, and often of a strict Calvinist persuasion, who deeply resented the imperialism of the Yankee missionaries, their schemes for temperance, Sunday Schools and other reforms, and the commercial system that sustained them.[34] The party's rhetoric of egalitarianism also secured it the support of those evangelicals alienated by what they considered to be Whiggery's "aristocratic," elitist outlook. George Fort was lured by Democrats' "great principles of equality"; James B. Walker considered them "a party from the people and for the people." George Bethune's loyalties can be similarly explained. He shared many of the perspectives commonly associated with Whiggery, including disquiet over mob violence and class antagonism, and concern for social brotherhood and "active benevolence"; but his self-perception as "a Christian and a democrat . . . a man who acknowledges his fellow-man as his equal, and is willing to give to every man the rights which God has given him" held him in a Jacksonian party that stuck to a single purpose, "the permanent good of the whole, unchecked by particular privileges, and unfettered by artificial restrictions."[35]

Desire for specific action by the state or for the political triumph of a party's broad, philosophical posture were by no means the only determinants of evangelical Protestant voting. The work of Benson and other "ethnocultural" historians has provided a clear indication that animosities both between evangelical and non-evangelical groups, and between the constituent elements of evangelicalism, profoundly affected party choice, particularly but not exclusively in the northern states.[36] In the earlier phase of the second party system especially, strict Calvinists' fears of Unitarianism, and its theological liberalism, elitism, moral paternalism, and sympathy for political action, placed many of them by reaction in the Jacksonian camp. When Ezra Stiles Ely called on evangelicals to rally around the theologically sound Jackson in 1828, he and his Old School Presbyterian sympathizers were moved by fears that Adams was tainted with the corrupt Boston creed.[37] The presence of Universalism, too, may have helped define voting allegiances, for the holders of this liberal heterodoxy were largely Democratic in sympathy and where they were strong on the ground the evangelically orthodox appear to have taken an opposite political stance.[38] But the most obvious evangelical animus against non-evangelicals, one which deeply and increasingly influenced political choice, was anti-Catholicism.

As has been noted, most Catholics, and almost all of the recent immigrant arrivals of that church, were strong in the Democratic faith. Only in a few exceptional cases were they Whigs. "That a very large portion of the members of the Catholic church are [Jacksonian] democrats" was a cause of embarrassment to some Catholic spokesmen; it was a matter of constitutional and moral outrage to their Protestant counterparts. "What other denomination called christian, ever go to the polls in a body?" asked Nathan Beman, terrified by the "fearful and desolating" action of "this ecclesiastico-political machine." Such perceptions controlled the voting habits of thousands of Protestants in New York, Boston, Philadelphia, Cincinnati, and other major centers of Catholic settlement. Even well beyond the immediate locus of Catholic influence, once men like William Brownlow had concluded that there existed "an unholy alliance between the leading Romanists and locofocos of this country" the whole pattern of their partisan career was set. George Marsden, writing of his childhood in thinly settled Wisconsin in the 1830s, recalled Catholics and Democrats as evil agents in evangelical Protestant demonology; his mother, a devout Congregationalist, lowered her voice to mention them.[39]

If "anti-voting" was so influential and anti-Catholicism so pervasive, why then did large numbers of evangelicals remain loyal to the Democrats? In fact that loyalty was significantly eroded through these years, but the question is nonetheless pertinent and points to the existence of antipathies within evangelicalism which more than outweighed the fear of Romanists. Some of the most potent of these tensions grew out of the historic conflict between those denominations which had enjoyed the benefits of legal establishment and those which had fought discrimination and prejudice in their struggle for equality before the law. Baptists engaged in fighting the Anglican establishment in the South, and the Congregationalist Standing Order in New England, were warmly sympathetic to the Democratic-Republican party, in view of Jefferson's and Madison's commitment to religious freedom and the clear identification of the Calvinist establishment with the Federalists. Their continuing antipathy to higher-status evangelical churches helped keep many Baptists out of Whiggery, the party of "church and state," through the 1830s. The Sabbath mails issue in particular picked unhealthily at all the old sores.[40]

The same story was as vividly clear and even more bitter in the case of Methodists, since here the relations between churches were additionally poisoned by the doctrinal challenge that Arminianism presented to Calvinist orthodoxy. In New England Methodists were obliged to pay taxes to support the Standing Order; poor ministers incurred heavy fines for performing marriage ceremonies for their own members; hostile mobs destroyed meeting houses, intimidated worshipers, and attacked itinerant preachers, whom they regarded as "incarnate demons" and "intruders into the land of steady habits." Even in areas where the early Methodists suffered no legal disabilities they experienced discrimination at the hands of socially entrenched Calvinists, as in the Western Reserve of Ohio, where the informal establishment of "Presbygationalists" worked to deny them access to preaching places. In self-defense they generally shunned Federalism, became, as William Winans described himself, "rather enthusiastic" Jeffersonians and even, like the ministers Jeremiah Stocking of Connecticut and Dan Young of New Hampshire, sought office as Republicans to fight for full and equal rights for their church. These same elements of Calvinist arrogance and bigotry, or the enduring memory of them, lured many Methodists into the ranks of Jacksonian Democracy, especially in its early years; it seemed to offer a home to those members of the denomination who continued instinctively to define themselves in politics as anti-Federalist, and who feared that John Quincy Adams's National Republicans and then the early Whigs represented the Calvinist establishment in new clothing. It was no accident that Solon Stocking turned to the Democracy when his efforts at revival ran into the full social weight of Connecticut's residual Standing Order in the 1820s. William X. Ninde recalled that even into the 1850s Democratic politicians continued to exploit the residual tensions between those two denominations in that state and "went in heart and soul to help the Methodists. It was a sort of 'you tickle me, and I'll tickle you' system, a kind of see-saw arrangement. When the Whigs and the Congregationalists went down the Democrats and the Methodists went up and *vice versa.*"[41]

The complex of status, class, and theology that lay behind inter-denominational conflict was nowhere more visible than in disputes over education. This was especially true where churches with only a limited commitment historically to higher education, notably Baptists and Methodists, enjoyed a growing numerical advantage over Presbyterians and others who disdainfully asserted that university education was not safe in their hands. In a number of western states, including Ohio, Kentucky, and Tennessee, Methodists believed that Calvinist educators enjoyed undue influence in the legislatures, and in Indiana in particular their sense of grievance boiled over into political action. The state university at Bloomington, nominally non-sectarian, was effectively under Presbyterian control. Methodists, who outnumbered Presbyterians in the state by more than four to one, were excluded from the board of trustees; according to Allen Wiley, students who did not subscribe to Calvinist teachings "were regarded as ignorant or fanatical." When the Indiana Methodist Conference petitioned the legislature in 1834 the Presbyterians, including the lawyer Samuel Bigger, ridiculed that church's educational pedigree and prevented any change in the board's composition. Presbyterians' political influence was re-emphasized when Wabash College secured a state loan. Though the college defaulted on its interest payments in 1842, an educational convention secured their suspension for four years. The principal officers of the convention were Presbyterians and included Henry Ward Beecher, pastor of Indianapolis's Second Presbyterian church, and Bigger, now Whig governor. Matthew Simpson, president of the Methodists' new Indiana Asbury college at

Greencastle, was invited to speak at the meeting, but in terms which Methodist educators regarded as contemptuous.[42]

This was the context in which Bigger ran for re-election in 1843. Though Methodists, like Presbyterians, were perceived in Indiana as preponderantly Whig, Bigger's "Presbyterian bigotry" made him an unhappy choice for that party, as many of its spokesmen realized. Whig worries were compounded when the Democrats opportunistically nominated a Methodist, James Whitcomb, and sought to exploit the unease of his Whig co-religionists. In this Simpson played a critical role. Probably the single most influential Methodist in the state, his commitment to Whiggery did not extend to supporting a gubernatorial candidate who he believed had slandered his denomination. During the campaign Simpson, on a speaking tour for Indiana Asbury, did nothing to prevent the opinion from growing amongst Methodists that "a man high in office" was an enemy of their aspirations. Whigs and Presbyterians, watching him "with a hawk's eye," concluded that he was stirring up preachers "to make votes for Whitcomb." Beecher himself rashly criticized Simpson in public, to the dismay of shrewder Whigs, who could see Methodist support for Bigger shriveling by the day. In the event Democrats won their first victory for a decade, thanks to Methodists' defecting from Whiggery and abstaining on a large scale. Whigs sought to repair the damage by offering Simpson a place on their ticket of presidential electors in 1844, but he refused. Frayed relations between the Presbyterians and the increasingly powerful Methodists continued to poison Indiana politics into the 1850s.[43]

Sourness also marked relations between these two churches in eastern Tennessee. Here the bad feeling had only in part to do with education, though David McAnally and Samuel Patton, Methodist leaders, were highly critical of the Presbyterian clique who exercised undue influence (as they saw it) over the board of trustees of East Tennessee University. Arminians and Calvinists had fought tooth and claw in the early decades of the century in southern Appalachia, and by the 1840s there existed a legacy of bitterness between Methodists and Presbyterians which in certain circumstances might damage slowly improving relations. When Frederick A. Ross and other New School men, unhappy about Methodism's extraordinary advance and growing influence throughout the region, launched a furious attack in the pages of the *Calvinistic Magazine*, the stage was set for a battle whose repercussions spilled beyond the churches and into party politics.

Ross, a minister of formidable intellect, charged Methodists with flawed theology and a despotic church structure that threatened republican freedom. Their ministers, he asserted, following the example of the Roman confessional, used furtive class meetings to debauch the women. Since "Arminianism leads to monarchy and tyranny," he called on

America's civil authorities to suppress the Methodist church. Samuel Patton and "Parson" Brownlow, who had sharpened his combative skills in an earlier controversy with Ezra S. Ely, rushed to join battle with "his African highness" (Ross was the son of a wealthy Scot and a mulatto).[44] Just as the Rossites played on fears of Methodism's becoming "a *politico-religious party*," so Brownlow and his allies asserted it was the Presbyterians who infringed the separation of church and state by looking to government to do Methodism down. Both sets of polemicists in fact largely shared party political affinities; each subscribed to the Whig-evangelical doctrine of "improvement." But this did not prevent Brownlow from seeking electoral revenge on those Presbyterian politicians who had morally and financially supported the publication of Ross's charges. The running controversy through the later 1840s and early 1850s threatened (but did not in fact destroy) Brownlow's friendship with Thomas A.R. Nelson, who had helped pay Ross's printing costs. It also prompted Methodists to threaten revenge at the ballot box; in the 1853 election in the second congressional district Brownlow threw the considerable influence of the *Knoxville Whig* behind the victorious Democrat instead of the Rossite Whig. As late as 1859 the Democrats were still seeking to benefit from residual Methodist anger at Nelson's association with Ross.[45]

Even more clear-cut in southern Appalachia were the conflicts between the two largest evangelical families, Baptists and Methodists. It is a mistake to believe that because the South enjoyed greater ethnic and religious homogeneity than the North "ethnocultural" conflicts did nothing to shape party politics there. Protestant evangelicals did not act as a harmonious mass. In parts of the South where social relations were not complicated by large plantations, or by the presence of a large black or Catholic population, conflicts between different evangelical traditions had the power to polarize whole communities. The population of southern Appalachia, overwhelmingly white, Protestant, modest in wealth, and geographically isolated, often divided along a fault line separating Arminian and Calvinist, and more particularly Methodist and Baptist. In the mutually abusive and unremitting battle for souls, Methodists ridiculed adult baptism and Baptists' standards of personal morality; their opponents, fearing Methodists' increasing strength and energy, denounced the "Romanist" theology, church polity, and political aspirations of the Arminians.[46] To some degree these sectarian dividing lines corresponded to attitudes towards community "improvement," with Methodists more strongly identified than Baptists with Whiggish enterprise in moral and economic affairs. Frank Richardson entered the itinerancy in Clinton circuit in eastern Tennessee in 1854; many years later, at the end of a long life as a preacher, he recalled that there he had found the animus between Methodists and Baptists "the bitterest denominational prejudice I have ever known anywhere." At Clinton itself, capital of Anderson County, "they had Methodist and Baptist Churches, schools, taverns, stores, blacksmith shops, and ferries across the river. Like the Jews and Samaritans, they had no dealings with each other whatever." Ambitious politicians sought to exploit these tensions, and very often party political and church lines coincided. Southern highland Methodists were in many instances strongly Whig, while Baptists more commonly gravitated towards the Democrats. The more nearly "pure" the conflict between the two religious groups (unmuddied, that is, by the cross-pressures of other loyalties), the more nearly complete was the church–party alignment. Significantly, in Clinton, according to Richardson, "Most of the Methodists were Whigs, and most of the Baptists were Democrats," and the preachers of both groups were also political leaders.[47]

The patterns of "reference group" politics were not shaped by religion alone. Men might feel a loyalty to their church, but they also belonged to an ethnic or racial grouping. That attachment, with its associated antagonism to other racial or ethnic types, generated its own partisan commitments. These sometimes reinforced the political thrusts of denominational allegiance and sometimes cut across them. In Jacksonian America the principal line of ethnic division was between those of English birth or descent, or who identified with Anglo-Saxon culture, on the one side, and the Anglophobes on the other. Evangelicals of English stock took it as axiomatic that "[w]hile the world stands, it will be a theme of gratulation, that [America] fell into the hands of the Anglo-Saxon race," for as Lucien Berry asserted, the country's "indomitable Anglo-Saxon spirit" would make it "the great leader and abettor of social progress throughout the world." Those like Calvin Fletcher who regarded England as "a great Christian nation from whom we sprang" found their natural home in the Whig party. Such men upheld the evangelical values of both Old and New England. Wherever they carried this Yankee culture the Whig party was assured a constituency, particularly through upstate New York, into the Western Reserve and other parts of the Old Northwest, and beyond. "New England is the salt of the United States," an Ohio Methodist remarked privately to his cousin: "her moral influences have preserved us, or our Government would not have stood till this time."[48]

Dislike of the English and Yankee mentality of the Federalists and of the party's nativism had tended to make both the Dutch and the German communities dependably Republican under the first party system. Similar patterns prevailed under the second, with the Anglophobia of the New York and New Jersey Dutch pulling them into the Jacksonian army; the more numerous and politically influential German electorate was also strongly Democrat, with the significant exception of the minority sects, the Brethren and the Moravians, who were strongly antipathetic to Catholics, Lutherans, and German Reformed.[49] Some of the deepest antagonisms towards the English, however, prevailed amongst the Irish and Scotch-Irish immigrants. The British establishment's historic injustices towards Ulster lay behind the massive eighteenth-century migration to North America, the overwhelming support that the Scotch-Irish gave to the Revolutionary cause, and their close identification with Jeffersonian Republicanism. Significantly, those areas in which they had settled most thickly (especially the Carolinas, Virginia, and the middle states, where they constituted over 40 percent of the white population by 1790) were sources of Republican strength; in Federalist New England, by contrast, nearly 80 percent of whites were of English origin. There were some important exceptions to the rule of Scotch-Irish Republicanism, especially in the Tory areas of North Carolina, but Yankee disdain for "bog trotters" alienated most Scotch-Irish voters. Democrats of the succeeding political era seemed the natural inheritors of their support. By birth, family experience, and military action, Jackson possessed ideal Anglophobic credentials, and although Polk lacked the same military glitter his hardy Scotch-Irish background and rhetorical aggression towards the English made him a plausible "Young Hickory" in the eyes of this constituency.[50]

This antagonism between Americans of Scotch-Irish and English-Yankee backgrounds rarely corresponded with the lines between denominations. It is true that the essentially English ethnicity of the Quakers connected them almost entirely with Federalism and, later, with Whiggery. But in far more cases these ethnic differences helped develop conflicting political allegiances as much within as between denominations or denominational families. Most pertinently, Presbyterians had long been internally divided between the majority, Scots and Scotch-Irish, and the minority of English, Welsh, and New England origin. The former, focused on Philadelphia but spread through the South and West, gloried in their strict attachment to the Westminster Confession. They looked suspiciously on the revivalistic warmth and doctrinal innovations of the New Englanders, especially after the Plan of Union had opened up the church to Congregational influence. As Robert Kelley has shrewdly explained, the Presbyterian "ultra" mentality of "new measure" revivalists, and the New School to which they gave rise, was naturally Whig, while the orthodox Presbyterianism of the stern Scotch-Irish Calvinists who opposed them looked to Jackson's Democracy. Even when their icy orthodoxy melted, Presbyterians of this stock remained largely frozen in their political loyalties. When James Barr Walker forsook the Scottish Covenanters for New School Congregationalism he held firm to his Democratic allegiance.[51]

Less noticed by historians, because less apparent and less consistent, was a similar alignment in Methodism. For every Allen Trimble, a Whig Methodist of Scotch-Irish ancestry, there seem to have been half a dozen or so of the same stock in the opposite camp. John Binns was a politically active Jacksonian in Philadelphia, sternly refusing to respond to Whiggish nativism and anti-Catholicism in 1844. Joseph H. Creighton remained a firm Democrat even though it meant losing the confidence of the Whig presiding elder on whom his ministerial preferment depended. John McFerrin slipped away from his parents' Presbyterianism but not from their devotion to Jackson. Another Tennesseean, John Mathews, offered a clear statement of the importance of Irishness in political loyalty. He recalled how once after preaching he took a baby on his knee while waiting for his supper. Having sung the first line of a Clay campaign song, he forbore to continue with the bastardized Democratic version that he favored and discreetly turned to a popular revival chorus. An old Methodist, failing to identify a fellow Democrat, complained to the presiding elder, who reprimanded him. "My Irish got the better of me and I resented the charge of singing Whig songs," Mathews recalled. "Bitterly denying the charge, I said, 'How could I sing Whig songs when I was born a Democrat!'" On the other side politically were those Methodists whose English (or Welsh) birth or ancestry made them more comfortable in a party that seemed to champion English or New England culture. It is significant that the general pattern of Methodist support for Jeffersonian Republicanism broke down most clearly in Delaware, where members of that denomination were of English stock and had been Anglicans before the Revolution, while the Republicans were seen as the Presbyterian, Scotch-Irish party. Under the succeeding party system the staunchest Whigs were often English born, like George Coles, or of English or Welsh stock, as in the cases of James Harper and Colin Dew James.[52]

The fact that partisanship was shaped by long-standing group loyalties and antagonisms suggests some degree of continuity in voting behavior from generation to generation. We have already noted a number of connections in evangelical political alignments between the first and second party systems. Many National Republicans, Antimasons, and Whigs had earlier been Federalists; ex-Jeffersonians made their way by various routes into the Jacksonian camp. There is considerable evidence that during the second party system children adopted the partisan enthusiasms of their fathers. At the Methodists' Wilbraham Academy in 1840, Gilbert Haven stood firm against the Whiggery of many of his fellow students largely out of loyalty to his father, an "old-line Democrat." Moses F. Odell's politics derived originally "[f]rom the associations of his childhood." Roeliff Brinkerhoff, as the son of a Democratic activist and an old friend of Van Buren, could have been nothing other than "a Jackson boy."[53] But to emphasize continuity can be to overlook the disjunctions in political allegiance through the period when the Jacksonian party system emerged and matured. During the early years in particular loyalties were in flux.

In the creation of firm new allegiances, especially in national elections, the party managers' choice of candidate became all-important. Both Jackson and Harrison were of critical significance to the Democrats' and Whigs' first national victories. Their candidacies encouraged a focus on attractive (in Jackson's case, charismatic) personalities at a time when their parties were heterogeneous coalitions. This emphasis on the candidate's character was most influential amongst those evangelicals whose pronounced antiparty attitudes embraced the view that a party's so-called "immutable principles" were "but little more than the watchwords of party" and that it was "of far greater importance that we have virtuous men, men of stirring energy and invincible integrity... in office." If, as William A. Scott argued, "[t]he example of a pious man in power is a living law to the people, and does more than ten thousand statutes... to mould and fashion public sentiment," then a candidate's righteousness was of far greater import than his party label.[54] It is clear that many evangelicals made their electoral choices as much on these grounds as any other, though of course a candidate's qualities often could not be disentangled from those of the party he represented.

Jackson's career had given him a wide acquaintance with evangelicals of all denominations, and he had many friends in the ministry. Amongst the most popular Methodists, Lorenzo Dow took the view that Old Hickory would be "the means, in the hand of Providence, of saving the country"; John Newland Maffitt, his devoted admirer, considered his defects of character to be "but spots upon the sun." A clutch of Presbyterian Democrats lauded the "far-reaching faith," piety, and benevolence of a "truly great" man; Tommy Rankin of east Tennessee, though otherwise staunchly National Republican and Whig, idolized "the greatest warrior and statesman who had ever lived"; Ezra Stiles Ely, of course, considered him the natural leader of a much-needed "Christian Party." Harrison, too, was widely admired by evangelicals for his "beautiful union of private excellence with public virtue." Of other candidates for whom there was enormous personal enthusiasm, none was more respected than Clay. T.N. Ralston, a Methodist preacher from Kentucky, considered him the "most far-seeing statesman and patriotic orator" the country had ever produced. Other friends and admirers included Henry Bascom, William Winans, John Broadus, and Gurdon Trumbull, a Connecticut Congregationalist made ill by sheer disappointment at Clay's defeat in 1844. Few, however, went quite so far towards "unbounded idolatry" of the Kentuckian as William Brownlow, who regarded him as "the greatest man now living" and who, he said, would have "willingly voted for Clay's last pair of pantaloons stuffed with straw!"[55]

Candidates' personal qualities could arouse anxiety as well as respect. In many cases evangelicals were moved to vote as much by hostility to one office-seeker as by positive attraction to another. Chauncey Hobart had real doubts about Jackson's religious belief; others were concerned about his horse-racing, cock-fighting, gambling, "profane swearing," and his Masonic connections. Clay's moral deficiencies, his dueling and card-playing, worried many of those concerned for the integrity of "vital religion"; James W. Alexander and William A. Scott were just two who saw good reason to be pleased at his failing to secure the presidency.[56]

Denominational attachments and party preferences

At first sight there are few signs of a consistent correspondence between evangelicals' denominational loyalties and their partisan sympathies. Interested contemporaries commonly testified to political divisions in the churches at both denominational and congregational level. "No party leader ever asks, 'How will the Presbyterians, or Baptists, or Protestant Episcopalians, or Methodists vote','" a New York editor wrote. "They are known to be divided on every leading question of policy, and to vote without reference to any religious creed, or dogma." A Baltimore Presbyterian minister, John Duncan, was typical in maintaining partisan discretion in the face of a politically variegated congregation. Disruptive animosities marred the life of many congregations and church gatherings. "Lord, deliver us from Whiggery!" implored a preacher at a Tennessee camp meeting; "God forbid!" responded another. Anecdotal evidence of this kind tallies well with Benson's correlations of aggregate religious and voting behavior in New York, where he discovered no clear relationship by 1844 between Protestantism and party loyalty; it corresponds, too, with the few available data relating to the known voting habits of identifiable individuals. It has to be remembered that men and women belonged to churches primarily to meet spiritual and social needs, not to pursue political ends; churches looked for conformity to doctrinal and moral standards, not for partisan uniformity. At the Tennessee Annual Conference John McFerrin suffered rebuke for publicly stating his political differences with a particular candidate for the ministry. Even more significant were his efforts to minimize their importance: "In spite of all this, I am for him – separated in politics, we are one in Christ. . . . I shall vote for him with both hands raised. Religion, thank God, is above all political combinations, and this day shows itself the very essence of love."[57]

Yet the relationship between church membership and partisan loyalty was by no means wholly random. That there were few examples of denominations being pulled overwhelmingly towards one or other of the parties reflected to a very large degree the influence of context in conditioning churchgoers' political stances. Historians have become increasingly conscious of what Harry Watson has described as "the intensely local character of American life and politics." Although the major denominations were important agents in the breaking down of American localism during the nineteenth century, in the Jacksonian and immediate antebellum period they were themselves shaped by those very community differences. Environment mattered. Political, social, and economic context varied considerably, as of course did denominational make-up and relative strength. When Yankee emigrants from the minority sects arrived in upstate New York they abandoned their Democratic Republicanism for what in the new context appeared a more congenial home, Antimasonry. In New Hampshire the much more positive attitudes of the Democrats to reform and the economy ensured the political affection of the majority in the same churches. Catholics in Louisiana were prosperous, French, and Whig; elsewhere, where the Irish dominated, they were poor and Democratic.[58] The importance of context can be demonstrated by a survey of the political associations of the major evangelical churches, denomination by denomination.

In one case, at least, a broadly consistent pattern existed. New England Congregationalists, very largely Federalist under the first party system, maintained a strongly Whig identity under the second.[59] Amongst the Congregationalists of Connecticut, where in the early nineteenth century to be a Jeffersonian in politics "was esteemed almost equivalent to being a blasphemer," the weight of opinion in the next generation took a similar view of Jackson's Democracy. The firm Whiggery of the church's luminaries in that state, including Joel Hawes, Noah Porter, and Nathaniel Taylor, was matched throughout New England by such men as James Meacham in Vermont, and Moses Stuart, Alfred Ely, and Hubbard Winslow in Massachusetts. Congregationalism and Whiggery also joined hands in areas settled by New England and British emigrants, in upstate New York, in the Western Reserve of Ohio, around the Great Lakes and further west into Iowa, and even in pockets of the South.[60]

Presbyterians never experienced denominationally the same close association with a single political party. Many, probably most, had put their faith in the Republicans in the 1790s and 1800s. A lack of partisan coherence continued to mark the church, taken as a whole, during the early years of the second party system. But Presbyterian attachments were not wholly random, as alignments after the denominational schism of 1837–38 demonstrate. New School men appear to have pulled heartily for Whiggery (even if one of their number, Benjamin F. Butler, served in Jackson's cabinet). Ministerial leaders, including Albert Barnes, Lyman Beecher, Nathan Beman, Thomas Brainerd, and George Duffield, were of that persuasion, as were a number of their children; so, too, were many prominent laymen active in the moral reform societies of the "benevolent empire." New School, "Presbygationalist" presence in New York and Ohio corresponded with areas of Whig strength. Whig Presbyterians also made their mark further west, as well as in Pennsylvania and the border states of Kentucky and Tennessee. Some of these were members of the Old School, for that section of the denominational family was less uniform in party political attachment than were New School men. Though the elite of Old School ministers, north and south, appear to have been disproportionately Whig (to do in part with their social conservatism and concern for social order), in general Whig Old Schoolers like Charles Hodge, Stephen Colwell, John Hall, Robert J. Breckinridge, and John L. Nevius were no more typical of the denomination than those of the stripe of Ashbel Green, Nathan L. Rice, Cyrus H. McCormick, Robert L. Dabney, or William A. Scott. The latter were often (but by no means exclusively) of Scotch-Irish stock, found their strength in the middle and southern states, regarded the New School and the institutions of the benevolent empire with some suspicion, and sought in the Democratic party refuge from "church and state" Whiggery.[61]

The similarity of Congregationalists' and New School Presbyterians' political postures seems to have derived in part from the theological beliefs that helped shape their view of the world. The modified Hopkinsianism and the "New Divinity" that sustained the evangelistic successes of the Second Great Awakening was an optimistic, activist creed. Excited by the achievements of theologically suspect Methodism, Finney and other revivalists within the Congregational and Presbyterian traditions sought to break out of the constraints of their churches' prevalent dry Calvinism. With varying degrees of coherence they stressed sinners' moral responsibility, their ability to choose between salvation and damnation, and God's intention that men and women use all means open to them to secure the operation of the Holy Spirit on their hearts. Once he was "hopefully converted" the regenerate individual had a Christian duty to cooperate with others similarly blessed to seek a more perfect world and introduce the millennium through disinterested benevolent action. Drawing on the Puritan theocratic tradition, the exponents of the new revivalism respected no lines of division between an individual's responsibilities to himself, his church, and the wider world, and recognized the importance of political engagement. The Whig party to which they were strongly attracted offered a number of striking parallels. It, too, sought to harness the activist, optimistic energies of America, believing that government had a positive, participatory role to play in the development of the country's economy and in the creation of a morally well-ordered society. If the typical Presbygationalist was a sort of spiritual engineer, the representative Whig favored a form of socioeconomic engineering. Both groups were composed of interventionists and "instrumentalists" who thought that public action was the means to a better society; their prevailing spirit was postmillennialist.[62]

By contrast, the conservative critics of Hopkinsianism and "modern" Calvinism, formally institutionalized into the Old School after the Presbyterian schism, stood loyally by the Shorter Catechism of the Westminster Confession. They were convinced that the starting point for all Christian activity was the individual's total depravity and moral inability: Finneyite "new measures" presumptuously encouraged human instrumentality and implicitly denied the sinner's dependence on the Holy Spirit and the rule of God. Like their opponents, they saw religion as an intensely personal struggle to achieve grace, but unlike New School thinkers they tended to back away from reforming the world, keeping their religious and secular activities carefully compartmentalized. In the most extreme cases their predestinarian heritage, submissiveness to God, and pre-millennialism led them to eschew all mission activity and any attempt to make morality a matter for the state. Many of these strict confessionalists felt a strong sympathy for the Democratic party, in whose *laissez-faire*, "hands-off" philosophy could be seen a secular equivalent to predestinarianism. They appeared to be comfortable in a party that thought leaving people alone was the highest virtue, and to find far more security in its negativism than in the Whigs' positive encouragement of a moral order.

Given the Jeffersonian attachments of the majority of Methodists, it is not surprising that in many instances the church's members held strongly to the Democrats during the 1830s and 1840s. In New England in particular there was a clear continuity, well represented by John Brodhead and the Gordon family in New Hampshire, the Stockings of Connecticut and the Havens of Massachusetts. Colonel Jesse Pierce, Bishop Edmund S. Janes, and "Father" Richard Libby, all prominent, New-England-born Methodists, further exemplify the Jacksonian presence in the region. Elsewhere in the North, numbers of influential Methodists carried a Democratic torch, including the editor Thomas Bond in New York, William N. Shinn, sometime member of Congress from New Jersey, Governor Robert Lucas, and the lawyer Thomas Drake in Ohio; a long roll of full-time ministers embraced Wilson Spottswood, John Binns, Joseph Creighton, W.W. Hibben and, most assertively, Edward R. Ames and Peter Cartwright. Luminous Methodists among southern Democrats included Henry Slicer and William Baker of Maryland, John McFerrin and John Mathews of Tennessee, the Dromgoole family in Virginia and North Carolina and, from Georgia, Augustus B. Longstreet and US Senator and preacher Walter T. Colquitt.[63] Taken together they seem to confirm Hugh McCulloch's contemporary assessment that up to the 1850s the general rule, with a few exceptions, was of Methodist identification with the Democrats. Certainly a number of historians have pointed to what appears to be the predominance of Jacksonianism amongst grassroots Methodists throughout the South and West, and some state-level voting analyses, particularly Formisano's study of Michigan and Cole's of New Hampshire, come to a similar conclusion.[64]

Yet it is evident from Methodists' memoirs and private papers that there was widespread hostility to the Democrats within the denomination. Few were as publicly indiscreet as the "violent Anti-Jackson preacher" in the Baltimore Conference who, when visiting the White House in 1831 with thirty or more of his colleagues, knelt and "prayed that the Gen[era]l might be converted," "which he did so loud, that he could be heard at the President's gate." But by the 1840s Whiggery had a firm grip on many of the church's influential figures, some of whom regarded it as a truer heir of Jeffersonian Democracy than locofocoism. Bishops James O. Andrew and George F. Pierce, Henry W. Hilliard, Greene Haygood, and William Winans upheld it in the lower South. In the northern tier of slave states Samuel Patton, William Brownlow, Henry Bascom, David Rice McAnally, Benjamin Northcott, William T. Senter, David Hazzard, and William McComas energetically preached both a Whig and a Methodist gospel.[65] Asahel E. Phelps, William Sprague (of Michigan), Alfred Brunson, Arthur Elliott, Samuel Brenton, Matthew Simpson, and Chauncey Hobart, who had to swallow hard before preaching his sermon on the occasion of Jackson's death, helped make Whiggery a respectable creed amongst western Methodists; indeed, it was claimed that most of the Indiana Conference was Whig by 1840.[66] So, too, were John Inskip, George Crooks, John McClintock, Jared Perkins, Thomas Stockton, and George Coles, who spoke for many in north-eastern Methodism. When the English Wesleyan James Dixon visited the United States in 1848 to attend the General Conference of the MEC, it was his clear impression that the vast majority of the Methodist ministers he met on his extensive travels were firmly in the Whig camp.[67]

Compared with the Congregationalists and New School Presbyterians the Methodist churches were far more divided in their allegiances. As the largest denomination, with a national constituency, encompassing an even greater variety of local and regional contexts, this was inevitable; for example its historic animosity towards legally established churches drove it towards the Democrats in New England, but away from them where it felt threatened by the call from Ezra Stiles Ely and other Jacksonian Presbyterians for a "Christian party." Nor did Methodist theology thrust as obviously as did the New Divinity towards one party alone. Both creeds shared an emphasis on individual salvation, of course, but the Methodists' understanding of their obligation as a church often seemed to go no further than saving the largest number of souls, whereas revival-conscious Calvinists pressed ahead to establish the kingdom of God by redeeming society. Many Methodists were reluctant to join the benevolent societies that constituted the "evangelical united front," and proved just as cool towards the political party through which socially concerned Calvinists sought to change the world. But by no means all of them were blind to the vision of the good society. These Arminians with Calvinist lenses came to regard Whiggery as the better political prospect.[68]

Baptists, too, a truly national denomination, and the second largest, displayed a far more divided political profile than they had in the days of Jefferson and the struggle for religious liberty. As has been suggested, many sustained through Jacksonianism their Jeffersonian Republican antipathy to any hint of state support for religion. John Leland carried the anti-Federalist, anti-Whig banner in Massachusetts, and throughout much of the rest of New England, especially New Hampshire, the connection between Baptist and Democrat was widely acknowledged. In New York, Pennsylvania, and further west in Ohio and the Great Lakes region there is evidence of a similar link. If Thomas Morris, US Senator and son of a Baptist preacher, typified the relationship in Ohio, John G. Landrum and Richard M. Johnson symbolized it in the South and West. Here, particularly where Primitive or "antimission" churches flourished, Baptists voted heavily for the party of Jackson and Van Buren. A product of long-term discord between "Arminians" and "Calvinists" within American Baptists, which culminated in open rupture in 1832, the Primitives were always a minority within the larger family.[69] Contemptuously dismissed as "iron-sided" and "hard-shell," they took pride in a term that acknowledged their "hard heads and sound hearts," that is, their strict and unyielding Calvinism in the tradition of Geneva and of John Gill, and their repudiation of more recent, watered-down Arminianized doctrine. Primitives emphasized the individual's depravity and sin, and God's stern plan of predestined salvation of an elect through grace alone. They regarded protracted meetings, anxious benches, and other "new measures" as "steam religion" and "priestcraft."[70] "Good works" they dismissed as diabolical encouragements to pride, self-righteousness, worldliness, and ostentation. They had no time, explained Elder Mark Bennett, for plans designed "for the improvement of the moral, intellectual, and physical, condition of mankind." Temperance societies, theological schools, tract societies, Sunday Schools, Bible societies, Freemasonry, and similar secret brotherhoods, railroads, banks, and protective tariffs – none were based on apostolic principles but rather were Yankee-inspired contrivances, instruments of New England cultural imperialism, tending towards a fusing of church and state, and fatal to religious and civil liberty. Their proponents were a "new race of Jesuits," "Mammonites," and "money-missionaries" who "would take from the poor man his last hard-earned fourpence half-penny."[71] Primitives' tenacity in defense of the "free right of conscience" and Jeffersonian republican forms expressed itself politically in an almost complete identification with Jacksonian Democrats and deep hostility to Whiggish elitism, enterprise, and "improvement."[72]

But these Democratic preferences do not exhaust the story. When George N. Briggs stood as Whig candidate for governor in Massachusetts he pulled many fellow Baptists with him. There were many similarly disposed Baptists in Vermont and Rhode Island, the most prominent of whom, Francis Wayland, stood firm for Clay in 1844. Formisano has discovered a Whig strain amongst Michigan Baptists. In Illinois there appears to have been a partisan division in the church corresponding to lines of Yankee and southern settlement, and the same may have been true in Indiana. Other northern states, too, including Pennsylvania and New Jersey, sheltered a number of Baptists hostile to a party that, through Richard M. Johnson, appeared to threaten true religion.

Historians have tended to regard southern Baptists as strongly Democratic in outlook, but there is a danger of reading forward into the second party system the affiliations of the first, or reading back those of the third. North Carolina Baptists, for example, harbored significant numbers of Whigs in the 1840s and 1850s. One of the most fervent of these, William D. Valentine of Hertford County, reflected sourly on the campaign tactics of a leading Democrat and Baptist layman, Godwin C. Moore, who thought Baptist Whigs sufficiently numerous to appeal to them "in the name of church fellowship" when running for state office in 1842.[73] Whiggish Baptists in the South tended to be found in that part of the denomination most sympathetic to moral and social reform. Primitive Baptists certainly regarded the Missionary, or New School, churches from which they had broken away, and with whom they maintained poisonous relations, as backsliders from the true standards of high Calvinism in religion and Jeffersonianism in politics. Fearing a convergence of Missionary Baptists with Methodism, Primitives like John Scallorn of Carroll County, Tennessee, predicted "a consolidation of the popular sects" into a new form of Popery and legislative despotism.[74] In Virginia, Edmund Broadus, a member of the Shiloh Baptist Association, enthusiastically espoused missions, Sunday Schools, temperance reform, and ministerial education – all objects of abuse from the strict Calvinists strong throughout the state's piedmont, mountains, and valley. In a county equally divided in politics they were Democrats, he an ardent Clay man. Significantly, too, it seems likely that the small numbers of southern Freewill Baptists, Arminian in theology, were predominantly Whig.[75]

Amongst the smaller denominations, the Quakers were overwhelmingly Whig. Although not integrated into Finneyite revivalist culture, their Whiggish ambitions for a moral society, their considerable English connections, and their pacifist objections to Indian-fighting kept them out of Jackson's party, though the presidential candidacies of both Clay and Taylor ("men of blood") caused them some anguish; only the minority of Hicksite Quakers in New Jersey, consumed with bitterness against Theodore Frelinghuysen for taking the side of the orthodox party in the Friends' property dispute, were unequivocally Democrat. Most Dutch Reformed and German Lutherans, on the other hand, traveled from Jeffersonian Republicanism into the Jacksonian party, sustaining a conservative theology, fears of Puritan blue laws, and antipathy to Yankee culture. Rather more problematic were the Episcopalians. Often of high social standing, concerned for the good order of society and agitated about "the follies of Jacksonism," they were naturally disposed towards the Whig party, but in New England some Democratic Episcopalians continued to be animated by the hostility to Congregationalists and the Standing Order that had controlled their political actions earlier in the century.[76]

The task of relating denominational to political loyalties is further confused by changes during the 1830s and 1840s in religious preoccupations, in relationships between ethnocultural groups, and in the make-up of political coalitions. The arrangements of the second party system were fluid, not static. Historians have properly stressed how impressively loyal voters were to their parties in the early years of American mass democracy, and how uncomfortable they felt when they switched party.[77] Yet it should be remembered that stable and near universal two-party competition did not exist before the late 1830s, and that even when it did political loyalties were not necessarily deep or immutable. Given the principled hesitancy of so many evangelicals about the new partisanship, it seems likely that they contributed out of proportion to their numbers to the ranks of the ticket-splitters, the party-switchers, and the genuine independents. William Crane often did not vote; he took pride in supporting the Whigs only "when any good to mankind seemed likely to be gained by their success." James Havens's Whiggery was similarly conditional on the character of the candidate; he often scratched or split his ticket.[78]

Many evangelicals switched allegiance from one major party to the other as old issues lost their significance and new ones replaced them. A Massachusetts Baptist, William Hague, noted that during the 1830s the "church and state" question ceased to operate on the political calculations of his denomination, and new issues gradually broke the historic connection between that church and the Democratic party. Methodists found the same processes at work. For some party-switchers, like Lorenzo Dow, the catalytic issues were economic. For Francis Wayland,

Gamaliel Bailey, and other defectors from the Democrats the principal agent of change was the slavery question. Paul Johnson describes how politically active Methodists in Rochester shifted allegiance from the Democrats to the Whigs over the parties' contrasting stances over working towards a Christian society. Alexander Campbell's increasing disillusionment with Jacksonian Democracy derived from concern about the party's tolerance of creeping atheism and social insubordination; in 1840, though still claiming loyalty to Jeffersonian principles, he threw in his lot with Harrison and Whiggery.[79]

Probably the single most influential issue in driving evangelicals out of the Democracy was the party's relationship with the Roman Catholic church. Despite the Whiggish outlook of John Hughes, John Power, other hierarchs and many native-born, well-to-do members of the Roman church, nothing seriously prevented the hardening of the glue that held the mass of Catholic immigrants to the Democratic party. As Catholics asserted their political influence, especially in eastern cities over the question of the public schools, many evangelicals lamented their own partisan divisions. "In the political dissensions of Protestants Rome even now holds the balance of power," Gardiner Spring reflected in New York. Throughout the early 1840s he and others looked for a "a more concerted union of Protestant influence" either through the existing Whig party or the creation of "new combinations." Tensions between Dutch and Yankee relaxed in the face of a common anti-Popery. Catholics' growing numbers and political muscle stretched the earlier tolerance and political cooperation between Protestant Scotch-Irish and Irish Catholics to breaking point, pushing Ulster Presbyterians towards Whiggery and the nativist American Republican party. The latter, with its uneasy but not wholly uncooperative relationship with the Whigs, acted as a sort of transit camp for some nativist ex-Democrats from various Protestant denominations.[80]

Shifts in evangelicals' political alignments were further encouraged by developments in theology and church practice on the one hand, and by changes in the churches' socioeconomic profiles on the other. First, the enormous popular appeal of democratic Arminianism during the Second Great Awakening imposed irresistible pressures on Calvinist churches to modify their doctrines of human inability, election, and limited atonement. Sometimes congregations revolted against a strict creed; sometimes ministers themselves were the popularizers of an Arminianized "new divinity" and Finneyite "new measures." As the Second Great Awakening drew to a close both Methodists and New School Calvinists came to reassess their theological position and to recognize their near-agreement on evangelical fundamentals in the face of threatening heterodoxies: Mormonism, Universalism, and Roman Catholicism. "[T]he times call for unity of spirit and effort among the evangelical churches," announced the *Christian Advocate and Journal* in 1842, at the very time when all orthodox Protestant denominations were involved in defending themselves against Catholic intrusions, through the American Protestant Union. At the Evangelical Alliance meetings in London in 1846, much applauded by his fellow Methodists, George Peck euphorically demanded: "Perish the Calvinistic and Arminian controversy." During the 1840s much of the past bitterness gave way to interdenominational efforts for revival ("giving no quarters to *bigot* or *pope*") and an emphasis on the agreed elements of belief, including on occasions a common attachment to perfectionist doctrine. George Coles looked back in the early 1850s to the time over thirty years earlier when he had arrived in America: "One thing is certain, the *evangelical* sects are more harmonious in their feelings toward each other than they were formerly. The Dutch Reformed, Presbyterians, Baptists, and Episcopal Methodists, are now on a very friendly footing with each other." Such theological softening and practical cooperation made it much easier for Arminians and Calvinists to sit side by side in the same political party.[81]

Secondly, changes in the social status and class make-up of the churches also appear to have affected their political attachments. The divisions between Whigs and Democrats were not straightforwardly class based, but Whigs were more commonly seen as the party of the "respectable" and the upwardly mobile. Many poorer evangelical churches, as they acquired greater wealth and standing, became part of the evangelical "establishment," one which tended towards Whiggishness. As urban Baptists in New England, for instance, rose in the social scale and acquired education and polish, they became estranged from the Jacksonianism of their rural counterparts and found the "Christian state" mentality of the National Republicans and the Whigs much more congenial.[82]

The most dramatic changes occurred within Methodism. Through the first half of the century Methodists progressed from being a socially despised sect of the poor, "the offscouring of all things," into a respected denomination of some power and influence. As they grew wealthier and built larger, more ornate churches with organs, rented pews, and steeples, as they demanded and secured a college-bred, more sophisticated and urbane ministry, as they preached before presidents and respected statesmen, and officiated as chaplains to Congress, so they left their persecuted past behind. When Selah Stocking transferred from the New England to the Oneida Conference in the 1830s he discovered that "his church members were among the leading citizens of the place; and he soon found himself associated with families of wealth and refinement." Southern and western Methodists reflected similarly. In all regions, including New England, Methodists grew in esteem, made converts amongst doctors, lawyers, and other professionals, gained access to the evangelical "establishment" and in some instances, as in Indiana, secured through their wealth and popularity the status of a state church in all but name.[83] Methodists were to be found in state governorships, in the United States Senate, and in the Supreme Court. Their improving status and attendant concern for social order helped secure their allegiance to the party most closely associated with "respectability."

The evidence from the mouths and pens of evangelicals themselves, and of those who observed them, suggests a multiplicity of divisions and antagonisms amongst evangelicals which, far from being superficial exceptions to an underlying Protestant unity, had significant implications for their political outlook. These religious conflicts were not based on economic differences, although issues of status and economic outlook certainly impinged, but revolved around profound cultural antagonisms. For this reason during the second party system no "evangelical Protestant vote" was cast consistently for one party or the other.

Whigs, however, enjoyed strong, even enthusiastic, support amongst religious and social "improvers," people sympathetic to the pursuit of economic progress, concerned to maintain social cohesion and traditional standards of moral behavior in a changing world, and ready to invite government action to secure those ends. Whigs appealed particularly strongly to Congregationalists and reform-minded New School Calvinists in the Presbyterian and Baptist churches. They attracted many, possibly most, Methodists – certainly in areas where the historic conflict between Arminian and Calvinist was yielding to new antagonisms between Romanist and Protestant. They also won over a significant and influential minority in some of the Old School denominations, men like the Presbyterian Charles Hodge, and Talbot W. Chambers amongst the Dutch Reformed.

Many contemporaries thought that Whigs were more strongly represented than the Democrats within the evangelical ministry. John England, Roman Catholic bishop of Charleston, concluded from his experience in the lower South and the border in 1840 that "very many Protestant clergymen prayed and preached chiefly for General Harrison, a few for Mr. Van Buren." A Marylander estimated at the same time that some "three-fourths of the clergymen of all denominations" were Whig, and the *Carrollton Jeffersonian* charged that the clergy "*truckled* so low as to ride *astride* of log cabins and *huzza for 'Tippecanoe and Tyler too'*." Such experiences seared themselves into Democrats' memories. During the excitement of the 1856 contest for the presidency Gideon Tucker bitterly recalled the activities of "demagogic parsons . . . in the disgraceful Log Cabin campaign": "Sunday-school children by the hundred were paraded in Hard Cider processions, and taught to sing 'Tip and Ty' songs, and otherwise to partake of the then prevalent tom-foolery."[84]

If, then, one party could claim more plausibly than another to be "the Christian party," it might seem to be the Whigs. But there were too many evangelically minded Democrats for the label to be wholly convincing. We need not take seriously William Brownlow's inimitably belligerent argument that evangelical Democrats were hypocritical scoundrels and that the Jacksonians were the party of the churchgoing moral dregs, the Whigs the home of the truly devout.[85] Democrats were to be found in all churches, many of them amongst the most active and engaged of the membership. They embraced those whose own churches' historic experience aroused fear and suspicion of priest and politician acting in concert, those who distrusted "improvers" as agents of Yankee cultural imperialism, and those who placed egalitarianism and individual freedom above social deference and political intrusion.

By the later years of the second party system, however, both Whigs and Democrats were suffering evangelical depletion. The community of the devout would go on sustaining one or other party for as long as they remained alert to churchgoers' ambitions and pursued acceptable policies. But when Whigs and Democrats responded unsatisfactorily to evangelicals' swelling concern over slavery, temperance, and the status of Catholicism in the republic, the demands for a genuine "Christian party in politics" grew more urgent. Ultimately, evangelicals created a pressure for change that helped explode the political arrangements of the second party system.

Role of evangelicals in breaking up the second party system

Chapter 5

Evangelicals, Slavery, and Sectionalism in the 1840s

National parties that cultivated nationwide constituencies were primary bonds of the American Union. Historians widely recognize that the series of tremors in the second party system in the 1850s, which removed the Whigs and grievously damaged the Democrats, left the antebellum Union severely if not mortally wounded. They are less clear about its causes. Most acknowledge two principal solvents of established loyalties through the 1840s and early 1850s: disputes about the boundaries and future status of slavery within the Union; and cultural conflicts over drink, education, and religious observance which accompanied mass immigration from Ireland and Germany. But there is no consensus on their relative significance.[1]

Evangelical Protestants actively participated in this process of political realignment, taking initiatives that forced politicians to address both sets of issues. Their concerns about the consequences of mass immigration for Protestant religion and American republicanism will be discussed in Chapter 7. For the present, the role of antislavery evangelicals in fostering a political momentum against slavery, and the reactive defensiveness of southern Protestants, demand two lines of analysis. Evangelical action can be seen, first, as a response to essentially secular developments, particularly to efforts to stifle public debate on slavery and to the federal government's pursuit of territorial annexation and conquest. Secondly, evangelicals' political thinking can be placed in the context of events in the churches themselves, especially the ecclesiastical schisms and their litigious, polarizing, abrasively sectional aftermath. Internal church conflicts had considerable implications for secular politics. The anger they generated went well beyond church walls and demonstrated how permeable was the membrane separating church membership from citizenship.

"A proper religious enterprise": the emergence of political abolitionism

The political crisis of 1819–21, when free and slave states confronted each other over the status of slavery in the proposed new state of Missouri and the rest of the Louisiana Purchase, appeared to bring the country to the verge of war. Over the next two decades chastened political leaders in Washington and the state houses sought to limit public debate on the South's peculiar institution. The most concrete expression of this mood was Martin Van Buren's creation of a national political organization – the Democratic Republicans – dedicated to a states-rights' philosophy that would remove the question from national politics and leave it as a domestic matter for the individual slave states.[2] It was a measure of Van Buren's success that, until the 1840s, the issues that dominated the political debates between the Democrats and their principal opponents had – ostensibly – little to do with slavery.

At the same time, outside the legislative chambers the South's peculiar institution was becoming a matter of heated and rancorous debate. In part this had to do with the changing realities of slavery itself: even as the issue was being marginalized in national politics the massive expansion of cotton culture into the Gulf states during the 1820s and 1830s confirmed slavery's growing centrality in southern economic and social life. For concerned critics of the institution, north and south, inheritors of the Founding Fathers' belief that slavery's days were numbered, this new reality threw up uncomfortable questions about the effectiveness of colonization and other schemes of gradual emancipation. But the debate was also affected by changing perceptions of the individual's moral responsibilities. The oft-told tale of the emergence and development of immediate abolitionism needs no extended rehearsal here. It need only be stressed that the movement that eventually found institutional expression in the American Anti-Slavery Society (AASS) from 1833 was profoundly influenced by that strain of millennialist, perfectionist revivalism associated with Finney, the Burned-over District of upstate New York, and other parts of the New England diaspora, as well as New England itself. There were, of course, liberal Protestant and antinomian embodiments of abolitionism, but it was the more orthodox evangelical expression of Protestantism that gave the movement its ballast. This new abolitionism shared with the revivalism that spawned it a romantic belief in the perfectibility of humankind in general and American society in particular, and a conviction that individual Christians had the duty and ability to separate themselves entirely from sin, avoiding all compromising connections with evil in any shape or form. For these men and women slavery was far more than a social evil to be endured stoically until it naturally withered away. It was a sin that corroded the moral fiber of everyone it touched, directly or indirectly. Every individual, slaveholder or otherwise, had a compelling moral obligation to sever all ties with the institution and begin immediately to work for its removal.[3]

It was from within this relatively small band of radical critics of slave society, particularly from the movement's orthodox evangelical wing, that the most determined efforts to politicize the slavery question emerged. From the outset the AASS, the majority of its members sympathetic to "Calvinistic" views of citizenship, called for political action to accompany moral suasion. Most respected the rights of slave states to jurisdiction within their own borders, but believed Congress could move against slavery wherever the federal government had sole jurisdiction, as in the District of Columbia. Abolitionists' political duties included petitioning Congress, questioning candidates for public office, securing pledges from voters, and voting only for reliably antislavery men. Evangelicals, not least clergy, so took to heart the plea to use the ballot box that unsympathetic ministers like Samuel Luckey regarded them as "the most decided and violent political party in the land."[4] From the mid-1830s a number of abolitionists – following William Lloyd Garrison and Henry C. Wright – moved further and further down the "no-human-government," non-resistant, perfectionist, Christian-anarchist road, refusing to vote or fulfill other conventional civic obligations.[5] But they were drenched in torrents of criticism from the more orthodox majority, who perceived such views "as the quintessence of transcendental nonsense."[6]

At first the political strategy of evangelical abolitionists was to act as a leaven on the two major parties and achieve an influence beyond their limited electoral numbers. They turned in particular to interrogating Whig and Democratic candidates on various issues relating to slavery and race. But early optimism yielded to disillusionment as politicians ignored the questionnaires or retreated on their promises once elected. Though some abolitionists optimistically remained loyal to the two major parties, particularly the Whigs, others increasingly came to regard them as "divisions of the pro-slavery party," each sacrificing principle for the reward of southern votes.[7] Conventional parties spinelessly acceded to black codes and gag laws, and pandered to "mobocrats" who attacked abolitionists, free blacks, and churches with impunity.[8] There was, it seemed, little to choose between Van Buren and Harrison in 1840. Both were dupes of the slave power. "Which ever of them is elected, and whatever policy prevails in regard to a National Bank, or an Independent Treasury, slavery will govern the nation."[9]

Against this background the idea of a separate antislavery party began to germinate, cultivated most effectively in the revival-enriched soil of upstate New York by Alvan Stewart and Myron Holley. Proponents of third-party action met resistance not only from non-voting Garrisonians but from many orthodox evangelical abolitionists like Nathan Beman and Lewis Tappan, afraid their movement's crusading idealism would be compromised and corrupted. Through 1839 the Executive Committee of the AASS continued to oppose the creation of a distinct antislavery party. But Holley (an ex-Congregationalist who had developed his own eclectic, liberal creed) and Elizur Wright, Jr, as editor of the *Massachusetts Abolitionist*, persisted in presenting separate political action as a compelling religious duty: "Both politics and religion will gain by it. Politics will be enobled, and religion will be *humanized.*" Once Joshua Leavitt, member of the Executive Committee and editor of the *Emancipator*, and the previously doubtful Gerrit Smith had thrown their influence behind the cause, there was every chance of securing independent antislavery nominations for the presidency and other elective offices. At Albany in April 1840 a convention of political abolitionists, unmoved by Nathan Beman's sneer that "they would always be known as the April fool party," nominated James G. Birney and Thomas Earle as presidential and vice-presidential candidates of what Gerrit Smith described as the "Liberty party."[10]

The new organization's lack of political success, and its own internal confusion about strategies, help explain why historians have rather neglected the party and been so uncertain over its precise nature. Some supporters, like Francis J. LeMoyne, Gerrit Smith, and Beriah Green, saw it as an "emphatically religious" minority pressure group uniquely engaged in "Bible Politics"; others perceived a permanent agency which would challenge the supremacy of Whigs and Democrats. These internal tensions, and the party's failure, have led some historians to interpret Liberty men as essentially "anti-politicians" and religious visionaries, while others treat them as realistic "reformer-politicians" driven by a mixture of conscience and knowing calculation. Put another way, the debate is over how far the party was a "pre-modern" or a "modern" political force. In fact the party was hybrid. In propaganda techniques, organizational structure, and campaign tactics the party copied many of the "modern" characteristics of Whigs and Democrats: to this extent they accepted the arrival of the new mass political parties. But the distaste of so many Liberty men for the compromises of conventional politics, their unyielding attachment to "one idea" in a pluralist society, and their anti-institutional temperament set them apart from the new political order.[11]

In program, *modus operandi*, and composition the new party was a quintessential product of socially concerned, revivalistic Protestantism. Its agenda sprang from seeing slavery as moral corruption, not just a social evil; from regarding government not as a neutral arbiter but as a vessel of righteousness. America's rulers, to avoid the judgment of the

Almighty, had to stand up squarely to slaveholders. Liberty party supporters (Alvan Stewart and a few others excepted) recognized that Congress had no direct authority over slavery in the states, but demanded it deploy its constitutional powers to keep it a municipal or local institution. This would involve abolition in the District of Columbia and in Florida territory, an end to the coastal and interstate slave trade, active protection of freedom of speech and petition against proslavery gag laws, and prevention of the annexation of Texas. In other words, the federal government, and indeed the governments of the free states, were morally obliged to make the interests of equality and free labor the controlling element in every legislative, executive, and judicial action.[12]

The party's *modus operandi* proceeded from an understanding that individual voters bore a personal responsibility for the actions of their government. Party leaders drove home the citizen's obligation, as Luther Lee put it, "to vote the Liberty ticket as a religious duty," supporting only candidates who would sustain Christian government.[13] Religious criteria should guide all political actions. Those who put party tickets before conscience should prepare for the Last Day, when "God will judge us as individuals, and not in parties." Liberty party meetings, especially when preceded or followed by essentially religious gatherings, took on a crusading, revivalistic character, to reassure the faithful and convince earnest seekers. At Oberlin, "after a sermon by Mr. Finney, about every Whig vote was given to the Liberty Party." Liberty men boasted a novel, uncorrupted, liberating, and uniquely scriptural form of politics. Austin Willey later recalled something of this sense of the movement's unique excitement: "The Liberty party, unlike any other in history, was founded on moral principles – on the Bible, originating a contest not only against slavery but against atheistic politics from which Divine law was excluded." Opponents found the crusading single-mindedness and self-righteousness of Liberty men "intolerant and denunciatory," but neither friend nor foe doubted the movement was, in the words of the critic Calvin Colton, "a proper religious enterprise."[14]

The movement's evangelical character was evident in its personnel. Though we lack systematic data regarding its membership and support, there is every reason to accept Colton's description of the party as "a religious brotherhood." Party leaders targeted clergy and their church members as the likeliest recruits. Where polling evidence exists, as for Smithfield, New York, the evangelical, revivalist, predominantly Yankee orientation of the party's followers is clearly discernible. The party elite presented a similar pedigree. Liberty leaders in Vermont included George Storrs, Benjamin Shaw, and Orange Scott, all Wesleyan Methodist ministers; Baptists and Congregationalists were also to the fore. Free Will Baptists assumed particular prominence in Maine, together with Baptists, Congregationalists, and some Methodists. A similar pattern – of strong "come-outer" representation supplemented by the support of a vigorous minority from mainstream evangelical denominations – was evident in New Hampshire, other New England states, and New York. Despite historians' tendency to dichotomize between "pragmatic," politically realistic westerners and religious, visionary New Englanders, the Yankee religious diaspora is indisputably evident in Ohio, where Free Presbyterians like John Rankin worked alongside Methodists such as Samuel Lewis and New School Presbyterians and Congregationalists like Oberlin's President Asa Mahan and James A. Thome. Even those like Gamaliel Bailey, who pursued a more coalitionist approach to antislavery politics, and whose pedigree was middle-state, Arminian, and Democrat, not New England, Calvinist, and Whig, brought an evangelical sensibility as well as a pragmatic temperament to the pursuit of moral ends.[15]

Theodore Foster later confirmed that "most of our leaders and political speakers have been and are ministers – not statesmen or politicians." His reflection indicated not satisfaction but regret: whatever evangelicals had contributed by way of crusading moralism had been offset, in his view, by their narrowness of political vision. Few expected the party to achieve much in the Log-Cabin campaign, but its advances in the early 1840s at state and local level had appeared to promise far more than its meager tally of 65,608 votes in the presidential contest of 1844. Its successes were largely negative: preventing the filling of numerous legislative seats in New England states where representatives had to secure over 50 percent of votes cast; discouraging major parties from putting up candidates known to have voted with the South; preventing the election of Clay in 1844 by attracting enough Whig votes to throw the pivotal state of New York behind Polk.[16]

As a one-idea movement with no reasonable hope of electoral success the Liberty party seemed to offer little to antislavery evangelicals aiming to prevent the return of a Democratic administration and pursuing other concerns besides abolition. Its problem in countering the fear of the "wasted vote" was evident in 1840. Jonathan Blanchard, Samuel Lewis, and John Rankin and other western evangelicals, for example, championed Harrison to prevent the re-election of Van Buren, regarded by Gamaliel Bailey as "par eminence the slaveholders' candidate."[17] For Rankin, supporting Harrison to keep Van Buren at bay was the most principled course of action in morally complex circumstances: "If they [Whig Abolitionists] do not vote for Harrison, they do as much for Van Buren as so many Democrats who put in their votes for him. I abhor the Whig party, and sustain it only because it is the best I can do for abolition, and for the country." Henry B. Stanton estimated that "19/20ths" of Massachusetts abolitionists were hostile to independent nominations in that year and that "49/50ths of our friends" there were Harrison

Whigs so hostile to Van Buren that they "would wade to their armpits in molten lava" to turn him out.[18]

The problem persisted after 1840, as it became clear that Liberty growth tended to weaken Whiggery and play into the hands of the Democrats. In fact the party did win a few Democratic recruits, principally Thomas Morris of Ohio, son of a Baptist preacher and US senator, who was to be the party's vice-presidential candidate in 1844.[19] But it was from evangelical Whiggery that the movement stole most of its support. Significantly, Blanchard, Lewis, and Rankin were all supporters by 1844. So too were Lewis Tappan and other lukewarm observers of 1840. In Michigan the party, as Ronald Formisano has told us, was "a splinter group of the Whig-Presbyterian-evangelical subculture."[20] As we have seen, Henry Clay directly attributed his defeat in 1844 to such losses. This tormented not only the Kentuckian himself but many of his antislavery supporters. They would remain skeptical about third-party action until the day (not far distant) when Democrats faced defections on a similar scale.

Rebuking abolitionism, castigating slavery: free-state evangelicals of the mainstream

One of the most evident, and unwanted, achievements of Liberty campaigning was to demonstrate that even within the free states most evangelicals held abolitionism and its political expression at arm's length, regarding it at best with distaste and more commonly with horror.[21] Though few clergy had directly encouraged physical attacks on AASS agents in the 1830s and early 1840s, the violence of their outpourings against "the whole tribe of lunaticks" and the "Radico-Abolitionists" was commonplace.[22] The sentiments of these free-state evangelical critics were not always grounded in a very clear understanding of the philosophical differences within abolitionism. They often polemically lumped non-Garrisonian abolitionists with Garrisonian anti-sabbatarians and non-resistants.[23] But it is possible to distinguish a number of coherent lines of argument in mainstream evangelicals' repudiation of abolitionist doctrine and methods.

What induced most of these critics to denounce abolitionist doctrine as "Jacobinical," "revolutionary," and "ultra" was not its implications for race relations but its appearing radically to threaten, first, scriptural orthodoxy and the ecclesiastical status quo and, secondly, political stability. Even those abolitionists who distanced themselves from Garrisonian attacks on the Scriptures, conventional sabbatarianism, the orthodox ministry, and the other "venerable, sacred, and time honored *institutions*" of New England, and who were amongst the most severe critics of Garrison's "infidelity," were vulnerable to the charge that in making slavery a sin in all circumstances they stood traditional Christian teaching on its head.[24] Abolitionists' demand for the end of all church fellowship with slaveholders, without regard to particular circumstances, revealed a want of Christian discrimination. "I am no abolitionist in one sense of the word," John McClintock explained. "I do not believe that all slaveholders are sinners; I know that some of them are pious men, so far as human judgment can go, and I would not harm them, even in my thoughts, for the world. I pity them." Asa Kent affirmed there was no sin in offering fellowship to a slaveholder "provided he will acknowledge that he disapproves the system &c but . . . believes it to be his duty – under the circumstances – for the good of the slaves to retain that relation." The unyielding stand of abolitionists on the sinfulness of slavery would set brother against brother, destroy *communitas*, delay the advent of the millennium, encourage church "convulsions," and tighten the bonds of slavery by undermining the work of evangelical churches amongst slaves and slaveholders.[25]

Abolitionism seemed equally subversive of political order. Here, too, Garrison's notorious, anarchist views cast a shadow over the reputation of the wider movement: even non-Garrisonian, political abolitionists looked like "revolutionists."[26] True Christians, Charles Elliott explained, could not subscribe to the "anarchy, rebellion and treason" to which political abolitionism must inevitably lead; they should rather respect the powers that be, "though they may be even in political error." The Union, and a unique political experiment, were at stake. In George Duffield's view, abolitionists jeopardized the God-given republicanism that underpinned America's prosperity and made her the envy of the world. Their principles, declared Nathan Rice, would rend "our civil union" through "a most dreadful civil war."[27]

Abolitionists' manner inspired as much evangelical criticism as did their matter. Immediatism seemed to be a system of heated agitation rather than rational discussion. Evangelical critics variously described abolitionists as reckless, self-righteous, and intolerant; they were "headstrong, fanatical, abusive, Pharisaical," "wanton" in their attacks on "the more sober and thinking portion of the Church," and driven by a "spirit of crimination, denunciation, and slander." "Do the Abolitionists go amongst slave-holders, and reason kindly with them?" asked Nathan Rice: "The notorious Leavit[t] talks of reasoning with slave-holders with 'cold steel.'" These imperious attitudes they carried into their own brand of intolerant politics. "The people . . . must vote as they dictate, and those who seek for office must look directly to them, and yield to their dictation," a Methodist complained. Political abolitionists, lamented George Duffield, resorted "to the polls rather than to the power of reason, to the genius of christianity and moral force of truth." This conviction that Liberty men had, in "a perversion of duty," abandoned their true religious vocation for the heated arena of politics where they now set Christian fanatically against Christian, was a common theme amongst their churchgoing critics.[28]

The most fundamental grievance free-state evangelicals entertained against abolitionists, however, was that they brought an excellent goal into disrepute. As Abel Stevens explained, "the noble cause of Human Emancipation" was "distracted, disgraced and frustrated by an amalgamation" with antislavery radicals.[29] Criticism of slavery was as near-universal in northern churches as was antipathy towards abolitionism. Though most refused to see slavery as a personal sin *per se*, it was widely regarded as a cruel and unjust evil whose removal would be "a godly deed." A Methodist from McConnelsville circuit, Ohio, reported in 1844 that "all our members are pretty heartily opposed" to slavery: though only four or five in the circuit considered themselves out-and-out abolitionists, over 250 called on the General Conference of the (MEC) to adhere resolutely to the church's historic antislavery posture. A long list of articulate and severe critics of abolitionism, including Leonard Bacon, Samuel W. Cozzens, George Duffield, Charles Elliott, Charles S. Porter, Nathan Rice, and Matthew Simpson, were equally forceful in their disapproval of slavery itself.[30]

For some the grounds of objection related less to principle than to specific abuses particular to the South. Old School Presbyterian James W. Alexander censured southern slaveholders for separating families, preventing legal marriage and restricting religious instruction, but was not convinced that slavery was unjust in all cases or that freedom was sanctioned by the Bible. More commonly, however, northern evangelicals drew on an amalgam of enlightenment philosophy and scriptural exegesis to present slavery as a national sin that violated the slave's natural rights on the one hand and "the equity of God's law" and the spirit and precepts of the Gospels on the other. The Christian's duty was to condemn a system which, while it did not always imply sin in the individual slaveholder, was a national crime, the "dark spot upon our national character."[31]

For most of these critics the solution lay not in violent and sudden emancipation, externally imposed on the South. They called for the voluntary manumission of slaves by their masters, followed by their settlement of west Africa through the efforts of "that most benevolent association," the American Colonization Society (ACS). In Liberia blacks would find opportunities for self-improvement and self-government that their unequal and dependent condition in North America would never allow. There they would provide a beacon for "that most benighted continent," extending Christianity and ending the slave trade along the African coast. Charles Elliott described colonization as the only possible approach for "true philanthropists." Slavery was the "peculiar business" of the South with which "we have no wish to interfere," but since good men in each section desired its end and southerners themselves had taken a prominent role in the ACS, "those in the north and middle states may safely and consistently unite with them." Thus, for reasons that combined religious mission and political conservatism, colonization won extensive support amongst northern evangelicals, especially Methodists and Old School Presbyterians.[32]

One of the most pivotal of antebellum political processes was that by which those who disliked slavery (as opposed to its passionate haters) became sufficiently aroused to stand publicly against it. An earlier school of historians saw this broadening of antislavery opinion in the 1840s and 1850s very much as the direct achievement of abolitionist agitation.[33] More recent historiography tends to see that change having developed in a more complicated way, from two related processes: violent reaction against abolitionism by southern leaders, and the consequent response of northerners to what they considered the over-reaction of an intolerant, militant "slave power" to a vocal but unrepresentative free-state minority. In other words, antislavery opinion amongst non-abolitionists in the North developed primarily in response to perceived southern aggressions, not to the cajoling of northern radicals.

As will be seen, the shifting relationship between the sectional halves of evangelical Protestantism in the 1840s and 1850s tends to sustain this view. But it is as well to understand that whatever separated immediate abolitionists from more cautious antislavery evangelicals, they shared (non-voting Garrisonians excepted) enough common perceptions of their public duty to cooperate in political action in the right circumstances. Disagree as they might over the sinfulness of individual slaveholders, both immediatists and their critics castigated slavery as the nation's sin, for which an angry God would punish the unrepentant republic. They were also agreed that the Christian could not countenance what Horace Bushnell called the separation of politics from the fear of God.[34] The exercise of the Christian conscience in politics was a basic obligation of every evangelical.

By the second half of the 1840s many evangelical critics of the abolitionists had come to moderate their hostility. John McClintock, an influential Methodist not known for mincing his words, continued to think of Garrisonians as actuated by the Devil, and was implacably opposed to cutting off slaveholders from church membership, but he confessed to Stephen Olin in 1846 that "my abhorrence of slavery grows apace." Early in the following year he publicly declared that "the division of Northern men into abolitionists and anti-abolitionists exists no longer." With few exceptions the northern public was "imbued with anti-slavery feeling; not the dormant, passive feeling which existed . . .

ten years ago, . . . but a living, even an aggressive, power, which not only refuses to strengthen the institution of slavery, but speaks ominously of its overthrow." Over the decade northern evangelicals had opened their eyes more fully to their nation's moral contamination. "In a word," McClintock suggested, "the CONSCIENCE of the great Northern race is aroused, and even the 'potsherds of the earth' do homage to it in Wilmot provisos and the like."[35]

Two sets of forces sharpened evangelical sensibilities, one originating outside the churches, the other within. Most obviously, "conscience" was conditioned by political developments – congressional gag laws, territorial expansion into Texas and Mexico – that intimated the enhanced power of the slavocracy. It was also shaped by evangelicals' experience as members of churches which found it impossible to duck the question of slavery, but whose institutional elasticity could not absorb the inter-sectional stresses to which their debates gave rise. These parallel experiences demand separate analyses.

Texas, Mexico, and America's religious destiny

The enthusiasm of the South's political representatives for measures which, legally or otherwise, restricted public discussion of slavery found little echo in northern evangelical circles. When planters sought through state and federal action to prevent the circulation of abolitionist tracts, to drive critics of slavery from the South, and to prevent discussion of the issue in the legislatures, it was not just radical critics of the peculiar institution who protested. The *Christian Advocate and Journal* was no friend of Joshua Giddings or the radical antislavery resolutions whose introduction had secured his censure in the House of Representatives. Yet this respected voice of Methodism deplored "the hasty and inconsiderate proceedings" that drove him from his seat. Such actions would "give error itself the advantage of awakening public sympathy by the cry of persecution." The prediction proved accurate: Giddings's Western Reserve constituency, peopled with transplanted Yankee evangelicals, re-elected him and so effectively destroyed the congressional gag and the bipartisan arrangements holding it in place.[36]

A principal theme of the antislavery petitions southerners sought to stifle was the contention that the slave power was engaged in a nefarious plot to annex Texas to the United States, to perpetuate and extend slavery. "Texas was dismembered from Mexico, by a band of robbers," George Allen asserted, "to be partitioned into numerous States, that slavery might thenceforth hold the sceptre of a nation where freedom should never reach its hand to molest it." Texas was the latest stage in a pattern of southern aggression that had won much of the

Louisiana Purchase and Florida for slavery and driven Indian tribes into the trans-Mississippi territory as a barrier to freedom. Further additions from Mexico would inexorably follow. Evangelical editors and pulpiteers, particularly in New England and the wider Northeast, offered dire prophecies of the national calamity, "a more terrific doom," that would follow this immoral act: war, butchery, destruction of commerce, and moral degeneracy. The Almighty would not easily forgive his special people for abandoning self-restraint and quenching "the flame of primitive freedom and Puritanism." Even conservative Old School Presbyterians like James W. Alexander considered the event "an enormity," though he wondered whether slavery might not be weakened in the border states as slaveholders descended on the Southwest.[37]

Evangelicals did not divide straightforwardly along sectional lines. Set against those who believed that territorial aggrandizement betrayed America's mission were those convinced of her providential duty to bring all of North America under Protestant influence.[38] American churches had begun missionary activities in Texas in the early 1830s, and after the republic had declared its independence Baptists, Presbyterians and, in particular, Methodists increased their efforts there. Both northerners and southerners saw a net balance of religious advantage in territorial acquisition. True, southern Christians could identify sectional as well as broader Protestant benefits. The *Southern Christian Advocate* spoke for southern Methodists who saw Texas not only as "the *point d'appui*, the key to the religious conquest of the vast regions beyond," but as a means of contributing "strength and consolidation to the M.E. Church in the South": from the Potomac and the Ohio to the borders of Mexico primitive Methodism would be "safe from fanatical intermeddling."[39] But northern – even some New England – Methodists, too, waxed enthusiastic about this further step towards fulfilling "the prediction of Edwards that America is to be the birth place of the Millennium," not least by thwarting Mexican efforts to impose on American settlers Catholic rites of baptism and marriage. John Clark presented Anglo-Saxon settlers as invulnerable targets of Mexican despotism: "Will Protestant Texans ever submit to being governed by the near-sighted and narrow policy of Papal Mexico? No. NEVER."[40]

The United States' subsequent war with Mexico generated an even greater passion in evangelical churches, eliciting a similar pattern of sectionalism modified by patriotic fervor and anti-Catholicism. Support for the war found its center of gravity in the South, especially amongst Baptists and Methodists; Old School Presbyterians there showed more muted sympathy. Southern evangelicals regarded Mexicans as "ignorant, idle and degraded": "The great mass of the population doze out their lives with no higher thoughts or purposes than the beasts which perish around them." Fed an idolatrous and priest-ridden religion, the country had floundered in darkness since the days of Montezuma. America's spirituality beckoned her to overturn what the Southern Baptist Convention considered "the withering reign of the Man of Sin." The United States army became a Christian force whose "every cannon ball is a missionary; and every soldier is a Colporteur." Amongst its ministers in the field was Richard Stuart of Louisiana, whose church gave him six months' leave to fortify American troops, children of Israel advancing on Canaan.[41]

Pro-war feeling amongst evangelicals extended beyond the South. If few northerners matched the unquestioning enthusiasm of ministers like John Chambers of Philadelphia and William Daily of Evansville, Indiana, staunch defenders of Polk and Democracy, many others did their bit to rally opinion behind the American forces.[42] Baptists, Methodists, and Presbyterians very widely took the view that patriotism demanded an embargo on political controversy and, more positively, that the conflict would yield rewards for American Protestantism. Stephen M. Vail, Methodist minister of Pine Plains, New York, represented those for whom war between republics was in most cases "a real calamity" but here was "enlightened, humane and liberal," since it sought to introduce Mexicans to a superior religion, morality, and education. Though believing slavery challenged the basic political and ethical values of America, he made no attempt to link the war with this issue. Even the *New York Evangelist*, firmly antislavery and opposed to the conflict, saw some benefit from the acquisition of parts of Mexico and the ensuing spread of Anglo-Saxon culture.[43]

Hostility to the war presented a denominational and geographical pattern similar to that prompted by the Texas issue. Congregationalists and New School Presbyterians in New England and its diaspora provided the spine of opposition, reinforced by Quakers, Unitarians, Freewill Baptists, and a determined minority of Baptists, Methodists, and Old School Presbyterians. Critics in the Northeast were vocal from the outset, their voices supplemented as time passed by those of churches and clergy in the Ohio Valley.[44] Open dissent was rare but not unheard in the South, articulated in the border regions by James Pendleton of Kentucky, Morgan Rhees of Delaware, and William Brownlow of Tennessee, and in the lower South by Robert L. Stanton of Louisiana and William Winans of Mississippi.[45] Some Old School ministers in the South harbored doubts, but on this, as on other political issues, silence and caution were their watchwords.

One thrust of argument took the theme of war as "dire calamity," fought at huge cost in lives and damage to the nation's economic and political fabric. Although by later standards the tally of American casualties was moderate, William Hill, Baptist itinerant of South Carolina, grieved that the conflict was "sweeping off . . . hundreds of our choice young men." Many believed the expense of the war – estimated at the outset to be costing half a million dollars a day – would lead to a huge increase in the public debt and taxation, and interrupt or derange commerce and industry. Politically, war would undermine American liberties as it had those of all republics. It tipped power towards the executive branch, disturbed the delicate balance between state and federal authority, encouraged what Milton P. Braman described as "an imperious, tyrannical spirit," and threatened a larger standing army. War infringed the citizen's rights without the people noticing, warned Samuel Harris of Conway, Massachusetts, alarmed as were so many New England ministers by the consequences of the war for Christian republicanism.[46]

War with Mexico was more than calamitous. It was "a piece of most atrocious wickedness," born in "the bowie knife style of civilization"; before God and the conscience of the world every lost life was murder. "Never," lamented James W. Alexander, "have I so much feared the judgments of God on us as a nation." What troubled evangelicals was not simply that all war corroded a society's moral integrity and increased the appetite for blood, but that this particular conflict inaugurated a "new national era." In a radical departure, the nation had abandoned peaceful, moral influence over others for a war of conquest. Many were contemptuous of the government's claim that Mexicans had provoked hostilities. Why, if the war were defensive, asked Samuel Burchard, were the Americans in Mexico City? Grand claims sought to mask the "vulgar robber passion of military adventure." Calvin Fletcher and other Whig evangelicals, north and south, explicitly blamed Polk, a weak, "compromising party candidate" for this "uncalled for & aggressive war" designed to increase Democratic prestige.[47]

American aggression was all the more reprehensible for its cowardliness and cruelty. John McClintock stood appalled by "the conduct of our troops in Mexico – barbarity upon barbarity – worse than Goths and Vandals." A chorus of Presbyterians protested against American attacks on "a half-civilized, . . . weak and defenceless people" who had "done as little against us as we could have expected." David Riddle asked scornfully of those who defended force as a means of extending Protestant, Anglo-Saxon civilization: "will christians be likely to pause and think of the heathen, or of sending them salvation, while engaged in dealing damnation to their brethren?" Samuel Burchard impatiently protested that no one had "an unqualified license to commit evil, that good may come": this was "papal dogma," wholly at odds with the professed intention of defeating Romanism.[48]

For many of these critics the ultimate proof of the moral wickedness of American policy was the murky but incontrovertible evidence that at its heart stood the slave power. Polk was the slaveholders' tool, and the extension of "the dark realm of slavery" their hidden ambition. Richard Tolman's view of the war as "a crusade against freedom and humanity" was commonplace amongst north-eastern Protestants.[49] Inflicting slavery on any conquered territory would combine with the weakening of social cohesion, the corollary of rapid territorial growth, to reduce further the influence of New England culture and religion in the republic. The spread of settlers (including a likely flood of Catholics) into millions of new acres (already churched by Rome) would secure "a departure from Social Purity," generate "a downward gravitation in morals, in social manners, in education, in religion," and turn the Mexican lands into a "great pasture ground of barbarism." Not all shared Burdett Hart's farsighted fear that acquiring new territory would engender "fratricidal conflict" over slavery, but his sense that Americans had embarked on a new phase of their moral journeying was widely recognized.[50]

True patriotism, critics contended, lay not in adopting the "corrupt and destructive" maxim "our country, right or wrong," but in peacefully engaging the nation's moral power to extend over the whole of North America "all the civilization, order, freedom, happiness, which Heaven would love to see established there." Warfare diverted Americans from "the high destiny to which God is calling us." What other lessons could He have intended by the cruel deaths of Secretary of State Abel Upshur and Secretary of War Thomas Gilmer? "The millennium will only come," a Pittsburgh Presbyterian insisted, "when war and all other works of the devil and forms of human sin, cease from the earth."[51]

"Baptised in this Free Soil principle": the third-party movement of 1848

The Mexican war achieved what abolitionism alone had signally failed to do. By raising questions about the intentions of the slave power and the moral direction of the nation, it sharpened the conscience of northern evangelicals previously hostile to "ultra abolitionists" and pushed them towards a new political consensus. Observers outside and inside Protestantism noted the sea-change. Orestes A. Brownson commented sadly in the summer of 1847: "Nearly all the young men from Protestant theological seminaries come out infected, and, wherever settled as ministers, seek to enlist their congregations in the [political antislavery] movement." The war had made "even the most moderate of the citizens of the Free States...resist the further extension of the slave system." Thanks to Mexico, explained a New England Methodist, "abolitionist" was no longer an abusive term in northern churches, where non-extension sentiment was general.[52]

Free-state ministers, especially in New England, boldly called on their members to exploit every political means to reverse the "regular and constant progression" of the slave power. "Too long ... has the North succumbed to the haughty and overbearing spirit of the South," Burdett Hart complained: "The period of forbearance and truckling slavishness has passed."[53] Christians did not have to "wait idly God's time": as voting citizens they could act at once.[54] The "dictates of an enlightened judgment and conscience" demanded dislodging politicians subservient to southern aristocrats, an end to unquestioning loyalty to party, and cooperation in support of the Wilmot Proviso, or some similar measure. For free soil, insisted Benjamin F. Morris of Indiana, was the "basis of all Progress"; "God himself consecrated the Soil of earth to Freedom ... to be tilled only by the Sons of Freedom." Free soil was a moral question "infinitely superior to all party considerations." Conventional political issues would pale into insignificance. Joshua Giddings provided a comforting text: "Who now speaks of a protective tariff? . . . [T]he old lines of demarcation [between parties] have become obscure and uncertain, and new political associations are gradually forming."[55]

Most ministers were, as ever, careful not to be heard publicly endorsing any particular party, though Democrats inevitably interpreted anti-war sermons as Whig propaganda and in 1848 both parties treated pulpit celebrations of free soil as barely disguised endorsements of Van Buren and Adams.[56] Politicians' sensitivity was understandable during a period of uncommon flux in churchgoers' party loyalties. The principal political question for free-soil evangelicals on the eve of the 1848 presidential election was how best to respond to the changing shape of parties in a contest that would turn on the question of slavery's extension.

Whigs in areas where free-soil sentiment was strong enjoyed some success in presenting themselves as firm supporters of anti-extension doctrine, while simultaneously casting Cass and Van Buren as unprincipled opportunists. The veteran Ohio Methodist Arthur W. Elliott, a confirmed free soiler, remained true to Whiggery: he lacked confidence in Van Buren and believed that Taylor, an honest man, would stand by his pledge to follow Congress's lead on the Wilmot Proviso. In New England, where Whigs strongly backed the proviso, they retained the support of many free-soil evangelicals. More conservative Calvinists, too, like James W. Alexander and William E. Dodge, looked to Taylor to follow a prudent anti-extensionist course. As in 1840 and 1844, tactical voters remained loyal to Whiggery, afraid a "wasted" third-party vote would let Cass slip in by default.[57]

Impressive numbers of anti-extensionist evangelicals, however, concluded that only the Free Soil party could be trusted to challenge "southern principles," whatever qualms they might have had over Van Buren's antislavery credentials.[58] Slavery had "fully triumphed" in the national conventions of Whigs and Democrats, whereas Free Soilers at Buffalo had adopted a platform which endorsed the Wilmot Proviso and called on the federal government to disengage from slavery wherever it had power to do so.[59] Sympathizers included some first-time voters who contributed to Free Soil youthful energy, enthusiasm, and an absence of prior party loyalties: men like Henry L. Pierce of Stoughton, Massachusetts, an active Methodist who "did more than any other citizen to give the lead . . . in his town."[60] But far more significant in shaping the party as an electoral force were the thousands of evangelicals who shifted from a previous allegiance.

Some were Liberty men, though the failure of the Free Soil party to nail its colors to the mast of racial equality and its explicit denial of congressional power over slavery in the states were unwelcome to the small minority of the old party who now formed the Liberty League. Most Liberty newspapers came out for the new third force. Oberlinites moved into the new camp with enthusiasm. From Iowa in the west to Maine in the east Liberty clergy coalesced with Free Soilers, though patterns of commitment varied. Austin Willey had resisted cooperation between Whigs and his own Liberty men in Maine in 1846–47, fearing a compromise of moral principle, but once he had met the impressive John P. Hale he threw his considerable influence and his newspaper, the *Liberty Standard*, behind Free Soil. In New Hampshire, by contrast, the fusion movement proceeded more smoothly, thanks to the earlier cooperation of Independent Democrats, antislavery Whigs, and Liberty forces to secure Hale's election to the US Senate. Here Oren B. Cheney, Free Will Baptist minister and Liberty man, was especially instrumental in bringing together these once bitterly opposed groupings; he himself later won election as a Free Soiler to the state legislature. One of the principal architects of the Liberty movement of 1840, Joshua Leavitt, was again active, ensuring unanimity behind Van Buren's nomination at Buffalo, organizing free-soil clubs in Massachusetts and taking the stump throughout New England.[61]

More significant, in the perspective of the longer-term fragmentation of the second party system, were the defections to Free Soil of evangelicals from the two main parties, particularly the Whigs. Having previously resisted association with the Liberty party, significant numbers of Whig evangelicals seriously questioned the premises on which they had remained aloof. First, the pragmatic Whig argument, that in a two-party system there was no real alternative to voting for the lesser of two evils, had been undermined by the experience of the last four years: voting for Clay had not prevented the annexation of Texas or the Mexican war. Joseph P. Thompson, Joshua Leavitt's less radical colleague on the New York *Independent*, and no Liberty man, moved firmly into the Free Soil column in 1848, arguing that though *principled* voting might lead to the victory of the more wicked party in the short term, "a re-action" would lead to the right outcome: be ready, he demanded, for "the greatest present evil, for the sake of a greater good in the end than can be secured by taking the lesser evil now."[62] Secondly, many questioned whether antipathy to radical abolitionism should take precedence over hostility to the slave power in shaping political allegiance. Calvin Fletcher, hearing the outcome of the Free Soil convention, resolved to abandon Whiggery for a third party that "makes an issue with slavery that I am willing to meet. . . . [T]he association with some of the old rank abolitionists . . . is not one particle more disagreeable than the association with either of the other parties."[63] Such men found the pull of an antislavery third party irresistible once it had jettisoned "one-ideaism" and shown itself serious about achieving power. Early in 1846 Theodore Foster found credible the claim of a Presbyterian antislavery minister, a Giddings man, that "there are many tens of thousands of religious men, who now vote with the Whigs because they have no other national party" but who longed for the chance to vote for a more broadly based party. Giddings himself, a New School Presbyterian, had by 1848 concluded he could not continue both to support Whig slaveholders for the presidency and represent the thousands of evangelical western Whigs who looked to Free Soil.[64]

The new party's potent combination of moral purpose and evangelical support helped Free Soil function as a religious crusade as much as a conventional political party. Its revivalist character immediately surfaced at the August Buffalo convention that united a diverse collection of Barnburners, Conscience Whigs, Liberty men, and abolitionists, white and black, into a coherent political force. While several hundred official delegates met privately in the Universalist church to make recommendations on nominees and platform, an estimated 20,000 gathered in the city park in a tent that Democratic opponents mockingly called "the great Oberlin canopy." Over three days, speaker after speaker, refreshed with prayer and not alcohol, committed the gathering to a "great moral revolution" founded on "the idea of right and justice and the truth of God." They had come "to be baptised in this Free Soil principle," one which derived as much from the Bible as from the Declaration of Independence. Free Soil was a Christian, purifying agency. The Lord would strike down its wicked political opponents: "God raised up a David of old to slay the giant of Gath. So hath David Wilmot with the sling of freedom and the smooth stone of truth struck the giant slavery between the eyes – he reels – let us push him over!" Hardened politicians, Democrats in particular, miraculously repented of past associations. Sherlock Bristol, Oberlin perfectionist, revivalist, and New York pastor, recalled his astonishment at hearing "old-line wire-pulling politicians . . . speaking all the Abolition language." As one dyed-in-the-wool Democrat spoke, amazed abolitionists cried out: "Is Saul also among the prophets?"[65]

Early morning gatherings for prayer confirmed the convention's character as a protracted revival meeting. Hymn-singing members asked God to guide the proceedings, to forgive the nation's complicity in slavery and racial intolerance, and to extend His kingdom. Hiram Wilson believed "God had determined to make the Convention . . . the medium of reviving . . . throughout this great . . . Nation, the pure principles of Free Government . . . ; and by founding here a real . . . Republic, to diffuse its light and truth to all Nations, until every member of the great human family shall know and rejoice in this great Salvation." On the last morning, nominations completed, the meeting choked with millennialist joy. After the adjournment many remained to sing: "DAUGHTER OF ZION! from the dust,/ Exalt thy fallen head;/ Again in thy Redeemer trust,/ He calls thee from the dead. /Awake! Awake!! put on thy strength/ Thy beautiful array;/ The day of Freedom dawns at length – / The Lord's appointed day!"[66]

Free Soilers left Buffalo convinced that God had called them to serve in a near-apocalyptic struggle between "the dark hellish principles of the past unholy war, and of slavery extended" and "those principles of righteousness . . . pointing us as a people . . . to the rights of man, the rights of God, and the claims of Jesus Christ on earth." Clergy and leading laymen took seriously their duty to be visible in the campaign, speaking out from the pulpit, taking the stump as "mushroom politicians," moving resolutions at state and local conventions, and even standing for office. Jonathan Blanchard was drafted onto the party's electoral ticket in Illinois; he had too much faith in Free Soil politics as the gateway to the Kingdom to decline the nomination, but only narrowly escaped the efforts of Whig trustees to remove him from the presidency of Knox College. Such were the enthusiasts who prompted Senator Thomas Corwin of Ohio to characterize Free Soilers as the most violent and hopeful men he had ever known.[67]

Bound by conscience, not "the trammels of party," third-party men saw themselves as political revolutionaries destined to overturn the existing order.[68] "Henceforth there will be . . . but two great political parties in this country – the party of the South, composed of Southern slaveholders, and a few Northern office expectants with Southern principles, on the one hand – and the FREE Democracy of the nation, and especially the North, on the other." Returning from the Buffalo convention by Hudson steamboat, Sherlock Bristol proudly fought a Tammany Democrat who had threatened to throw overboard any passenger he saw signing an antislavery petition. The incident was emblematic of Free Soilers' contempt for Democratic "bulldozers" and spineless Whigs, of their conviction that their new force was the only dependable defender of freedom. The vote for the Buffalo nominees in November did not, of course, mortally wound the second party system. Van Buren secured little more than 14 percent of the poll in the free states, and there is nothing to suggest that Free Soilers' intervention changed the outcome of the election. One skeptical observer, an antislavery Presbyterian in Missouri, thought the party's failure entirely the result of putting political ambition before philanthropy. But many of its more committed supporters well understood that political realignment would take a series of elections. They were greatly cheered by a fivefold increase in third-party support since 1844 and the many congressional, state, and local victories it secured throughout the fall. Matthew Simpson confidently judged that politicians could not long delay party realignment.[69]

The free-soil campaign demonstrated more clearly than ever the unstable party loyalties of antislavery voters. It also drew a response from southern evangelicals that suggested a similar instability in that section too. Antislavery in general, and Free Soil in particular, appeared to the Georgia Methodist Augustus B. Longstreet a "disorganizing monster" whose policy of non-extension was "an outrage upon all decency and all propriety"; William Valentine called Van Buren "the abolition fanatic, and every other *ism* candidate," driven by unchristian dogma. Free Soilers were "a heterogeneous compound of religious and political fanatics" whose standing before heaven, William Brownlow gleefully noted, was revealed at the meeting where a speaker who declared "God is on the side of the Barnburners!" promptly collapsed and died. Thus Longstreet, though he had "very decided" views on the presidential candidates mooted by the two major parties, determined to submerge his preferences to avoid having "an Abolitionist fastened upon us for any time."[70] Though Iveson L. Brookes, Baptist preacher and substantial planter in Georgia and South Carolina, voted for Taylor, he was soon to cut his ties to Whiggery, believing southerners "at the present crisis should know but one party" and "as one man stand forth in defence of southern rights."[71]

Evangelicals' responses to expansionism, then, as raised by government policy over Texas and Mexico, had shown that political loyalties under the second party system were not unquestioning but conditional, and that the system itself was vulnerable to aroused sectional feelings. Enhanced sectionalism did not, however, derive solely or straightforwardly from events in the political sphere. Developments within as well as outside the evangelical churches also encouraged churchgoers to stare suspiciously and even angrily across a blurred line that separated northern from southern Christians.

"God's Institution": southern evangelicals and slavery

Determining the churches' proper Christian relationship to slavery proved a nagging, divisive, and irrepressible issue for antebellum evangelicals. Conflict within and between churches was a feature not only of the rancorous years from 1837 to 1845, when the major denominations experienced agonizing schisms deriving at least in part from the slavery agitation, but of the whole period before 1861.[72] This persisting debate and its associated stresses profoundly shaped the political perspectives of American churchgoers, including those who believed slavery an improper matter for discussion in ecclesiastical bodies. Polarization of church communities encouraged in each section destructively negative perceptions of the other. The images so created gave meaning to political as well as ecclesiastical events. Hundreds of thousands of evangelicals, thanks to their churches' unprecedentedly effective communications system of traditional pulpit and revolutionary steam press, were made to feel part of a widely extended denominational community; they enjoyed swift access to church news and the developing views of appointed or self-appointed opinion-formers; they achieved their own understanding of who and what had caused the breakdown of national consensus in the churches. At the same time, through the political columns of their weekly religious newspapers or through the secular press, these same men and women interpreted political events that appeared to parallel or follow a pattern already established in the churches. Methodist families that subscribed, for example, to the *New York Tribune* and *Western Christian Advocate* (as did William F. King's in Ohio) were typical of evangelical households countrywide which took seriously both ecclesiastical and political affairs, and for whom the conceptual understandings formed in one sphere shaped judgements in the other. Precisely because church conflicts over slavery could not be tidily compartmentalized in the minds of evangelical citizens, there was every reason why – as a Virginian Methodist declared in 1848 – "the eye of the whole political world" should be fixed on the warring parties.[73]

Before looking at precisely how these church conflicts shaped political attitudes we must consider first the shifting patterns of southern evangelicals' thinking on slavery.[74] The sea-change in their outlook in these years contributed to the North–South polarization that made church division likely and was itself quickened by that experience of schism. In the early years of the century southern Christians widely understood that slavery was not destined to last and was, as the Charleston Presbyterian John B. Adger put it, "at least injudicious as far as the happiness of the master was concerned."[75] Yet by mid-century there existed in the same circles something of a proslavery consensus which regarded the institution as neither transient nor evil. Iveson

Brookes recalled how as a student at Chapel Hill from 1816 to 1819 he wrote speeches against slavery, considering slavery "a moral wrong to the African race . . . [and] justified only upon the ground of necessity," but later became convinced that it was "God's Institution." Another Baptist, Jeremiah B. Jeter, described in later life how his own thinking, under Thornton Stringfellow's influence, had been pulled away from a negative understanding of slavery as necessary but "uncongenial" to one in which it might in certain circumstances "belong to the best order of society that human, or even divine, wisdom can devise."[76] As with all glacial shifts in collective thinking there was no single pivotal moment of change. Brookes's own writings suggest that he reached his new perception late in the 1840s. Yet Basil Manly and others clearly adopted this more sanguine view at least a decade earlier. What is beyond dispute is that by 1850 southern churches had come widely to see slavery as a Christianizing agent and an institution that would continue to improve as the millennium approached.[77]

The South's deepening economic stake in slavery and its pursuit of social cohesion in the face of threatened slave revolts had forced all white southerners into reappraising the institution. Amongst evangelicals, however, it was widely believed that the most important catalyst of change had been the abolitionists' harsh criticisms of the South. John Adger was in no doubt of the effect of the "furious anti-slavery crusade." "I do believe," he mused to Robert L. Dabney, "that if these mad fanatics had let us alone, in twenty years we should have made Virginia a free State. As it is, their unauthorized attempts to strike off the fetters of our slaves have but riveted them on the faster." Adger's view, that "[w]e are less inclined to do that which we know to be our duty because persons, who have no right to interfere, demand it of us," was a more muted version of William Winans's belief that the South invited "turbulence" and "evil" for the tenacity with which it held "its chivalric notions in regard to foreign interference in domestic concerns." Winans's view suggests the tension between, on one side, the honor code which Bertram Wyatt-Brown has encouraged us to see at the heart of the Old South's social and political relations, emphasizing shame, the rule of tradition and conformity to community will, and on the other, an evangelical ethic that nourished individualism, conscience, self-scrutiny, and guilt. Amongst those southerners who subscribed implicitly to the code of honor "antislavery polemics evoked feelings, not of guilt, but of anger and indignation." Evangelicals responded differently. While they had no truck with northern abolitionist "fanaticism," aimed at "infecting the consciences of weak minded good Christian people of the South," they were equally conscious of the sins associated with southern conceptions of honor: pride and egotism, traits at odds with Christian "humility and a proper estimate of one's self." For such southerners it was essential that any defense of slavery should be grounded not on "false honor" ("those fictitious and absurd sentiments ... [which give] to the duel a character of exalted chivalry"), but on respect for the sovereignty of the individual conscience.[78]

Successfully challenge the abolitionists' premise that slavery was a sin before God, they believed, and the Christian's conscience could be engaged in its defense. Scripture provided the forensic weapon, for on closer scrutiny it appeared in both letter and spirit directly to sanction the institution. Old Testament society was founded on it. God had incorporated into the Jewish polity "negro slavery, or the [hereditary] bondage of the Canaanitish descendants of Ham," recognizing that it would provide the basis of "the preservation of true liberty, civil and religious, among the Jews."[79] The explicit reference to servants in the final commandment of the decalogue evidently legitimized slaveholding by "the most eminent Old Testament saints." Slavery was equally recognized under the new dispensation. Christ and his apostles, living and working where it existed under Roman law, failed to denounce it, even though they rebuked all kinds of sin; indeed, they received into the church as Christians in good standing both slaves and slaveholders, who were "spoken of in the highest terms of approbation"; they indicated the duties of masters and slaves as precisely as they did those of parents and children, rulers and subjects. They were fools or rogues who argued that the spirit of the New Testament ("All things whatsoever ye would that men should do unto you, do ye even so to them") demanded the freeing of slaves. The Golden Rule merely meant, according to a Georgia Baptist, "that it is our duty to do unto others as it would be *reasonable* for us to wish others to do unto us, were our situations reversed"; it called on the slave to be obedient to his master, and the master to act with humanity. Ferdinand Jacobs reminded his fellow Presbyterians that Christ described the Golden Rule as the *sum* of the law and the prophets, which should never be applied to subvert any of the orders or relations they had established; northern applications of the rule invited "agrarianism and communism."[80]

Since slave-free societies were unknown to Scripture, any polity which sought to exclude slaves must be "an artificial state." This logic convinced some evangelicals of a profound dichotomy between the imperatives of Holy Writ and the natural rights philosophy of the Declaration of Independence. The doctrine of the equality of all men was "manifestly erroneous." Jefferson had been "a noted old infidel." Those who appealed to his writings in preference to Scripture were rank blasphemers. Whitefoord Smith scorned those who pursued an atheistic equality that sprang from "a jealousy of all who seem more favored than ourselves." Another South Carolinian asserted: "INEQUALITY is now the law of our being. In innumerable forms, it determines the conditions and relations of life." He was by no means alone in his Calhounite belief that equality and freedom were not "born with man" but were "high prizes to be won."[81]

If the Bible commanded acceptance of the natural inequalities of human society it also imposed on the rich and powerful a responsibility for the poor and enslaved. Recognizing this obligation, evangelicals in the mold of Robert L. Dabney, Presbyterian minister and Virginia slaveowner, and the wealthy Methodist A.L.P. Green, called for the removal of "the most erroneous abuses" of "the grosser form of slavery"; they urged masters to put their relationship with their slaves on the highest moral basis, preparing themselves, in the words of the Alabama Baptist Convention, "to give an account to their master in heaven."[82] In material terms this meant providing for the blacks' physical welfare, but even more did it entail nurturing their spiritual development. Some Christian masters, anxious that no man should put asunder those whom God had joined together, took this to demand careful protection of the slave family as a moral regulator. At the heart of their concern lay the slave's salvation. Thus missions to the slaves burgeoned through the 1840s and 1850s as planters' earlier fears of the movement's crypto-abolitionism melted away. Even in South Carolina, where chronic white alarm over slave rebelliousness was most evident, most of the slaves were under religious instruction by the eve of the Civil War, thanks to the vigorous leadership of such slaveholding ministers as Charles Colcock Jones and William Capers, and supportive politicians.[83] As their efforts bore fruit, so those involved in missions regarded slavery as a great Christianizing influence, providing "a most merciful deliverance" from the "savage idolatry," warfare, and butchery of unredeemed Africa.[84]

God's blessing on missions was one confirmation of the scriptural basis of slavery. So too was the South's social harmony. Those "riotous outbreaks" that commonly endangered northern life and property were almost unknown below the Mason-Dixon line, since slavery sustained republican peace and safety by uniting labor and capital, cultivating "the mutual good feeling" of master and servant, and preventing the strife inherent in a free labor system. In Iveson Brookes's view the non-slaveholding states, "ignorantly fighting against God & the Bible," contained the elements of their own destruction, since the ballot box was open to the control of agrarians and anarchists: "None other than a monarchical and military despotism can ultimately control the populace, and secure the rights of the property-holders, where slavery is not the basis of society." In contrast, southern slaves, except when deluded by "diabolical inter-meddlers," were "the most contented and happy people on earth," while whites enjoyed "equality of social and political intercourse" unparalleled in the civilized world.[85]

The logic of southern Protestants' near-universal conviction that slavery was scripturally sound and could be sustained in good conscience, was to elevate it into a positive blessing ordained to be permanent in America. This certainly was the view of an articulate few who staunchly declared it an absolute good, and called for the removal from church regulations of all references implicitly criticizing it.[86] It is hard to know how fully these public apologists internalized their proslavery thinking. What is beyond dispute is that surface agreement within evangelicalism on the scriptural basis of slavery masked wide variations in attitude, and that, as Calhoun was told in 1849, "many religious people at the South" had "strong misgivings on this head."[87]

Some of these doubters, of course, were emancipationists, largely from the border states, who never subscribed to the prevailing scriptural defense; for them slavery was a rank sin against God and man. New School Presbyterians in Kentucky and eastern Tennessee, for instance, included those who declared that "the gospel, & slavery cannot flourish in the same field" and that no one "could be a christian who did not pray earnestly that the Lord would hasten the day when American Slavery would come to an end."[88] But far more representative of evangelical unease were those in both upper and lower South who, though refusing to describe slavery as a moral evil or sin, were prepared to categorize it as a "curse" or, as Thomas Meredith termed it, a natural evil.[89] Some, like William Winans, William Brownlow, and Moses D. Hoge, were supporters of schemes of colonization which aimed at the longer-term removal of an impolitic institution.[90] More common were such critics as William Valentine, who regarded slavery as "an evil to the whites and a curse to the blacks," but who could see no better alternative. John Witherspoon, a slaveholding Presbyterian minister of North Carolina, believed slavery, though "*lawful & not unchristian* and . . . better for . . . [blacks], on the whole, *than liberty*," had "prostrated our Southern country in point of domestic improvement." Few expressed deeper anguish than his fellow Presbyterian, Benjamin M. Smith of Virginia, personally trapped in selling, hiring, and disciplining slaves. "O what trouble, running sore, constant pressing weight, perpetual wearing, dripping, is this patriarchal institution!" he lamented. "What miserable folly for men to cling to it as something heaven-descended." Even James Thornwell, one of those South Carolinian Presbyterians most closely involved in developing a scriptural defense of slavery, conceded that "Slavery is a part of the curse which sin has introduced into the world, and stands in the same general relation to Christianity as poverty, sickness, disease or death."[91]

What nagged at these evangelicals were not simply the day-to-day cruelties and ignominies of slavery, its debilitating moral effects on slaveholder and non-slaveholding white alike, and its impoverishing economic effects. There was also the uncomfortable fact of the slave's humanity, a reality recognized in the broad evangelical acceptance of the unitary origins of the races and in Protestant missions to the enslaved. In practice they accepted slavery not because it was a positive good, but because it was consistent with Scripture and involved fewer evils than would result from emancipation. Henry Bascom, Kentucky Methodist and a founder of the MECS, spoke for these ambivalent southerners when, stoutly defending the withdrawal of southern Christians into their secure sectional fastnesses, he denied that he and those he represented were pro-slavery. We go, he wrote, "as far *against* slavery as christianity teaches, and no further *for* it than christianity allows."[92]

The critical point, however, is that whatever divisions existed amongst southern evangelicals over whether slavery was an absolute good, a relative benefit, or a tolerable evil, there was near-universal agreement that southern institutions were wholly consistent with Scripture, that slaveholding was not in and of itself a sin, and that owning slaves should not be a barrier to church membership. There was a broad consensus, too, that strategic questions relating to slavery's future were no direct concern of the churches. "Christian men may discuss them as citizens and patriots," pronounced James Thornwell, "but not as members of the Church of Jesus Christ." The robust and combative William A. Smith described Church efforts *"to give both policy and laws to the State"* as a popish betrayal of the Founding Fathers' and John Wesley's stand against "Ecclesiastical combination" in civil affairs. When churchmen did speak out on slavery they insisted they intended no erosion of the doctrine of ecclesiastical non-interference. Iveson Brookes, in his defense of the South against Free Soil attack, was anxious not to be thought "intermeddling in politics"; clergy had a duty as "God's heralds of Bible doctrine" to do what politicians were ill equipped to do, to present the scriptural defense of slavery. Even the Lexington pastor, Robert J. Breckinridge, who in 1849 out of "religious duty" stood as an emancipationist for the new Kentucky convention, was adamant that he had no right to involve the church itself in the campaign.[93]

These certainties – that slaveholding was not a sin *per se*, and that churches had no role in determining matters of social policy – lay at the heart of the sectional conflict within the three major Protestant denominational families. They collided not only with the peremptory demands of the abolitionist minority for the removal of all slaveholding in the churches, but with the more common northern conviction that slaveholding was *prima facie* evidence of iniquity, that the onus of proof for his untainted character lay on the slaveholder himself, and that only those who were doing all they could to cut their ties with slavery should be allowed into communion.[94] The Presbyterian schism of 1837 had only partly to do with incompatible perceptions of slavery's place in the church, but the fracturing of Baptist and Methodist structures in the mid-1840s followed directly from the hammer blows of angry debate between the spokesmen of increasingly alienated sections. Numerically larger than the Baptists, more comfortable than they with centralized coordination and discipline, and proud of their nationally integrated structure, the Methodists suffered even greater trauma from the division of their church. For these reasons they deserve particular attention in the analysis that follows.

"Tirade of abuse": Methodist rupture and sectional antagonism

Abolitionist agitation to secure an end to all slaveholding within the MEC seemed at first to unite against it most northern ministers and their southern brethren.[95] Fearful that internal conflict would divert the church from its declared function as the engine-room of American revivalism, and sharing the general aversion to "fanaticism," conservatives drew together to silence debate in Conference, censure radicals and close the columns of the church's principal newspaper to abrasive critics of the South. But in practice such action served to raise uncomfortable questions amongst non-abolitionist northerners about the rights of Christians to freedom of speech and private judgement. Once suspension and expulsion of antislavery Methodists had been followed by the secession of Orange Scott, La Roy Sunderland, and other leading abolitionists to form an independent Wesleyan Methodist Church in 1843, the authorities in northern conferences of the MEC moved to soften their line to pre-empt the membership drive of the new church.[96]

Delegates met in New York for the General Conference in May 1844 aware that concessions to the South would recruit for the come-outers, but that a firm stand against Methodist slaveholding risked a schism along sectional lines.[97] The issue was soon tested, first in the case of Francis Harding, a minister suspended for slaveholding by the Baltimore Conference, and more critically in the debate over Bishop James O. Andrew of Georgia.[98] The "Finley resolution" called on the bishop, who had recently married a slaveowning widow, to "desist from the exercise of his office" for as long as he remained "connected with slavery." Andrew was a decent, pacific man whose personal feelings were overridden as the issue became "a matter of conscience on both sides." Northern critics found irrelevant Andrew's record as a scrupulous Methodist who, in a state where manumission was forbidden by law, had tried to avoid direct ownership of slaves: to accept a slaveholder as an officer exercising nationwide authority would concede that slavery was a national, not local, institution. For their part, most southerners insisted that Andrew draw back from his intention to resign in the interests of harmony. This would be a surrender to the false doctrine of the sinfulness of slaveholding in all cases and an admission of the moral inferiority of the South.[99] When delegates decided against Andrew, southerners moved down the road to schism. The General Conference overwhelmingly adopted a Plan of Separation under which resources would be divided and the annual conferences in the slave states would establish an independent church. Representatives of those conferences met under the presidency of Bishops Soule and Andrew in Louisville in May 1845 and organized the Methodist Episcopal Church, South (MECS).

The action of southern delegates elicited warm approval from their members at home. Throughout the summer and fall and on into 1845 camp meetings, quarterly conferences, and other gatherings passed resolutions attacking the unscriptural and "revolutionary" action at New York as "an outrage against our civil, social, and religious compact, to which we ought not, cannot, and will not submit!" In legislating on slavery the General Conference had "stepped out of their sphere" into a secular sphere "with which they had nothing to do." The MEC "had got into Cesar's province," William Capers protested: separation was the only proper response. Southern Methodist editors dismissed northern calls for restraint. William M. Wightman of the *Southern Christian Advocate* thought it "a matter of small moment to the Southern people just now, whether he who takes ground against them is a *moderate* or an *ultra* abolitionist." Both parties were *"politico-religious agitators . . .* wield[ing] *ecclesiastical* weapons for extra-ecclesiastical purposes." Only division would offer protection against "the rapacious juggernaut of *Northern Fanaticism"* and establish confidence in southern Methodists' social orthodoxy, essential to their job of saving southern souls.[100]

Significantly, protests spilled beyond churches into angry public meetings whose character was as much political as ecclesiastical. A gathering in Russel County, Alabama, unanimously declared the action against Andrew an "outrage to the people of an entire section of this Union" to which the only honorable response for southern Methodist ministers was separation. In Houston County, Georgia, a large public meeting chaired by Democratic Congressman Howell Cobb mixed religious exercises with clerical addresses and a resolution calling for separation. Lorenzo Waugh described the events of 1844–45 with some bitterness. "Politicians were busy," he recalled, "and some of our leading ministers of the gospel were about equal with the politicians in fanning up the spreading flames." Texas annexation and the Andrew case proved an unlikely but potent combination of issues. In his own state of Missouri most Methodist preachers sought to lead the member-ship into a southern church, using tactics "some of which would not have been exceeded if they had been managed by Jefferson Davis or John C. Calhoun."[101]

A few southern voices were raised in opposition. The experience of simmering revival in Mount Sidney, Virginia, prompted the view that the only division that would benefit Christians was "the separation of the sinner from his sins." Methodist church members in Lawrenceville, Georgia, met in April 1845 to call for unity and compromise instead of sinful division, though according to William Wightman the demand was the only one of its kind in the south-eastern states. Conciliatory feeling was stronger in the border conferences of Baltimore, Holston, Kentucky, and Missouri than in the lower South, but even there, according to Henry Bascom, there were only some 3,000 supporters of the MEC. This was at least in part due to a sense amongst Methodist emancipationists of the border that the founders of the new church were acting in good faith. Though he came later to regret it, John Stewart, presiding elder of the Kanawha District, Virginia, initially swallowed the view that a southern church, cleansed of northern agitators and "foreign inter-ference," would have unique opportunities to advance a moderate antislavery program. In consequence an estimated 95 percent of the southern branch of the original MEC supported the division of the church. Only three ministers in the whole South expressed their opposition when the Plan of Separation was put to a ballot.[102]

By contrast, northern Methodists proved far more seriously divided than had been evident from the vote at New York. Though there was wide approval of the action against Andrew, from abolitionist and non-abolitionist alike, there was no unanimity on the wisdom of voluntary division of the church. Abolitionists and those whom southern action had shocked into less conciliatory positions welcomed the severing of ties. "Why compromise with evil? Why concede what is right?" John McClintock asked. "The moral vision of the South is blinded and darkened." These hardliners found unlikely allies in the small minority of warm southern sympathizers in the North who encouraged voluntary division to save the South from further ill treatment.[103]

At the same time a growing body of opinion pulled in a quite different direction. "In this section the prevailing feeling seems to be – resistance to any division of the church," Robert Emory reported from Pennsylvania. Like many others, Emory had approved the firmness of the General Conference action but not of their "suffering themselves to be frightened . . . [into] measures which look to a division." Many took the view that voluntary separation would unnecessarily strengthen the hands of "immediatism" on one side and "slaveism" on the other by severing the strongest of the "golden chains binding [the country] . . . together in the bonds of love." Those of a more irenic disposition, like John Durbin and Stephen Olin, looked for compromise. Many others, more steely, resolved neither to compromise their antislavery heritage nor to cooperate in a voluntary separation. If southern Methodists were unhappy, let them secede – but without the blessing of the MEC. Consequently, when the annual conferences voted on the Plan of Separation there were almost as many northern ministers against peaceful schism as there were for, and constitutional division failed for lack of a sufficient majority.[104]

The separation of 1844, far from removing the aggravation between northern and southern Methodists, served only to generate new and persisting tensions between them. Southerners were incensed as influential conservative northerners like Charles Elliott and George Peck reneged on their initial commitment to support the Plan of Separation, seemingly under pressure from northern abolitionists. When the MEC Conference of 1848 described the Plan as unconstitutional and "null and void," and added insult to this injury by unanimously refusing to receive Lovick Pierce as a fraternal delegate from the MECS, southern Methodists bitterly excoriated northern "nullification" and betrayal. Equally aggrieved, the spokesmen of the MEC replied that the Conference of 1844 had too hastily conceded the Plan, as the sovereign fact of its rejection by the annual conferences indicated, that the actions of the MECS itself had "practically nullified" it, and that to have received Pierce would have signified the existence of fraternal relations when in fact the two churches were at war over the disposition of assets and the status of the border.[105]

The border conflict that followed the setting up of the MECS and persisted in a variety of guises until the civil war has rarely received its due in the historiography of developing sectionalism, no doubt in part because its Methodist label suggests a parochial collision of essentially ecclesiastical significance. But the events in this conflict were far-flung, dramatic, often ugly, and of great significance for the development of wider sectional antipathies. The Plan of Separation had sought to establish the basis for drawing a 1,200-mile line through those "border conferences" of the MEC which held jurisdiction over non-slaveholding territory but which also penetrated into the slave states of Maryland, Virginia, Kentucky, Arkansas, and Missouri. Here men and women of foreign and northern descent, and ordinary southern folk of antislavery pedigree, faced devoted members of the southern church. "Societies, stations, and conferences" along the slaveholding/non-slaveholding line (but not "interior charges") could by majority vote decide their allegiance, and once that loyalty was established the authorities of the other church would not attempt to form their own societies.[106]

From the first, MEC hardliners were unhappy about terms which seemed likely to leave most if not all the South to the operations of a "slavery church." There should, they argued, be no restrictions on MEC ministrations in the slave states: there were thousands of its members who, absolutely refusing to join the MECS, were deprived of freedom of religious choice. William Fee, stern critic of the Plan, was a convinced free-marketeer: allow both churches to function wherever they could secure local support, and the MEC would reach many sympathizers amongst those in slave territory who refused to join the MECS despite persecution and abuse. In Missouri, though many MEC ministers left their posts, Lorenzo Waugh stayed on to minister to the minority of loyal members who petitioned the General Conference for the reinstatement of the MEC in the state.[107]

The Plan left much unclear. In particular, if the dividing line between churches were redrawn as a result of a vote was the society or station newly abutting the border also allowed to express its collective will? This was the implication of Henry Bascom's view, common in the South, that the Plan, in providing a scheme rather than a fixed line, looked to the emergence of a line through *"adherence"* and that the border was neutral common ground until allegiances were established. In that case, what was to prevent a perpetual, unsettling campaign of recruitment? According to Thomas H. Busey of Port Republic, Virginia, the authorities of the MECS, in breach of the spirit of the Plan, were sending out aggressive proselytizers: "they have declared the border a movable line, so that when they have procured the secession of a society, station, or circuit, from the Methodist E. Church, the next one north becomes a border, and so on, *ad infinitum*."[108]

In practice, then, the Plan gave rise to mounting aggravations and frustrations, each side seeing the other as nullifiers and predators bent on violation of rights and invasion of territory. In Missouri, while MEC loyalists complained of obstruction and mischievous inclusion of part of Illinois into the St Louis Conference, southern sympathizers blamed the conflict on Illinois preachers who, disregarding the vote of the Missouri Conference to "go south," had crossed the state line "to commence the work of distraction and division." Throughout the border area split congregations and complaints of injustice were rife. In a setting where one Methodist's "popular majority" was another person's "dissatisfied minority" charges of manipulation and irregular voting proliferated. A presiding elder in the southern limits of the Philadelphia Conference bitterly complained that while MEC ministers were absent at conference "one of the southern members went into Ocohonock Neck ... where then no vote had been taken. He made his own efforts & representations and took the vote and reported that a majority was for the South. The southern preacher forthwith took possession." Formal procedures were similarly disregarded elsewhere. In the main the areas suffering greatest friction were in slave states, though Cincinnati provided its own discordant, free-state variation on the wider theme. Here southern sympathizers had established a minority society, later to become Soule Chapel. Though not immediately adjacent to the line of division, Bishop Andrew recognized it as part of the MECS on the grounds that there had been no formal vote on the Plan in the Ohio Conference. Northerners of even a conservative temperament, including Bishop Elijah Hedding, regarded this as an aggressive violation of the Plan, and more cautious southerners, too, feared this overt challenge to the "sacred" demarcation line of 1844.[109]

As sectional temperatures rose, the language of the warring parties gained in violence what it lost in charity. What southern Methodists had once reserved for radicals they now lavished on the whole of the MEC, an "abolition Church" composed of "incendiaries" driven by "malignity" and "fanatical excitement." Northerners complained of "reckless," "revengeful" language, inappropriate in those professing "a high state of grace and perfect conformity to the law of love." But to many in the MECS it seemed that the "tirade of abuse" emanated principally from the northern churches. William Winans explicitly laid the breakdown of comity at the door of the editorial fraternity, principally Thomas Bond and Charles Elliott, whose ecclesiastical invective and "implacable hostility" to the South had shriveled the "primitive spirit and character" of Methodism. Their newspapers, the *Christian Advocate and Journal* and the *Western Christian Advocate*, regarded as the two most powerful in the church before the schism, came to be seen as hostile and even incendiary publications in much of the border. On the eastern shore of the Chesapeake and in the Kanawha Valley these newspapers were regularly burned by magistrates under a Virginia act of 1836 giving justices of the peace and postmasters power to suppress and destroy incendiary materials.[110]

Anger and fear translated into intimidation and actual violence. Preachers in Weston and Hermon circuits, Missouri, were "threatened hard," seized and told to go north; when Lorenzo Waugh stubbornly resisted he worked in fear of his life. Armed southern sympathizers in Clarksburg, Maryland, camped out in the church to prevent MEC loyalists holding services there. Citizens of Independence County, Arkansas, threateningly called on the MEC to withdraw its missionaries. In the Virginia circuits of the Baltimore Conference preachers whose churches initially declared for the MEC were personally confronted, while meeting places in Warrenton circuit and Leesburg were forcibly entered and the congregations locked out.[111]

These disturbances were modest when compared to events in two other districts of Virginia, which saw violent excitement unparalleled in the border. In the Kanawha Valley region support for the MEC remained strong among many of the non-slaveholding mountain folk, though not amongst the poorest whites. At Parkersburg the Methodist community had narrowly voted to join the MECS. When the Ohio Conference nonetheless chose to send a preacher, John Dillon, the trustees there closed the church against him. His supporters forced an entry but Dillon was driven from town, though not before he had delivered a sermon in the besieged church. In other circuits of the Kanawha District the presiding elder John Stewart and his fellow ministers faced threats of violence, locking out of congregations, and seizure of property by a "dictatorial and tyrannical" MECS apparently determined to drive out the northern church.[112]

More dramatic still were events on the eastern shore, in Northampton and Accomac Counties, where social prestige and judicial power united against the northern church. An MEC minister of the Philadelphia Conference, Valentine Gray, was pulled out of the pulpit on the second Sunday of July 1846 and dragged from the church; when he presented himself at the county court at Eastville the following day to seek redress, a mob drove him away and warned him to leave the county. Later that year a mob at Guildford surrounded the church where another MEC minister, James Hargis, was preaching, and began shooting, throwing missiles, jeering, and shouting; the congregation was broken up and Hargis threatened with a millpond ducking if he returned. On each occasion the mobs were egged on by the *Richmond Christian Advocate* and the local magistracy. Thomas Bond concluded that the only rule operating on the eastern shore was "Mob law."[113]

The tussle for territory and church property led in some cases to legal action. Missouri Methodists in Hannibal and St Louis began suits to recover meeting places physically lost to the MECS. In the bitter conflict at Maysville, Kentucky, where the county court had instructed rival preachers to use the church jointly, the state court on appeal ruled in favor of the South. The judgment in this case delighted the South since it held that the MECS was not, as some northerners contended, a secession from a continuing MEC; rather, the General Conference of 1844 had authorized a division and reorganization into two new churches, leaving the old MEC defunct. This gave heart to southerners in their efforts to secure a share of the biggest prize of all, the capital and income of the two Book Concerns in New York and Cincinnati, which oversaw the publishing, storage, and distribution of Methodist literature. Once the annual conferences had failed to authorize the Plan of Separation, with its intended pro rata division of these church assets, the initiative seemed to lie with those elements in the MEC who would do nothing to strengthen a proslavery church and who thought "disunionists" and "seceders" had no legitimate claim to a share in the Book Rooms or any other property. Southerners unanimously attacked the dishonesty, selfishness, and illegality of those who sought to "swindle" them out of their proper share. Henry Bascom, leading the demand for justice, insisted that when the General Conference in 1844 had granted southerners the right to establish an independent church, its action "necessarily implie[d] the *right* to divide the common funds and property." Torn between the claims of constitutionality on the one side (could the voice of the annual conferences properly be ignored?) and their sense of fair play on the other (superannuated preachers, their wives, and children had a just claim to the funds of the Book Concerns, regardless of section), many northerners looked to conciliation. The General Conference of 1848, equivocating, thus called for legal arbitration. But the MECS, angered by what it considered northern Methodist evasion, brought suits against the MEC in the US circuit courts of New York and Ohio in the summer of 1849. Not until 1854 would the separation of 1844 be formally legalized.[114]

Presbyterian and Baptist schism

No other church suffered the abrasions of sectionalism as intensely as the two halves of the MEC, but aspects of their experience recurred across the range of evangelical denominations. The Methodist Protestants managed to prevent schism in the 1840s by leaving each annual conference to determine its own approach to slaveholding, but they could not avoid stormy passages in the General Conference, recriminatory petitions, and chronic animosity between conservatives and radicals. The staunchly antislavery Wesleyan Methodist Church suffered no internal sectional stresses, of course, but the experience of its southern missionaries – arrested, mobbed, and hounded out – served to shape and confirm its sectional stereotypes.[115] Beyond Methodism, the trauma of division and persisting sectional animus was experienced most profoundly by the denominational families of Presbyterians and Baptists.

The schism of 1837–38 in the Presbyterian church had ostensibly to do with the advance of what its conservative leaders considered a false theology, a corrupt revivalism, and a degenerate alliance with liberal Congregationalists. These at least were the grounds on which the General Assembly excluded four synods in New York and Ohio in 1837, and blocked New School efforts to secure their readmission in the following year. But some historians have pointed to persuasive – if largely circumstantial – evidence which suggests that the slavery issue was integrally bound up in the dispute.[116] Following the strong antislavery pronouncement of the General Assembly in 1818 conservatives had prevented reconsideration of the issue until 1835 and 1836, when they took fright at the rapid spread of abolitionist sentiment in the New School synods; the four excluded synods were those where abolitionists had been most vocal. At the heart of the theological quarrel was a

New School view of the "moral ability" of the individual which had implications for human freedom. Southerners certainly regarded abolitionism as the offspring of New School heresy and seem to have reached an unspoken understanding with orthodox northerners, who were afraid a southern exodus would leave them in a minority, to drive out the radicals. Though some historians have sought to minimize the issue of abolitionism in the schism, for many contemporary Presbyterians the reality was clear enough. New Schoolers regarded themselves as victims of "the desire to get rid of Northern Anti-slavery brethren. It was avowed without scruple – 'If we get rid of the New School, we get rid with them of Abolition.'" Robert J. Breckinridge, centrally involved in these events, spoke for many Old School men when he concluded that although the schism grew out of doctrinal conflict "yet the question of abolitionism was so far mixed with it, that nearly the entire mass of abolitionists . . . sloughed off with the schism itself."[117]

Each of the two new branches of Presbyterianism continued to harbor both slaveholders and widely divergent views on slaveholding. Neither was able wholly to eliminate internal friction. The Old School developed as a more conservative church than its undivided predecessor, northerners largely cooperating with the minority of southerners to choke off discussion of slavery in church councils. But it faced the constant sniping of Thomas E. Thomas and other Old School radicals in western New York and Ohio who accused the church of backsliding from its antislavery commitment of 1818. Their pressure through the 1840s to establish the "inalienable sacred right" of free speech in the General Assembly alarmed Old School southerners. "The churches at the South feel that they are standing on a volcano," their commissioners told the General Assembly in 1841. "They need to be assured that the Assembly will let the subject of slavery alone." That assurance came in 1845 when, by a clear-cut vote of 168 to 13, the church appeared to retreat from its position of 1818 and resolved that, though there were evils connected with slavery, the General Assembly as a spiritual body could not legislate on slavery or bar slaveowners from membership. These resolutions, the work of Nathan Rice, demonstrated the anxiety for consensus not just between northern conservatives like Joshua L. Wilson and Charles Hodge and border state emancipationists such as Robert Breckinridge and Henry Ruffner, most of whom looked to colonization and regarded their church as essentially antislavery; but between both these groups and those southerners who, like James Thornwell, were moving to a less defensive stance on slavery. The action of 1845 helped keep the Old School church largely intact for the rest of the antebellum period, a self-conscious but far from secure symbol of national unity.[118]

New School Presbyterians had to contend with a potentially more explosive chemistry. From the parent church they had gathered in not only most of the abolitionists but also enough southerners to form six synods. Some of these were moderate, Hopkinsian Calvinists of the border, centered on eastern Tennessee, but they also included staunchly proslavery "states-rights" Presbyterians fearful that the exclusion of New School presbyteries in 1837 marked a perilous step towards ecclesiastical centralization. Conservatives sought, successfully at first, to keep the slaveholding issue a matter for local jurisdiction. Radical antislavery opinion, however, wanted to see all slaveholders removed from the church, and had some success in western presbyteries. Their influence was felt at the General Assembly of 1846 when, by a vote of 86 to 27, it was agreed that slavery was "intrinsically an unrighteous and oppressive system . . . opposed to the prescriptions of the law of God, to the spirit and precepts of the Gospel, and to the best interests of humanity." All the southern members voted against. In 1850 the General Assembly took an even sterner line, but still stopped short of declaring voluntary slaveholding "presumptive evidence of guilt." This slow hardening of the church's position did nothing to reassure Presbyterian slaveowners but left more radical northerners "deeply grieved and mortified" by the General Assembly's balking at the final step.[119]

These sectional frictions within the New School were aggravated by similar pressures within the American Home Missionary Society (AHMS) and the other national benevolent societies under the sway of moderate Calvinism. AHMS efforts were largely based in the free states. Of its 1,006 agents in 1848 only 54 worked in the South. There its operations were focused mainly on the border, in Missouri, Kentucky, and eastern Tennessee, though a few missionaries did penetrate into the deep South, where they encountered the suspicion and outright hostility that also prevented the agents of the American Tract Society, American Bible Society and American Sunday School Union gaining access to the slaves. What disturbed the New School antislavery forces was not so much the modest scale of benevolent efforts in the South as that the AHMS agents maintained silence on slavery and ministered to slaveowners. Benjamin Mills, agent in Kentucky, vainly tried to persuade the society's critics that he and his AHMS colleagues were better placed to secure emancipation than "ultra antislavery" missionaries imposed from outside. They were more likely to heed the criticisms of another Kentuckian, John G. Fee, who resigned his AHMS commission in protest against the society's using agents ready to "defend & apologize for American slavery." Presbyterian tolerance of slaveholding in New School and AHMS churches drove William W. Blanchard to reflect sadly: "Free soil politics are far in advance of free church principles. Ministers will go into, and participate in a free soil meeting, who most violently oppose as mad fanaticism the same principles when applied to the church."[120]

Baptists too had to face the issue of slaveholding in the church. On the face of it their decentralized structure and commitment to local congregational autonomy should have freed them from the institutional pressures that fractured more centralized and hierarchical denominations. But their missionary operations were coordinated by two voluntary bodies, the Baptist Triennial Convention, established in 1814 to supervise foreign missions, and the more recently instituted American Baptist Home Missionary Society (ABHMS). Both became the targets of Baptist abolitionists who sought an end to all connection with slaveholders.

Matters came to a head at the very time that the MEC was fracturing.[121] In November 1844 Alabama Baptists sought to test the commitment of the Board of Foreign Missions to a policy of neutrality on slavery, as declared by the Triennial Convention earlier in the year. The board sought to tread a diplomatic path between abolitionist and proslavery positions, declaring it could not appoint a slaveowning missionary but insisting it could continue to embrace slaveholding members and contributions. Meanwhile the Executive Board of the ABHMS had refused to commission the Reverend James Reeve of Georgia, not on the grounds that he was a slaveowner but because his application was presented as a test case. Radical Baptist voices in the South saw both developments as evidence of "Romish usurpation" and the iron grip of abolitionism. The call for an end to all connection with existing missionary and other benevolent bodies culminated in the formation of the Southern Baptist Convention in May 1845, when not only ministers but governors, congressmen, judges, and other public figures, overwhelmingly from the states of the deep South, gathered in Augusta, Georgia. Northern Baptists consequently reorganized their own missionary bodies.[122]

The "acerbity and vituperation" that accompanied these events severely upset moderates on each side, ministers like John M. Peck, Rufus Babcock, and Thomas Meredith, who sought to keep Baptists from "the state of bickering and interminable quarreling, into which the Methodists have fallen."[123] In that they enjoyed some success, for Baptists avoided much of the blood and fury that marked the sectional relationships of their principal evangelical rival. Even so, the abrasions caused by a continuing ABHMS presence in the South and by persisting newspaper wars gives the lie to any thought that the Baptist split terminated inter-sectional conflict in that church.[124]

"Frittering away the bonds of national union": denominational schism and sectionalism

These suppurating intradenominational conflicts were to have a profound effect on evangelicals' political perspectives. It was not that the schisms directly helped restructure party political loyalties: the case of the anonymous, tobacco-chewing, poor white Missourian who regarded MEC preachers as abolitionist Whigs "tryin' to git the niggers sot free right hur among us," suggests how the Methodist split actually strengthened the faith of Jackson "dimocrats" in the South; meanwhile William Brownlow's Whiggery remained equally unshaken by the conflict in his church, which he regarded as a battle between treacherous antislavery Democrats and loyal Whig defenders of southern values.[125] But if denominational schism left partisan allegiances largely unaffected, or even reinforced, in the short term, its longer-term effect was to dissolve the glue that bound national parties together. Separation bequeathed a legacy of bitterness and sectional stereotyping that seriously corroded evangelicals' sense of belonging to a political and ecclesiastical Union based on common values.

This was precisely what conservative evangelicals, north and south, feared as they faced the prospect and then reality of division. Nathan Bangs warned in 1840 against the potentially catastrophic effects of schism. The political nation, he asserted, owed its strength to the invisible bonds cultivated by national religious bodies. "[T]he cohesive tendency of a religious community, moving around a common centre of union" helped contain "the centrifugal tendencies inher[ent] in the disorganizing workings of . . . irreligious and ambitious men." Bangs and others inside and outside the MEC, including Henry Clay, attached particular importance to holding Methodism together, most obviously because it was the largest denomination, more shrewdly because its system of itinerancy, involving ministerial interchange from one section to another, had a "natural tendency to do away with those prejudices which grow out of local circumstances and habits." Other denominations showed a similar understanding of the political dangers inherent in ecclesiastical rupture. Thomas Meredith shuddered as Baptists moved towards a separation whose proponents were employed "in frittering away the bonds of national union, and in exasperating and incensing one half of this republic against the other," and so inviting "the horrors of civil war."[126] The Richmond Presbyterian William S. Plumer predicted in 1837 that ecclesiastical division along sectional lines would "rend the star-spangled banner in twain . . . and the Potomac will be dyed with blood."[127]

Not all shared these alarmist views. Many on both sides of the Mason-Dixon line believed that separation would be more likely to reduce aggravation than to culminate in apocalyptic climax.[128] William A. Smith told southern Methodists that a national connection only served to stir agitation and countrywide excitement: "Our separation therefore is highly important to the union of these states." The *New York Baptist Register* took the view that, freed from strife, Baptist churches would pursue missionary and benevolent work "with renewed zeal and increased liberality." Sterner southern voices argued that separation alone would show intelligent northerners that there were limits to southern tolerance: if the North learnt that it must stand up to the actions of "a restless abolition cabal" or forfeit the affections of the South, then good would follow ecclesiastical rupture.[129]

Alarmists regarded these advocates of schism as either fools or knaves. In the first place, rupture played into the hands of the abolitionists. As one slaveholding southern Methodist explained: "While the union continues, all the reasons that make the North averse to division, operate ... to ... repress the violence of abolition; but let division take place, and ... [t]he motives to induce moderation no longer exist." In consequence "the excitement of abolition will increase tenfold." Secondly, schism strengthened southern disunionists. Hardliners who shared the view of the Baptist editor Joseph Baker that they "would rather see the community severed into its integral parts, and the universe itself reduced to its original atoms, than sacrifice one moral principle" seemed not simply to engage in dangerous bravado, but to encourage southern states-rights radicals who looked to the churches to take the first steps towards the sundering of the Union.[130]

Those who believed that at the very least there existed an informal understanding between states-rights politicians and separatist clergy to establish an independent southern confederacy, and that they might even have conspired secretly to engineer the ecclesiastical ruptures to that end, found highly suspicious any evidence of connections between the two parties. The cry of treason was soon raised once it was known that John C. Calhoun, then secretary of state, had written to William Capers during the 1844 General Conference in New York inviting him, Judge Longstreet, and other prominent southern Methodists to visit him in Washington on their way home. Capers originally intended to accept the invitation but on reflection declined – according to his biographer because he feared it would prompt the charge of conspiracy. Not long after the conference John Durbin encountered widespread rumors in the west of Calhoun's collusion with the southern delegations in a plan to split the church. The accusation was made more publicly in the columns of the New York *Christian Advocate and Journal*. Capers protested against the "crazy" insinuations, charging the editor, Thomas Bond, with flaunting his "Whig prejudices" to advance Clay's presidential claims: the affair was no more than the "story of a coon-skin hung up in a parlour." Bond accepted that Capers might have been an unwitting ally of Calhoun, but accomplice he had been in a grand design to undermine the American Union.[131]

However far-fetched these charges of conspiracy, evangelical concern that church rupture weakened the Union was well founded. Throughout the 1840s evangelicals in each section developed increasingly anti-pathetic and hostile images of the other. Southerners' experience of schism led them to identify northern churchmen with fanatical, irreligious, anti-republican, revolutionary abolitionism. "Mischievous and disorganizing" forces lay behind the "ungodly" attack on the ecclesiastical status quo; abolitionists' success in winning support from a majority of northern clergy indicated the creeping degeneracy of religion in that section. Many who had once seemed allies of the South had shifted their ground and "out abolitionized the abolitionists themselves." Rupture had been thrust unwillingly on orthodox southerners, who had no means other than conservative, constitutional separation with which to defend true religion and the social order. In their "war of extermina-tion" against the South northern churchmen sought to remove slave-holders from membership and, after schism, embarked on offensive, even conspiratorial, action to deprive the southern churches of their constitutional rights. "We are compelled to repel invasion and assault," Henry Bascom complained, "or be overthrown and trodden upon by the assailants." Their battle was not local but cosmic. The world, as the South Carolinians James Thornwell and Whitefoord Smith saw it, was "the theatre of an extraordinary conflict of great principles" between true Christianity and social stability on the one side and false religion and "a spirit of insubordination and lawlessness" on the other. The Lord's allegiance was plain. Why else would He provide new south-western mission fields and separate ecclesiastical organizations? Why else bless the South with revivals while Mormonism, Millerism, come-outerism, German rationalism, and the other absurdities of "Free Soil Morality" engendered crime, drunkenness, and the wasting of orthodox churches in the North?[132]

For southern evangelicals it was a small, logical step to extend these perceptions into the political realm. Renegade former colleagues in northern churches had not only betrayed the nation's unique religious mission: their attack on the South's civil institutions converted them into collaborators in a political scheme to deny southerners their con-stitutional rights. Addressing a southern camp meeting in 1847, the president of Randolph-Macon College presented the Wilmot Proviso as a logical political sequel to the break-up of the three main Protestant denominations: all were expressions of northern aggression. Henry Bascom explained the conflict in Methodism as "the result of party spirit and party organisation," the party being "the great Northern Abolition and Antislavery party" in which "the politician, the demagogue, and the religionist all unite." Southern Methodists stood firm by federal and ecclesiastical law. Conversely, the MEC had become "a pander to political agitation."[133]

Northern evangelicals similarly attached political significance to the ecclesiastical traumas of the 1840s. Schism itself was at bottom designed "to continue and protect slavery," not to defend doctrine or polity, and the emergent churches, seeking to conciliate not only Calhoun but all southern-rights politicians, took their place alongside the other agencies of the slave power. The MECS, readers of the *Christian Advocate and Journal* were told, had become "a great politico-ecclesiastical party, for the defense and support of the peculiar political institution of the South." Why else would the MECS have selected only slaveholding bishops at its first General Conference? If anyone were the victim of offensive hostility it was not southern but northern evangelicals. "Southern Aggression" had engineered the schisms. It was southerners who had "practically nullified" the terms of separation. It was their "ecclesiastical demagogues" who had sought, with some success, to drive out northern religious newspapers. It was they who had acted to remove the antislavery section from the Methodist Discipline; they who had denied freedom of speech, liberty of conscience, and religious toleration in the "border wars"; they who had encouraged mobs and violence in a war of conquest against representatives of the northern churches. Northern evangelicals were faced with a slave power and a battle against "rebels and secessionists" in their ecclesiastical operations at the very time (and in some instances well before) they had to confront them in the political arena.[134]

The 1840s, then, saw the hardening of evangelical attitudes on both sides of the border. Abolitionist demands for the severing of every church connection with slaveholding elicited in response a more coherent and thought-out scriptural defense of slavery from southern radicals. But of far greater significance for the future of the Union was the wedge that schism inserted between the more conservative or moderate forces on each side. Some, like Alfred Griffiths, an MEC minister in the Baltimore Conference who deprecated "all blending or uniting of sacred with political and worldly things," fought stoutly to hold the middle ground against the "politico-ecclesiastical" combinations of the North (the abolitionist churches) and South (the MECS).[135] But as southerners who tried to ward off advancing sectionalism discovered, keeping open the channels of communication was not easy when surrounded by more suspicious, hardline colleagues and when addressing northern moderates whose own position was gradually hardening.[136]

This shift in northern moderate opinion was arguably the most profound result of the events of the 1840s. A deepening aversion to slavery amongst those who were declared enemies of abolitionism, and the severing of bonds of comity with the South, were necessary preconditions for the emergence of a broad-based, antislavery political party.[137] Ecclesiastical rupture promoted these conditions. As Donald Mathews has emphasized, "After the schism, Methodist leaders who had previously tried to keep agitation about slavery out of the church even began to write antislavery tracts of their own." Enoch Mudge, no friend of abolitionism, lamented "the folly and extavigance [*sic*] we [northern Methodists] have been guilty of which has done much to excite ... [southern] jealousy, needless fear and violent opposition"; but he was unyielding in his view that it was "too late to put a prop to Slavery. The World & the Church will not countenance & endure it." It was the developing orientation of men of this outlook which would shape northern politics. At the end of the decade a shrewd New Englander stood back to analyze the broad categories of opinion in northern churches, particularly the MEC. There were, he argued, four groups of people in its orbit: hardline abolitionists, who had seceded; equally hardline immediate abolitionists who had remained to exercise influence from within; a much larger element composed of those who regarded slavery, but not necessarily all slaveholders, as always sinful; and conservative advocates of gradual emancipation. The last three groups, he maintained, shared a much greater mutual respect than they had once done. His explanation pertinently sustains the theme developed here. The convergence had been occasioned "by a better understanding of each other, by changes in ecclesiastical relations, by the division of the M.E. church, and particularly by the recent movements in the political world."[138]

Chapter 6

Evangelicals and the Resolution of Political Crisis, 1850–52

The elections of 1848 resolved none of the questions raised by the Mexican cession. When Congress gathered in December 1849 a Whig president faced a Democratic House of Representatives, and excited southern-rights men confronted unyielding free soilers. There was no consensus on the terms of entry into the Union of newly acquired California, into which thousands of gold-seekers were pouring. The organization of the rest of the Mexican acquisition presented an equally divisive issue, for on its resolution too hung the future status of the South and slavery in the Union. Three other issues filled the caldron of sectional bitterness: the South's demand for a more stringent Fugitive Slave Law, the future of the slave trade in the nation's capital, and Texan claims to more territory on her western boundary. Civil war loomed.

A compromise, or more accurately an armistice, eventually emerged around proposals first brought forward by Henry Clay. This was secured only after the deaths of Calhoun in March 1850 and the stubbornly free-soil President Taylor in July had eased the way for Stephen A. Douglas's brilliant maneuverings. Congress admitted California as a free state; left the issue of slavery in New Mexico and Utah to the decision of the territorial legislatures (with the possibility of appeal to the federal courts); passed a stricter Fugitive Slave Law; abolished the slave trade in the District of Columbia; and by means of a debt-relieving sweetener persuaded Texas to accept a more limited boundary. It took time to mollify, or at least marginalize, the settlement's critics, particularly in the South, where Unionists and southern-rights men fought a series of tumultuous electoral battles in 1851. Candidates' stands on the Compromise became one of the salient issues in 1852. Whigs' equivocal response to the settlement, which so many of their northern activists had opposed, underlined the fragility of the ties binding together the sectional halves of the party; they entered the campaign seriously, though not fatally, wounded. Democrats emphasized their conservatism and acceptability to both North and South. Their victory and the subsiding of political passions briefly suggested that the Union was secure.[1]

Evangelical Protestants, their political antennae well developed over the previous decade, were neither uninterested nor passive observers during this period of high drama. Both as individuals and through their church bodies, evangelicals widely sought to influence the direction of events. The triumph of Compromise and Unionism (at least in the short term) owed much to the work of conservatives in the churches. Yet at the same time free-soil evangelicals' moral outrage at the Compromise measures, and the evident disaffection of the minority of southern-rights Protestants, suggested the limitations of the political peace. These radical elements within northern and southern churches had ominously given notice they would tolerate no further loss of sectional advantage.

Free-soil evangelicals and the higher law

"The hour of trial is upon us," Matthew Simpson declared in April 1850. The Methodist editor articulated the view of tens of thousands of antislavery Christians for whom the gathering crisis pitched the lovers of liberty, humanity, and conscience against a scheming slave power and its northern spaniels. From pulpit and press in these troubled months free-soil evangelicals spared neither Whig nor Democrat, thundering against "the pro-slavery spirit" and elastic consciences of "time-serving politicians" who would "stifle the cries of humanity" in return for office and personal advance. Southerners and their "bullying arrogance" offered a natural and easy target, particularly while tempers flared violently in Congress. When the Mississippian Henry S. Foote drew his pistol on Thomas Hart Benton of Missouri during the Senate debate on the California bill, he seemed literally on the point of murdering the spirit of freedom. But free soilers reserved particular venom for "truckling" northern politicians who had sold their souls to the "all-controlling south." They castigated Lewis Cass, Daniel S. Dickinson, Stephen Douglas, and other Democrats for allying with Henry Clay to become "the oppressors of the suffering sons and daughters of Toil." As for northern Whigs, two in particular stood condemned: Millard Fillmore, for his renegade acquiescence as president in the Compromise measures, especially the Fugitive Slave Act, and Daniel Webster, whose plea for the Union on 7 March had earlier provoked even greater anger. Charged with putting ambition before conscience, Webster encountered a barrage of invective and hisses on his return to Boston, where one Congregationalist minister grieved that "the very Samson of New England" was now "grinding in the prison house of the Philistines." Most of the New England Protestant press censured Webster's backsliding, and well beyond his home constituency evangelicals protested against his sneers at the clergy's moral absolutism.[2]

Few free-soil evangelicals took seriously the premise of Webster's speech, that the Union was in mortal danger unless concessions were made to southern interests. Most regarded the South's disunionist threats as bluster, or moral blackmail, designed to alarm northern Unionists and secure for slaveholders what the strict standards of justice and religion would deny. Bogus alarm, according to free soilers, also served the interests of northern politicians who had to propitiate the South to secure the presidency or cabinet office, but needed to justify to northern voters their willingness to compromise. If there *were* a threat to the Union, it was the passage of Compromise measures which, if enforced, "must rend the Union asunder, or save it only at the cost of blowing the slave system to atoms." A Brooklyn Presbyterian asserted that the greatest danger to the Union was not southern disunionism but slavery itself, an obsolete system and "the fretting sore of our institutions."[3]

Consequently, it was those standing up most squarely to disunionist threats who won the eulogies of antislavery evangelicals. Whatever misgivings some had had about the election of a Louisiana slaveholder to the presidency, Zachary Taylor soon earned plaudits for the "practical wisdom and heroic firmness" with which he confronted the slave power. More predictable was free-soil evangelicals' approval of Joshua Giddings, John G. Palfrey, John P. Hale, and Charles Sumner, though the most admired of the central actors in the congressional drama was William Seward. The senator's "higher law" speech on 11 March 1850 earned him a widespread reputation in the North for "Christian manliness."[4] Arguing that no political society could survive without respecting the moral sentiments of its citizens, and that most civilized people now condemned slavery, Seward insisted there should be no concessions to the South. What Seward understood by the "higher law" was much less radical than many of his interpreters, then and since, supposed. But free-soil evangelicals, determined to square political action with God's law, drew him to their bosom as one of them.[5]

The political crisis and its resolution elicited widespread reflection on the citizen's duty to human and divine law. Antislavery clergy demanded that all human enactments be tested against the law of God, the higher law, by the measure of Scripture and conscience. They dismissed arguments based on Romans 13. 1: "Let every soul be subject unto the higher powers. For there is no power but of God; the powers that be are ordained of God." That command, they explained, was a time-bound product of early Christianity, designed to contain new converts' natural instincts towards sedition. Far more relevant to nineteenth-century Christians was Peter's order "to obey God rather than men" (Acts 5. 29) and Daniel's response to Darius' iniquitous law forbidding him to name his God. The Union and the Constitution deserved respect but did not provide the supreme standard for action. Human government was indeed authorized by God but, as Wooster Parker asked, "does it therefore follow that Congress may amend the ten commandments, or reverse the principles of Christ's Sermon on the Mount . . . ?" Man could not, by any law, make right what God and his own conscience declared wrong.[6]

In these circumstances, when human government denied higher law, there were limits to Christian obedience. Properly constituted governments should be treated respectfully, John Morgan agreed, even if they engaged in occasional acts of tyranny. But it could never be right for citizens to assist in the enforcement of an unrighteous law. In that instance God expected His people to refuse cooperation. This, too, was Nathaniel Colver's conclusion, as he applauded those who had disregarded Nebuchadnezzar's call to idolatry. Few were ready openly to advocate violent resistance, though the example of the American Revolutionaries gave nourishing food for thought. But many recognized that overt passive disobedience was an appropriate response to bad laws, for which Christians should, as William De Loss Love argued, "peaceably suffer the penalty."[7]

What made discussion of the higher law and the proper limits to civil obedience particularly urgent was the passage of a new Fugitive Slave Law. This was deeply unpopular in northern churches and more than any other element of the Compromise drove evangelicals into political action. Even amongst those who called for the law's full-hearted enforcement there was widespread dislike of its terms. The evangelical press thundered in protest, while church bodies and informal gatherings of ministers met to express their outrage. Robert Hall recollected vividly the sad day when his father assembled the family, devout New School Presbyterians, to announce the bill's passage into law. Antislavery evangelicals' "utter astonishment" derived principally from the law's suspending habeas corpus, denying a jury trial to "runaways," prescribing higher fees to commissioners for finding in favor of the slaveholder, levying taxes for its enforcement, and commanding all citizens, at risk of fine and even imprisonment, to assist in slave-catching. Deeply angered, Matthew Simpson accused the government of turning the whole North into "a hunting-ground for kidnappers." Northerners, who had held slavery at arm's length, were now made complicit in an institution they abhorred.[8]

Most evangelical critics were sure the new law flagrantly violated the

Federal Constitution, by depriving citizens of their freedom without due process of law.[9] Webster and other northern politicians who argued otherwise, by alluding to the "compromises of the Constitution," seemed to play into the hands of Garrisonian ultra-abolitionists: "Only persuade the people of the free states that the Constitution . . . makes it their duty to become slave-catchers for the south, and from that hour multitudes will feel . . . [a duty] to resist and disavow so base a compact." But even if the political compromisers were – implausibly – correct on the score of its constitutionality, the new law lacked all moral force by being, as William Carter described it, "the first ever passed by Congress commanding all good citizens to do what the Divine law forbids." Did not Scripture call on Christians "to deliver him that is spoiled out of the hand of the oppressor"? How else should they interpret the Lord's command to the Israelites (Deuteronomy 23. 15–16) not to surrender a runaway slave to his master, but give him refuge? Luther Lee considered complicity in the law "treason against God and humanity, . . . guilt equal to the guilt of violating every one of the ten commandments."[10]

What, then, was the Christian's duty? Few opponents jibbed at open political protest. Ministers dispatched memorials to their representatives. Gilbert Haven and others leapt to deliver their first political sermons. But what of passive disobedience, or even forcible resistance? Here the critics' voices were confused and ambiguous, for though most accepted their duty to seek the overthrow of a godless law there was no consensus on the proper boundaries to disobedient action. Radicals like Daniel Foster, Congregationalist minister of Boston, declared he would "actively disobey" the law by placing obstructions in the way of the "abominable kidnapper." Amongst Reformed Presbyterians, William L. Roberts of Auburn similarly believed the law should be resisted "by every means within our power," which included shelter to fugitives through the underground railroad and, by implication, physical force. Such men believed that since the law was itself an act of violence against natural rights, sustained by slave-catchers and lawless mobs, its opponents could justly use all means to help the escaping slave.[11] Other critics scrupulously distinguished between passive disobedience to unchristian laws, which God allowed, and active resistance, which one Methodist editor regarded as "not only unchristian, but, in a democratic country, . . . wholly unwise."[12] Henry Ward Beecher equally disavowed any wish to attempt to rescue fugitives from imprisonment or to collide with federal officers, but insisted he would shelter, conceal, and speed slaves north at whatever cost in fines and imprisonment. A wide range of fellow clergy expressed their willingness to suffer the full penal consequences of passive disobedience to secure repeal of the hated law.[13]

Free-soil evangelicals found little in the other Compromise measures to assuage their anger. California's admission as a free state and the abolition of the slave trade in the District of Columbia might have been cause for celebration in themselves, but these gains were neutralized by territorial arrangements for New Mexico and Utah that might open the way to slavery. Throughout the crisis months a barrage of conference resolutions, sermons, and newspaper editorials called for a free-soil solution, essential to gospel advance in the expanded republic. The bitter lesson of the churches' recent warfare in the border South was clear enough: "let New Mexico be made slave territory, and it will be, to a great extent closed against the Churches and ministers of the north."[14] The emergent legislation had the merit of not formally imposing slavery on the new territories and of leaving open the possibility of its exclusion, but free soilers remained anxious.[15]

The events of 1850 generated amongst free-soil Protestants an anger and resentment which enhanced their sense of unity and encouraged the prospect of a new political alignment. As protest meetings spread, predictions of party disintegration swept through the ranks of evangelicals. Politicians, they warned, should "tremble for their places." A New York Methodist, claiming to speak for thousands of his brethren, threatened to abandon the Whigs if they embraced Webster's position on compromise. Others expected the first efforts at enforcing the "execrable kidnapping law" to "shock into confusion all our present party relations" and impel the public mind towards "an attempt to annihilate, at any consequence, the slave power of the land." The effects would be "irresistible by any party management." Isaac Collyer confidently called to action men of conscience: "in the future let us elect such men to office as will properly regard 'THE HIGHER LAW!' "[16]

"The Palladium of our National happiness": northern conservatives defend the Union

In fact, free-soil evangelicals were much too sanguine about northern evangelical unity and the imminence of party realignment. Many nominally antislavery evangelicals in the northern states welcomed the Compromise and threw their substantial weight behind it. Staunch Unionists, committed to political consensus and the Constitution, they feared the consequences of unyielding free soilism and were shocked by disobedience to the law. On the whole they saw slavery as a social and political evil, to be regretted and wished away. But they insisted that slaveholding, sanctioned by the Scriptures, was not a personal sin. They mostly saw colonization as the only legitimate, socially acceptable, and politically realistic escape. These conservatives tended to belong to an older age group and to come from the higher-status churches in their area and from denominations which placed less emphasis on individual conscience. Many of the most vocal ministered to prosperous, often Old School Presbyterian, churches in New York City, Philadelphia, and other cities with southern commercial and cultural links. Their pleas on behalf of social stability, and their lashing of political agitators in the pulpit, endeared them to their conservative congregations. Henry Boardman's Unionist sermon at Thanksgiving in November 1850 was significantly published at the behest of "fellow-citizens . . . representing the commerce of our city, and the learned professions."[17]

For these evangelicals the Union represented more than a utilitarian political arrangement. It was the handiwork of God. It had originated not in flawed secular wisdom but in "the special illumination of Divine Providence," without which the Founding Fathers could never have reconciled the conflicting interests of the new nation and fashioned a political structure "clothed with majesty and honor, radiant with celestial beauty." With the sole exception of the confederated republics of Israel, there had never been a government "so beautifully adapted to the great wants of human society." American freedom, republicanism, and political stability contrasted poignantly with the 1848 convulsions in Europe. The political Union, with the country's God-given material resources, provided the context for her unprecedented economic prosperity. It sustained religious liberty, educational progress, moral improvement, and the advance of Protestant Christianity. "Who can be ignorant," asked George Duffield, "that by the good providence of God, the national Union of these confederated States, bound together under the same constitution, forms the elements, the life and soul, of that civil, political and social prosperity, distinguishing us as a people, from all the nations of the earth?"[18]

There could be no greater calamity or impiety than the destruction of this Union, "the Palladium of our National happiness." One minister warned that the dissolution of the new Israel would shatter the hopes of political freedom "over the entire globe," another that it would mean "Freedom herself proclaiming that Freedom is a chimera." Just as surely would disunion betray America's trusteeship of "the ark of religious liberty," snuffing out the Christian progress of the last three-quarters of a century, splintering churches and foreign missions, and encouraging atheism and crime. "[T]he dismemberment of this Union would be one of the most appalling calamities which could befall the world," warned Henry Boardman, adopting the apocalyptic tone then resonating throughout conservative circles.[19]

For these evangelicals slavery was a relatively minor blemish in the perfection of the Union: no sane system of moral accounting could justify jeopardizing it out of concern for the slave. Northern agitators and southern disunionists, they argued, forgot that without some compromise between slave and free states at the republic's birth, the glorious Union would never have come into being. Persisting commitment to compromise and respect for southern constitutional rights was the only honorable and prudential strategy. Slavery was gradually disappearing, aided by the lesson God offered slaveholders in blessing the free states. Radical approaches that split the Union would do nothing to help the slave: the southern states would adopt more stringent slave laws, impose a system of greater surveillance, and put back the day of freedom.[20]

Conservative evangelicals, unlike antislavery hardliners, who tended to regard politicians' scare stories as manipulative fiction, proved much more credulous of threats of imminent disunion. They agreed with George L. Prentiss of Newark that the Union was "a rope of sand, unless it be cherished and consecrated in the hearts of the people"; its perpetuity depended not on force but on bonds of affection. Some, like William W. Eells, blamed political dangers almost entirely on "the ravings of moon-struck fanatics" in the North: southern disunionism was an inevitable reaction to external provocation. Most were more even-handed, pointing the finger of guilt at both northern zealots and southern "demagogues and traitors." Early in 1850 James W. Alexander believed that the danger of national schism emanated primarily from Garrisonian abolitionists; but after visiting Virginia and South Carolina the following December he was shocked to encounter those who "not merely look[ed] on secession as a possible evil, but pray[ed] for it as a real good." Even after the Compromise measures had passed into law, conservatives remained fearful the country was at "the very verge of a fearful vortex."[21]

Political disunion, according to these conservatives, would bring appalling destruction in its train. They dismissed as misguided visionaries those who advocated peaceful separation or imagined that the conflict could be limited. "Disunion and desolation are synonymous terms," William P. Breed asserted: "how long would northern and southern troops [along a garrisoned border], in the spirit enkindled by the slave question, look each other inactively in the face?" North-westerners would fight for access to the lower Mississippi; Europe would intervene; northern-inspired slave rebellions would heap black and white southerners together "in one common ruin." Secondary fissure would follow the initial schism. "[C]onflagration, rapine and violence" would turn the country into "ALCEDAMA and GOLGOTHA, a field of blood – a place of skulls."[22] The consequences for religious life did not bear contemplation.

This prudence derived not so much from evangelicals' political pragmatism as from their conservatism in temperament, in social philosophy – and in theology. Many had developed their unyielding views on the supremacy of the law during the 1830s and 1840s, when the nation had appeared to face a variety of irreverent challenges to its institutional integrity. Nullifiers, Dorrites, anti-sabbatarians, anti-abolitionists, anti-Catholics, debt repudiators, lynchers, congressional duelists and brawlers: all had demonstrated the country's chronic affliction by anarchist and lawless elements. When in 1850 "higher-law" clergy called for disobedience and even resistance to the Fugitive Slave Law, their conservative brethren regarded them as simply the most recent exponents of this endemic "ultraism." Their doctrine of political nullification, George Peck declared, "has no limits ... [and] sweeps away all the barriers of social order" since by disregarding one law a person adopts a position "which may apply to all laws whatsoever, and which all others have as good a right to occupy as he has." This explains why higher-law advocates earned a reputation as "wild," "anarchical," and "lunatic" amongst those who saw themselves as guardians of a stable society.[23]

Even more often, however, the critics' charges against higher-law evangelicals related to their licentiousness, wickedness, and "flexible morality," for at the heart of their indictment was the conviction that higher-lawism was a perversion of scriptural Christianity. Drawing particularly on Matthew 22. 17–21 ("Render unto Caesar ..."), Romans 13. 1–5 ("Let every soul be subject unto the higher powers ..."), and Titus 3. 1 ("be subject to principalities and powers"), they maintained that all authority was of God and "the action of civil governments within their own appropriate jurisdiction is final and conclusive upon the citizen." Government, Charles Hodge explained, was not a mere voluntary compact to be made or unmade at the whim of the individual: "those who resist the magistrate, resist the ordinance of God, and ... shall receive unto themselves damnation." Private judgment and conscience were unrealistic instruments for measuring the moral worth of any law. As George Prentiss remarked, "there are some twenty millions of consciences in these United States, and probably no two of them are practically just alike." Though governments could make mistakes, Christians' remedy lay in judicial appeal and electoral action. It was one thing for a majority of citizens "under circumstances of aggravated oppression and upon a reasonable assurance of success" to engage in organized resistance to tyranny, as had American patriots in 1776; it was quite another for an individual or faction forcibly to resist the law, while professing obedience to other enactments of the same government. Christ had not counseled resistance. Early Christians had only refused obedience over matters of belief and worship. If men and women could not in conscience submit to a law then their only proper action was peacefully to submit to the penalty.[24]

The particular focus of these conservatives' concern, of course, was the "truce-breaking, men-stealing, and perjury" of radicals who incited runaway slaves and sought to nullify the new Fugitive Slave Law. Representative voices in each of the major denominational families counseled full obedience to the new law, from patriotic duty. Some agreed it was an unattractive, even oppressive, measure and looked for a final ruling to the federal courts, but they joined with other conservatives to assert its essential consistency with Constitution and Scripture. Abel McEwen, Congregational minister of New London, Connecticut, lamented that provision for fugitives had been a necessary part of the Compromise of 1787, but insisted that the law was entirely legitimate and binding. Legal regulation of slavery derived its authority from the experience of the Hebrew commonwealth; the return of runaways, from Paul's treatment of Onesimus. Those troubled by the Israelites' obligation to provide a haven for fugitives (Deuteronomy 23. 15−16) could turn to Moses Stuart, who explained that the command applied only to refugees from heathen nations, not to runaways from other tribes of Israel.[25]

The true patriots of 1850, for these evangelicals, were the politicians who engineered the Compromise and outwitted contemptuous ultraists. They included Clay and Fillmore, of course. President Taylor, respected when alive for rebuking disunionism, was elevated by his death into a symbol of harmony. But Unionist evangelicals' principal hero was Daniel Webster. Both during the crisis and again at his death in October 1852 conservatives lionized him and applauded his understanding of the divinity of American government. Nehemiah Adams and William Eells honored him as "an instrument in the hands of God," a latter-day Joshua chosen to pass on unharmed to the next generation the legacy of a new Israel bequeathed by the Founding Fathers.[26]

For their part, pro-Compromise northern politicians sought to harness the support of these Unionist evangelicals. The governor of Illinois and members of the state's legislature invited John Peck, one of the most influential western Baptists and a known critic of law-breaking, to address them in the State House on "The Duties of American Citizens." The Union Committee of Safety in New York warmly recommended Ichabod Spencer's sermon, "The Religious Duty of Obedience to Law," as well as John Krebs's Thanksgiving appeal for public compliance with the Fugitive Slave Law. Conservative members of Congress used their franking privileges to distribute John Lord's stern rebuke to the higher-law party, endorsed by the Union Committee. At the same time Democratic politicians and publicists sought to foster the fear amongst some evangelicals that the higher-law clergy were attempting "to substitute the laws of Moses, interpreted by themselves, in place of those of their country." These Negro-loving fanatics, according to one Democrat, were the heirs of conformist New England Puritans, a "maturing combination" intent on establishing "the Divine right of the church in place of the divine right of kings." Stephen A. Douglas, speaking in Chicago's City Hall, asked where, if the Constitution of the

United States were repudiated as repugnant to divine law, the Christian friends of freedom should seek a better framework of government: "Who is to be the prophet to reveal the will of God and establish a theocracy for us?" John Peck echoed Douglas's theme by rebuking his fellow Baptists for tolerating the recent stealthy spread of "Puritan dogma" and "Jewish theocracy" in the northern states.[27]

By no means all pro-Compromise clergy were happy about the semi-partisan use of their writings, or about some of the interpretations imposed upon them. Whiggish ministers like Ichabod Spencer were uneasy when they saw their sermons "prostituted" for party purposes by northern Democrats. They were equally troubled when they understood the Union Committee of Safety to be denying the citizen's right to any private judgment in public affairs. Nonetheless, their anxiety over the future of the country, and their sense of commanding the support of majority sentiment in northern churches,[28] led many conservative evangelicals to cooperate in the public campaign to sustain the Compromise.

In this they left themselves open to attack from free-soil evangelicals irritated by what they considered double standards and inconsistency. For at the very time conservatives were letting themselves be enlisted politically in the cause of the Union, many of their number were castigating free soilers for "politico-religionism" and protesting vociferously when religious bodies passed "political" resolutions on slavery.[29] When the Old School Presbyterian General Assembly discussed sending a memorial to Congress in May 1850, expressing Presbyterians' concern about the crisis, a blocking majority protested that it was not the Assembly's proper business. New Schoolers likewise declined to act over the Fugitive Slave Law. Gatherings of Cumberland and Associate Reformed Presbyterians declared slavery a political institution outside the churches' concern. Though many local bodies of Methodists took a formal stand on the question, in the broader forum church leaders were much more cautious: George Peck, as editor of the official organ of the MEC, the New York *Christian Advocate and Journal*, kept the fugitive issue out of the paper and restricted discussion of slavery generally.[30]

In fact, conservatives were not asking evangelical citizens to be wholly uncritical in politics. They distinguished carefully between the individual's rights and obligations, and those of the church as a corporate body of worshipers. Thus George Peck in his capacity as private individual condemned the Fugitive Slave Law, even though as denominational editor he believed he carried a responsibility for the harmony of the MEC, and hence the Union, which meant not giving ammunition to its opponents in the sensitive border states.[31] This is what essentially distinguished conservative from free-soil evangelicals. Whereas the latter celebrated the primacy of conscience (at any cost to the unity of church and country, it seemed to their critics), conservatives put a higher premium on social and ecclesiastical cohesion. Presbyterians in particular, both New School and Old, regarded themselves (despite the schism of 1837) as genuinely national bodies. "We believe," wrote David McKinney, referring to Presbyterian Unionists, "that the fraternal unity of the Northern and Southern portions of the churches is one of the strong bonds which hold the States together."[32] Those bonds of Union would be severed if Presbyterians went the way of Methodist and Baptist churches by taking up the agitating question of slavery. When the Union survived the crisis of 1850–51 conservative evangelicals in all the northern churches, but especially within Presbyterianism, had good reason to believe they had been instrumental in shaping the public and political opinion that kept the country together.

Radicals and Unionists in the South

The most vigorous attacks on the "politico-religious ravings" of free-soil evangelicals emanated not from northern but from southern churches, most of whose members denounced the "higher-law fanaticism" for jeopardizing the Union. The southern consensus on the source of the crisis, however, masked a range of opinions about the appropriate response to northern provocation. While most southern evangelicals tried to shield the Union and use their influence to prevent a secession of unreconciled states, a small minority of proslavery radicals advocated disunion.

This latter group, fusing Calhounite states-rights ideology with a conception of slavery as a holy institution, created a radical doctrine that authorized disloyalty to existing, and corrupt, political arrangements, whether political parties or the Union itself. Its authentic voices included those of Iveson Brookes, planter and Baptist preacher; the Methodist local preacher and ex-United States senator from Georgia, Walter T. Colquitt; and John C. Coit, Presbyterian minister and self-professed disciple of John C. Calhoun. They found their audiences mainly in the states of the deep South, particularly South Carolina. Brookes demanded an end to conventional partisanship. "Let us ... drop party names and party intrigues, and rally without division to the standard of Southern rights and Southern institutions," he urged in April 1850, responding to Clay's proposals ("submission projects") with a radical critique which friends thought would prove too strong for the public at large. Colquitt, too, sought to shape, not follow, public sentiment, directing his extraordinary intellect and silver tongue to the task of turning fellow Georgians against the emergent Compromise. Both called on the

Nashville Convention (which Colquitt attended) to take the ultimate step of secession if necessary.[33]

What especially troubled these southern-rights evangelicals was the likely implementation of the Wilmot Proviso in fact if not in name. They feared the Compromise Acts relating to California and New Mexico would "smuggle" in some seven or eight free states, distorting the nation's political balance and leaving a harsh choice between the Union's dissolution or its conversion into "the instrument of unheard of oppression."[34] Clay's predatory measures, "yielding all to the North," ignored the South's contributions to the nation in blood and treasure, and added to the injury of pecuniary loss the insult of political degradation.[35]

Southern radicals drew several lessons from the political crisis. Most evidently, northerners' appeals to the higher law demonstrated the appalling advance of rotten theology and "moral and political heresies" in the free states in recent years. Though conscience might have been an infallible counselor before the Fall, to Adam's posterity it was "a blind guide, or a parasitical and crafty sophist, or a servile pander, or a 'dumb dog,' or a lawless, fanatical raging tyrant." Higher-law doctrine developed in Seward and other "moral monsters" an elastic conscience over their oath to the Constitution; their "Luciferian" free-soil plans trampled on their Christian obligation to use political power for the common, not sectional, welfare. Less evident, but almost as worrying, was the threat these southern evangelicals identified from what John Coit called the "sober North": those who, like Daniel Webster, appeared loyal to federal covenants, but who spoke of slavery as a moral evil and only held back from abolitionism for reasons of policy. Then there was the alarming lesson of Taylor, Clay, and other cloven-footed southerners ready to sacrifice their section's interests in return for national office.[36] Put together, the evidence of 1850 suggested to southern-rights evangelicals that they could no longer depend on their sacred Federal Constitution for protection.

For these evangelicals, political separation assumed a godly character: it was the ultimate antidote to northern atheism. At the same time secession presented the only honorable course when all other reasonable strategies had failed. In this instance evangelical and honor codes fused. There could be no compromise with "the fanatical empire of the monk and the crusader," insisted Coit: "The things that touch a people's honor and independence do not admit of compromise." William A. Scott, not an out-and-out secessionist, nonetheless believed that the South in the later part of 1850 faced a simple choice between separation and abolition. "[M]uch as I love the Union, & much as I wish the negroes to be free," he declared, "yet I am for dissolution rather than dishonor & shame to the South and a forced emancipation." These men saw no contradiction between insisting on free soilers' scriptural duty to obey the civil power and their own toying with disunion as a last resort. "Free white men" had delegated certain powers to federal and state governments, but had retained "their own, sovereign and supreme political dominion." "The political right of sovereignty to draw the sword in its own defence," Coit maintained, "is . . . a moral right, and may become a moral duty." In fact, few thought a literal sword likely. Dismissing predictions of revolutionary carnage, Brookes found an appropriate analogy in the bloodless disruption of the Jewish kingdom after Solomon's death. Though professing a readiness to resist to the death, most separatist evangelicals expected a peaceful secession.[37]

The vast majority of southern evangelicals, however, rallied to the Union. The tide of opinion in the upper and central South, articulated by John T. Hendrick, William Brownlow, Thomas Meredith, and other denominational spokesmen, flowed strongly in favor of compromise. "Disunion indeed!" protested Moses Hoge. "Disunion of these United States! I wish Old Hickory was alive – I just wish Old Hickory was alive." In the lower South, too, influential evangelical leaders counseled against the folly of secession. In South Carolina, a group of respected slaveholding, conservative Presbyterians, including John Adger, Ferdinand Jacobs, Benjamin M. Palmer, and James Thornwell, feared the worst if the state withdrew from the Union. The Methodist bishop, William Capers, though a states-rights advocate, called on South Carolinians not to act unilaterally. Likewise James Andrew urged caution. Few hoisted their Unionist colors more publicly than the Mississippi Methodist minister William Winans, who ran unsuccessfully for Congress in 1849 so there would be in Washington "one less fire-brand to light up the fires . . . to dissolve the ties of our most important Union."[38]

Southern Unionist evangelicals shared with like-minded northerners a common belief in the providential origins of the Union, the sublimity of its design, and the uniqueness of its purpose. They too suffered a heightened sense of threatening catastrophe. They too dismissed peaceful separation as "a mere dream of the fancy." They too insisted that a "cruel, bloody, ferocious war" must follow disunion, terminating "in a hatred more intense than any which ever yet disgraced the annals of any people." They too feared war's effect on morals and religious enterprise. In Thornwell's mind, "the dissolution of the Union is synonymous with ruin; ruin to us, ruin to the North, ruin to all parties. It is another name for war, cruelty, political experiments, licentiousness, irreligion, atheism, anarchy."[39]

Consequently, their eulogies of Clay, Webster, Douglas, Fillmore, and other political compromisers paralleled those delivered by their northern brethren. They had spoken in similar terms of Taylor's death in 1850, as an act of Providence designed to energize the Union. They too dismissed free soilers and abolitionists as "hell-bound fanatics" and infidel "nullifiers" of the Word of God. But their sharpest contempt was reserved for the radicals in their own midst, the southern-rights secessionists. Bitterly they condemned "these Southern Ahethophels" ("John Catiline Calhoun," Robert B. Rhett, John A. Quitman, William L. Yancey, and their clerical supporters) not just for their folly and desperation, but for religious dereliction. The doctrine of non-submission "was introduced into the world by the Devil" when he encouraged the eating of forbidden fruit: "rebellion strikes at the foundation of the Eternal Throne." William Brownlow lambasted southern ultras, doubting if there were "a solitary good man in the *Bible meaning* of the term . . . who believes that it would be right to destroy the Union for the sake of establishing slavery in regions where it never existed." Such wickedness could never triumph. Those attending "the *Hartford* Convention at Nashville, in search of *political salvation* will find . . . POLITICAL DAMNATION!" When secessionists failed at the polls in 1851, especially in South Carolina, Unionist evangelicals rejoiced at the fate of these latter-day Corahs, Dathans, and Abirams.[40]

Most evangelicals, then, north and south, threw themselves behind the settlement of 1850 and did much to mobilize Unionist public opinion. A reflective southern anti-secessionist doubted if there were "a true minister of the Gospel or christian of any denomination . . . not in favor of the compromise and preservation of the Union." Conservatives enjoyed some success in pushing to the margins the more radical dissenters in the churches. Events in New York Methodism were symptomatic. There Davis Clark, author of the Mulberry Street preachers' resolution criticizing the 1850 settlement, incurred the wrath not only of his well-connected church members but of his conservative Annual Conference, who no longer wanted him to represent them at the General Conference. Robert Hall Morrison was convinced that the Union owed much to the like-minded conservatism of evangelicals across the nation; he particularly rejoiced that Old School sermons in the winter of 1850–51 proved "so sound in political matters." Preaching on the return of sectional peace, Charles W. Shields, pastor of Philadelphia's Second Presbyterian church, celebrated the new mood as a triumph for Christian principles: the Bible and pulpit had silenced "the clamors of treasonable men," reversed the advance of "unrighteous dissension," and rebuked the alliance of "infidelity and disunionism."[41]

Behind the return of political placidity, however, lurked a number of potential threats to the Union. A sharp-eyed observer would have seen that the Unionism of many southern evangelicals was conditional on the North's standing by the constitutional rights of the South, especially full enforcement of the Fugitive Slave Law. Southern evangelicals underestimated the potential of northern antislavery forces to harness the growing dislike of slavery in northern society, and overestimated the North's readiness to acquiesce in the return of runaways. Likewise northern evangelical Unionists deceived themselves by overestimating the extent of hostility to slavery in the South. As events unfolded over the following decade evangelical conservatives on both sides would find it increasingly difficult to secure common ground. Within months of the passing of the Compromise measures southern evangelicals could be heard regretting the persistence of the "fanatical virus" of higher-lawism amongst northern clergy and politicians engaged in rescue attempts on fugitive slaves.[42]

Persisting *denominational* frictions also haunted sectional harmony. For the time being Presbyterians effectively marginalized agitation (the New School General Assembly of 1851 successfully foreclosed discussion of antislavery memorials), but in the largest family of churches, Methodism, border conflicts continued to simmer. Southern Methodists complained of the MEC's sending "disorganizers and agitators" into Missouri and Arkansas, and creating a new Kentucky Conference in 1852 as a platform for driving into the slave states. Meanwhile the MEC eyed southerners' operations in Virginia with deep suspicion, fearing for the Baltimore Conference; MEC preachers faced threats of mobbing, tarring, and feathering in Missouri and west Virginia.[43] When the South Carolina Conference issued an amended Discipline which expunged the "taboo" of the historic antislavery section, northern Methodists felt all the more justified in standing up to the ecclesiastical nullifiers in what appeared an unblushingly proslavery MECS.[44]

Similarly chafing were the legal irritations associated with the church property question. In November 1851 Judge Samuel Nelson ruled in the New York case, filed two years earlier in the United States circuit court. Nelson declared that the MECS was not a secession and was entitled to its share of the church's assets. Southerners exulted. Northern Methodist opinion railed against "southern aggression" in Methodist affairs, and treated Nelson's decision as the inevitable result of cotton influence and the "despotic spirit of slavery" at work in politics and the judiciary. When the MEC refused to accept Nelson's ruling (thoughts of appeal to the United States Supreme Court eventually yielded to success-ful arbitration under the Methodist Judge John McLean) southern Methodists bitterly denounced the northern church's disgraceful "jugglery." Yet they themselves, faced in 1852 with Judge Humphrey H. Leavitt's ruling in support of the MEC over the Cincinnati Book Concern, declared that decision sinfully unjust and chose to appeal to the United States Supreme Court. In 1854, under Chief Justice Roger B. Taney, and with McLean disqualifying himself, the Supreme Court ruled without dissent in favor of the MECS. Once again Justice Nelson wrote the opinion. Once again northern Methodists expressed their anger, both at the southern church for its bitter litigation, and at the court's political bias. Granville Moody called the proslavery decision "astonishing and unparalleled and unjust," but his surprise melted when he reflected that the majority of the court's judges were southerners.[45] The significance of his assessment should not be lost. For thousands of northern Methodists the outcome of the Western Book Concern suit exposed the pro-slavery coloring of Taney's Supreme Court. Three years later antislavery forces exploited the historic Dred Scott ruling to show that the slave power controlled the highest judicial body in the land. But well before then a strategically placed body of opinion-formers in northern Methodism had already taken that bitter lesson to heart.

"Higher-lawism" and the election of 1852

The presidential election of 1852 gives credibility to this picture of broad, but by no means universal, evangelical support for the Compromise and the Union. Despite the reservations of free-soil and southern-rights minorities in their ranks, both Whigs and Democrats adopted pro-Compromise platforms and candidates obligingly free of strong opinions, and avoided open rupture. The Free Democrats (as the Free Soilers now called themselves) made every effort to challenge the emerging orthodoxy that the Compromise provided a final settlement. But they faced an uphill struggle in the face of public apathy and a widespread desire to close the book on sectional wrangling after nearly a decade of bitterness.[46]

The battle over the Compromise of 1850 had demonstrated Whig fragility, for a substantial proportion of the party in the North (probably a majority) sympathized with the free-soil position. Its leaders knew that to win crucial northern states in 1852 they would have to prevent defections to an antislavery third party capable of holding the balance of power. For a while, indeed, antislavery Whigs hoped to persuade Free Soilers that a third-party campaign was unnecessary. These hopes evaporated once their party had adopted a platform acquiescing in the recent settlement, including the Fugitive Slave Law, and their candidate, Winfield Scott, had endorsed the Compromise. This, though, did not prevent Sewardites serenading free-soil evangelicals, stressing both the Democrats' two-facedness over slavery and the Whigs' determination not to accept the finality of the Compromise.[47]

Northern Democrats, too, made some attempt to woo Free Soilers. They exposed Whig efforts to present Scott to the South as its undying friend. They made much of their own candidate's ramrod integrity: Franklin Pierce stood up to overbearing southerners. But this was a minor theme. In the main Democrats believed victory would lie in presenting themselves, north and south, as the only dependable friends of the Union and Compromise. Whereas an "essential sectionalism" vitiated Whiggery, evident in the Whig party convention's choice of an "anti-finality" candidate, the Democratic platform and dark-horse nominee promised to abide by and enforce the settlement of 1850. Pierce, they boasted, had never made any concessions to the "politico-religious fanaticism" of the abolitionists and their political allies. In the 1840s, at some personal cost, he had stood firm with the conservative or "Hunker" Democracy in New Hampshire against his friend Senator John P. Hale and the senator's antislavery cronies. Through the dark days of 1850 he had rebutted clerical protests against fugitive slave legislation, dismissing the hisses of Baptist ministers and their allies at a public meeting in New Hampshire as the quintessence of higher-law argument. According to one biographer, his "steadfast moral strength" was wholly at odds with Whig do-goodery and benevolent activism: he regarded slavery "as one of those evils which divine Providence does not leave to be remedied by human contrivances, but which, in its own good time . . . it causes to vanish like a dream."[48]

The real test for the two major parties' competing claims to be the best guarantor of Union lay in the South, where both sought to engage the moral sensibilities of the electorate. Dismissing as preposterous Whig charges that Pierce was a crypto-abolitionist who loathed the fugitive slave bill, Democrats directed their main fire at Scott. Had he not spoken of the "high moral obligation" of the slave states "to meliorate slavery even to EXTERMINATION"?[49] Though Pierce and other northern Democrats shared a common southern view that slavery was a social evil, Scott regarded it, unacceptably, as "a great *moral* evil – leprosy on the *conscience* of the master," to be removed regardless of constitutional guarantees. Whigs, they claimed, sought through Scott to absorb into the party abolitionists and higher-law fanatics repelled by the statesmanship of Fillmore and Webster. Despite his endorsement of the Whig platform, he did not see the Compromise as a final settlement. He was unsound on the fugitive slave question. As a weak, vain, and silly man he would be under the control of Sewardite puppeteers. His election would seal the South's doom.

Democratic arguments gained additional credence from the public disaffection of leading southern Whigs. Appalled by the ungenerous casting aside of Fillmore, hero of 1850, Alexander H. Stephens, Robert Toombs, Meredith P. Gentry, Thomas L. Clingman, and others came to see Scott's defeat as necessary to the defeat of free soilism. Understandably concerned, Whig loyalists rallied with claims of Scott's independence, kindness, and humanity. Just because free soilers had supported his nomination did not make him one himself. Giddings and other northern radicals treated him with contempt. Fillmore had endorsed him. He was "one of the great pillars" of the republic. In a sophisticated but over-subtle argument, Bartholomew F. Moore reminded North Carolina Whigs that the major parties had a responsibility for neutralizing free soilism, which was "capable of concentration into the highest intensity of zeal, and of becoming the *one* and *only* idea of humanity"; that was best done by quarantining free soilers in both parties "to manage them – to divide them, and thus conquer the danger." Whigs counterattacked by reminding voters that the real threat to the republic lay not in their party's tolerating a few free soilers but in the Democrats' harboring disunionists and lawless expansionists with their eyes on Cuba and central America. William Valentine contended that the two parties differed principally not over the Compromise but in their attitudes towards lawless, piratic filibustering.[50]

Whigs found the hemorrhage of southern support over Scott's alleged free soilism all the more galling when they considered the threat of continuing losses on their other flank to the Free Democrats. Though free-soil Whigs worked hard to prevent a separate Free Soil ticket and found some Free Soil leaders ready to delay nominations in case an acceptable Whig candidate and platform emerged, the Free Soil party contained a core of inflexible evangelicals who believed that neither of the "Hunker" parties *"can ever be . . .* true to liberty, while organized with slaveholders." "Politicians are playing a game deeper than ever," Samuel Lewis told Lewis Tappan, insisting that *"Christian principles must guide every action in so holy a cause,"* not expediency. After carefully examining the Whig and Democratic candidates and platforms, the Boston *Congregationalist* concluded: "There is little to choose between them. . . . We could not vote for Gabriel himself upon such a platform as either of these two."[51]

Significantly, when the Free Democrats convened in Pittsburgh in August, Samuel Lewis (along with Joshua Giddings) was one of its moving spirits. Far fewer gathered than in 1848, due in part to the return of the Barnburners to the Democratic fold. The 2,000 made up in moral earnestness what they lacked in numbers. According to Austin Willey, there was "less hurrah than . . . in '48, but in every element of real moral force . . . and *principle*, Pittsburgh far exceeded Buffalo." Though Free Democrats rejected full-blooded abolitionism and failed to advocate the equal rights of free blacks, their platform denounced slavery as a sin, stood by the Wilmot Proviso, called for the complete separation of the federal government from slavery, and castigated the Fugitive Slave Law as "repugnant . . . to the spirit of Christianity." Gerrit Smith and a small minority of former Liberty Leaguers, looking for stronger meat, launched their own ticket. But the idealism of the Free Democratic platform, combined with the adoption as candidate of a reluctant, upright John P. Hale instead of the tainted Martin Van Buren, pushed the party beyond the standards of 1848. Indeed, there was far less political manipulation of the convention than at Buffalo, though Salmon P. Chase and Henry Wilson successfully blocked a move to make Samuel Lewis vice-presidential candidate, believing him too much of an abolitionist, and secured George W. Julian as Hale's running mate.[52]

Staunch antislavery evangelicals both inside the convention and beyond took pride in the outcome, delighted at the persisting union of old Liberty men and Free Soilers in "God's righteous cause." Hale confirmed his image as an instrument chosen of the Almighty "to shake the stagnant elements of political and moral death" by breaking convention and actively campaigning with Julian, addressing cadres of the free-soil regenerate in churches and meeting halls, and pressing home the duty of churches as well as government to drive out slavery. As in 1848, the party boasted the support of ministers of all evangelical families, especially Congregationalists and other New School Calvinists. The contest, according to one voice from Augusta, New York, was more than a prosaic political competition: it was a battle "between the powers of light, and the powers of darkness – between righteousness and truth, and spiritual wickedness in high places."[53]

In the event the Free Democrats faced much greater difficulty in stirring the public's imagination than in 1848. Free-soil evangelicals' bold predictions, in the angry days of 1850, that existing parties would disintegrate looked increasingly misplaced as Whigs and Democrats successfully capitalized on prevailing Unionist and pro-Compromise sentiment, inside and outside evangelicalism.[54] Free Democrats' leaders complained that the major parties conspired to ignore the third party's challenge and (as will become clear) to divert attention from slavery-related issues by stirring up religious sectarianism. On polling day their popular vote fell to half the Free Soil total of 1848. This was especially due to the Barnburners' return to the Democrats' embrace. Significantly, Free Democrats suffered their most grievous loss in the state of New York, where a decline of nearly 100,000 votes since 1848 resulted mainly from the Van Burenites' departure. Hale secured over 10 percent of the vote in only four states, and Free Democrats' congressional candidacies (apart from those of Joshua Giddings, Edward Wade, and Gerrit Smith) achieved markedly less than in 1848. The party's hopes of eating into Whig support were largely disappointed. Many free-soil evangelicals continued to see Whiggery as the best practical hope of blocking the territorial ambitions of the slave power. Calvin Fletcher feared Pierce's election would give license to the "mad spirit" of expansionism into Cuba and Mexico; the young Henry Clay Trumbull brought to Scott's cause all the earnestness that might have been expected of a recent convert of Charles Finney.[55]

For all this, evangelical Free Democrats were remarkably heartened. Joseph Bent told Jonathan Blanchard that the election gave antislavery Christians good reason for encouragement. The departure of the Van Burenites had left a purer metal, "gold tried in the fire." In the western states, an Oberliner claimed, compared to 1848 "the vote is . . . every way far *better*. It is the vote of truer and more reliable men, on better and more enduring principles." The party had kept the support of most of its Liberty and Whig elements from 1848, secured the "political somersault" of some prominent Whig evangelicals, and attracted a number of first-time voters repelled by the major parties, men like the young Methodist itinerant and disciple of Finney, De Witt Clinton Huntington of Thetford, Vermont.[56] Though they would have preferred to have thwarted Pierce and the Democrats, third-party forces had shown their power to inflict serious damage on the Whigs.[57] Indeed, some of them, including Joshua Leavitt, took heart from what they considered the effective death of that party.[58] They took the view that once conscientious Whigs had lost faith in their party's capacity to win elections for free soil, they would seek to replace it with an unyielding antislavery force, and evangelicals of conscience would never again have to choose the lesser of two evils.

In fact the presidential campaign in the North proffered ambiguous evidence for predicting the future of Whiggery. Events in the slave states, on the other hand, proved starkly discouraging. Here Scott suffered the worst rout of any candidate since 1832. He won only one southern state, Tennessee. Tens of thousands of Whigs refused to vote for him, many staying at home in the firm belief that his victory would hand the national government to anti-southern interests. Evangelicals figured prominently in the ranks of the disillusioned, most notably Whiggish Methodist preachers who had longed for the nomination of the "fearless, self-sacrificing" Fillmore, as Lovick Pierce described him. The elderly Methodist minister, in a letter to the *Milledgeville Recorder*, asked to be excused his public meddling in a presidential election: no true southerner, he wrote, could vote for a representative of Seward Whiggery; and since Franklin Pierce threatened the other "dreaded evil of our age," an expansionist foreign policy, he urged voters to support the independent Unionist ticket of Daniel Webster and Charles Jenkins. William Brownlow, outspoken as ever, shared this sense of desperation. "The nationality of the Whig party is destroyed," he declared on news of Scott's nomination. He had not forgiven the General for thwarting Clay's presidential ambitions in 1840 and 1848. Repelled by Scott's higher-lawism and his vanity, the Methodist editor urged all southern Whigs and Democrats to rise above party (both now controlled, he claimed, by free soilers) to support Webster. Undaunted by the New Englander's death just before the election, which the more conventionally minded might reasonably have supposed removed the ticket's vestigial credibility, Brownlow invited posthumous votes for the candidate so his electors could vote for Charles Jenkins or some other dependable Whig in the electoral college.[59]

According to Brownlow, such anti-Scott sentiment was rife amongst southern Methodist ministers, who were as a body overwhelmingly Whiggish. In the Holston Conference (embracing portions of Virginia, Kentucky, Tennessee, the Carolinas, and Georgia), where, he claimed, five out of every six Methodist clergy were Whigs, two-thirds of Whig ministers were alienated Fillmorites. Though Brownlow's figures should be treated cautiously, the thrust of his argument carries. Methodists certainly agonized over internal developments within Whiggery, their sensitivity to higher-law advances in this bond of Union heightened by parallel events within another, the Methodist church, both before and after the schism of 1844. "[T]he same Free Soil States that sent 90 delegates to the Gen[eral] Conference of 1844 . . . sent 66 Free Soilers to the Whig National Convention at Baltimore who made President Fillmore the *Andrew* of the South." No Methodist preacher who approved the Plan of Separation, Brownlow contended, could support Scott, a candidate who had replaced "that great *Bishop of Southern Rights and Southern Interests*, MILLARD FILLMORE!"[60]

So the events of 1852 suggest that the party's stand on slavery profoundly alienated many erstwhile Whig evangelicals, north and south. While southern Fillmorites feared Scott's "unholy alliance" with the higher-law men and the "*free nigger crew*," northern Sewardites proved unable to choke off the challenge of a third party which comprised many ex-Whigs and which believed that the future lay with those who would "burst off party shackles and vote for conscience and liberty." Whig managers were learning that in neither section could they expect unquestioning allegiance from many of the devout Protestants who had done so much to shape the party's character. Even the staunch Brownlow had come by 1851 to view his once-beloved Whigs, not just the loathed locofocos, as "drifting, unsettled and divided, corrupted and selfish, reckless of fundamental principles, dignity and self-respect." Both parties were breaking into fragments, he observed, as expediency and not principle became the watchword of their leaders. "But, as we sometimes sing at our camp-meetings, 'a better day is coming'. . . . [T]he people are casting off the shackles of dictation." Events proved him partially correct. Following further traumatic defeats in southern state elections in 1853, southern Whigs appeared on the verge of extinction. They could only hope to survive as part of a national party, but their union with northern Whiggery seemed to make them dangerously inadequate defenders of southern interests. They would not survive the excitement over the Nebraska bill in 1854.[61]

The preceding two chapters invite the conclusion that the public discourse of evangelicals had changed during the 1840s and early 1850s in reaction to the combined force of political and ecclesiastical events. Northern evangelicals, postmillennialist protectors of the republic against ungodly conspiracy, treated the annexation of Texas, the conquest of Mexico, and the paroxysms that followed church schism as related developments, as individual and collective obstacles to the promised advent of Christ's kingdom. Their southern counterparts, with their own vision of a godly republic and sharing the paranoid temper, reacted in alarm at the advance of infidel abolitionism in the North, evident in the spread of free-soil sentiment inside as well as outside the churches. They felt a special sense of betrayal as sometime "conservative" allies in the free states now appeared to cast in their lot with radical abolitionists in the moral condemnation of the South. The sectionalism that would put such strains on the two major parties in the 1850s was thus grounded in conflict over moral perceptions and what "true" conscience required.

It seems clear, too, that Whigs and Democrats developed their political ethics from different assumptions, and that the Whigs' ethic was partly rooted in a certain kind of evangelicalism that made them more unstable and more exposed to disintegration than their opponents. The higher law, with its roots in natural law and the precepts of the eighteenth-century Enlightenment, and consistent with the Christian emphasis on measuring behavior against divine commands, exercised a powerful influence on many Whiggish evangelicals: those, that is, for whom politics was not essentially about pursuing the utilitarian or the pragmatic, but about advancing a new world order rooted in New Testament values. Government's duty as a moral, Christian agent was to advance that order. Democrats, in contrast, not only tended to emphasize government inaction and the citizen's right to freedom from political intervention, but more populist Democrats' stress on the sovereignty of the people and on right democratic process led them to locate political morality in listening to amassed individual sentiments as expressed through the ballot box. The voice of the people – of individual moral agents – provided the moral authority and justification of government action. Whigs, seeing individuals as members of a corporate moral body, the nation, were less interested in process than outcome. A godly nation would be judged less by its democratic process (only a means to an end) than by the congruence of government action and scriptural command. Whigs' emphasis on the government as an *active* agent, and evangelicals' concern that the state behave as a *righteous* agent, suggest that the party's disintegration was inevitable once it lost the confidence of those postmillennial evangelicals who had done so much to shape it.

The Whigs' enfeeblement, as we have seen, derived considerably from the party's failure to prevent the alienation of northern and southern evangelicals over the issue of slavery and free soil. We shall never know whether the party could have survived had it faced the tensions generated by that question alone. For, as the next chapter will demonstrate, there were other, equally potent, moral and religious issues current in the early 1850s. Their agitation damaged both major parties, but worked most dramatically to dissolve the threads weaving evangelical Protestants into the fabric of Whiggery.

Chapter 7

The Collapse of the Second Party System: Protestant Insurgents and Know Nothing Millennialism

The three million immigrants who arrived in the United States between 1845 and 1854 posed a real threat to the republic's social cohesion. Taking the longer perspective, the historian can reflect on the relative ease with which those new arrivals, almost 15 percent of the population of the mid-1840s, took their place in American life. But at the time the indigenous population of Boston, Cincinnati, New York, and other towns and cities facing this foreign tide took a less sanguine view.[1] The immediate threat to the values and way of life of the Protestant native-born in the free states, where most of the newcomers settled, troubled evangelicals far more than did the evils of slavery and the slave power. When neither Whigs nor Democrats provided a satisfactory vehicle for Protestant schemes of social control, the days of the second party system were numbered.

"This threatening darkness of hell": evangelical responses to Catholic immigration

Outraged Protestants regularly denounced the immigrants' moral degeneracy. Francis D. Hemenway warned of a "refuse population" from the "moral pest-houses of the old world," and Eugene Levert of "the basest specimens of human character." That these waves had begun to "tinge and corrupt the whole mass of waters" seemed only too evident from the multiplication of brothels, prisons, and poor-houses, which offered a crude but alarming measure of the increase in prostitution, crime, and improvidence. More threatening still was the proliferation of grog shops, "the dens of thieves, idlers, drunkards, blacklegs, strumpets, assignations, and of the vicious, lazy, fierce, and profligate of both sexes." The "dominion of Alcohol" engendered most of the nation's crime and debauchery, and imposed a terrifying tax burden on the industrious and virtuous.[2]

In essence, evangelicals ascribed the newcomers' immorality not so much to a general godlessness or secular radicalism (though the immigrants included "Red Republican" refugees from the failed revolutions of 1848) as to Roman Catholicism.[3] Irish and Germans, predominantly Catholic in religion, made up the two largest sub-groups in the aggregate body of immigrants. The alarm evangelicals had expressed in the early and mid-1840s took on even more force as Catholic churches swelled and proliferated.[4] At one level Protestant volleys against Antichrist assaulted traditional targets in the Roman church's creed, liturgy, and ceremonial: its denial of justification by faith alone, its doctrine of human merit, its elevation of the priesthood, and its appeal to "the external senses" through "mummeries" and superstitious rites.[5] At another, their attacks had to do with the social and political implications of Catholicism's growing power. For in a number of ways an increasingly assertive papacy seemed intent on severing the sinews of American republicanism.

In the first place, evangelicals believed that Romanism corroded the high standards of personal behavior essential to virtuous citizenship. Instead of rebuking their members' moral laxity, priests used the privacy of the confessional to condone drunkenness, fraud, theft, and sexual immorality. What else could be expected of shockingly licentious clergy, wielding untrammeled authority over the hearts and minds of female churchgoers – not to mention the bodies of vulnerable novitiates in the shielded confines of Catholic convents? Priests flaunted their perverted moral code by openly encouraging the rivers of Irish whiskey and German lager that drowned any sense of personal Christian responsibility. A church that could accommodate drunken worshipers, coffee-house keepers, and the owners of liquor stores, and castigate total abstainers as fanatics and "Maineacs" (advocates of the prohibitionist Maine Law) was no friend of republican sobriety. According to some, the Roman church's small number of temperance advocates, even the celebrated Father Theobald Mathew, encouraged provident habits simply to fill Catholic coffers. Far more honest were those who smiled benignly as their members replaced family prayer with Sabbath-day grog-drinking. According to their critics, Romanist clergy had no scruples about turning Sunday into a day of drunken pleasure, gun practice, marching, loud music, and "din infernal to quiet ears." Their aim was treason. "[T]o destroy the Sabbath," Charles Elliott told his readers, "is to pull down at one raw pull the pillars of the republic."[6]

Secondly, republics depended on an educated citizenry, but Romanists appeared to hate free inquiry and free schools. In the early 1850s Archbishop Hughes and other Catholic leaders resumed the bitter struggle for state support to parochial institutions and against the reading of the Protestant Bible in public schools.[7] In New York, Philadelphia, Detroit, Cincinnati, St Louis, Baltimore, and other communities with substantial numbers of Catholics, they called on parents to withdraw their children from public schools and petition the legislatures for a division of the school fund. The campaign, more assertive and far-reaching than that of a decade earlier, drew down the wrath of an army of evangelicals who regarded Bible-centered common schools as the *"the nurseries of free principles."* A common Christian education for all children would promote social integration and responsible citizenship. Rome, fearing the light of the Bible, and loving darkness because *"ignorance* is the mother of devotion," had only two ways of conquering the American people: "by brute force, and . . . by *pulling down our schoolhouses."* An alarmed western Methodist pondered Catholic efforts to impose the Douay Bible on Cincinnati schools. "Blot out the Bible from the American mind," he wrote, "and cut loose all the restraints which it imposes on man, and how long would this republic last?"[8]

By corrupting personal morality and warping Christian education Rome sought to reduce the United States to the degraded condition of Mexico, Spain, Ireland, and other Catholic countries. Evangelicals considered it axiomatic that "the development of material wealth and prosperity can never be long or safely dissociated from intelligence, morality and a pure religion." Thus Popery would always obstruct social and moral advance. "[W]hat a clog to progress in any direction is Romanism," remarked a visitor to Brazil, blaming the underdeveloped economy of a naturally rich country on 300 years of Catholic influence. "The Pope," concluded a correspondent of the *Christian Watchman,* "has a natural dread of railroads and the other great enterprises of modern civilization." He was "bent on reviving the darkness and barbarism of the Middle Ages."[9]

Poignantly for evangelicals, since it symbolized the very republican values they sought to defend, the ballot box appeared to be Catholics' principal means of subverting civic order in the United States and establishing a political and spiritual despotism. Rufus W. Clark spoke both for fellow Massachusetts Congregationalists and a much wider constituency when he pointed to "a deep, systematic, and extensive plan," which would use Catholic voting power "to overthrow our institutions, and bring this nation under the blasting and withering influence of Romanism." The conspiracy's guiding genius, of course, presided in Rome. Pius IX's reputation as a bigoted reactionary and "supreme dictator" sprang principally from his role in the Italian uprisings in 1848 and 1849, when Louis Napoleon and French troops sustained him against Mazzini and the "popular party."[10] It derived too from the case of Francisco and Rosa Madiai, two Tuscan peasants imprisoned for possessing and reading a Protestant Bible, and from other cases of persecution.[11] Constitutional liberties languished wherever the autocrat in the Vatican held sway.[12] Now he was set on smothering Protestant republicanism in the United States.

The Pope's plan, according to staunch Protestants, depended in the first instance on his lieutenants: his archbishops, bishops, and parochial priests. Disciplined, well organized and obedient, they were the "sworn officers of the Papal crown," many of them foreign-born, all of them owing primary loyalty to Rome, not the United States. These church-men, Protestants declared, shared the Pope's autocratic temperament and antipathy to political liberty.[13] This was starkly evident in their hostility to the triumphal American tour of Louis Kossuth, Hungarian patriot, hero of republicans, victim of Austrian Catholic despotism and darling of enthusiastic evangelicals, who regarded him as the herald of a new age of Christian liberty.[14] It emerged in their bitter determination in Buffalo and elsewhere to control church property, and in Archbishop Hughes's efforts to secure a New York state law removing all ownership from the hands of lay trustees. It was apparent in their warm wel-come to Gaetano Bedini, the papal nuncio sent to settle these property disputes – a man whose flaying alive of Ugo Bassi and other Italian republicans did not augur well for more enlightened American Catholics who wanted "the Pope's Nancy" to support them against priestly authority. It surfaced in the chilling boast of the editor of the St Louis Catholic newspaper, the *Shepherd of the Valley*, that once Romanists had achieved their inevitable numerical superiority, "religious freedom is at an end."[15]

Lieutenants needed troops. The Pope, evangelicals insisted, had encouraged thousands of Europe's Catholic paupers to emigrate to the United States. Here he taught them to sponge on the public purse while they gathered strength to outvote Protestants and establish the Roman church by law. Ignorant and illiterate, they proved easy prey for conniv-ing priests. The confessional, "the most formidable of all engines of oppression," provided the hierarchy with a powerful political machine: it encouraged control of believers' "thoughts, desires and emotions." This explained why Romanists, unlike Protestants, voted as a bloc; why they resorted to physical brawling to return sympathetic candidates; why they voted "with reference to their Church, and not with reference to the state." All in all, the Pope's iron grip over his church meant, as Nicholas Murray sneered, that "a man can no more be a Papist, and a true and loyal American citizen, than he can serve two masters."[16]

Protestants reached greater agreement on the character of the papal threat than on the likely outcome of the struggle for supremacy. The growth of the Catholic population in North America gave that church at mid-century an assertive self-confidence which Archbishop John Hughes ebulliently expressed in November 1850 in his lecture, "The Decline of Protestantism and Its Causes."[17] Hughes implicitly repudiated Orestes Brownson and other Romanists who advocated Catholic accommodation with native Protestants and sought the immigrants' cultural assimilation.[18] Instead he dismissed Protestantism as an inherently decadent force which, despising authority, tended doctrinally to rationalism and infidelity, and institutionally to fragmentation. The way beckoned for the Catholic church "to convert the world – including the inhabitants of the United States."[19] Hughes's words and Catholic variations on his theme resounded menacingly amongst Protestants. Both Nathan Bangs and Henry Clay Fish pointed to the relative decline of evangelical numbers in many cities during the later 1840s and early 1850s, and to an absolute drop in New York's Methodist and New School Presbyterian membership at a time when the city's Catholics were doubling in strength. Daniel Eddy spoke apocalyptically of America's sitting "on a volcano, which threatens to send out its overwhelming tides of lava, to consume every vestige of beauty and holiness." Many doubted that the republic would survive.[20]

More commonly, however, evangelicals believed that they could survive the crisis. There might indeed have to be, as William Nast predicted, "a civil war, . . . a *bloody, religious war* . . . against this threatening darkness of hell!" But all the signs pointed to Protestants' victory in "the great Battle" pending. Romanism, they argued, grew only through foreign immigration or the conversion of native reprobates and "perverts," particularly high-church Episcopalians. It could not flourish amidst freedom of thought and accessible Bibles. Witness Protestant missionaries' impressive conversions amongst German, Irish, and French immigrants whom they had prized from their priests' clutches. Once Catholics became convinced of sin, a Cincinnati Methodist exulted, they "find no comfort in beads, holy water, praying to the Virgin Mary, etc." The Irish in particular were vulnerable: "They become Americans too readily, and sink their nationality in the newly adopted character with too much facility."[21]

Evangelicals, then, saw the American republic standing at a crossroads. Romanists sought to drive it towards despotic papal rule and crush its unique identity. The Lord called on Protestants to recognize what Charles B. Boynton and Francis Hemenway respectively called America's role as "a prophet of a new dispensation" and the nation's "lofty and peculiar destiny" to maintain free institutions in conformity with an untrammeled Gospel. The crisis presented a breathtaking, cosmic opportunity as well as a challenge. For Nathan Beman recent events heralded the death of paganism, the tarnishing of Islam and, now, the final testing of the papal world. Despite papal threats and intrusions, Benjamin F. Crary knew who controlled the future. "Let us feel the impulse of a new power," he urged fellow Methodists. "I am distinctly in favor of a new instauration. . . . We must all throw off the shackles of old forms, and old, mean ways, and work to bring [in] the glorious millennium."[22] Romanism had no place in this brave new world.

"Driving back the demon of intemperance to his native hell": drink as a political issue

From the later 1840s growing numbers of evangelicals called on their fellow churchgoers to engage single-mindedly and imaginatively in politics to defend the republic against Romanism and its attendant evils. They warned candidates against the consequences of succumbing to the concentrated Catholic vote. They demanded state and municipal action to defend the traditional Sabbath, either by enforcing existing laws or passing new ones. They urged elected authorities to sustain common schools and the Bible against an unholy combination of papists, freethinkers, and treacherous Protestants. Above all, they sought to regulate the country's liking for drink, first by overturning the licensing system, and later through prohibitory laws to prevent the manufacture, sale, and consumption of all alcohol. Their crusade against liquor demands particular attention since it tells much about their changing political perceptions and tactics. As frustration turned to anger, many moved away from lobbying the major parties towards independent political action, further weakening the structure of the second party system.

The antipathy amongst middle-class evangelicals to the self-help, Washingtonian movement in the early 1840s had operated, as Albert Barnes put it, "to *throw off* a considerable portion of the churches, and the religious community" from the temperance effort.[23] But from the mid-1840s a combination of foreign immigration, mounting fears of social disorder, and a widely articulated teetotal millennialism drew evangelicals firmly into renewed activity.[24] "The work of purification from the giant vice of the world is going on," Nathan Beman reflected in 1846, "and it will be rendered perfect, under God, by the simple principle of total abstinence from everything that can produce intoxication." Convinced that removing alcohol would make "the wilderness . . . bud and blossom as the rose," evangelical Protestants strained earnestly after stricter standards. Home missionary boards drew closer to the American Temperance Society; Methodists restored Wesley's strict rule at the MEC General Conference in 1848, despite the huge commercial pressures on western farmers to sell their corn to distilleries; new interdenominational organizations in New York City and Philadelphia yoked teetotalism and evangelical recruitment.[25] In the South many regarded total abstinence as another Yankee "ism": there the triangular relationship of drink, social tension, and immigrant culture was less evident and threatening than in the North, and the distinctive cultures of subsistence farmers, poor whites, and the planter class gave alcohol a valued role in work and relaxation. Even so, a growing minority saw the social value of temperance. Southern professionals, merchants, skilled tradesmen, entrepreneurs in the towns, and commercially minded farmers, seem to have been drawn to orders like the Sons of Temperance by their ethic of moral and economic improvement. Often members of Baptist (though not Primitive Baptist), Methodist, and Presbyterian churches, they enjoyed the support of at least some of their clergy, who believed no drunkard could enter the Kingdom of Heaven, and that without teetotalism no free, Christian nation could survive.[26]

As they redoubled their temperance efforts evangelicals turned more and more to political means. In the earlier days of the movement the conventionally wise had understood that "for every moral evil God . . . provided one only and sure remedy, a moral one." A persisting fear of "religious laws" and the union of church and state led many to resist political action. These included not only Primitive, or hard-shell, Baptists and other staunch antimission groups in the southern and western states, but many from mainstream Methodist and Baptist churches who re-membered blue laws, suspected Presbyterians and Congregationalists of seeking to reconstruct their Calvinist imperium, and hated any sugges-tion of "meddling in politics." When in 1834, as a young man of twenty-three, Jonathan Blanchard urged his audience in Plattsburg, New York, to work for the legal restraint of the liquor traffic, he regarded himself as one of an eccentric minority. So too did Luther Lee, when a little later he called in print for the prohibition of the trade.[27]

Such demands multiplied in the next few years, though the significant leap in clerical and public support for political action came only in the mid and later 1840s, assisted by changing attitudes within both the Washingtonian movement and the Sons of Temperance. Increasingly evangelicals came to share the view of Matthew Simpson, that "moral suasion alone will not answer. Criminals have never been restrained by moral suasion alone." "Enlighten the mind of the rum-seller?" Davis Clark scornfully asked. "You may as well attempt to reason with the midnight assassin, or the pirate on the high seas." Moral victories over sinning individuals, even when achieved, left the structural problem untouched. Seeking to assuage persisting fears of a return to blue laws and "religious legislation," advocates of legal action stressed the utilitarian argument: the drink trade cost the state money, raised taxes, impoverished its human resources, and even threatened the lives of its citizens.[28] Since sobriety advanced the economic and social interests of the state, as well as its moral standing, it was a political as well as a moral issue. Politicians had a duty to act.

Reformers' particular target in the mid and later 1840s was the licensing system. Though intended to limit retail sales of alcohol and promote sobriety, licenses seemed in practice to do little to stem the rising tide of alcohol: one Presbyterian minister dismissed them as "a cob-web around the brawny limbs of a giant." They were also morally flawed: they temporized with sin and tempted the weak, in chimerical pursuit of an impossible outcome, "a holy Sodom."[29] The cry of "no license!" thus rang out from evangelical platforms across a number of northern (and a few southern) states which by the early 1850s had moved to repeal or modify their licensing arrangements. But evangelical reformers found the resultant mix of old and new laws scarcely more satisfactory. After the license elections across the state of New York in 1846, inhabitants of the non-licensed towns could still slake a thirst in neighboring licensed ones; the Wisconsin statute to make sellers responsible for the harm they inflicted failed when juries proved unable to estimate that damage with precision; the Illinois law of 1851 only forbade retailers from selling in quantities of under a quart, and seemed unlikely to limit consumption, even by under-age drinkers.[30] Altogether the no-license campaign did little to stop the possession or manufacturing of liquor, or prevent its sale for consumption off the premises.

For those most committed to securing a dry millennium it was a short, logical step from such complaints to a demand for thoroughgoing prohibition. When Maine introduced its celebrated prohibitory statute in June 1851, one sustained both inside and outside the legislature by the state's single-minded Protestants, evangelicals from all parts of the country called for its universal adoption.[31] Aimed at securing an end to the manufacture and sale of all intoxicating drink within the state, under threat of fearsome fines and imprisonment, Neal Dow's uncompromising law seemed to these churchmen entirely consistent with the constitutional powers of the states, with social utility and with the moral obligation on all government to promote virtue, happiness, and general thrift. Above all, fusillades of evangelical opinion extolled the law for being "as agreeable to true republicanism as it is to the spirit of the Gospel."[32]

In these campaigns to overturn the licensing system and extend the Maine Law, temperance evangelicals sought to maintain relentless pressure on their political representatives. Ministers collected thousands of signatures for no-license petitions and memorials aimed at state assemblies. Influential church presses listed worthy candidates, while leading evangelicals interrogated those of doubtful credentials. In all this they exuded a growing confidence. When, for example, in 1851 the Ohio constitutional convention submitted to popular vote a separate anti-license clause, ministers excitedly welcomed a unique chance for dry Protestants to outvote wet Irish and Germans (even in their strong-hold of Hamilton County) "without becoming entangled with the party feuds of the political canvass." They called for temperance lectures in every schoolhouse and church, and for all pulpits to address the issue the Sunday before the election. "Ministers of the Gospel; fear not the charge of meddling in politics," urged Matthew Simpson, suggesting they set up special committees to encourage a good turnout, especially of the infirm, the elderly, and customary non-voters. "Presidential, congressional, and political questions of every grade, sink into in-significancy, when compared with this great moral question." Indiana witnessed a similar fusing of political practicality and revivalist enthusiasm in a prohibition campaign which one Methodist minister boasted would drive back "the demon of intemperance . . . to his native hell."[33]

Temperance evangelicals at first generally disclaimed any wish to establish "formal combinations." Many considered a Christian, tem-perance party, running separate tickets for local and state offices, to be far more problematic than lobbying primary meetings and marching up to the polls to select "the most respectable, decent and honest men" from the lists of the Whigs and Democrats. Third-party action would set up tensions amongst evangelical loyalists of the major parties: far better for the temperance constituency to wield the balance of power within the two party system.[34] But attitudes changed as prohibitionists met ambivalent and even hostile responses from mainstream politicians. Suitable candidates were not always on offer, and even when they were, and won office, legislatures could not be trusted to pass the right measures. The truth was that not only in matters of drink but across the whole range of issues connected with the new immigration, includ-ing Catholic schooling and the naturalization of foreigners, neither Democrats nor Whigs responded with the energetic commitment which evangelicals considered vital to a Protestant republic. Their confused and deficient responses demand a brief examination.

Two-faced Whigs and equivocal Democrats

By the early 1850s many of the economic issues that had deepened party cleavage in the high Jacksonian period no longer animated voters. The decline in sectional antagonism following the Compromise of 1850 limited another potential source of party conflict. Worried by creeping consensus, which reduced the parties' distinctiveness and electoral magnetism, Whigs and Democrats sought to sharpen their differences.

The conflicts generated by mass immigration, of course, offered them a glut of issues capable of arousing powerful passions amongst the electorate. Yet they deliberately equivocated, believing these questions – especially prohibition and political restrictions on foreigners – so divisive that any unambiguous stand would cost them electorally far more than they would gain. Though tactically understandable, such equivocation proved, for Whigs at least, strategically disastrous.[35]

The drink question seriously divided both parties.[36] Democrats knew they invited damaging defections if they openly defied the no-license and Maine Law movements. But the party generally embraced a smaller proportion of dry voters than its opponents, and its leaders had to balance the demands of evangelical reformers against those of other grassroots supporters, native and foreign-born, who argued, in the words of a Tennesseean, "If we are to have laws that shall tell us what we must drink and what we must not drink, we had better belong to grate britton at once, for queen victorys subjects are allowed to drink what they please."[37] A number of Democratic publicists boldly attacked the reformers, warning voters against "pseudo-philanthropists" and preachers "whose vocation of moderators is forgotten in their efforts to fan the flames of the most dangerous partizan fire ever kindled among us"; some local parties formally stood by the Jeffersonian and Jacksonian principles that "legislation will not make men honest, moral, temperate or religious"; others denounced the Maine Law as an unconstitutional attempt "to lay the iron hand of a gigantic governmental control upon the conscience and habits of a whole people."[38] Yet in practice the party, under pressure from its teetotal supporters, could not hold unflinchingly to this stern line. In Maine itself, for example, Democratic moral reformers and political realists united to pass the path-breaking law. Significantly, the issue ruptured an already factionalized state party.[39]

Whigs were even more torn. In many areas the party had a deserved reputation as a truer friend of temperance than their opponents. Some saw in the burgeoning of anti-drink enthusiasm a chance to break up the Democrats by wholeheartedly endorsing the crusade. At the same time others threatened to bolt if Whigs championed strict prohibition. Many strategists, well aware that the party suffered electorally when it took up the issue, cautioned against risky action that would at the very least destroy its hopes of winning over foreign-born voters. As a result the party's leaders hesitated, including its non-drinkers. When, for instance, Alfred Dockery, a Baptist teetotaler, ran as the party's candidate for the governorship of North Carolina in 1854, he tried to duck the issue to avoid alienating the many Whigs opposed to legal prohibition.[40]

Whigs' ambivalence about drink has to be set in the context of their uneasy oscillation over other immigrant-related local issues. For the whole of the party's history it had faced a dilemma which it never completely resolved: how might it satisfy the demands of nativists and anti-Catholics, and so prevent their running independent candidates, without incurring the electoral wrath of the increasingly powerful foreign-born population? In the 1830s and 1840s the party's self-projection as the best guarantor of "Protestant" values and respectability helped see off the periodic challenges of nativist third parties in New York, Boston, and Philadelphia. But this stance worked to confirm foreign-born voters in their Democratic loyalties, as Whigs bitterly reflected in the aftermath of Clay's defeat in 1844. Whig concern deepened as the naturalization of the burgeoning immigrant population brought new Democrats cascading to the polls and threatened to consign Whiggery in many states, and in every presidential election, to permanent minority status. Some Whigs, centered on William Seward, had long looked sympathetically on the needs and ambitions of the foreign-born. Seward himself developed close ties with the Catholic hierarchy and sought the full political integration of the foreign-born: in this his purpose was not just to make them Whigs but to engage them as allies in the defense of American republicanism, self-government, and public virtue. A hard-nosed political pragmatism drew others to see the merits of Seward's approach. Thus, for instance, Cotton Whigs allied with the Catholic Irish in Boston in the early 1850s to defeat the more liberal and democratic (and temperate) order sought by the Democrat–Free Soil alliance, while in Brooklyn and other parts of New York in 1852 Whigs conspicuously failed to take up the militant nativists' demand for radical changes in the immigration laws. In similar fashion, when the common school issue boiled over in Detroit, Baltimore, Cincinnati, and elsewhere in 1853, Whigs widely sought to distance themselves from nativist extremism.[41]

Whigs and Democrats employed this equivocal approach both locally and nationally. It attracted most widespread attention in the presidential campaign of 1852. In that election the two major parties inconsistently projected their candidates as determined both to defend all that was best in "Protestant" America and to respect in equal measure the rights of the electorally pivotal immigrant voters. This was not a new approach, as the analysis of the three presidential campaigns of the 1840s has already made clear. But in 1852 the parties' ambivalence proved more acute and – given the context in which it emerged – more damaging.

In Franklin Pierce Democrats had a candidate whose good looks and relative youth compensated for a modest political and military career. Party propagandists presented the New Hampshire man as a sober product of steady New England religion. Brought up by a devout mother, "deeply impressed by the truths of religion" as a Bowdoin student, and married to the daughter of a Congregational minister, Pierce found his campaign biographers (including his friend Nathaniel Hawthorne) praising his kindheartedness in religious causes, his service as a Sunday School teacher, and his "steadiness and sobriety." Though not formally a church member, he "generally attends worship at the Congregational Church in Concord." Perhaps fearing this might offend non-Calvinists, Pierce's biographers hurried to celebrate his youthful friendship with the devout Methodist, Zenas Caldwell, and to coo their paeans to the Methodist church. Then for good measure, lest other denominations should feel slighted, they stressed Pierce's appetite for "the most evangelical preaching" regardless of source. It was this religious sensibility that made him an honest lawyer, a gallant and dutiful brigadier-general in the Mexican war, and a modest statesman. Together with the party's vice-presidential nominee, the morally upright and patriotic William R. King, Pierce would bring a tone to the White House wholly superior, they declared, to that offered by his hypocritical Whig opponent, Winfield Scott. In the event, Pierce's biographers spoke more prophetically than they knew. The tragic death of the couple's twelve-year-old son in January 1853 plunged Mrs Pierce into four years' black mourning and the distressed President-elect into deep soul-searching. Convinced that God had punished him for his spiritual shortcomings, Pierce instituted a regimen of strict Sabbath observance and twice-daily family prayers for the whole of his period in the White House.[42]

At the same time, thanks to an Irish father, Pierce's religious sense was rooted, not in "illiberality, but a wide-embracing sympathy for the modes of Christian worship, and a reverence for individual belief." For this reason, his champions explained, he had worked untiringly if ineffectually to remove from the New Hampshire state constitution the religious test that excluded Catholics from higher public office. Recognizing that "Catholics have always been found in the advance-guard of freedom," Pierce would maintain the Democrats' traditional defense of religious and political minorities. Throughout the campaign the party's presses enthusiastically championed the exiled "Irish Patriot," Thomas Meagher, now freed from British imprisonment, and demanded that he be given immediate citizenship. A Democratic administration would be a more dependable guarantor of immigrants' rights than one headed by Scott. The Whig candidate's sympathetic response to nativist approaches in the 1840s certainly provided a useful store of damaging material. His letter *"concurring fully in the principles of* the Philadelphia movement" (the Native American Republican party), shortly before the church-burning riots of 1844, allowed Democrats to claim that, despite his later renunciation of nativism, *"Scott hates the foreigner"* and that he sought to exclude the immigrant from citizenship. The Irish should understand that the general had hanged or branded a whole Legion of St Patrick for desertion in the Mexican war. Though Whigs sought their votes in elections, at all other times they dismissed the Irish as "the offscouring of all God's creation."[43]

Whigs, too, played this double game, attending to evangelicals' concerns while courting the foreign-born with unprecedented ardor. Extolling Scott's personal qualities, as they had Harrison's and Taylor's before him, Whigs presented him as an uncorrupted warrior, whose valor contrasted luminously with his opponent's cowardice: Pierce "fainted and fell" at Cherubusco and "got the gripes" at Chapultepec. But Scott's courage blended with integrity, justice, and humanity. His "pure, noble and affecting philanthropy" showed in attentiveness not only to his own men but to his enemy. When removing 15,000 Cherokees from the south-eastern states in 1838 he had evinced a potent "spirit of Christian humanity." Whigs blessed with more enthusiasm than literary sensibility might choose to sing: "And when the Cherokees were moved,/ According to the Congress law,/ SCOTT did it: and it can be proved/ He didn't kill one single squaw!" In private life, too, Scott (an Episcopalian) evinced "a lofty tone of morals and an uprightness of personal character and habits." On the burning issue of temperance, Whig pamphleteers insisted, an abstemious (though not teetotal) Scott had long sought to limit the damage liquor-drinking inflicted on military discipline. By way of contrast they made much of tales of Pierce's heavy drinking, particularly as a United States senator – when, according to the *New York Tribune*, he had been "almost continually intoxicated." Such stories did nothing to help Democrats counter the related charge that their candidate was "not a professor" ("by which is . . . meant," the *New York Freeman's Journal* scornfully remarked, "that he has never sat on the anxious-bench of a prayer-meeting, and does not sharpen his wits by a prayer previous to trading horses"). Democrats continued to complain of insinuations "secretly and industriously circulated" against their candidate, and published evidence from named Baptist and Methodist preachers intended to show that Pierce was no drunkard.[44]

These were familiar Whig campaign themes, which irritated rather than threatened their opponents. Much more alarming to Democrats were Whigs' concerted efforts to woo the foreign and Catholic vote, especially by turning their candidate into a friend of Catholicism. Whig campaigners explained that one of Scott's daughters had been converted to the faith. They dressed the General himself in Jacksonian garb, praising his self-sacrificing exploits against the British and his fellow-feeling for "warm-hearted Hibernians" during the war of 1812: combining bathos with enthusiasm, they told the tear-stained story of his successful intercession with the enemy for the return of twenty-three Irishmen destined to hang. More recently, in his Mexican campaigns, he had ordered his men not to interrupt religious processions and had guaranteed the religious freedoms of surrendering forces. Campaigners insisted that

Scott had recanted his earlier dallyings with nativism. In a much-quoted letter, to William E. Robinson in 1848, he had renounced his support for tougher naturalization laws in view of the patriotism of German- and Irish-born troops. Traveling the extra mile to outbid the Democrats, Scott announced in June 1852 that he favored actually reducing the naturalization requirements for immigrants who served their adopted country in wartime. Then, in September, the Whig candidate set off on an extensive tour of Pennsylvania, Ohio, Indiana, Kentucky, and New York. Speaking at over forty places, he regularly flattered the Irish and Germans, even attending a Catholic service in Madison, Indiana. "I detect in these cheers," he told an audience in Auburn, New York, "a brogue I am always happy to hear. I have been in many tight places in my life, but I have never been deceived by that brogue." To further cheers he continued: "[T]he natives of the glorious Emerald Isle . . . have always been on hand in every emergency."[45]

Robinson himself, the Irish-born recipient of Scott's renunciatory letter, played an active and enterprising part in the canvass as a pamphleteer, seeking to blacken Pierce's name by associating him with the Catholic exclusion cause in New Hampshire. Examining the state's constitutional convention and subsequent ratification campaign, in 1850–51, the Irishman insisted that the Democrats' presidential candidate had done less to remove the test than "a humane man would undergo to save a blind puppy from drowning in a pond" and concluded "no *good Catholic*" could vote for him. The issue appeared a promising one, and Whigs diligently exploited it, distributing pamphlets in English and German not only in the East but as far west as Iowa and Wisconsin, and twisting Archbishop Hughes's studiedly neutral public letter on the issue into a recruiting appeal for Scott.[46] Worried Democrats took the challenge seriously, aware of anxieties amongst Catholic spokesmen, whom they regarded as their customary supporters. Dismissing Robinson as a New England Presbyterian, fruit of the accursed "Orange tree," they devoted gallons of ink to establishing Pierce's "noble" course, alleging "Federal-Whig" responsibility for the original test, and reminding voters of Scott's association with Philadelphia natives and Boston convent-burners.[47]

Democrats ridiculed Whigs for being two-faced and determined to win Catholic votes at any cost. They enjoyed a warm glow of satisfaction at Scott's crushing defeat. The fact was, however, that Democrats too suffered significant electoral damage in the early 1850s because of their tenderness towards those who seemed to threaten the Protestant republic. As the anger of native evangelicals towards the existing leadership of both parties heated to boiling point, reform-bent Protestants became ever more open to the idea of independent political action.

"Blowing both political parties to the Devil": evangelicals and independent political action

Clearly, Scott's campaign in 1852 had backfired. His overtures to Catholics had done little to prize rank-and-file members of that church from the Democracy and much to alienate Protestant Whigs especially sensitive to immigrant intrusions. William Brownlow, for instance, deserted Scott not just for keeping abolitionist company, but for his "devotion" to Catholicism, his friendship with John Hughes, and the two-facedness of "Roman Scott Whiggery" in attacking the New Hampshire Test; he considered the General's electoral rout "a God-send to the Whig party." In Pennsylvania the brogue-lover's "waterloo defeat" appeared thoroughly to vindicate pre-election predictions of massive defections or abstentions amongst the state's Whig Methodists and Presbyterians. In New York possibly as many as one-third of the state's Presbyterians, strongly Whig in 1848, withheld their votes. Concessions to the Catholic church, moaned Calvin Fletcher during the campaign, "are made by the corrupted politicians – the infidals & debachers [*sic*] of the political parties & they drag the masses, the pro-testants along with them. Party fanaticism is such that each is bound to make any vile concessions to the Pope & the evil one to get votes." He had once thought better of the Whigs, but they "at this day have abandoned many of the *ways* of former adherents & care but little for the principles if they can be elected to office."[48]

The contest of 1852 undoubtedly damaged Whigs' credibility amongst numbers of evangelical Protestant voters and did little to improve the reputation of Democrats. But the election took on significance less because of the idiosyncrasies of Scott's and Pierce's appeals than because their parties' conduct conspicuously reinforced an existing and wide-spread political disenchantment. Evangelicals' stern antipartyism in the earlier years of the second party system had yielded to a more tolerant acceptance of parties' utility. But they remained profoundly fearful about Whigs' and Democrats' openness to abuse by self-seeking can-didates and "wire-pulling" managers who treated recently naturalized and electorally pivotal immigrants as "objects of flattery and dread." Stephen Colwell's and Elisha L. Cleaveland's blistering attacks on the degeneracy of political parties, the lack of patriotism amongst office-seekers, and "the moral dereliction" of every legislative body in the Union coincided with the Pierce–Scott campaign but pointed to a malaise far deeper than the ills of a single presidential election. Evangelicals directed ever more acerbic tirades at local and state office-holders ("atheists, drunkards, libertines, gamblers and demagogues") who "outraged their consciences, betrayed their constituents and insulted

God at the mandate of party." What confidence could Protestant republicans place in elected representatives who arrested anti-Catholic preachers, fêted Catholic dignitaries (including the notorious Bedini), and stalled on politically delicate issues like drink and schooling? What could be expected of lower-level politicians when Franklin Pierce himself appointed James Campbell, a Catholic, to cabinet office as postmaster-general? Though aware that, once in office, the "narrow-souled" Philadelphian would turn Protestants out of postmasterships, suppress patriotic anti-Catholic newspapers, and subordinate American interests to those of Pius IX, the new president had happily sold his soul in return for the foreign vote.[49]

Protestant anger at prevailing political practice created a receptive environment in which disillusioned ministers like Colwell could urge "the great Evangelical Denominations of this country" to take independent political action. Prohibitionists' efforts at working within the major parties retreated before a conviction that success would come only through third-party action. In Ohio, for instance, the 1851 election on the license issue had shown anti-drink evangelicals the shortcomings of "time-serving politicians" in both parties. The Democrat-controlled legislature in 1852 and 1853 successfully resisted the efforts of the Maine Law lobby. Whigs, sensitive to the political influence of lager-drinking Germans, tried to avoid a clear stand. In the 1853 state election drink was the salient issue. Charles Elliott and other evangelicals pointedly chided Whigs and Democrats for hypocrisy in bewailing the evils of intemperance while refusing to endorse the Maine Law. But in the Free Democrats' candidate for governor, Samuel Lewis, they had a figure to whom they could rally with enthusiasm. Drawing on a reform-minded Protestant constituency, Free Soilers in Ohio and elsewhere, unlike the main parties, had no difficulty with prohibition: far from being divisive, the drink issue might even boost their electoral fortunes.[50] Ohio evangelicals threw themselves feverishly into the campaign. Methodists' numbers gave them particular influence (Lewis himself, of course, was one of their local preachers). Members of Chester circuit, for example, "in the present crisis, when party drill is attempting to coalesce with the whisky interest," resolved "to rebuke the perversion of party, and . . . [to] sacrifice all personal and party ties, and . . . to support no man . . . who is not the known friend of the cardinal principles of the 'Maine law'."[51] Other quarterly conferences took similar stands. Technically speaking, this was not an independent political movement: no separate prohibition party was established and Lewis himself received no formal endorsement from the temperance forces. But a limited fusion movement between prohibitionist Whigs and Free Democrats enjoyed some success, and many temperance men certainly considered Lewis and his party's other candidates to be as much exorcists of drink as of slavery. Though Lewis ran a poor third, with less than 18 percent of the vote, he drew considerable numbers of temperance men from the Whigs; the injection of the Maine Law issue helped him improve not only on John P. Hale's performance in the previous year, but on his own earlier bid for office in 1851. Mass demonstrations, revival enthusiasm, and prohibition sermons had given Free Soil in Ohio a new energy.[52]

In a variety of other settings, too, Maine Law evangelicals rallied with great enthusiasm to third-party and fusion movements. When Rhode Island prohibitionists advanced an independent slate in January 1854 the *Temperance Union Journal* predicted a victory that would throw off the chains of King Alcohol and "that which for fifty years, has been the most tyrannical and galling of all – the yoke of party politics."[53] In Detroit the Friends of Temperance called for the cutting of all party ties in the city election in February 1854, and in the April county and township elections Maine fusion tickets helped shape the outcome in many places across the state. The previous year's gubernatorial election in neighboring Wisconsin, strongly Democratic, had already seen prohibitionists joining with Free Democrats and Whigs to support Edward Holton, pious Congregationalist and Milwaukee merchant, and a People's ticket which was firm on the Maine issue and which would draw its most significant support from the Yankee Protestant settlements of the south and center of the state.[54] In Indiana a similar fusionist People's party emerged in 1854, succored by thousands of antiparty prohibitionists whose vituperative language offered some measure of their righteous fury. As in Ohio, Methodists across the state led the way in advising their 80,000 members and those of other churches to set aside "all merely party alliances" and expel the "serpent tongued" political trimmers who bowed and scraped "to the whisky fiend." Calvin Fletcher, elected chairman of the Central Temperance Committee, worked energetically to secure a ticket composed of "temperance men sober" and hailed the People's party's October triumph over the Democrats as primarily a victory for prohibition.[55]

Developments in Maine and other free states reverberated amongst evangelicals in the South and loosened the ties of party there, too. Thomas Stringfield, William Brownlow, W.E. Caldwell, John McFerrin, and other Tennessee churchmen resolved in 1853 to vote only for dependable temperance candidates: the fall election saw substantial defections from Whiggery and "a very general determination to drop all party names till the Temperance question is settled," even "if it blow both political parties to the Devil." Many Kentucky evangelicals took a similar position; Robert J. Breckinridge's determination to make the 1853 elections turn on the license question drew him into bitter conflict with his sometime Whig allies, who were terrified that the issue would split their vote and hand victory to a Democratic opposition that enjoyed greater "party tenacity." In both Delaware and Maryland temperance forces' loss of confidence in the major parties prompted a separate prohibition ticket. In Baltimore in 1853 they nominated a Maine Law slate of delegates drawn from both parties, which swept to victory and shattered the existing two party structure; in the state at large they won sufficient seats to hold the balance of power in the House of Delegates and secure the passage of a prohibition bill early in 1854. Further south, Alabama temperance men supported independent "fusionist" candidates in 1853 and 1854; North Carolina prohibitionists were at the same time setting up independent tickets calling for public referenda and a Maine Law; when the Georgia legislature resisted calls for prohibition, evangelicals and others ran Basil H. Overby, a Methodist local preacher, as a third-party candidate for governor in 1855.[56]

There was no greater tribute to the power of evangelical prohibitionists to shape state and local politics in the early 1850s than the course pursued by Thurlow Weed, the legendary Whig boss in New York, during the state election of 1854. In the previous year Horatio Seymour, the Democratic governor, had vetoed a strict Maine Law that dry Whigs, led by Myron Clark and other prohibitionists, had steered through the legislature. Weed was no dry, but once the Democrats had renominated Seymour as their gubernatorial candidate (seeking to divert electoral attention from the revived slavery question) he regretfully concluded there was little he could do to stop the issue dominating the canvass. Seymour's veto had spurred the state's Maine Law evangelicals, the "religiously earnest" as George Coles called them, into furious action; at the American Temperance Union anniversary, in May, Theodore Cuyler and Henry Ward Beecher told them to go home and work for the triumph of a prohibitionist ticket. The threat of independent temperance nominations, remote in years past, Weed now saw to be real enough. Making the best of a Whig convention which he barely controlled, he acceded to Myron H. Clark's nomination for governor. Evangelicals turned the campaign into a pivotal battle in the worldwide war for prohibition. Upstate Baptists in convention at Syracuse eagerly resolved to give their support to Clark; Theodore Cuyler joined Greeley and others at an intensely excited mass meeting in the Broadway Tabernacle just before polling day.[57] Clark's victory by just a few hundred votes out of 450,000 cast seemed providential. "We felt it to be a great moral as well a political triumph," recalled John Marsh, "and we felt disposed to give God the glory." William E. Dodge organized a day of rejoicing, speeches, and prayer to mark the glorious event. Once Clark had signed a prohibition bill into law in April 1855 (and added New York to the roster of seven states which had already traveled the same road) Dodge, Beecher, George Peck, Stephen H. Tyng, and others gathered for further celebrations. By no means all Maine Law men had voted for Clark, since a nativist, third-party candidate, Daniel Ullman, had split the Whig vote and seems to have won support from some temperance men in the Burned-over District as well as from anti-prohibitionists elsewhere. But a majority of prohibitionists (a fusion of most dry Whigs and the complete army of Free Democrats) rallied to the candidate they had helped force on Weed.[58] On this occasion evangelical prohibitionists' threat of an independent course, not its reality, had brought about the result they desired.

Evangelicals did not confine their appetite for independent political action to promoting the Maine Law. New political coalitions also emerged in response to the Catholic bishops' call for public funding of their parochial schools, a campaign which produced confusion in the major parties and fury amongst the most anti-Romanist of Protestants and nativists. In the March 1853 city elections in Detroit, not long after Bishop Peter Paul Lefevre had demanded a Catholic share of public school money, an "Independent" ticket of Whigs, Protestant immigrants, and nativist Democrats confronted Democratic "Regulars." All the evidence suggests that voting largely followed religious fault lines: Elizabeth Stuart reported during the campaign that "the cry now is Protestantism against Popery." As the Independents swept to victory she exulted, "We can begin to see the goodness of God in scattering or annihilating the Whig party." Evangelicals observed with satisfaction that similar religious configurations, also growing out of the school issue, replaced older loyalties in the state elections in Maryland later in the year.[59]

Even more remarkable was the upheaval in Cincinnati, where the funding question became the principal campaign issue in the city election of April 1853, despite the attempts of regular Democrats and anti-nativist Whigs to ignore or marginalize it. The electorate faced a choice of four tickets. One comprised candidates of an Independent Free School movement, whose nominee for mayor, James D. Taylor, was a demagogic ex-Whig and editor of the zealously anti-Catholic, nativist *Cincinnati Times*. Taylor drew the support not only of working-class Protestant laity but of middle-class ministers like Charles Elliott, who warmly welcomed Taylor's appeal that voters set aside "all party trammels, and meet openly and boldly, the issue presented by the Roman, or Church and state party." Though David T. Snelbaker, the Democrat, won the mayoral contest, victory came on a minority vote and by so narrow a margin over second-placed Taylor that it severely damaged the political authority of his once-unassailable party. Undaunted by the mayoral result, Elliott and his fellow evangelicals celebrated the "Defeat of the Pope in Cincinnati" as Free School men swept to victory in the elections for council and school visitor.[60]

The concern of hundreds of thousands of reform-minded evangelical Protestants to protect the republic from Catholicism, secure a temperate society, defend the public education system, and remove unprincipled party manipulators from positions of public influence thus found dramatic outlet in fusion movements and independent political action in the early 1850s. In a variety of state and local settings regular Democrats and Whigs came to fear the electoral potential of evangelicals driven as much by righteous indignation as by a pragmatic political calculus. Those regulars had every reason to fear. For during 1854 and 1855 evangelicals went beyond crusades focused narrowly on drink or common schooling to give spectacular expression to uninhibited anti-Catholicism. This they did in a political organization still regarded as the quintessence of Protestant evangelicals' full-blooded intrusion into political life: the Know Nothing party.

"The hand of God is visible in this thing": the Know Nothing Order

For over a decade some nativist Protestants had been prophesying a realignment in politics. "[T]he time is not likely far distant when the political parties will be, not Democratic and Whig, but Popish and Protestant," a western Methodist asserted in 1841. In 1844, when American Republican and Native American parties were active in Boston, New York City, and Philadelphia, William Buck, a Louisville Baptist editor, expected to see "new political combinations" developing nationally, through which, as he put it, "Whigism and Democracy will be merged into Nativeism and Anti-nativeism." Electoral victories like that of Joseph Barker, who as the "People's and Anti-Catholic" candidate ran ahead of regular Whigs and Democrats in the Pittsburgh mayoral contest of 1850, appeared portents of political earthquakes to come.[61]

Know Nothing origins are shrouded in the secrecy that made the party attractive to so many native-born Protestants. Charles B. Allen's Order of the Star Spangled Banner was at first, in 1849–50, little more than a covert patriotic society in New York City designed to support the nativist candidates of existing parties. But within a few years, under the new leadership of James W. Barker, a staunch New York Methodist, class-leader, Sunday School teacher, and dry-goods merchant, it was well on the way to becoming an independent, national political force. Formally known as the American party, it was more commonly referred to by the name invited by its members' feigned ignorance of its existence. Its most stunning early victory – in the Philadelphia municipal election in June 1854 – gave notice of an imminent political revolution. In the ensuing fall elections in the North the party sometimes fought as an independent force, sometimes in fusion with other parties. In every case it seriously wounded at least one of the major parties; in many instances it inflicted mortal damage on the Whigs. Know Nothings performed astonishingly well in New England, New York, New Jersey, Pennsylvania, and several western states, including Indiana. In Massachusetts, it seemed miraculously, their candidates won the governorship and all the congressional seats, and filled most of the places in the state legislature. By the end of 1854 the Order had taken institutional root in every northern state and was advancing rapidly in the South; insiders put total membership at about a million. Throughout the following year Americans won southern victories in Texas, Kentucky, and Maryland, principally by providing a refuge for homeless Whigs. Henry Wise, Whig-turned-Democrat, halted the Know Nothing tide, but not before they had fought "the greatest political contest" in Virginia for a quarter of a century against Democrats who saw themselves battling against "Temperance societies and Know-Nothings and every damnable ism." In Tennessee, too, and further south in Georgia, Alabama, Mississippi, and Louisiana, Americans ran a close second to their Democratic opponents.[62]

Evangelicals watched with wide-eyed wonderment what Daniel Eddy called a "political earthquake" and James W. Alexander a "political rage." Denominational presses carefully reported each step of Know Nothings' electoral progress, in many cases departing from their customary studied neutrality at election time. A northern correspondent of the *Southern Christian Advocate* marveled at this "strange and wonderful" chapter of the country's history.[63] William Brownlow declared "the hand of God ... is visible in this thing. Divine Providence has raised up this new Order to purify the land."[64] In Indiana, where according to Edward R. Ames Know Nothings were "thick as the locusts in Egypt," an eloquent millennialist regarded the "new and strange order" as an indication of humankind's entry into the " 'latter days,' while the earth is groaning with age, and struggling for deliverance." For Samuel D. Baldwin, who regarded the United States as God's agent in the final days and His instrument for the destruction of Romanism, Know Nothings took on a very special significance.[65]

The American party, like all electorally successful parties, sought to build up an effective coalition by appealing to a variety of interests by multiple means. At a time of serious upheaval in a number of local economies, particularly those connected with the river trade, Know Nothings played on the anxieties of native working men fearful of immigrant competition.[66] Alfred B. Ely described "foreign ignorance" as a real threat to "American intelligence" and the dignity of labor: impoverished and strike-prone immigrant workers tended "to reduce the rate of wages to less than a living price." The party simultaneously proffered itself as a reliable serum against the rising poison of sectionalism in the bitter aftermath of the Kansas–Nebraska bill. Entry into the so-called "third degree" of the Order's membership, which cleared the way to office-holding in the party itself, depended on an oath of allegiance to the American Union. Party spokesmen declared they would "bring back the nation to its original American platform" and "establish a pure and elevated nationality . . . undisturbed by sectional politics." Their words were meant for those like the Virginia Presbyterian minister, James Morrison, who looked to God to raise up a new breed of politicians "who will strive to promote the prosperity of our Country and the perpetuity of our union." More than one historian has explained Know Nothings' advance in these terms, not only in Morrison's Virginia but in other parts of the South and in the North.[67]

At the heart of the American party's appeal, however, lay not economic nativism or Unionism, important as these were, but manipulation of the nation's profound anti-Catholicism, and a call for social and political reforms to protect Protestant republicanism.[68] Know Nothings undoubtedly played on popular fears of the Catholic religion *per se*, that is on prejudice against its creed, its priests, and its ecclesiastical institutions, especially its nunneries and confessionals. They also exploited a widespread animus against the numerically dominant group within American Catholicism, the Irish. (While campaigning in Mississippi in 1855 the Reverend William H. Holcombe jeered that *"he would as soon preach to a jackass as an Irishman."*)[69] But primarily Know Nothings emphasized the political consequences of mass Catholic immigration, the secular ambitions of the Pope and his American hierarchy, and the unique role Protestant America had to play in the present phase of a 300-year struggle against the papacy. Anna E. Carroll boasted that the American party's principles "dated their origin with Luther," and had descended to the present generation via the Huguenots, the Pilgrim Fathers, and the Declaration of Independence. Know Nothings of course denied any intention of depriving Catholics of their specifically religious rights: they insisted that there be no infringement of Romanists' constitutional guarantees. But their political privileges were quite a different matter. James Campbell's elevation to cabinet rank and Roger Taney's influence over the Supreme Court indicated the progress towards a seamless union of church and state, driven forward by the "unholy combination" of Archbishop Hughes and President Pierce. The *Milwaukee Daily American* concluded darkly: "The man who is a Roman Catholic cannot be an American." His political exclusion could come at a legislative stroke, party leaders explained, by extending the residency requirement for naturalization to a full twenty-one years. The Know Nothing editor and Methodist minister, John H. Power of Cincinnati, denied any wish to restrict "open asylum and bountiful hospitality to the refugees of all nations," but adamantly stood by the party's rallying cry, "America to be governed by Americans." The book of Deuteronomy offered comforting support for this doctrine, Charles Elliott noted: "The

Almighty, in conceding that Israel might choose a king, laid down the law that they must not choose a *stranger*, but a Hebrew of their own nation."[70]

Such attitudes were by no means restricted to the northern states. Southern Know Nothings also wove anti-Catholicism into the fabric of their party with considerable success – far more so than some historians have been inclined to recognize. It is true that Catholics were thicker on the ground in the North: the slave states were overwhelmingly (about 95 percent) Protestant, and less than 20 percent of Catholic church accommodations in 1860 were located there.[71] But there were significant numbers of Catholics in Louisiana, Maryland, and Texas, and the church also had a notable institutional presence in Kentucky, South Carolina, and Missouri. According to likely sympathizers of the American party, the South sheltered quite enough papal agents (aided by Democratic party quislings) to give substance to fears that Rome's power had increased, was increasing, and ought to be diminished. The great connexional denominations in particular, the Presbyterians and Methodists, through their assemblies, conferences, itinerant preachers, and presses, helped spread news and heighten fears of Catholic advance. Southern newspapers carried regular reports from the North and West on Catholic "aggressions," from which impressionable Protestants would have concluded that the Pope intended Cincinnati as the epicenter of Roman despotism in the United States. American party politicians seized hold of this anti-Popery, even where Catholics were few in number.[72] Only seventeen of Virginia's 2,386 churches belonged to that church, but this did not prevent Thomas S. Flournoy, Know Nothing candidate for the governorship in 1855, from waving a nativist, Protestant flag and emphasizing that in a "sisterhood of States" Virginia should *"not act . . . for herself alone."* Henry Wise and the Democrats dismissively rebuked him for "The Absurdity of Being Afraid of the Catholics." But James Morrison unhesitatingly blamed the defeat of Flournoy ("a christian . . . without a stain on his reputation") on Wise's appeal to Catholics and foreigners; "the drunken priest" in Augusta County, he instanced, had delivered 450 Democratic votes, bringing to the polls "a railroad car full of low ignorant Roman Catholics."[73]

As this suggests, the American party's anti-Catholicism was closely linked to the widespread distrust of established parties in the early 1850s. Know Nothings fully exploited popular disenchantment with those whom a Louisville Baptist dismissed as "the old party hacks and broken-down politicians, who swarm like locusts over the land."[74] They promised a new moral order in politics. An Indiana Methodist spoke of a "moral and political thunderstorm" that would "purify the elements." The old parties were driven by plunder and spoils, but Know Nothings sprang "fresh from the uncorrupt and uncorruptible virtue of the people." Daniel Eddy promised a new order of politicians, *"temperate, intelligent, and pious men"* who would act consistently with "their consciences, their liberties, their country, their religion, their souls." Alfred Ely, who helped carry the antiparty philosophy of the Order of United Americans into Know Nothingism, expected a return to Washingtonian integrity. "Many contend that there must be two great parties in this country," wrote one enthusiast, "but why one national party should not answer all the requirements of the nation, is, as yet, an unsolved question." Similarly, George Robertson, a party leader in Kentucky, promised "to break the *rusty ties of nominal and fruitless partyism*, and to unite in a devoted band of patriotic *Americans*." All in all, a deep and pervasive political millennialism informed the thinking and language of the new party leaders.[75]

Many Know Nothings expected this new political order to repair the republic's Protestant foundations by protecting the Sabbath, defending the Bible and the common school system, monitoring all Catholic institutions, particularly convents, and encouraging sobriety. Prohibition was not formally incorporated into the party's platforms, since its leaders feared alienating its urban, working-class sympathizers, many of whom enjoyed a dram.[76] But mostly their supporters showed great enthusiasm for the Maine Law. Brownlow's declaration, "We are for *Know Nothingism* and a *Prohibitory Liquor Law*," held true not only for the American party's candidates in his home state, but for its office-seekers in many of the state elections in 1854 and 1855.[77] Analysis of Ohio and Pennsylvania voting patterns points to a strong kinship between the two crusades at grassroots level.[78] A similarly strong connection existed between northern Know Nothingism and hostility to slavery and its territorial expansion. Through the political crisis over the repeal of the Missouri Compromise, much earnest antislavery and free-soil sentiment found an initially comfortable home in the American party, though the movement was eventually to split over the issue. Know Nothingism was indeed a vehicle for poisonous bigotry against foreigners and Catholics. But its pursuit of political and social reform indicates that it engaged not only the dark underside of nativism, but also the purifying, optimistic millennialism of Protestant culture.[79]

These Christian troops fought for a godly republic under leaders proud of their evangelical credentials and church connections. Protestant clergy were involved from the outset, not only as furtive organizers of the new order, but as public spokesmen and office-seekers. "The secular papers from East and West, and South and North tell us that Methodist preachers, and Presbyterian preachers, and Baptist preachers and those of other sects, are foremost and most active in the conclaves of the dark lantern fraternity," complained the *New York Freeman's Journal*. A bitter Massachusetts Whig viewed the order as "a race of spavined ministers, lying tooth pullers, and buggaring [*sic*] priests"; following its victory in the 1854 state election Boston Catholics dubbed the newly assembled General Court the "Praise-God Barebones Legislature." Alexander K. McClure judged that in Pennsylvania the movement "pulled an unusual number of ministers into politics, largely from the Methodist and Baptist churches." In Louisville, Kentucky, opposition papers asserted that most of the Protestant ministers took a prominent part in the city elections of 1855.[80]

Behind all such claims, even those dressed in the most extravagant language, stood a solid stanchion of truth: the moral urgency of Know Nothingism did indeed draw many ministers, religious editors, and leading laymen into an unaccustomed, high-profile role in public life. According to John R. Graves, the influential editor of the *Tennessee Baptist*, the emergence of the Order made it "the duty of the *minister*, as well as the *member*, to become a politician." Political neophytes, including the Massachusetts ministers Daniel C. Eddy and Mark Trafton, ran successfully for state and national office; the astute and eloquent Otis H. Tiffany, Methodist minister, played a critical diplomatic role in negotiations amongst Whigs, Americans, and Republicans in Pennsylvania electoral politics in 1855; a number of clergy, including Thomas Goodwin in Indiana and D.J.H. High of St Louis, edited Know Nothing papers.[81] The emergence of this clerical phalanx prompted understandable hyperbole. Benjamin F. Butler later declared that the Massachusetts legislature of 1855, for example, was "very largely composed of the lower class of sectarian preachers." In fact only 24 of the 419 legislators were ministers.[82] An even smaller proportion reached the Connecticut General Assembly of 1855–56: 3 out of the 248 representatives of the party. And only 12 of the successful American party candidates elected as representatives to the 34th Congress in 1855 were clergymen. But the absolute numbers were far less significant than the relative increase in ministerial representation (Massachusetts in 1855 saw a doubling of ministers in public office compared with the average over the previous seven years) and the fact that evangelical leaders were now actively pursuing a higher public profile.[83]

The new order's mass membership, too, showed a significant evangelical orientation. Combining as it did both economic and religious protest, the party of course secured the support of many who, as Frederick R. Anspach explained, were "not intimately nor professionally associated with any denomination"; but, he insisted, Know Nothings "have that religious consciousness which lives in the bosom of every American." Charles Elliott, too, boasted that American party supporters largely comprised "the great body of the intelligent, moral, religious, and reliable portions of citizens." Know Nothingism showed that if Roman Catholicism were defined as the common enemy, old partisan and denominational antagonisms could melt sufficiently to encourage evangelical Protestants into an unprecedented (if incomplete) display of political unity.[84]

Know Nothings tended to poll extremely well amongst previous non-voters, an indication of its strength amongst the young and its power to rouse the politically apathetic.[85] But most of its evangelical support came from massive Protestant defections from Whiggery and, to a lesser degree, from the Democracy. Sometime Whig enthusiasts like George Coles in New York, Lucien Berry in Indiana, Charles Elliott in Ohio, James L. Chapman and William Brownlow in Tennessee, William Valentine in North Carolina, and James Morrison in Virginia found a comfortable home in the new party. Ex-Whigs were easily the most important element in the party's strong showing in the New York state elections in 1854, and in all places they played an essential role in the movement's dramatic emergence.[86] But so too did many staunchly Protestant and prohibitionist Democrats like "Father" Richard Libby, shoemaker and elderly Methodist, who presided over the Massachusetts Senate in 1855, Anson G. Phelps, wealthy New York merchant and devout Presbyterian, and W.H. Goodwin, Methodist minister and Maine Law advocate, elected as a Know Nothing to the New York Senate. In Virginia Charles Dabney was especially concerned about possible defections of Christian Democrats (including his brother Robert) from Henry Wise's ticket in 1855. In particular, Pennsylvania, Massachusetts, and Maryland Democrats all suffered serious losses to the new party.[87]

The American party also acted as something of a denominational, as well as a political, melting-pot. William Brownlow, disappointed in his ambition of harmonizing all evangelicals within Whiggery, looked to the American party for the creation of "a union of the *Protestant Freemen* of the country, irrespective of parties, in a grand Republican, Protestant, and Native movement" which would result in a simple political division between "the *Foreign and Catholic Party*, and the *American and Protestant Party*."[88] Know Nothingism went some way towards realizing these hopes: all the major Protestant churches – especially Methodists, Baptists, Presbyterians, and Congregationalists – proved fertile territory for the recruiting officers of the movement.

The evidence suggests that Methodists' contribution to the party was fully in keeping with their status as the largest Protestant family in the nation. Augustus B. Longstreet, a Democrat, believed seven out of every ten of his fellow southern Methodists had joined, contributing in total perhaps as many as 200,000 of its staunchest supporters. From within the party, too, William Brownlow announced that he would "be surprised to learn that less than *two thirds* of all the Preachers and members of the Methodist church, are not in full fellowship with the Order, wherever they are working!" Aaron V. Brown, no friend of Brownlow, also pointed to the contribution of the MECS, and its ministry in particular, to Know Nothing advance in Tennessee. Virginia Democrats rebuked "political" Methodist class-leaders, stewards, and itinerant preachers ("Protestant Priests kneeling at . . . our LOVE FEASTS") for their general and active participation.[89] Further north, Indiana Democrats blamed Methodists for their defeat in 1854: one (Joseph A. Wright, himself a Methodist) reported bitterly that two-thirds of the church's ministers in the state were active in the secret order; another claimed preachers had secretly exerted great influence in pre-election meetings "in cornfields and ravines." William Gienapp estimates that Indiana rank-and-file Methodists were almost evenly divided between a "People's Party" (largely controlled by the secret order) and the Democrats. His figures for Pennsylvania suggest that perhaps 60 percent of the church's voters supported the American party there in 1854.[90] In Ohio the party's German opponents regarded "Methodist" and "Know Nothing" as interchangeable terms. The judgment was understandable in view of the Ohio Conferences' implicit endorsement of Know Nothingism and the open sympathy of denominational papers. In New York City editors, clerks, printers, and agents at the Methodist Book Concern were said to be members, actively engaged in printing and distributing Know Nothing documents. In New England, Freewill Baptists regarded Methodists as widely involved in the work of the secret societies. Mark Trafton's election to Congress owed much to their support.[91]

There is some evidence to suggest that the Order exerted a particularly strong influence over Methodists of Irish extraction. In 1855 there were over 250 Methodist preachers who had been born in Ireland; many more had Irish parents; tens of thousands of members had Irish connections; almost all inherited an animus against Catholics. William Barnes, of the Philadelphia Conference, an Irishman who "refused to be called one," showed a "hearty hatred of the Pope, Romanism and the Devil, and generally classed them together." Feelings were mutual. Charles Elliott, Irish-born himself, believed that "the prejudices of the Romanists against Irish Protestants are stronger than against Americans." Leonard Bacon noted that Know Nothings were "widely suspected to be, in large proportion, native Ulstermen." Democrats certainly judged "Orange Irishmen" to be at the heart of the party. Catholic spokesmen, including John Hughes and Orestes Brownson, echoed this opinion, noting the resemblance of the secret societies to the Protestant lodges of Ulster and claiming that they comprised far fewer American Protestants than English, Scots, and Irish. The Order of United Americans, explained the *New York Freemen's Journal*, "talk about foreign influence, when the society is composed entirely of foreign influences, being nothing more or less than the revival of . . . Orangeism in this country."[92]

This led many to link the secret orders even more with Presbyterianism than with Methodism. "Know-Nothingism is of puritan origins," explained the *Catholic Vindicator*, "and is to be traced to the Scotch Presbyterians." The victory of James Pollock, a Reformed Presbyterian and "severe Roundhead in his religious views," in Pennsylvania's gubernatorial election in 1854, seemed to offer clear evidence of Presbyterians' seminal role in the birth of the new movement, though in fact Presbyterians were much less likely to be Know Nothings in that state than they were in New York and Indiana, where a majority of members supported the Order at the polls in 1854. In the Virginia contest of 1855 prominent Presbyterians were known supporters of Flournoy, whom Wise sneeringly dismissed as *"the Presbyterian Elder."* Robert J. Breckinridge and Andrew B. Cross represented the most influential of a substantial Presbyterian contribution to the American party in Maryland.[93]

Baptists also delivered considerable support to the new Order. As the second-largest family of Protestant churches, and enjoying the support of plain farmers and working people, Baptists – like Methodists – were a natural target for Know Nothing recruiters. Gienapp indicates that they gave substantial support to the party in the Indiana and Pennsylvania elections of 1854. In Tennessee, where a number of Baptists endorsed the Order from the outset, Know Nothings made much of Meredith Gentry's Baptist roots in his contest against Andrew Johnson for the state governorship in the following year.[94] Congregationalists, too, inside and outside New England, contributed both leaders and members in considerable numbers. In Connecticut Know Nothingism's make-up reflected Congregationalist hegemony in the state. For more urbane members of the denomination, however, the movement's proletarian roughness could act as a deterrent: Josiah B. Grinnell felt considerable sympathy for its aims but regarded the Order as vulgar.[95]

These four denominational groupings provided the weight of Protestant support. But the new party also drew on other evangelical churches and on elements within churches whose evangelicalism was more muted. The former included members of German Reformed churches: like German Methodists, they harbored some of the strongest anti-Catholic and anti-Irish sentiment, and their presence indicated the complex and unpredictable relationship between anti-foreign sentiment and anti-Roman feeling in the movement. Other "foreign" elements included those Lutheran church members whose dislike of Irish Catholics outweighed their suspicion of prohibition and their concern about the Order's xenophobia.[96] The party also recruited Episcopalians.[97] Their presence alongside Lutherans indicates Know Nothings' capacity to draw from denominations commonly categorized as "liturgical" or "ritualist," though it seems likely that those so attracted were from the evangelical wing of their denominations.

In practice, resort to the concept of a "liturgical"–"evangelical" continuum within American churches is of only limited value in elucidating the sources of Know Nothings' religious support. Certainly, the party's strength derived especially from the evangelical wing of American Protestantism. But this did not mean that all, or even a majority, of voting evangelicals fell in behind it. Whatever the ambitions of Brownlow, Anspach, and others for Protestant political unity, and whatever the accusations of the party's Democrat and Whig opponents regarding the evangelicals' electoral cohesiveness, the reality was very different. A much-neglected question, just as important as why evangelicals sustained the American party, is why so many others either remained consistently opposed to Know Nothingism or demonstrated an initial enthusiasm which was quickly dissipated.

Evangelical opposition to Know Nothingism

Churchgoers who resisted the Know Nothings' overtures could be found in all evangelical denominations. Amongst Methodists, a substantial minority in Pennsylvania and Indiana, for example, withheld support in 1854; in New York most stayed aloof; John McFerrin, Augustus B. Longstreet, and a variety of other influential southern Methodists backed off. Baptists were in general even more suspicious, with some of their leading spokesmen and editors, like Elder John R. Graves of the *Tennessee Baptist*, denouncing the movement. A number of Baptist churches split, as in Masontown, Pennsylvania, where the meeting suffered a hemorrhage of members when its pastor joined the Order. Amongst hard-shell or Primitive Baptists hostility was almost universal, and members known to be connected with Know Nothingism suffered ostracism or expulsion. Congregationalists and Presbyterians, both Old and New School, harbored stern critics. Henry Ward Beecher, Joshua Leavitt, and the *Independent* were firmly opposed. The *Puritan and Recorder* believed the movement "wrong in principle." In Pennsylvania, Scotch-Irish coolness towards the order kept many (perhaps most) Presbyterians Whig in 1854.[98]

William Brownlow blamed what he regarded as the perfidy of these evangelical critics on their moral deficiency. They were "the hypocritical and profligate portion of the Methodist, Presbyterian, Baptist and Episcopalian membership" who were "in love with the *loose moral code* of Romanism" and who consequently held firm to its agent, the Democratic party. "Backslidden, unconverted, or unprincipled members of Protestant Churches," he insisted, "find in Popery a *sympathising irreligion*, adapted to their vicious lives."[99] His explanation suggests the frustration he and other Know Nothings felt when confronting established party loyalties. Though they offered Protestants a new vision of politics, they found it hard to dislodge evangelicals long entrenched in the Jacksonian coalition. Indeed, once southern Democrats saw that the new Order was nothing more than "Whiggery in disguise" many retreated warily from their initial interest and even enthusiasm.[100] At the Holston Annual Conference in 1854 Brownlow spent much of his time initiating as many preachers as he could into the secret order. Most were Whigs, and succumbed. The few Democrats were far more suspicious and backed away from swearing allegiance.[101]

Where these established political loyalties meshed with denominational ones, Know Nothings like Brownlow faced the stiffest of tasks. In Tennessee, for example, many of the "best" Baptists, according to John R. Graves, were Democrats; concerned to secure and defend the equality of all before the law in matters of religion and conscience, they remained true to the party of Jefferson and Jackson. Methodists, on the other hand, were well represented in the American party. In the state elections of 1855 Andrew Johnson, Democratic candidate for governor, sought to exploit well-developed interdenominational antipathies. Johnson claimed that Brownlow and the Methodists (*"Reverend hypocrites"* and *"scribes and Pharisees"*) sought through the American party to extend their church's political and ecclesiastical power, and to humiliate the state's Baptists and Presbyterians.[102] The charge would at other times have been seen as little more than a campaigning ploy. But in 1855 relations between Calvinist and Arminian churches, not only in Tennessee but in much of the South and West, were as abrasive as they had ever been.

A powerful chorus of Baptists in the mid-1850s asserted that Methodism was essentially at odds with Scripture and with American republicanism, egalitarianism, and democracy. Graves's *Great Iron Wheel*, the most influential expression of the argument, circulated amongst tens of thousands, principally in Tennessee and southern Appalachia, but also further afield, east to Maryland and west to Texas.[103] Throughout 1855 and 1856, and on into 1857, the controversy and its accompanying ecclesiastical billingsgate (which involved Graves in a libel suit) dominated the columns of Baptist and Methodist newspapers. Methodist preachers, according to a correspondent of the *Biblical Recorder*, were belligerent and boastful; "their domineering spirit" made them "as bitter persecutors as ever grew up in the bosom of Papal Rome." Many blamed these attitudes on an episcopal system which encouraged "intolerance, bigotry and persecution" and threatened both religious and political freedom. Methodist ministers' control over church property matched that of the papal hierarchy. Like Romanists, Arminians operated a *"false system of theology."* All in all, Baptist critics agreed with the New School Presbyterian, Frederick A. Ross, that *"[t]he Methodist system is* ANTI-CHRIST.*"*[104]

Methodists fought fire with fire, denying charges of despotism, satirizing their opponents' baptismal rites, and rebuking the confusion and anarchic tendencies of the Baptists' church polity.[105] In William Brownlow and James Chapman they had two especially doughty religious pugilists, who together produced a number of influential anti-Baptist works; these included Brownlow's notorious *Great Iron Wheel Examined*, spread far and wide by Methodist itinerants.[106] Both men were, of course, not only Methodists but principals in the American party: their defense of their church fused with their campaign to advance "Americanism." On the other hand, Baptists who were also Democrats were hardly likely to join the new movement once it was clear that Methodists and Whigs were steering it. They were as stern in their hostility to Rome as the most enthusiastic Know Nothing, but saw no inconsistency in sustaining their anti-Catholicism within the Democracy.[107] The timing of Baptists' outpourings against Methodism indicates how closely they were linked to the appearance of the American party. The *Southern Christian Advocate* certainly believed that fear of Methodist control over the new party, and hence government, lay at the heart of the controversy.[108] Baptists' language, too, turning Methodists into surrogate papists, indicates their desire both to underscore their integrity as anti-Romanists and to link Methodists with the threat from abroad.[109] It was in this setting that Andrew Johnson and other Tennessee Democrats made their well-timed pitch for Baptist votes. They saw very well, for instance, the significance of the week's public debate in June 1855 between Graves and Chapman over *The Great Iron Wheel*, when Baptist and Democrat confronted Methodist and Know Nothing.[110] It is not clear whether this element in Johnson's constituency voted for him primarily as Baptists who feared Methodists, or as Democrats who saw the American party as Whigs under another name. But without doubt both considerations were in play.[111]

Important as they were, persisting party loyalties of this kind cannot alone explain Know Nothings' failure to win wider support amongst evangelical Protestants. The new party's equally profound weakness was that, though it paraded as the guardian of the nation's evangelical and republican identity, its methods, goals, and rhetoric appeared to undermine the very values it sought to defend. In the first place, though the movement's mystery, its secret ceremonies, signs, handshakes, and pledges, created an allure and excitement that helped attract members, at the same time they alienated a powerful stratum of evangelicals passionately opposed to all secret societies. Hostility to secret organizations ran deep within portions of American evangelicalism. Freemasonry had formed the target of an evangelical counter-culture in eighteenth-century Virginia; the Antimasonic explosion of the 1820s had demonstrated the continuing destructive power that fear of conspiracies could generate within certain churches, particularly in New England and its

Calvinist diaspora.[112] Along with newer orders, like the Odd Fellows and Sons of Temperance, Masons continued to arouse suspicion and even loathing into the 1840s and 1850s. Some smaller denominations which prided themselves in standing prophetically apart from the world rebuked these secret organizations: Primitive Baptists, for example, generally expelled members who joined them; Associate Presbyterians, Associate Reformed Presbyterians, Freewill Baptists, and Wesleyan Methodists were also vigorously opposed. Larger denominations, however, embracing a broad cross-section of opinion, tended to be more equivocal. In the South, for instance, as Methodists and Baptists, no longer a counter-culture, secured social acceptance and even dominance through the first half of the nineteenth century, many ministers and members not only dropped their earlier hostility but confirmed their new standing by becoming active Masons, regarding them (as a Georgia Baptist explained) as "second only to the church, in everything, *moral and social.*" Others, however, persisted in treating Freemasonry as the second whore of Babylon. Despite the emollient diplomacy of church leaders and editors, few evangelical denominations in these years avoided conflict, recrimination, and even schism over secret societies.[113]

Critics found sustenance in both Scripture and political theory. Christ's words, "In secret have I said nothing," and Paul's injunction to "have no fellowship with the unfruitful works of darkness" seemed to Jonathan Blanchard, a lifelong opponent of secret bodies, a clear argument for their proscription; so too did blasphemous oaths to remain silent and closed ceremonies incorporating "popish mummeries." True Christianity operated openly and directly, and shrank "instinctively from every scheme which proposes to work underground like a mole." Secret societies, insisted Thomas Smyth, "are in their origin pagan, in their tendency popish, and in their spirit anti-christian." Equally, true republicanism and democracy rebelled against the principles and practices of secret organizations. "The genius of our free institutions abhors secrecy," explained a writer in the *Oberlin Evangelist*: "Leave secret movements to despots." Republics depended on the unconstrained operation of the individual citizen's reason in "open and fair discussion"; closed debates in hierarchical organizations implied control and political enslavement. Secrecy paved the way for favoritism and intrigue; it encouraged furtive influence over courts and juries, and political corruption.[114] Ultimately, complained an Associate Presbyterian minister of Smyrna, Pennsylvania, centralized secret associations invited conspiracy against the legitimate government.[115]

Well aware of the animus against secret orders, the American party sought to establish a line of distinction between "jesuitical" secrecy in the service of a foreign master and its own philanthropic, fraternal association; between the voluntary and aggressive secrecy of Romanists, and the "unavoidable," defensive, and legitimate – though covert – response of Know Nothings, who would happily disband once Rome had opened its doors to the revealing light of day.[116] Many Know Nothings were also members of Masonic or Odd Fellows' lodges (in whose buildings party meetings were often held).[117] Conversely, their evangelical critics included a number of former Antimasons who saw in Know Nothingism a revived danger to the republic.[118] Many who shared Know Nothings' ambitions emphatically disapproved of their "midnight conspiracies" and induction ceremonies in church basements. John McClintock feared the "dangerous tendencies" of the party's covert *modus operandi*, which also led Oberliners to retract their initial, qualified welcome. Richard Beale, a Virginia Democrat, touched a raw nerve amongst the more devout Methodists around him when he reflected that "at the mere behest of men bound alone by loose ties of party – to swear upon the holy Bible to do thus & so . . . was wrong in principle, and demoralizing in its effects, and I knew the class leaders, and stewards around me did this." Well aware of the damaging hostility it provoked amongst hoped-for allies, Know Nothings formally gave up their secrecy oath in the summer of 1855.[119]

The American party drew evangelicals' further criticism for encouraging a hatred of the foreigner. Though many Know Nothings denied that theirs was a crusade against the immigrant as such, that every man "should be measured by his intrinsic worth" and that "American principles neither demand nor imply the slightest . . . prejudice" against European newcomers, in practice the movement played quite consciously upon popular xenophobia. "The hostility of the Know-nothings against all people of foreign birth is blind, bigoted and unreasonable," maintained the *Oberlin Evangelist*: "It is opposed to benevolence, which affirms the *brotherhood of man*."[120] As well as unchristian, exclusion of all foreign-born citizens was un-American, for it sabotaged the republic's God-given role as an asylum for the oppressed of all nations. The policy, too, was impolitic and shortsighted, since it would alienate valuable citizens and "divide . . . the nation into hostile camps." Foreigners could be assimilated without damaging the character of the host, the Reverend Charles Wadsworth explained: "This nation is already, in all its grand elements of character, permanently Anglo-American; and a wise man would just as sincerely fear to dine on salmon, lest he . . . should become a great fish . . . as have a fear lest this American nationality be essentially or injuriously modified by any foreign" influx. Henry Ward Beecher extended the gastronomic metaphor: "When I eat chicken, I don't *become* chicken. *Chicken becomes me!*"[121] It was on this assimilative principle that evangelicals multiplied their missions to the foreign-born and foreign-language communities, particularly the Germans and Scandinavians, in the 1840s and 1850s.[122] The Reverend Harvey Miller saw a millennial design in "this gathering of the nations within our borders": following the immigrants' exposure to America's religious advantages "a reflex influence shall go out from this land to bless the nations of the earth."[123]

By the mid-nineteenth century most Americans held it as an article of faith that the legal separation of church and state was in the best interests of religion and republican freedom. Know Nothings' attempts to exclude Catholics from political life consequently exposed them to fellow evangelicals' taunts of "religious persecution" and of tugging together the two worlds which their freedom-seeking ancestors had successfully separated. American party sympathizers strove to explain that proscription of Catholics was not *religious* persecution, strictly defined: the political ambitions of Rome and her ultramontane allies made control of Catholics' political action the only safe course for responsible Protestant citizens.[124] But a chorus of distinguished evangelical voices, some long concerned to prevent Protestants emulating "the persecuting spirit of Romanism," cried out against a proscriptive policy which evangelicalism was sufficiently vigorous not to need.[125] Moreover, the principle at work was double-edged. "When the work of crushing churches is begun," Augustus B. Longstreet warned, "it is not going to stop with the overthrow of one." A more apocalyptic voice predicted: "Next we shall have a similar crusade against the High Church Episcopalians – some of whom it is even now affirmed, are but a step removed from the Catholics – then the Low Church Episcopalians will share the same fate; – then the Presbyterians and so on until the country shall become the scene of a religious, civil and social war." Amongst evangelicals whose own churches had historically fought against Standing Orders for full legal equality there remained great residual distrust of anything that smelt of a union of religion and politics.[126]

The American party's attempts to put its anti-Catholic program into effect also brought it into disrepute. Though institutional inertia and its own political inexperience considerably explain its failure to enact many laws, there were other, more inglorious factors at work.[127] Soon after Know Nothings had taken office in Massachusetts, the charges of "corruption" and "hypocrisy" which they had used to wrest power from the political establishment were echoing in their own ears. Exposures of their own political chicanery written by expelled members of the Order could possibly be brushed aside.[128] It was less easy for the party to defend itself against charges of abusing power when it was revealed that the "nunnery" or "smelling" committee of the Massachusetts legislature had misspent public funds while investigating the state's Catholic institutions, and that its chairman, Joseph Hiss, had used his position to frighten novices, make sexual propositions to nuns, and charge to the state hotel expenses incurred while enjoying the company of a prostitute.[129]

Know Nothing secrecy, nativism, and hostility to Catholics made the party an obvious scapegoat when ugly mob action stained American urban life in 1854 and 1855. The "Angel Gabriel," one of a number of violent anti-Catholic street preachers, stirred up regular violence against the Brooklyn Irish throughout the summer of 1854, and incited a mob in Bath, Maine, to break open the doors of the Catholic church, display the American ensign from its belfry and set the building ablaze. Know Nothings themselves regarded the Cincinnati election-day riots in April 1855, in which poll boxes were seized and a member of the American party killed, as the fault of provocative Germans who had engaged in voting fraud; they blamed foreigners and Catholics for the murderous riot the following August in Louisville, when on "Bloody Monday" over twenty died and hundreds were wounded. But many respectable (and not just middle-class) evangelicals were deeply distressed by brute force of this kind, especially when the targets were churches and worshipers. Mob action was not only wrong: it was bad policy, since it manufactured for Catholics and foreigners "scores of friends and sympathisers where they had none before," insulated them from true Protestant and republican example, and encouraged them to fashion a united "foreign party" out of heterogeneous cultural elements which, left alone, posed no serious threat to the Anglo-American, Protestant republic.[130]

It was not through law, political action, violence, or "raising a crusade against Romanism" that Catholic immigrants would be rendered powerless. Confrontation of that kind, a Baptist wrote, only strengthened "the Scarlet Woman's bands." Rather, as Horace Bushnell had urged a few years earlier, "[w]e must rise upon [Romanism] . . . as the morning in the tranquillity of love. We must rain righteousness upon it, as a genial shower."[131] In a battle conducted in pentecostal spirit, and relying on the Gospel, religious education, and moral suasion, American Protestants would surely triumph over "the myrmidons of Jesuitism." Revivals of religion would, according to Alexander T. McGill, be "the bane of Antichrist." Romanism simply could not survive in a free environment fostering free inquiry. "Protestantism has the advantage of freedom of will, and thought, and action; it appeals to reason and the common sense of man."[132] A combination of kindness and truth would overwhelm Catholic error.

"It is full time," announced Charles Elliott in September 1854, "that the moral and truly religious men of the country . . . unite and carry out the principles of morality in civil life, as well as in social." The doughty editor of the *Western Christian Advocate* captured the mood sweeping through much of American evangelicalism as church members questioned the ability of the existing parties to act as channels of political conscience. A little over six months later another of his editorials proclaimed that the old political parties had been "dashed to pieces": hundreds of Democrats "despise the *thing* now called by this name"; Whigs were "careless about their former designation." A new era had dawned, the Methodist warhorse rejoiced, "a time of great *conflict* between the right and the wrong, truth and error, the service of God and conformity to the world." That battle focused on three issues, one of them "intemperance and its kindred vices" and another "the introduction of a foreign spiritual power to regulate civil matters for the good of the Church."[133]

Elliott spoke for those who saw much to welcome in Know Nothingism and hoped it could become the vehicle for evangelical conscience in political life. The initial auguries seemed good, for the secret Order shattered the old political arrangements by harnessing profound evangelical anger. It seemed for a while that it might become the principal political force in the nation. But the American party proved a flawed instrument. Instead of uniting the nation's evangelicals, it divided them. We have examined several reasons why. But one explanation remains. The party failed to address convincingly the third issue on Elliott's moral agenda: slavery, particularly as it presented itself in the repeal of the Missouri Compromise in 1854 and subsequent events in "bleeding" Kansas. At first the local and state focus of Know Nothing electoral activity allowed sympathetic evangelicals, north and south, to regard the Order as consistent with their own strong, sectional reactions to the crisis over the Nebraska bill. But many antislavery evangelicals were suspicious of the party's commitment to Unionism on southern terms and the diversionary effects of nativism on the cause of the slave; Protestant critics of the party in the South were equally, and realistically, suspicious of free soilers who had thrown in their lot with the northern wing.[134] Eventually, similar anxieties were to afflict Know Nothings themselves, and the party split in two in June 1855. Quite another third force was to pick up the mantle of "the evangelical party in politics."[135]

Chapter 8

The Emergence of the Third Party System: Evangelicals and Sectional Antagonism, 1854–56

By 1856 a new, essentially sectional, party had established itself as the second force in American politics. The Republicans owed their emergence and consolidation to the efforts of shrewd political leaders who creatively exploited geological shifts in northern public opinion. In that process of party-building evangelical churches took an active role, shaping and expressing popular attitudes to the fast-moving events that followed the introduction of the Kansas–Nebraska bill, and contributing much of the moral energy and many of the members of the new organization. At the same time, deteriorating ecclesiastical relations between free-state and southern evangelicals served to harden sectional attitudes. Denominational, sectional, and party political lines of division in the 1856 presidential election did not in fact coincide, but conservative evangelicals, north and south, well understood what would happen if and when they did. The Union would not easily survive the fusing of sectional chauvinism and Christian self-righteousness.

"Hot times": northern evangelicals and the Nebraska bill

That the political storm following the introduction of the Nebraska bill in January 1854 took its author by surprise shows Stephen A. Douglas's remoteness from the world of northern evangelicals, where the significance of the proposed repeal of the Missouri Compromise and its likely political ramifications were clearly understood. "[T]here will be hot times over it," predicted a Cincinnati Methodist, at the moment when fellow Ohioans Salmon P. Chase and Joshua Giddings, and the other authors of the Appeal of the Independent Democrats, were confidently calling on like-minded Christians "to interpose" in the cause of human freedom.[1] Most northern evangelicals had acquiesced in the terms of Compromise in 1850, which they regarded as the necessary price for a final settlement. But Douglas's bill, with its doctrine of popular sovereignty, radicalized many political moderates by threatening to introduce slavery into territories regarded since 1821 as forever free. According to the *Presbyterian of the West*, "clergymen and college professors, who, in by-gone days of technical abolitionism, stood conservative, now stand up and solemnly protest."[2] Ministers preached to overflowing congregations, addressed political meetings, peppered their representatives with private and public protests, and filled the columns of church newspapers with diatribes against an abomination.[3] Never since the days of the Sabbath mails issue, reflected Lorenzo Dow Johnson, had there been "such an uprising of the clergy." Remonstrances and memorials flooded Congress: over 500 signatories from the Old Northwest, 25 from Chicago, 150 from New York City, and – most flamboyantly – over 3,000 from New England, their names recorded on a 200-foot scroll which Edward Everett (with little enthusiasm) presented to the Senate.[4]

Pro-Nebraska editors "unkenneled and unleashed" their presses "to howl on the path of the recreant clergy"; Democrats' repudiation of activist clergy briefly gave the long session of the 33rd Congress "the semblance of an ecclesiastical council more than that of a legislative assembly."[5] Deeply concerned about ministers' potential for political mischief, Douglas and his allies complained of the petitioners' discourtesy and arrogant presumption in acting as "viceregents of the Almighty"; they sneered at the clergy's ignorance of political affairs and inconsistency in upholding the Missouri Compromise while undermining the Fugitive Slave Law; they denounced them for leaving "their high vocation . . . to mingle in the turbid pool of politics," and bringing "our holy religion into disrepute." But these were peripheral adornments on the main body of the argument: anti-Nebraska clergy, by protesting as a class, sought to re-establish a theocracy. Here was a "left-handed attempt," Democrats explained, "to put the State in subordination to the dictates of the church." Douglas feared that anti-Nebraska clergy, drawing "the whole religious community into their schemes of political aggrandizement," would organize "a great political sectional party for Abolition."[6] Events were to strengthen his apprehensions.

What embittered Douglas and other critics were the moral absolutes in which ministers couched their arguments. Supporters of the bill were not simply advocates of misguided policy: they were morally flawed. The bill was "a great national crime," "a measure fraught not only with political evil, but dishonorable, unjust, wicked, ungodly; contrary to the laws of God and to every unbiased moral judgment of man." Clergy widely accepted the view set out in Chase's Appeal that Douglas's bill represented "a gross violation of a sacred pledge": it was "an act of perfidy," a nullification of a "solemn compact," and "a cowardly betrayal of sacred trust." The breach of faith was twofold. The bill reneged on guarantees to the "poor red men" of permanent, undisputed, and unmolested settlement in territories to which they had already been brutally driven. Ministers tapped a reservoir of evangelical sympathy they had helped create in the days of Jackson. "The crimes of Georgia," predicted one commentator bitterly, "are to be re-enacted on the soil of Kansas and Nebraska." "Shall the savage red man and the grizzly bear," asked another, "make room for the more savage white man and his human prey?"[7]

Even more treacherous was the overturning of the Missouri Compromise. According to Richard H. Richardson, a young, Kentucky-born, Old School Presbyterian minister of Chicago, the Nebraska bill assailed a political settlement that was "virtually a part of the Constitution, . . . a covenant the same in nature and obligation" as that between Abraham and Lot. Douglas's claim that the 1850 Compromise had set aside the imperatives of the earlier compact appeared preposterous and flimsy. George F. Magoun bewailed a triple treachery: the betrayal of the people by Congress, of northern states by southern, and of future states by existing ones. Radical critics of the Nebraska bill saw in the measure not only faithlessness but a "providential retribution to the north" for successive accommodations with slavery. A sequence of compromises "where we settle[d] points of conscience by contract," starting with the first Fugitive Slave Law in 1793, had rotted the free states' moral sense and encouraged the South to expect another surrender of principle: "Because we have reckoned 'niggers' as nothing, we ourselves are now justly reckoned as 'niggers.'"[8]

Herein lay the primary villainy of the bill: it put freedom and pure religion on the defensive, and altered the moral orientation of the republic. Though Douglas's supporters claimed that favoring citizens' independence in the territories made it effectively a free-soil measure, in reality, critics argued, the formula of popular sovereignty would encourage slavery and neutralize congressional authority. According to the *Presbyterian of the West*, "the question is completely changed, and no longer reads, *shall slavery be abolished?* but, 'shall liberty be abolished?'" At a stroke Douglas had opened up an area "wide as an empire, and beautiful as Eden": half a million square miles of enormous strategic importance, "destined to hold the central sceptre of power in the . . . country," much larger than the original thirteen colonies, seven times the size of New England, ten times that of New York, and capable of sustaining twelve slave states as big as Ohio.[9] In 1850 most antislavery evangelicals had accepted the Compromise because at heart they considered slavery's days numbered. William Wisner had pronounced the peculiar institution "decrepit with age": "The time is not far distant when it will be sepulchered for ever." George Duffield, too, had reassured his congregation, "The balance of power has been turned in favor of freedom."[10] On the very eve of the introduction of the Nebraska bill, sanguine northern evangelicals speculated that the free settlement of the western territories, joined with the influence of Illinois, Iowa, and other free states, would end slavery in Missouri and other border states. Douglas's measure – irresponsible, morally flawed, revolutionary – fundamentally challenged these perceptions. Charles Bulkley, George Magoun, and other critics of the Kansas–Nebraska Act saw themselves as essentially conservative. They labeled Douglas and the Pierce administration the real revolutionaries, who had removed the "ancient landmarks," torn up the principles of natural law and republicanism embodied in the Federal Constitution, and violated the "fundamental policy" of the Founding Fathers, "the conservation and extension of liberty."[11]

Critical evangelicals believed that the spread of slavery would not only blight the economic prospects of the new territory, but would transform it into a moral and religious wilderness. Charles Beecher and others spoke of Kansas and Nebraska becoming a vast "dungeon-brothel," where under slavery's moral code Bible-reading, education, marriage vows, and Christian family life would be obliterated, and where human beings would be bred and sold like cattle. Heathenism and brute violence would hold dominion in a region which should have become a "favored land with Bibles, preachers, temples, schools, arts, sciences, industry, and all that marks a great, a pious, a prosperous and happy people." A free Nebraska proffered Heman Humphrey a vision of a Gospel "preached in ten thousand pulpits," a land where, "as the millennial dawn opens and 'shines more and more,' songs of salutation will make the arches of the sky ring with the joy of numbers almost numberless, uninterrupted by the wailings of a single slave." But handing the territory over "by quit-claim deed to the Devil," and extending slavery, the Antichrist would shatter this dream, and with it America's world-wide hopes. How could friends of overseas missions carry on Christian work in pagan lands with heathenism corrupting the fabric of domestic society?[12]

Evangelicals blamed this moral revolution on the slaveholders' control of the federal government. Though slavery was at odds with the democratic, free-labor spirit of the age, it survived and grew because, as Joseph B. Bittinger explained, the slave power benefited from northern division and its own unity, "always mov[ing] to the conflict with the steady, heavy tread of the Macedonian phalanx." Manipulative, conspiratorial, aggressive, and power-loving, the political leaders of 300,000 slaveholders aimed to hold sway over a nation of 30 million. Thus, for Francis Wayland, "The question ceases to be whether black men are forever to be slaves, but whether the sons of Puritans are to become slaves themselves." The Kansas–Nebraska Act was simply the boldest of a sequence of advances by this "ever sleepless and encroaching" slavocracy, from the purchase of Louisiana, through the Missouri Compromise, Texas annexation, and the Mexican war to the settlement of 1850. Slavery had to expand to avoid economic suffocation: "it cannot breathe in its own atmosphere more than 100 years.... [S]hut up slavery to a limited territory and it dies of atrophy." The Nebraska bill was an "entering wedge" for further expansion into the north-western and south-western territories, into Cuba, Haiti, central America, Mexico, the Sandwich Islands, Canada, and other lands yet to be seized – and into the free states. Granville Moody farsightedly raised the specter of the Supreme Court's asserting a master's right to hold slaves in any of the nation's territories, and *"in transitu* in any state"; Charles Beecher, even more alarmed, predicted the imposition of slave law in every state of the Union.[13] The reopening of the African slave trade would complete the revolution.

Determined as the slave power was, it could not succeed on its own. Southerners, evangelical critics insisted, depended on subservient northern "doughfaces" and "gamblers," vulnerable to browbeating and bribery. The passage of the Nebraska bill required a northern man with southern principles in the presidential chair, ready to use his patronage to buy votes. Pierce commonly appeared as a latter-day Ahab, deaf to the warnings of his Elijahs, the anti-Nebraska clergy, and bent on leading the nation "into deep and disgraceful sin." In this he was sustained by the party loyalty of congressmen like Lewis Cass and Isaac Toucey, men who assumed, as Leonard Bacon put it, that "the will of a Democratic president is the true democracy."[14] But the northern pulpit reserved its greatest contempt for the perfidious Douglas himself, married to a slaveholding wife, protected by an Irish-Catholic praetorian guard, and variously likened to Pontius Pilate, Benedict Arnold, and Judas Iscariot. Churchwomen of Alliance, Ohio, sent him thirty three-cent pieces sewn between two pieces of gauze. Alexander C. Twining sarcastically dismissed him and other doughfaces as "ultra-calvinistic, in their acceptance of the doctrine of total depravity."[15]

As well as threatening an expansion of slavery the Nebraska bill seemed also to imperil the Union through its *"wanton disturbance of national peace and tranquility."* Rather than "put a final end to agitation," as its supporters claimed, it would create destructive new conflicts. With more bleakness than most, Eden B. Foster blamed the bill for generating a "bitter and eternal" sectional feud between a South whose sense of honor could not allow a shameful retreat and a North which could not yield Nebraska territory to slavery: disunion and a fratricidal war seemed the only logical and likely outcome. Charles Beecher predicted that Douglas's measure would result "sooner or later . . . [in] anarchy, civil war, and all the horrors of servile insurrection and massacre."[16]

Dire predictions were balanced by more sanguine views. Horace Bushnell, reflecting on the country's long experience of disunionist threats and "political fictions," saw not "the least real danger of a rupture," despite present tensions. Francis Wayland maintained that "intelligent and rightminded" slave-owners who regarded slavery as a wrong "form a large portion of the best men at the South . . . and will in their hearts rejoice if our opposition be successful." Optimistic or not about the Union's future, all critics of the Nebraska bill insisted on their right to speak out. Better to be "sectional" and right, than "national" and complicit in evil. Indeed, true nationality meant standing up for "truth and justice and liberty," not acquiescing in "a common dishonor" and a "national crime" which exposed the Union to "the curse of an angry Judge."[17]

Fear of a righteous God undergirded the stand of anti-Nebraska evangelicals: He called for crusading resistance against a moral enormity and proffered the crisis as an opportunity for American churches to erase their reputation as "the bulwarks of slavery." The Reverend John Nelson of Leicester, Massachusetts, insisted that the bill's "repudiating and nullifying principles" released the North from "the neutralizing and embarrassing restraints" on antislavery exertions; it opened the way not only to limiting slavery's advance but to destroying it completely. God would sustain His latter-day Israelites. He demanded action by Christian means: by petitions, prayers, conversation, personal example, and "the quiet, peaceful, faithful exercise of the Ballot-box." Evangelical reformers' proper course beckoned clearly: "To the Polls then let us hie to do our duty . . . to the God of righteousness, as men of faith and piety."[18] Steeled by such appeals, anti-Nebraska evangelicals helped transform American political topography over the next two years.

"Thank God, the people are waking up": fugitives, bleeding Kansas, and the crime against Sumner

The introduction of the Kansas–Nebraska bill shattered the modest sectional harmony briefly inaugurated in 1850; its passage through the House and signature into law in May 1854 proved only the first phase of a two-year crescendo of anger amongst northern churchgoers over slavery and slave-power aggression. Renewed protests about fugitive slaves provided one measure of the changed climate in northern churches.[19] Evangelicals who since 1850 had suppressed their qualms about the fugitive issue in the interests of the Union were especially bitter about the deceit of the Nebraska bill and insisted that the measure absolved them from all moral obligation to abide by the iniquities of 1850.[20] If Douglas could render the Missouri Compromise "inoperative," so could they the odious Fugitive Slave Law. Public uproar following the arrest of the fugitive Joshua Glover in Milwaukee in March 1854 indicated the change in opinion wrought by "southern aggressions." More dramatic still were the scenes surrounding the return from Boston of the escapee Anthony Burns. Hundreds of clergy, gathered for the annual meetings of the New England benevolent societies, watched appalled as armed troops streamed into the city to carry out President Pierce's enforcement order. An estimated 50,000 furious citizens lined the streets as soldiers escorted Burns onto a Virginia-bound ship. "What a shame for Boston! And what a scandal to Christianity!" lamented a Methodist minister, appalled that Burns, "a preacher in the same [Baptist] church . . . of which his master . . . is a member," had fallen victim to the slave power. But, like Edwin Leonard, of Milton, Massachusetts, he thanked God that, following recent events, "the people are waking up."[21]

The ominous developments in Kansas, where the future of freedom in North America appeared to hang in the balance, proved more potent still in hardening attitudes in northern churches. Free-state evangelicals took a deep interest in the settlement of the new territory. They saw its strategic importance for the spread of the Christian Gospel. Given its rich lands and raw materials, none doubted its economic potential. But its prosperity would depend on blending evangelical Protestant institutions and a system of free labor. Charles Boynton and Timothy B. Mason, agents of the American Reform Tract and Book Society, hurried to investigate Kansas in the fall of 1854 and returned to proffer an exciting vision of Kansas as "a 'city set on a hill'," whose rich combination of small farms, manufacturing industry, benevolent institutions, schools, and churches would allow it to function as "a genuine Puritan state." Allow slavery a toehold, and these hopes would shatter.[22]

The blighting influence of the peculiar institution on southern society and economy was a byword amongst northern evangelicals. Horace Bushnell's view that "wealth is the natural fruit of free labor, poverty of slave labor" had become by the 1850s a staple of their discourse. Slavery was synonymous with not only moral degradation but "indolence," "lethargy," and "dishonor to honest toil." As such it directly contradicted the law of God. It demoralized white laborers even more than black, keeping them illiterate and debased. A northern Methodist visitor to Georgia wrote home to tell of "indolent, improvident, and overbearing" whites who had kept as an agricultural desert land around

Savannah which under Yankee cultivation would have flourished. Put St Louis in a free state, James Finley insisted, and it would double its prosperity. Granville Moody pointed to the steady increase in productive industry, in population, and in the number and cash value of farms on the journey from the Texas frontier to the free states.[23]

Slaveholders' influence had thus to be minimized in Kansas. The southerners who moved there, explained Henry Ward Beecher, were "without organizing tendencies, without the creative force which builds up new societies." What was needed was the "peaceful march of freedom's armies": the systematic emigration of whole Christian communities from the free states. When Eli Thayer, a member of the Massachusetts legislature, organized the New England Emigrant Aid Company to help settle Kansas with antislavery colonists he located his earliest and most reliable supporters amongst anti-Nebraska clergymen and their congregations. The Reverend Edward Everett Hale of Worcester wrote the first handbook for the company's emigrants; many ministers became life members, subscribing $20 each, and made their churches available for Thayer's meetings.[24]

The armed incursions and illicit voting of so-called "border ruffians," land-hungry and proslavery Missourians, gave particular urgency to these efforts. Out of the instability bred by this violence emerged two competing Kansas legislatures: one proslavery, sustained by the President, and the other free-soil, supported by the majority of settlers. Though the free-state men were driven less by high-minded abolitionism than by fear of "Africanization" and a determination to keep Kansas free of *all* blacks, here was a mix of elements which allowed full scope to the moral outrage of the northern pulpit and church presses.[25] At one level evangelicals saw in "bleeding" Kansas an expression of the original sin of southerners and their allies, and a bleak celebration of their personal shortcomings: the drunkenness and blasphemy of the border ruffians, the unprincipled conduct of Senator David R. Atchison of Missouri, and the delinquency of Pierce and the national administration.[26] But the lessons ran deeper than this. The slave power's inflicting "monstrous fraud" on Kansas through "the utter burlesque of *squatter sovereignty*," and its employing the bayonets of the federal government to crush the rights of free citizens, indicated that slavery unchecked would crush God-given free government and, as the *Oberlin Evangelist* feared, pervert "all our Republican Institutions . . . to the worst purposes of despotism."[27]

A burning sense of injustice and a fear that southerners would cut the republic's jugular vein drove on the army of clergy and evangelical laymen recruiting pilgrims for Kansas. When Charles G. Finney, Jr, returned from the territory to report, Oberliners could barely contain their outrage; only the strenuous efforts of the professors prevented the whole sophomore class from enlisting in the armed struggle. Henry Ward Beecher's notorious call for emigration supported by Sharps rifles in no sense reflected the policy of mainstream northern evangelicals (and invited conservatives' rebuke as a sacrilegious act of "idio-sin-craziness"), but his insistence that "the destiny of souls, of ages, of a hemisphere, is pending in this doubtful contest" captured the predominant mood. At a celebrated meeting in the North church, New Haven, in March 1856, Leonard Bacon, Joel Hawes, and other luminaries blessed a company of emigrants who, their ears ringing with cheers and stirring songs, might have believed they were off to recapture Jerusalem from the infidel. Similar appeals inspired other churches and country prayer meetings throughout New England, and beyond.[28]

Early in 1856 James Harlan predicted to Matthew Simpson that by May the efforts of the proslavery men to drive their opponents from Kansas would end in cataclysm in the town of Lawrence; he prayed that God would "direct the storm." Though the subsequent "sack" of the free soilers' headquarters, like many other incidents in the history of "bleeding Kansas," was much less serious than reported, free-soil churchmen concluded in the summer of 1856 that the territory faced an apocalyptic crisis. "Kanzas is now passing through the furnace," lamented the Reverend Samuel Young Lum from Lawrence itself: "This is the darkest hour that Freedom has ever seen [here]." Edward N. Kirk told his Boston congregation, "Justice and oppression have now met in the field of contest. Kansas is our Sebastopol." The war would be one "such as the world has not seen." And war there, Henry Ward Beecher predicted, "will be war all over the land." Even conservatives raised voices and pens to demand northern unity in the face of injustice. "If Ohio had done to Kentucky what Missouri has done to Kansas," protested Charles Hodge, "the South would have risen as one man and redressed the grievance." Though a new governor, John W. Geary, applied a tourniquet to the territory from late summer, leading the religious press to report a decline in violence during October, the sectional animosity aroused in northern churches by bleeding Kansas contributed powerfully to party realignment.[29]

So, too, did church reactions to Representative Preston S. Brooks's retribution on Charles Sumner in the Senate chamber on 23 May 1856. A two-day speech on "the crime against Kansas" – which included an invective against the state of South Carolina and tasteless personal remarks about one of its senators, Andrew P. Butler – drew down on the Massachusetts senator's head thirty blows from Brooks's gutta percha cane. Seriously hurt, Sumner would not resume his seat for three years. Northern churchmen explained to thousands in packed churches and "Sumner indignation meetings" why they had every reason to be angry. Brooks's action was, first, an "unholy outrage" –

one which indicated the vast gulf in moral understanding between northerners, whose canons of right behavior were largely nourished by the tenets of evangelical Christianity, and southerners guided by a code of chivalry which inculcated a false sense of honor.[30] Sumner's Christianity, unlike his attacker's, was "too real and profound" to engage in a duel. Indeed, measured by the logic of St Paul's words, that "where the spirit of the Lord is, there is liberty," Brooks's action was nothing less than an attack on the Christian religion. Thus the unarmed, defenseless Sumner – "the purest, loftiest, most loved man" – was transmogrified into a Christ-like figure, in part because of the widespread but mistaken belief that he had narrowly escaped death. The Reverend W.D. Haley of Alton, Illinois, likened Brooks's assault to the "same cowardly *expediency* [that] crucified the Son of God." In Westfield, Massachusetts, Gilbert Haven interpreted the suffering of the senator as part of the experience of Christ's disciples, who participated in Jesus' suffering "though falling infinitely below it."[31]

The incident, secondly, confirmed slavery as the enemy of republican liberties. Slaveholders had already trampled down freedom of speech and press in the South. Brooks now attacked them in the nation's capital. Henry Clay Fish asked his congregation to remember a lesson which the slave power had not forgotten, that "Rome lost her liberties by suffering encroachment on the Senate." To achieve its ends, the South had to use violence and blood, means to which the brutalizing and life-cheapening effects of slavery had predisposed them. Brooks's action – "murderous in its design" and akin to the methods of the slave overseer – was not the spontaneous work of a political isolate. Premeditated, it was part of a process by which the slave power aimed to inaugurate "the *code of blood, and the reign of brute force*" and make "ruffianism" and "plantation manners" the order of the day in national affairs; such means were "part of a general system of tactics for nationalizing slavery and oligarchizing the government." The Brooks–Sumner incident helped impress on potential Republicans the evils of the slave power much more forcibly than did the territorial warfare. But Sumner's regrettable experience took on serious significance for northern evangelicals only because they could place it in a broader pattern of violence, coercion, and contempt for political rights. That the caning coincided with Pierce's sending troops to Kansas to assist proslavery "ruffians" signified to Calvin Fletcher "the death knell of our republic." Others, too, contemplating the conjunction of events, concluded bleakly that "in the great struggle between Slavery and Freedom . . . the reign of terror and anarchy is upon us."[32]

"An ecclesiastical as well as a political war raging": sectional antagonism in northern churches, 1854–56

The Nebraska bill and its political fallout lie at the heart of historians' explanations of the reawakened sectional antagonism on which the emergent Republican party built its appeal. But the deterioration in North–South relations in the mid-1850s was not solely a product of political conflict, narrowly defined. The poison of sectionalism seeped along various channels. As in the past, evangelical churches were not only vulnerable to its effects but actually assisted its workings. Indeed, evangelicals' experiences help explain how the issues raised nationally by slavery and the slave power took on meaning in local settings. Not surprisingly, sectional warfare in churches reached unmatched levels of drama and notoriety in Kansas and Missouri, but elsewhere a variety of new and established ecclesiastical frictions over slaveholding also set evangelical against evangelical. Northern denominational presses and polemical preachers kept all these aggravations before the widest possible audience.

Determined to win Kansas for liberty and Christ, missionaries from the free states – especially agents of the AHMS, the MEC, the American Baptist Home Missionary Society, and the abolitionist American Missionary Association – pushed into the territory early on. From the outset they faced the abuse and violence of the proslavery party, who sought to drive them out. Samuel Young Lum, an AHMS missionary, told eastern sponsors how his church members had rescued fellow Christians from "banditti" and how after the sack of Lawrence he had fled those who threatened to hang him. "Ruffians" (sometimes lower-class men, but by no means always so) tarred and feathered the Reverend Pardee Butler in Atchison. Missouri "law and order men" also intercepted William Moore, a local preacher of the MEC, on his way to Kansas City, forced alcohol down his throat, and threatened to kill him. The presiding elder of the South Kansas mission district lost all his possessions, including his horses, to southern "outlaws."[33] Such incidents, broadcast widely through northern churches, suggested not only the bravery of antislavery churchmen ready to die "in the cause of God and the right," but the complicity of southern Christians in persecuting them. The activities of the Kansas missions of southern Baptists and Methodists attracted the particular venom of northern evangelicals: they were especially troubled by the role of the violently pro-slavery Thomas Johnson, superintendent of the MECS operations amongst the new settlers. Johnson had used his influence in Washington in support of the Nebraska bill. He afterwards took an active role in Kansas politics and his mission became the headquarters of the proslavery party, where government officers and the proslavery legislature met.[34]

These conflicts spilled over into Missouri, where proslavery mobs, drawing moral support from southern churches, set upon northern ministers. Frederick Starr, New School Presbyterian minister of Weston, Platte County, was threatened with the rope and then expelled for teaching slaves. He was the most visible victim of the state's Old School Presbyterians' constant insinuations that New Schoolers were abolitionists as well as heretics. But the principal targets of "Mobocracy in earnest" in the state's western areas were the itinerant preachers of the Missouri Conference of the MEC, whose area of operations extended across both Kansas and Missouri. "Ruffians" charged ministers with circulating antislavery documents and inciting slaves to run away. Vigilance committees and their supporters broke up quarterly meetings, blocked access to camp-meeting grounds, interrupted sermons, and drove preachers from the state. At Independence prominent citizens successfully prevented the gathering of the Missouri Annual Conference under Matthew Simpson's presidency in October 1855. As free-state Methodists called ever more confidently for the exclusion of slave-holders from the MEC, and as Kansas grew bloodier, so the dangers to northern preachers increased. A young minister, one C.H. Kelly, was ejected from his pulpit and forced to ride through bitter December winds, without protective clothing, to Fort Madison, Iowa. He subsequently died. In Rochester, Andrew County, slavery supporters set upon the Reverend William Sellers, filled his mouth and smothered his head with tar, left him to fry in the sun, and shot Benjamin Holland, an elderly class leader. Blaming southern churchmen for creating the climate for these attacks, the *Central Christian Advocate* lamented: "There is an ecclesiastical as well as a political war raging, and we are shamelessly attacked and falsely represented as well by political demagogues and false-hearted slavery-defending preachers."[35]

At the same time relations between the two branches of Methodism ulcerated in other parts of the border where the MEC maintained an active presence, including Arkansas, Kentucky, and particularly Virginia. Two MEC annual conferences embraced parts of the Old Dominion: Baltimore, which extended into the valley of Virginia and a large portion of the upper area of the state, and West Virginia. Reporting from the valley in 1855, C.B. Davidson bewailed the growth of painful sectional bitterness, which he blamed on the malign influence of the MECS and which without emollient would sever the Union: "Then will follow civil war inevitably."[36] In parts of west Virginia, too, accusation, counter-claim, and paranoia raised public opinion to fever pitch throughout the mid-1850s. Charged by MECS leaders with incendiarism, infidelity, and treachery to the Constitution, Wesley Smith and other

MEC preachers took their case to the people through press and pulpit. In West Milford circuit Smith's four-hour public lecture filled the church to overflowing and halted the harvest and weekday business. He contemptuously dismissed proslavery ministers' efforts "to brand as abolitionists every non-slaveholder in the slave States who will not adopt the nullification doctrines of Drs [William A.] Smith and [Henry] Bascom." Ultras north and south sought the same end, he warned: a dissolution of the Union through dissolution of the churches. The result would be "a border war without a figure of speech – a war of bloodshed and carnage." He concluded: "If any future historian shall be called upon to write the history of the dissolution of the Union, he will trace it to the action of the southern Methodist preachers . . . [since 1844]. We hold them accountable before Heaven and earth for the exasperated state of feeling which exists at present between the North and South, and which is constantly increasing."[37]

The mutual alienation of the two branches of Methodism offers only the most acute example of festering sectionalism between and within denominations. In the aftermath of the Nebraska bill, the ecclesiastical landscape was strewn with the debris of battles over slavery's proper place in the churches. Methodist Protestants, split over their Book Committee's refusal to address in its publications the moral implications of slavery, established two competing book concerns in 1854. This left George Brown weeping over what he considered an accommodation with the slave power, and by no means quieted northern demands for an end to all connection with tainted southerners.[38] Within the MEC itself, an increasingly influential group of radicals tried to end slaveholding in the border conferences, declaring it a departure from Wesleyan standards and a symptom of the same moral slackness that fed northern complicity in the 1850 Compromise and the Nebraska bill. At the fraught 1856 General Conference at Indianapolis, in session while Sumner and Lawrence bled, the radicals made plain their contempt for the alleged equivocation of MEC ministers and members in slaveholding conferences, who were in turn aggrieved that no allowance was made for their border trials with the MECS. Following ill-tempered debates ("We cuss and discuss," as one delegate put it), the more radical group won control of several of the church's newspapers and secured a simple, but not the constitutionally necessary two-thirds, majority for a change in the General Rule to make non-slaveholding a test of church membership.[39]

Meanwhile, northern Baptists watched with alarm as southern colleges and churches discontinued the use of Francis Wayland's *Elements of Moral Science* because it propounded a system of ethics at odds with slavery. Here, insisted the *New York Examiner*, was the same slave-power intolerance that had strong-armed freedom of speech from the Senate chamber.[40] The failure of the New School Presbyterian General Assembly to do what antislavery westerners demanded – declare slavery a sin *per se* and make slaveholding a ground of church discipline – helped maintain church unity, but only at a cost of painful internal friction, an increase in northern presbyteries' suspicion of southern devices, and the steady withdrawal of New England Congregational associations from fellowship, correspondence, and exchange of delegates with their former New School brethren. The Old School's even fiercer refusal to discuss slavery yielded an equally unequivocal Congregationalist refusal to fraternize. These animosities surfaced damagingly in several of the national benevolent societies, which Congregationalists and northern New School Presbyterians regarded as the creatures of proslavery southerners. Following the Nebraska bill they were all the more determined to insist, under threat of withdrawal, that the American Tract Society (ATS) address slavery unflinchingly in its publications and that the AHMS and the American Board of Control for Foreign Missions cease to support slaveholding missionaries or those who ministered to slaveowners.[41]

"Combine and array a party of freemen": northern evangelicals and the Republican coalition

By 1856 events inside and outside the churches had driven tens of thousands of northern evangelicals to conclude that America faced two kinds of tyranny: the despotism of southern planters over their black laborers and that of the slave power over the white friends of human freedom. Slavery, in giving planters absolute power locally, nourished in them a corrupting ambition for national control. Edward N. Kirk conceded that white southerners were tainted with no more original sin than northerners, but concluded that slavery's irresistible temptations added a further layer of corruption. "That the three hundred thousand slave owners should have among them as many depraved men as we have," he told his fashionable Boston congregation, "is not surprising; that they should have more bad men, and even worse, is natural; that those worst men should aim to control the mighty forces of our General Government for their own purposes, is not wonderful; that they are doing it, I do not question."[42] The actions of southern Christians and politicians in the mid-1850s revealed to George W. Perkins and others an "utterly *faithless*" slave power seeking to turn northern freemen into the "white serfs of southern nobility"[43] and to establish an expanded slave republic in the Gulf of Mexico.[44]

But good might come from evil. The aggression of the slavocracy, the *Oberlin Evangelist* explained, in "giving the free men of the North a little of what it has for ages given the slave so much," was God's way of engaging their sympathy for those in bondage. More practically, He was teaching northern Christians to create a rival political force whose members would, in Heman Humphrey's words, "march shoulder to shoulder, just as they do in the slave states, on every question between liberty and slavery"; wrest the federal government from planters' control; and throw its influence unequivocally onto the side of liberty. Minister after minister called on their congregations to abandon the politics of "coaxing and smiles," and to cultivate what Nathaniel P. Bailey termed "a correct public conscience" that would eliminate "party prejudices, party names, and all demagogueism." "You must be something more and better than mere Whigs or Democrats or Free Soilers," Joseph Bittinger insisted. He and others urged Christians to "combine and array a party of freemen," united "in one solemn, conscientious and decided protest." Alexander Twining looked specifically to northern religious youth to form the backbone of the new agency, young men who had demonstrated their moral vigor in the temperance cause. Non-voters, too, were encouraged to sacrifice their political virginity. The Reverend Edwin Leonard, a customary abstainer (except for a solitary temperance vote), declared that southern aggression had stiffened his resolve "to vote as a *religious* no less than as a *political* duty." The message to evangelical Christians was clear: "Let ... the war against slavery be a *holy war*" – one in which "a united northern ballot" would be a principal weapon.[45]

In actively encouraging church members' widespread disenchantment with Whig and Democratic parties, northern evangelical clergy played a midwife's role in the birth of the anti-Nebraska coalitions that reshaped northern politics in 1854 and 1855. Antislavery ministers and editors of church papers, though harboring a residual distrust of all political parties, hailed what seemed the dawn of a new political era.[46] The pattern of politics following the passage of the Nebraska bill, one which they helped to shape, was complex and intricate. In essence the picture is one of new coalitions attempting to draw together those revolting against the old order: prohibitionists, anti-Catholics, nativists, and anti-Nebraskaites. The shape of the new organizations varied from state to state and locality to locality, depending on the extent of fusion and the relative strengths of Whigs, Democrats, Free Soilers, and Know Nothings. In Michigan a "Republican" movement, a radical forerunner of the fully-fledged party of 1856, emerged at an early date, but in most northern states during 1854 and 1855 the Free Soil/Republican forces played second fiddle to the Know Nothing party.[47]

Know Nothings were particularly strong in New England, and took an influential, sometimes commanding, role in fusion movements in other parts of the North. This reflected not just the Order's powerful nativist appeal but northern Know Nothings' evident hostility to the extension of slavery, their outrage at the Nebraska bill, and their warm embrace of former Free Soilers. Seekers of the party's nomination had commonly to demonstrate the purity of their antislavery credentials. Significantly, two-thirds of the anti-Nebraska congressmen elected in 1854 were members of the Order. "I was elected as a 'Native American', but I was as thoroughly anti-slavery as Garrison himself," explained Mark Trafton of Westfield, Massachusetts. In this the Methodist minister overstated his radicalism but effectively suggested the flavor of Know Nothingism in a state where the most significant result of the party's electoral triumph of 1854 was the passing of a Personal Liberty Law and where the Baptist Speaker of the House, Daniel Eddy, held that the party's "threefold principle" was "Temperance, Liberty and Protestantism."[48]

Eddy's remarks help explain northern evangelicals' rallying to the Know Nothing and fusion movements of 1854 and 1855. As these churchgoers saw it, Protestant Americans were locked in battle against three dark forces: "the whiskey power, the power of the Romish hierarchy, and the power of the slave demon." Each curse enjoyed the protection of political demagogues whose war cries, Benjamin F. Crary jeered, were "slavery now and forever . . . ; Roman Catholicism the preserver of the rights of man . . . ; rum and whisky the keystone of Democracy, and the hope of our country." Evangelicals jumped aboard, and even drove, the anti-Nebraska coalitions and People's parties because they promised to resist not one but all the demonic forces threatening the republic.[49]

In the minds of these evangelicals – whose Trinitarian theology attuned them to the notion of the "Three-in-One" – the evils they faced were not discrete, independent forces of wickedness but three aspects of a single satanic influence, three matched elements fusing "to destroy truth and righteousness from the earth." We have seen how the experience of mass immigration encouraged evangelicals to link the poison of drink directly with Romanism. At the same time they identified a powerful philosophical and institutional affinity between that church and southern slavery. To some extent evangelicals argued from direct political experience. Not only did most Catholic immigrants sustain the Democratic party and the "proslavery" administrations it had furnished, but the Irish were amongst the most vocal and muscular defenders of the nation's racial arrangements. John Hughes and the Roman hierarchy in North America, and their Catholic organs, adopted an ambivalent stance towards slavery, treating it as an unavoidable economic and social evil, but not a personal sin. They contemptuously dismissed all varieties of antislavery, from abolition to free soil, as expressions of fanatical Protestantism and atheistic republicanism. The "higher-law" party's radicalism, especially its violent resistance to the Fugitive Slave

Law, affronted their social conservatism. The *New York Freeman's Journal* consistently treated defiance of government and Constitution as the natural fruit of Protestantism: the higher law was "nothing more nor less than 'private judgment' extended from the Church to the State." During the political storms of the mid-1850s few Catholics signed, and most condemned, the clerical protests against the Nebraska bill. Their spokesmen generally supported Pierce's Kansas policy and blamed abolitionists for the territory's civil war. Most felt little indignation at Sumner's injuries, given the failure of "Yankeedom" to rebuke nativist violence against Catholics.[50]

As well as regarding the Roman church as a buttress of the slave power, evangelicals saw in slavery a secular expression of Romanism's worst evils. Comparing the two institutions, Eden Foster concluded: "Their spirit is one, ... the spirit of dictation over the conscience and over politics. Their principles are in perfect harmony, principles which establish an aristocracy, ... which perpetuate the power of caste." Slaveholders shut out the Bible from slave quarters as effectively as the papacy controlled its reading in Catholic lands. Both robbed their victims: by its penances, masses for the dead, and indulgences, Joseph Gordon sighed, "popery extorts money without rendering an equivalent; slavery robs men of their earnings, their wives and children, and their own souls and bodies." Slaves' confinement and openness to sexual abuse directly paralleled the plight of young Catholic novices. Slavery blighted economic and social progress, and destroyed the spirit of human enterprise, as thoroughly as Romanism. Any abolitionist who spoke out in the South, declared Henry Clay Fish, "would not be less liable to lose his life than ... a sojourner in Rome, if he made bold to traduce the Pope." Southern "political popes" demanded nationwide homage to the "sacred toe" of the slave power. The characteristics of "organic unity and permanent existence," which both the slavocracy and papacy enjoyed, not only suggested philosophical kinship but presaged a formal alliance between "the foulest despotisms of the world ... [,] on the one side to establish spiritual bondage, on the other to perpetuate physical."[51]

Evangelicals completed their triangulated schema of evils by directly linking the curse of slavery to that of drink. Many saw these as the two greatest sins facing the nation, equal in iniquity and, because sustained by law, liable to invite God's wrath on the nation. The language and metaphors of slavery ran through their discussion of liquor's effects. Though a victim of the "bondage of drink," the degraded drunkard was still "a man and a brother" who needed help to break his chains. Alcohol resulted in an "expulsion of judgment, conscience and self-control; and a surrender ... into the possession of a demon" just as slavery blunted the conscience and undermined rational, moral behavior in slave and master. As slavery violated family life, so liquor warred "ruthlessly upon Home and all that sacred circle of interests of which Home is the centre." Both depended on an elaborate commercial system driven by selfish and reckless traders, "men bankrupt in conscience and humanity." Both reined back national prosperity and spread "thriftlessness and dilapidation." And, in an argument holding together all three points of the triangle, reformers stressed that both the whiskey power and the slave power were sustained by Catholic votes.[52]

These connections within evangelical opinion profoundly influenced the direction and outcome of party realignment in the free states between 1854 and 1856. Indeed it was largely because of their respective relationships with assertive Protestantism that Know Nothings failed and Republicans succeeded in establishing themselves as the principal anti-Democratic party. Republicans knew that they would win elections only by tapping the moral energy of evangelical free soilers who were also, almost by definition, anti-Catholic and prohibitionist. But they also knew that if they were associated too closely with nativist extremism they would lose credibility with two electorally influential groups: foreign-born Protestants, especially German Reformed and Lutherans, hitherto Democratic in allegiance but much distressed by the repeal of the Missouri Compromise; and native-born liberal Protestants dismayed by proscriptive Know Nothingism. Through strategic shrewdness and good fortune the Republicans managed to cement a powerful coalition of native and foreign-born evangelicals, and cleverly outmaneuvered the American party throughout 1855 and 1856.[53]

In this they were very much aided by the Know Nothings' split over slavery in their National Council in June 1855, which led the party's free-soil sympathizers to view southern members as proslavery agents and the northern wing (the "North Americans") as a nativist diversion from the cause of freedom. These developments encouraged Sewardite Republicans who believed that their party could achieve an electoral majority without concessions to nativists. But continued Know Nothing electoral successes – as in Massachusetts and New York – suggested the limitations of a Republican strategy that emphasized slavery to the exclusion of (and even in direct opposition to) nativism. Instead the party came to adopt Salmon P. Chase's accommodationist approach first employed by Ohio Republicans to secure his election as governor in 1855. This involved privately recognizing Know Nothings' power and publicly avoiding outright repudiation of the American party, even trimming where necessary on nativist issues, yet giving slavery primacy over all other issues and reaching out to foreign-born Protestants.[54]

What particularly helped Republicans in this strategy, which they successfully extended to other states and to national politics, was the decreasing potency of prohibition as an issue. In the summer of 1854,

Nebraska bill notwithstanding, Thomas Eddy could announce, "Prohibition is becoming the one great question," and northern church resolutions regularly yoked intemperance and slavery as evils crying out equally for political remedy. Yet by the later part of 1855 and throughout 1856 evangelicals widely regarded the Maine Law movement as running out of steam. In the face of successful legal challenges to prohibitory laws in various state courts, and against a background of stiffening (and sometimes violent) public resistance, many supporters, as a writer in the *Oberlin Evangelist* complained, had "grow[n] weary of everlasting struggle."[55] Diminishing enthusiasm led a western Methodist ruefully to conclude in October 1856 that "the rum-sellers, rum-suckers, and rum-politicians are having it all their own way."[56] Republican leaders, with some exceptions, contributed to prohibition's decline by seeking to avoid or play down the issue in view of its associations with nativism and its capacity to alienate German Protestants. In some cases, to avoid a clear stand on the substantive issue, they called for referenda and local option. Where necessary, to keep anti-liquor forces sweet, prohibition appeared in the party's platforms, but defeats as galling as those in Maine in the fall of 1855 and in the Chicago municipal election the following March, in both of which Republicans were seen as Puritanically dry, only increased their determination to ignore the question as far as possible. Thomas A. Goodwin recalled bitterly how in 1856 Indiana Republicans adopted a prohibitory resolution in convention, but then never mentioned it again during the rest of the campaign.[57]

Historians of the early Republican party, whatever their disagreements, are of one opinion with Eric Foner in refusing to see it straightforwardly as "the political expression of pietistic Protestantism." William Gienapp's magisterial study treats the new force as the product of impressive political calculation and not as a spontaneous creation of evangelical fervor.[58] As Gamaliel Bailey's *National Era* put it, "a political party is not a church nor a philanthropic association." Republicans benefited initially from the destabilizing influence of evangelical moralism and antipartyism, but they were no exception to the rule that to develop and grow successful parties need managers, discipline, and professional politicians as much as ideological enthusiasts. The party's builders had to bring together and conciliate a variety of disparate interests. Protestant evangelicals formed just one element in their construction. Thus Republican leaders sought to mute the voices of nativism; advised radical clergy "not to go too far" in pressing the party to the limits of the Constitution "to satisfy the demands of . . . moral principle"; worked to prevent evangelical ministers running for office where they might counterproductively arouse sectarian opposition and fears of the union of church and state; and retreated from the higher moral ground that the party had staked out in Maine, Iowa and a number of other states in 1855 through the passage of laws to limit drunkenness, gambling, Sabbath-breaking, and other threats to good Protestant order.[59]

Yet, as this suggests, Thurlow Weed and other Republican managers were not, in their relations with antislavery evangelicals, all-powerful bosses marshaling passive, biddable troops. Ministers and committed laymen were themselves active leaders and organizers at local and state level.[60] Some pulled together disparate antislavery elements into a coherent force, as did Owen Lovejoy and Ichabod Codding with the "rag-tag and bob-tail gang" of anti-Nebraskaites in Illinois. The Reverend John Jones worked to recruit politically neutral fellow clergy into the Republican organization he had established in New Bremen, Ohio. A number, like Samuel Brenton and James Harlan of Iowa, and Ebenezer Knowlton of Maine, ran successfully for national office. Others played the role of king-makers. In Iowa the Republican party's candidates, who especially courted the evangelical voters of New England origin, benefited measurably from the work of the state's Congregationalist ministers, particularly Josiah Grinnell, Simeon Waters, and Asa Turner, in shaping public sentiment. Throughout the free states, antislavery evangelicals through press and pulpit acted as sympathetic secondary propagandists for the anti-Nebraska and Republican coalitions. Altogether they played a vital role in sustaining the new movement, not least in providing the energy, moral earnestness, and meeting places essential to a party still without a strong institutional framework. When Jonathan Blanchard remarked in May 1856, "The Anti-Nebraska force, not having organized must rely on enthusiasm," he implicitly recognized his fellow evangelicals' special contribution to the party.[61]

Their ostentatious political involvement drew down on the heads of "meddling priests" ("Rev. Dr. Schreecher" and his crew) a torrent of obloquy from furious Democrats and their ecclesiastical allies. The Catholic press castigated "Puritans" for bringing the country to the verge of disunion and war, while dissident Protestant voices joined with the Reverend William C. Larrabee, Indiana Methodist, in rebuking those who took a stand on "matters concerning which they know not whereof they affirm." Conservative Whigs, too, fretted over what Edward Everett regarded as the prostitution of the pulpit and its complicity in agitation and social upheaval. James W. Alexander mourned the loss of true piety in New England, where "Politics, Abstinence, and Slavery, usurp the 'sacred desk'," and other Presbyterians lamented the more general ecclesiastical disrespect for political authority.[62] Within the Protestant Episcopal church the minority of antislavery evangelical clergy were vulnerable to the wrath of outraged vestries; Dudley A. Tyng resigned from the Church of the Epiphany, Philadelphia, when he lost a congregational vote of confidence.[63]

Republican clergy stood undaunted in the face of these attacks, maintaining their right as citizens to a voice in public affairs and denying that they were political dolts. They were duty bound to measure the actions of government against the standards of God. Charles W. Clapp agreed that issues such as banks, internal improvements, tariffs, or land distribution had no place "in the temple of God . . . because they are *not* moral," but it was another matter when politicians were ready to defy the Lord Almighty.[64] "Caesar is to have the things that are Caesar's," William T. Dwight explained. "But when God's authority is invaded, when any political measure [violates] . . . His precepts, then Caesar has no right."[65] An Indiana Methodist drily remarked: "The object of demagogues is to establish the rule, that preachers have no right to meddle with politics, and . . . then to call every vice a political matter, and thus exclude every virtuous man from any party in our government." By this doctrine parties could without protest legislate away the Sabbath, the Bible, and the churches. Besides, as Calvin Kingsley observed, hostile politicians operated a double standard: preaching in the aftermath of the Nebraska bill was no more "political" than the pro-Compromise, Union sermons that political committees had rushed to circulate in 1850 and 1851. In fact, antislavery ministers argued, America's whole historical experience vindicated an involved pulpit. What freedoms would nineteenth-century Americans enjoy had colonial clergy not thundered against George III and British tyranny?[66]

"Disgust, mortification and sorrow": southern evangelical responses

Southern churches watched these national political developments with mounting alarm. Their spokesmen in the main aimed to avoid commentaries on overtly political issues, reminding their members that Christ's kingdom was not of this world. In practice they found such self-censorship impossible, not least because of the stance of the northern pulpit. Though reluctant to address government actions, they could not sit silent in the face of the free-state clergy's "phrenzied fanaticism."[67] And as they excoriated their northern brethren so they found themselves addressing the substantive issues that had driven anti-Nebraska clergy to speak out. Southern clergy generally desired political quiescence but their response to events in the mid-1850s did little to secure it.

The Nebraska bill drove a further wedge between northern and southern churches. Most evangelical spokesmen in the South considered it just and ridiculed the inconsistency of northern clerics who had resisted the extension of the Missouri Compromise line in 1850, but now deemed it sacred. A small southern minority of more Whiggish preachers considered Douglas's measure a misguided, impolitic, and even infamous act: it threatened the Union, threw conservative northern friends of the South on the defensive, and encouraged further Catholic immigration. But these voices were lost in the storm of protest against northern clerics turned clamorous party politicians. Anti-Nebraska preachers' "politico-religious" preaching sought a union of church and state, replaced scriptural obedience to civil authority with clerical dictation in secular affairs, and brought ever closer the threat of civil war.[68]

Thus, just as northern evangelicals posed as conservative defenders of the republic against Douglas's revolutionary proposals, southern churches perceived themselves as equally staunch defenders of law, civilization, and moderation in the face of northern preachers' unbiblical initiatives. Southern Baptists watched despairingly as Francis Wayland, long regarded as a model of sobriety, joined in the denunciation of the Nebraska bill. Joshua J. James, forceful editor of the *Biblical Recorder*, concluded that Wayland's mounting unfriendliness to the South, evident in his controversy with Richard Fuller, had now developed into outright enmity. For the rest of the decade southerners associated his name with northern fanaticism, threatened to burn his books, and dropped his writings from college use.[69] Such reactions only exacerbated the sectional war of words and increased the danger that southern pessimism about the future of the Union would act as a self-fulfilling prophecy.

Southern anxiety over the unremitting "abolition epidemic" seemed further justified in the aftershock of the Nebraska crisis, as free-state ministers encouraged the rescue of fugitives, promoted armed free-soil emigration to Kansas, and defended violent attacks on proslavery settlers there.[70] When Bishop George F. Pierce visited southern Methodists in the territory in August 1856 he blamed the troubles on the blind zeal of "the Beecher Sharpe's Rifle Tribe," characterized the "border ruffians" as "quiet, polite, orderly" and humble farmers exasperated by numberless provocations, and presented the South as victim not aggressor.[71] Baptist opinion, too, concluded that the sack of Lawrence was "a merited chastisement" for abolitionist-inspired and church-supported violence.[72]

Southern evangelicals offered a less coherent judgment on the caning of Sumner. All agreed that the Massachusetts senator had been insolently offensive, and many held that only *"clubs* and *cowhides"* could "loosen the hide of a vagabond philanthropist," but a significant number condemned Brooks's response as foolish or wicked. Robert L. Dabney, no admirer of the pride of southern political leaders, accused the South Carolinian of turning the South's righteous cause into a "stench in the nostrils of all moderate men."[73] But as northern clergy joined the clamor against Brooks and the slave power, so the majority of southern voices were moved by "disgust, mortification, and sorrow" (as a South Carolina Baptist put it) to condemn Yankees' double standards towards violence and their intolerable self-righteousness.[74]

Southern evangelicals' hardening sectional antipathies derived also from more narrowly ecclesiastical developments. Slave-state Methodists watched, with gleeful self-vindication and a *frisson* of horror, as "Hosmerites" and other "rabid abolitionists" (ecclesiastical counterparts of the hated "Black Republicans") challenged the MEC's conventional stand on slavery and brought the church to the verge of further schism. Baptists, aggrieved by their exclusion from free-state pulpits for conniving at human suffering, told northern ministers to remove the mote in their own eye and attend to the needs of the urban poor and free blacks. Southern Presbyterians viewed with alarm the increasing pressure within the New School General Assembly to declare slavery a sin *per se*. The debate in the ATS on the society's proper stance over slavery only reinforced an ominous conviction that "miserable fanatics of the North ... seek through such mediums to press upon the South their gratuitous dictation and rant," and that it was "impossible for the North and South to combine in any national benevolent enterprise, and act together with any harmony."[75]

As the political and ecclesiastical atmosphere became ever more charged, a number of influential southern churchmen moved to act in the interests of national unity. In 1855 John Lansing Burrows established the *American Baptist Memorial* in Richmond, Virginia, which by avoiding all "local, sectional, or controversial" matters would draw together "all sections of our land." Similar ambitions prompted the setting up of the *Central Presbyterian* soon afterwards, also in Richmond. Its editors, who included Moses Hoge and Benjamin Gildersleeve, saw themselves as peacemakers in church and state, holding "faithful to those great conservative principles that underlie all our institutions." Calls for political moderation rang out during the frenzied summer of 1856. "Seldom, if ever, have we observed a more exciting and general interest in political subjects," reported one editor, eager to stop his readers succumbing to the "high party feeling." Robert L. Dabney warned against "reckless faction mongers" in both sectional camps.[76]

But the efforts of southern conservative evangelicals to sustain national harmony through political silence were never entirely convincing. For northern Methodists like Erwin House and Charles Elliott, by no means radical opponents of slavery, southerners' creed of political quiescence was "sublime nonsense": silence meant winking favorably at the Nebraska bill, the arrangements of slavery, and the status quo. For every text ("Let every soul be subject to the higher powers") there was a subtext ("Yield yourselves up body and soul, for time and eternity, to the slaveholders"). As Seagrove W. Magill sarcastically put it: "To preach against slavery is of course political preaching; but to preach for it ...

is ... preaching the Gospel." In their calmer moments southerners, too, recognized how untenable was the doctrine of silence, since it not only put politicians – fallible human beings – beyond reproach but seemed logically to demand that churches acquiesce in congressional action to abolish slavery, should that day dawn. A group of twenty-three influential ministers implicitly acknowledged the deficiencies of mute acceptance when in June 1856 they issued their "Richmond Appeal," widely circulated in the secular and religious press. The signatories, who included Jeremiah Jeter, William A. Smith, Moses Hoge, and other leading Baptists, Methodists, and Presbyterians, insisted that they were not transcending their proper sphere by addressing "conservative remarks" on the "alarming crisis in our national affairs." Patriotism and Christianity jointly compelled them to defend the Union and good order against "lawless" physical and verbal violence that set "[t]he flames of civil war ... kindling on our borders."[77]

Southern evangelicals, then, who sneered at the "meddling" northern pulpit were by no means all political innocents. True, many clergy could claim – with some justice – to have remained non-partisan in public and broadly to have kept clear of the rough and tumble of electoral politics. Yet even here their record was not spotless. If most had kept their Whig or Democratic loyalties private, they had been less strenuous in containing their public diatribes against the party of northern "ultras": the Free Soilers and their successors, the Republicans. The religious press did not dare engage in Whig-bashing or Democrat-baiting for fear of giving offense. But when, for instance, the *Southern Christian Advocate* alluded to the "fanaticism" of Seward, no subscribers threw up their hands in alarm, nor did any cancel their subscriptions when it described John C. Frémont as "the sectional candidate of an extreme ultra fanatical party." Noting that John McFerrin's "holy horror" of politics did not prevent allusions to "Black Republicans" in his *Nashville Christian Advocate*, a northern editor sarcastically denied that these words had a "sly slur for any political party. O, no! but if *we* should say the Black Democracy, it would be construed as being violently partisan."[78] Such inconsistency, conscious or not, increasingly angered northern evangelicals as the presidential campaign of 1856 built to its climax.

"We've truth on our side – We've God for our guide": the 1856 election in the North

Historians of antebellum politics confer on the presidential election of 1856 a special significance, for it witnessed the emergence of the Republican party as the second party in the nation, signaled the end of the first phase of a profound electoral realignment, and launched the

Republicans on the road to a portentous victory in 1860.[79] Contemporaries, too, recognized the special character of the campaign and compared its intensity of excitement to that of 1840. While some evangelical Protestants sought to avoid what a Philadelphia Methodist described as "almost continual uproar" and tried to keep church attention on higher things, many others worked to make moral and religious themes paramount in politics, and ensure that party spokesmen addressed religious sensibilities more directly than ever before.[80]

Kansas, the implications for the stability of the Union of extending or restricting slavery, and the character of American republicanism provided the staple issues of public debate, as did the persisting questions raised by foreign immigration. True to the pattern of earlier presidential elections, that of 1856 comprised two different campaigns, one aimed at the slaveholding states, the other at the free. But whereas previously the same two major parties had competed in both sections, each modifying its message to fit the audience, in 1856 the victorious party, the Democrats, faced a different principal challenger north and south. In the slave states their candidate, James Buchanan, comfortably outran Millard Fillmore and the American party, though the ex-president was by no means disgraced: he secured nearly half a million ballots, over 40 percent of the popular vote, winning Maryland and doing very well elsewhere in the border. But in the free states Fillmore came a poor third, running behind both Buchanan and the Republicans' John C. Frémont, who carried the section overall with 1.3 million votes, 45 percent of those cast there.[81]

The character and outcome of both these campaigns were deeply influenced by the preoccupations of evangelical religion. This was most evident in the North. There Democrats, consistent with their philosophical commitment to civil libertarianism and cultural pluralism, appealed to the fears of immigrant and many native-born Americans that fanatical ultra-Protestants controlled both the American and Republican parties.[82] Delegates at their national convention in Cincinnati, and Buchanan in his letter accepting the party's nomination, set up their standard against political distinctions based on "religious opinions and accidental birthplace."[83] Party leaders trumpeted news of Democratic accessions from conservative "Old Line Whigs" repelled by the nativist, anti-Catholic stand of the American party. They presented Republicans as religious hypocrites whose pious pratings concealed a "profoundly concerted plot" to destroy orthodox Christianity and the Union that sustained it. By what system of moral calculus could Republicans justify sending Sharps rifles to Kansas? Democrats, committed by their platform to congressional non-interference in territorial affairs, offered a morally acceptable recipe for national harmony and the return to peace. But Frémont's unyielding sectionalism, threatening the pillars of the republic, made him *"the instrument of vice, and the foe of God and of Freedom."* The party's "conjoined fanaticisms" derived from a motley of moral eccentrics. These included "infidel" abolitionists like Theodore Parker and Wendell Phillips, and such perverted Protestants as Horace Greeley and the *New York Tribune*, who had "passed through all the phases of Fourierism, Socialism, and Freeloveism, up to the sublime heights of Rifleism."[84]

Democrats were particularly concerned to discredit the phalanx of orthodox evangelical clergy who, they complained, had thrown themselves with unwonted energy into anti-Democratic campaigning, mainly on behalf of Frémont. A Kentucky Episcopalian traveling through the free states reported that the contest, "more than any one preceding, [is] one in which the religious portion of the North takes an active part." Buchanan's lieutenants berated "[h]ypocritical Church and State men," "pulpit schreechers," and "clerical *cobblers*" whose ecclesiastical rule over biddable Christian women and children made them "arrogant, impatient of contradiction, and intolerant," and whose political activities turned them into "the most dangerous class in [the] community to the peace of society." One clear index of Democrats' concern about clerical power was the launching in Philadelphia of a new campaign paper, *Political Priestcraft Exposed*. Their banners in New York City, portraying a priest standing on a Bible, with a rifle in one hand and a revolver in the other, bore the legend: "Beecher's Command – kill each other with Sharp's Rifles."[85]

At the same time Democrats adopted a more positive approach to retain their customary evangelical supporters. Known Protestants, like Jeremiah S. Black (a Campbellite who was to become Buchanan's attorney-general), emphasized the positive benefits of religious tolerance. John L. Dawson assured Methodist Democrats that their party would protect them against proscriptive Protestants who asserted that Episcopal Methodism was un-American. Stephen A. Douglas, in giving Chicago Baptists ten acres of land for a new college, provided party propagandists with a handy (if lightweight) counterbalance to his Nebraska bill and his association with Irish Catholics.[86] Most of all, Democratic spokesmen sought to reassure orthodox evangelicals of Buchanan's soundness in religion and his pure moral character. With devout Scotch-Irish immigrant parents, a religious upbringing, a brother in the ministry, a reputation for Sabbath strictness, and a pew in each of the Presbyterian churches in Lancaster, Pennsylvania, the candidate possessed safe credentials, even if he was not yet a full church member. His Calvinism in religion, like his Unionism in politics, they insisted, gave credibility to the claim that the parties were divided by a moral chasm, not narrow political issues. To vote for Buchanan would be to sustain principles forming "the basis of the entire standing of society."[87]

With Millard Fillmore as leader, the American party lost some of its earlier crusading anti-Catholicism, suffered defections amongst anti-slavery nativists alienated by the party's apparent endorsement of the Kansas–Nebraska Act, and became essentially a focus for Whig Unionists. Its strength lay principally in the South, where many had wanted Fillmore on the Whig ticket in 1852, but it retained significant support in parts of the North strategically important to the Republicans. Though Fillmore was not personally consumed with nativist bitterness, insisting publicly that he had "no hostility to foreigners," and though the party dropped the most proscriptive of earlier Know Nothing policies, anti-Catholicism remained a considerable element in its propaganda arsenal. Its platform stipulated that no one should serve in political office who recognized allegiance "to any foreign prince, potentate or power." "Ours is a Protestant government," one polemicist wrote; "our President should be a Protestant. Our Protestant laws and constitution need Protestant officers to enforce and execute them."[88]

In view of its strong Whig pedigree, it is hardly surprising that the American party directed at the outgoing administration all the anti-Romanist animus Whig propagandists had launched at an earlier date at Van Buren, Polk, and other Democratic contenders for high office. The Americans' managers pointedly played on the collective memory of Whig defeat in 1844, quoted from Fillmore's letters to Clay stressing the damage done by Catholic and foreign votes, and presented their candidate as the avenger of past wrongs. They attributed the corruption and errors of the Pierce administration to Catholic influence; Buchanan, if elected, would bring the republic even further under the destructive sway of Rome.[89]

More interestingly, however, Fillmorites turned the same guns on the Republicans, accusing them of covert sympathy for the Pope and the foreign-born. This tactic reflected the American party's determination to weaken Frémont's standing with Know Nothing voters whose support he badly needed (and indicated the secret funding of Fillmore's northern campaign by Democrats anxious to keep the opposition's vote divided).[90] It was indeed the case that Republicans recognized the need to win the votes of the foreign-born, or at least the Protestants amongst them. The nativist who claimed, "The Republican party is pre-eminently a foreign party . . . [which] bids high for the foreign and Roman Catholic vote," indulged in electoral hyperbole. But he was not wide of the mark when he added, "Its plan is to rise to power through the aid of the foreign population and the abolitionists."[91] The most audacious element of the Americans' attack, however, was the claim that the Republicans' presidential candidate was a closet Romanist.

This charge against Frémont was part of a broad-based effort to blacken the name of "the Pathfinder," the glamorous explorer and adventurer, and prove him "a thoroughly bad man." As well as the outright fictions that he had killed a dozen men in duels, owned and hired out nearly two dozen slaves, and had taken the side of proslavery southerners during his stint as a United States senator, Frémont faced the murky claim that during the conquest of California he had defrauded the public treasury. More serious was the incontrovertible evidence of his court martial in 1848 for mutiny, disobedience, and conduct prejudicial to military discipline. In fact Frémont had been the victim of the Stockton–Kearny quarrel over the location of authority in the new territory, and was pardoned by Polk, but the abbreviated story was more valuable to Know Nothings than the more complex truth.[92] However, the most damaging, though wholly fictitious, charge he faced was the unequivocal assertion that he was, as the editor of the *New York Day Book* insisted, "a bigoted and proscriptive Roman Catholic."[93]

From the uncontested evidence that Frémont and his beloved Jessie Benton had been married secretly by a Catholic priest (after Protestant ministers, fearing the wrath of her father, had declined), and that his adopted daughter had attended a Catholic seminary, American leaders embroidered an imaginative tapestry so finely detailed that Republicans remained handicapped by the issue throughout the campaign. Amongst other claims, it was alleged that Frémont was the son of a French Roman Catholic; that he had been educated by Catholics in preparation for the ministry; that he had recruited for their church; that he and his Protestant wife were at odds over religious worship; that he regularly attended mass, "going through all the crosses and gyrations, eating wafer, and so on"; that he believed in transubstantiation; that he had refused a Protestant hymn-book; and that he and Bishop Hughes had been seen, arms linked, drunkenly reeling home from church.[94]

Behind these harmful claims, and implicit in their mischievous banners depicting Frémont as a tiaraed Pope, lay Fillmorites' even more damaging charge that the Republican party as an institution had become the tool of "Romish tyranny": Frémont's nomination allegedly followed a bargain struck by Bishop Hughes, Seward, and the candidate. Seward's public friendship towards Romanists ruled him out of contention, while the "Massachusetts Puritan," Nathaniel P. Banks, and the Methodist John McLean were unacceptable to the Catholics. Lacking known political antecedents, and superficially acceptable to native-born Protestants, the covert Romanist Frémont was the ideal choice. Only the operations of this Jesuitical double game could explain the support of the German press for the Republican candidate.[95]

. These allegations struck an icy chill into many evangelical hearts. John Inskip, staunch in the anti-Catholic cause in Brooklyn and a warm admirer of Republican free-soil principles, was sent into a dithering spin by stories of Frémont's Catholicism: "If this should prove true," he despaired, "I cannot vote for him." Even those who doubted that the Republican strategy would secure many Catholic votes feared that the party would attract enough "red" foreigners to adulterate its moral purity. Hiram Ketchum drew loud applause when he warned fellow New England evangelicals not to support Frémont out of blind zeal for antislavery. True liberty, he insisted, must be harnessed to evangelical Christianity. The anti-sabbatarian, freethinking Germans' liberty " is not our liberty.... It is a liberty which seeks freedom from the restraints of God and man. It may be red republicanism, or it may be black republicanism, but it is not American republicanism."[96]

In these circumstances, American leaders insisted, Fillmore and his running mate, Andrew Jackson Donelson, were the only candidates whom Protestant voters could trust. Fillmore had been a Unitarian for most of his adult life, but this did not stop his biographers lauding his evangelical Yankee pedigree, his tenuous family connections with Methodism, and his marriage to the devout daughter of a Baptist minister. They wrote of "the purity of his life," his "active benevolence," total abstinence from alcohol and tobacco, and philanthropic concern for the Indians. His moral perspectives provided the foundation of his watertight anti-Catholicism, evidenced in his support for Kossuth and efforts on behalf of the persecuted Madiai. They undergirded his staunch defense of the Union ("the palladium of our civil and religious liberties," as the party's platform put it) and his lofty record as a compromiser. According to Erastus Brooks, "The Creator of the Universe planted... [the] principle of Compromise in the heart of every Christian man. It is one of the great attributes of Mercy witnessed in the redemption of the world."[97] Christianity and patriotism linked hands in Millard Fillmore.

From the moment Albert Barnes offered prayers to open their national convention in June, the Republicans' campaign took on the character of a quasi-religious crusade.[98] At that Philadelphia gathering the more conventional politics of calculation fused with a distinctive evangelical ethos, moral energy, and revivalist enthusiasm to suggest the party's direct lineage from Free Soilers and Liberty men. One participant found the proceedings reminiscent of a "Methodist conference rather than a political convention." Ministers and radical antislavery evangelicals like Owen Lovejoy and Joshua Giddings worked assiduously to ensure that the party's platform remained true to "God's revealed Word" and to Jeffersonian imperatives on equal rights. Giddings deceived himself when he declared that what emerged was "ahead of all other platforms ever adopted," but the party took unequivocal ground against the extension of slavery, a "relic of barbarism." The scheming but inflexibly antislavery Henry Wilson asserted that with a platform that "embraces freedom, humanity and Christianity, ... all that is required is that we organize the Christian Democratic sentiment of America, and place that ticket in power." John P. Hale exhorted every party activist to be "not only a soldier, but a missionary," broadcasting the news that "in the good Providence of God" the moment of decision for the future of freedom had arrived. Delegates left Philadelphia fired up to sing "The Fremont Crusader's Song," with its stirring couplet: "We've truth on our side – /We've God for our guide."[99]

Republicans insisted that the Democrats' deliberately ambiguous formula of congressional non-interference in the territories would make Kansas a slave state, and predicted that Buchanan ("the choice of the Virginia Slave-breeders") would smile indulgently on the acquisition of a slave empire in the Caribbean.[100] Fillmore, too, had already shown himself "a most subservient instrument of the slave power," and his party's straddling platform (offering a form of popular sovereignty) guaranteed that he would remain so.[101] In contrast, the Republicans' antislavery posture and their call for slavery restriction brilliantly exploited a variety of northern aspirations and phobias: it harnessed anti-southern feeling, fear of a furtive slave power, faith in the material and moral benefits of free labor, Negrophobic concern over the spread of slavery into the territories, and alarm about the future of republicanism itself. But what gave Republicans' efforts such *élan* was their ability to sustain over several months the idea of the campaign as a "holy endeavor" in "fealty to the law of God" against the sin of slavery and the morally deficient schemes of their political opponents.[102] In shaping this crusade, the party depended enormously on the contributions of evangelical Protestants. Before assessing evangelicals' role, two particular features of the Republicans' electoral message deserve notice: its deliberate attention to church aggravations that bore on the sectional conflict; and its treatment of the Catholic issue.

Republican presses seized every opportunity to exploit free-state Protestants' bitterness about the harsh censorship and physical attacks their border and slave-state antislavery brethren were suffering at the hands of the slave power. Proslavery vigilantes' assaults on brave preachers in Kansas and the border, the silencing of "unsound" southern pastors and college professors, the banning and burning of suspect religious books and newspapers, and the imposition by northern ecclesiastical "doughfaces" of "safe" editors on denominational papers: these provided graphic evidence of the slave-power conspiracy at the heart of the republic and gave meaningful context to the party's call for "free speech." The *Albany Evening Journal* drew the shocking Sellers–Holland incident in Missouri to the notice of those "of our Methodist friends as are still disposed to cling to the Pro-Slavery Party." A northern minister working in the South feared physical assault for subscribing to the *New York Tribune*: "He who says there is a Free Press or Free Speech in the Slave States is, in plain Saxon, a LIAR." Such stories served not only to reinforce antislavery evangelicals' anti-southernism. They allowed Republicans to question whether any party comprising southern and "doughface" interests could serve the needs of antislavery churchgoers. This was the lesson drawn by Chauncey Shaffer, a Methodist lawyer and influential New York Know Nothing who declared for Frémont when Fillmore failed to rebuke the slave power for its treatment of border-state Methodists.[103]

While the slave power took pride of place in the party's demonology, Republicans also continued to exploit popular fear of Romanism as they had done in the previous year. They had been successful, through brilliant sleight of hand, in forcing Frémont on the North Americans as their presidential candidate (following the withdrawal of the stalking-horse, Banks), but the price of this merger had been concessions to the Know Nothings at a lower level.[104] Thus, while the Republican national convention adopted a deliberately ambiguous resolution on citizens' rights and liberty of conscience, many state and local platforms took up explicitly nativist and anti-Catholic themes.[105] In general, party presses played down the temperance issue (though they listed Frémont's abstinence as one of his Protestant virtues) and other matters that could alienate antislavery foreigners. But since Republicans had little hope of winning Catholic votes, and since Protestant German and Scandinavian immigrants shared their anti-Catholicism, they had little to lose by reiterating the established themes of the antislavery evangelical pulpit and linking southern and Roman despotism: one made people slaves in fact, the other slaves in effect.[106]

As the candidate of the northern antislavery Know Nothings, the North Americans, Frémont might have expected a clear run at the anti-Catholic vote. But Fillmorites' scare stories of the Pathfinder's Romanism proved enormously damaging, and Republicans did not help their candidate by their uncertain response. Some wanted Frémont himself publicly to declare his Protestantism. Many others took Greeley's view that the Fillmore men had set a trap, and that ignoring the charge would do less damage than repudiating it – which would antagonize Catholics and betray the principle of equal political rights. Frémont's religion was "a private matter, with which we have no business," Henry Ward Beecher told a mass Republican meeting. In the event party leaders decided that Frémont should remain silent, though Republican presses would continue to print testimonies to his strict Protestantism. A clutch of pamphlets and newspaper reports affirmed that the candidate was a communicant in the Episcopal church, the denomination of his mother, his children, and his wife; that his father had been a Huguenot; that his education had been exclusively Protestant; and that a second, quite other, Frémont, who was an army officer and resembled the Pathfinder, had worshiped at the Catholic church where the Republican candidate had supposedly been sighted.[107] To help put the record straight various groups of distinguished Protestant professors, editors, and clerics visited Frémont at home in New York, and declared the charges against him utterly baseless.[108]

One index of Frémont's and the Republicans' Protestant orthodoxy, party spokesmen maintained, was the antagonistic stance of the Romanist press. The *Boston Pilot* denounced free soilism, linked the Republicans with Know Nothingism, backed Buchanan, and called on the South to secede if Frémont were elected. James A. McMaster, a zealous states-rights Democrat, used his *New York Freeman's Journal* to laud Buchanan's patriotic wisdom, while denying that his support amounted to a conventional partisan endorsement. In Cincinnati the *Catholic Telegraph* remained publicly neutral until the Republican press began to extol Frémont's Protestantism. Then it firmly attached its colors to the Democrats, berated free soilers for "savage animosity" towards Rome, an asserted that Republicans found their mainstay in the "Protestant associations and Irish Orangemen." Horace Greeley reflected that he did not know a single Catholic paper, out of the thirty or forty in the country, that supported Frémont's election: "There is certainly no other denomination half so adverse [sic] to him as the Roman Catholics."[109]

As a final if more desperate tack, Republicans impugned the faith of Millard Fillmore and accused the American party of hypocrisy over the Catholic issue. One pamphleteer reminded voters that "FILLMORE *is a* UNITARIAN," and insinuated a lack of patriotism in his shunning *"the American Protestant faith that Jesus Christ is the Son of God."*[110] Another pointed out, in what was more than an objective sociological observation, that the candidate's creed "is quite as obnoxious to the great majority of Christians as is the Roman Catholic." At the same time other Republican propagandists asked "Is Mr. Fillmore a Catholic?" In drawing to public notice Fillmore's personal connections with the Roman church (he had educated his daughter at a Catholic convent, and recently visited Rome, conversed with Bedini, and secured a private audience with the Pope) they hoped to plant in voters' minds the thought that the politics of the American party were not all they purported to be and were ultimately directed from Rome. What else explained the presence of Romanist delegates from Louisiana at the American party's national convention? "[I]t may be," fretted one alarmist, "we are on the eve of another St Bartholomew's massacre."[111]

As will be seen, this Republican strategy for enticing northern Know Nothings into Frémont's column did not wholly succeed. Fillmore was able to hold onto enough conservative nativists to deprive Frémont of victory in critical states. It may be, as William Gienapp has argued, that Frémont's failure to convince nativist doubters of his Protestantism was "fatal" to his hopes; but there were too many other influences on this group of voters for this one element to be isolated with any certainty. For instance, when the Reverend Allen Steele and several other Methodist ministers visited Frémont and emerged to declare the charges against him groundless, a war broke out in Albany Methodism. Seventy-seven Methodists signed an article in the *Evening Statesman*, a Fillmore paper, criticizing Steele for entering politics. This prompted a further one hundred Methodists to defend Steele and Frémont in the *Evening Journal*.[112] It is not clear whether the Fillmorites were genuinely open to Republican persuasion. They more probably represented that wing of Albany Methodism for whom Fillmore's urbane ex-Whiggery and Unionism offered a more attractive home, regardless of Frémont's religious credentials.

Whatever the shortcomings of Frémont's campaign, its message and style nonetheless generated enormous enthusiasm amongst mainstream evangelical Protestants in the free states. With some justice Republicans boasted of their popularity within the major denominational families, as well as amongst Unitarians and Quakers. They celebrated the supportive work of church women and enthusiastic youth. Theological students called on Frémont. James M. Buckley, then a student at Wesleyan University, took the stump for him. Lyman Abbott, some weeks short of voting age, spent polling day with his brothers in New York City distributing Republican tickets and identifying fraudulent Irish voters.[113] Most significantly, the campaign drew in thousands of local and national luminaries from the evangelical churches. Though some Republican clergy, like Francis Wayland, believed partisan activity inconsistent with Christian ministry, many more gave visible support to what an octogenarian Methodist, James Finley, called the party of "free grace, free seats, free speech, a free press, [and] free territory."[114] It was the clergy's involvement above all that prompted Charles Francis Adams to conclude that Frémont had found his "chief support in this canvass . . . in the religious element." Clerical endorsement, rejoiced sympathetic editors, showed that Republican activists were not conventional politicians driven by "the lucre of office;" unlike the Democrats they did not comprise rowdies, border ruffians, "nine-wived Mormons," and slave-catchers; when their opponents did find a preacher willing to support Buchanan they "cackle[d] over the event like a hen over a new laid egg."[115]

The Republican campaign blurred the conventional line between party politics and church life. Party members, so often church members too, gathered in meeting houses and church basements for rallies or ward meetings. Mass gatherings convened in churchyards. Ministers presided over Frémont clubs, offered prayers at party conventions, and even manned the polls to encourage right voting. At least one, Ichabod

Codding, produced a campaign manual.[116] Illustrious clergy-politicians like Jonathan Blanchard took the limelight at mass meetings. Many took to the stump. From Bradford County, Pennsylvania, Democrats complained of "the fanatical Methodist and Baptist preachers . . . hurling their anathemas at us from their pulpits on Sundays and from the stump on week days." The most celebrated and inspiring of all stump preachers, Henry Ward Beecher, taking semi-leave from Plymouth church, was employed by the party's national committee to speak twice or three times a week; sometimes speaking for three hours at a time, he reached tens of thousands, indoors and out. Well represented amongst the hearers as well as the speakers, devout Protestants gave a novel ethos to Republican gatherings, combining enthusiasm with good order. Even stern evangelical judges noted the relative absence of drunkenness and applauded the contrast with the "degrading" influences of the hard-cider campaign.[117]

Ostensibly religious occasions and institutions, too, took on a partisan character. Ministers whose Republicanism was a public fact – George B. Cheever, Nathan Beman, George Duffield, Jr, Joseph P. Thompson, for instance – delivered sermons on the slave power, Kansas, the extension of slavery, the citizen's political responsibilities, and other themes which only occasionally endorsed the Republicans by name, but whose elec-toral import was clear.[118] Beecher used his Sunday pulpit to advance Frémont's claims amongst those deaf to more conventional political approaches; when on the eve of the election the candidate and his wife attended the "Church of the Holy Rifles," as Beecher's Brooklyn base had become known, the congregation practically burst into cheers. Through the weeks immediately before polling day, numerous denomi-national gatherings at state and regional level resolved to resist by all means, including political, the slave power's threat to free territory, free speech, and the Union. The broad anti-Democratic bias of their resolu-tions was clear, and while they usually left undiscussed the relative claims of Frémont and Fillmore, this was not invariably so. Delegates from all but three of the free states gathered in Ohio for the General Conference of Freewill Baptists: having called for the victory of "the cause of civil and religious liberty," they closed the session with an open-air Frémont and Dayton meeting addressed by the Reverend Ebenezer Knowlton, member of Congress from Maine. Similar em-phases characterized the northern evangelical press: though only a few newspapers (most prominently the Boston *Congregationalist*, the New York *Independent*, the *Oberlin Evangelist*, and the *American Baptist*) unequivocally declared for Frémont, many more gave him their implicit endorsement.[119]

Evangelicals' most powerful contribution to politics in this election year was perhaps to the Republican cast of mind. Republicanism incorporated many of the dichotomies of evangelical thought and language. Charles Boynton, in a sermon early in 1856, articulated not only a cosmology universally held by fellow Congregationalists but a credo well suited to the emergent Republican coalition. "[T]ruth and falsehood, liberty and tyranny, light and darkness, holiness and sin, were," he said, "the two great armies on the battlefield of the universe, each contending for victory. There could be no cessation of hostilities . . . till righteousness triumphs." George B. Cheever drew similar antitheses firmly into the electoral battle, which he described as "a decisive struggle . . . between freedom, and Slavery, truth and falsehood, justice and oppression, God and the devil." For evangelical Republicans, 1856 represented a crux in the nation's history. There could be no surrendering compromises with the slave power. According to Lyman Abbott, America would imminently choose either to "remain in God's service, an exponent of individual freedom," or to "go over to Satan's, and relapse into oligarchy and thence to monarchy." The election gave Christians the clear-cut chance actively to work for God. As Benjamin Adams, a Methodist preacher and paid agent of the New York State Republican party, explained, there was no tension between religious and political action: campaigning for Frémont was an extension of gospel preaching and revivalism. Unlike previous campaigns, this one would strengthen piety. One religious paper called the contest "a religious movement, a revival of religion, 'a great awakening' to be classified among the moral reformations of the world." Election day was a sacred occasion when Christians would pray for Frémont's victory, and voters obey the imperative of the Republican song: "Think that God's eye is on you;/ Let not your faith grow dim;/ For each vote cast for Fremont/ Is a vote cast for Him!"[120]

"Reverend Hypocrites", "uncircumcised Philistines," and Locofoco "Judases": the 1856 election in the South

The primary question at issue in the southern states in the 1856 campaign was how best to protect the South's peculiar institution in a Union that had given birth to a dangerous sectional party. With an acrimony reminiscent of earlier Whig–Locofoco battles, Know Nothings and Democrats fought for the title of surest guardian of southern interests.[121] Their conflict raised issues that engaged the religious loyalties and moral perspectives of southern voters, and ensured that evangelicals played a shaping role in the politics of 1856.

Southern Know Nothing leaders aimed to attract previous Whig voters and disaffected Democrats.[122] They presented themselves as staunch Unionists sustained by conservative Protestant values. They

blamed their opponents' dangerous policies, whether proslavery disunionism or radical free soilism, on moral and religious deficiency.
William Brownlow, Thomas A.R. Nelson, Anna E. Carroll, and other
Fillmorite publicists accused the Democrats of propitiating papists,
infidels, and deficient Protestants. In language similar to their northern
counterparts' they declared the party of Pierce and Buchanan a "bogus"
or "bastard" democracy which had "degenerated into a *Semi-Papal*
organization." Democrats had infiltrated Romanists into cabinet and
Supreme Court; they had denounced as "Reverend Hypocrites" those
God-fearing Protestant clergy who committed no sin greater than rallying
to the American party; they had watched with criminal indifference as
the Catholic church in the Mississippi Valley encircled Protestants "with
a wall of fire." At the same time the party had blended fanatical new
notions with the crazy legacies of the Jacksonians to create a poisonous
stew of Fourierism, Millerism, "women's rightism," "mobbism,"
Mormonism, deism, and spiritualism. It had also attracted "all the
assassins, cut-throats, thieves and hypocrit[e]s in the country." Know
Nothings thus called on orthodox Protestants to forget their doctrinal
differences and unite against Romanist, freethinker, and infidel. On
the premise that no pious minister could ever be a Democrat, they
mercilessly attacked Protestant preachers who publicly worked for
Buchanan. William Brownlow turned his invective on these Locofoco
"Judases" with his customary combative flair. He accused a Georgia
Baptist minister of adultery, and a Missouri Campbellite of assault
and murder. He berated liquor-loving, "brawling tobacco-mouthed"
preachers who edited Democratic papers. He charged the Primitive
Baptist preacher in Newbern, Tennessee, with stealing from the post
office and deserting his destitute wife. The whole catalogue of Democratic moral degeneracy fused in "this Reverend, Foreign, Locofoco,
Judas Iscariot, Hard-Shell Baptist, Roman Catholic, Dry-Rot, Forging
and Stealing, Lying, Pierce and Reeder, Nebraska and Kansas, Johnson
and Liberty-loving old villain."[123]

Democratic radicals, insisted their Know Nothing critics, drank at this
well of irreligion and lax morality. Wicked southern fire-eaters wanted
the fanatical and unchristian Frémont to defeat Fillmore and thus create
a disturbed climate for southern secession. To these disunionists the *New
Orleans Bee* issued a scriptural warning: "lay not thine unhallowed
hands upon the ARK of our country." Northern free soilers, too, had
deeply infected the party and secured office in Pierce's double-dealing
administration. Foreign voters, who gave breath to the party, were
mostly freethinkers, Catholics, and "thoroughgoing Abolitionists."[124]
Romanists' social philosophy tended to erode slavery, asserted a North
Carolinian: wherever there have been social revolutions "the Church of
Rome has invariably thrown the whole weight of her moral influence in

favor of emancipation." It abhorred caste distinctions and slavery, he maintained with more ingenuity than conviction, because it ascribed to every priest "a mysterious spiritual dignity which entitles him to the unqualified reverence of every layman" and leveled every individual before the confessional. Free soilism served Rome's purposes in another way, too, for the sectional quarrels it provoked would open a weakened Union to papal conquest. For that reason, Anna Carroll explained, the Pope aimed "to drench our country in . . . vinegar and gall."[125]

Though in reality Frémont constituted no threat in the South, beyond a few pockets in the border states where emancipationists were strong,[126] he proved an extremely important whipping boy for both sets of opponents, by which their own southern orthodoxy could be measured. Southern Fillmorites linked Frémonters to the Catholic church, claiming that Archbishop Hughes had fused the Irish and the Black Republican vote, and had successfully imposed Frémont himself, a Roman emissary, as candidate instead of the good Methodist, Judge McLean.[127] At the same time Republicanism was based on the "villainous piety" of the "uncircumcised Philistines of New England," unsexed females like Harriet Beecher Stowe, and blasphemous, fanatical preachers.[128] When people went to church in the North, sneered the *Columbus Enquirer*, they had no chance of hearing Christ crucified. As a Louisiana Know Nothing insisted, "Abolitionism, religious fanaticism and Black Republicanism" were synonymous.[129]

Only the American party, its leaders declared, would conscientiously defend the Protestant Bible, the American Constitution, and the liberties of the South within the Union. As in the North, Fillmore emerged as Clay *redivivus*. Much was made of the support offered him by Theodore Frelinghuysen, Clay's evangelical running mate of 1844. The Reverend Lovick Pierce, a patriarch of southern Methodism, saw "the hand of God" in the movement. Party presses openly associated themselves with revivals and other religious causes. Tennessee Know Nothings claimed the overwhelming support of Methodist, Presbyterian, and Missionary Baptist ministers. "For a Protestant minister now, to make genuine Know Nothing speeches," a Fillmorite contended, "is only another name for preaching the Gospel of the Son of God."[130]

Southern Democrats, too, exploited the fears and prejudices of slave-state evangelicals. They matched the American party's publicists in stigmatizing the Republican clergy and their introduction of "the *Northern Puritan* Compass" into political life. But they proceeded to accuse Fillmorites themselves of direct involvement with these fanatics in a northern fusion of Know Nothingism, Black Republicanism, and Maine Lawism. Fillmore, they declared, opposed slavery extension, the Kansas–Nebraska Act, and southern rights generally.[131] His party's nativism was a smokescreen for its abolitionism. In 1855 Augustus B.

Longstreet had appealed explicitly to fellow southern Methodists not to join a party through which they would be associated with the anti-slavery clergy of the North.[132] Charles Dabney, tobacco planter and active Virginia Democrat, sought to persuade his brother Robert, Presbyterian minister and nativist sympathizer, that foreigners and Catholics constituted no serious threat to slave interests: "The true fanatic is the Yankee, and he persecutes the foreigner, and the Southern K[now] N[othing] helps him." To similar ends Alexander H. Stephens had earlier asked why, in view of Yankee Protestants' warfare against slavery, "we Southern men [should] join the Puritans of the North to *proscribe* from office the Catholics on account of their religion?"[133]

Fillmorites' elitism, religious intolerance, and fusion of church and state remained constant themes of Buchanan's southern supporters throughout 1856. As ministers made Know Nothing speeches, Democrats reflected sarcastically, "There can . . . be but few revivals going on. . . . What a good thing there are no heathens to convert nor devils to fight!" The editor of the Democratic *Nashville Union*, a scourge of "clerical politicians," cheered when the members of Buck Run Baptist church expelled their Know Nothing minister. "No man can serve God and the Devil at the same time," he purred. The *Montgomery Advertiser* derided Lovick Pierce's declaration for Fillmore.[134] Yet for all their sneering, Democrats themselves appealed openly to denominational loyalties and welcomed the support of evangelical clergy. They reminded Presbyterians that Buchanan and his running mate, John C. Breckinridge, were of that persuasion. In Tennessee Governor Aaron Brown, presenting himself as "the son of a now sainted father, late a Methodist minister," urged all Fillmorite Methodist preachers to defect to the Democrats. At an outdoor meeting, at Mossy Creek, composed mainly of Baptists, the Democratic speaker flourished a copy of Brownlow's *Great Iron Wheel Examined*, offensive to the Baptist church for its harsh criticisms of Elder Graves and "obscene pictures" of baptismal candidates, and castigated it as a Fillmorite production. A variety of southern Protestant ministers, particularly Baptist and Methodist, edited Democratic papers, attended the national convention at Cincinnati, and addressed party meetings. Their activities allowed Brownlow to jeer that Democrats had no principled objection to political preachers, merely a grievance against their overwhelmingly pulling for Fillmore.[135]

Changing patterns of Protestant partisanship

On election day, 4 November, the Old School pastor of the First Presbyterian church in Trenton, New Jersey, entered briskly in his diary: "I did not vote for Fremont, because &c nor for Buchanan, because &c

nor for Fillmore, because &c." But John Hall's reaction was unusually dismissive, and set him apart from the vast majority of his fellow evangelicals, north and south. Even the previously apolitical attached a special significance to the contest.[136]

In northern evangelical churches this deep engagement with politics reflected increasing unity of outlook and coherence of action. The double threat of slave power and Roman church encouraged political convergence. A writer in the *Democratic Review* jeered at Massachusetts divines "who, though they never agreed in one single point of faith, have become miraculously amalgamated in political doctrines." He rather missed the point that issues of doctrine and ecclesiastical practice no longer poisoned relations between evangelical churches as they had once done. Joel Hawes, Congregationalist minister of Hartford, Connecticut, reflected contentedly in 1854 on the unprecedented catholicity drawing the different churches into common projects. An Ohio Methodist rejoiced that a new generation of younger Methodist ministers had no experience of the "vauntings & thrusts" of despotic Calvinists.[137] Fearing Rome's ambitions, all evangelicals – whether Arminians or Calvinists, adult baptizers or pedobaptists – tended to bury their religious differences.[138] Social relations thawed, too, as Baptists and, especially, Methodists became more self-consciously respectable and influential citizens, through determined self-improvement and commitment to education.[139]

These changes smoothed the way for members of all evangelical groups, and of a variety of previous political orientations, to enter the Republican coalition. Most evangelical Free Soilers moved behind Frémont, many via the experience of Know Nothingism, others more directly through anti-Nebraska, Republican initiatives. Though a number of radicals took the chary view of William Crane, that the new party embraced far more unprincipled office-seekers than its pioneering fore-runners, many fiercely antislavery ministers, including Theodore T. Munger (Congregationalist), William N. Rice (Methodist), John Rankin (Presbyterian), and Oren Cheney (Freewill Baptist), cheered for Frémont as loudly as they had for Hale and Julian in 1852.[140] Even more important to the Republican cause were the votes of ex-Whigs from all evangelical denominations, whether they traveled, as did the Methodist local preacher Chauncey Shaffer, via Know Nothingism; or in a single hop like Charles Hodge, William Salter, and Colin Dew James.[141] Evangelicals also took their place amongst the relatively small proportion of ex-Democrats who contributed directly to the Republican amalgam.[142] The new party successfully severed the Democratic ties of many Methodists and Baptists in Massachusetts and elsewhere in New England, in Pennsylvania, and in parts of the Midwest.[143] Anson R. Graves's family, sincere Ohio Methodists, fled the party after the

Kansas–Nebraska Act. Roeliff Brinkerhoff, editor and Congregationalist, turned to the Republicans in 1856 as the only true guardians of the Jeffersonian tradition. German Methodists and Scandinavian Lutherans also defected.[144] Finally, of course, Frémont drew the support of many first-time evangelical voters. Sheldon Jackson, James Buckley, and others were only just of age. More significant still were those like Alvaro D. Field, who had shunned previous opportunities to vote, but now braved the first snow of winter and "voted the Republican ticket clean through."[145]

But just how complete was the Republican grip on the northern evangelical vote? Republican presses insisted that the party comprised "the great protestant body in America." The high public profile of activist Republican clergy, together with many evangelicals' private and public ruminations, appeared to confirm this claim. Observers reported near-unanimous Republicanism amongst the clergy in various Methodist conferences, Presbyterian synods, Congregational associations, and Baptist conventions. Greeley's *Tribune* judged the clergy of New York, city and state, to be overwhelmingly Frémont men. Similar claims were made for church members. Calvin Fairbank described a sea-change between 1850 and 1856 that turned Methodists from critics of antislavery radicalism into Republicans. According to a Presbyterian minister of Wyoming County, New York, every male member of his church was a Frémonter, as were all voting Baptists. An unsystematic poll in the Methodist Book Concern revealed a two-thirds majority for Frémont. Canvasses at Wesleyan Methodist and Freewill Baptist picnics yielded even better returns. Republicans laid claim to the support of Quakers, Moravians, Mennonites, Shakers, and others who had not voted for years.[146]

In reality, however, the picture was much less straightforward. Support for Frémont amongst northern Protestant clergy was indeed impressive, and amongst the membership of the more radical antislavery churches – Wesleyan Methodists, Freewill Baptists, Free Presbyterians, Associated Reformed, and Quakers, for instance – Republicans enjoyed overwhelming support.[147] The deacon of Sparta, Michigan, whose Freewill Baptist church expelled him for voting for Buchanan, knew all about a Republican monolith. But ministers' support for Frémont, which was by no means unanimous, more commonly tended to run ahead of their members'. Most clergy faced politically divided congregations. When the AHMS agent arrived at his new charge, in Middleport, Illinois, at the height of the campaign, he became the subject of a recruiting campaign by the churches' warring political factions.[148]

Many Whig-American evangelicals resisted Republican overtures. Alfred B. Ely, James W. Barker, Hiram Ketchum, and other nativists joined with political conservatives like William E. Dodge, James W.

Alexander, and Hugh Hodge to support Fillmore, whom they judged to be the most plausible sectional conciliator. Though Frémont in the main ran well amongst Congregationalists and New School Presbyterians, a small minority of them voted for the American party as the better anti-Democratic option. Other denominations furnished considerable numbers for Fillmore: Old School Presbyterians in New York and parts of the Midwest, Methodists in Pennsylvania, and Baptists and Methodists in Ohio, Indiana, and Illinois.[149] Many traditionally Democratic evangelicals, too, remained deaf to Republican entreaties and played a part in Buchanan's victory. Some of these, in Pennsylvania, Ohio, and especially Indiana, were Old School Presbyterians: conservative Unionists, they included such men as Nathan Rice, William A. Scott, Cyrus McCormick, and others with family or other ties to the slave states and southern Jacksonianism. Amongst the Dutch Reformed, traditionally anti-Yankee in outlook, few smiled on the Republicans. George Bethune, staunch Democrat, friend of Buchanan, and fierce defender of religious freedom, voiced his church's deeply felt hostility to the "petty popes" of Frémont's party. In New York state the denomination's vote split between Fillmore and the Democracy, with the Americans winning the larger share.[150] In Illinois and Indiana, Methodists and Baptists were more likely than not to be Democrats. Matthew Simpson teased his fellow Methodist, William Larrabee, president of the state institution for the blind and editor of an Indiana Democratic paper, that he was "the head of two blind institutions, the State Asylum, and the Democratic party," but the joke was on Simpson as the Indiana Republican party trailed behind Democrats and Americans in garnering evangelical Protestant support.[151] Further east, in Ohio, Pennsylvania, and New York, Baptists were far less likely to be Democrats and were markedly more committed to the Republican party than any other. Methodist Republicans outside New England, however, seem rarely to have predominated over Methodists of other political persuasions. Even in New England, where Methodists (and Baptists) were cutting their Democratic ties, older loyalties persisted. In Westfield, Massachusetts, the Methodist society, suspicious of Gilbert Haven's radical antislavery views, was "pretty evenly divided politically."[152]

As this picture suggests, local context continued to matter in shaping the ties between denomination and political party, just as it had done during the years of the second party system. But some generalizations are possible. Republicans enjoyed particular strength where New England religion and culture were most vigorous. In the main, Congregationalists were Republican. So too were most New School Presbyterians. In a number of states Republicans secured the lion's share of the temperance vote.[153] The dissenting churches of New England – Baptists and Methodists – had begun to shake themselves free of the chains of bitterness against the Congregationalist Standing Order. Their Democratic loyalties were melting fast in the region itself and in its diaspora. However, where southern and foreign migration into the free states had shaped church and local culture, and where hostility to "Yankeedom" remained strongest (especially in the lower counties of Pennsylvania, Ohio, Indiana, Illinois, and Iowa), Republicans made less headway against persisting Democratic influence.[154]

The volatility of northern politics in the mid-1850s went unmatched in the slave states. Party names changed, but the South experienced no fundamental shifts in loyalties on the scale of the free-state realignment. The American party's vote corresponded very largely to that of the defunct Whigs. Whatever initial interest southern Democrats took in the Know Nothing order largely evaporated once it had evidently become the refuge of their old enemies. In 1856 southern evangelicals remained very largely tied to their customary moorings. Sometime-Whig evangelicals like William Winans of Mississippi, Jacob Bachtel of Maryland, and Atticus Haygood of Georgia rallied to the sometime-Whig candidate, Fillmore. Meanwhile, John Mathews of Tennessee, Trusten Polk of Missouri, S.D. Hopkins of Virginia, and other Democratic loyalists remained determinedly true to Buchanan. Southern Americans claimed, in much the same way as Republicans in the North, to be the party of the pious in general and the clergy in particular. But in reality Democrats both held on to significant support amongst mainstream rank-and-file evangelicals and, in so far as loyalties were switched in the highly charged climate of 1856, successfully won over a number of doubting ex-Whigs. The Reverend Abraham Hagaman, Old School Presbyterian of Jackson, Louisiana, considered southern rights safer in Democratic hands, now that the old Whig party had yielded up the ghost. Concern over Know Nothing proscription of foreigners, as well as sectional defense, caused James Davidson, a Presbyterian of Fayetteville, North Carolina, to make a similar political journey. Whatever joy William Winans might have tasted at the religious conversion of his son turned to ashes as the young man voted for Buchanan.[155] Buchanan's victory elicited a deep sigh of relief from conservative evangelicals, north and south. In the words of a young Methodist lawyer, Robert Beale Davis, Democrats welcomed the new President as "the Savior of the country, and the only man who could have saved it." Fillmorites, too, took comfort in Frémont's defeat, and hoped conservative Unionism would set the tone of the new administration.[156] Yet amongst these same conservatives there remained considerable unease. "The signs of the times are dark and foreboding," sighed Robert Hall Morrison, less than two weeks after the election. "Our only hope for the Country is, that God can restrain the wrath of men, and defeat the counsels of the ungodly." Davis himself, taking a states-rights perspective on events, feared that "the South and the Conservatism of the Nation will be unable to curb the fanaticism of the North ... [;] before 4 more years have rolled around the Union will be dismembered." At the same time northern Democrats like George Bethune entered an ominously different caveat over Buchanan's success: the party's victory would only bring stability if the new President used his influence "to arrest the march of the slave power, and repress the violence of its reckless propagandism."[157]

While victory for Democrats was marred by defensive misgivings, Frémont's defeat could not shake a fundamental optimism amongst his evangelical supporters – though many of their initial reactions suggested otherwise. Gilbert Haven marked the occasion with a sermon on the "national midnight," which took as its text Ezekiel 2. 9, 10 ("lamentations, and mourning, and woe") and treated the result as a victory for Antichrist. Slavery, he now believed, might even advance into the free states.[158] While some pointed the finger of blame at the traditional scapegoats – Catholics and foreigners – evangelical Republicans widely took Buchanan's victory to be a measure of their own shortcomings. Antislavery northerners, Calvin Fletcher believed, "have so far participated in the wickedness of Slavery that God intends we shall suffer by it." The party as a whole had still not embraced full equality for black and white, radicals complained. In its concern for free white labor and suffering Kansas it had lost sight of the suffering slave. Anxious to win at all costs, Republicans had undervalued election prayer meetings and failed to maintain religious momentum.[159] Frémont's defeat was the Almighty's judgment on Republicans' fitness for power.

But defeat nourished hope. God, though reproachful, was evidently still speaking to his people. An organized antislavery party had carried whole states – eleven of them – for the first time. That party was unprecedented in having "so much of the life and power of religion flowing through its veins." Christians had "voted as they prayed, and prayed as they voted – for Christ and Caesar ... for eternal as well as for temporal good." The whole North, Haven marveled, had been "moved by the Spirit of God." Now the Lord demanded four more years of devotion. In return for study, discussion, and hard work, radical Oberliners insisted, "God will yet save a *remnant* at least of this nation." Frémont, or his successor, would surely win in 1860.[160]

These remarks, seen in the wider context of the emergence and consolidation of the Republican party, sustain the view that northern evangelicals were involved in the creation of a striking new fusion of religion and politics, through the agency of postmillennialism. Those historians who deny that the Republican party was "the political expression of pietistic Protestantism" are of course correct in a statistical sense, but they have tended to miss the point that northern evangelicals had over twenty years or so been developing a public discourse and a way of looking at political issues that would profoundly shape the way in which Republicans thought, and without which the party would have been a very different and much less effective force. Throughout the 1820s and 1830s evangelicals, north and south, had very largely expected to achieve the millennium through the agency of mission and Christian influence. Gradually, however, as political issues became thoroughly moralized during the 1840s and 1850s, an influential and growing body of northern evangelicals came to see the state itself as a means of introducing the millennial order. A form of postmillennial political evangelicalism, with its roots in Antimasonry and sabbatarianism, nourished the Whig, Free Soil, temperance and Know Nothing parties, and reached its apotheosis in the Republicans. That party, a political fusion of elements – sectional alienation and postmillennial aspiration – which originated outside electoral politics, became for many northerners the route to the Kingdom of God. Southern evangelicalism did not lack its postmillennialists, or its church members who invested partisanship with moral meaning, but they generally remained hostile to the open fusing of politics and religion, did not gravitate so strongly towards one political party rather than another, and crucially avoided identifying the advance of the Kingdom with a party triumph. The full implications of this disparity, however, were not yet clear in 1856.

Chapter 9

Houses Divided: Evangelical Churches and the Sundering of the Union, 1857–61

Hindsight allows historians of late antebellum America to impose the inevitability of a Greek tragedy on the accelerating events that between 1857 and 1861 swept the country into the vortex of civil war. The sequence of damaging and overlapping political developments between the election of Buchanan and the firing on Fort Sumter takes on the character of a litany. It begins with the Supreme Court's ruling in the Dred Scott case that Congress could not exclude slavery from the national territories, and continues with the open conflict between Buchanan's administration and southern interests, on one side, and Douglas Democrats and Republicans, on the other, over the proper locus of authority in Kansas and over the proposed proslavery constitution. There follows John Brown's conspiracy to seize the federal armory at Harper's Ferry and his abortive attempt to launch a slave uprising; and the victory in the 1860 presidential election, against a divided opposition, of a sectional candidate representing a party committed to the restriction of slavery and its ultimate extinction. The narrative concludes with the subsequent secession from the Union of seven states of the deep South and President Lincoln's stern defense of the Union's interests, which in turn provoked a violent response from southern nationalists manning the Charleston battery.

In this developing tragedy evangelical voices, north and south, have generally been treated as offstage noises rather than principals in the drama. Evangelicals' own providentialist language to some degree encourages this perception. Early in 1860 Robert L. Dabney expressed the view, especially common in the South, that "the omnipotent ruler of the Universe will . . . shape our destiny for his own wise ends – and that we should with supplication and submission look there for the result."[1]

In practice, however, evangelicals were hardly passive victims on the anvil of sectionalism. As well as working actively themselves to mold moral sensibilities in response to national political events, church leaders were also players in religious developments that would have profound implications for the Union. Bruising and persistent ecclesiastical conflicts – and, more surprisingly perhaps, the revival of 1857–58 – were deeply to influence evangelical thinking on secular, not just religious matters. In 1857 almost all evangelicals, north and south, regarded themselves as trustworthy guardians of a peaceable Union. Yet by April 1861 most southern Protestants were ready to rally to an independent Confederacy, while their northern counterparts vigorously supported a forcible reconstruction of the nation. Their allegiances to the gray and the blue sprang from their respective, and very different, moral visions.

From "*the* tawny *decision*" to "*the gospel of John Brown*"

Buchanan had barely settled into the White House before the modest political calm was again disturbed, by the Supreme Court's ruling in the case of the slave, Dred Scott. In response to Scott's claim that residing with his master in the free state of Illinois and the free territory of Wisconsin had made him a free man, Chief Justice Taney delivered an opinion that exposed him to charges not just of bad law but of moral dereliction. His declaration that American blacks could not be citizens drew down the wrath of antislavery evangelicals as an "inhuman and antichristian" ruling, one which removed constitutional privileges from half a million free blacks, many of whom, John Dixon Long protested, "are our brethren in Christ, and ambassadors from the Court of Heaven to sinful men." James Finley angrily preached on "the corruptions of . . . the *tawny* decision – crushing out a whole race, and at one dash of his pro-slavery pen reducing men to mere chattels."[2] But even more troubling was Taney's ruling that the Missouri Compromise was unconstitutional because Congress had infringed the slaveowner's constitutional right to carry property unimpeded into any of the national territories. The northern evangelical pulpit, presses, and denominational gatherings at once launched a sustained attack on what they regarded as the slave power's most shameless attempt yet to make slavery a national institution.[3]

Tancy's decision, according to the Baptist voice of the *Cincinnati Journal and Messenger*, showed that slavocrats had bound "the Supreme Court in submissive chains." A correspondent of its Methodist sister paper declared that the highest judicature had "licked the feet" of the slave power, its obeisance a further step towards reducing "every body and every thing" to the "sovereign sway" of the monster. The enslavement of free blacks and even poor whites would soon follow, and slaveholders would be allowed to transport their slaves without restriction through free states. Shortly, Robert Toombs and other planters would be seen "calling a roll of [their] . . . slaves on Bunker Hill." Yet Scripture nor Constitution nor history legitimized the Court's removing black rights and erecting slavery as the keystone of the republic. A differently composed court, they predicted, would eventually set aside Taney's judgment and revert to the Founding Fathers' position, that slavery was local and freedom national.[4]

A small minority of northern evangelicals demurred at this widespread attack on the Court, but to little effect. A few readers of Thomas Eddy's *Northwestern Christian Advocate* canceled their subscriptions in protest at the editor's stand.[5] The conservative *New York Observer* dismissed as "ravings" the asperities of George B. Cheever and other critics. Indeed, some of Cheever's own church members tried to remove him for his "violent objurgation" against defenders of slavery, but they were conspicuously absent when the matter was put to a church meeting.[6] Critics of the Court were of course open to the charge of playing party politics, given the Democratic connections of the chief justice ("the mere caterer of a political party," as the Reverend Abram Pryne dismissed him), and the Republican credentials of Justice John McLean (the "Christian-like" author of a "truly constitutional" dissenting opinion). But the firm stand of free-state clergy against Taney's ruling did them little harm with their members.[7]

Those, like Benjamin Crary, who wondered in the aftermath of the Dred Scott case "what iniquity . . . is to be on the carpet next" soon found their attentions tugged towards the miasmic politics of Kansas. For a while, in the winter of 1856–57 and the summer following, free-soil churchmen had expressed their modest confidence that under Governors James W. Geary and Robert J. Walker order was returning and Kansas would duly become a free state. "We have enjoyed the longest term of peace that we have [experienced] at any one time," the *Western Christian Advocate*'s Kansas correspondent wrote from Sugar Mound in July 1857. But those who counseled caution, fearing a plot to force slavery on the territory, were soon vindicated. An unrepresentative constitutional convention gathered at Lecompton, following elections marked by fraud and boycotted by free soilers. The emergent scheme nominally observed the principles of popular sovereignty but in fact protected slaveowners already living in Kansas and gave voters a choice only about the introduction of new slaves. Buchanan stood by the Constitution, deserted by Governor Walker and facing the combined forces of Republicans and alienated Douglas Democrats in Congress.[8]

For most free-state evangelicals, reading the writing on the wall, it was the President who had been weighed in the balance and found wanting. Church leaders were quick to conclude that the Lecompton scheme was "a most wicked trick and a fraud," a "high crime against God and liberty," perpetrated by a president who was the puppet of southern fire-eaters. Once more the slave power had engineered a plan marked by *"oppression, hypocrisy, deceit, falsehood, and violated faith."* James Gilpatrick, a Kansas Baptist minister, complained to eastern colleagues that the repealers of the Missouri Compromise in 1854 had got their way only by promising popular sovereignty; now they could see that local democracy in Kansas would result in peace, religious prosperity, and "freedom and equal rights to all" they sought to obstruct it. The fact was, declared the outraged *Christian Watchman and Reflector*, the President's policy towards Kansas derived from a "premeditated purpose to strike down liberty."[9] Douglas, by contrast, for successfully preventing congressional acceptance of the Lecompton constitution, basked in the unprecedented esteem of those who had previously treated him with suspicion or disdain.[10] Jonathan Blanchard, an old antagonist, continued to regret that the senator was no Christian but told him that his heroic efforts had expunged the worst memories of the fugitive slave and Nebraska bills, and placed him "'By act of God' on the side of freedom . . . against all the unconstitutional demands of the slave power."[11]

Dred Scott and Lecompton, then, appeared to offer the clearest evidence yet of the South's concerted plan to make slavery a national institution. And there seemed to be other elements in the strategy. Though Buchanan had declared his intention of suppressing filibustering in central America, those who believed that slave-power expansionists aspired to the annexation of Cuba and Nicaragua were kept in a high state of alarm by reports that hundreds of men in the Gulf states were preparing to sail into the Caribbean.[12] Just as disturbing were the southern proposals for reviving the African slave trade, which emanated especially from the Southern Commercial Convention, an annual talking shop for slave-state nationalists.[13] In reality only a small number of southern rights advocates desired the repeal of prohibitive laws, and most southern evangelicals, including a largely unanimous body of editors, found the proposals "monstrous" and "wicked." James Thornwell, slaveowner by marriage, summarized the prevailing objections when he fretted that reopening the trade would change the domestic-patriarchal character of slavery, dehumanize the system, endanger the South by importing "lawless savages," reduce the value of existing slaves, and encourage man-stealing and warfare in Africa. Nonetheless, antislavery evangelicals professed to detect a growing opinion in the South "that the foreign slave-trade is not piracy." When in the summer of 1858 the MECS expunged the historic General Rule that outlawed the buying and selling of men, women, and children with

the intention of enslaving them, northern Methodists mistakenly interpreted this as a major step towards reopening the traffic with Africa. A
New England Congregationalist concluded early in 1860 that the South's
growing "fever" on the subject indicated a growth in illicit importations,
which would soon be pronounced legal by a Supreme Court shameless
in advancing southern interests.[14]

While the course of political events drove northern evangelicals to
cultivate ever higher moral ground in the face of slave-power aggression,
their southern counterparts grew increasingly alarmed at what they
judged to be the intransigence and hypocrisy of the free states, and their
cavalier attitude to American law and institutions. Resistance to the
Dred Scott decision and Lecompton meant studied deafness to constitutional imperatives and willful sabotage of efforts to restore sectional
harmony in religion and politics So, too, did personal liberty laws
and underground railroads, which amounted to "nullification" of the
Fugitive Slave Law and "practical disunion." None of these, however,
operated to antagonize southern evangelicals nearly as effectively as
John Brown's raid on the federal arsenal at Harper's Ferry.[15]

Whether or not Brown intended the seizure of the armory as a
prelude to a massive slave uprising, evangelicals experienced the collective shudder of fear that ran across the South. They joined in calls for
vigilance: a fearful Virginian Methodist recommended "regularly drilled
volunteer companies, for any immergency [sic] that may . . . seriously
threaten our civil institutions." They shared too a general southern view
that the raid was the logical result of the Republicans' "inflammatory
denunciations of slavery," and that retribution should be swift: Brown
should be hanged for his "appalling wickedness" and "blasphemous"
act.[16] But what rather set apart slave-state evangelicals' experience
from their fellow southerners' was the deep betrayal they felt when an
ambivalent northern pulpit refused to declare Brown's actions unequivocally evil.

Many northern clergy of impeccable antislavery credentials took
the view that the raid had been foolhardy and wrong. The Michigan
Methodist, William Crane, conceded that Brown might be far more
innocent than Buchanan, but he could not accept that "these violent
massacres were calculated to benefit the slave or reform the slaveholder"; to avoid fueling sectional hatred he refused to preach on the
affair. For George Bethune, friend of Buchanan and staunch Democrat,
Brown's action had shown "what madness it would be to precipitate
changes by violence which the progress of the Gospel will bring about
peacefully"; to combat "appeals to the wildest fanaticism" he swallowed
his lifelong reservations about the public mixing of religion and politics
and stirringly addressed one of the great Union meetings in New York.
Amongst Republicans, Henry Ward Beecher disapproved of Brown's

"mad and feeble schemes" and shrank "from the folly of the bloody foray." Eden B. Foster considered Harper's Ferry the product of a "wild, misguided, perverted conscience": "I am living under the same constitution with the Slave States," he declared; "it does not allow me to incite slave rebellion." Like Bethune, he judged that "[a]rgument, love, and persuasion are all the weapons that we ... can employ."[17]

At the same time, however, other northern clergy, some of whom knew Brown personally, glorified him as an antislavery hero.[18] Nathaniel Colver wrote to Governor Wise of Virginia to declare that Brown's death would elevate him into "a pure and noble martyr to liberty, – to sympathy for poor, crushed, degraded and wronged humanity." Ten thousand Browns would rise up to take the place of "a good man, a noble man, ... no traitor to any law which God sanctions." Erastus O. Haven rejoiced that Brown, a "pure-hearted" liberator of the oppressed, had shown the world "that not all the blood in Northern arteries was water." Many, like the Congregationalist William W. Patton, distinguished between the raid itself (a "rash undertaking") and Brown's "nobility of character," which incorporated "[t]he sternest integrity, the highest sense of justice and honor, the most tender and womanly compassion, and yet the coolest daring and most unflinching fortitude." As a professing Old School Presbyterian and a man of prayer known for "the reality and fervency of his piety," he possessed "all the moral and mental qualities of a martyr and hero." William Salter called him "a Cromwellian Puritan" who more resembled "the warriors and saints of the Old Testament than the humble confessors and martyrs of the New."[19] At his death, church bells tolled and rousing church meetings gathered in his honor. Many rejoiced that the whole episode marked "the beginning of the end of American slavery."[20]

Fervent Unionists in southern churches attempted to salvage some message of hope out of northern evangelical reactions.[21] Nathan Lord's denunciation of Brown's enterprise, in his *Letter to J.M. Conrad*, first published in Virginia, was well received. Old School Presbyterians took comfort from their northern colleagues' disapproval of the raid.[22] The *North Carolina Presbyterian* commended the message to Congress of the nation's Old School President, in which Buchanan hoped that Harper's Ferry would be the means "under Providence" of reminding the nation of the value of the Union. None of this, however, significantly allayed the widespread alarm and betrayal aroused by northern paeans to Brown and his cause. The "vagabond philanthropists" and "*raving-pious pulpit* leaders," who cast Governor Wise as Pontius Pilate and turned a horse thief into a sainted, Christ-like "protomartyr," delivered a message, according to a Baltimore Methodist, "in which it was hard to decide which elements predominated, treason to our social compacts or blasphemy to God." Their "gospel of John Brown" was a gospel of "rifles, of revolvers, of pikes, of fire, murder, insurrection, and all the horrors of civil war." Augustus B. Longstreet concluded that "ultraism" and religious heterodoxy now dominated the North; a truly Christian society would have experienced "one spontaneous burst of indignation from Pennsylvania to the Lakes" and defrocked the ministers who took Brown's part.[23] Brown himself, regarded as a product and symptom of the North's flawed religion, had supposedly told Methodist preachers who visited him in prison: "I don't believe in . . . [Christ] as a Savior; I don't want any body else to bear my sins."[24]

Shortly after Brown's execution on 2 December 1859, the Reverend Theodore Munger reflected gloomily on the whole affair. "No single event, probably, within the generation has so deeply moved the people North and South," he wrote. "Never was there such danger of disunion." Many southern Unionists agreed with the Massachusetts clergyman. "No language can express my love for the Union," protested Richard Fuller, Baptist minister of Baltimore. "Hitherto I have smiled at all croaking about disunion; now I feel that the Union is in imminent danger." Despite the efforts of northern Unionists, he complained, "the South is denounced for not at once immolating four thousand millions of property guarantied [*sic*] to them by the Constitution; . . . for not breaking up their entire social system"; murderous northern fanatics created fears that prevented educational efforts to the slaves. Fratricidal warfare loomed, unless heaven interposed.[25]

"Good, and only good"?: slavery, church conflicts, and the Union under strain, 1857–60

Southern evangelicals of all denominations in the later 1850s commonly endorsed the view that the bonds of Union were "as sacred as those of the marriage relation, and as important as our life." The Union had brought liberty, religious toleration, educational progress, material prosperity, and geographical expansion to the republic. Its citizens, Augustus B. Longstreet told South Carolinian students, were "the greatest, the richest, the happiest, the holiest, the most Heaven-favored people on the globe." Many believed that a splintered republic would mean rivers of blood, economic disorder, turmoil for slaves, the interruption of Christian enterprise, and "the perishing of the hopes of freedom all over the world." Southern churchgoers had a clear sense of Christian duty in the face of these dangers. "My poor prayers," a Virginian Methodist, Anne Davis, told her stepson, "have been, and shall continue to be offered up to the throne of Heavenly grace in 'behalf of our beloved country.'" The Union for which they were prepared to contend, however, was one from which they expected in return the vigorous and willing protection of southern values and institutions – a Union which recognized the necessity and (now) the moral worth of slavery, and which exerted a "conservative christian influence" through orthodox Protestantism.[26]

By the later 1850s the idea of slavery as (in John Adger's words) "good, and only good" had taken even deeper root in the South's churches. "The dogma that slavery is sinful, or always an evil to both parties, is completely exploded," declared the *North Carolina Presbyterian*: Henry Ruffner, Robert J. Breckinridge, and earlier critics "find no supporters now in this section." A clear orthodoxy existed, centered on the propositions that slavery, consistent with both natural law and Scripture, was "justifiable in the sight of man and God"; that the system had yielded "untold and inconceivable blessings to the negro race"; and that political leaders had a duty to execute laws "for the protection of their property . . . and the punishment of intermeddlers."[27] Doubts remained, but in the main these were overridden. Anne Davis confessed that she "would gladly hail the day, when every son and daughter of Ham were free and independent in some country of their own." But, significantly, she added that "until that can be peacefully effected, . . . they had better remain in bondage under the care of good masters, than be free in the United States."[28] William Goff Caples recognized that evils existed in the relationship between slave and master, but these he judged inherent in the relationship between capital and labor, whether slave or free, and derived from "the evil that is inherent in the depravities of a fallen world." Many shared the view of the pugnacious Leroy M. Lee, the editor of the *Richmond Christian Advocate*, who pointed to the financial collapse, unemployment, and destitution of the northern states in 1857 and 1858 as evidence of the shortcomings in the free labor system. By contrast, he boasted, the South enjoyed "comparative prosperity, harmony in . . . social organization, and quiet and good order among all classes." In brief, the black slave was "the happiest class in society."[29]

But, complained southern evangelicals, far from respecting the South's social system and the scriptural Christianity that sustained it, the North had traveled further and further down the abolitionist road. And by definition that was the road of flawed religion. Caples asserted that abolitionism "bred disrespect for the Bible" and led ultimately to infidelity; a contributor to James Thornwell's *Southern Quarterly Review* exchanged cause for effect and declared abolition doctrine "a foul exhalation out of the Serbonian bog of New England Theology." Apply strict construction to the interpretation of Scripture as consistently as to the Constitution, insisted Elder John Clark, a Virginia Primitive Baptist, and there would be no antislavery fanaticism. Southerners widely believed that northern religion had set its course away from the "sound practical morality" of the slave states, from an emphasis on the Bible-focused morality and piety of the individual, towards heresy, humbug, and every "crazy *ism* known to the annals of bedlam."[30] Returning from New York City to the "conservatism, order and respect for religion" of North Carolina, George McNeill rejoiced to leave the "craziologists" and "strange exotics" behind him.[31]

Southern evangelicals, then, more and more resented being preached at by what they regarded as self-righteous Yankees whose corrupt theology and disrespect for social order increasingly threatened the Union's stability. John Brown's raid, though alarming in itself, was far more terrifying for being part of a larger process of northern aggression. That aggression impinged on southern Protestants not only through the sequence of political crises, but through persisting religious conflicts over the place of slaveholding in the churches.

The southern leaders of the Methodist Protestant church, for example, had fought for several years to prevent any antislavery modification to its Constitution and Discipline. Their life was made easier by successive defections of frustrated antislavery members into more radical bodies. But matters came to a head in 1858, when the General Conference at Lynchburg faced the demand of increasingly restive northerners and westerners that slaveholding and slave trading become formal barriers to church membership. After years of seeking to hold the denomination together, ministers like the alarmed William H. Wills of North Carolina now accepted schism, rather than make unacceptable concessions: "if they [free-state members] will not be content with the system as it is – why let them go."[32] As they saw it, yet another evangelical denomination had split as a result of northern hostility.

Episcopal Methodists' experience proved even more damaging to sectional harmony. Well before Brown's raid MECS spokesmen regarded abolitionism as "the *monomania* of the Northern Methodist Church" and froze with alarm when MEC preachers in the border conferences described their church as "the most powerful and systematic organization on earth against slavery." The resolutions of MEC annual conferences throughout 1858 and 1859, calling for resistance to slavery and encouraging slaves to run away, prompted southern Methodists to assert their right to drive "abolition emissaries" out of their territory. This explains the angry expulsion of lone individuals like the Reverend Solomon McKinney in Dallas, and the forced adjournment of MEC gatherings, especially the Arkansas Conference meeting under Bishop Janes in Bonham, Texas. "The M.E. Church invades our borders," complained the *Southern Christian Advocate* in the summer of 1859: "it comes on a crusade against our rights of property and our political institutions."[33]

After the volcanic rumblings of October 1859 the border operations of the MEC appeared all the more menacing. "It is a curious fact," ruminated William Brownlow, "that John Brown and his secret advisers selected a portion of Virginia lying within the bounds of the Baltimore Conference, as the most appropriate theatre of their operations." Here the MEC admitted black testimony against whites in church trials and refused to ordain slaveholders as local preachers. The church's influence was more dangerous to slavery than a dozen Harper's Ferry insurrections. Not only in western Virginia, but throughout the MEC's areas of operations in the slave states, vigilant southern Methodists took guard against its provocation and "sedition." In the summer of 1860, in a climate of increasing paranoia and fear, a Texan mob seized and hanged the Reverend Anthony Bewley, a member of the Arkansas Conference stationed at Hamilton Valley. Spokesmen for the MECS declared him complicit in "murderous abolition plots of insurrection and bloodshed," one of "the advance guard of . . . [the] Black Republican party." He had, they claimed, no legitimate business in Texas, which under the Plan of Separation was MECS territory. If, as northerners insisted, he really was a pious man, then no harm had been done: "hanging was 'a short cut' to the Kingdom of God."[34]

Events within the northern church during the summer of 1860 appeared to the leaders of the MECS only to confirm the wisdom of their independent existence. The MEC General Conference of 1856 had failed to resolve the issue of communicant slaveholders, since when the church had suffered the defection of several upstate New York radicals.[35] The border conferences enjoyed no respite from the taunts of the denomination's fiercer antislaveryites, who were determined to force the issue at the 1860 General Conference in Buffalo.[36] Their efforts to change the General Rule on slavery narrowly failed to secure the necessary two-thirds majority. But the conference did agree an alteration in the chapter on slavery (an advisory declaration of sentiment), which deemed the institution "contrary to the laws of God and nature" and against the rule requiring Methodists "to avoid evil of every kind."[37] In the South, this outcome deeply unsettled MEC preachers in the border states, threatening secessions in the Baltimore Conference in particular, while MECS leaders interpreted events in Buffalo as the triumph of "rampant Abolitionism." Northern Methodists had clearly become the ecclesiastical agents of William Seward and the Black Republican party.[38]

Similar anxieties shaped the thinking of many southern Presbyterians, principally within the New School branch. The General Assembly of 1857 "earnestly condemned" the presbytery of Lexington for declaring that ministers, elders, and ordinary members often held slaves "from principle" and "of choice." The Assembly did not criticize all slaveholders, believing that they included those who sought the well-being and ultimate emancipation of their slaves. But many southern Presbyterians and their allies in other denominations protested angrily at a resolution which they regarded as the culmination of years of abolitionist agitation and which "degraded" the southern church, jeopardized New School Presbyterian harmony, and "add[ed] to the peril of the union of these United States." Some 15,000 communicants seceded, most of them to form the new United Synod of the Presbyterian church.[39]

Other southern ecclesiastical bodies enjoyed a less fraught relationship with their northern counterparts. Baptists exulted that they had "suffered less from the slavery agitation than any other denomination of equal size" because of their churches' autonomy and the lack of fellowship between northern and southern branches. Old School Presbyterians, conscious that only they, Episcopalians, Catholics, and Primitive Baptists could claim to be truly national denominations, rejoiced in the "good sense, piety and conservatism" of their church, and contrasted the harmony of their 1860 General Assembly at Rochester with the bitterness of the recent MEC General Conference in nearby Buffalo.[40] Nonetheless, Old School southerners were uneasily aware that the church contained those who wanted it to follow the antislavery road taken by the New School Assembly in 1857, and that even anti-abolitionist ministers like Nathan Rice refused to accept the notion of slavery as a God-given good. Equally, the annual, if unsuccessful, attempts of northern radicals to get the ATS to address slavery (having brought the AHMS largely into line) created chronic southern anxieties.[41] And in the late 1850s the sizeable abolitionist defection from the Disciples of Christ, who had prided themselves on escaping the worst of the sectional bitterness in the churches, signaled their vulnerability, too.[42]

Northern evangelicals' commitment to American nationality – no less heartfelt than southerners', but different in goal – was inspired by a vision of the Union as a crucible of republican liberty. Casting their country in the role of God's appointed guardian of freedom and Christianity, most free-state evangelicals rebuked Wendell Phillips, William Lloyd Garrison, and other radical antislavery disunionists for pursuing a strategy which would surely cut slaves adrift from liberating influences. Their freedom would more certainly come through a Union that encouraged the gradual working of benevolent Protestant influences, possibly aided by colonization of freed blacks and perhaps the financial compensation of the emancipators.[43] But, to the mounting anxiety of northern evangelical leaders, southern churches were no longer proving trustworthy allies in that campaign and seemed instead to have become an adjunct of proslavery aggression.

Many northern clergy tried to believe the best of their southern counterparts. Some optimistically insisted that the efforts of slave-state

Evangelicals and Politics in Antebellum America

Christians would in time remove the peculiar institution. Others noted, in mitigation of church inaction, that the voice of humanity was "drowned by the outcry of wicked men and interested politicians." But more commonly free-state evangelicals reached the unmistakable conclusion, as a contributor to the *Christian Watchman and Reflector* put it, "that the sentiments of southern Christians have been misinterpreted, or are undergoing a singular revolution." Leonidas Hamline had no doubts. "Thirty years ago scarcely a man in the South justified, but simply excused, slavery. Now," he lamented, "nobody there excuses but justifies it – and *'O tempora! O mores!'* – by the Bible, perverted to that base end." Abel Stevens reflected bitterly on this "great apostasy," by which the South's moral sense had been "overthrown and confounded." Southern preachers, bewailed another, had come to rival politicians in their capacity for "twaddle about its [slavery's] benign influence."[44]

Evidence crowded in from all sides. The new United Synod, formed by the arch-supporter of slavery Frederick A. Ross and other New School seceders, was clearly "organized for the simple purpose of giving the sanction and support of Christianity to southern slavery." The "time-serving policy" of the "ultra conservative and ultra timorous" ATS showed it had succumbed to the grip of "horrible modern pro-slaveryism."[45] James Thornwell and his fellow Old School Presbyterian theologians produced formulations on the proper province of the church that denied the "Calvinistic," theocratic traditions of Puritanism and celebrated a more private devotionalism: many northerners, radical and moderate, believed they thereby aimed to remove existing formulations on slavery, including the declarations of 1818 and 1845, and to open the door to "radical Pro-Slavery ultraism."[46] Similar northern reactions followed southern Methodists' expunging all testimony to the evil of slavery from the MECS Discipline in 1858.[47] When slaveholding members of the Philadelphia Conference of the MEC brought to trial their colleague John D. Long for publishing attacks on their "mercenary" slaveholding, it seemed clear that the revolution in sentiment was not restricted to the lower margins of the South.[48]

Northern evangelicals watched in shock as southern churches condoned a more physical aggression to supplement their doctrinal muscularity. Free-state delegates absented themselves from the Lynchburg Methodist Protestant General Conference in 1858 in part because they feared mob violence and forcible imprisonment. The 200-strong mob, armed with revolvers and bowie knives, that broke up the Arkansas Conference and drove it out of Texas was headed by a prominent MECS layman. Again and again in border areas, claimed the *Christian Advocate and Journal*, southern Methodists cooperated with secular authorities to persecute the MEC and force her members into the southern church.[49] A northern Methodist itinerant in western Virginia complained of the debilitating effects of hostile scrutiny and persistent questioning: "if you do not become half proslavery at least you are set down as an *Abolitionist* and consequently your influence is destroyed." From Baltimore, after the Brown affair, Thomas Sewall reported intense pressure on the city churches to separate from the MEC: this made the preacher's position ever less tenable and turned his people "into the ranks of martyrs." Grimmest of all, Anthony Bewley's dangling corpse cast a morbid shadow across northern Methodism and beyond, his murder the "diabolical deed" of a religious community under slave-power control.[50]

The historian Bertram Wyatt-Brown has shown how southern politicians' appeals to the honor code in the later 1850s encouraged southerners to suppress "higher-law" politicians and preachers. Though many southern evangelicals were ambivalent in their reactions to the demands of that code, particularly towards dueling, the compatibility of the Manichean perceptions of the world of honor with the dualisms of evangelical Protestant theology helps explain the ease with which southern churchgoers accepted tarring, feathering, whipping, and even hanging to protect southern civilization.[51]

This "extremism" of southern churches induced northern observers to see a crisis approaching, "when it will be impossible for any Christian to occupy neutral ground." Southern politicians, they argued, had step by step forced northern allies to accept the universality of slavery: Southern Christians, in league with the slave power, expected similar compliance from free-state churches. "They will not be content with non-interference but will demand strict approval" of slavery as "a blessing to both races," declared the *Christian Watchman*. In this crisis, though "many will make the needed concession" and yield conscience to expediency, "the great body of northern Christians will . . . take higher ground." Northern Christians had to act. Edward N. Kirk described the sea-change in his attitude once he had heard Benjamin Palmer of New Orleans announce that the South's glorious mission was to construct a church and a state around the cornerstone of slavery: he would compromise and delay no longer.[52] An intransigent South, diverging from the republic's historic and divinely sanctioned course, must be challenged and drawn back into the enlightened community of the wider English-speaking world.

A substantial minority of northern evangelicals, conservative Unionists worried about the centrifugal forces around them in church and state, feared confrontation and sought strategies for sectional cooperation. Such, for instance, were the men who fashioned the Southern Aid Society in protest at the other northern-based mission societies' antipathy towards slaveholding churches. Founded in 1853 by Henry Rowland, Ansel D. Eddy, Samuel H. Cox, and other conservative ministers and laymen, some of them politically active Whigs and Democrats, and sustained financially by merchants, bankers, and manufacturers with southern connections, the society sought to help struggling Calvinist churches throughout the South and Southwest. Its operations and finances remained limited, ostracized as it was by antislavery Christians. Though attractive to a small number of Unionist evangelicals and even non-churchgoers who admired its "national attitude," it became a victim of the very sectionalism it sought to remove, and disbanded itself in 1861.[53]

More commonly, northern evangelicals failed to understand that what they considered their defensive protection of the republic's original values (that is, restoring the nation's antislavery consensus) seemed to southern churches aggressive interference with traditional ways. They professed a conservative intent, unmoved by the charge that their rhetoric and actions would alienate the South and jeopardize the Union. Many took Asa Turner's view, that disunion was a necessary and manageable risk to be run: excising slavery demanded the knife, even if it meant the shedding of blood. In fact, the most firmly antislavery of northern clergy tended to treat the warnings of southern disunionists as mere bluster. Outside South Carolina and a few earnest individuals in the Gulf states, disunion seemed to be "a mere game of the politicians ... to frighten the ... Yankees." Given the ties of religion, family, commerce, and geography, the *Christian Advocate and Journal* reassured its readers, "we no more fear for the Union than for the moon."[54]

"*A precursor to some great event*": the revival of 1857–58

As the sense of national crisis deepened in the later 1850s American churches experienced what they judged to be a remarkable outpouring of God's spirit. The extraordinary revival of 1857–58 found its immediate origins in the midday interdenominational prayer meetings set up in the business district of New York City in September 1857 to call down God's mercy at a time of financial panic. Similar union meetings and more conventional revival services soon spread to other cities and towns across the country. By the end of the following year the main evangelical denominations had recruited several hundred thousand new members.[55] At the height of the excitement, in the spring of 1858, George Duffield judged that, though the millennium itself might not be immediately at hand, "it is a great and wonderful day in the Ch[urches] of Christ, and a precursor to some great event." After the Civil War evangelicals kept faith with the millennialist tone of earlier reflections when they wondered, in Anna R. Eaton's words, whether "the baptism of holy fire [was] then preparing our beloved land for the baptism of blood so soon to follow?"[56] Modern historians of antebellum America, too, though not entirely confident about the precise connection between the "awakening" and the momentous events that followed, sense a significant relationship between the two.[57]

Lyman Abbott's life-changing involvement in the movement led him years later to agree with James Ford Rhodes that the revival was "the most extensive and thorough ever experienced in America." The teenage Anson Graves, on the other hand, recalled three months of nightly meetings on the Illinois prairie which made him "earnest and happy" for a while but left him "a downright atheist." A revival that so variously affected its subjects does not encourage facile generalizations. Men and women – as converts, counselors, and engaged bystanders – developed a variety of often conflicting expectations from their personal and collective experiences. As James Moorhead has sensibly remarked, the revivalists' encouragement to converts to "stand up for Jesus" and obey his trumpet call gave them enormous leeway to decide for themselves what kind of society the Lord wanted them to build.[58]

In some ways the revival deserves to be seen as the expression of an evangelical impulse towards harmony and Christian reconciliation. The businessmen's prayer-meetings and other revival services drew together in the simple Gospel of repentance and salvation thousands who, like Nathan Bangs, had "laid aside the polemic armour." The *New York Observer* rejoiced that the revival had created an "era of good feelings" between Christians who had forgotten "all past alienations and distractions." Even Episcopalians and Unitarians responded with some enthusiasm.[59] The occasional Catholic accession to evangelical ranks encouraged anti-Romanists to conclude that Catholic belief would dissolve in the heat of Protestant revivals and that Popery could only survive in the New World through immigration.[60]

The revival also offered the hope, and even the reality, of social harmony at a time when banking collapses and economic recession threatened the loss of jobs and financial ruin. Fearful that widespread poverty might generate "some uncontrollable and fearful storm," middle-class evangelicals watched with evident relief as revival meetings seemed to foster class harmony. In the New York City meetings lawyers, physicians, bankers, and manufacturers knelt alongside clerks, mechanics, butchers, bakers, porters, and wagonmen. "Old men and young men, men of all conditions and social standings, here meet as equals and as brethren," reported an impressed observer at the Dutch Reformed church in Fulton Street. In this and similar gatherings across the Union, evangelicals demanded – and briefly secured – gospel standards in behavior. "Prayer never was so great a blessing to me as it is in this time!" exclaimed one New York businessman. "I should certainly either break down or turn rascal, except for it!" Merchants confessed to extortion and pledged themselves to gospel practice in future. For a while a harmonious Christian republic beckoned, as theaters closed, grocery keepers poured away their liquor, and prostitutes lost custom.[61]

Most significant of all, many evangelicals in the mid-1850s looked for a nationwide revival of religion, and celebrated its ultimate arrival, as an antidote to destructive political excitement. Henry C. Fish insisted that only a revival could prevent the country's being "rent asunder by internal divisions"; George Bethune regarded the Gospel as the only suppressant of current political jealousies. But a precondition for revival was the very political harmony its promotion was designed to achieve. Political calm depended on revival, but revival depended on peace. Evangelicals widely complained that what one Methodist in 1856 called "the moral desolation of our Zion" was a direct result of political excitement and sectional antagonism. After the November election of that year many hoped for new vigor in the churches. "Now that the political strife is over," a Methodist explained, "we are looking, in New England, . . . for a season of general revival." The conservative Unionists of the *New York Observer* expressed the hope in the summer of 1857 that the God who had safely led the country through the perils of the last twelve months would now bless "a happy, peaceful and united people."[62]

Once the revival was under way many of its architects worked diligently to ensure that it would, as a Philadelphian put it, "harmonize sectional differences."[63] New York City prayer meetings carried notices forbidding the discussion of "controverted points," to keep slavery off the agenda. Given the Unionism and southern commercial connections of those who provided the backbone of the revival in its earlier phase, the city's merchant class, the prohibition was especially comprehensible.[64] To avoid stirring partisan feelings, whenever revival meeting leaders were asked to pray for named politicians they studiously passed over the requests in silence.[65] Southern ministers, so often treated as pariahs in the North, found a welcome there. The revival's conservative inclusiveness attracted the scorn of some radical abolitionists. Significantly, Garrison condemned the movement as "an emotional contagion" which diverted attention from reform and "practical righteousness" into "a pharisaical piety and sectarian narrowness."[66]

Ultimately, however, the revival did little to allay the sectional controversy and, as Leonard W. Bacon later reflected, "it may have deepened and intensified it." The movement certainly reinforced ethical perspectives and conflicting sectional images that did nothing to further national harmony. In the North, Garrison's dismissive criticisms notwithstanding, the revival generated a highly charged sense of social responsibility in many of its converts, a passion to carry the message of life and love to others, including the slaveholder and the drunkard.

Henry Ward Beecher's revival meetings in Plymouth church electrified Lyman Abbott, then working as a young lawyer in New York City. Helped to an understanding of the "new Calvinism" of Charles Finney, the Beechers, and Albert Barnes as a doctrine intended to shape "life and conduct," he abandoned law for the ministry, to devote himself to "a new and divine life of faith, hope and love." He was firmly convinced of the revival's invigorating contribution to antislavery and temperance movements.[67] Younger still than Abbott were the tens of thousands of Sunday School and Bible class scholars, male and female, very often children of church members, who constituted so large a proportion of the new converts. Their instructors included those who looked to Sunday Schools and other institutions as nurseries of the nation's "future statesmen and patriots," where the ethical instruction of boys and young men would prevent their becoming "compromisers and slave-catchers."[68] In due course the Union armies would draw many of their recruits from amongst these young Christian scholars.

Northern evangelicals concluded that the Almighty had picked them out for special favor. Few doubted that the "awakening" was a genuine and spontaneous blessing from on high, as opposed to a manufactured excitement "got up" by human technique. Significantly, God's "blessed flood of light" had illuminated northern churches in particular. The revival's origins in the north-eastern cities, its spread into the small towns and villages of the free states, and its belated, imitative, and seemingly ineffectual progress through the South indicated to northern churches God's approval of the free states' social arrangements and confirmed their belief that slavery had corrupted the quality of southern religion.[69] According to a New Hampshire Congregationalist, writing before the outbreak of revival, the moral sense of people in the South was "exceedingly obtuse"; religion there was "severed from morality." John D. Long insisted that southerners' attachment to slavery made them deaf to God's commands. Sharp social distinctions in churches worked against the egalitarianism essential to religious progress. When revivals did occur, slavery destroyed their fruits, since it was "opposed to . . . personal effort to attain perfection."[70] Abram Pryne denounced a religion "that prays – and steals negroes; that sings psalms – and whips women." Slavery's practices explained to Finney, the high priest of revivals, why "the Spirit of God seemed to be grieved away from" southern churches. It was doubtful if the millennial day would ever arrive while "Christian slaveholding" flourished.[71]

Southerners, however, while welcoming evidence of northerners' turning to Christ, showed no sense of inferiority. They refused to fret unduly about southern churches' relative exclusion from the religious excitement during the early months of 1858. The *Southern Christian Advocate* offered a climatic explanation: the North's longer winter offered more leisure for religious services; southern efforts would come later, reaching their climax at the end of summer, the customary season for camp and protracted meetings. Throughout the spring and summer months all the South's evangelical bodies sought to emulate northern churches.[72] Their meetings in general had little of the drama, novelty, and inventiveness of the Union arrangements in northern cities, but their more conventional methods still yielded enough conversions for celebration.[73] Some believed the South uniquely blessed, convinced that the revivals allowed her churches to look forward to the day when, as an Alabama Methodist predicted, "millennial glory shall fill the world." They saw the southern awakening as a vindication of slavery and missions to the blacks. The presbytery of Fayetteville, North Carolina, reporting large additions "from the colored people," concluded that "God is calling us to more enlarged and earnest efforts" for the improved religious condition of the slave population. At the same time southerners, having initially welcomed the revival in the free states as evidence of the North's enhanced religious feeling, soon retreated to repeating their previous criticisms of deficient Yankee theology and morality. A southern Methodist visitor to New York in September 1858 lamented the Sabbath-breaking, drunkenness, and other vices which, despite the recent revival, still scarred the city's face. New England's capacity for "appalling apostasy" from religious truth remained an issue.[74] By 1860 hopes of a revival-inspired *rapprochement* between northern and southern evangelicals had withered, and the moral chasm separating them was wider than ever.

Speaking to the conscience of the nation: the election of 1860

When Americans went to vote for their President in November 1860 politics had become irretrievably sectional. At its national convention in May the Democratic party had split over whether Congress should positively protect slavery in the territories. It had subsequently fielded two separate tickets: one headed by Stephen A. Douglas, hero of those (mainly northern) Democrats who admired his defense of popular sovereignty and his stand against the proslavery antics of the Buchanan administration; and another, headed by John C. Breckinridge, nominee of the Charleston seceders, who advocated a protective federal "slave code" for the territories. The campaign in the South had principally pitted Breckinridge against John Bell and his running mate Edward Everett, candidates of the newly fashioned but distinctly traditionalist Constitutional Union party, barely camouflaged heirs of the Fillmorite Whig-Americans. In the most meaningful contest in the free states Douglas had faced Abraham Lincoln and a Republican party confidently united on a platform similar in its antislavery orientation (though not its tone) to that of 1856.[75]

In the North three issues in particular, all at the heart of the election debate and all with a perceived bearing on the course of American republicanism, engaged the moral sensibilities of evangelical Protestants: the spread of slavery, Catholicism, and political corruption. This was the terrain on which, as one religious paper put it, each party sought "to establish itself in the conscience of the nation" as the voice of truth and righteousness. As in 1856, the Republicans worked hardest to be seen occupying the highest moral ground, flavoring their national, state, and local conventions with prayer, and engaging clergymen in their cause. Although Republican gatherings in 1860 were less militantly temperate than they had been during the Frémont campaign, Democrats still jeered at "the party that claims ... all the piety." Bell–Everett forces, too, described it as working "in the very vein and spirit of a religious Sect," with a "holy zeal for its one idea."[76] They were, in fact, mistaken in seeing Lincoln's campaign as a one-idea exercise: Republicans exploited a range of issues, including a protective tariff and a homestead act, with the interests of the pivotal states of Pennsylvania and Illinois firmly in mind. But they were nonetheless correct to imply that the foundation of Republicans' strategy lay in exploiting popular fears about slavery's becoming a national institution.

The Republicans' antislavery message converged with the trenchant and simultaneous demands of evangelicals' sermons and church resolutions that government block the "steady and tireless march" of aggressive slaveholders. Though the party's platform dropped the harsher language of 1856 and denounced John Brown's raid, it stood unequivocally against the extension of slavery, the revival of the African slave trade, and disunionism, and included an endorsement of the Declaration of Independence.[77] Republicans set the antislavery battle in a gospel context and, persisting with the Whig style of "hurrah" campaigning they had enlisted in 1856, appealed for Christian soldiers to rush to arms in what George W. Julian described as "a fight ... between God and the Devil – between heaven and hell!" William Burleigh told the Brooklyn "Wide-Awakes" (as Republican clubs were called) that Seward's celebrated "irrepressible conflict" speech of 1858, asserting a fundamental antagonism between free and slave labor and the societies erected upon them, was in essence "Christ's doctrine of righteousness conflicting with evil." Republican songs, including the "Freedom Battle Hymn," encouraged voters to march "On for freedom, God, our country, and the right."[78]

Party leaders also appealed directly to denominational loyalties and, as in 1856, exploited the indignities suffered by free-state churches at the hands of the slave power and its ecclesiastical sympathizers. They condemned the "gag rule" that northern "doughfaces" imposed on the ATS to sustain the southern oppressor. They rebuked slavery's allies in southern Illinois for burning an "abolitionist" Sunday School library, dismissing the school's teachers, and cutting the ministers' salaries to punish their supposed Republicanism.[79] They exploited the trial and four-month imprisonment of Daniel Worth of North Carolina, a sixty-two-year-old Wesleyan Methodist minister and an agent of the abolitionist American Missionary Association, who had been arrested for "incendiary" activity: circulating copies of *The Impending Crisis*, a notorious critique of slavery's economic effects by a North Carolina non-slaveholder, Hinton Rowan Helper. Following Worth's release on bail he fled to New York, where Lewis Tappan arranged a speaking tour that allowed the party to laud the "estimable clergyman" as a "martyr of freedom."[80] Anthony Bewley's murder elicited a highly charged response from Republican publicists, especially after Thomas Eddy, the editor of the Chicago *Northwestern Christian Advocate*, had written a public letter to President Buchanan calling for government protection of MEC ministers in slave states. "Is our blood," he asked, "to be shed like water to appease the insatiable Moloch of Slavery?" The one million Methodists of the North had previously been politically divided but "'oppression maketh a wise man mad'" and would, he predicted, unite them behind any party willing to "protect the rights of conscience and the freedom of worship." Republicans eagerly turned Eddy's letter into a campaign document and badly disconcerted the Democratic press.[81]

Douglas Democrats adopted three lines of response to the Republicans' attempt to seize the moral ground. First, they denied that slavery was unequivocally against God's law. Where were the signs of the Lord's wrath? "What nation on the globe has been so wonderfully and bountifully blest as this people under our Constitution[?]" An omnipotent God would provide the means for the removal of slavery, John L. Dawson told a party gathering, "at the very moment when it shall be to the advantage of the negro." Secondly, the real evil in the nation was not slavery but the sinful violations of the principle of self-government. Douglas's doctrine of popular sovereignty, Democrats insisted, embraced the fundamental tenet of American republicanism, that (white) people everywhere had the right to make their own laws. Republicans' opposition was immoral as well as impolitic.[82]

Thirdly, and most insistently, Douglasites warned against Lincoln and his party as an avowedly sectional force which would destroy the "sacred ties" of the Union. Douglas and congressional "non-intervention" in slavery were "the *only* true and safe" means of sustaining a Union that guaranteed the nation's religious progress, and civil and religious liberty for all. The Bell–Everett camp argued to the same end.

The Republican party's "frenzied belief" that it was "the minister of a higher law than govern[ed] anybody else" gave it the character of an exclusive sect inimical to a society like the United States, "where all opinions, moral, religious and political, not in violation of the Constitution, must be free." A substantial number of Unionists, including the Alabama congressman, Methodist preacher, and ex-Whig, Henry W. Hilliard, called for a righteous fusion of Douglas, Breckinridge, and Bell forces, and this is what occurred in New York, New Jersey, and Rhode Island.[83]

That Bell's sometime Know Nothings could agree on fusion with the party of the Irish, the Catholics, and immigrants' rights dramatically signified their highest priority: preventing the election of a sectional, antislavery President.[84] But while nativism and Protestant–Catholic hostility were of secondary importance in national politics in 1860, they still helped shape the election result. To win the presidency Lincoln needed to capture a large part of Fillmore's free-state nativist vote of 1856. His victory owed much to Republicans' being able and willing to hum a Know Nothing tune with as much conviction as Frémont four years earlier – indeed with more.

Democratic opinion-formers certainly insisted that the Republican party was under the thumb of nativists, and contrasted its "hypocrisy" with Douglas's "bold and manly" stand against Know Nothingism. The Little Giant, they declared, professed the Jeffersonian doctrine that government had a duty "to establish social and political equality among the varieties of religious faith."[85] Republicans, by contrast, were the natural allies of "blue-light puritans" and "fanatical Sabbatarians." As one Democrat complained, the Republican party sought to impose New England morality on the whole society: if it "had not slavery for a hobby, it would be vexing us about some other questions of morals or of social arrangement." In New York, for instance, the party "delight[ed] in Prohibitory liquor bills and intollerant [*sic*] Sabbath laws." It had joined with illiberal Presbyterianism to pass new restrictions on Sunday drinking and entertainment, saying to the poor: "No music but psalms; and no drink but water."[86]

In fact, Republican leaders were concerned to consolidate and even to extend their hold over immigrant – especially antislavery, Protestant immigrant – voters. Though Horace Greeley was reluctant to issue appeals to the Germans or Irish as such, since "[h]e who votes in our elections as an Irishman or German has no moral right to vote at all," Republican strategists were generally less squeamish. They invited delegations of German Republicans from each of the free states to the national convention in Chicago. They established a special campaign bureau under Carl Schurz to win over the immigrant vote.[87] The party nominated a candidate not tainted with Know Nothingism and rejected another (Edward Bates of Missouri), who was. It adopted a platform which explicitly condemned legal efforts to abridge or impair the rights of citizens, and included a homestead law offering benefits to immigrants. Further, wherever Bell and Douglas forces moved towards fusion, "cuddling under the same dirty bed-clothes," Republicans denounced "the confusion ticket" for deceiving the foreign-born: though Douglasites protested that the alliance drew in only those ex-Fillmorites "who were never tainted with the . . . proscriptiveness" of Know Nothingism, in reality "British Whigs" and nativists dominated the partnership. Irish Wide-Awake clubs catered in a number of cities for "Irish friends" who did "not like to wear the *Orange* uniforms of the 'Little Giants.'"[88]

But wooing immigrants was only one side of the Republican strategy. The party courted strict Fillmore Americans as assiduously and successfully as it had in pivotal local and state contests throughout 1858 and 1859.[89] During the later 1850s Republicans' support in many areas for nativist, especially anti-Catholic, legislation (including voter-registration and sabbatarian laws, though rarely prohibition) fostered their image as an anti-Romanist party. So, too, did their nominating known nativists for political office. Though in 1860 the party kept its national platform clean, many of its nominees for office, including the electoral college, were known nativists.[90] William Seward's bid for the presidential nomination failed in part because his record when governor of New York on the public school issue, and his persisting closeness to the Catholic hierarchy, "made him an impossible candidate."[91]

The Republicans' propaganda machine studiously kept the Catholic issue before native and foreign-born voters, not least because of the persisting conviction that the Roman church was in cahoots with the slave power. The Catholic press had defended the Dred Scott decision; lauded popular sovereignty; linked the "revolutionizing" Republicans to a "seditious" Protestant pulpit; rejoiced in the Democratic doctrine "that it is not the business of the political power to settle moral questions"; and declared Douglas "the *true* 'Union candidate'."[92] That Catholics, and especially John Hughes's *New York Freeman's Journal*, widely endorsed Douglas made all the more plausible what some Republican editors falsely whispered about his relationship with Rome. Recently married to a Catholic wife, the senator (they alleged) had himself converted and become, in Hughes's words, "a good and faithful member" of the church. Insisting to the foreign-born that Douglas was a furtive nativist, Republicans simultaneously alerted nativists to the Little Giant's closet Romanism.[93]

Closely linked to the Republicans' use of anti-Catholicism was their emphasis on corruption in the Buchanan administration. Whigs in 1840 had exploited a popular sense of moral malaise in an Augean national government, after twelve years of Democratic rule, and presented Harrison as a purifying agent. In 1860 the Democrats once more faced the charge that, after a decade and a half in which they had controlled the Senate and formed three of the four national administrations, corruption stalked the land.[94] Through the later years of the decade Republicans had responded with a Whiggish sensitivity to evangelicals' belief that the revival of 1857–58, and the Panic itself, had been God's response to immorality in government and public life, and that (Democrat-controlled) foreigners and Catholics had perverted the course of elections to sustain a "swarm of vampires" in municipal office.[95] A Cincinnati Republican wrote of the nation's standing at the edge of a "perilous abyss" and facing a moral crisis like those the world faced just before Christ's advent and the Reformation. Republicans' promise to encourage "a revival of *moral honesty and integrity*, in all departments of life" took on added moment in June 1860 when the congressional Covode Committee wounded the Buchanan administration by demonstrating its dishonesty in Kansas affairs and in government contracts. "The venal, the vicious, the unprincipled," declared Greeley's *Tribune*, "inevitably gravitate toward a party that has achieved a prestige of even unqualified invincibility." The times demanded a new Messiah, a new Luther.[96]

Abraham Lincoln met that need. Joshua Giddings told a ratification meeting in Oberlin that "every beat of 'honest Abe's' heart was a throb of sincerity and truth." The career of the Illinois lawyer, declared another, showed "no crooked turns, no evasions, no duplicity in his past life, official or private. All is plain, manly, straightforward and consistent." He would restore the federal government to "its pristine purity and vigor" by bringing simple personal habits to the White House. His eulogists described a paragon who drank no liquor of any kind ("not even a glass of wine"), avoided tobacco, never used "profane language" or gambled, and was generous and scrupulously honest in all financial dealings. Above all, his integrity was that of the "religiously honest" – which was more than could be said of some of his promoters, who implied, misleadingly, that he professed a conventional evangelical faith. Lincoln was extolled as "a regular attendant upon religious worship, and though not a communicant, . . . a pew-holder and liberal supporter of the Presbyterian Church in Springfield," who had taught in, and continued his love for, Sunday Schools. "Orthodox in his belief," he had the confidence of the religious community. As "a man God made, and one of his best jobs at that" he was the leader "to deliver us from the rule of a God-less and pro-slavery Administration." He enjoyed the support of a devout wife who was "a strict and consistent member of the Presbyterian Church" (unlike Douglas, whose papist, gallivanting spouse had left her domestic duties to pursue her husband around the country). Republicans could point to the women who packed the galleries of party conventions, gathered at local pole-raisings, and sewed the party's flags, as visible evidence that Lincoln's probity made him wholly acceptable to the nation's wives, mothers, and daughters.[97]

No other challenger to the Buchanan–Breckinridge forces, Republicans earnestly insisted, had Lincoln's moral power. John Bell claimed to be a respectable Christian, but this was a respectability tarnished with wine-drinking; he called himself a Presbyterian, but this was a tenuous connection conveniently broken when he wanted Baptist support. Douglas's morals conformed to those of a party which both encouraged Catholicism and corrupted Protestants. If the northern Democracy could shelter William Daily, expelled from the MEC "because of his fondness for liquor and loose women," it would hardly jib at running a sinful Jeroboam, Stephen Douglas, as its presidential candidate.[98] "Little Doug," according to Republican versifiers, liked "lots of drink in his jug" and, as one clergyman maintained, found his most enthusiastic supporters amongst "the stews and grog-shops of the country." Others reported him drunk and incapable in a railroad car. Democrats tried to respond in kind: Republicans were liars, drunkards, and Sabbath-breakers, while Douglas, who placed "firm reliance upon Divine Providence," possessed a "puritan devotion to the sense of duty," untainted by the fanatical religion of Republicans.[99] But this line of attack came less naturally to them and their ripostes lacked the imagination and finesse of Republicans' charges.

By addressing slavery, Catholicism, and government corruption Republicans sought to establish themselves as the party of Christian witness – "the *decency, moral* and *Christian party*," as Democrats sneered. To this end they encouraged the visible support of distinguished ministers and the religious press. Some Democrats maintained that northern churches had been more energetically committed to the Republicans in the previous presidential contest, and that the religious backwoods had switched allegiance from Frémont to Douglas. But in this there was a distinct element of whistling to maintain flagging spirits. It is true that more radical antislavery evangelicals believed that the party should have adopted higher ground and a better candidate: had it done so, sighed the editors of the *Oberlin Evangelist*, "our zeal and enthusiasm would have felt a summons to action they have not heard in the present campaign."[100] But even so they endorsed the party, believing it capable of reform. As in 1856, although only a small number of religious papers formally supported the Republicans, Lincoln had many allies amongst the editorial fraternity. And as in 1856 the substantial involvement of Beecher, Grinnell, and other influential clergy drew down upon their heads the wrath of Democratic leaders.[101]

The sense of exhilaration and excitement felt by so many northern (and Republican) evangelicals during the contest of 1860 was much less evident in the South. There a mood of alarm about the future of the Union, by no means absent in northern churches, gripped the Protestant community. An agitated wife of an Alabama Presbyterian minister resolved to set aside the first Friday in October "as a day sacred to the duty of pleading... [that] our beloved country... be delivered from civil war and faction." On the eve of poll many anxious churches observed a day of fasting, humiliation, and prayer for national reconciliation.[102]

Fear of the Republicans' "madness and fury," nourished by New England infidelity and perverted Protestantism, ran deep within southern evangelicalism.[103] Lincoln seemed to threaten both an irrepressible conflict and, through the "dissipating effect" of the Wide-Awake clubs, the perversion of the country's young Christians.[104] The Democratic schism reinforced the belief that the country stood on the brink of ruin.[105] The lieutenants of the two principal candidates seeking the southern vote, Breckinridge and Bell, played differently on these apprehensions but together raised the level of alarm to a new pitch. As in the North, the place of slavery within the Union dominated southern evangelicals' political agenda – though not to the exclusion of all other issues with a moral and religious bearing.

Breckinridge Democrats knew that, whatever blame they might attract for splitting the only truly national party, no southerner could doubt their firmness as defenders of the section's interests. Robert L. Dabney was by no means the only minister to rally to the Kentuckian because he considered his stand on southern rights the "most theoretically correct." Bell, by contrast, had opposed the Nebraska bill and, later, the interests of Kansas slaveholders in the Lecompton crisis; Everett's part in presenting the petition of the 3,000 New England clergy left him vulnerable to charges of poor stewardship of southern interests. Constitutional Unionists fought back with a defense of the slaveholding Bell and his conservative running mate as true heirs of Henry Clay, emphasized their endorsement of domestic slavery as a religious institution, and tried feebly to link John Breckinridge to the emancipationism of his uncle, the Presbyterian minister Robert J. Breckinridge.[106]

The Bell–Everett men were less convincing when posing as the staunchest guardians of slavery than they were in the guise of full-blooded defenders of the Union against the "crazy antics" of southern radicals.[107] They tapped a deep yearning amongst southern churchgoers like Overton Bernard for "a President whose course may be conservative and allay sectional strife." Throughout 1860 a rising clamor from pulpits and religious presses (most ostentatious in Robert Breckinridge's public letter to his nephew) demanded the defense of a perpetual Union and dismissed as a "suicidal absurdity" calls for secession in the event of the election of a "treasonable" Republican president. While not all southern Democrats were radical disunionists, it was widely believed that all disunionists and fire-eaters supported Breckinridge and Joseph Lane – a view which leaders of the Constitutional Union party did much to cultivate. William Brownlow insisted that "the pernicious heresy of Disunion" was confined to Democratic ranks, and that William L. Yancey and his hot-headed followers had deliberately broken up the Charleston convention to provoke a chain reaction of Republican victory and southern secession. Taking the oneness of Bell supporters and evangelical nationalists as self-evident, he devised a Unionist prayer for Methodist local preachers to use publicly in Tennessee against Breckinridge and his "organized band of traitors and hell-hounds." These disunionists included a vigorous and influential minority of southern evangelicals who judged that launching a southern Confederacy would in certain circumstances be a moral necessity. Augustus B. Longstreet reached this view in 1859, convinced that no war would follow a united secession of the slave states.[108] The Methodist minister, P.P. Neely, took the stump for Breckinridge in Alabama and won Democratic plaudits for declaring that "whilst he was not a disunionist *per se*," yet "*he would go down on his knees to every man in the South*, and beseech him not to submit to the inauguration of a Black Republican."[109]

Constitutional Unionists had, of course, to fight on a second front. Facing the challenge of Douglas Democrats for the southern Unionist vote, especially in the border states, they mixed argument with scurrility to alert Protestant sensibilities to the senator's political and personal shortcomings. The Little Giant offered a "bogus Democracy" whose squatter principles, sustained by "*Patrick and Hans*," ultimately slithered into Republican free soilism.[110] Though Bell's supporters could not use the "stench of corruption" against Douglas as effectively as they did against the administration Democrats, they revived familiar charges that he was "a profane swearer, a gambler, and a brawling drunkard," the leader of a party whose three "great principles" were "drunkenness, adultery and stealing."[111] They also reminded ex-Know Nothings of Douglas's Catholic connections.[112]

Bell's appeal to the evangelical conscience did not go unrewarded: impressionistic evidence suggests that his victories in Tennessee, Kentucky, and Virginia, and his respectable performance in Missouri, Maryland, North Carolina, Louisiana, and Georgia, benefited from the support of those who fused conservative Unionism with an "improving" evangelical outlook. Brownlow's claim that southern Methodists were far more committed to Bell than to any other candidate was plausible for the border slave states, and even further south his denomination's strong Clay/Know Nothing tradition carried over into the Constitutional Union party: James O. Andrew, George F. Pierce, and Atticus Haygood represented Methodist luminaries in Georgia who looked for a way of remaining true to old-time Whiggery. Anti-Democratic Presbyterians and United Brethren like George McNeill, David Coulter, George Junkin, Jacob Bachtel and, of course, Robert Breckinridge also held firm.[113] Bell's support was not necessarily deeply rooted. For Sterling Y. McMasters of Palmyra, Missouri, who "felt little attachment to any political party since the death of the noble old Whig[s]," the choice lay between the Unionism of Douglas and Bell, and reduced itself to a question of who was more likely to win; Henry Hilliard, having supported Breckinridge at the Charleston Convention, ultimately voted for Bell as the likelier victor and "for the good of the Union." Showing more positive enthusiasm, James K. Stringfield, son of a Whig Methodist preacher, attended the party's rallies in eastern Tennessee and earnestly cast his first presidential vote. Younger still, and delighting his Methodist grandfather, Overton Bernard's little grandson stood on a box on the porch and loudly rang his bell as the party's faithful processed by.[114]

Yet, as we have seen, evangelicals continued to lend their support actively and in large numbers to the Democratic party. No southern church presented so uniform a picture of loyalty as the Primitive Baptists, who saw in Breckinridge (and to a lesser degree Douglas) the best antidote to the "priestcraft" of ex-Whigs like Bell and the whole of the Republican movement. There is no reason to believe that missionary Baptists' previously extensive support for the Democracy weakened at all in 1860: even when, for example, Samuel Boykin of the Atlanta *Christian Index* encountered the wrath of southern fire-eaters, he still kept faith with Breckinridge. So, too, did leading southern Presbyterians like Robert L. Dabney, who voted for the proslavery Democrats as a principled gesture in the face of Lincoln's likely victory, and Thomas Smyth.[115] Methodist supporters of Breckinridge included recipients of government patronage; some local preachers and ex-ministers like Landon C. Haynes and James D. Thomas were candidates for office. They confirmed the implicit faith of a Virginian Democrat who, well before the onset of the campaign, believed that itinerant Methodist ministers would be reliable advocates of the southern-rights position.[116]

In the North, too, split political loyalties within denominations continued to characterize most of Protestantism in 1860, though the process by which evangelicals cleaved ever more to the Republicans advanced an important stage further.[117] Republicans maintained their strength amongst Congregationalists and New School Presbyterians;[118] amongst the smaller, earnestly antislavery denominations, including Quakers, Freewill Baptists, Wesleyan Methodists, and Free Presbyterians; and amongst very large numbers of Methodists and Baptists, especially in New England and its diaspora – western New York, the Western Reserve of Ohio, the Northern Tier of Pennsylvania, and the northern counties of the Midwestern states.[119] To these they made important additions from two separate sources. Compared with Frémont's vote in 1856, Lincoln ran impressively well amongst German Reformed and indeed other German Protestant voters, and won particularly important support from them in the key state of Pennsylvania.[120] Even more important were the accessions from the American party, conversions which were part of an election-winning recruitment in the vital states of Illinois, Indiana, New York, and Pennsylvania.[121] Theodore Frelinghuysen and Shepherd Knapp, Presbyterians, and James W. Barker and Chauncey Shaffer, Methodists, all old-line Whig-Americans and influential community figures, declared for Lincoln. So, too, did the cautious William E. Dodge, a conservative colonizationist with many southern friends, who was initially attracted to Bell's camp but who finally voted Republican. Lincoln also made converts amongst long-time Democrats, including Evan Johnson, the oldest minister in Brooklyn, but these were probably less instrumental in his victory than the rush of support from young, first-time voters into what Seward described as "a party chiefly of young men." John Wanamaker, twenty-two-year-old secretary of the Philadelphia YMCA, cast his ballot for Lincoln, having become an enthusiast at the time of his public debates with Douglas in 1858: significantly, he rejected the Democratic certainties of his pastor, John Chambers.[122]

Recent historians have been at pains to qualify the picture of a uniform Republicanism within the northern evangelical churches in 1860. Quite apart from those ex-Whig and ex-Know Nothing churchgoers who turned to Bell rather than Lincoln in 1860, large numbers of traditionally Democratic evangelicals remained true to the party of Jackson. Despite the Charleston schism, many conservative Unionists persisted in seeing the party as the best hope for national harmony. Cyrus McCormick represented those Old School Presbyterians for whom that church and the Democracy were "the two hoops that held the Union together." Though some contemporaries believed that the MEC, as "the largest and most influential denomination in the land," had exerted "a most control[l]ing power in electing Mr. Lincoln," it should be remembered that it was in the interests of the church's leaders to overstate their popular influence when pursuing favors and public office from the President-elect. Democratic Methodists included George Fort, and his brother Jacob, who believed that Douglas occupied the "truely [sic] national conservative and safe position for all sections and interests."[123] The similar stance of Peter Cartwright and William Daily indicated continuing loyalty to the party of Jackson amongst western Methodists. In New England, where some Methodists had moved rapidly to Republicanism, others remained stubbornly opposed. While the Reverend John Allen of Farmington, Maine, judged Lincoln's victory to be the triumph of "the Lord's side," a minority of his congregation protested in dismay. Even amongst Congregationalists, Republicanism might struggle where New England influence was attenuated. Lyman Abbott took up a Congregational pastorate in Terre Haute, Indiana, early in 1860, where he found few New Englanders and little antislavery sentiment: the "best people" were from the middle states and some from the South. "Yankee" was a term of abuse. He bit his Republican tongue and remained silent on political issues through the campaign.[124]

These qualifications to monolithic evangelical voting patterns in the North are, however, less significant than the extraordinary achievement of the Republican party: harnessing the moral energies of evangelical churches unprecedentedly and so effectively in the cause of political antislavery. What mattered more than evangelicals' partisan homogeneity, which was not realized, was the disproportionate commitment of the churches' ministers, editors, and lay leaders to Republican politics, which was. Republicans most evidently achieved this in New England, but their success was by no means restricted to that region. A buoyant New Yorker took heart in 1860 from an awareness "that a large majority of the clergymen of all denominations, and the teachers in our schools and colleges, are wide-awake Republicans." Driven by a burning sense of Christian duty, these evangelicals embraced a public, active form of politics in the cause of "freedom." For some that meant above all securing liberty for the slaves. For many others, perhaps for most, a multiple vision drove them on: freedom from the slave power's impositions on white freemen as well as black slaves, in both church and state. It would be a distortion to treat the Republican party as primarily an instrument of the works-focused, reform-minded evangelicalism fashioned through the Second Great Awakening. A party that wins a presidential election, albeit on a minority vote, must do so as an institutional coalition and a philosophical amalgam. But without evangelical Protestantism and its moral imperatives the party would have been less energetic, less visionary, less indignant, less self-righteous – and less successful. Lyman Abbott attended Lincoln's Cooper Union speech in February 1860 and heard him conclude, "Let us have faith that right makes might, and in that faith let us dare to the end to do our duty as we understand it." For Abbott this was a call to Christian action. "That faith I had inherited from my father, and my pastor [Henry Ward Beecher] had kindled it into a passion." Lincoln gave that faith "steadfastness of courage."[125] The Republican party may not have been in any simple sense "the Christian party in politics." But for northern antislavery evangelicals it deserved that mantle far more than any other party in the republic's history.

"God be with the right!": the winter crisis, 1860–61

Lincoln's election initially elicited an exultant response – "a flood of ecstasy," as Gilbert Haven put it – from antislavery evangelicals. "Our hearts are jubilant, our lips overflow with praise to God," trumpeted the *Congregational Herald* of Chicago. "As Christians we rejoice at the auspicious result of the portentous struggle, even as Christians we labored and prayed to secure it." The Republican victory seemed to mark the beginning of a new era. Power would pass to those who would put slavery in the way of ultimate extinction. The many southerners who thought similarly would be emboldened to act. The New York *Independent* believed that "the most critical point in the struggle between Freedom and Slavery" since 1787 had been "*safely, decisively, finally passed.*" Even organs less closely tied to the Republican party and antislavery radicalism took heart. The New York *Christian Advocate* celebrated Lincoln's victory not as a party triumph but as a repudiation of southern disunionism by lovers of the Constitution.[126]

But while northerners widely celebrated the passing of crisis, southern evangelicals' predominant mood was one of anxiety, alarm, and anger. Far from settling a national crisis the election seemed to have created one. "*Sectionalism has triumphed,*" declared the *North Carolina Presbyterian*; the Republicans' victory was "an outrage on southern sentiment." As fire-eaters called for the South's withdrawal from the Union even the most politically quietist ministers, like Eugene Levert of Marion, Alabama, confided their "most intense anxiety" and contemplated the horrors of civil war.[127] Robert L. Dabney feared that the threatened convulsion would "damn more souls than all the evangelical agencies of the Presbyterian Church can save in one year."[128] He watched with mounting alarm as South Carolina seceded from the Union on 20 December, to be followed over the next month and a half by the withdrawal of six other states of the lower South and the launching of a southern confederacy. Lincoln's determination to maintain federal authority occasioned a denouement at Fort Sumter that launched an exodus of further slave states and four years of bloody warfare.

This winter of crisis in government became a winter of crisis for the churches. Religious leaders, north and south, encouraged by Buchanan's call for a national fast on 4 January, commonly treated the emergency as a "work of chastisement" for national sins meted out by a stern Father, though their agreement on this broad principle concealed profoundly different understandings of the sins in question: while northerners' catalogue frequently culminated in what James Smart called "the great crime . . . against another race," slave-state clergy like C.H. Read, a Richmond Presbyterian, and James Thornwell emphasized, without challenging the institution itself, the South's unfulfilled duties to black "servants."[129] Some of these evangelicals (especially in the South) held a view of Providence which ascribed to God alone the power to remove the punishment He had inflicted. "It seems that God is teaching the nation that no reliance can be placed upon human aid," the Methodist minister Albert S. Hunt reflected at the time of the national fast, adding later, "May the God of our fathers bless & keep us from civil war." The fellow New Yorker who exclaimed, "God save the Republic!" took a similarly pessimistic and restricted view of human effort, as did southern Presbyterians who cried, "There is no help but in God." For such people the only proper church action was prayer to implore the Lord's guidance. Political interventionism, as well as being divisive to churches, was philosophically flawed.[130]

Nevertheless, what was remarkable about churches in the winter crisis was how readily so many ministers of a politically quietist outlook abandoned their hesitation for "active interposition" and engaged in debates on the nature and permanence of the Union.[131] They were as aware as elected politicians – whether the instigators of the secession movement, the southerners who opposed them, members of Buchanan's lame-duck administration, or northern Unionists – of the importance of shaping public opinion throughout the crisis months at a time when conventional channels of political control were impaired. While politicians tried (with some success) to gain access to the churches' leverage on public opinion, clergymen themselves took political initiatives and sought to pressurize their political representatives. The unprecedented national danger, and its implications for Christ's kingdom, legitimized a new code of ministerial behavior. Samuel B. Wilson of Union Theological Seminary, Richmond, insisted that "clergy as well as politicians, may properly express their views," and use their influence "to avert evil." Provided Christian ministers avoided the emotional appeals of "noisy politicians" they had every right to instruct citizens in their proper duties.[132]

The churches' response to this time of crisis was, then, by no means simply reactive. As northern and southern evangelicals confronted the conflicting demands of maintaining the Union or staying true to their respective understandings of republican liberty, they actively took initiatives to shape political agendas. It is also clear that, in keeping with the experience of ecclesiastical conflict over the past two decades, sectional abrasions within the churches (especially in the MEC and the Old School Presbyterian church) played their part in the final break-up of the Union.

The northern pulpit and religious press spoke with a multitude of voices between the 1860 election and the outbreak of hostilities.[133] The historian's difficulty in detecting a clear sense of direction in their outpourings is compounded by their swirls of opinion as the crisis moved from phase to phase. But it is evident that, except for a small number in sympathy with the South, evangelicals' immediate, consensual reaction to the secessionist threats after Lincoln's election was one of adamantine Unionism.[134] "There is no party in the North, either in Church or state, which desires the dissolution of the Union," declared one Methodist editor. South Carolina's moves towards separation generated a chorus of protest from all sides: Republican and Democrat, antislavery radical and conservative Unionist. "Don't let the Union be dissolved," John McClintock wrote home from Paris to his friend George Crooks. "What more dreadful calamity could befall the great American nation than a dissolution of their republic[?]" asked another.[135]

As the pace of secession increased, as the Buchanan administration floundered, as national disintegration became a reality, and as schemes of political compromise were floated, signs of a fracture appeared in northern churches. To stiffen the resolve of Unionist southerners and pave the way for some form of accommodation between hostile sections, conciliatory evangelicals explained why preservation of national unity was the ultimate good, and why disunion should be seen as "a crime against the country" and against God himself. "Our prosperity depends upon our Union," insisted the elderly Methodist Heman Bangs: "The South and the North cannot live without each other." Their interdependence was in part cultural: as Charles Hodge reminded them, "a common language, a common religion, and a common history" cemented the Union. It was also in part physical (Edward Thomson mused sarcastically about the difficulties of dividing the Mississippi) and economic: the South's predictions of burgeoning prosperity through the rule of King Cotton were damagingly self-deluding. Constitutionally, too, the Union was an organic whole, a mixture of confederation and consolidation: secession represented an attack on law, freedom, republicanism, and the moral bonds of "covenants and oaths." Yield the right of secession and further divisions, "anarchy and confusion," would follow. A deep respect for "the powers that be" had led conservative Unionists to sustain southern interests against northern radicals in 1850 (and since) through a defense of the Fugitive Slave Law and other constitutional protections of slavery; that same conservatism now threw them just as energetically against the radicals of the South. But most distressing of all, disunion delivered a dreadful blow to the kingdom of Christ. "We lose our position as one of the foremost nations of the earth," warned Charles Hodge, "the nation of the future – the great Protestant power, to stand up for civil and religious freedom." Angels would weep, warned a Pennsylvania Methodist, at the collapse of America's millennial dream and the destruction of "the most splendid achievement of man since the foundation of the world."[136]

Preoccupied by the need to protect this sacred trust, and convinced that the present crisis derived as much from northern as from southern extremism, many evangelicals began to push for political compromise. The agitation over the spread of slavery seemed to Henry Boardman "the work of desperate politicians" who had grasped the issue as "a convenient lever for stirring up the sediment of party feeling."[137] Many shared Horace Bushnell's view that population growth in the free states would exert economic pressures to which slavery would finally succumb; the contribution of abolitionist agitators to its eventual demise, he sneered, would turn out to be like adding a drop of water to the Mississippi. If slavery were doomed, asked Samuel J. Baird, what was the point of formally restricting it? In fact Baird, an Old School Presbyterian previously scrupulous about not interfering in politics, asked John T. Nixon, his newly elected Republican congressman, to pursue compromise: "the great mass of the people, Republicans, as well as others," he argued, "would sustain heartily any reasonable settlement" and nothing would be lost.[138] Like Hodge, George Bethune and many others, Baird was sympathetic to reintroducing the Missouri Compromise line as a permanent settlement of the territorial issue. When Senator John J. Crittenden made proposals on this basis, they enjoyed considerable support from conservative evangelicals, some of whom had voted for the Republican party which was now adamantly setting its face against concessions.[139]

Staunchly antislavery evangelicals reacted with alarm at the possibility of humiliating compromise. At one level, of course, they found sweet satisfaction in the "refreshing" change in conservative northern pulpits, rejoicing that "the squeamishness which would banish politics from the pulpit has been displaced by a more manly and Christian sentiment." But they had no sympathy for any approach which, instead of squarely blaming the South for the crisis, identified northern guilt. The Fugitive Slave Law, Nebraska bill, Kansas warfare, Dred Scott decision, and other "paroxysms of madness" which had culminated in secession were entirely the product of a mischievous slave power and the "political atheism" of the God-defying South. The aged Ezra S. Ely, quoting Webster, hoped God would never ask him to choose between liberty and Union, but his conclusion took a distinctly un-Websterian turn: ultimately the Union was the means to the end of republican freedom, not an end in itself. By late December Joseph Bittinger of Cleveland, Ohio, had concluded that Union sentiment amongst Christians was waning: "The feeling is gaining ground that it would be good riddance if the South went out.... God's people ... favor ... secession rather than ... any more political compromise with slavery." The New York *Independent* moved from a mid-January declaration of full-blooded Unionism at whatever cost, to a mid-February statement of the un-wisdom of coercion. John McClintock similarly shifted ground. By early

February he thought it best for the Gulf states peacefully to leave the Union: "Civil war will do no good. Compromises of principle will do no good. The Free States will be a great power by themselves." The lesson was clear: sever the cords of Union, for northern benefit.[140]

The bombardment of Fort Sumter radically altered the terms of debate, of course. Lincoln's call to put down the rebellion removed all possibility of peaceful secession and swiftly re-cemented the fracturing consensus of northern Protestants. Conservative conciliators and higher-law evangelicals, as James Moorhead has demonstrated, now united against the demonic slave power in "a great people's war for Christian democracy" and for a Union that "had been rehabilitated and suffused with new moral vitality." "The great irrepressible conflict between liberty and slavery has at last broke in war, and a war of no ordinary magnitude it may yet be," reflected Matthew Simpson to his nephew, the Methodist bishop. "But the Lord reigns," he continued, in a letter whose millennialist expectations captured the wider mood of northern Protestantism:

> let the Earth rejoice, for bad as war is He can cause good to follow. Therefore it may be that the agitation of the slavery question both in church and state is about to be put to rest forever by the destruction of the peculiar institution itself. Millions of negroes have been murdered by that institution. Does retributive justice require that blood must now flow for the sins of the past? . . . In the book we read of one who said when you hear of wars and rumors of wars be not troubled for these things must be.[141]

Southern evangelicals, too, were to enjoy in April 1861 a similarly euphoric closing of ranks behind a righteous objective, but before that they had to pass through their own even more testing time of confused and conflicting responses to Lincoln's election.[142] In the panic and fear that followed Republican victory, secession-bent politicians did not hesitate to exploit Christians' anxieties as a means of speeding an independent southern republic. Often driven themselves by a highly developed sense of religious obligation (William L. Yancey believed Christ's command to destroy heresy meant it was "our bounden duty to agitate"), advocates of secession presented the crisis as the work of diabolical northern priests. When Howell Cobb, for example, accused northern religious leaders of fomenting bitter sectional hatred and threatening, "in company with . . . [their] political handmaid, Black Republicanism, to overthrow our once happy and glorious Union," he directly addressed the concerns of southern churchmen who blamed events on "priest-craft," "abolition priests," and "Antichrist." At the same time, disunionists emphasized the corruption of national politics and, as Kenneth Greenberg has shown, offered secession as an act of

purification, encouraging the view that delegates to the secession conventions, unlike northern politicians, "would bow to no authority but
what they believed to be the authority of God." In due course the
Confederate constitution-makers would reverentially invoke "the favor
of Almighty God," in conscious contrast to the impious silence of the
men of 1787.[143] Throughout the winter crisis leading secessionists sought
the churches' help in molding public sentiment and clothing the movement in the garments of righteousness. They recognized, as Charles
Dabney wrote, that "the clergy are the most respected and respectable
of our citizens, and for acting on an issue already joined, for voting on a
question fully digested and put, . . . do enjoy great influence."[144]

In fact secession-minded clergy needed little prodding to act in
defense of southern interests. Prepared by their own pre-election
rhetoric to see Lincoln's victory as legitimate grounds for separation,
they lost no time in asserting the political folly and moral negligence of
waiting impotently for his inauguration. Whatever Lincoln's personal
integrity, he was only "a figure upon the political chess-board," manipulated by a morally blind, atheistic party. Republicans' victory had led
them to believe that "the whole land belongs to them."[145] Letting
Lincoln exercise power over the South would be the "death-knell of
slavery." Seceding was lawful. It would bring relief from "such strife &
injustice as we have suffered for many years past." It would free the
churches, already liberated by denominational schisms, to achieve even
greater religious prosperity. It would prevent the South's "degradation."
It would maintain her "self-respect, justice, and honor."[146] Above all,
secession was an act of religious and moral duty. Independence provided
the only way of defending what Benjamin Palmer of New Orleans called
the South's "providential trust": the "duty *to ourselves, to our slaves, to the
world, and to Almighty God . . . to preserve and transmit our existing system of
domestic servitude, with the right, unchallenged by man, to go and root itself
wherever Providence and nature may carry it.*" In this moment of crisis in
the millennial advance, he declared, "God be with the right!"[147]

These views took secessionist clergy into the secular arena with all the
zeal of the Know Nothing or Republican ministers they had themselves
once denounced for mixing religion and politics. The irony was not lost
on friend or foe, but this did nothing to inhibit their appetite for political
engagement. Contemporary observers saw them, as have some historians since, as prime movers in the first wave of secession and in the
gathering momentum towards war.[148] In South Carolina, for example,
church bodies enjoying considerable public respect moved to support
political separation before the state actually adopted its ordinance of
secession: Presbyterians in Synod, previously very much a force for
conservative Unionism, called on the people to "stand up for their
rights," while the MECS Annual Conference declared its support for

those "resisting Northern domination." Many of the state's preachers used the day of fasting, humiliation, and prayer on 21 November to press the case for secession, "though our path to victory be through a baptism of blood."[149] Ministers were equally active in other states of the lower South. The Alabama Baptist Convention unanimously proclaimed their state's "sacred right as a sovereignty" to withdraw from a Union that had failed to provide "justice, protection or safety." Secessionist appeals rang out on Thanksgiving Day, one of which – Benjamin Palmer's – was reprinted as a pamphlet and circulated by the thousand throughout the South.[150] Clergy who stumped for election to secession conventions included the wealthy slaveholder and leading Alabama Baptist, Basil Manly, later chaplain at Jefferson Davis's presidential inauguration; the North Carolina Methodist, Charles F. Deems; and, in Mississippi, Thomas Caskey of the Disciples of Christ. The 169 delegates at the South Carolina secession convention included a dozen ministers, most notably the Baptist James C. Furman, president of Furman University.[151] At a less elevated level numerous younger evangelicals rallied to the separatist cause. If, as a North Carolina editor declared, the most determined secessionists were mainly "young men, of hot and impulsive natures," many of these were members of deeply evangelical families.[152] George Gilman Smith, a young Georgia Methodist preacher, later wished he had been "wiser and more thoughtful" in these feverish days, but at the time he wrote and spoke with great passion.[153]

Even so, not all southern Christians, in Robert L. Dabney's words, "lost their senses with excitement, fear and passion." When church bells pealed in joyful celebration of independence many evangelicals felt a silent shiver of apprehension, and others erupted in angry rebuke. Unionist religious leaders, shedding their anxieties about entering politics, worked hard to combat separatism in church and state. Often (but not exclusively) former Whigs, they located their particular strength in the upper South, especially in Maryland, west Virginia, Kentucky, western North Carolina and eastern Tennessee. Richard Fuller and other Marylanders issued a Unionist appeal "To the Baptists of these United States of America"; Dabney's influential pen called on fellow Presbyterians and all southern Christians to save the country from political convulsions.[154] Most of the religious journals in Virginia and North Carolina remained instinctively cautious and distanced themselves from the secession movement of the lower South, though less vociferously than preachers like Simeon Colton, John Tillett, Brantley York, Thomas B. Hughes, and John Lanahan.[155] Further west, William Brownlow, James K. Stringfield, and other representative eastern Tennessee preachers attended Union meetings, passed anti-secession resolutions, and used the 4 January fast day to rally loyal opinion. Robert J. Breckinridge's sermons and articles circulated influentially in Kentucky and further afield.[156] In the deep South Unionists found themselves much more on the defensive, but even here ministers like the Georgia Methodists James Andrew and Lovick Pierce, the Baptists John A. Broadus and James P. Boyce in South Carolina, and the Mississippi Presbyterian James A. Lyon held out fiercely until the act of separation itself and, in some cases, beyond.[157]

Such people regarded the Union "with little less than an ardent *religious* veneration," as one North Carolinian put it, and like most northern evangelicals viewed with horror a disruption which would destroy a "glorious government" and sabotage Christian endeavor. Dabney could not have been more clearly contemptuous when he described South Carolina's unilateral secession as "treacherous, wicked, insolent, and mischievous," and declared his opposition to Virginia's joining such "a dirty, slave-holding, filibustering, proslavery, cotton league." For such men secession was an unconstitutional deed, "an act of wicked rebellion" entirely unjustified by Lincoln's election.[158] Disunionist intriguers, they insisted, deliberately exaggerated the threat the President-elect would represent once in office, and misjudged the unity and radicalism of his party. They aimed to frighten fellow southerners into over-hasty action, and to use the upper South as a buffer: South Carolinians, according to Dabney, wanted other southern states to "shield her from the chastisement which she most condignly deserves." In fact, Lovick Pierce and others argued, the South's rights were best secured within the Union by the common, united action of all the slave states. "Precipitate action by separate States, is unwise, because it destroys the strength of the South; and it is unjust to the border States," explained Samuel B. Wilson. It would also consume the country in civil war. While many southern evangelicals regarded war as only a distant – but tolerable – prospect, the specter of a bloody, internecine conflict made farsighted and pessimistic Unionists all the more earnest in their support of compromise efforts, and explains the urgency of their rhetoric. Crittenden's proposals for a settlement were "holy work"; "ungodly" secessionists obstructed the restoration of national harmony; secession itself became an "unholy diabolical vortex."[159]

What added to Unionist evangelicals' righteous indignation was their conviction that secession, as well as springing from the intrigues of secular politicians, owed far too much to the energies of separatist clergy who should have known better. "Presbyterian, Methodist, and Baptist preachers... [who] have stuck their *Disunionist Cockades* upon their bosoms... deserve to be hung!" fumed William Brownlow. The *North Carolina Christian Advocate* rebuked the ministers of the South Carolina Conference of the MECS for formally supporting secession; it warned them to tread with care in that part of western North Carolina which remained under their jurisdiction but which, following secession, was "under no more necessity to import foreign preachers from South Carolina, than Yankee cabbages from New England."[160] At the same time, Unionist Methodists in Virginia regarded with withering contempt those who tried to split the Baltimore and East Baltimore Conferences from the essentially northern MEC and incorporate them into southern Methodism.[161] Loyalists like John Lanahan were convinced that Maryland and Virginia dissidents were covertly plotting with disunionist politicians like John B. Floyd of Virginia to take the state into the Confederacy. Their "deep, dark & infamous" agitation threatened political as well as ecclesiastical catastrophe.[162]

The Unionism of southern evangelicals was not, of course, a monolithic doctrine, consistently held. A number of anti-secessionists in the border states, and an even smaller number further south, maintained an unequivocal attachment to the Union even after events at Fort Sumter had drawn their states into the second round of secession. Simeon Colton, the elderly, disabled Presbyterian minister of Asheboro, North Carolina, persisted in treating the seceders as rebels, and blamed the war on southern provocation.[163] Brownlow and his allies, who warmly endorsed Lincoln's inaugural address, kept the Union flag flying in eastern Tennessee. "Southern man and slaveholder as I am, if the South in her madness and folly will force the issue on the country, of slavery and no Union, or a Union and no Slavery," Brownlow proclaimed in Philadelphia, "I am for the Union, though every other institution in the country perish."[164]

Significantly even Brownlow's convictions seem to have wavered momentarily in private. But while he was to keep faith with the Union, many others who sternly rebuked the secessionists in the final weeks of 1860 were to succumb over the next four or five months to the pressures of southern nationalism. Much southern Unionism was highly conditional. Rufus T. Heflin, editor of the *North Carolina Christian Advocate* and critic of the initial thrust to disunion, still conceded that the Union he loved was only a means to an end: securing Christ's kingdom. Its days would be numbered if it lost sight of that. Many secessionists and conditional Unionists were agreed that southern social arrangements were scripturally based, that the real source of the crisis lay in "the infidel teachings of the [northern] pulpit and the press" on slavery, and that the principal point at issue was not the legitimacy but the expediency of secession in the present crisis. Only a minority of southern Christians would have demurred at Burwell Temple's declaration: "I am in favor of the Union of the strict principles of our Constitution; and if the Southern States, in their sovereign capacity, shall be debar[r]ed of their just and equal rights, I am for secession as a last resort – though I much prefer the Union, if it be indeed a Union of rights, interest and honor."[165]

The point at which conditional Unionists acceded to secession varied according to their location and their reading of events. In the lower South, once the secession conventions had proclaimed independence, many saw little option but to acquiesce and declare their allegiance to the new governments. Robert Paine, the Methodist bishop, who had done nothing to advance secession in his home state of Mississippi, declared he "breathe[d] more freely" since it had occurred. In the upper tier of slave states, too, once-vigorous Unionists like Calvin H. Wiley had by the end of February, following the formation of the Confederate States of America, come to believe that division of the nation was God's will. His and other Old School Presbyterians' shift in opinion was hastened by their growing lack of faith in northern conservatism in general and the northern wing of their denomination in particular. When the long-respected *New York Observer*, which still circulated quite widely in the South, endorsed Lincoln's position on slavery, southern Presbyterians considered the change of tone "significant of evil." Charles Hodge's article on "The State of the Country," written before South Carolina's secession and published in the *Princeton Review* in January 1861, confirmed their worst fears. A bitter opponent of abolitionism, Hodge had long been admired in the South as the best kind of northern conservative. But South Carolina's drive to independence snapped his patience, and he denounced southern disunionists for their "perversion of historical truth" in declaring slavery a national institution. George McNeill, himself a graduate of Princeton, was aghast at Hodge's "heartless and unfair" attack and maintained that the *Princeton Review* had "gone over to the enemy of our country's peace and happiness." Northern and southern Old Schoolers had taken pride in being the only remaining evangelical church able to claim full nationality. Now the bonds of respect (no longer of affection) frayed to breaking point and snapped apart with the onset of war.[166]

But the most potent influence on the behavior of Unionist southern evangelicals was the mounting fear that the new Republican administration would use physical force. These churchmen commonly accompanied their expressions of concern about the lower South's actions with fierce warnings to the President-elect and northern religious conservatives not to seek reunion by military means: they would resist "to the last extremity" the "injustice or dishonor" of coercing the seceded states.[167] Thus Overton Bernard, a staunch Unionist when Lincoln was elected, believed that Lincoln's inaugural address increased pro-secession feeling by raising the specter of coercion; and attacked his "most shameful duplicity" in his response to the crisis at Charleston. Robert L. Dabney's Unionism also melted in face of the failure of compromise efforts, the bombardment of Fort Sumter ("an act of *strict self-defence*") and Lincoln's subsequent call for 75,000 volunteers. More than any other single act, this appeal converted into secessionists thousands of evangelical Unionists in Virginia, Arkansas, Tennessee, and North Carolina, who considered it "a declaration of war." "Lincoln's proclamation was written on *Sunday* the 14th of April," lamented James K. Stringfield within a week of its issue. "How much better to have gone to church on that day, to have first made it the subject of prayer. I do not believe that God will prosper any cause thus recklessly and sacreligiously [*sic*] inaugurated." Abandoning his former loyalties, he was soon to vote for "the immediate, unconditional, and eternal separation of the State of Tennessee from the miserable yankee union."[168]

Thus by April 1861 an overwhelming majority of southern evangelicals regarded an independent Confederacy as the only realistic response to an aggressive and encroaching infidelity. Crusading northern Unionists who viewed Lincoln's call to arms as the prelude to a holy war would face southern troops equally convinced that they marched under the banner of God. In the initial frisson of excitement Confederate clergy suppressed their doubts, blessed company battle flags, declared that the Almighty had ordained the coming conflict, and assured the departing soldiers that the Lord of hosts would shield their heads in the day of battle. In Prince Edward County, Virginia, the Presbyterian minister Robert L. Dabney and a Methodist colleague were asked to address a rifle company, the Prospect Greys. After drilling, the company gathered in the packed church, surrounded by wives, sisters, children, and neighbors, to create a tableau common throughout the Confederacy in the early summer of 1861. Dabney, in his own words, offered "various good advices, seeking rather to quiet than to agitate their feelings." Delivering up a prayer, he dismissed them "among universal tears and sobs." The company, he reflected, "is composed of middle-class men; most of them Presbyterians or Methodists, and a few gentlemen. They are a stalwart set of fellows, sun-burned, raw-boned and bearded; but they all wept like children. They will fight none the less for that. Such a people," he declared, "cannot be conquered."[169]

Conclusion: "God Prosper the Right"

The Union and the Confederacy that invoked the aid of the same God in their awful struggle had been brought to the point of conflict by a potent mix of social, economic, cultural, and political forces. For the historian much of the war's fascination lies in the sheer complexity of its roots and the possibility of refracting the events of the antebellum years through a number of different lenses. But despite the variety of focus in scholarly analyses, despite historians' increasing awareness of religion in their treatments of antebellum politics, and despite their current disposition to emphasize cultural antipathies in dividing the two sections, attention still focuses very largely on the secular dimensions of what is commonly treated as a secular political crisis.[1] That crisis was, of course, shaped by politicians seeking to advance secular interests and material ends. But as this book has indicated, it was more than that. American evangelical churches acted as forcing-houses for a theology that had considerable implications for public discourse; they spawned an ecclesiastical sectionalism. Their members instigated political discussion, mobilized voters, pressured vote-seeking politicians, and variously made their marks on the political cultures of the different parties. Evangelicals thereby made their own distinctive contributions to political life and to the processes that alienated North and South.

Friends and critics of evangelical religion had no doubt that the churches played active, and not reactive, roles in the coming of war. "This unholy and fratricidal war," declared the editor of the New York *Freeman's Journal* on the eve of southern secession, "*began* with your hard-shell Reformed Presbyterians, and your soft-shell new-school Presbyterians, and with your Baptists, Methodists, and such like. *You,* Protestant religionists were the very first to begin this game of disunion." The Republican party, he sneered, the aggressors in the struggle, were "the children of Northern Protestantism": "The fundamental curse of the Republican party" – as of its parent, Calvinist evangelicalism – was "its irrepressible disposition to *meddle* with other people's business, and to impose its notions, and its will, on people who do not freely accept them." Differing only over the value, not the effect, of northern evangelicals' actions, the Cincinnati Methodist, Granville Moody, agreed. "I believe it is true that we did bring it [the war] about," he told Salmon P. Chase soon after Lincoln's call to arms, "and I glory in it, for it is a wreath of glory around our brow."[2] They oversimplified the churches' role, but Moody and his Catholic contemporary were correct in recognizing evangelicals' power and eagerness to shape the world beyond their meeting places, and in identifying their contribution to the Republican party as a determining element in the coming of war.

The emergence and ultimate success of the Republicans were dependent on a particular understanding of politics, one which evangelicals had played a major role in shaping. That political ethic was rooted in the moderate or "Arminianized" Calvinist theology of the Second Great Awakening, marked by an optimistic postmillennialism and an urgent appeal to disinterested action. In the early decades of the century evangelicals' strenuous doctrines of duty, moral uplift, and benevolence underpinned the countrywide promotion of temperance, Sabbath observance, education, and Protestant nurture. At first Protestants' efforts to cultivate and sustain a Christian republic developed through voluntary organizations outside the arena of party politics. But as the young nation moved from a more restricted, deferential form of republicanism towards a discernibly modern mass democracy, the worlds of evangelicalism and politics found themselves bound together in a process of cultural symbiosis. Professional politicians and party managers realized the churches had much to teach them about how to organize, communicate, and persuade, both nationally and locally; evangelicals, exposed to a pervasive "Calvinist" doctrine of political engagement, came to see that mass politics, despite being open to abuse and corruption, could also be an agency for Christianizing the republic. The sabbatarian and Antimasonic crusades, though narrowly based, demonstrated evangelicals' potential for mobilizing pious voters behind a program of political purification. The significance of this lesson was not lost on the organizers of the heterogeneous amalgam of anti-Jacksonians that made up the Whig party. Not all sabbatarians and Antimasons would necessarily become enthusiastic Whigs, but a doctrine of moral improvement gave the party an ideological glue, and this, along with Whiggery's emphasis on social and economic modernization, ensured the adherence to the party of more than its fair share of postmillennialists. With some success Whig propagandists addressed evangelicals' concern for moral order and appealed to their Manichean mentalities, not least by their elaboration and repetition of a religiously charged political language that identified Whigs as purifiers and their opponents as moral dregs.

Harsh reality, however, prevented Whigs from establishing themselves as the "Christian party" which would monopolize the evangelical Protestant vote. Evangelicals' perspectives and social aspirations were too varied, their ethnicity too diverse, their relationships too persistently sectarian to present a monolithic partisan front. Moreover, the very characteristic of Whiggery that made it so attractive to many evangelicals – its evident concern to judge political action against a higher moral standard – would prove a source of weakness. The more northern Protestants fashioned an antislavery imperative and expected Whig politicians to obey the voice of conscience in all their dealings with the peculiar institution, the more impossible it became for the party leaders, who needed southern votes, to respond as energetically as the "higher-law" people demanded. They survived the electoral inroads of the conscience-driven Liberty and Free Soil movements. But when they also failed to measure up to evangelicals' expectations over prohibition, the Bible in common schools, and other strategies for defending the republic against Catholic intrusions, the party's days as the vehicle for postmillennialist northerners were numbered. For a brief period it seemed as though the American party might provide evangelicals with a lasting basis for moral politics, but it too proved a flawed instrument.

Northern political postmillennialism – which had, then, taken a variety of forms in the sequence of sabbatarian, Antimasonic, Whig, Liberty, Free Soil, Maine Law, and Know Nothing parties – reached its apotheosis in the Republican party. Like these earlier parties, the Republicans acquired their essential moral energy from evangelical Protestantism, and their unique fusion of religion and politics drew on established modes of mobilizing revivalist enthusiasm. Republicans also drew on the public discourse of evangelicals as it had been elaborated over a quarter of a century. To some extent this was a discourse that hinted at paranoia. Fears of Freemasons and Catholics as conspirators against the Christian republic seem to have provided many evangelicals with the initial impulse towards political engagement. Antimasonic and Know Nothing parties certainly mobilized many new voters, and the concern of their evangelical supporters about conspiracy carried over into the fear of the slave power that formed so potent an element of Free Soil and Republican appeals. But evangelical discourse also brought to the practice and program of politics a less defensive emphasis on conscience, obedience to the higher law, Calvinistic duty, self-discipline, and social responsibility – a postmillennialist creed that reached its fullest expression in the expectant and triumphalist early years of the Republican movement. Most strikingly, that movement's pious Protestant supporters went further than evangelicals had ever done before in identifying the arrival of the kingdom of God with the success of a particular political party. When during the climax of the campaigns of 1856 and 1860 ministers officiated with equal enthusiasm at revival meetings and at Republican rallies, it was clear that religion and politics had fused more completely than ever before in the American republic.

The religious meaning that Republican evangelicals attached to political action moved well beyond what most southern Christians could understand or tolerate. Evangelicals in the slave states were not, of course, as apolitical as most of them publicly insisted: while northern churchgoers fashioned an antislavery imperative many southern Protestants simultaneously developed a justification and framework for proslavery action. Nor were southern evangelicals untouched by postmillennialism, or unwilling to invest partisanship with moral meaning. They also shared northern evangelicals' dichotomized world view (one reinforced by the honor code that still flourished in the South and to which they responded with some ambivalence). But most southern evangelicals resisted the explicit fusing of politics and religion, and remained divided in their partisan allegiances. Most critical of all, they deplored Republican evangelicals' linking of the inauguration of God's kingdom with the triumph of a party. When southern evangelicals continued to protest that the North had breached the conventions surrounding the proper relationship between church and state, they may have overstated their political purity but they identified a point of real distinction between the evangelicals of the two sections.

Thus by the eve of the Civil War there existed at least two evangelical solutions to the question of how to be a citizen of the republic. There was no uniform evangelicalism in either of the two sections, of course: sectarianism and cultural diversity kept many northern evangelicals resistant to the party of Lincoln, while similar forces ensured the complex reaction of southern Protestants to the events of 1860 and early 1861. But the impetus of the North's evangelical thinking moved it towards the Republicans' postmillennial nationalism, which linked moral and economic progress. At the same time, evangelical southerners, some more assertively and confidently than others, were elaborating a Christian apology for slavery and its related social arrangements. Many southerners saw these philosophical differences at an early date and pressed, successfully, for separation. For others it was the painful, alarmingly abrasive, aftermath of church schisms that drove home the meaning of sectionalism. Even those whose churches had not split and who believed they shared with their northern co-denominationalists a common understanding of American nationality, discovered with anguished surprise on the eve of conflict just how wrong they were.

The experience of America's evangelical Protestants argues for the existence of deep cultural and ideological fissures separating the North from the South in 1861.[3] Although the Civil War had to do with the defense of vested material interests, we may reasonably doubt whether concern over economic interests could of itself have launched that conflict. What engaged the passions of both sections was the moral meaning men and women gave to being "southern" and "northern" and to the systems of free and slave labor each had developed. Evangelicalism, more than any other element, provided the core of these divergent moral perceptions of the appropriate social and economic direction of the Union. Henry Clay understood something of the power of ideology when he reflected with foreboding on the sundering of national denominations. "If the Churches divide on the subject of slavery," he told the editor of the *Presbyterian Herald*, "there will be nothing left to bind our people together but trade and commerce. . . . [W]hen the people of these states become thoroughly alienated from each other, and get their passions aroused, they are not apt to stop and consider what is to their interest. . . . Men will fight if they consider their rights trampled upon, even if you show them that ruin to themselves and families will be the probable result."[4] He did not live to see it, but by the later 1850s the prevalent fears on each side of the Mason-Dixon line were exacerbated by abrasive relations between sectional churches. By 1861 northern and southern evangelicals could barely communicate across the sectional divide. But they addressed the same God, and in confidence and sincerity implored Him to prosper the right.[5]

Abbreviations Used in Notes

AHMS	American Home Missionary Society
AHR	*American Historical Review*
AQ	*American Quarterly*
BDAC	*Biographical Directory of the American Congress* (Washington, DC, 1961)
CAJ	*Christian Advocate and Journal* (New York)
CWH	*Civil War History*
DAB	*Dictionary of American Biography*
DU	Methodist Archives, Drew University
GTS	Garrett-Evangelical Theological Seminary, Evanston
JAH	*Journal of American History*
JER	*Journal of the Early Republic*
JSH	*Journal of Southern History*
Kallenbach	Joseph E. and Jessamine S. Kallenbach, *American State Governors, 1776–1976* (3 vols, Dobbs Ferry, NY, 1977)
LC	Library of Congress
MVHR	*Mississippi Valley Historical Review*
NEC	New England Conference Archives, Boston University
OCL	Oberlin College Library
PHS	Presbyterian Historical Society, Philadelphia
SCA	*Southern Christian Advocate* (Charleston, SC)
SHC	Southern Historical Collection, University of North Carolina at Chapel Hill
WC	Wheaton College, Illinois
WCA	*Western Christian Advocate* (Cincinnati)
WEGT	Transcripts provided by Professor W.E. Gienapp

Notes

Introduction

[1] Henry F. May, "The Recovery of American Religious History," *AHR*, 70 (Oct. 1964), 79–92; Mark A. Noll (ed.) *Religion and American Politics: From the Colonial Period to the 1980s* (New York, 1990); Garry Wills, *Under God: Religion and American Politics* (New York, 1990). See also Samuel P. Huntington, *American Politics: The Promise of Disharmony* (Cambridge, Mass., 1981); Furio Colombo, *God in America: Religion and Politics in the United States*, trans. Kristin Jarratt (New York, 1984). For other literature on the theme of church–state relations (in the broadest sense) in American history and on the intersection of religion and politics over the past fifteen years in particular, see the works cited in Mark A. Noll, "Introduction," Robert Wuthnow, "*Quid Obscurum*: The Changing Terrain of Church–State Relations," Lyman A. Kellstedt and Mark A. Noll, "Religion, Voting for President, and Party Identification, 1948–1984," in Noll, *Religion and American Politics*, 3–15, 337–79.

[2] John M. Murrin, "No Awakening, No Revolution? More Counterfactual Speculations," *Reviews in American History*, 11 (June 1983), 161–71; Daniel Walker Howe, "The Evangelical Movement and Political Culture in the North during the Second Party System," *JAH*, 77 (March 1991), 1216.

[3] Daniel Walker Howe, *The Political Culture of the American Whigs* (Chicago, 1979); William E. Gienapp, *The Origins of the Republican Party 1852–1856* (New York, 1987).

[4] The path-breaking proponents of an "ethnocultural" interpretation of Jacksonian and antebellum electoral behavior include Lee Benson, Ronald Formisano, and Paul Kleppner, whose works are discussed more fully below and in the bibliographical essay.

[5] Jean Baker, *Affairs of Party: The Political Culture of Northern Democrats in the Mid-Nineteenth Century* (Ithaca, NY, 1983), 22–24 and *passim*, imaginatively discusses the process by which "the family, the school, and the party inculcated public habits" amongst northern Democrats, but oddly offers little discussion of the role of religion.

[6] Donald M. Scott, *From Office to Profession: The New England Ministry* (Philadelphia, 1978), 147; Robert H. Wiebe, *The Opening of American Society: From the Adoption of the Constitution to the Eve of Disunion* (New York, 1984), 306. For a seminal study of the politically

energizing power of religion, see Michael Walzer's study of the "Calvinist saintliness" of the English Puritans, "the first of those self-disciplined agents of social and political reconstruction who have appeared so frequently in modern history." Michael Walzer, *The Revolution of the Saints: A Study in the Origins of Radical Politics* (London, 1966), ix and *passim.*

7 C.C. Goen, *Broken Churches, Broken Nation: Denominational Schisms and the Coming of the American Civil War* (Macon, Ga., 1985).

8 In some "ethnocultural" history, notably the writings of Joel Silbey, the discovery of religious and ethnic conflicts has tended to the deliberate de-emphasizing of sectional issues in the politics of the 1840s and 1850s. The quintessential statement is Joel H. Silbey, "The Civil War Synthesis in American Political History," *CWH*, 10 (June 1964), 130–40. But, as this book will demonstrate, there is no necessary antithesis. For some wise observations see, for example, Don E. Fehrenbacher, "The New Political History and the Coming of the Civil War," *Pacific Historical Review* 54 (May 1985), 117–42; William E. Gienapp, "Nativism and the Creation of a Republican Majority in the North before the Civil War," *JAH*, 72 (Dec. 1985), 529–32. In later work Silbey himself has sought to elucidate some of the connections between sectionalism and religious antipathies. Joel H. Silbey, *The Partisan Imperative: The Dynamics of American Politics before the Civil War* (New York, 1985).

9 For the synthesis of ethnocultural and economic interpretations of political behavior see in particular Howe, *American Whigs*; William R. Brock, *Parties and Political Conscience: American Dilemmas, 1840–1850* (New York, 1979); Harry L. Watson, *Liberty and Power: The Politics of Jacksonian America* (New York, 1990); Daniel Feller, "Politics and Society: Toward a Jacksonian Synthesis," *JER*, 10 (Summer 1990), 135–62.

10 *The Presbyterian*, 17 Oct. 1840.

11 For an especially persuasive working out of the argument that a moral chasm separated North and South, see Bertram Wyatt-Brown, *Yankee Saints and Southern Sinners* (Baton Rouge, La., 1985), 1–10 and *passim.*

12 Lewis O. Saum, *The Popular Mood of Pre-Civil War America* (Westport, Conn., 1980), xxii, 3–104. Bruce Laurie, *Working People of Philadelphia, 1800–1850* (Philadelphia, 1980), xii, 33–52, 115–24, 139–47, 168–203, demonstrates that evangelicalism was by no means a narrowly middle-class phenomenon and "identifies religion as a major component of worker culture."

Chapter 1 *Protestant Evangelicals in an Age of Mass Political Parties*

1 On the Second Great Awakening, see especially: William G. McLoughlin, *Modern Revivalism: Charles Grandison Finney to Billy Graham* (New York, 1959), 3–121; Nathan O. Hatch, *The Democratization of American Christianity* (New Haven, Conn., 1989). McLoughlin, concerned with the theological reorientation within Calvinism, considers the Awakening to have been over by 1835. Statistically, however, the escalating sequence of revivals only reached its climax in 1843. Richard Carwardine, *Transatlantic Revivalism: Popular Evangelicalism in Britain and America, 1790–1865* (Westport, Conn., 1978), 48–52.

2 Donald G. Mathews, "The Second Great Awakening as an Organizing Process 1780–1830: An Hypothesis," *AQ,* 21 (Spring 1969), 23–43; Tobias Spicer, *Autobiography . . .* (Boston, 1851), 33. See also William G. McLoughlin, "Introduction" to Charles G. Finney, *Lectures on Revivals of Religion,* ed. William G. McLoughlin (Cambridge, Mass., 1960), viii–ix; George M. Marsden, *The Evangelical Mind and the New School Presbyterian Experience: A Case Study of Thought and Theology in Nineteenth-Century America* (New Haven, Conn., 1970), 31–58.

[3] Donald G. Mathews, *Religion in the Old South* (Chicago, 1977); Gordon S. Wood, "Evangelical America and Early Mormonism," *New York History*, 61 (Oct. 1980), 359–86; Hatch, *The Democratization of American Christianity, passim*. For case studies that contextualize evangelical religion within the new social and economic order see Whitney R. Cross, *The Burned-Over District: The Social and Intellectual History of Enthusiastic Religion in Western New York, 1800–1850* (Ithaca, NY, 1950); Paul Johnson, *A Shopkeeper's Millennium: Society and Revivals in Rochester, New York, 1815–1837* (New York, 1978); Lawrence Foster, *Religion and Sexuality: Three American Communal Experiments of the Nineteenth Century* (New York, 1981); Mary Ryan, *Cradle of the Middle Class: The Family in Oneida County, New York, 1790–1865* (Cambridge, UK, 1981); Randolph A. Roth, *The Democratic Dilemma: Religion, Reform, and the Social Order in the Connecticut River Valley of Vermont, 1791–1850* (Cambridge, UK, 1987).

[4] Robert Baird, *Religion in America; or, An Account of the Origin, Relation to the State, and Present Condition of the Evangelical Churches in the United States* (New York, 1856), 370. See also Perry Miller, *The Life of the Mind in America: From the Revolution to the Civil War* (New York, 1965), 43–8.

[5] Ernst Tuveson, *Redeemer Nation: The Idea of America's Millennial Role* (Chicago, 1968); Sacvan Bercovitch, *The American Jeremiad* (Madison, Wisc., 1978); Ruth Bloch, *Visionary Republic: Millennial Themes in American Thought, 1756–1800* (Cambridge, UK, 1985); Timothy L. Smith, *Revivalism and Social Reform: American Protestantism on the Eve of the Civil War* (Harper Torchbook edn, New York, 1965), 103–47, 225–37 and *passim*; Marsden, *Evangelical Mind*, 182–92; E. Brooks Holifield, *The Gentlemen Theologians: American Theology in Southern Culture 1795–1860* (Durham, NC, 1978), 141. James L. Moorhead, "Between Progress and Apocalypse: A Reassessment of Millennialism in American Religious Thought, 1800–1880," *JAH*, 71 (Dec. 1984), 524–42, argues that even the prevailing optimistic postmillennialism incorporated apocalyptic elements.

[6] Smith, *Revivalism and Social Reform*, 33; Robert B. Mullin, *Episcopal Vision/American Reality: High Church Theology and Social Thought in Evangelical America* (New Haven, Conn., 1986), 106–13. However, Kathleen Kutolowski, "Identifying the Religious Affiliations of Nineteenth-Century Local Elites," *Historical Methods Newsletter*, 9 (Dec. 1975), 9–10, suggests that there were fairly frequent changes in denominational allegiance within the elites of frontier or post-frontier communities like those of Genesee County, NY, in the first half of the nineteenth century. These shifts seem to have been largely due to a lack of churches and to the non-sectarian character of Protestantism there. Vernon Burton explains that the limited availability of preaching in Edgefield County, South Carolina, "meant that when a preacher was available people of different denominations would attend the same church: hence the values of the different denominations were mingled" (Orville V. Burton, *In My Father's House Are Many Mansions: Family and Community in Edgefield, South Carolina* (Chapel Hill, NC, 1985), 22. For a discussion that places the centrifugal, atomistic tendencies of American Protestantism within the context of the shared Biblicism, millennialism, and providentialism of popular religion, see Hatch, *The Democratization of American Christianity*, 162–7.

[7] *Christian Watchman and Reflector*, 8 Oct. 1857; *SCA* (Charleston, SC), 6 May 1858.

[8] William L. Muncy, *A History of Evangelism in the United States* (Kansas City, 1945), 111; Robert Baird, *Religion in the United States of America . . .* (Glasgow, 1844), 600–3; *idem*, *Religion in America*, 530–2; Henry C. Fish, *Primitive Piety Revived, or the Aggressive Power of the Christian Church* (Boston, 1856), 25–6; *CAJ*, 2 June 1853, 26 Jan., 22 June 1854,

9 Oct. 1856; Carwardine, *Transatlantic Revivalism*, 27–8, 30–1.

[9] Sydney E. Ahlstrom, *A Religious History of the American People* (New Haven, 1972), 483, 615–32; Walter H. Conser, *Church and Confession: Conservative Theologians in Germany, England, and America, 1815–1866* (Macon, Ga., 1984), 217–309.

[10] M.J. Heale, *The Making of American Politics, 1750–1850* (London, 1977), 116–62; Ralph Ketcham, *Presidents above Party: The First American Presidency, 1789–1829* (Chapel Hill, NC, 1984); Michael Wallace, "Changing Concepts of Party in the United States: New York 1815–1828," *AHR*, 74 (Dec. 1968), 453–91.

[11] For the origins and characteristic features of the second party system, see Richard P. McCormick, *The Second American Party System: Party Formation in the Jacksonian Era* (Chapel Hill, NC, 1966); see also William N. Chambers and Philip C. Davis, "Party Competition and a Mass Participation: The Case of the Democratizing Party System, 1824–1852," in Joel H. Silbey, Allan Bogue, and William H. Flanagan (eds) *The History of American Electoral Behavior* (Princeton, NJ, 1978), 174–97. Gerald Ginsburg, "Computing Antebellum Turnout: Methods and Models," *Journal of Interdisciplinary History*, 16 (Spring 1986), 579–611, doubts that the antebellum electorate was as fully mobilized as is commonly claimed. For a riposte, see Walter Dean Burnham, "Those High Nineteenth-Century American Voting Turnouts: Fact or Fiction?" *ibid.*, 613–44.

[12] Ronald P. Formisano, "Political Character, Antipartyism and the Second Party System," *AQ*, 21 (Winter 1969), 683–709; Ronald P. Formisano, *The Birth of Mass Political Parties: Michigan, 1827–1861* (Princeton, NJ, 1971), 56–80; Howe, *American Whigs*, esp. 43–68; John Ashcroft, *"Agrarians" & "Aristocrats": Party Political Ideology in the United States, 1837–1846* (London, 1983), 205–18.

[13] John C. Lord, *Signs of the Times: A Sermon*... (Buffalo, NY, 1837), 5–7; Nathaniel Gage, *Sins and Dangers of the Times: A Sermon*... (Haverhill, Mass., 1838), 21; La Roy Sunderland to E. Kibby, 9 Sept. 1835, NEC; Hugh H. Davis, "The Reform Career of Joshua Leavitt, 1794–1873" (PhD diss., Ohio State University, 1969), 115–16; John W. Nevin, *Party Spirit: An Address*... (Chambersburg, Pa., 1840), 9 and *passim*; Theodore Appel, *The Life and Work of John Williamson Nevin* (Philadelphia, 1889), 117–25.

[14] Alexander T. McGill, *The Presence of God a People's Prosperity: A Sermon*... (Philadelphia, 1841), 7; *WCA*, 25 Dec. 1840; Benjamin Labaree, *A Sermon on the Death of General Harrison*... (Middlebury, Vt., 1841), 14–15; Stephen Colwell, *Politics for American Christians*... (Philadelphia, 1852), 52–5; *Oberlin Evangelist*, 20 Nov. 1844; James C. Watson, *Oration on the Death of William Henry Harrison* (Gettysburg, Pa., 1841), 19.

[15] Ketcham, *Presidents above Party*, 157, sees antipartyism "[d]eriving in part from a Winthropian sense of an organic society knit together in brotherly affection for the good of the whole, and imbued with an Edwardsian vision of a worldwide 'pious union' of Christian love." See also Formisano, "Political Character," 707–8 (stressing the influence of New England town culture on the development of antipartyism); Heale, *Making of American Politics*, 151–2, 159; Richard Hofstadter, *The Idea of a Party System: The Rise of Legitimate Opposition in the United States, 1780–1840* (Berkeley, Calif., 1969), 8–9, 12, 20, 199, 266–7; Daniel W. Howe, *The Unitarian Conscience: Harvard Moral Philosophy, 1805–1861* (Cambridge, Mass., 1970), 207.

[16] Leonard Bacon, *The Duties Connected with the Present Commercial Distress: A Sermon*... (New Haven, Conn., 1837), 12–14; Cornelius C. Cuyler, *The Signs of the Times: A Series of Discourses*... (Philadelphia, 1839), 261; William Ramsey, *A Sermon Occasioned by the Death of William Henry Harrison*... (Philadelphia, 1841), 14; Frederick J. Jobson, *America, and American Methodism* (New York, 1857),

30; John Wheeler, *A Discourse, Occasioned by the Death of Gen. William Henry Harrison* ... (Burlington, Vt., 1841), 12–15, 30–2; William T. Dwight, '*A Great Man Fallen': A Discourse* ... (Portland, Me., 1841), 17–19; William C. Crane, *A Discourse Occasioned by the Death of William Henry Harrison* ... (Ann Arbor, Mich., 1841), 24–5; Chauncey Hobart, *Recollection of My Life: Fifty Years of Itinerancy in the Northwest* (Redwing, Minn., 1885), 202–3; John Mason Duncan, *A Discourse Delivered on the Fast Day* ... (Baltimore, 1841), 21, 24–30; Nathaniel Hewit, *Discourse at the Funeral Solemnities* ... (Bridgeport, Conn., 1841), 12–13; George W. Bethune, *Sermon on Thanksgiving Day* ... (New York, 1856), 9. Wallace, "Changing Concepts," 481–91, examining the developing theoretical defense of party in the 1820s, shows how the new party men of the Albany Regency argued that the consensual ideal encouraged vacillation, trimming, despotism, and other moral evils: the truly virtuous, moral man was the partisan.

[17] Labaree, *Harrison*, 16; *WCA*, 18 Dec. 1840.

[18] Bacon, *Commercial Distress*, 12; Edward A. Lawrence, *A Discourse on the Death of ... Daniel Webster* ... (Boston, Mass., 1852), 14; Silas McKeen, *God Our Only Hope: A Discourse* ... (Belfast, Me., 1837), 20–2; E. Stearns, "Christian Politics," *Quarterly Christian Spectator*, 10 (1838), 437; *WCA*, 30 July, 17 Dec. 1841.

[19] Calvin Fletcher, *The Diary of Calvin Fletcher*, ed. Gayle Thornbrough, Dorothy L. Riker, and Paula Corpuz (6 vols, Indianapolis, 1972–77), III, 80; *Oberlin Evangelist*, 13 Oct. 1852; Alfred Brunson, *A Western Pioneer; or Incidents of the Life and Times of Rev. Alfred Brunson* ... (2 vols, Cincinnati, 1880), II, 140–2; Horace Bushnell, "American Politics," *American National Preacher*, 14 (Dec. 1840), 201; George Lewis, *Impressions of America and the American Churches* ... (Edinburgh, 1845), 394–6; *WCA*, 10 Jan. 1840, 17 June 1842; McGill, *Presence of God*, 7. See also Charles White, "Political Rectitude,"

American Biblical Repository, 3rd ser. 2 (Oct. 1846), 602–12.

[20] *SCA*, 16 March 1855; *Olive Branch and Weekly Messenger*, quoted in *WCA*, 4 June 1841; *Pittsburgh Conference Journal*, 5 Sept. 1839; *WCA*, 25 March 1842, 21 July 1852, 21 Dec. 1853, 14 March 1855; Labaree, *Harrison*, 13, 19; George Duffield, *A Thanksgiving Sermon: The Religious Character of a People the True Element of Their Prosperity* (Detroit, 1839), 12–13; Mark Trafton, *Scenes in My Life: Occurring during a Ministry of Nearly Half a Century in the Methodist Episcopal Church* (New York, 1878), 232; Cuyler, *Signs of the Times*, 75–81; R. Emory to J. Emory, 26 May 1832, Emory Papers, DU; J.C. Bontecou to S.L. Pease, 17 Aug. 1844, NEC; Charles White, *A Sermon ... May 14, 1841, the Day of the National Fast* ... (Owego, NY, 1841), 33–4; *CAJ*, 25 Dec. 1844; Ramsey, *Harrison*, 12; Jonathan Blanchard, *A Perfect State of Society* ... (Oberlin, Ohio, 1839), 12.

[21] Davis W. Clark, *The Problem of Life* ... (Cincinnati, 1861), 19; Matthew Simpson, "Reasons for Building a Metropolitan Church in Washington," n.d. (*c.*1854), M. Simpson Papers, DU. See also John A. Roche, *The Life of J.P. Durbin* (New York, 1889), 60–1. Kutolowski, "Religious Affiliations," 11–12, shows how local political leaders in upstate New York were often only nominally attached to churches; many were drawn to the Episcopal church, which offered status without the rigors of strict evangelical piety.

[22] *WCA*, 7 July 1852, 22, 29 July 1857; Glyndon G. Van Deusen, *William Henry Seward* (New York, 1967), 37–8; Peyton C. Hoge, *Moses Drury Hoge: Life and Letters* (Richmond, Va., *c.*1899), 94; *SCA*, 29 June, 10 Aug. 1849; Robert and Elizabeth Stuart, *Stuart Letters of Robert and Elizabeth Stuart, 1819–1864*, ed. Helen S.M. Marlatt (2 vols, New York, 1961), I, 422; *Oberlin Evangelist*, 24 Nov. 1852; *New York Observer*, 12 June 1856. For evangelicals' mixed assessments of Daniel Webster's religion, see Nehemiah Adams, *A Sermon Preached ... the Sab-*

bath after the Interment of Hon. Daniel Webster... (Boston, 1852), 14–19; Henry A. Boardman, *A Discourse on the Life and Character of Daniel Webster* (Philadelphia, 1852), 51–61; Roswell D. Hitchcock, *A Eulogy on Daniel Webster*... (Brunswick, Me., 1852), 42–3.

[23] William L. Breckinridge, *Submission to the Will of God: A Fast Day Sermon*... (Louisville, 1841), 24–7; Artemus Bullard, *A Sermon Preached... on the Death of William Henry Harrison* (St Louis, Mo., 1841), 15–16; Heman Humphrey, *Death of President Harrison: A Discourse*... (Amherst, Mass., 1841), 16; Joshua L. Wilson, *A Sermon, in Memory of the Death of William Henry Harrison*... (Cincinnati, 1841), 8; Hewit, *Funeral Solemnities*, 6–8; Joshua Bates, *A Discourse on the Character, Public Services, and Death of John Quincy Adams* (Worcester, Mass., 1848); Stedman W. Hanks, *A Sermon on the Occasion of the Death of John Quincy Adams*... (Lowell, Mass., 1848), 20–22; *New York Freeman's Journal*, 12 Feb. 1848; *Oberlin Evangelist*, 13 March 1844; Moses M. Henkle, *The Life of Henry Bidleman Bascom* (Nashville, Tenn., 1856), 135–9; Howe, *American Whigs*, 58–9; *Memorials of Philemon H. Fowler* (New York, 1881), 10, describing Adams as a Unitarian "with a decided leaning towards Puritanism"; William Hague, *A Discourse Occasioned by the Death of John Quincy Adams*... (Boston, 1848), 20–21; Leonard E. Lathrop, *A Discourse on the Death of John Quincy Adams*... (Auburn, NY, 1848), 24–7.

[24] Wheeler, *Harrison*, 26–7; *WCA*, 16 April, 16, 30 July 1841; James L. Reynolds, *A Discourse Delivered at the Furman Theological Institution*... (Winnsborough, SC, 1841), 12; Colwell, *Politics for American Christians*, 59; Fletcher, *Diary*, IV, 487; V, 533; Labaree, *Harrison*, 29–30; Henry A. Boardman, *A Sermon Occasioned by the Death of William Henry Harrison*... (Philadelphia, 1841), 18–24; John Richards, *Eulogy Pronounced Before the Citizens of Windsor*... (Windsor, Vt., 1841), 16–18; *Pittsburgh Christian Advocate*, 17 March, 5 May 1841; Cornelius

C. Vanarsdale, *Lessons of Wisdom for a Mourning People*... (Philadelphia, 1841), 16; William R. De Witt, *A Discourse on the Life and Character of Francis R. Shunk*... (Harrisburg, Pa., 1848), 26; Ebenezer P. Rogers, *Religion in Public Life: A Discourse*... (Albany, NY, 1860), 19–24.

[25] John M. Krebs, *Righteousness the Foundation of National Prosperity: A Sermon*... (New York, 1835), 21; Edward N. Kirk, *An Oration on the Occasion of the National Fast*... (New York, 1841), 25; John Codman, *The Importance of Moderation in Civil Rulers: A Sermon*... (Boston, 1840), 14; Cuyler, *Signs of the Times*, 289; *Oberlin Evangelist*, 9 Oct., 20 Nov. 1844; *CAJ*, 23 Oct. 1856; Colwell, *Politics for American Christians*, 57–8; *WCA*, 30 July, 17 Dec. 1841; Boardman, *Daniel Webster*, 36; Horace Bushnell, *Politics Under the Law of God: A Discourse*... (Hartford, Conn., 1844), 11–12; Henry A. Boardman, *Moral Courage: A Sermon*... (Philadelphia, 1856), 22–3.

[26] Mary Riggs to her brothers, 20 Jan. 1841, Riggs Papers, PHS; White, *National Fast*, 37; *Zion's Advocate and Wesleyan Register*, quoted in *WCA*, 25 Dec. 1840; *WCA*, 2 Aug. 1848; T.M. Eddy to A. White, 2 Aug. 1844, Eddy Papers, GTS; R. Emory to C. Emory, 13 Nov. 1844, Emory Papers, DU.

[27] *SCA*, 23 Oct. 1856. See also John Marsh, *Temperance Recollections: Labors, Defeats, Triumphs: An Autobiography* (New York, 1866), 298; *WCA*, 14 Oct. 1842; *Pittsburgh Christian Advocate*, 14 Aug. 1844; *Knoxville Whig*, 20 Nov. 1852; William G. Hawkins, *Life of John H.W. Hawkins* (Boston, 1859), 181–2; Ian R. Tyrrell, *Sobering Up: From Temperance to Prohibition in Antebellum America, 1800–1860* (Westport, Conn., 1979), 206–7. The Methodist preacher Dan Young led a successful campaign against election treating in New Hampshire. Southern Methodists were less successful, even less ambitious: one of them won a Mississippi election by outdoing his opponent in dispensing drink. Dan Young, *Autobiography*... (New York, 1860), 233–5; W.J. Rorabaugh, *The*

Alcoholic Republic: America 1790–1840 (New York, 1979), 152.

[28] *Pittsburgh Christian Advocate*, 20 Nov. 1844; *Biblical Recorder*, 16 Nov. 1844.

[29] *WCA*, 21 Aug. 1840, 28 July 1852, 6 and 20 Aug., 17 Sept., 8 Oct. 1856; *CAJ*, 20 Dec. 1860; *Northwestern Christian Advocate*, 12 Nov. 1856; William Wisner, *Incidents in the Life of a Pastor* (New York, 1852), 267–70; *New York Evangelist*, 21 Nov. 1844; *Christian Watchman and Reflector*, 8 Jan. 1857; David Lewis, *Recollections of a Superannuate*... (Cincinnati, 1857), 295–6; James E. Welch, *Diary*, 7 Oct. 1840, PHS; William B. Sprague, *A Sermon on the Danger of Political Strife*... (Albany, NY, 1844).

[30] *WCA*, 19 March, 1 June 1841, 15 Nov. 1854, 7 Jan. 1857; *SCA*, 14 July 1848; Fletcher, *Diary*, IV, 437; *CAJ*, 4 Nov. 1840; Thomas S. Sheardown, *Half a Century's Labors in the Gospel*... (Lewisburg, Pa., 1865), 24–42.

[31] *WCA*, 5 June 1840, 29 Jan. 1841, 20 Aug. 1856; John D. Lang, *Religion and Education in America*... (London, 1840), 320–1; *Pittsburgh Conference Journal*, 16 April 1840; *Oberlin Evangelist*, 16 Dec. 1840; Heman Bangs, *The Autobiography and Journal of Rev. Heman Bangs*... (New York, 1872); *CAJ*, 27 Nov. 1844.

[32] Dwight, *"A Great Man Fallen,"* 17–19; Daniel S. Doggett, *A Sermon on the Occasion of the Death of General William Henry Harrison*... (Richmond, Va., 1841), 22; Reynolds, *Discourse May 14, 1841*, 12; Erskine Mason, *God's Hand in Human Events: A Sermon*... (New York, 1850); Abraham B. Van Zandt, *God's Voice to the Nation: A Sermon*... (Petersburg, Va., 1850), 15–16; David Magie, *God's Voice and the Lessons It Teaches: A Sermon*... (New York, 1850), 10–11; Jacob West, *Our Nation's Refuge – The Chamber of Solemn Reflection: A Sermon*... (Schoharie Court House, NY, ?1850), 10–12.

[33] Tryon Edwards, *God's Voice to the Nation: A Discourse*... (Rochester, New York, 1841), 9–10; Boardman, *Daniel Webster*, 35–6; *Oberlin Evangelist*, 13 Oct. 1852; F. Hemenway, "Oration for 4 July 1851," F. Hemenway Papers, GTS.

[34] Joseph L. Blau, "The Christian Party in Politics," *The Review of Religion*, 11 (Nov. 1946), 18–35; J.T. Crane, "Party Politics," *Methodist Quarterly Review*, 20 (Oct. 1860), 584; "Party Spirit in America," *Christian Review*, 20 (1955), 96–108; Joseph P. Thompson, *Duties of the Christian Citizen: A Discourse* (New York, 1848), 15–16. Ronald P. Formisano, *The Transformation of Political Culture: Massachusetts Parties 1790s to 1840* (New York, 1983), 93–101, documents shifting attitudes to party amongst the Massachusetts clergy from 1800 to 1844 and notes the explicit and controversial acceptance of the benefits of party in the 1840s. See also South Middlesex Conference of Churches, *The Political Duties of Christians: A Report*... (Boston, 1848), 22: "parties... must not only be expected and endured, but depended upon."

[35] I have followed George M. Marsden, *Fundamentalism and American Culture: The Shaping of Twentieth-Century Evangelicalism: 1870–1925* (New York, 1980), 7, 85–93, 252, in using the term "pietist" in this context, aware that it is charged with a number of different meanings and nuances. This usage draws on Troeltsch: "Pietism does not seek to reform the world.... [It makes] life... more personal and inward.... When it does influence civilization at all, particularly on the political and social side, it does so reluctantly and almost involuntarily" (Ernst Troeltsch, *The Social Teachings of the Christian Churches*, trans. Olive Wyon, 2 vols, London, 1931, II, 718–19). Yet Troeltsch identified several kinds of pietism, and contrasted the quietist, Continental model with the Puritan pietism of England, activist and reformist, seeking to transform the culture. William G. McLoughlin, drawing also on H.R. Niebuhr and E.S. Morgan, has described this dynamic pietist-perfectionism as one of the bases of American civilization, and the tensions within it (between conservatives seeking to maintain perfect moral order and an organic state, and

antinomians primarily concerned to attain perfect moral freedom) as continuous throughout American history. McLoughlin, "Pietism and American Character," *AQ*, 17 (Summer 1965), 163−86. A number of historians have drawn with profit on Lenski's study of Detroit in the 1950s, where he related political behavior to two broad religious orientations, "doctrinal orthodoxy" (compartmentalizing the sacred and secular) and "devotionalism" (stressing the oneness of life). Gerhard E. Lenski, *The Religious Factor: A Sociological Study of Religious Impact on Politics, Economics and Family Life* (New York, 1961), 22−4, 50−5, 182−7. Paul Kleppner, *The Third Electoral System, 1853−1892: Parties, Voters, and Political Cultures* (Chapel Hill, NC, 1979), esp. xix−xx, 185−97, offers a significant reformulation and refinement of the religious categories he adopted earlier in *The Cross of Culture: A Social Analysis of Midwestern Politics, 1850−1900* (New York, 1900): he distinguishes between *"evangelical pietists,"* who saw conversion as only part of a broader obligation to sanctify society, and *"salvationist pietists,"* who felt no responsibility to transform the wider culture. His categories correspond respectively to Marsden's "Calvinists" and "pietists," which I prefer as less cumbersome and which are no less theologically nuanced. See also Richard Jensen, "Religion, Morality, and American Politics," *Journal of Libertarian Studies*, 6 (1982), 321−8. For a thoughtful discussion of the persisting "Calvinist" or "Reformed" approach to American politics, see Mark A. Noll, *One Nation Under God? Christian Faith & Political Action in America* (San Francisco, 1988), 14−31 and *passim*.

[36] Emerson Andrews, *Living Life: or, Autobiography*... (Boston, 1872), 242.

[37] Mathews, *Religion in the Old South*, 98, 197; Kleppner, *Third Electoral System*, 186; David E. Harrell, Jr, *Quest for Christian America: The Disciples of Christ and American Society to 1866* (Nashville, 1966), 54−8; George F. Magoun, *Asa Turner: A Home Missionary Patriarch*

(Boston, 1889), 283−4; Thomas B. Miller, *Original and Selected Thoughts on the Life and Times of Rev. Thomas Miller, and Rev. Thomas Warburton* (Bethlehem, Pa., 1860), 17; Bangs, *Autobiography and Journal*, 316; J.H. Davis to R.B. Davis, 26 March 1856, Beale−Davis Papers, SHC. See also A.T. Davis to W.F. Davis, 29 Nov. 1855; A.T. Davis to J. Davis, 22 March 1858, *ibid.*; E.V. Levert to F.J. Levert, 10 Oct. 1860, Levert Papers, SHC; I.L. Brookes to Mr. Wood, 14 Jan. 1857, Brookes Papers, SHC; T.M. Eddy to A. White, 9 Nov. 1844, 1 and 21 March 1845, T.M. Eddy Papers, GTS; Walter C. Palmer, *Life and Letters of Leonidas L. Hamline, D.D.* (New York, 1866), 88; William Warren Sweet, *Religion on the American Frontier* (4 vols, Chicago, 1931−46), IV, 455. For a blistering Antimission attack on "law religion" and "priestly influence" in politics, see *WCA*, 6 Aug. 1851; but in the main the preoccupation of Baptist and other Antimissionists with individual salvation did not prevent them from adopting an ardent Jacksonian stance. Byron C. Lambert, *The Rise of the Anti-Mission Baptists: Sources and Leaders, 1800−1840* (New York, 1980), v−vi. Harry L. Watson, *Jacksonian Politics and Community Conflict: The Emergence of the Second American Party System in Cumberland County, North Carolina* (Baton Rouge, La., 1981), 240−1, identifies a high proportion of political abstainers amongst the Baptists and Methodists of that part of the state. For the apolitical orientation of early nineteenth-century foreign missionaries, see Bertram Wyatt-Brown, *Saints and Sinners*, 68−74.

[38] *Pittsburgh Christian Advocate*, 11 Nov. 1840, 5 June 1844; *CAJ*, 28 Oct. 1840; E. Mudge to B. Pitman, 22 Oct. 1844, NEC. See also Gideon B. Perry, *Two Discourses on the Occasion of the Death of William Henry Harrison*... (Alton, Ill., 1841), 5.

[39] *WCA*, quoting from *Signs of the Times*, 28 Aug. 1840; Jonathan K. Peck, *Luther Peck and His Five Sons* (Cincinnati, 1897), 216. For Millerism and its proph-

ecies of the world's end, first in 1843 and then in March and October 1844, see Cross, *Burned-Over District*, 287–321.

[40] H.K. Carroll, *The Religious Forces of the United States Enumerated, Classified and Described on the Basis of the Government Census of 1890* (New York, 1893, 309–12; Robert E. Thompson, *A History of the Presbyterian Churches in the United States* (New York, 1895), 75, 102–4; James B. Scouller, *A Manual of the United Presbyterian Church of North America 1751–1887* (rev. edn, Pittsburgh, 1887), 155–6; Samuel B. Wylie, *The Two Sons of Oil; or, The Faithful Witness for Magistracy & Ministry upon a Scriptural Basis*, (3rd edn, Philadelphia, 1850), 47–71.

[41] John R. McKivigan, "Abolitionism and the American Churches 1830–1865: A Study in Attitudes and Tactics" (PhD diss., Ohio State University, 1977), 167; Luther Lee, *Autobiography...* (New York, 1882), 281; Lewis Perry, *Radical Abolitionism: Anarchy and the Government of God in Antislavery Thought* (Ithaca, 1973), 52, 78, 162 and *passim*; Aileen S. Kraditor, *Means and Ends in American Abolitionism: Garrison and His Critics on Strategy and Tactics, 1834–1850* (New York, 1968), esp. 78–140.

[42] Scott, *From Office to Profession*, 27–35; Bloch, *Visionary Republic*, 214–20; Howe, *American Whigs*, 158; Mark Tucker, *A Discourse Preached on Thanksgiving Day, in the Beneficent Congregational Meeting-House, Providence, July 21, 1842* (Providence, RI, 1842), 4.

[43] Marsden, *Fundamentalism and American Culture*, 85–93 and *passim*; David Moberg, *The Great Reversal: Evangelism versus Social Concern* (rev. edn, Philadelphia, 1972), 28–45; Donald W. Dayton, *Discovering an Evangelical Heritage* (New York, 1976), 121–41 and *passim*. However, for the argument that postbellum Methodism lost little of its pre-Civil War disposition towards public engagement and social action, see Donald G. Jones, *The Sectional Crisis and Northern Methodism: A Study in Piety, Political Ethics and Civil Religion*

(Metuchen, NJ, 1979). 1–5 and *passim*.

[44] Finney, *Lectures on Revivals*, 297; *WCA*, 6 Jan. 1843; Augustus B. Longstreet, *Letter from President Longstreet to the Public...* (n.p., n.d. [c.1855]), 5; *Northwestern Christian Advocate*, 12 Nov. 1856; Calvin Fairbank, *Rev. Calvin Fairbank During Slavery Times...* (Chicago, 1890), 168; Granville Moody, *A Life's Retrospect: Autobiography of Rev. Granville Moody* (Cincinnati, 1890), 306–8; *Madison Courier*, undated cutting, T.M. Eddy Papers, GTS; *CAJ*, 14 Aug. 1844; *Oberlin Evangelist*, 11 Sept. 1844, 13 Sept. 1848; McGill, *Presence of God*, 7–8; *Christian Watchman and Reflector*, 10 April 1856; Fletcher, *Diary*, IV, 46.

[45] H.H. Green, *The Simple Life of a Commoner: An Autobiography* (Decorah, Iowa, 1911), 51–2; D.R. McAnally, *Life and Times of Rev. S. Patton, D.D., and Annals of the Holston Conference* (St Louis, Mo., 1859), 239; Jacob Osgood, *The Life and Christian Experience of Jacob Osgood...* (Warner, NH, 1873), 31–2, 61–5, 84, 114–16.

[46] Fred J. Hood, *Reformed America: The Middle and Southern States, 1783–1837* (University of Alabama, 1980) argues persuasively for the influence of the Reformed tradition on the political thinking of many early nineteenth-century Baptists, Methodists, and Episcopalians. For the convergence and reciprocal reinforcement of classical republican and Protestant traditions in the era of the American Revolution, see Bloch, *Visionary Republic*, 63–4, 109–10 and *passim*.

[47] George Peck, *National Evils and Their Remedy: A Discourse...* (New York, 1841), 31–2; Alfred B. Ely, *A Eulogy on the Life and Character of Zachary Taylor...* (Boston, 1850), 4; T.H. Skinner, *Religion and Liberty: A Discourse...* (New York, 1841), 22–4; *WCA*, 19 Feb. 1841; *CAJ*, 29 Nov. 1848; Bela B. Edwards, *Address Delivered on the Day of the National Fast...* (Andover, 1841), 22–5; Mark Hopkins, *A Sermon, Delivered at Plymouth...* (Boston, 1847), 14–16.

[48] Dwight, "A Great Man Fallen,"

14–15; *WCA*, 19 Feb. 1841; Bushnell, "American Politics," 199–200; Theodore J. Frelinghuysen, *An Inquiry into the Moral and Religious Character of the American Government* (New York, 1838), 143; Robert Turnbull, *The Mighty Fallen! A Sermon* . . . (Boston, 1841), 19–20; Benjamin F. Tefft, *The Republican Influence of Christianity: A Discourse* . . . (Bangor, Me., 1841), 1–8; Charles B. Boynton, *Oration* . . . *Before the Native Americans of Cincinnati* (Cincinnati, 1847), 19; Michel Chevalier, *Society, Manners and Politics in the United States: Being a Series of Letters on North America* (Boston, 1839), 368; Lyman Beecher, "Republicanism of the Bible," *The Hesperian: or Western Monthly Magazine*, 1 (1838), 47–53 ("our own republic, in its constitution and its laws, is of heavenly origin. It is not borrowed from Greece or Rome, but . . . from the Bible."); J.V. Moore, "Republican Tendency of the Bible," *Methodist Quarterly Review*, 6 (April 1846), 202–26; Enoch Pond, "Republican Tendencies of the Bible," *American Biblical Repository*, 3rd ser. 4 (April 1848), 283–98; John M. Peck, *The Principles and Tendencies of Democracy: An Address* . . . (Belville, Ill., 1838), 11.

[49] *CAJ*, 28 Jan. 1846; Colwell, *Politics for American Christians*, 51; *WCA*, 16 Oct. 1840, 29 Jan., 24 Sept. 1841; Wilson, *Harrison*, 3; Krebs, *Righteousness*, 6; Nathaniel Bouton, *The Good Land in Which We Live: A Discourse* . . . (Concord, NH, 1850), 9–10; Thomas Williams, *Eulogium on the Life and Character of William Henry Harrison* . . . (Harrisburg, Pa., 1841), 29–30; Joseph Abbott, *A Sermon Preached on the National Fast* . . . (Salem, Mass., 1841), 13 Vanarsdale, *Lessons of Wisdom*, 37; Walter Clarke, *Shimei and Abishai, or the Extreme Politicians* . . . (Hartford, Conn., 1851), 6–8; John N. Murdock, *The Signs of the Times* . . . (St Louis, Mo., 1855), 3–23, 144–84; Skinner, *Religion and Liberty*, 38–9, 50–1; Henry Clay Northcott, *Biography of Rev. Benjamin Northcott* . . . (Cincinnati, 1875), 93; Charles B. Boynton, *Our Country, the Herald of a New*

Era: A Lecture . . . (Cincinnati, 1847), 4–13, 20; Edwards, *National Fast*, 22–8; B.F. Morris, *Our Country: Three Discourses* . . . (Lawrenceburgh, Ind., 1848), 3–21; James Rowland, *The Glorious Mission of the American People: A Thanksgiving Discourse* . . . (Circleville, Ohio, 1850), 5–6; Charles W. Shields, *A Discourse on Christian Politics* . . . (Philadelphia, 1851), 25–9.

[50] Tefft, *Republican Influence*, 6; *SCA*, 6 July 1849; Hood, *Reformed America*, 7–112; Cuyler, *Signs of the Times*, 291; *WCA*, 16 Oct. 1840, 19 March 1841, 14 Jan. 1848; Doggett, *Harrison*, 16–17; M. Simpson, "Sketch of a Sermon," 18 Dec. 1859, M. Simpson Papers, DU; Boynton, *Our Country*, 12; Skinner, *Religion and Liberty*, vi, 74; Frelinghuysen, *Inquiry*, iii–iv, 184–98, 200–1, 207; Duncan, *Discourse on the Fast Day*, 6–7; Bushnell, *Politics Under the Law of God*, 10–11; J. Alden, "Baird's Religion in America Reviewed," *American Biblical Repository*, 3rd ser. 1 (July 1845), 492; Edward W. Hooker, "Political Duties of Christians," *American Quarterly Observer*, 1 (July 1833), 14; "The American State and Christianity," *Presbyterian Quarterly Review*, 8 (April 1860), 571–93; Lyman H. Atwater, *The Importance of Good Rulers* . . . (New Haven, Conn., 1844), 3–8.

[51] Boardman, *Harrison*, 19–20; Wheeler, *Harrison*, 26–7; Samuel D. Burchard, *Causes of National Solicitude: A Sermon* . . . (New York, 1848), 5; Brunson, *Western Pioneer*, II, 140; Philip D. Jordan, *William Salter, Western Torch-bearer* (Oxford, Ohio, 1939), 58; *WCA*, 29 Jan., 12 Nov. 1841; Breckinridge, *Submission*, 27–9; David H. Riddle, "The Morning Cometh"; *or, the Watchman's Voice: A Discourse* . . . (Pittsburgh, 1841), 3; William B. Sprague, *Voice of the Rod: A Sermon* . . . (Albany, NY, 1841), 5–6; *SCA*, 20 Dec. 1844, 13 July 1849; *CAJ*, 19 Nov. 1845; *Oberlin Evangelist*, 25 April 1849, 24 April 1850; Bethune, *Sermon on Thanksgiving-Day*, 5–6; Robert Bellah, "Civil Religion in America," *Daedalus*, 96 (Winter 1967), 1–21. For the more limited attention to Thanksgiving in

the South, particularly in its religious dimensions, see William D. Valentine, Diary, 16 Nov. 1849, SHC; S. Colton, Diary, 24 Nov. 1853, 25 Oct. 1855, SHC.

[52] *WCA*, 19 April 1848, 25 Feb. 1852, 11 Jan. 1854; *SCA*, 16 Dec. 1853, 7 Feb. 1856; Lorenzo D. Johnson, *An Address to the Pastors and People of These United States on the Chaplaincy of the General Government*... (Washington, DC, 1857), 3–9. Opponents of government chaplains, including Antimission Baptists in the South, forced the 33rd Congress to address the issue in 1853–54: the office was retained. Lorenzo D. Johnson, *Chaplains of the General Government, with Objections to their Employment Considered* (New York, 1856), 5–23.

[53] *WCA*, 16 Oct. 1840, 4 Feb., 2 Sept. 1842; *New York Evangelist*, 7 March, 19 April 1844; McGill, *Presence of God*, 9; Brunson, *Western Pioneer*, I, 285–6; Gage, *Sins and Dangers*, 6–9; Cuyler, *Signs of the Times*, 293.

[54] Doggett, *Harrison*, 1–16; Roche, *Durbin*, 76; *WCA*, 19 March 1841; Krebs, *Righteousness*, 6 and *passim*; Ramsey, *Harrison*, 6, 14; Sprague, *Voice of the Rod*, 21–2; Wilson, *Harrison*, 9–10; Labaree, *Harrison*, 8–11; *SCA*, 14 May 1847; Vanarsdale, *Lessons of Wisdom*, 34–6; William B. Sprague, *A Sermon Addressed to the Second Presbyterian Congregation in Albany*... (Albany, NY, 1838), 7.

[55] Abbott, *Sermon on the National Fast*, 20; Tefft, *Republican Influence*, 12.

[56] "During the Second Great Awakening... the evangelical Protestant denominations became a kind of national church dedicated to enforcing the moral law upon everyone in the nation either by revivalistic religion (which produced voluntary obedience) or by a majority vote of the regenerate (which compelled obedience of the unregenerate)." McLoughlin, "Pietism," 168.

[57] *SCA*, 14 May 1847; Colwell, *Politics for American Christians*, ii–iii, 20–1, 51; *Oberlin Evangelist*, 4 Dec. 1844, 5 Jan. 1848; *WCA*, 2 Jan. 1850, 28 July 1852. For the "conservative" power of evangelical revivalism and its protection of the republic, see Miller, *Life of the Mind*, 66–72. Donald Scott describes how early nineteenth-century New England clergy moved from stressing external discipline as the means of securing social order and came to emphasize the self-discipline of the individual; thus revivals became "an essential instrument of public guardianship" (Donald M. Scott, *From Office to Profession: The New England Ministry 1750–1850*, University of Pennsylvania, 1978, 36–51). For the evangelical's stress on self-control and for its political significance see also Howe, "The Evangelical Movement and Political Culture in the North," 1217–22; Holifield, *The Gentlemen Theologians*, 141–2, 145; Louise Stevenson, *Scholarly Means to Evangelical Ends: The New Haven Scholars and the Transformation of Higher Learning in America 1830–1890* (Baltimore, 1986), 114–16.

[58] Humphrey, *Harrison*, 22–3; *WCA*, 7 Aug., 25 Sept. 1840, 24 Sept. 1841; *CAJ*, 2 Aug. 1848; William C. Anderson, *The Republic and the Duties of the Citizen: A Sermon*... (Dayton, Ohio, 1847), 15; William A. Scott, *The Duty of Praying for Our Rulers: A Discourse*... (New Orleans, 1843), 3 and *passim*. For the argument that "the habits of praying for [public men of the opposing party] would soften the asperities of party strife," see Thompson, *Christian Citizen*, 11–13.

[59] *CAJ*, 28 Oct. 1840, 14 Aug. 1844; William G. Lewis, *Biography of Samuel Lewis, First Superintendent for Common Schools for the State of Ohio* (Cincinnati, 1857), 369; Moody, *Life's Retrospect*, 311; *WCA*, 30 Oct. 1840, 26 March 1841, 6 Aug., 8 Oct. 1856; *SCA*, 10 May, 15 Nov. 1844; *Ohio State Journal*, 23 Oct. 1848; John Rankin, *The Duty of Voting for Righteous Men for Office* (n.p., n.d.), *passim*; Crane, "Party Politics," 587; *Christian Watchman and Reflector*, 17 Sept. 1857; *Oberlin Evangelist*, 13 Oct. 1852.

[60] Ashbel Green, *The Life of Ashbel Green*... (New York, 1849), 470; Abraham R. Van Nest, *Memoir of Rev.*

Geo. W. Bethune, D.D., 361; George Coles, Diary, 8 Nov. 1842, 5 Nov. 1844, DU; *The Autobiography of Lyman Beecher*, ed. Barbara Cross (2 vols, Cambridge, Mass., 1961), II, 267; James E. Pilcher, *Life and Labors of Elijah H. Pilcher* (New York, 1892), 116; Northcott, *Northcott*, 93; J.J. Fleharty, *Glimpses of the Life of Rev. A.E. Phelps and His Co-laborers* ... (Cincinnati, 1878), 330; Lewis, *Recollections*, 294–5. See also A. Wood to L. Smith *et al.*, Aug. 1860, M. Simpson Papers, LC.

[61] *WCA*, 7 Aug. 1840, 4 June 1841, 9 Dec. 1842, 8 Oct. 1856; Sweet, *Religion on the American Frontier*, IV, 428, 436; *CAJ*, 8 Nov. 1848; *SCA*, 18 Feb. 1848; *Pittsburgh Conference Journal*, 26 March 1840; *Baptist Banner*, quoted in *WCA*, 5 July 1848; *Oberlin Evangelist*, 4 Aug. 1852; Charles S. Porter, *A Discourse Occasioned by the Death of William Henry Harrison* ... (New York, 1841), 23; Bushnell, *Politics Under the Law of God*, 16; *Christian Watchman and Reflector*, 20 Nov. 1840; Lewis, *Samuel Lewis*, 325, 342; *New York Observer*, quoted in *WCA*, 14 Oct. 1842; Fairbank, *Rev. Calvin Fairbank*, 167–8; T.M. Eddy, "Sermon on the Death of General Zachary Taylor," July 1850, Eddy Papers, GTS; Davis W. Clark, *An Alarm to Christian Patriots: A Thanksgiving Sermon* ... (Hartford, Conn., 1843), 15–16, 20.

[62] Stuart Blumin's study of the ten Protestant churches in Kingston, NY, in the 1850s [2 Dutch Reformed, 2 Presbyterian, 2 Methodist, 2 Baptist, 1 Episcopalian and 1 German Evangelical Lutheran] suggests that the churches' lay leadership tended to be active in the wider life of the community, and constituted 28.6 percent of Kingston's party political activists (committee men and convention delegates). Blumin, "Church and Community: A Case Study of Lay Leadership in Nineteenth-Century America," *New York History*, 56 (Oct. 1975), 404–5. For the view that evangelicals and "good men" had a duty to involve themselves in party primaries and other meetings see, for example, Samuel T. Spear, *The Politico-Social*

Foundations of Our Republic: A Sermon ... (New York, 1845), 12; Thompson, *Christian Citizen*, 16–17.

[63] *CAJ*, 28 Oct. 1840, 30 Oct., 13 Nov. 1856; *Pittsburgh Conference Journal*, 26 March 1840; Fletcher, *Diary*, V, 550; R. Emory to C.W. Emory, 9 Nov. 1844, Emory Papers, DU; Sweet, *Religion on the American Frontier*, IV, 643; Magoun, *Asa Turner*, 325; Sprague, *Voice of the Rod*, 14–15.

[64] See, for example, Riddle, "Morning Cometh," 18–20; Humphrey, *Harrison*, 20–1; Doggett, *Harrison*, 16–18. See also Adams, *Webster*, 11–14; Van Zandt, *God's Voice to the Nation*, 13–14: "Perhaps there are no people more prone than we to worship the idol of the hour.... There is in this modern apotheosis of individuals an atheistical contempt for Jehovah, which may be well supposed to provoke his displeasure."

[65] M. Simpson to M. Simpson, 25 May 1841, M. Simpson Papers, LC.

[66] Harriet Martineau, *Society in America*, ed. Seymour M. Lipset (New York, 1962), 352.

[67] Wilson L. Spottswood, *Brief Annals* (Harrisburg, Pa., 1888), 39. See also David H. Mickey, *Sunset on the Prairie: Life of DeWitt Clinton Huntington* (Lincoln, Neb., 1977), 37; Helen Nevius, *The Life of John Livingston Nevius* (New York, [1895]), 66–7. For a discussion of the great variety in American voting laws and procedures, and the persistence of viva voce voting in some states (especially in the South) into the second half of the century, see Paul F. Bourke and Donald A. DeBats, "Identifiable Voting in Nineteenth-Century America: Toward a Comparison of Britain and the United States before the Secret Ballot," *Perspectives in American History*, 11 (1977–8), 259–88. For ministers' confidently voting with an open or unfolded ballot paper, see *Knoxville Whig*, 2 Dec. 1846 (for the Cincinnati Presbyterian, Joshua Wilson), 7 June (for William G. Brownlow). The Whiggish George Duffield, aware of public scrutiny and confident Zachary Taylor would win,

cast his vote for Lewis Cass, the Democratic candidate, in the 1848 presidential election, out of "[p]ersonal attachment & to prevent him and his family from harbouring feelings toward myself which might in any degree impair my usefulness" (Lewis G. Vander Velde, "Notes on the Diary of George Duffield," *MVHR*, 24, June 1937, 59).

68 R.N. Price, *Holston Methodism: From Its Origin to the Present Time* (3 vols, Nashville, Tenn., 1908), III, 284; Bethune, *Sermon on Thanksgiving Day*, 30; John Codman, *The Signs of the Times: A Sermon* . . . (Boston, 1836), 7; *SCA*, 1 June 1849; Edward P. Humphrey and Thomas H. Cleland, *Memoirs of the Rev. Thomas Cleland, D.D.* . . . (Cincinnati, 1859), 189; Ichabod S. Spencer, *The National Warning: A Sermon* . . . (New York, 1841), 8; G.C. Cookman, "Watchman, what of the night?," 18 May 1839, G. Coles letterbook, DU; Adam Wallace, *The Parson of the Islands: A Biography of the Rev. Joshua Thomas* (Philadelphia, 1861), 324–5; *CAJ*, 3 Aug. 1842; William M. Wightman, *Life of William Capers* . . . (Nashville, Tenn., 1902), 514; *WCA*, 26 March 1841; Jacob B. Moore, *The Contrast: or, Plain Reasons Why William Henry Harrison Should Be Elected President of the United States* . . . (New York, 1840), 5; H.L. Chapman, *Memoirs of an Itinerant: An Autobiography* (n.p., n.d.), 132–4; L.W. Berry to M. Simpson, 30 July 1844, M. Simpson Papers, LC.

69 *Pittsburgh Conference Journal*, 21 May 1840; Anson Phelps Stokes, *Church and State in the United States: Historical Development and Contemporary Problems of Religious Freedom under the Constitution* (3 vols, New York, 1950), I, 622–8; Clark, *Alarm to Christian Patriots*, 16; *WCA*, 4 Sept. 1840, 30 April 1851, 9 Aug., 13 Dec. 1854; Lewis, *Impressions of America*, 100; *SCA*, 3 Aug. 1849, 23 Oct. 1856; Bethune, *Sermon on Thanksgiving Day*, 31–34; *Independent*, 6 April 1854; Pilcher, *Elijah H. Pilcher*, 116; William W. Crane, *Autobiography and Miscellaneous Writings of Elder W.W. Crane* (Syracuse, NY, 1891), 72, 114–15. See also Alexis de Tocque-

ville, *Democracy in America*, ed. J.P. Mayer (New York, 1969), 290–301, 448–9. Ralph A. Wooster, *The People in Power: Courthouse and Statehouse in the Lower South 1850–1860* (Knoxville, Tenn., 1969), 13, 25, 54, 98, 123, 131, 141, 146, notes that the bar on ministerial office-holding at state level in much of the South did not necessarily extend to county offices.

70 Wesley Norton, *Religious Newspapers in the Old Northwest to 1861: A History, Bibliography, and Record of Opinion* (Athens, Ohio, 1977), 26; *WCA*, 25 June, 6 Aug. 1856; *Pittsburgh Christian Advocate*, 14 April 1841, 20 Nov. 1844; *CAJ*, 27 Oct. 1841, 13 July 1842, 25 Dec. 1844, 21 Jan., 1 July, 11 Nov. 1846, 17 Jan. 1856; John F. Wright, *Sketches of the Life and Labors of James Quinn* (Cincinnati, 1851), 201; *SCA*, 10 May 1844.

71 *Oberlin Evangelist*, 4 Aug. 1852; *SCA*, 29 June 1844, 14 Sept. 1849; *Stuart Letters*, I, 496; II, 657. Elizabeth Stuart recognized her ambivalence. She wrote to her godly son-in-law: "I catch myself quarrelling because you are interested in Politics, yet every day of my life I pray to God to give us Rullers [sic] who fear God, and will keep his commandments" (II, 758).

72 See, for example, J.W. Lawrence to E. Osborn, 24 Jan. 1846, DU, and *WCA*, 3 April 1850 [correspondence on the Mexican war, Wilmot Proviso]; J. Leavitt to R.H. Leavitt, 17 May 1841, Leavitt Papers, LC, and J.A. Wright to M. Simpson, 7 Feb. and 23 Nov. 1844, M. Simpson Papers, LC [lobbying and patronage]; George Prentice, *American Religious Leaders: Wilbur Fisk* (New York, 1890), 253–4 [aid to denominational colleges]; *WCA*, 3, 17 Jan. 1840 [Ohio bill for the protection of religious assemblies].

73 *Christian Watchman and Reflector*, 11 Aug. 1840; Northcott, *Northcott*, 93.

74 Eden B. Foster, *Four Pastorates: Glimpses of the Life and Thoughts of Eden B. Foster, D.D.* (Boston, 1883), 70; Lyman Abbot, *Reminiscences* (Boston, 1915), 202; Lewis, *Impressions of America*, 394; Thomas

Nichols, *Forty Years of American Life* (2
vols, London, 1864), II, 232; *Oberlin
Evangelist*, 25 Sept. 1844, 22 Oct. 1856;
Erastus O. Haven, *Autobiography of Erastus
O. Haven, D.D., LL.D.* ... (New York,
1883), 133–5; William E. Griffis, *John M.
Chambers: Servant of Christ and Master of
Hearts and His Ministry in Philadelphia*
(Ithaca, NY, 1903), 111–17; Frances
M.B. Hilliard, *Stepping Stones to Glory:
From Circuit Rider to Editor and the Years in
Between: Life of David Rice McAnally, D.D.
1810–95* (Baltimore, 1975), 55–61; E.
Merton Coulter, *William G. Brownlow,
Fighting Parson of the Southern Highlands*
(Chapel Hill, NC, 1937), 42–3; Price,
Holston Methodism, III, 156–7, 347;
McAnally, *S. Patton*, 239–47; Oscar P.
Fitzgerald, *John B. McFerrin: A Biography*
(Nashville, Tenn., 1888), 255–6; *Highland
Messenger*, 5 June, 3 July 1840.

[75] Foster, *Four Pastorates*, 242; William
H. Lawrence, *The Earnest Minister: A
Record of the Life, Labors and Literary
Remains of Rev. Ruliff S. Lawrence* ...
(Philadelphia, 1873), 29; Lewis, *Samuel
Lewis*, 366; Ray Holder, *William Winans:
Methodist Leader in Antebellum Mississippi*
(Jackson, Miss., 1977), 184–90; Haven,
Autobiography, 127; *SCA*, 3 Aug. 1849;
WCA, 30 April 1851. See also W. Stanley
Hoole, "The Diary of Dr. Basil Manly,
1858–1867," *Alabama Review*, 4 (April
1951), 142. B.F. Tefft, *Methodism Success-
ful, and the Internal Causes of Its Success*
(New York, 1860), 197, estimated that
about a hundred lay Methodists served
in the US Congress in the 1850s, and
some twenty ministers.

[76] J. Harlan to M. Simpson, 27 April
1847; D. Reynolds to M. Simpson, Aug.
1843; L.W. Berry to M. Simpson, 16 Dec.
1851, M. Simpson Papers, LC; T.S. Parvin
to S.J. Baird, 15 April 1857, S.J. Baird
Papers, LC; Norton, *Religious Newspapers*,
102; *WCA*, 6 Aug., 3 Sept. 1851, 20
Oct. 1852. See also W.H. Daniels (ed.)
*Memorials of Gilbert Haven, Bishop of the
Methodist Episcopal Church* (Boston, 1882),
50; Jacob P. Fort, "Reminiscences," 233,
DU; Carl Kaestle, *Pillars of the Republic:
Common Schools and American Society, 1780–
1860* (New York, 1983), 113–15, 155, 157.

[77] Brunson, *Western Pioneer*, II, 140;
WCA, 8 Oct. 1851, 20 June 1855; William
J. Cotter, *My Autobiography* (Nashville,
Tenn., 1917), 116–17; *New York Evangelist*,
4 Jan. 1844; Lewis, *Impressions of America*,
99–100. This evidence of ministerial
pursuit of political office modifies
Tocqueville's judgment that "the
American clergy stand aloof from public
business." As a French Catholic he was
understandably impressed by the separation of church and state in the United
States; the stark contrast between the
public role of Christianity in Europe and
America led him to overstate his case
(Tocqueville, *Democracy in America*, 9–10,
291–301, 448–9).

[78] William McDonald and John
E. Searles, *The Life of Rev. John S.
Inskip, President of the National Association
for the Promotion of Holiness* (Chicago
and Boston, 1885), 49; *WCA*, 25 June
1856. See also Oscar P. Fitzgerald, *Judge
Longstreet: A Life Sketch* (Nashville, Tenn.,
1891), 58. Paul Johnson stresses the relatively limited involvement of evangelical
church members in political activity
in Rochester in the later 1820s, even
when sabbatarianism and Antimasonry
were the dominant issues (Johnson,
Shopkeeper's Millennium, 75–6). By
the 1850s, however, there was a very
much stronger relationship between
church membership and party activism.
For a discussion of the relationship
between southern churches, especially
the Presbyterians, and politics before
1861, and the pursuit of Christian community and even theocracy during the
war itself, see Jack P. Maddex, "From
Theocracy to Spirituality: The Southern
Presbyterian Reversal on Church and
State," *Journal of Presbyterian History*, 54
(Winter 1976), 438–57; Holifield, *The
Gentlemen Theologians*, 154; James O.
Farmer, *The Metaphysical Confederacy:
James Henley Thornwell and the Synthesis
of Southern Values* (Macon, Ga., 1986),
256–9; James O. Farmer, "Southern
Presbyterians and Southern Nationalism:
A Study in Ambivalence," *Georgia His-
torical Quarterly*, 75 (Summer 1991),
292–4. Kleppner's emphasis on the

"*salvationist*," apolitical pietism of the South is more appropriate for the post-bellum period than for the 1850s (Kleppner, *Third Electoral System*, 187).

[79] Richard D. Shiels, "The Feminization of American Congregationalism, 1730–1835," *AQ*, 33 (Spring 1981), 46–62, estimates that 69 percent of all new members of New England Congregational churches were women. The denominational figures for 1859 indicate a nearly identical figure of 67 percent for that section and something very similar (66 percent) nationwide. In some cases, as in Vermont, over three-quarters of the membership was female. *Congregational Quarterly*, 2 (Jan. 1860), 139; *New York Observer*, 3 Sept. 1857. See also Leonard I. Sweet, *The Minister's Wife: Her Role in Nineteenth-Century American Evangelicalism* (Philadelphia, 1983), 35–7.

[80] *Christian Watchman and Reflector*, 15 Oct. 1857. Barbara Welter argues that during the Second Great Awakening "[r]eligion...became the property of the ladies...[It] became more domesticated, more emotional, more soft and accommodating..., more 'feminine'" (Welter, "The Feminization of American Religion: 1800–1860," in Barbara Welter, *Dimity Convictions: The American Woman in the Nineteenth Century*, Athens, Ohio, 1976, 84). For the alliance between women and the clergy (liberal and evangelical) see Ann Douglas, *The Feminization of American Culture* (New York, 1977); Sandra S. Sizer, *Gospel Hymns and Social Religion: The Rhetoric of Nineteenth-Century Revivalism* (Philadelphia, 1978), 85–9. Recent American historiography on women and religion tends to overstate the contrast between the American experience during the Second Great Awakening and the experience of Christian churches throughout history: the energetic involvement and numerical dominance of women in religious life was hardly new.

[81] *Christian Watchman and Reflector*, 2 April 1841; *WCA*, 26 Feb. 1841; *New York Observer*, 13 March 1856. A Methodist minister in eastern Georgia reflected in

1852 on the additions to his church over the previous ten years: of a total 204 revival converts, 58 were backsliders from previous revivals, and 45 of these (77 percent) were male (*SCA*, 23 July 1852). See also R.D. Shiels, "The Scope of the Second Great Awakening: Andover, Massachusetts as a Case Study," *JER*, 5 (Summer 1985), 236. Mary P. Ryan, "A Woman's Awakening: Evangelical Religion and the Families of Utica, N.Y., 1800–1840," *AQ*, 30 (Winter 1978), 602–3, demonstrates that in Utica women not only formed the majority of church members and revival converts but became active orchestrators of domestic and church revivals.

[82] Harriet Beecher Stowe, "Appeal to the Women of the Free States of America on the Present Crisis in Our Country," 3 March 1854, quoted in Ronald G. Walters, *The Antislavery Appeal: American Abolitionism after 1830* (Baltimore, 1976), 103; Bushnell, "American Politics," 198–9; William G. McLoughlin (ed.) *The American Evangelicals, 1800–1900* (New York, 1968), 18; Colleen McDannell, *The Christian Home in Victorian America, 1840–1900* (Bloomington, Indiana, 1986), 143–4. For the prevailing ministerial view of the proper place for women during the Second Great Awakening in New England, see Nancy F. Cott, *The Bonds of Womanhood: "Woman's Sphere" in New England, 1780–1835* (New Haven, Conn., 1977), 157–9.

[83] Ann Braude, *Radical Spirits: Spiritualism and Women's Rights in Nineteenth-Century America* (Boston, 1989), 3–7, 56–81 and *passim*.

[84] Barbara Berg, *The Remembered Gate: Origins of American Feminism: The Woman and the City, 1800–1860* (New York, 1978), 167–8; Lori D. Ginzberg, *Women and the Work of Benevolence: Morality, Politics, and Class in the Nineteenth-Century United States* (New Haven, Conn., 1990), 71–9. Ginzberg notes (p. 77) that, by making financial contributions to political campaigns, and enhancing the reputation of certain politicians, whom they might invite to social events to meet

like-minded constituents, elite women "participated in the complex informal process by which politicians maintained the patronage of their constituents."

[85] Ginzberg, *Women and the Work of Benevolence*, 67–97. Henry Ward Beecher, in pursuit of full political rights for women, found it argumentatively expedient to stress their political impotence even in the domestic sphere (Henry Ward Beecher, *Women's Influence in Politics: An Address . . .*, Boston, 1860, 13 and *passim*).

[86] Mary P. Ryan, *Women in Public: Between Banners and Ballots, 1825–1880* (Baltimore, 1990), 132–41; *Ohio State Journal*, 25 May 1844; 17 May 1860; *Harrison Medal Minstrel: Comprising a Collection of the Most Popular and Patriotic Songs . . .* (Philadelphia, 1840), 25; *Albany Argus*, 6, 11, 16 July 1844; *Albany Evening Journal*, 21 July, 1, 14 Aug. 1856; *New York Tribune*, 8, 21 Aug., 8, 27 Sept. 1860; John S. Littell, *The Clay Minstrel: or, National Songster . . .* (2nd edn, Philadelphia, 1844), 261; Fletcher, *Diary*, III, 85; R. Emory to C. Emory, 13 Nov. 1844, Emory Papers, DU; Robert G. Gunderson, *The Log-Cabin Campaign* (Lexington, Ky., 1957), 135–9; Keith E. Melder, *The Beginnings of Sisterhood: The American Women's Rights Movement, 1800–1850* (New York, 1977), 118–19. For the suggestion that in parts of the South women's salience in election campaigns was a relatively late development, see W. Davis to R. Davis, 29 May 1859, Beale–Davis Papers, SHC.

[87] *Pittsburgh Christian Advocate*, 11 Nov. 1840; Thomas B. Alexander, "Presidential Election of 1840 in Tennessee," *Tennessee Historical Quarterly*, 1 (March 1942), 36; *Cincinnati Telegraph*, 29 June 1844; M. Theophane Geary, *A History of Third Parties in Pennsylvania, 1840–1860* (Washington, DC, 1938), 104; *WCA*, 20 Oct. 1850, 16, 23 April, 3 Sept. 1851; *Christian Watchman and Reflector*, 25 Feb. 1858; Tyrrell, *Sobering Up*, 279–80; *Albany Evening Journal*, 5, 13 Aug., 3 Sept. 1856; *Oberlin Evangelist*, 19 Dec. 1849; *Knoxville Whig*, 7 Jan. 1854;

Valentine, Diary, 17 Nov. 1852, SHC; M.M. Lewis to R.L. Dabney, 22 Sept. 1844, C.W. Dabney Papers, SHC; H. Bent to M. Blanchard, 15 Nov. 1844, C.A. Bent to M. Blanchard, 2 Sept. 1846, S.B. Eustis to M. Blanchard, 9 March 1847, M. Bent to M. Blanchard, 1 Jan. 1849, Blanchard Papers, WC; Keith Melder, "Ladies Bountiful: Organized Women's Benevolence in Early Nineteenth-Century America," *New York History*, 48 (July 1967), 247; S.W. Dearborn to J.H. George, 29 Oct. 1856, John H. George Papers, New Hampshire Historical Society [WEGT].

[88] *Scott and Graham Melodies; Being a Collection of Campaign Songs for 1852 . . .* (New York, 1852), 27; *Ohio State Journal*, 6 Nov. 1860; Spottswood, *Brief Annals*, 39–40, 135–6.

[89] William E. Gienapp, "Politics Seem to Enter into Everything," in Stephen E. Maizlish and John J. Kushna (eds) *Essays in American Antebellum Politics, 1840–1860* (University of Texas at Arlington, 1982), 16–17.

[90] Bushnell, *Politics Under the Law of God*, 9.

[91] Brock, *Parties and Political Conscience*, 68–9. See also Formisano, "Political Character," 705–6.

[92] The argument for status decline, particularly in the case of New England Calvinist and liberal churchmen, is to be found in John R. Bodo, *The Protestant Clergy and Public Issues, 1812–1848* (Princeton, NJ, 1954); Cole, *Social Ideas*; Charles I. Foster, *Errand of Mercy: The Evangelical United Front, 1790–1837* (Chapel Hill, NC, 1960); Clifford S. Griffin, *Their Brothers' Keepers: Moral Stewardship in the United States, 1800–1865* (New Brunswick, NJ, 1960); Douglas, *Feminization of American Culture*. For a telling critique, see Lois W. Banner, "Religious Benevolence as Social Control: A Critique of an Interpretation," *JAH*, 60 (June 1973), 23–41.

[93] *Christian Watchman and Reflector*, 12 Nov., 10 Dec. 1857; *WCA*, 26 March, 17 Dec. 1851; 16 Feb., 20 April, 17, 24, 31 Aug., 21 Dec. 1853; 1 Feb., 7 June 1854,

13 Feb. 1856; *SCA*, 3 June 1856; Sweet, *Minister's Wife*, 70; Ernest T. Thompson, *Presbyterians in the South* (3 vols, Richmond, Va., *c.*1963–73), I, 461; Martineau, *Society in America*, 348; Holifield, *The Gentlemen Theologians*, 15–23, 29–36. See also S. Williston to J. Blanchard, 15 Feb. 1851, Blanchard Papers, WC. Edward N. Kirk turned down a New School Presbyterian pastorate in Philadelphia despite the inducement of an annual salary of $5,000; the Old School minister Nathan Rice, in receipt of a salary of $3,000 in St Louis, was supposedly offered one of $7,000 to move to New Orleans. At the other end of the spectrum, salaries of $3–400 were not uncommon in the early 1850s. A survey of 1,500 ministers of all denominations in New York and New England in 1854 indicated an average of about $500 p.a. In urban churches the figure was considerably higher. For congregational use of financial pressure to silence ministers, see B. Mills to D.P. Noyes, 2 Feb. 1857, AHMS Papers.

[94] Douglas, *Feminization of American Culture*, 29–30; Abbott, *Reminiscences*, 202–3; O.A. Brownson, "Catholicity Necessary to Sustain Popular Liberty," *Brownson's Quarterly Review*, 2 (Oct. 1845), 523–4; Scott, *New England Ministry*, 112–32, 155 and *passim*.

[95] Robert P. Swierenga, "The Ethnic Voter and the First Lincoln Election," in Robert P. Swierenga (ed.) *Beyond the Civil War Synthesis: Political Essays of the Civil War Era* (Westport, Conn., 1975), 99–115; Richard L. McCormick, "Ethno-Cultural Interpretations of Nineteenth-Century American Voting Behavior," *Political Science Quarterly*, 89 (June 1974), 369–70.

[96] William W. Sweet, *Religion in the Development of American Culture, 1765–1840* (New York, 1952), 139, quoting Thomas Ford, later state governor. See also Mathews, "Second Great Awakening," 40.

[97] Douglas, *Feminization of American Culture*, 22; Winthrop S. Hudson, *The Great Tradition of the American Churches*,

(rev. edn, New York, 1963); Baird, *Religion in America*, 278; J.R. Lowell to C. Sumner, 23 March 1854, Charles Sumner Papers, Harvard University [WEGT]. For a perception of the minister's "prodigious weight in the community," see C.W. Dabney to R.L. Dabney, 1 Dec. 1844, C.W. Dabney Papers, SHC. See also Allan Nevins, *Ordeal of the Union*, (2 vols, New York, 1947), II, 130; James Rowland, "Range of Topics for the Pulpit," *American Biblical Repository*, 3rd ser. 3 (Oct. 1847), 721; Miller, *Life of the Mind*, 42–3. For reflections on the pressures on American clergy to follow rather than to lead public opinion on slavery and other controversial issues, see Goen, *Broken Churches, Broken Nation*, 141–90, esp. 187–8; Marsden, *Evangelical Mind*, 89ff.

[98] *WCA*, 4 Jan. 1854, 10 Jan. 1855, 14 May 1856, 27 May 1857; *CAJ*, 10 July 1856; William I. Fee, *Bringing the Sheaves: Gleanings from Harvest Fields in Ohio, Kentucky and West Virginia* (Cincinnati, 1896), 228–9; Valentine, *Diary*, 1 Jan. 1850, SHC; R.A. Keller, "Methodist Newspapers and the Fugitive Slave Law: A New Perspective for the Slavery Crisis in the North," *Church History*, 43 (Sept. 1974), 319–20; Henry S. Stroupe, *The Religious Press in the South Atlantic States, 1802–1865* (Durham, NC, 1956), 26–7; Hatch, *The Democratization of American Christianity*, 125–6, 141–6. By 1860 the *Independent* had a circulation of 45,000. Louis Filler, "Liberalism, Anti-Slavery and the Founders of the Independent," *New England Quarterly*, 27 (Sept. 1954), 302–3. For the salience of religious titles amongst the newspapers and periodicals circulating in communities as disparate as upstate New York and small-town North Carolina in this period, see Cross, *Burned-Over District*, 104–8; Helen R. Watson, "A Journalistic Medley: Newspapers and Periodicals in a Small North Carolina Community, 1859–1860," *North Carolina Historical Review*, 60 (Oct. 1983), 457–85.

[99] Heman Humphrey, *Revival Sketches and Manual* (New York, 1859), 281–2, reflected on the revolution that had

occurred in New York City: in the 1830s "it was difficult to get even a short paragraph of religious intelligence into a secular city newspaper," but the same papers spontaneously devoted columns to the Union revival meetings in 1857 and 1858. See also *Memoir of Rev. Austin Dickinson* (n.p., 1854), 8–10.

[100] Thomas A. Morris to M. Simpson, 16 Aug. 1848, M. Simpson Papers, LC; South Middlesex Conference of Churches, *Political Duties*, 28–31. For a newspaperman's view that the editor's influence in the 1850s was greater than that of the pulpiteer, see William S. Robinson, *"Warrington" Pen Portraits: A Collection of Personal and Political Reminiscences from 1848 to 1876* (Boston, 1877), 54.

[101] J.C. Chambers to M. Simpson, 2 May 1850; J.L. Smith to M. Simpson, 23 May 1850; W. Daily to M. Simpson, 5 Dec. 1850, M. Simpson Papers, LC; *Indiana State Sentinel*, quoted in *WCA*, 20 Nov. 1850; Robert D. Clark, *The Life of Matthew Simpson* (New York, 1956), 158–60; *WCA*, 9 June 1852.

[102] Henry Clay Dean of Iowa, whose Democratic sympathies secured his election as chaplain to the Senate, was recognized as a raw westerner out of his depth in Washington; the bitter speakership election of the 34th Congress spilt over into a partisan contest for chaplain to the House, resolved only by appointing the ninety-four-year-old patriarch, Daniel Waldo, politically anodyne but a near-disaster by any conventional measure of chaplaincy. Lewis, *Impressions of America*, 98–9; *WCA*, 21 Dec. 1853, 3 Jan. 1855, 2 Sept. 1857; J. Harlan to M. Simpson, 11 Jan. 1856, M. Simpson Papers, LC; Johnson, *Chaplains of the General Government*, 63 and *passim*; Henry Clay to James Gallaher, 8 Oct. 1851, Posey Papers, PHS; *Knoxville Whig*, 8 Jan. 1853; James Dixon, *Personal Narrative of a Tour through a Part of the United States and Canada* ... (New York, 1849), 40; Roche, *Durbin*, 60–1; Elbert Osborn, *Passages in the Life and Ministry of Elbert Osborn, an Itinerant Minister of the Methodist Episcopal*

Church ... (New York, 1847), 167; *CAJ*, 1 Aug. 1901; *SCA*, 16 March 1855; Stokes, *Church and State in the United States*, I, 499–507.

[103] Fee, *Bringing the Sheaves*, 178–85; J. Emory to R. Emory, 28 Sept. 1832, Emory Papers, DU; Clark, *Problem of Life*, 19–25; *WCA*, 14 Jan. 1848, 24 Nov. 1852; John Hall (ed.) *Forty Years' Familiar Letters of James W. Alexander, D.D.* ... (2 vols, New York, 1860), II, 76; Talbot W. Chambers, *Memoir of the Life and Character of the Late Hon. Theo. Frelinghuysen, LL.D.* (New York, 1863); *Oberlin Evangelist*, 25 April 1849; *Sketch of the Life and Character of George N. Briggs, Late Governor of Massachusetts* (Boston, 186?), *passim*. See the entries for Briggs, Frelinghuysen, and Haines in *DAB*.

[104] W. Daily to Simpson, 11 Feb. 1845; M. Simpson to E. Simpson, 1 Feb. 1856; S.P. Chase to M. Simpson, 26 April 1850, M. Simpson Papers, LC; *WCA*, 20 April 1853, 17 June 1857; Sweet, *Religion on the American Frontier*, IV, 449; *CAJ*, 19 June 1856; William B. Sprague, *Annals of the American Pulpit* ... (9 vols, New York, 1857–69), VII, 205; William C. Smith, *Pillars in the Temple; or, Sketches of Deceased Laymen of the Methodist Episcopal Church* (New York, 1872), 16–36, 127–50. Other politically distinguished evangelicals included Seth Gates of New York and Joshua Giddings of Ohio, and a number of Methodist governors: Allen Trimble and Robert Lucas (Ohio) and Joseph Wright (Indiana). James Brewer Stewart, *Joshua Giddings and the Tactics of Radical Politics* (Cleveland, Ohio, 1970); Gilbert Hobbes Barnes, *The Anti-Slavery Impulse, 1830–1844* (1933; repr. New York, 1964), 181–2; Allen Trimble, *Autobiography and Correspondence of Allen Trimble, Governor of Ohio* ... (n.p.[?Columbus, Ohio], 1909).

[105] J. McLean to A. Trimble, 4 Dec. 1828, quoted in Trimble, *Autobiography*, 177. See also Chambers, *Frelinghuysen*, 157–9. On his arrival in Washington in 1843 Joseph Wright immediately sought out fellow Methodists to organize prayer and class-meetings, remarking that "a man can select his society here as well as

any place in the world" (J. Wright to M. Simpson, 23 Dec. 1843, M. Simpson Papers, LC).

[106] *WCA*, 1 Feb. 1857; William L. Smith, *Fifty Years of Public Life: The Life and Times of Lewis Cass* (New York, 1856), 585–6. See also *The Christian Lawyer: Being a Portraiture of the Life and Character of William George Baker* (New York, 1859), 256–7.

[107] Marsh, *Temperance Recollections*, 30–3, 46–7, 117–18; *CAJ*, 25 May 1842; *Sketch of Briggs*, 9–13; Hawkins, *Hawkins*, 179–81, 191–3, 223ff. The Congressional Temperance Society was at its most influential in the early 1840s, when some eighty congressmen, drawn from all sections but especially from New England, attended meetings. It had declined into inactivity by the late 1850s (Keith L. Sprunger, "Cold Water Congressmen: The Congressional Temperance Society Before the Civil War," *Historian*, 27, Aug. 1965, 498–515).

[108] Tyrrell, *Sobering Up*, 91; *WCA*, 4 March 1842; John A. Krout, *The Origins of Prohibition* (New York, 1925), 176; *SCA*, 4 May 1849; Hawkins, *Hawkins*, 173.

[109] George G. Smith, *The Life and Times of George Foster Pierce* (Sparta, Ga., 1888), 324; C.L. Woodworth, "Edward Norris Kirk," *Congregational Quarterly*, 20 (April 1878), 260; Griffis, *John Chambers*, 112; George Peck, *The Life and Times of George Peck, D.D.* (New York, 1854), 299; John D. Wade, *Augustus Baldwin Longstreet: A Study of the Culture of the South* (Athens, Ga., 1969), 123–4; Roy F. Nichols, *Franklin Pierce: Young Hickory of the Granite Hills*, (2nd edn, Philadelphia, 1958), 75, 225, 243–4, 322, 527–8; *WCA*, 23 Feb., 9 March, 17 Aug. 1853, 25 Jan. 1854; Edmund Fuller and David E. Green, *God in the White House: The Faiths of American Presidents* (New York, [1968]), 81–6; Fitzgerald, *John B. McFerrin*, 91, 116, 168–9, 196–9, 243. For other examples see R.W. Landis, Journal, unpaginated, PHS; Albert H. Redford, *Life and Times of H.H. Kavanaugh, D.D., One of the Bishops of the Methodist Church, South* (Nashville, Tenn., 1884), 315–16; J.

Blanchard to T. Stevens, 9 April 1842, 13 March 1850, T. Stevens to J. Blanchard, 24 May 1842, Blanchard Papers, WC.

[110] Lewis, *Impressions of America*, 82; *WCA*, 6 April 1853; Leonard W. Levy, "Satan's Last Apostle in Massachusetts," *AQ*, 5 (Spring 1953), 16–30; Tocqueville, *Democracy in America*, 293.

[111] *CAJ*, 20 Oct. 1847, 21 Feb. 1850, 12 June 1856.

[112] *WCA*, 27 Feb. 1850, 30 April 1856; Alonzo F. Selleck, *Recollections of an Itinerant Life* (New York, 1886), 154–5; Andrew Jackson, *Correspondence of Andrew Jackson*, ed. John Spencer Bassett (7 vols, Washington, DC, 1926–35), VI, 84; Pilcher, *Elijah H. Pilcher*, 115–16.

[113] G.W. Ames to M. Simpson, ?29 Nov. 1850, M. Simpson Papers, LC; *WCA*, 29 Jan. 1851; *Memoir of John C. Lord, D.D., Pastor of the Central Presbyterian Church for Thirty-Eight Years* (Buffalo, NY, 1878), 30–1; J. Jay to C. Sumner, 28 Aug. 1852, Sumner Papers [WEGT]; *New York Observer*, 31 Oct., 7 Nov. 1840.

[114] Baird's estimates in 1856 were based in most cases on lower ratios than he had used in 1844. The *American Almanac* put the ratio in the Calvinist churches even higher than did Baird. Charles Elliott, anxious to assert his denomination's primacy in Ohio, claimed a Methodist population of six or eight times the membership in a period when the more cautious amongst his colleagues offered a figure half that amount. In the Dutch Reformed church, the ratio of hearers to members in 1850 stood at 2.3:1; it held steady in the mid-1850s, but in the years after the revival of 1857–8 fell to 1.7:1. Roeliff Brinkerhoff, *Recollections of a Lifetime* (Cincinnati, 1900), 83–4; *Methodist Quarterly Review*, 5 (Oct. 1845), 497; *WCA*, 22 Jan. 1841, 26 April 1854; Dixon, *Personal Narrative*, 321; *CAJ*, 25 Dec. 1844, 15 May 1856; *The Acts and Proceedings of the General Synod of the Reformed Protestant Dutch Church in North America . . .* (New York, 1850, 1855, 1860); Paul Goodman, "A Guide to American Church Membership Data before the

Civil War," *Historical Methods Newsletter*, 10 (Fall 1977), 184–5.

[115] *CAJ*, 10 July 1856. Baird's estimate of total evangelical strength in the early 1840s was, unrealistically, 15 million, over 80 percent of the population. *CAJ*, 3 July 1856, and Fish, *Primitive Piety*, 23, offer less heady assessments.

[116] Saum, *The Popular Mood of Pre-Civil War America*, xxii, 3–104.

[117] *Christian Watchman and Reflector*, 10, 17 April 1856; *New York Observer*, quoted in *WCA*, 14 Oct. 1842.

[118] David O. Mears, *Life of Edward Norris Kirk, D.D.* (Boston, 1877), 49; *WCA*, 18 Oct. 1848, 26 Feb. 1851; *Oberlin Evangelist*, 13 Oct. 1852.

[119] C. Cushing to N.D. George, 26 Dec. 1836, NEC.

[120] William Salter, *Life of James W. Grimes, Governor of Iowa, 1854–1858; A Senator of the United States, 1859–1869* (New York, 1876), 3–4, 26, 31, 120, 197, 237–8, 260, 392; G.A. Thomas to W. Salter, W. Salter Papers, Iowa State Hist. Dept, Des Moines (transcript supplied by Dr R.J. Cook).

[121] William J. Wolf, *The Almost Chosen People: A Study of the Religion of Abraham Lincoln* (New York, 1959), 34–51, 68.

[122] *Ibid.*, 69–79, 89–114; Roy P. Basler (ed.) *The Collected Works of Abraham Lincoln* (9 vols, New Brunswick, NJ, 1953–55), I, 319–21. Lincoln's statement, "If slavery is not wrong, nothing is wrong" derived from his reading of Bacon's *Slavery Discussed in Occasional Essays* (1846). See "Leonard Bacon," in *DAB*.

[123] Henry Steele Commager, *Documents of American History* (2 vols, 7th edn, New York, 1963), I, 329–31.

[124] Dixon, *Personal Narrative*, 143 and *passim*. See also *SCA*, 15 June 1849 ("'the States' are not so Puritanical and Evangelical as he imagines"); Achille Murat, *America and the Americans* (New York, 1849), 13; Smith, *Revivalism and Social Reform*, 18, 34–44; Philip Schaff, *America: A Sketch of the Political, Social, and Religious Character of the United States*

of North America . . . (New York, 1854), 76 and *passim*.

[125] See notes 1, 3 and 5 above, and also Charles C. Cole, *The Social Ideas of the Northern Evangelists 1826–1860* (New York, 1954); Ronald G. Walters, *American Reformers, 1815–1860* (New York, 1978); Cott, *Bonds of Womanhood*; Welter, "Feminization," 83–102; Joseph F. Kett, "Growing Up in Rural New England, 1800–1840," in Tamara K. Hareven (ed.) *Anonymous Americans: Explorations in Nineteenth-Century Social History* (Englewood Cliffs, NJ, 1971), 1–16; Albert J. Raboteau, *Slave Religion: The "Invisible Institution" in the Antebellum South* (New York, 1978); Ray Allen Billington, *The Protestant Crusade: A Study of the Origins of American Nativism* (New York, 1938).

Chapter 2 *Presidential Electioneering and the Appeal to Evangelicals: 1840*

[1] Paul Goodman, *Towards a Christian Republic: Antimasonry and the Great Tradition in New England, 1826–1836* (New York, 1988), 3, 53, 56, 106–9, 122, 152–3, 169, 235; Richard R. John, "Taking Sabbatarianism Seriously: The Postal System, the Sabbath, and the Transformation of American Political Culture," *JER*, 10 (Winter 1990), 517–67.

[2] Brock, *Parties and Political Conscience*, 35–52, considers the elements of rationalism, romanticism, and revivalism that made up the intellectual framework in which the second party system developed. R. Laurence Moore, "The End of Religious Establishment and the Beginning of Religious Politics: Church and State in the United States," in Thomas Kselman (ed.) *Belief in History: Innovative Approaches to European and American Religion* (Notre Dame, Ind., 1991), 237–64, offers some thoughtful reflections, generally consistent with what is argued here, on the reciprocity of politics and revivalist religion in this era, and on the important role of evangelical religion in

the formation of the country's political system.

³ Chevalier, *Society, Manners and Politics*, 317–21; J. Campbell to W.B. Campbell, 4 Feb. 1840, quoted in Alexander, "Presidential Election of 1840," 26–7; *The Life and Public Services of... J.K. Polk* (Baltimore, 1844), 5; *WCA*, 7 Aug. 1840. For evangelicals' borrowing from the organizational strategies of secular politics, and vice versa, see Bertram Wyatt-Brown, "Prelude to Abolitionism: Sabbatarian Politics and the Rise of the Second Party System," *JAH*, 58 (June 1971), 322, 329–30, and *CAJ*, 29 Sept. 1841.

⁴ Peck, *George Peck*, 293–4; *Harrison Medal Minstrel*, 3, 21, 65; Littell, *Clay Minstrel*, 235–6; Hatch, *The Democratization of American Christianity*, 146–61; Helen Grant, *Peter Cartwright: Pioneer* (New York, 1931), 153–5. See also Joe L. Kincheloe, Jr, "Similarities in Crowd Control Techniques of the Camp Meeting and Political Rally: The Pioneer Role of Tennessee," *Tennessee Historical Quarterly*, 37 (Summer 1978), 155–69.

⁵ Littell, *Clay Minstrel*, 143, 208; *Harrison Melodies...* (Boston, 1840), 10; *The Coon Dissector* [Dayton, Ohio], 31 May 1844; *Ohio State Journal*, 5 Sept. 1848; *Fremont & Dayton: Campaign Songs for 1856...* (Cleveland, Ohio, 1856), 12; William H. Harrison, *Gen. Harrison's Speech at the Dayton Convention, September 10, 1840* (Boston, [1840]), 7; Calvin Colton, *The Life of Clay. By Junius* (New York, 1843), 14; *The Wide-Awake Vocalist; or, Rail Splitters' Song Book...* (New York, 1860), 31; B.F. Martin to W.B. Campbell, 10 Feb. 1840, quoted in Alexander, "Presidential Election of 1840," 34, *Albany Argus*, 25 Sept. 1848; George F. Fort, "Reminiscences," 55, DU; M.J. Heale, *The Presidential Quest: Candidates and Images in American Political Culture, 1787–1852* (London, 1982), 226–8.

⁶ Littell, *Clay Minstrel*, 290–1; *Ohio State Journal*, 27 May, 17 June, 1 Sept. 1844; C.S. Brown, *Memoir of Rev. Abel Brown...* (Worcester, Mass., 1849), 102.

⁷ James Phelan, *History of Tennessee* (Boston, 1889), 391, quoted in Alexander, "Presidential Election of 1840," 36; Coulter, *Brownlow*, 112; Gunderson, *Log-Cabin Campaign*, 258; *Ohio State Journal*, 13 Nov. 1848; R. Emory to C. Emory, 13 Nov. 1844, DU.

⁸ Brock, *Parties and Political Conscience*, 40–1; Richard P. McCormick, *The Presidential Game: The Origins of American Presidential Politics* (New York, 1982), 12.

⁹ Carwardine, *Transatlantic Revivalism*, 45–53; Gienapp, "Politics Seem to Enter," 17–32.

¹⁰ Gunderson, *Log-Cabin Campaign*, 123 (citing Hone's diary entry for 21 March 1843); W.N. Chambers, "Election of 1840," in Arthur M. Schlesinger, Jr and Fred L. Israel (eds) *History of American Presidential Elections*, (8 vols, NY, 1985), I, 673–744.

¹¹ Michael F. Holt, "The Election of 1840, Voter Mobilization, and the Emergence of the Second American Party System: A Reappraisal of Jacksonian Voting Behavior," in William J. Cooper, Jr, et al. (eds) *A Master's Due: Essays in Honor of David Herbert Donald* (Baton Rouge, La, 1985), 16–58; William J. Cooper, Jr, *The South and the Politics of Slavery 1828–1856* (Baton Rouge, La, 1978), 102–3, 132–48; Richard P. McCormick, "New Perspectives on Jacksonian Politics," *AHR*, 65 (Jan. 1960), 296–301.

¹² For the character of presidential campaign propaganda and the use of religious themes in earlier elections during the second party system, see Heale, *Presidential Quest*, 50–1, 69–70, 78, 81, 111, 117, 207.

¹³ Cuyler, *Signs of the Times*, 1–4, 7–9, 76; Carwardine, *Transatlantic Revivalism*, 48–52; Roche, *Durbin*, 76; Bacon, *Commercial Distress*, 4–11 and *passim*.

¹⁴ Cuyler, *Signs of the Times*, 89–108, 191–240, 289; John Mitchell, *A Sermon Preached Before the First Church and the Edwards Church, Northampton...* (Northampton, Mass., 1837), 4–6; Duffield, *Thanksgiving Sermon*, 12–16; McKeen, *God Our Only Hope*, 7–20; Gage,

Sins and Dangers, 6–17; Mark Tucker, *Public Sins, a Cause for Humiliation; a Sermon . . .* (Providence, RI, 1838), 13–17; *WCA*, 15 May 1840, 22 Jan. 1841; *Pittsburgh Conference Journal*, 9 July 1840; Lord, *Signs of the Times*, 6–7, 12–15; Bacon, *Commercial Distress*, 14–15; Krebs, *Righteousness*, 20; Magoun, *Asa Turner*, 136.

[15] Stearns, "Christian Politics," 437; Lord, *Signs of the Times*, 8–15; Frelinghuysen, *American Government*, 10–12, 124–8; Hood, *Reformed America*, 104.

[16] Cuyler, *Signs of the Times*, 63–86, 241–64; Codman, *Importance of Moderation*, 18; *Pittsburgh Conference Journal*, 8 March 1838; McKeen, *God Our Only Hope*, 5–7, 22; Sprague, *Sermon to the Second Presbyterian Congregation, passim*; Duffield, *Thanksgiving Sermon*, 12–13; Tucker, *Public Sins*, 7–10; O. Hutchins to E. Curtis, 12 Dec. 1838, DU.

[17] *WCA*, 30 Oct. 1840, 8 Jan. 1841; Lord, *Signs of the Times*, 11.

[18] Goodman, *Towards a Christian Republic*, 30–3, shows how the idea of nominating a model Christian statesman and moralist for the presidency had been prefigured by Antimasons' running the devout Presbyterian William Wirt in 1832. For other earlier examples of "recognition politics" (that is, appealing to particular denominational groups by nominating prominent church leaders for political office), see *ibid.*, 118.

[19] Howe, *American Whigs*, 11–42, 150–70 and *passim*; Heale, *Presidential Quest*, 129–32, 182–3, 222; Brock, *Parties and Political Conscience*, 56–7; Formisano, *Mass Political Parties*, 128–36; John M. McFaul, "Expediency vs. Morality: Jacksonian Politics and Slavery," *JAH*, 62 (June, 1975), 38; Ashworth, *"Agrarians" & "Aristocrats,"* 193–205.

[20] Caleb Cushing, *Outlines of the Life and Public Services, Civil and Military, of William Henry Harrison of Ohio* (Boston, 1840), 24; *Albany Argus*, 3 June 1840; *Ohio State Journal*, 3 June 1840; *Highland Messenger*, 12 June 1840; Isaac R. Jackson, *The Life of William Henry Harrison* (2nd edn, Philadelphia, 1840), 206–8; James

A. Green, *William Henry Harrison: His Life and Times* (Richmond, Va., 1941), 444–5; Freeman Cleaves, *Old Tippecanoe: William Henry Harrison and His Times* (New York, 1939), 325.

[21] Maxwell P. Gaddis, *Footprints of an Itinerant* (Cincinnati, 1855), 281–2; Tefft, *Methodism Successful*, 195–6, which misdates the occasion by a year.

[22] *Pittsburgh Christian Advocate*, 19 May 1841; Nichols, *Forty Years*, II, 175.

[23] *Harrison Melodies*, 9; Richard Hildreth, *The People's Presidential Candidate . . .* (Boston, 1839), 198. See also Jacob B. Moore, *The Contrast: or, Plain Reasons Why William Henry Harrison Should be Elected President of the United States . . .* (New York, 1840), 5.

[24] Cleaves, *Old Tippecanoe*, 321; J. Wheelwright to W.H. Harrison, 15 Aug. 1840, H. Kingsbury to W.H. Harrison, 12 Nov. 1840, W.H. Harrison Papers, LC; *Albany Argus*, 26 June 1840; *Ohio State Journal*, 7, 28 Oct. 1840.

[25] Hildreth, *People's Presidential Candidate*, 197; *Harrison Medal Minstrel*, 2; Cushing, *William Henry Harrison*, 24. In areas where temperance concern was muted Harrison's advocates were ready to celebrate his appetite for hard cider. See, for example, George E. Badger, *Speech Delivered at the Great Whig Meeting in the County of Granville, on Tuesday, the Third Day of March, 1840* (Raleigh, NC, 1840), 15.

[26] *Iowa Territorial Gazette and Advertiser*, 22 Aug. 1840; *Albany Rough Hewer*, 30 April 1840, quoted in Gunderson, *Log-Cabin Campaign*, 235; *Albany Argus*, 26 May, 15, 20 June 1840; *The Letters of Stephen A. Douglas*, ed. Robert W. Johannsen (Urbana, Ill., 1961), 86–91; *Ohio State Journal*, 2 Sept. 1840; *Harrison Medal Minstrel*, 2, 8.

[27] *Albany Argus*, 20, 28 May 1840; *Pittsburgh Conference Journal*, 28 May 1840; E.W. Chester to L. Burnell, 27 July 1840, Finney Papers, OCL; Mrs S.R. Riggs to her brothers, 20 Jan. 1841, PHS.

[28] Tyrrell, *Sobering Up*, 109–10, 237–8; Richard Hildreth, *Strictures on Governor Morton's Message . . .* (2nd ed, Boston,

1840), 6 and *passim*; Lee Benson, *The Concept of Jacksonian Democracy: New York as a Test Case* (New York, 1961), 198–207; Johnson, *Shopkeeper's Millennium*, 128–33; Formisano, *Mass Political Parties*, 116–17.

[29] Wheeler, *Harrison*, 22; White, *National Fast*, 9; L. Beecher *et al.* to W.H. Harrison, n.d., W.H. Harrison Papers, LC. William Metcalfe, teetotaler and "Bible Christian" minister, together with his son, turned his Philadelphia printing office over to the production of the *Morning Star*, a paper established in 1838 to secure the nomination and election of Harrison. After Old Tip's death Metcalfe published the weekly *Temperance Advocate*. Joseph Metcalfe, *Memoir of the Rev. William Metcalfe, M.D., Late Minister of the Bible-Christian Church . . . Philadelphia* (Philadelphia, 1866), 24–5. To deflect teetotalers' criticisms of Harrison's campaign William G. Brownlow called on Whigs to use cider "made of this years apples" at their gatherings (*Tennessee Whig*, 22 July 1840).

[30] Peleg Sprague, *Remarks of the Hon. Peleg Sprague at Faneuil Hall . . .* (Boston, 1839), 18; *General Harrison in Congress* (Washington, DC, 1840), 32; *Harrison Medal Minstrel*, title page.

[31] Jackson, *William Henry Harrison*, 60–1; Moore, *The Contrast*, 6.

[32] William Henry Harrison, *A Discourse on the Aborigines of the Valley . . .* (Boston, 1840), 38–9; *Harrison Medal Minstrel*, 115–16; *Harrison Melodies*, 13; *New York Evening Express*, 29 Sept. 1840; *Ohio State Journal*, 7 Oct. 1840; *CAJ*, 10 March, 14 April 1841.

[33] Moore, *The Contrast*, 16; Heale, *Presidential Quest*, esp. 224–8, discusses the perceived fragility of republican forms.

[34] Van Deusen, *William Henry Seward*, 44; M. Fillmore to C.A. Reppier *et al.*, 23 June 1840 in *Millard Fillmore Papers. Publications of the Buffalo Historical Society*, vols X and XI, ed. Frank H. Severance (Buffalo, NY, 1907), XI, 211; *Wherefore Change? More Than One Hundred Reasons Why William Henry Harrison Should and Will Have the Support of the Democracy . . .* (Boston, 1840), 3, 5; *New Orleans Bee*, quoted in *Ohio State Journal*, 16 Sept. 1840; Robert Mayo, *A Word in Season; or, Review of the Political Life and Opinions of Martin Van Buren . . .* (3rd edn, Washington, DC, 1840), 9, 13–16; *Albany Argus*, 26 May 1840; Wheelock S. Upton, *Address Delivered before the Tippecanoe Club, of New York* (n.p., 1840), 5; Waddy Thompson, *An Examination of the Claims of Mr. Van Buren and Gen. Harrison to the Support of the South . . .* (n.p., 1840), 2; Valentine, Diary, 21 March, 16 May, 15 Sept. 1840, SHC; *An Address to the People of North Carolina* ([n.p.], 1840), 1, 25. Whigs themselves faced the charge of being little more than a wicked, ill-assorted, and corrupt coalition united only by their desire for political power. J.S. Swift to J.F. Speight, 25 June 1840, J.F. Speight Papers, SHC.

[35] *Wherefore Change?*, 14; Thompson, *Claims of Van Buren and Harrison*, 11; *Harrison Medal Minstrel*, 3; *Fillmore Papers*, XI, 212. Samuel Swartwout, Van Buren's Collector of the Port of New York, absconded to Europe with a million dollars.

[36] See, for example, Formisano, *Mass Political Parties*, 56–80; Heale, *Presidential Quest*, 130–2, 139–41; Edward L. Mayo, "Republicanism, Antipartyism, and Jacksonian Party Politics: A View from the Nation's Capital," *AQ*, 31 (Spring 1979), 3–20; Stephen E. Maizlish, *The Triumph of Sectionalism: The Transformation of Ohio Politics, 1844–1856* (Kent, Ohio, 1983), 17–20.

[37] Harrison, *Speech at the Dayton Convention*, 7; Moore, *The Contrast*, 3–4, 7, 10, 13; *Wherefore Change?*, 11; Mayo, *A Word in Season*, 7.

[38] Gunderson, *Log-Cabin Campaign*, 11, 167; *Ohio State Journal*, 14, 21 Dec. 1839, 16 Sept., 7 Oct. 1840; Joseph Badger, *A Memoir of Joseph Badger; Containing an Autobiography . . .* (Hudson, Ohio, 1851), 127, 135, 173–4; Sprague, *Remarks at Fanueil Hall*, 19; *Harrison Medal Minstrel*, 3, 21; *Albany Argus*, 28 May 1840; Formisano, *Mass Political*

Parties, 129–31; White, *National Fast*, 30; Calvin Colton, *The Crisis of the Country. By Junius* (Philadelphia, *c.*1840), 16. The name "Loco-focos" initially referred to radical New York Democrats but opponents came to use it to embrace all Jacksonians.

[39] For the Democrats' promotion of a "negative liberal state," see Benson, *Concept*, 86–109. Benson regards the Jacksonian/anti-Jacksonian alignment in New York as having been determined in the first instance by reactions to the Antimasons – the Christian party in politics and the forerunners of the Whigs. The party allegiances then established were maintained until the 1850s. In that state at least "the Whigs were the 'religious party' and the Democrats the 'free thought party'." *Ibid.*, 193–7, 300–12. See also Levy, "Satan's Last Apostle," 16–30.

[40] *Ohio State Journal*, 17 June, 5 Aug. 1840; *Albany Argus*, 19 June 1840; *The Diary of George Templeton Strong*, ed. Allan Nevins and Milton H. Thomas, (4 vols, New York, 1952), I, 147; Mayo, *A Word in Season*, 9; *Correspondence of Andrew Jackson*, VI, 61.

[41] Gunderson, *Log-Cabin Campaign*, 132; Mayo, *A Word in Season*, 7; *Tennessee Whig*, 22 Oct. 1839; *Harrison Medal Minstrel*, 65, 126; Moore, *The Contrast*, 11; *Hawkeye and Iowa Patriot*, 29 Oct., 12 Nov. 1840; *Ohio State Journal*, 27 May, 17 June, 23 Sept. 1840; Calvin Colton, *American Jacobinism. By Junius* (New York, 1840), *passim*; "Catholicism," *Boston Quarterly Review*, 4 (1841), 320–38.

[42] Billington, *Protestant Crusade*, remains the essential starting point for early and mid-nineteenth-century anti-Catholicism.

[43] Benson, *Concept*, 187, 321–2; he estimates (p. 171) that by 1844 in New York state 95 percent of the Catholic Irish voted Democrat.

[44] *Letters of Douglas*, 85, 95–6; B. Maguire to J. England, 3 Sept. 1840, M. Van Buren Papers, LC; *Ohio State Journal*, 28 Oct. 1840; Orestes A. Brownson, *An Oration before the Democracy of Worcester*

and Vicinity . . . (Boston, 1840), 20, 35; *Albany Argus*, 16 May 1840. For Whig nativism in the 1830s see, for example, Leo Hershkowitz, "The Native American Democratic Association in New York City, 1835–1836," *New York Historical Society Quarterly*, 46 (Jan. 1962), 41–59; Richard J. Purcell and John F. Poole, "Political Nativism in Brooklyn," *The Journal of the Irish Historical Society*, 32 (1941), 26–7; Louis Dow Scisco, *Political Nativism in New York State* (New York, 1901), 21–38.

[45] *Ohio State Journal*, 12 Feb., 12 Aug., 14 Oct. 1840; A. Lincoln to J.T. Stuart, 20 Jan. 1840, *The Collected Works of Abraham Lincoln*, ed. Roy P. Basler, (9 vols, New Brunswick, NJ, 1953–55), I, 184; *Harrison Medal Minstrel*, 6–7; *Harrison Melodies*, 66–7; A.C. Flagg to M. Van Buren, 7 March 1840; J. Power to N. Devereux, 31 March 1840; P. Sharp to J. England, 1 July 1840; J. England to P. Sharp, 14 July 1840, M. Van Buren Papers, LC; John R.G. Hassard, *Life of the Most Reverend John Hughes* (New York, 1866), 227–38.

[46] Geary, *Third Parties in Pennsylvania*, 16; William G. Brownlow, *A Political Register, Setting Forth the Principles of the Whig and Democratic Parties in the United States* . . . (Jonesborough, Tenn., 1844), 77, 109–16; *The Works of the Right Reverend John England* (5 vols, Baltimore, 1849), IV, 69–73, 77–83; Thomas R. Hazard, *Facts for the Laboring Man* . . . (Newport, RI, 1840), 44–6; *Tennessee Whig*, 9 April, 15, 22 July 1840.

[47] Brock, *Parties and Political Conscience*, 55–63; Colton, *Crisis of the Country*, 6–13; Calvin Colton, *Sequel to the Crisis of the Country* (New York, 1840), 1–6. See also Howe, *American Whigs*, 16–21; William G. Shade, *Banks or No Banks: The Money Issue in Western Politics 1832–1865* (Detroit, 1972), 18–19, 173–4, 253; John M. McFaul, *The Politics of Jacksonian Finance* (Ithaca, NY, 1972), 213–15; Thomas Brown, "Southern Whigs and the Politics of Statesmanship, 1833–41," *JSH*, 46 (Aug. 1980), 373–4. Whigs' efforts to link Democrats' anti-Bank

posture to their alleged atheism were helped by the attacks of Fanny Wright and others on "the Banker's system" as the "adjunct and agent" of Protestant Christianity. Celia M. Eckhardt, *Fanny Wright: Rebel in America* (Cambridge, Mass., 1984), 252–3, 258, 271; *Tennessee Whig*, 9 April 1840; Henry R. Mueller, *The Whig Party in Pennsylvania* (New York, 1922).

[48] J. Wheelwright to W.H. Harrison, 15 Aug. 1840, W.H. Harrison Papers, LC; Dwight, *"A Great Man Fallen,"* 3–4; Breckinridge, *Submission,* 15; *WCA,* 16 April 1841.

[49] C.W. Dabney to R.L. Dabney, 12 April 1841, C.W. Dabney Papers, SHC; Green, *Harrison,* 513; Kirk, *National Fast,* 25; Hewit, *Funeral Solemnities,* 8; Sprague, *Voice of the Rod,* 9–11.

[50] Green, *Harrison,* 513; Kirk, *National Fast,* 25; Hewit, *Funeral Solemnities,* 8; Sprague, *Voice of the Rod,* 9–11.

Chapter 3 *Presidential Electioneering and the Appeal to Evangelicals: 1844 and 1848*

[1] For the presidential election of 1844 see Charles G. Sellers, *James K. Polk: Continentalist 1843–1846* (Princeton, NJ, 1966), 67–161; Charles Sellers, "Election of 1844," in Schlesinger and Israel, *American Presidential Elections,* II, 744–861.

[2] *Ohio State Journal,* 22 June, 22 Aug., 14, 24, 28 Sept. 1844; William Winans, *A Funeral Discourse on Occasion of the Death of Hon. Henry Clay . . .* (Woodville, Miss., 1852), 15; Nathan Sargent, *Brief Outline of the Life of Henry Clay . . .* (Washington, DC, 1844), 1–2; Chambers, *Frelinghuysen,* 180; Noyes Wheeler, *The Phrenological Characters and Talents of Henry Clay, Daniel Webster, John Quincy Adams, William Henry Harrison, and Andrew Jackson . . .* (Boston, 1844), 5–7; Littell, *Clay Minstrel,* 12, 134–5. The flavor of campaign rhetoric, and the salience of moral issues, is well captured in John E. Haynes, "Politics in 1844: Being a Choice Selection of the Most Important Points Contended for throughout the Campaign," a substantial collection of nationwide newspaper clippings, dated 1 May 1845, in the North Carolina Collection, Wilson Library, University of North Carolina at Chapel Hill (hereafter cited as "Haynes").

[3] Sargent, *Henry Clay,* 9; Cortlandt Parker, *A Sketch of the Life and Public Services of Theodore Frelinghuysen* (n.p., 1844), 3–4, 12; *Ohio State Journal,* 27 April, 28 Sept. 1844; Colton, *Life of Clay,* 12, 16; Wheeler, *Phrenological Characters,* 7, 13.

[4] *Albany Argus,* 17, 25 July, 3 Aug. 1844; *Coon Dissector,* 11 Oct. 1844; *Maysville Eagle,* 25 Sept. 1844 [Haynes].

[5] George C. Collins, *Fifty Reasons Why the Honorable Henry Clay Should Be Elected President of the United States . . .* (Baltimore, 1844), 21–2; John White, *Speech . . . in Defence of Mr. Clay, upon the Charge of "Bargain and Sale" . . .* (Washington, DC, 1844), 1; Littell, *Clay Minstrel,* 380; Lynn Boyd, *Speech . . . in Reply to the Hon. John White . . .* (Washington, DC, 1844), *passim.*

[6] *Albany Argus,* 2, 4 Sept., 24 Oct. 1844; *Behold the Man!* (n.p. [1844]); *Henry Clay's Duels* (n.p. [1844]); *A Full Account of Henry Clay's Duels, Compiled from Official Documents . . .* (Philadelphia, [1844]); *Clay and Frelinghuysen's Views on Duelling* (n.p. [1844]); Thomas L. Clingman, *Speech . . . on the Principles of the Whig and Democratic Parties, Delivered in the House of Representatives, March 7, 1844* (Washington, 1844), 171–8; Bushnell, *Politics Under the Law of God,* 16–17; *Ohio State Journal,* 13, 25 April, 4 May, 8, 13 Aug., 19 Sept. 1844; *Coon Dissector,* 16 Aug. 1844; Sargent, *Henry Clay,* 41; Colton, *Life of Clay,* 15; *Clay or Polk. By an Adopted Citizen, having twenty-one years residence in the United States* (New York, 1844), 10–11; Glyndon G. Van Deusen, *The Life of Henry Clay* (Boston, 1937), 49–55, 219–23. Liberty men, of course, also exploited the issue: see Joshua Leavitt, *The Great Duellist* (Boston [1844]). For Clay's pursuit of self-mastery, see Howe, *American Whigs,* 125–9. For dueling in southern culture, see Kenneth S. Greenberg, *Masters and*

Statesmen: The Political Culture of American Slavery (Baltimore, 1985), 23–41. For evidence that Clay's dueling did indeed damage his cause, see Neal Dow, The Reminiscences of Neal Dow: Recollections of Eighty Years (Portland, Me., 1898), 126, 138; Beecher, Autobiography, I, 108.

[7] Albany Argus, 13 July, 5, 27, 29 Aug. 1844; B.A. Bidlack, Speech . . . in Reply to the Political Attacks . . . upon the Nominees of the Democratic Convention . . . (Washington, DC, 1844), 8, 11–12; Coon Dissector, 9 Aug., 18 Oct. 1844.

[8] Van Deusen, Clay, 24–6; Coon Dissector, 28 June, 6 Sept., 11 Oct. 1844; Albany Argus, 16 July 1844.

[9] Clay or Polk, 9–10; Albany Argus, 16 July 1844; Ohio State Journal, 22 June 1844; Sargent, Henry Clay, 80; Chambers, "Election of 1840," 657.

[10] Albany Argus, 13, 26 July, 25 Oct. 1844; A Nut for the National Clay Club to Crack (Philadelphia, 1844), 2; Clay or Polk, 9; That Same Old Coon, 12 April 1844; John Wentworth, Speech of Mr. Wentworth of Illinois [House of Representatives, April 1844] ([Washington, DC], 1844), 3; Bidlack, Speech, 9, 12; The Coon Hunter, 26 Oct. 1844 [Haynes]; Columbian Register [New Haven], 9 Nov. 1844 [Haynes]; Sellers, Polk: Continentalist, 141.

[11] Life and Public Services of Polk, 3–4, 48; Fitzgerald, John B. McFerrin, 219–23, 230–2; Charles G. Sellers, James K. Polk: Jacksonian 1795–1843 (Princeton, NJ, 1957), 22–4, 45–6, 94, 111, 210–11, 329; Fuller and Green, God in the White House, 81–6; Albany Argus, 1, 4, 9, 24, 26, 29 July, 9 Sept., 31 Oct. 1844; Nashua Telegraph [NH], 24 Aug. 1844 [Haynes]; Ohio State Journal, 6 July 1844; The Political and Public Character of James K. Polk, of Tennessee (New York, 1844), 2–4.

[12] Wentworth, Speech, 6; Chambers, Frelinghuysen, 70, 88–90, 170–1, 176.

[13] Ohio State Journal, 7, 16 May 1844; Parker, Theodore Frelinghuysen, 1–9.

[14] Ohio State Journal, 23 May 1844; New York Evangelist, 9, 16 May, 19 Sept. 1844; Albert H. Redford, Life and Times of H.H. Kavanaugh, D.D. . . . (Nashville, Tenn., 1884), 388; CAJ, 2 Oct. 1844.

[15] Albany Argus, 16 July 1844; Cincinnati Gazette, 8 July 1844; Hill's New Hampshire Patriot, 28 Sept. 1844 [Haynes].

[16] Bushnell, Politics under the Law of God, 10; Littell, Clay Minstrel, 11–12, 59–60, 222–8, 251, 257, 289; Colton, Life of Clay, 16; Political and Public Character of Polk, 3; Ohio State Journal, 16 May, 8 Aug. 1844; Collins, Fifty Reasons, 6–9, 25, 35–6, 41; Sargent, Henry Clay, 8; Calvin Colton, Democracy. By Junius (New York, 1844), 5, 9 and passim.

[17] Parker, Theodore Frelinghuysen, 3, 9; Colton, Democracy, 16; Collins, Fifty Reasons, 34; Ohio State Journal, 23 May 1844; Sargent, Henry Clay, 61. For examples of sabbatarian reform efforts through the period of the campaign and the calling of a National Lord's Day Convention in November, see Pittsburgh Christian Advocate, 1 May, 28 Aug. 1844.

[18] Calvin Colton, Labor and Capital. By Junius (New York, 1844), 16; Parker, Theodore Frelinghuysen, 4–5; Collins, Fifty Reasons, 11–14, 38–9; Ohio State Journal, 3, 8 Oct. 1844; Sargent, Henry Clay, 80; Colton, Democracy, 14.

[19] Calvin Colton, The Currency. By Junius (New York, 1843), 5–15; Colton, Labor and Capital, 11; Address of the Democratic Hickory Club, for the City and County of Philadelphia, Recommending Martin Van Buren . . . (Philadelphia, 1844), 8; Albany Argus, 31 July 1844; That Same Old Coon, 25 May 1844; Sargent, Henry Clay, 80. In fact, realizing that his known preference for minimal duties would hurt him in the key state of Pennsylvania, Polk risked alienating his southern supporters by endorsing protection in his famous letter to the Philadelphian, John K. Kane (Sellers, Polk: Continentalist, 116–28, 160).

[20] Clay or Polk, 12–13; Sargent, Henry Clay, 5, 63, 68, 76; Parker, Theodore Frelinghuysen, 8, 10–11; Collins, Fifty Reasons, 19.

[21] Sellers, Polk: Continentalist, 145–50; Ohio State Journal, 25 April, 6, 13 June, 8 Aug., 19, 26, 28 Sept., 1 Oct. 1844; Albany Argus, 5 Aug., 21 Sept. 1844;

Calvin Colton, *Political Abolitionism. By Junius* (New York, 1843), 6–7.

[22] *WCA*, 8 April, 2 Sept. 1842; Bloch, *Visionary Republic*, esp. 57–60, 153, 160; R. Emory to J. McClintock, 22 May, 3 Dec. 1841, DU; Gardiner Spring, *The Danger and Hope of the American People: A Discourse . . .* (New York, 1843), 21–5; R.H. Morrison to J. Morrison, 20 Feb. 1843, R.H. Morrison Papers, SHC.

[23] For the Protestant Reformation Society and the American Protestant Union (New York City), the American Protestant Union (Phildelphia), the Society of the Friends of the Reformation (Baltimore) and similar organizations, see Billington, *Protestant Crusade*, 166–92.

[24] *New York Evangelist*, 4 July 1844; *Pittsburgh Christian Advocate*, 15 May 1844; William A. Baughin, "The Development of Nativism in Cincinnati," *Bulletin of the Cincinnati Historical Society*, 22 (Oct. 1964), 244–9; Billington, *Protestant Crusade*, 193–4, 211; Michael Feldberg, *The Philadelphia Riots of 1844: A Study of Ethnic Conflict* (Westport, Conn., 1975), 20.

[25] James E. Welch, Diary, 17 Dec. 1840, PHS. For the concept of the Catholic as scapegoat, see David Brion Davis, "Some Themes of Counter-Subversion: An Analysis of Anti-Masonic, Anti-Catholic, and Anti-Mormon Literature," *MVHR*, 47 (Sept. 1960), 205–24; Seymour M. Lipset and Earl Raab, *The Politics of Unreason: Right Wing Extremism in America, 1790–1970* (New York, 1970), 47–67. See also Howe, *American Whigs*, 163–4.

[26] Billington, *Protestant Crusade*, 142–65, 220–37; *WCA*, 19 Feb. 1841; *CAJ*, 3 Feb. 1841; Vincent P. Lannie and Bernard C. Diethorn, "For the Honor and Glory of God: The Philadelphia Bible Riots of 1844," *History of Education Quarterly*, 8 (Spring 1968), 50–1; Feldberg, *Philadelphia Riots*, 87–96.

[27] Feldberg, *Philadelphia Riots*, 35, 47–9, 57–8, 67, 113.

[28] *Cincinnati Telegraph*, 8 June, 27 July 1844; *New York Freeman's Journal*, 10 Aug. 1844. Feldberg could not find in Protestant church membership rolls the names of any of the known nativist rioters; he is sympathetic to David Montgomery's view that the conflict between Orangemen and Catholics was much exaggerated. But the case for an Orange dimension to the conflict is strong in the light of Catholic descriptions of events, Philadelphia's earlier history of sectarian warfare, and the evident alarm in Protestant quarters over the accelerating movement for repeal of the Act of Union. Feldberg, *Philadelphia Riots*, 27–9, 35, 112, 118–19; David Montgomery, "The Shuttle and the Cross: Weavers and Artisans in the Kensington Riots of 1844," *Journal of Social History*, 5 (Summer 1972), 411–46. See also Billington, *Protestant Crusade*, 196.

[29] *WCA*, 19 Nov. 1841, 4 Feb. 1842; Fletcher, *Diary*, III, 56, 58; *Pittsburgh Christian Advocate*, 15 May, 17 July 1844; *Oberlin Evangelist*, 18 Dec. 1844; *New York Evangelist*, 23, 30 May, 13, 20 June, 8 Aug. 1844; *Cincinnati Telegraph*, 7 Sept. 1844. For a discussion of the nativist bias of evangelical working men in Philadelphia, see Laurie, *Working People of Philadelphia*, 52, 168–203.

[30] Henry A. Boardman, *The Intolerance of the Church of Rome* (Philadelphia, 1844), 13; *New York Evangelist*, 20 June 1844; *WCA*, 2 July 1841 (quoting the *New York Baptist Almanac*), 10 Sept. (quoting the *New York Observer*), 4 Feb. 1842; McDonald and Searles, *Inskip*, 49; *CAJ*, 16 Feb. 1842.

[31] Duncan, *Discourse on the Fast Day*, 42; *WCA*, 12 March, 12 Nov. 1841, 16 Sept. 1842; *CAJ*, 10 Nov. 1841; *New York Evangelist*, 25 April 1844; Bullard, *Sermon in the First Presbyterian Church*, 10–11.

[32] *New York Evangelist*, 20 June 1844; *WCA*, 12 Nov. 1841, 18 Nov. 1842; *New York Freeman's Journal*, 10 Aug. 1844; *Pittsburgh Christian Advocate*, 24 July 1844; *CAJ*, 16 Feb. 1842, 21 Aug. 1844.

[33] Boardman, *Intolerance of Rome*; *CAJ*, 5 May 1841, 16 Feb. 1842; Scisco, *Political Nativism*, 39–51; Billington, *Protestant Crusade*, 200–4; *New York*

Evangelist, 20, 27 June 1844. Feldberg, *Philadelphia Riots,* 59–60, 69, stresses the secular, non-sectarian emphases of the Philadelphia American Republican party, with which only a handful of the city's clergy were publicly and formally associated. For the apparently contrasting experience of the Native American party in Cincinnati, see Alfred G. Stritch, "Political Nativism in Cincinnati," *Records of the American Catholic Historical Society* (Sept. 1937), 241.

[34] *Cincinnati Telegraph,* 22 June 1844; Brock, *Parties and Political Conscience,* 184–5; Sellers, *Polk: Continentalist,* 152.

[35] *New York Evangelist,* 16 May 1844; *That Same Old Coon,* 31 Aug. 1844; *New York Freeman's Journal,* 24 Aug. 1844.

[36] Brownlow, *Political Register,* 11–12, 111; *New York Freeman's Journal,* 24 Aug. 1844; *Coon Dissector,* 9 Aug. 1844; *Albany Argus,* 26 July 1844; Betty Fladeland, *James Gillespie Birney: Slaveholder to Abolitionist* (Ithaca, NY, 1955), 238.

[37] *Ohio State Journal,* 16, 18, 23, 25 July, 9, 23 Nov. 1844. David Tod, Democratic candidate in the Ohio gubernatorial election, had opposed in the state senate a bill to protect Methodist camp meetings from drink sellers and other sorts of disturbance.

[38] Fleharty, *Rev. A.E. Phelps,* 161–3; Thomas J. Bryant, "Autobiography of Rev. Thomas J. Bryant, 35 Years a Member of the Illinois Conference of the Methodist Episcopal Church," 11–13, typescript, DU. After the arrival of the Mormons in Illinois in 1839 Whigs had initially and successfully sought their votes. But it was Democratic legislation that effectively made Nauvoo independent of the state government and from 1842 it was the Democrats who benefited electorally from Mormon support. Robert W. Johannsen, *Stephen A. Douglas* (New York, 1973), 104–10, 149–50.

[39] *Albany Argus,* 2, 15, 23 Aug., 3 Sept., 3, 10, 11, 12, 28 Oct. 1844; *Coon Dissector,* 31 May, 14 June, 5 July 1844; Henry Riell, *An Appeal to the Voluntary Citizens of the United States . . .* (New York,

1844). Democrats more readily appealed to anti-Romanist sentiment in areas where there were few Catholic voters to be alienated. In eastern Tennessee Polkite pamphlets called for the annexation of Texas in order to rescue the independent republic from Romanism and secure the Pope's overthrow. *Knoxville Whig,* 24 June 1846.

[40] The union of Native and Whig forces in Philadelphia secured the Democrats' defeat in the city and substantially reduced Francis Shunk's statewide majority. Sellers, *Polk: Continentalist,* 152–3.

[41] *Albany Argus,* 19 July, 14 Aug., 1844; *That Same Old Coon,* 22 June 1844; *Ohio State Journal,* 20 Aug., 26 Oct. 1844; *Coon Dissector,* 2 Aug. 1844; William G. Brownlow, *Americanism Contrasted with Foreignism, Romanism, and Bogus Democracy* (Nashville, Tenn., 1856), 96 (quoting the *Boston Pilot,* 31 Oct. 1844); *Cincinnati Gazette,* 1 July 1844. Edward Norris Kirk (1802–74), Boston Congregationalist, and Spencer Houghton Cone (1785–1855), Baptist, were amongst those ministers on whose staunch anti-Catholicism was shortly to be erected the evangelical alliance.

[42] *Albany Argus,* 12, 15, 16, 30 Aug., 12, 18 Oct. 1844; *WCA,* 8 July 1842; *CAJ,* 10 March 1841, 27 April 1842; *New York Evangelist,* 3 Oct. 1844; *Nut for the National Clay Club,* 2; *New York Freeman's Journal,* 3 Aug. 1844.

[43] Whigs also attacked "the Jacobin Democracy of New Hampshire" for sustaining a state religious test that prohibited Catholics from holding office. *Clay or Polk,* 18–20; Collins, *Fifty Reasons,* 4–5; *Ohio State Journal,* 11, 18 and 23 May, 27 June, 6, 16, 27 July, 15, 17 Oct. 1844; *That Same Old Coon,* 20 July, 3 Aug. 1844.

[44] *Clay or Polk,* 6, 14; Collins, *Fifty Reasons,* title page and 14–15, 19–21, 28; Sargent, *Henry Clay,* 11; *Ohio State Journal,* 11 April, 27 June, 27 July, 28 Sept. 1844; Littell, *Clay Minstrel,* 42.

[45] Collins, *Fifty Reasons,* 31–2; *Ohio State Journal,* 17 Oct. 1844. For Whigs

who succeeded in persuading Catholics they were sincerely committed to the cause of Repeal, see Thomas J. Curran, "Seward and the Know Nothings," *New York Historical Society Quarterly*, 51 (April 1967), 141–42; *New York Freeman's Journal*, 6 July, 17 Aug. 1844.

[46] Littell, *Clay Minstrel*, 40–1, 256–7; Sargent, *Henry Clay*, 23; Parker, *Theodore Frelinghuysen*, 10; *Baltimore Patriot*, 19 Oct. 1844 [Haynes]; *Georgia Constitutionalist*, 24 Oct. 1844 [Haynes].

[47] *The Private Correspondence of Henry Clay*, ed. Calvin Colton (1855; repr. New York, 1971), 495–520 (see 507–9 for Hone's anguished letter to Clay, 28 Nov. 1844); Chambers, *Frelinghuysen*, 177–80; Brownlow, *Americanism*, 95–6; *Boston Daily Atlas*, 11 Nov. 1844 [Haynes]; Brock, *Parties and Political Conscience*, 185.

[48] For the presidential election of 1848, see particularly Joseph G. Rayback, *Free Soil: The Election of 1848* (Lexington, Ky., 1970); Holman Hamilton, *Zachary Taylor: Soldier in the White House* (New York, 1951), 38–133.

[49] *Ohio State Journal*, 23 June, 15 Sept. 11 Oct. 1848; *General Taylor's Moral, Intellectual and Professional Character . . .* (Washington, DC, [1848]), 4; Fuller and Green, *God in the White House*, 87–8; *Reasons Good and True for Supporting the Nomination of . . . Z. Taylor* (Washington, DC, 1848), 2, 7–8; *Jonesborough Whig*, 12 July, 1 Nov. 1848; Hamilton, *Zachary Taylor*, 24, 397.

[50] *Albany Argus*, 2, 3, 22, 30 Aug., 18 Sept., 2 Nov. 1848; Joseph R. Fry, *A Life of Gen. Zachary Taylor . . .* (Philadelphia, 1847), 60–6; *Ohio State Journal*, 11, 15 Sept. 1848; *A Sketch of the Life and Public Services of General Zachary Taylor, the People's Candidate for the Presidency* (Washington, DC, 1848), 23–5; *WCA*, 21 Jan. 1848; S. Horn (ed.) *All the Letters of Major General Z. Taylor: Anecdotes of Rough and Ready . . .* (New York, 1848), 10–12; Joseph Gales, *A Sketch of the Personal Character and Qualities of General Zachary Taylor* (Washington [1848]), 1–7. For non-resistants' bitter criticism of Taylor as a "hired assassin" whose election to the presidency by a professedly Christian people and their ministers would be a mockery of true religion, see Henry C. Wright, *Dick Crowningshield, the Assassin, and Zachary Taylor, the Soldier; the Difference Between Them* (Hopedale, Mass., 1848). In the West, whiskey jugs with no bottom were known as "Taylor jugs." Marsh, *Temperance Recollections*, 226.

[51] Rayback, *Free Soil*, 244–5; Owen Peterson, *A Divine Discontent: A Life of Nathan S.S. Beman* (Macon, Ga., 1986), 162–3; Smith, *Lewis Cass*, 585–6; Henry R. Schoolcraft, *Outlines of the Life and Character of Gen. Lewis Cass* (Albany, 1848), 27, 31, 45; Frank B. Woodford, *Lewis Cass: the Last Jeffersonian* (New Brunswick, NJ, 1950), 158–62, 165–6.

[52] *Ohio State Journal*, 19, 25, 27, 31 Oct. 1848; *Jonesborough Whig*, 25 Oct. 1848; Forrest Conklin, "Parson Brownlow Joins the Sons of Temperance: Part I," *Tennessee Historical Quarterly*, 39 (Summer 1980), 182; *Albany Argus*, 15 Sept. 1848.

[53] *To the People of North Carolina* ([published at the request of the Central Rough and Ready Club] n.p. [1848]), 6–7; *Jonesborough Whig*, 16, 23 Aug., 6 Sept. 1848; Rayback, *Free Soil*, 41, 44, 238–59; Cooper, *The South and the Politics of Slavery*, 244–68; *Ohio State Journal*, 17 April, 23 June, 11 July, 8, 14, 26 Aug., 4, 5, 7, 20 Sept., 9 Oct. 1848; *Reasons Good and True*, 8; *New York Tribune*, 18 July 1848. Though many northern Whigs were disappointed by Taylor's nomination they eventually rallied to him as the best hope for restricting slavery. See, for example, *New York Tribune* through the campaign, esp. 28 Sept. 1848.

[54] *Ohio State Journal*, 4, 7 Aug., 30 Sept. 1848; *Albany Argus*, 5, 22, 28 July, 23 Aug., July, 11 Sept. 1848; Rayback, *Free Soil*, 240 (for the *Cleveland Plain Dealer*); *General Taylor's Two Faces . . .* (n.p., 1848), 1–8.

[55] Rayback, *Free Soil*, 3, 7, 54, 165–6, 169, 266–7; Michael F. Holt, "The Winding Roads to Recovery: The Whig Party from 1844 to 1848," in Maizlish and Kushma, *Essays on American Antebellum Politics*, 141–3, 163; *New York Tribune*, 2

June 1848. For Seward's generous attitudes to Catholics, see William H. Seward, *The True Greatness of Our Country: A Discourse* . . . (Washington, DC, 1848), 12, 24 and *passim*.

[56] Kerby A. Miller, *Emigrants and Exiles: Ireland and the Irish Exodus to North America* (New York, 1985), 280–312; *New York Tribune*, 22 May, 27 Oct., 2, 3, 7 Nov. 1848; *Taylor Anecdote Book*, 73–4; *Ohio State Journal*, 24 June, 12 Aug. 1848; *General Taylor's Moral, Intellectual and Professional Character*, 5.

[57] *Albany Argus*, 1, 4, 28, 31 July, 2, 3, 12 Aug., 2 Sept., 3 Nov. 1848; *Ohio State Journal*, 12, 16 Sept. 1848; *New York Freeman's Journal*, 25 March 1848.

[58] *Albany Argus*, 5, 21, 27 July, 3, 9, 23 Aug., 23 Sept., 18 Oct., 4 Nov. 1848; Lewis Cass, *Remarks of General Lewis Cass on the late French Revolution* . . . (Washington, 1848), 1–2; Schoolcraft, *Cass*, 62.

[59] Heale, *Presidential Quest*, 124–7; Holt, "Winding Roads," 123; Rayback, *Free Soil*, 50–3, 154–8, 234–5, 274–5; V.M. Queener, "William G. Brownlow as an Editor," *East Tennessee Historical Society Publications*, 4 (Jan. 1932), 73–4; *The Taylor Text-Book, or Rough and Ready Reckoner* (Baltimore, 1848), 8–15; Gales, *General Zachary Taylor*, 5; *Ohio State Journal*, 15 June 1848; Horn, *All the Letters of Taylor*, 15.

[60] Fry, *Zachary Taylor*, 326–7; *Ohio State Journal*, 21 March, 2, 8 June, 3, 8 Nov. 1848; Horn, *All the Letters of Taylor*, 21; *Taylor Platform*, (Columbus, Ohio, 1848), 2; *A Review of the Life, Character and Political Opinions of Zachary Taylor* (Boston, 1848), 13–14; Valentine, *Diary*, 14 Sept., 14, 22 Nov. 1848, SHC; *Jonesborough Whig*, 30 Aug., 1 Nov. 1848.

[61] William Salter (ed.) "Letters of John McLean to John Teasdale," *Bibliotheca Sacra* (Oct. 1899), 719; Maizlish, *Triumph of Sectionalism*, 80–3; *Political and Public Character of Polk*, 20.

[62] Wentworth, *Speech*, 1–3; *Knoxville Whig*, 30 Dec. 1846. For similar Democratic anger over "Pharisaical" Whigs' claims to a monopoly of religious and moral truth, see the Baton Rouge *Democratic Advocate*, 23 Oct. 1844 [Haynes].

Chapter 4 *Patterns of Electoral Response: Evangelicals and Partisan Allegiance during the Second Party System*

[1] Benson, *Concept*, particularly 288–328. The most influential of the subsequent ethnocultural analyses of antebellum politics include Formisano, *Mass Political Parties*, Michael F. Holt, *Forging a Majority: The Formation of the Republican Party in Pittsburgh, 1848–1860* (New Haven, Conn., 1969) and Kleppner, *The Cross of Culture*. William Brock's illuminating *Parties and Political Conscience*, 63–8, also accords ethnic and religious factors a greater significance than class or occupation in party choice. For a bravura attempt to interpret the whole of United States political history along ethnocultural lines, see Robert Kelley, "Ideology and Political Culture from Jefferson to Nixon," *AHR* 82 (June 1977), 531–62, and *The Cultural Pattern in American Politics: The First Century* (New York, 1979).

[2] Arthur M. Schlesinger, Jr, *The Age of Jackson* (Boston, 1945), presents the classic expression of the view that socioeconomic questions lay at the heart of the Whig/Democratic divide. Amongst the most vigorous of the economic interpretations are J. Mills Thornton, *Politics and Power in a Slave Society: Alabama, 1800–1860* (Baton Rouge, La., 1978) and Watson, *Jacksonian Politics and Community Conflict*. Ashworth, *"Agrarians" & "Aristocrats,"* argues that Whigs (capitalist and meritocratic) and Democrats (leveling, agrarian, and pre-capitalist) adopted fundamentally different attitudes to the changing economy. See also Marc W. Kruman, *Parties and Politics in North Carolina, 1836–1865* (Baton Rouge, La., 1983), 15–16; Donald B. Cole, *Jacksonian Democracy in New Hampshire* (Cambridge, Mass., 1970), 140–59; T.B. Alexander *et al.*, "The Basis of Alabama's Two-Party

System," *Alabama Review*, 19 (Oct. 1966), 243–76; Thomas E. Jeffery, "National Issues, Local Interests, and the Transformation of Antebellum North Carolina Politics," *JSH*, 50 (Feb. 1984), 43–4, 49, 71. For the political divisiveness of economic issues, see James Roger Sharp, *The Jacksonians versus the Banks: Politics in the States after the Panic of 1837* (New York, 1970); Maizlish, *Triumph of Sectionalism*, 1–37, 411–12; Donald J. Ratcliffe, "Politics in Jacksonian Ohio: Reflections on the Ethnocultural Interpretation," *Ohio History*, 88 (1979), 5–36. In contrast, Shade, *Banks or No Banks*, 18–19, 173–4, 253, argues that partisan conflict over state banking measures was "essentially a cultural one based on ethnic and religious differences." Harry L. Watson, *Liberty and Power: The Politics of Jacksonian America* (New York, 1990), offers an impressive synthesis of economic and ethnocultural approaches.

³ That ethnoculturalists threaten to replace economic with religious determinism and that some of their evidence and multivariate techniques leave much to be desired is the burden of Eric Foner, "The Causes of the American Civil War: Recent Interpretations and New Directions," in Swierenga, *Beyond the Civil War Synthesis*, 15–32; McCormick, "Ethno-Cultural Interpretations," 351–77; James E. Wright, "The Ethnocultural Model of Voting," *American Behavioral Scientist*, 16 (May-June, 1973), 653–74; Richard B. Latner and Peter Levine, "Perspectives in Antebellum Politics," *Reviews in American History*, 4 (March 1976), 15–24; J. Morgan Kousser, "The 'New Political History': A Methodological Critique," *Reviews in American History*, 4 (March 1976), 1–14. See also Goodman, "Guide to American Church Membership Data," 183–5.

⁴ Some incomplete and scattered data survive on how individuals voted during the antebellum period. Poll books from communities that voted viva voce, and canvassers' and newspapers' lists form the basis of Bourke and DeBats, "Identifiable Voting in Nineteenth-Century America," 259–88, and Paul Goodman, "The Social Basis of New England Politics in Jacksonian America," *JER*, 6 (Spring 1986), 23–58.

⁵ Goodman, "Social Basis" and Howe, *American Whigs*, 9–10 and *passim*, stress the complexity of the impulses behind voting. Even those who give primacy to cultural factors recognize the influence of status and economics. Ronald P. Formisano, "Federalists and Republicans: Parties, Yes – System, No," in Paul Kleppner *et al.*, *The Evolution of American Electoral Systems* (Westport, Conn., 1981), 60–1; Kelley, *Cultural Pattern*, 163.

⁶ *WCA*, 3, 17 Jan., 13 Nov. 1840, 22 Oct. 1841.

⁷ Theodore Frelinghuysen, *Speech of Mr. Frelinghuysen on His Resolution concerning Sabbath Mails in the Senate . . .* (Washington, DC, 1830); J. Wheelwright to W.H. Harrison, 15 Aug. 1840, H. Kingsbury to W.H. Harrison, 12 Nov. 1840, W.H. Harrison Papers, LC. For quintessential sermons, see ch.2 n.15 above and Charles S. Porter, *Sermon Delivered in the First Presbyterian Church, Utica, NY* (Utica, 1844), 8; Lavalette Perrin, *The Nation in Perplexity* (New Haven, Conn., 1844), 10–23. The radical religionists of upstate New York generated much of the enthusiasm for aggressive sabbatarianism. See Cross, *Burned-Over District*, 132–6; Johnson, *Shopkeeper's Millennium*, 74–5, 83–94. For southern sabbatarians' support for political action, see Thompson, *Presbyterians in the South*, I, 308.

⁸ Charles Hodge, "The American Quarterly Review on Sunday Mails," *Princeton Review* 3 (Jan. 1831), 86–134; *North American Review*, 31 (July 1830), 155–6; *Niles' Register*, 24 Jan., 7, 28 Feb. 1829, 30 March 1830; *Cincinnati Telegraph*, 24 Sept. 1842; Leland W. Meyer, *The Life and Times of Colonel Richard M. Johnson of Kentucky* (New York, 1932), 299–303; William Hague, *Life Notes; or, Fifty Years' Outlook* (Boston, 1888), 148–9; George W. Bethune, *Our Liberties: Their Danger, and the Means*

of Preserving Them (Philadelphia, 1835), 8–19; David MacDill, *An Address, Occasioned by the Opposition which Originated in Cincinnati, Ohio, against the Attempts to Stop the Sabbath Mails* (Newburgh, NY, 1830), *passim*; "Thomas Morris," in *DAB*; McFaul, "Expediency vs. Morality," 24–39; Wyatt-Brown, "Prelude to Abolitionism," 335–7. James R. Rohrer, "Sunday Mails and the Church-State Theme in Jacksonian America," *JER*, 7 (Spring 1987), 53–74, also emphasizes the fears and resentments *within* Protestantism against an increasingly assertive "evangelical united front." See also Phineas T. Barnum, *Struggles and Triumphs: or . . . Forty Years' Recollections of P.T. Barnum . . .* (London, 1869), 136–8 (recollecting his youthful alarm in 1831 "lest a great religious coalition should be formed in this country, which would carry out the desires of certain fanatics," and describing the divisions amongst professors of religion). Significantly, the executive committee of the interdenominational National Lord's Day Convention in 1844 thought it prudent to repudiate "the coercive fear of human legislation," since "laws unsustained by public sentiment are but cobwebs; and . . . a healthy public opinion on the sabbath would render all laws unnecessary." (*CAJ*, 30 Oct. 1844).

⁹ Lewis, *Samuel Lewis*, 200–2, 211; Howe, *American Whigs*, 36; David X. Junkin, *Rev. George Junkin D.D., LL.D: A Historical Biography* (Philadelphia, 1871), 158; Nathan S.S. Beman, *The Claims of the Country on Young Men: An Address* (Troy, NY, 1843), 24; H.W. Mann, *Atticus Greene Haygood* (University of Georgia, 1965), 11; Edmund J. James, "Reverend Colin Dew James: A Pioneer Methodist Preacher of Early Illinois," *Journal of the Illinois State Historical Society*, 9 (Jan. 1917), 451; John B. Weaver, "Calvin Henderson Wiley and the Problem of Slavery, 1850–1865," (MA diss. University of North Carolina at Chapel Hill, 1975), 1–3, 37–9; Francis R. Flournoy, *Benjamin Mosby Smith, 1811–1893* (Richmond, Va., 1947), 40–7; Benjamin

M. Palmer, *The Life and Letters of James Henley Thornwell . . .* (Richmond, Va., 1875), 325; "James Harlan," "Samuel Lewis," "David Rice McAnally," in *DAB*; Hilliard, *Stepping Stones to Glory*, 63; Kaestle, *Pillars of the Republic*, 153–6. For other Whig "improvers," see Fletcher, *Diary*, IV, 59; *A Memorial of Samuel Barstow, of Detroit, Who Died July 12, 1854* (Detroit, 1854), 9, 12–13; Valentine, *Diary*, 1 June, 1 Aug. 1839, SHC. For examples of Democratic evangelicals who sought the widening of opportunity, see "Daniel Haines" and "Thomas Morris," *DAB*.

¹⁰ Marsh, *Temperance Recollections*, 70; Anne C. Loveland, *Southern Evangelicals and the Social Order* (Baton Rouge, La., 1980), 145–6; Tyrrell, *Sobering Up*, 56, 146–7, 230, 236, 266; *WCA*, 19, 26 June, 17 July 1840; *CAJ*, 14 Aug., 2 Sept. 1840; Bertram Wyatt-Brown, "The Anti-Mission Movement in the Jacksonian South and West: A Study in Regional Folk Culture," *JSH*, 36 (Nov. 1970), 501–29; Marsden, *Evangelical Mind*, 100.

¹¹ Cross, *Burned-Over District*, 131, 216; Thompson, *Presbyterians in the South*, I, 309–11; Wade, *Longstreet*, 141; Palmer, *Life of Thornwell*, 376–7; Tyrrell, *Sobering Up*, 57–8, 237–8.

¹² Archibald T. Robertson, *Life and Letters of John Albert Broadus* (Philadelphia, 1901), 14–16; Jordan, *William Salter*, 112; Duffield, *Thanksgiving Sermon*, 12–13; Grant, *Peter Cartwright*, 152; Kallenbach, III, 208; Van Nest, *Bethune*, 109–15; Clifford M. Drury, *William Anderson Scott: "No Ordinary Man"* (Glendale, Calif., 1967), 85; *Christian Lawyer*, 258–60.

¹³ Bodo, *Protestant Clergy and Public Issues*, 85–111; Brunson, *Western Pioneer*, II, 139; Crane, *Autobiography*, 79; "The Life of Robert McCutcheon Hall," 27, typescript, PHS; George W. Bethune, *Truth the Strength of Freedom: A Discourse . . .* (Philadelphia, 1845), 28–9; Joseph G. Smoot, "A Presbyterian Minister Calls on Presidential Candidate Andrew Jackson," *Tennessee Historical Quarterly*, 21 (Sept. 1962), 288; Kelley, *Cultural Pattern*, 168; Holder, *Winans*, 103–4, 108; Howe,

American Whigs, 40–2. For support amongst northern Baptists and Dutch Reformed for the policy of removal, see Bodo, *Protestant Clergy*, 101–3, 105.

[14] For an exception to this southern rule, see the appeal of the Methodist local preacher and US congressman from Georgia, Walter T. Colquitt, *Circular. To the People of Georgia, and Especially to the States Rights Party* (n.p. [1840]).

[15] Paul R. Grim, "The Reverend John Rankin, Early Abolitionist," *Ohio State Archaeological and Historical Quarterly*, 46 (May 1937), 254; Peterson, *Divine Discontent*, 194; Davis, "Joshua Leavitt," 216; Lewis, *Samuel Lewis*, 286.

[16] Fletcher, *Diary*, III, 28, 35, 68, 82–3, 86; Theodore T. Munger, *Horace Bushnell, Preacher and Theologian* (Boston, 1899), 44–5; Hall (ed.) *Forty Years' Familiar Letters*, II, 51, 73–6; G.R. Crooks to J. McClintock, 21 Oct. 1848, DU; Jordan, *William Salter*, 112; Dwight L. Dumond (ed.) *Letters of James Gillespie Birney, 1831–1857* (2 vols, New York, 1938), II, 1002–3. See also Richard Lowitt, *A Merchant Prince of the Nineteenth Century: William E. Dodge* (New York, 1954), 201–2; McDonald and Searles, *Inskip*, 66–7, 75–6; *Ohio State Journal*, 3 Oct. 1848 (for A.W. Elliot). Michael Holt suggests that in Pittsburgh in the late 1840s strong Presbyterian representation among the Whig leadership might have had to do with the party's more categorical antislavery stand than that of their opponents (Holt, *Forging a Majority*, 46). For Democrats see, for example, Brinkerhoff, *Recollections*, 30–66; McKivigan, "Abolitionism and the American Churches," 417–18 (for Nathan Rice).

[17] E. Ames to M. Simpson, 26 June 1841, M. Simpson Papers, LC; *CAJ*, 30 June 1841; Clark, *Alarm to Christian Patriots*, 20; Brownlow, *Political Register*, 29; Ralph W. Haskins, "Internecine Strife in Tennessee: Andrew Johnson versus Parson Brownlow," *Tennessee Historical Quarterly*, 24 (Winter 1965), 327–8; Atwater, *The Importance of Good Rulers*; *Pittsburgh Christian Advocate*, 1

May 1844; *WCA*, 12 Aug. 1842; Bacon, *Commercial Distress*, 4–5. For a discussion of Yankee thinking on wealth, the economy, and the emergent factory system, see Cole, *Social Ideas*, 164–91.

[18] Robert Kelley, "Presbyterianism, Jacksonianism and Grover Cleveland," *AQ*, 18 (Winter 1966), 627. See also Marvin Meyers, *The Jacksonian Persuasion: Politics and Belief* (Stanford, Calif., 1957); John McFaul, *The Politics of Jacksonian Finance*, esp. 210–16.

[19] Cushing Strout, *The New Heavens and New Earth: Political Religion in America* (New York, 1974), 111–12; Osgood, *Life and Christian Experience*, 114–15; J.P. Fort, "Reminiscences," 51–60, 79–92, DU. See also J.S. Swift to J.F. Speight, 25 June, 4 Sept. 1840, J.F. Speight Papers, SHC.

[20] Potts, "Presbyterian Minister," 289–90; James Walker, *Experiences of Pioneer Life in the Early Settlements and Cities of the West* (Chicago, 1881), 97–8. William Shade posits a connection between Jacksonian economic conservatism and the doctrinal orthodoxy of German Lutheran, Catholic, and Reformed churchgoers. William G. Shade, "Pennsylvania Politics in the Jacksonian Period: A Case Study, Northampton County, 1824–1844," *Pennsylvania History*, 39 (July 1972), 332–3.

[21] Lucien W. Berry, *An Address Delivered by the Rev. L.W. Berry, D.D., upon His Installation as President of the Indiana Asbury University, July 16, 1850* (Indianapolis, 1850), 29–36. See also Howe, *American Whigs*, 9–10, 18; Kelley, *Cultural Pattern*, 165–6.

[22] Archibald A. Hodge, *The Life of Charles Hodge . . .* (New York, 1880), 245; Philip E. Howard, *The Life Story of Henry Clay Trumbull: Missionary, Army Chaplain, Editor and Author* (New York, 1906), 28–30; *CAJ*, 23 June 1841; *WCA*, 21 Jan. 1842; Norton, *Religious Newspapers*, 97–9; A. Hagaman to D. Barkalow, 9 Aug. 1837, 21 April 1840, Hagaman Papers, PHS; R.H. Morrison to J Morrison, 14 June 1837, 20 Dec. 1838, 6 March 1840,

Morrison Papers, SHC; Bacon, *Commercial Distress*, 8; Bela B. Edwards, *National Fast*, 20–1; Duncan, *Discourse on the Fast Day*, 38–40; Duffield, *Thanksgiving Sermon*, 14; Crane, *Autobiography*, 72–3; Brunson, *Western Pioneer*, II, 138; George Brown, *Recollections of Itinerant Life: including Early Reminiscences* (3rd edn, Cincinnati, 1866), 269–70. See also Holder, *Winans*, 134. For evangelical attacks on the Independent Treasury scheme, see Brownlow, *Political Register*, 29; Toccoa Cozart, "Henry W. Hilliard," *Transactions of the Alabama Historical Society*, 4 (1904), 279.

23 *New York Evangelist*, 4 Jan., 15 Feb. 1844; Spring, *Danger and Hope*, 12; M. Simpson to H. Marshall, 15 Nov. 1841, M. Simpson Papers, LC; Holder, *Winans*, 134–5; Moses Stuart, *Mr. Webster's Andover Address and His Political Course while Secretary of State* (Essex County, Mass., 1844), 9–10; "Stephen Colwell," in *DAB*; Lewis, *Samuel Lewis*, 57. See also Palmer, *Life of Thornwell*, 479; George Duffield, *The Death of Gen. William Henry Harrison, President of the United States . . .* (Detroit, 1841), 14–16; Spear, *Politico-Social Foundations*, 13–16; Porter, *Sermon*, 8; Perrin, *Nation in Perplexity*, 15; Beman, *Claims of our Country*, 24; Brownlow, *Political Register*, 11; Norton, *Religious Newspapers*, 100; Cole, *Social Ideas*, 171–2.

24 Crane, *Autobiography*, 84–5.

25 *Tennessee Whig* 22 Oct. 1839; *CAJ*, 8 Sept. 1847; D. Maguire to unidentified correspondent, 4 Aug. 1843, M. Simpson Papers, LC; Fletcher, *Diary*, III, 82–3; Cross, *Burned-Over District*, 117; Michael F. Holt, "Antimasonic and Know Nothing Parties," in Arthur M. Schlesinger, Jr (ed.) *History of United States Political Parties*, (4 vols, New York, 1973), I, 587–8; William H. Brackney, "Expedience versus Conviction: The Baptist Response to the Antimasonic Impulse 1826–1830," *Foundations*, 21 (April–June 1978), 171; William Preston Vaughn, *The Antimasonic Party in the United States 1826–1843* (Lexington, Ky., 1983), 21–3. For a convincing portrayal of Antimasonry as a defense by conservative, uncompromis-

ing Calvinists of strict standards of Christian faith and behavior in the face of Freemasonry's "non-sectarian tolerance, its doctrinal vagueness, its affinity for natural religion, and its Arminian notion that good works and benevolence formed essential tests of moral worth," see Goodman, *Towards a Christian Republic*, esp. 53–78, 129–39, 163–76. Goodman also concludes that "Nothingarians" (i.e. freethinkers, secularists, and those only loosely attached to churches) in New England in the early and mid-nineteenth century were more likely to be Democrats, while identifiable church members were disproportionately Whig. "Social Basis," 37–8, 55.

26 M. Simpson to H. Marshall, 15 Nov. 1841, M. Simpson Papers, LC; Brock, *Parties and Political Conscience*, 50–51, 55–6; Cross, *Burned-Over District*, 270; Holder, *Winans*, 132–3; Hall (ed.) *Forty Years' Familiar Letters*, II, 88; William Wisner, *Nations Amenable to God: A Fast Sermon . . .* (Ithaca, NY, 1841), 6–8; Fleharty, *Rev. A.E. Phelps*, 330; Perrin, *Nation in Perplexity*, 23; Valentine, *Diary*, 21 March, 9 July, 15 Sept. 1840, 12 July 1844, SHC; *Tennessee Whig*, 21 Nov. 1839, 14, 27 May 1840; Holt, "Antimasonic and Know Nothing Parties," 578, 580–2. Harrison's pleasure may have been tempered by the Lord's instruction, as interpreted by Crane, "to make his organ – that is myself – President of the United States for the approaching term of office"; Harrison could console himself with the choice of "whatever other office in the Government you may think proper." G. Crane to W.H. Harrison, 1 Sept. 1840, W.H. Harrison Papers, LC. See also Johnson, *Shopkeeper's Millennium*, 75, which argues that in Rochester, NY, Antimasonic political leaders "had little use for religion, and even less for coercive moral reform." For an explanation of why Rochester was untypical, see Kathleen Smith Kutolowski, "Antimasonry Re-examined: Social Bases of the Grass-Roots Party," *JAH*, 71 (Sept. 1984), 290.

[27] *Albany Argus*, 21 Aug. 1852; Brock, *Parties and Political Conscience*, 63–8; Goodman, "Social Basis," 43–4; Howe, *American Whigs*, 10; Kelley, *Cultural Pattern*, 168–70; Fletcher, *Diary*, III, 82–3; Valentine, Diary, 24 May, 19 Oct., 3 Dec. 1844, SHC; *Jonesborough Whig*, 2 Aug. 1848; P. Hone to H. Clay, 28 Nov. 1844, in *Private Correspondence of Clay*, 508–9; Robert Doherty, "Social Bases for the Presbyterian Schism of 1837–1838: The Philadelphia Case," *Journal of Social History*, 2 (Fall 1968), 76–9; Laurie, *Working People of Philadelphia*, 48–52. Howe, "The Evangelical Movement and Political Culture," 1217–22, shrewdly considers the connections between Whiggery, evangelicalism, self-discipline, social control, humanitarianism, and capitalist development. For the argument that both major parties recruited from all social classes, but that "the reckless, ostentatious servitors of vice" and the "master-spirits" of "all the haunts of debauchery in the land" were overwhelmingly Democrats, see Horace Greeley, *Why I Am a Whig: Reply to an Inquiring Friend* (New York, 1852), 13. Kutolowski, "Antimasonry Reexamined," 269–93, concludes that in Genesee County, western New York, Antimasonic voters were proto-Whigs, distinguished not by poverty or socioeconomic class, but by their identification with improving, market-oriented communities and with the values of the Second Great Awakening. But Goodman, *Towards a Christian Republic*, 34–53, 122–5, 152–62, 235, 238, finds New England Antimasons ambivalent towards the market-place and an industrial society, and concerned about the consumerism and "wordliness" of the emerging new economic order: they did not enthusiastically embrace modernization. This leaves one asking why Whigs rather than Democrats were the greater beneficiaries of Antimasonry in the later 1830s. That Antimasons, faced with an unattractive choice between "secular" Democrats and "modernizing" Whigs, chose the latter suggests that their

religious concerns were more profound and more durable than their economic anxieties. For Antimasonic voters who later joined Democratic ranks, see also Holt, "Antimasonic and Know Nothing Parties," 591–2.

[28] *Knoxville Whig*, 11 Dec. 1850 (quoting the *Holston Christian Advocate*), 1 March, 5 April 1851.

[29] *Highland Messenger*, 5 June 1840. Whiggery was strong in these mountain areas. *Jonesborough Whig*, 21 Oct. 1846.

[30] *Jonesborough Whig*, 2 Feb. 1848. See also *ibid.*, 7, 21 July, 29 Sept. 1847; *Knoxville Whig* 19, 26 May, 2 June, 14 July 1849, 2 Feb., 23 March 1850, 29 Dec. 1851, 11 Sept. 1852. According to an inhabitant of Stewart County, "A spirit of evangelical enterprise has gone out into society, prompting Christians to the performance of the most noble deeds, and preparing many for the moral Revolution of an enslaved world" (*Jonesborough Whig*, 26 May 1846).

[31] *WCA*, 21 Jan. 1842; Spear, *Politico-Social Foundations*, 13–16; John Maltby, *Characteristics of the Times: A Sermon . . .* (Bangor, Me., 1838), 21–2; Spring, *Danger and Hope*, 17–21; William Goodell, *The Rights and Wrongs of Rhode Island . . .* (Whitesboro, NY, 1842), 3–4, 81–120; Porter, *Sermon*, 8–11; George S. Merriam, *Noah Porter: A Memorial by Friends* (New York, 1893), 125; Samuel W. Cozzens, *The Prominent Sins of the Times: A Sermon* (Boston 1844), 10; Tucker, *A Discourse Preached on Thanksgiving Day*, 16; Duncan, *Discourse on the Fast Day*, 21, 24–30; Humphrey, *Harrison*, 16; Valentine, Diary, 19 May 1852, SHC.

[32] David H. Fischer, *The Revolution of American Conservatism: The Federalist Party in the Era of Jeffersonian Democracy* (New York, 1965), 48–9; Bloch, *Visionary Republic*, 202–3; Scott, *From Office to Profession*, 24–7; Hodge, *Charles Hodge*, 233, 346; Goodell, *Rights and Wrongs of Rhode Island*, 92, 119–20; G. Coles to G. Cubitt, 21 Feb. 1845, DU; *Weekly Tropic* (New Orleans), 4 Nov. 1844 [Haynes].

[33] Greeley, *Why I Am a Whig*, 12–13; Cole, *Jacksonian Democracy in New*

Hampshire, 174–5; Cross, *Burned-Over District*, 135–6. The quintessential example of this outlook was the aged and popular Massachusetts Baptist John Leland, for whom see William G. McLoughlin, *New England Dissent 1680– 1833: The Baptists and the Separation of Church and State* (2 vols, Cambridge, Mass., 1971), esp. II, 926–38, 1099–101, 1112–13, 1141–2.

[34] Wyatt-Brown, "Antimission Movement," 501–29; *idem*, "Prelude to Abolitionism," 334; William T. Hutchinson, *Cyrus Hall McCormick* ... (2 vols, New York, 1930–35), II, 5; Kelley, *Cultural Pattern*, 161. For the appeal of Democratic egalitarianism amongst the temperamentally defensive migrants from the South in the Old Northwest, and that culture's clash with the commercially oriented Whiggery of Yankee evangelicals, see Howe, *American Whigs*, 162–3.

[35] Fort, "Reminiscences," 59, DU; Walker, *Pioneer Life*, 98; Bethune, *Our Liberties*, 8–15; Van Nest, *Bethune*, 313; Bethune, *Truth the Strength of Freedom*, 27. See also Crane, *Autobiography*, 85.

[36] Benson, *Concept*, esp. 284–6, drawing on Robert K. Merton, *Social Theory and Social Structure* (Glencoe, Ill., 1957).

[37] Wyatt-Brown, "Prelude to Abolitionism," 323–6. For the elements of Unitarian thought and the strong ties of that denomination to Federalism, National Republicans, and Whiggery, see Brock, *Parties and Political Conscience*, 44–9, 190–201; Howe, *Unitarian Conscience*, 8, 205–11; Octavius B. Frothingham, *Boston Unitarianism 1820–1850: A Study of the Life and Works of Nathaniel Langdon Frothingham* (New York, 1890), 197; Philip A. Nordquist, "The Ecology of Organized Religion in the United States: 1850" (PhD diss., University of Washington, 1964), 40.

[38] Cross, *Burned-Over District*, 323–34; McKivigan, "Abolitionism and the American Churches," 432. As well as provoking the opposition of Congregationalists and New School Calvinists,

Universalists became a prime target for Methodist attack during the 1830s and 1840s: these critics tended to Whiggery.

[39] Howe, *American Whigs*, 35; *Cincinnati Telegraph*, 28 Dec. 1844; Beman, *Claims of Our Country*, 22–3; *WCA*, 10 Sept. 1841; Feldberg, *Philadelphia Riots*, 30–1; Holt, *Forging a Majority*, 46–7; Brownlow, *Political Register*, 75–7, 116–17; M.G. Marsden, *Marsden*, 92.

[40] James H. Broussard, *The Southern Federalists, 1800–1816* (Baton Rouge, La., 1978), 394; MacDill, *Sabbath Mails*, 11; McLoughlin, *New England Dissent*, II, 1198–9; Paul Goodman, *The Democratic-Republicans of Massachusetts: Politics in a Young Republic* (Cambridge, Mass., 1964), 86–96; Formisano, "Federalists and Republicans," 63; McKivigan, "Abolitionism and the American Churches," 166.

[41] George C. Baker, *An Introduction to the History of Early New England Methodism 1789–1839* (Durham, NC, 1941); Brunson, *Western Pioneer*, I, 27–30, 35–43, 171–3; A. Hunt, "Reminiscences," 22 March 1847; J.B. Thomas to A. Stevens, 8 Oct. 1860; D.D. Kilburn, ms. recollections: G. Pickering to E. Kibby, 19 Dec. 1798, DU; Daniel De Vinne, *Recollections of Fifty Years in the Ministry* ... (New York, 1869), 14–15, 31–2; *CAJ*, 23 Oct. 1856; Holder, *Winans*, 36; Selah Stocking, "A Brief Biographical Sketch of the History of the Rev. Jeremiah Stocking", 4–6, and *idem*, "A Brief Historical Sketch of the Life of the Rev. Solon Stocking", 4–12, NEC; Young, *Autobiography*, 4, 101–3, 278–90; Cole, *Jacksonian Democracy in New Hampshire*, 39–40, 56; Mary L. Ninde, *William Xavier Ninde: A Memorial* (New York, 1902), 50–1. Under the Plan of Union of 1801 Presbyterians and Congregationalists cooperated in the work of evangelizing the West: hence "Presbygationalist."

[42] *WCA*, 23 Dec. 1842; John Stewart, *Highways and Hedges; or, Fifty Years of Western Methodism* (Cincinnati, 1870), 195–7; Pilcher, *Elijah H. Pilcher*, 28; Junkin, *Rev. George Junkin*, 422–7; J. McLean to J.P. Durbin, 20 April 1842,

DU; Brownlow, *Americanism*, 42; Allen Wiley, *Life and Times . . .*, ed. D.W. Clark (Cincinnati, 1873), 69–73, 128; T.M. Eddy, "Influence of Methodism upon the Civilization and Education of the West," *Methodist Quarterly Review*, 17 (April 1857), 291–4; Elsmere, *Henry Ward Beecher: The Indiana Years, 1837–1847* (Indianapolis, 1973), 181–2; Clark, *Matthew Simpson*, 72, 105–6.

43 W.W. Hibben, *Rev. James Havens* (Indianapolis, 1872), 183–4; M. Simpson to J. Stryker, 7 July 1843, DU; M. Simpson to J. Stryker, 3 July 1843, I. Grover to M. Simpson, 15 Sept. 1843, L.W. Berry to M. Simpson, 26 July 1843, 29 Jan. 1844, D. Reynolds to M. Simpson, 29 July 1843, J. Stryker to M. Simpson, 10 June 1843, W. Terrell to M. Simpson, 16 Aug. 1843, M. Simpson Papers, LC; Elsmere, *Beecher*, 184–7; Clark, *Matthew Simpson*, 106–11; *CAJ*, 21 Feb. 1850. For persisting frictions, over the appointment of a Methodist sympathizer to the Indianapolis postmastership, over the funeral ceremonies for ex-Governor Noah Noble, and over the Presbyterians' successful efforts to get the legislature to write off the Wabash College debt, see L.W. Berry to M. Simpson, 10 Jan. 1844, 12 Jan. 1844 [misdated 1843], 23 Feb. 1844, 26 Dec. 1844, 15 Nov. 1845, 23 March 1847, W.J. Burns to M. Simpson, 19 Jan. 1847, A.W. Harrison to M. Simpson, 15 Jan. 1847, M. Simpson Papers, LC; Elsmere, *Beecher*, 268–9. Interdenominational tensions did not necessarily conduce to partisan polarity, even when those involved implied that they should. George Duffield and other Plan of Union Presbyterians sneered at separatist Congregationalists in Michigan in the early 1840s, particularly for their "Finneyistic preferences," and dubbed their brand of religion "Loco Focoism in the church." But both groups were staunchly Whig. Vander Velde, "Diary of George Duffield," 32–4.

44 *Tennessee Whig* 14 May 1840; *Jonesborough Whig*, 22 Sept., 13 Oct. 1847, 14 June, 20 Dec. 1848; *Knoxville Whig*, 8 Sept. 1849, 12 Oct. 1850. Brownlow launched a journal, the *Jonesborough Quarterly Review* specifically to respond to Ross's attacks.

45 *Jonesborough Whig*, 29 Sept., 6, 20 Oct., 10 Nov. 1847, 13 Sept. 1848; *Knoxville Whig* 25 Aug., 1, 8 Sept. 1849; Thomas B. Alexander, *Thomas A.R. Nelson of East Tennessee* (Nashville, Tenn., 1956), 60. See also John Bell Brownlow's handwritten marginal notes in *Jonesborough Whig*, 29 Sept. 1847 (file in LC).

46 See, for example, *Biblical Recorder*, 15 March 1845, 20 Jan. 1854. These points of conflict were of course not restricted to the highland region: see *Christian Index*, 29 March, 17 May, 18 Oct. 1844.

47 Frank Richardson, *From Sunrise to Sunset: Reminiscence* (Bristol, Tenn., 1910), 107–8; *Tennessee Whig*, 19 Sept., 14 Nov. 1839, 8 Jan. 1840, 29 July 1840; *Jonesborough Whig*, 14 Oct. 1846; *Knoxville Whig*, 27 Sept. 1856. Gary R. Freeze, "The Ethnocultural Thesis Goes South: Religio-Cultural Dimensions of Voting in North Carolina's Second Party System" (unpublished paper delivered at the Southern Historical Association Convention, Nov. 1988), 2–18, indicates a positive correlation between areas of Methodist strength and Whiggery (the north-eastern coastal counties, the central piedmont and the western mountains), and between Baptist strength and Democracy (the coastal plain and the north-western mountains), and concludes that in North Carolina "religion was significant in the alignment of the second party system, and . . . was a force largely independent of economic forces." Freeze notes (16–17), however, that the congruence between denomination and party was stronger in the poorer "subsistence" counties than the richer "market" ones. For instances of *Democratic* Methodists in the highlands, see *Tennessee Whig* 12 Aug. 1840; for conflicts between Methodists and Baptists *within* Whiggery, see Brownlow's successful defense in a libel suit brought by the Baptist Lewis Reneau. *Jonesborough Whig*, 26 Aug., 14 Oct. 1846. In contrast,

William G. Shade's study of Prince Edward County, Virginia, links Methodists more closely with the Democrats, the party of the "physically and psychologically peripheral areas," than with the Whigs; but his evidence sustains the view that religious loyalties played a shaping role in the local party politics of the South. William G. Shade, "Society and Politics in Antebellum Virginia's Southside," *JSH*, 53 (May 1987), 163–93.

[48] Beman, *Claims of Our Country*, 8; Lucien Berry, *Address*, 29; Fletcher, *Diary*, V, 326; Kelley, *Cultural Pattern*, 165–6; Howe, *American Whigs*, 155; M. Simpson to H. Marshall, 15 Nov. 1841, M. Simpson Papers, LC. For examples of the dispersal of New England evangelical culture and its association with Whiggery, see George H. Wilcox, *A Christian Philanthropist: A Sketch of the Life of Mr. Daniel Hand*... (New York, 1889), 9–19; Jordan, *William Salter*, 112 and *passim*; Thomas A. Flinn, "Continuity and Change in Ohio Politics," *Journal of Politics*, 24 (Aug. 1962), 527; Herbert Ershkowitz, *The Origin of the Whig and Democratic Parties: New Jersey Politics, 1820–1837* (Washington, DC, 1982), 216–18. John M. Rozett's study of individual voting records in Green County, Illinois, indicates that 74 percent of the county's Methodists, who were mainly of English stock, voted Whig. Ronald P. Formisano, "Comments," on Kelley, "Ideology and Political Culture from Jefferson to Nixon," 573.

[49] Kelley, *Cultural Pattern*, 64–5, 127–8, 175; Alfred F. Young, *The Democratic-Republicans of New York: The Origins 1763–1797* (Chapel Hill, NC, 1967), 275; Formisano, "Federalists and Republicans," 64–5; Fischer, *Revolution of American Conservatism*, 223–4; William G. Shade, "Political Pluralism and Party Development: The Creation of a Modern Party System, 1815–1852," in Kleppner et al., *Evolution of American Electoral Systems*, 102. For the suggestion that Dutch–Yankee asperities softened over time, see David M. Ellis, "Yankee–Dutch Confrontation in the Albany Area," *New England Quarterly*, 45 (Sept. 1972), 262–9. Tully argues that the fissure between an English core and Scotch-Irish, German, and Dutch outgroups was not a major element in colonial politics, whatever may have been the case in the era of emergent mass democracy. Alan W. Tully, "Ethnicity, Religion and Politics in Early America," *Pennsylvania Magazine of History and Biography*, 107 (Oct. 1983), 494, 530–6.

[50] Thompson, *Presbyterians in the South*, I, 20–1, 31, 42–3, 81–96; Kelley, *Cultural Pattern*, 70–5, 101–5, 146–7; DeVinne, *Recollections*, 14–15; Forrest McDonald and Ellen Shapiro McDonald, "Ethnic Origins of the American People," *William and Mary Quarterly*, 37 (April 1980), 182–3, 195, 198–9; Broussard, *Southern Federalists*, 399–400; Manning J. Dauer, *The Adams Federalists* (Baltimore, 1953; paper edn 1968), 29; Jeffrey P. Brown, "The Ohio Federalists, 1803–1815," *JER*, 2 (Fall 1982), 281; James M. Porter, *Eulogium upon James Knox Polk*... (Easton, Pa., 1849), *passim*. Donald J. Ratcliffe, "The Role of Voters and Issues in Party Formation: Ohio, 1824," *JAH*, 59 (March 1973), 862–3. Harry Watson argues that by the 1840s in Cumberland County, North Carolina, the rivalries between the descendants of Scottish immigrants and their non-Scottish neighbors, which had been important, were no longer significant so far as party alignment was concerned. Watson, *Jacksonian Politics and Community Conflict*, 101, 147–8, 211–13, 228–9, 278–9. Grady McWhiney regards the line between southerners of English stock and Celtic "Crackers' as the fundamental cleavage in the Old South. Grady McWhiney, *Cracker Culture: Celtic Ways in the Old South* (Tuscaloosa, Ala., 1988), *passim*.

[51] Kelley, *Cultural Pattern*, 128, 167; Kelley, "Presbyterianism, Jacksonianism and Cleveland," 615–20; Shade, "Pennsylvania Politics," 325; Thompson, *Presbyterians in the South*, I, 353–61; Marsden, *Evangelical Mind*, 39–67; Walker, *Pioneer Life*, *passim*. For Scotch-

Irish Presbyterians of Whig persuasion, see "The Life of Robert McCutcheon Hall," 27, typescript, PHS; Weaver, "Calvin Henderson Wiley," 1–2; R.H. Morrison to J. Morrison, 6 March 1840, Morrison Papers, SHC; R.C. Colmery, *Memoir of the Life and Character of Josiah Scott* (Columbus, Ohio, 1881), 30–1; Oliver P. Temple, *Notable Men of Tennessee from 1833 to 1875: Their Times and Their Contemporaries* (New York, 1912), 88–9 (for William B. Carter). Scotch-Irish Presbyterians tended to be Whigs in those New Hampshire towns where they were the socially dominant group. Goodman, "Social Basis," 43.

[52] Brown, "Ohio Federalists," 281–2; John Binns, *Recollections of the Life of John Binns* (Philadelphia, 1854), 325–35; Joseph H. Creighton, *Life and Times of Joseph H. Creighton, A.M. of the Ohio Conference* (Cincinnati, 1899), 24, 67; Fitzgerald, *John B. McFerrin*, 11–27, 39, 91, 116, 168–9, 196–9, 243; John Mathews, *Peeps into Life: Autobiography of Rev. John Mathews, D.D., A Minister of the Gospel for Sixty Years* (n.p. [1904]), 21–2; William W. Williams, *The Garden of American Methodism: The Delmarva Peninsula, 1769–1820* (Wilmington, Del., 1984), 174–5; Smith, *Pillars in the Temple*, 230–6; Sean Wilentz, *Chants Democratic: New York City and the Rise of the American Working Class, 1788–1850* (New York, 1984), 316–24; James, "Colin Dew James," 452–3, 463–4. For Jacksonian Methodists of Huguenot stock, see for example Smith, *Pillars in the Temple*, 68ff. [Moses Odell]; *WCA*, 3 July 1850; *BDAC*, 1041 [William Hendricks].

[53] Daniels, *Gilbert Haven*, 30–1; Smith, *Pillars in the Temple*, 73; Brinkerhoff, *Recollections*, 16; Elijah E. Hoss, *David Morton: A Biography* (Nashville, Tenn., 1916), 6, 19. Goodman, "Social Basis," 33–4, concludes that in New England party preferences and loyalties were strong within families and across generations: sons "almost invariably" followed their fathers. See also Benson, *Concept*, 283–4. Ronald P. Formisano, "Deferential-Participant

Politics: The Early Republic's Political Culture, 1789–1840," *American Political Science Review*, 68 (June 1974), 481–2, cautions against assuming that voter loyalty and popular partisanship under the first party system was comparable to what existed under the second: institutionalized parties "reified in the public mind" do not seem to have emerged until the late 1830s.

[54] Clark, *Alarm to Christian Patriots*, 20; Scott, *Duty of Praying*, 33.

[55] Lorenzo Dow, *The Dealings of God, Man and the Devil; as Exemplified in the Life, Experience and Travels of Lorenzo Dow* ... (New York, 1854), 181–2; William B. Sprague, *Annals of the American Pulpit; or, Commemorative Notices of Distinguished American Clergymen of Various Denominations* ... (9 vols, New York, 1857–69), VII [Methodists], 839; Smoot, "A Presbyterian Minister Calls on Jackson," 290; Bethune, *Truth the Strength of Freedom*, 24–5; Drury, *Scott*, 63–9; Wheeler, *Harrison*, 3–4, 21–3; Edwards, *God's Voice to the Nation*, 8; Dwight, "A Great Man Fallen," 6–11; Redford, *H.H. Kavanaugh*, 530; Henkle, *Bascom*, 105–7, 135–9, 281–5; Holder, *Winans*, 143–5, 158–9; Robertson, *John Albert Broadus*, 40–2; Howard, *Henry Clay Trumbull*, 30–2; Coulter, *Brownlow*, 119; Brownlow, *Political Register*, v, vii.

[56] Hobart, *Recollections*, 204; Hall (ed.) *Forty Years' Familiar Letters*, II, 10; "The Life of Robert McCutcheon Hall," 27, typescript, PHS; *Documents Relating to Certain Calumnies against the Hon. Henry Clay, and ascribed to the Rev. W.A. Scott* ... (New Orleans, 1845), *passim*; *Memorial to the Members of the Presbytery of New Orleans* (n.p., 1845), *passim*; Drury, *Scott*, 99–109.

[57] *CAJ*, 4 Nov., 23 Dec. 1840, 17 Nov. 1841; Wright, *James Quinn*, 201; Duncan, *Discourse on the Fast Day*, 4–5; Coulter, *Brownlow*, 122–3; Fee, *Bringing the Sheaves*, 134–7; James D. Anthony, *Life and Times of Rev. J. D. Anthony: An Autobiography* ... (Atlanta, Ga., 1896), 80–1; Benson, *Concept*, 290; Richard H. Rivers, *The Life of Robert Paine, D.D., Bishop*

of the Methodist Episcopal Church, South (Nashville, Tenn., 1916), 99 (for McFerrin). Goodman, "Social Basis," 38, examines the political loyalties of 600 individuals in Littleton, New Hampshire, between 1770 and 1870: within each of the evangelical denominations there were clear party splits.

58 Watson, *Jacksonian Politics and Community Conflict*, 23–4; Cross, *Burned-Over District*, 79; Cole, *Jacksonian Democracy in New Hampshire*, 170–4; Howe, *American Whigs*, 35. See also Goodman, "Social Basis," 29; Wright, "Ethnocultural Model of Voting," 664; Paul Kleppner, "Partisanship and Ethnoreligious Conflict: The Third Electoral System, 1853–1892," in Kleppner *et al.*, *Evolution of American Electoral Systems*, 369–70.

59 Fischer, *Revolution of American Conservatism*, 224–5; Dauer, *The Adams Federalists*, 25–6; Richard D. Shiels, "The Second Great Awakening in Connecticut: Critique of the Traditional Interpretation," *Church History*, 49 (Dec. 1980), 401–15; James M. Banner, *To the Hartford Convention: The Federalists and the Origins of Party Politics in Massachusetts, 1789–1815* (New York, 1970), 152–7. For the minority of Jeffersonians amongst Congregationalists, see Goodman, *The Democratic-Republicans of Massachusetts*, 90–2; Banner, *op. cit.*, 197ff.

60 Merriam, *Noah Porter*, 125; *CWR*, 3 Dec. 1857; Munger, *Horace Bushnell*, 44–5; *BDAC*, 1317 [for Meacham, who served as a Whig congressman from December 1849 to his death in 1856]; C. Hammond, "Alfred Ely," *Congregational Quarterly*, 9 (April 1867), 137–47; *The Ballot Box a Remedy for National Crimes: A Sermon, Entitled "The Remedy for Duelling," by Lyman Beecher, Applied to the Crime of Slave-holding* ... (Boston, 1838), 4–6; Jordan, *William Salter*, 112; Howard, *Henry Clay Trumbull*, 28–32; John C. Holbrook, *Recollections of a Nonagenerian Life in New England, the Middle West, and New York* ... (Boston, 1897), 32–3; Marsden, *Marsden*, 92; Truman A. Post, *Truman Marcellus Post,*

D.D.: A Biography, Personal and Literary (Boston, 1891), 94; Wilcox, *Christian Philanthropist*, 14; David M. Ellis, "The Assimilation of the Welsh in Central New York," *New York History*, 53 (July 1972), 326–7. See also Donald B. Cole, "The Election of 1832 in New Hampshire," *Historical New Hampshire*, 21 (Winter 1966), 40–4; Formisano, *Mass Political Parties*, 147; Benson, *Concept*, 192, 279–80; Nordquist, "The Ecology of Organized Religion," 39–61. According to Goodman, Whigs commanded over 90 percent of the Congregationalist vote in Hallowell, Maine, and over 86 percent in Portland; everywhere in New England that church was unmistakably Whig. Goodman, "Social Basis," 36–7: For the staunch Whiggery of New Haven scholars, see Stevenson, *Scholarly Means to Evangelical Ends*, 5–6, 114–16.

61 Bloch, *Visionary Republic*, 153–4, 157–8, 178; Victor B. Howard, "Presbyterians, the Kansas–Nebraska Act, and the Election of 1856," *Journal of Presbyterian History*, 49 (Summer 1971), 142; *New York Evangelist*, 1 Aug. 1881; *Independent*, 28 Sept. 1871; Mary Brainerd, *Life of Rev. Thomas Brainerd, D.D.* ... (Philadelphia, 1870), 222; Vander Velde, "Diary of George Duffield," 33; *idem*, "Notes on the Diary of Duffield," 55–6; D. Stuart Dodge (ed.) *Memorials of Wm. E. Dodge* (New York, 1887), 72; Lowitt, *A Merchant Prince*, 194; Walter Carter, *Walter Carter; Autobiography and Reminiscence, 1823–1897* (New York, c.1901), 34–52; Holt, *Forging a Majority*, 46, 326; Brock, *Parties and Political Conscience*, 51; Shade, "Political Pluralism and Party Development," 102; Alexander, *Thomas A.R. Nelson*, 52–3; Howe, *American Whigs*, 166–9; *Albany Argus*, 23 Oct. 1844; *Ohio State Journal*, 14, 17 Sept. 1844; Hodge, *Charles Hodge*, 230, 346; John Hall, "Journals," 7 Nov. 1848, PHS; Robert J. Breckinridge, *Speech ... Delivered ... on the 12th Day of October, 1840, in Reply to "The Speech of Robert Wickliffe"* ... (Lexington, Ky., 1840), 6–7; *Dr. Breckinridge and the "Commonwealth"* (n.p., c.1853), 6; Nevius,

John Livingston Nevius, 66–7; Kelley, *Cultural Pattern*, 146–7, 164; Peterson, *Beman*, 78–9; McKivigan, "Abolitionism and the American Churches," 417–18; David H. Overy, "Robert Lewis Dabney: Apostle of the Old South" (PhD diss., University of Wisconsin, 1967), 6, 26–7; M.M. Lewis to R.L. Dabney, 22 Sept. 1844, 4 Dec. 1845, C.W. Dabney to R.L. Dabney, 22 Nov. 1848, 12 April 1849, Dabney Papers, SHC; Drury, *Scott*, 99–109; H.C. King to M. King, 31 July 1848, Mitchell King Papers, SHC; Wyatt-Brown, "Prelude to Abolitionism," 327–8; Humphrey and Cleland, *Rev. Thomas Cleland*, 189; E.R. Ames to M. Simpson, 5 Jan. 1849, M. Simpson Papers, LC; Ershkowitz, *Origin of the Whig and Democratic Parties*, 218; David Montgomery, *Beyond Equality: Labor and the Radical Republicans, 1862–1872* (New York, 1967), 49–50; *New York Freeman's Journal*, 18 Dec 1852; *DAB*, for Albert Barnes, Jonathan Blanchard, Anna E. Carroll, Stephen Colwell, George Duffield, Charles Hodge, Elijah Lovejoy, Cyrus McCormick, and Nathan Rice. For further illustration of substantial Whig representation amongst Old School ministers in the South, see *Jonesborough Whig*, 22 Sept. 1847; *Knoxville Whig*, 16 Aug. 1856; M. de L. Gohmann, *Political Nativism in Tennessee* (Washington, DC, 1938), 22–3; J. Witherspoon to W.D. McDowell, 5 Aug. 1849, Witherspoon–McDowell Papers, SHC; R.H. Morrison to J. Morrison, 6 March 1840, Morrison Papers, SHC; Farmer, *The Metaphysical Confederacy*, 245–6. A correspondent of the Jackson (Mississippi) *Southron* noted in 1845: "The Presbyterian clergy, & indeed I believe the great body of clergy of all denominations, are Whigs, not because they are aristocrats but because they are opposed to radicalism, and in favor of conservatism." Margaret Des Champs Moore, "Religion in Mississippi," *Journal of Mississippi History*, 22 (Oct. 1960), 235.

⁶² For this and the next paragraph, see Carwardine, *Transatlantic Revivalism*, 4–18; Marsden, *Evangelical Mind*, 41–2,

66–103; Howe, *American Whigs*, 159–67; Kelley, *Cultural Pattern*, 168–9; Kelley, "Presbyterianism, Jacksonianism and Cleveland," 620–6; Brock, *Parties and Political Conscience*, 49; David T. Bailey, *Shadow on the Church: Southwestern Evangelical Religion and the Issue of Slavery 1783–1860* (Ithaca, NY, 1985), 207–80; Wyatt-Brown, "Anti-Mission Movement," 501–29. Significantly, the one area of the South where the New School theology took deep root, eastern Tennessee, was also an area of Whig strength. Thompson, *Presbyterians in the South*, I, 353–5; T.C. Anderson, *Life of Rev. George Donnell, First Pastor of the Church in Lebanon* (Nashville, Tenn., 1859), 150–80. For the argument that Congregationalists and New School Presbyterians were "goal-oriented" denominations, moved by achievement and guilt, while the Old School was "rule-oriented" and influenced by demonstrations of honor and shame, see Richard Jensen, "Religion, Morality, and American Politics," *Journal of Libertarian Studies*, 6 (1982), 321–8.

⁶³ *WCA*, 30 April 1851, 7 June 1854; *BDAC*, 600–1 [Brodhead], 723 [Colquitt]; W. Gordon, "Autobiography," 1–3, NEC; Septimus Stocking, "A Brief Historical Sketch of the Life of the Rev. Solon Stocking," NEC; James M. Bugbee, "Memoir of Henry Lillie Pierce," *Massachusetts Historical Society Proceedings*, 31 (1896–97), 387; Thomas H. Pearne, *Sixty-One Years of Itinerant Christian Life in Church and State* (Cincinnati, 1898), 49; John Raymond Mulkern, "The Know-Nothing Party in Massachusetts" (PhD diss., Boston University, 1963), 123; Peck, *Luther Peck*, 120; J.P. Fort, "Reminiscences," 200–1, DU; Kallenbach, III, 208; T.M. Drake to R. Emory, 22 Dec. 1845, DU; Spottswood, *Brief Annals*, 39–40; E.R. Ames to M. Simpson, 21 Jan. 1845, 5 Jan. 1849, M. Simpson Papers, LC; *North Carolina Christian Advocate*, 13 Nov. 1860; *Christian Lawyer*, 244–50; *Knoxville Whig*, 23 June 1849; Edward Dromgoole Papers, SHC (for Edward Dromgoole, Jr, preacher and planter,

and George Coke Dromgoole, Democratic member of Congress from Virginia); Wade, *Longstreet, passim.*

[64] Hugh McCulloch, *Men and Measures of Half a Century* (New York, 1888), 74–5; Wyatt-Brown, "Prelude to Abolitionism," 336; Strout, *New Heavens and New Earth*, 113; Brock, *Parties and Political Conscience*, 51; Latner and Levine, "Antebellum Pietistic Politics," 21–2; Formisano, *Mass Political Parties*, 153–5; Cole "Presidential Election of 1832," 40–2, 49. For Democrats amongst Methodist Protestants, see J.S. Swift to J.F. Speight, 25 June 1840; T. Ruffin to J.F. Speight, 14 Jan. 1860, J.F. Speight Papers, SHC. In Cumberland County, NC, Methodists tended to the Democratic column. Watson, *Jacksonian Politics and Community Conflict*, 24–41. Ershkowitz, *Origin of the Whig and Democratic Parties*, 218, finds no clear partisan preference amongst Methodists.

[65] R. Emory to J. Nichols, 11 April 1831, DU; George G. Smith, *The Life and Letters of James Osgood Andrew, Bishop of the Methodist Episcopal Church, South* (Nashville, Tenn., 1883), 436; Smith, *George Foster Pierce*, 324; Cozart, "Hilliard," 278–82; Mann, *Haygood*, 1–12; McAnally, *S. Patton*, 239–47; Hilliard, *Stepping Stones to Glory*, 55–61; Northcott, *Northcott*, 93, 110; Andrew Manship, *Thirteen Years' Experience in the Itinerancy* ... (Philadelphia, 1872), 373–4; Stewart, *Highways and Hedges*, 143; *Highland Messenger*, 5 June 1840; Brownlow, *Americanism*, 82; Temple, *Notable Men of Tennessee*, 118–19, 182–3, 198–9. For Senter (Tennessee) and McComas (Virginia), Methodist preachers and US congressmen, see *Jonesborough Whig*, 6 Sept. 1848; *BDAC*, 1287, 1581. Hazzard served as governor of Delaware. Kallenbach, II, 153. James B. Finley, significantly, described William Harrison as "a Democrat of the Jeffersonian school." *WCA*, 21 May 1841. For Whigs amongst Methodist Protestants, see J.C. Whitaker to G.A.T. Whitaker, 1 Sept. 1845, W.H. Wills Papers, SHC.

[66] Fleharty, *Rev. A.E. Phelps*, 330;

New York Tribune, 25 Oct. 1848; *Ohio State Journal*, 3 Oct. 1848; *WCA*, 21 March, 8 Oct. 1851, 27 May 1857; *BDAC*, 594 [for Brenton, US representative from Indiana]; Hobart, *Recollections*, 200–2; Hibben, *James Havens*, 182; L. Berry to M. Simpson, 9 Aug. 1849, M. Simpson Papers, LC. For other western Whig Methodists, see *DAB* (for John McLean and James Harlan); Francis P. Weisenburger, *The Life of John McLean: A Politician on the United States Supreme Court* (New York, 1937; repr. 1971), 84, 101, 127; Fletcher, *Diary, passim*; John Burgess, *Pleasant Recollections of Characters and Works of Noble Men* ... (Cincinnati, 1837), 196–7; William F. King, *Reminiscences* (New York, 1915), 10, 53–4, 63, 97.

[67] McDonald and Searles, *Inskip*, 66–7, 75–6; G.R. Crooks to J. McClintock, 21 Oct. 1848, DU; *BDAC*, 1445–6 (for Perkins); *WCA*, 30 April 1851; *Ohio State Journal*, 23 May 1844; Dixon, *Personal Narrative*, 62–3. For confirmation of Dixon's judgment, see *Tennessee Whig*, 29 July 1840; *Jonesborough Whig*, 5, 19 Jan. 1848. Even in some parts of New England, where Democratic Methodists were well represented, the church was dominated by Whigs. Goodman has estimated that 75 percent of Methodists in Providence, RI, were of that party. (Goodman, "Social Basis," 55).

[68] John W. Kuykendall, *Southern Enterprise: The Work of National Evangelical Societies in the Antebellum South* (Westport, Conn., 1982), 82–3; Thompson, *History of the Presbyterian Churches*, I, 96–7.

[69] The best study of the Primitive Baptists in these years is Lambert, *Rise of the Anti-Mission Baptists*; also useful is R.H. Pitman (ed.) *Biographical History of Primitive or Old School Ministers of the United States* (Anderson, Ind., 1909). There were 69,653 Antimission Baptists in the United States in 1844, one for every nine regular Baptists; by 1854 Primitives' numbers had fallen to 66, 507. *Biblical Recorder*, 24 Feb. 1854.

[70] Edward Dumas (Georgia), Allen

Ellis (Mississippi), C.T. Echols (Tenn.), W. Hyman (NC), J. Mickle (South Carolina) in *Primitive Baptist*, V, 26, 54, 98, 165–6, 233 (28 March, 11 April, 13 June, 25 Aug., 12 Sept. 1840).

[71] *Christian Index*, 22 March, 12 April 1844; *Primitive Baptist*, V, 223, 282, 324 (25 July, 26 Sept., 14 Nov. 1840), IX, 241–3, 274, 289–92 (24 Aug. 1844), X, 8–9 (11 Jan. 1845), XXV, 92–3 (24 Feb. 1861); *Knoxville Whig*, 21 Dec. 1850; H. Harvey, *Memoir of Alfred Bennett, First Pastor of the Baptist Church, Homer, N.Y. ... and Senior Agent of the American Baptist Missionary Union* (New York, 1852), 153–7; Joseph H. McCullagh, *'The Sunday-School Man of the South': A Sketch of the Life and Labors of the Rev. John McCullagh* (Philadelphia [1889]), 89–90.

[72] *Primitive Baptist*, V, 348 (E.O. Hawthorn of Georgia, 28 Nov. 1840); Freeze, "The Ethno-Cultural Thesis Goes South," 15. For an indication of divisions within the Primitives, see A. Edwards (Troup Co., Ga.) in *Primitive Baptist*, VI, 25 (23 Jan. 1841).

[73] Bodo, *Protestant Clergy and Public Issues*, 40–59; McLoughlin, *New England Dissent*, II, 1113; Goodman, "Social Basis," 39, 41, 43, 55; Wyatt-Brown, *Yankee Saints and Southern Sinners*, 69–70; Kelley, *Cultural Pattern*, 217–20; *DAB* for Leland; Brisbane, *An Eulogium on the Life and Character of the Late Hon. Thomas Morris ...* (Cincinnati, 1845), *passim*; H.P. Griffith, *The Life and Times of Rev. John G. Landrum* (Philadelphia, 1885); F.M. Jordan, *Life and Labors of Elder F.M. Jordan for Fifty Years a Preacher of the Gospel among North Carolina Baptists ...* (Raleigh, NC, 1899), 272; *Ohio State Journal*, 28 Oct. 1840; England, *Works*, IV, 85; Kruman, *Parties and Politics in North Carolina*, 15–16; Johnson, *Chaplains of the General Government*, 36; Bailey, *Shadow on the Church*, 207–8; George Allen, *Reminiscences of the Rev. George Allen of Worcester ...* (Worcester, Mass. 1883), 93; James O. Murray, *Francis Wayland* (Boston, 1891), 269–73; Formisano, *Mass Political Parties*, 142–3, 147; *New York Tribune*, 25 Sept. 1848; Fletcher, *Diary*, II, 188–9;

Ershkowitz, *Origin of the Whig and Democratic Parties*, 218; Thomas P. Hunt, *Life and Thoughts of Rev. Thomas P. Hunt ...*, comp. S.C. Hunt (Wilkes-Barre, Pa., 1901), 345–6; George W. Clark, *Struggles and Triumphs of a Long Life ...* (Philadelphia, 1914), 52; Wyatt-Brown, "Prelude to Abolitionism," 335–7; Brock, *Parties and Political Conscience*, 51; Robertson, *John Albert Broadus*, 7–16; Valentine, Diary, 8, 10 Aug. 1842 (see also 19 May 1852), SHC. Kelley, *op. cit.*, 179, overstates the case when he suggests that southern Baptists may in general have leaned to Whiggery. But for examples of Whiggish "improvers" amongst Baptists, see I.L. Brookes to Messrs Greene and Orme, 20 March 1849, I.L. Brookes Papers, SHC; C.C. Pearson and J.E. Hendricks, *Liquor and Anti-Liquor in Virginia, 1619–1919* (Durham, NC, 1967), 99–100; Valentine, Diary, 19 May 1852, 5 April 1854 and *passim*, SHC; *Tennessee Whig*, 20 May 1840 (for Nathan Shipley); *The Spectator. Extra. Asheville, Saturday, July 15, 1854*, broadsheet; *Dictionary of North Carolina Biography*, ed. William S. Powell (Chapel Hill, NC, 1986), II, 87–8 (for Alfred Dockery). Harry Watson discovered many Whigs – and no clear party preference overall – amongst the Baptists he traced in Cumberland County. Watson, *Jacksonian Politics and Community Conflict*, 240–2.

[74] *Primitive Baptist*, V, 120–1, 125–6, 279 (25 April, 26 Sept. 1840). See also J. Hardie (Wilkinson County, Ga.), S.I. Chandler (Person County, NC), J.M. Lauderdale (Ala.), C.B. Hassell (Williamston, NC) in *Primitive Baptist*, V, 70–1, 74–8 (14 March 1840), X, 131–2, 135 (1845); Burwell Temple, "To the People of Wake County [North Carolina]," broadsheet.

[75] Freeze, "The Ethno-Cultural Thesis Goes South," 15.

[76] *Albany Argus*, 1 Aug. 1844, 18 Sept. 1848; *Ohio State Journal*, 24 Sept., 9 Nov. 1844; *Coon Dissector*, 18 Oct. 1844; Ershkowitz, *Origin of the Whig and Democratic Parties*, 159–62; Donald J. Ratcliffe,

"The Experience of Revolution and the Beginnings of Party Politics in Ohio, 1776–1816," *Ohio History*, 85 (Summer 1976), 213; Kruman, *Parties and Politics in North Carolina*, 16; McKivigan, "Abolitionism and the American Churches," 165; Kelley, *Cultural Pattern*, 127–8, 163, 167, 175, 217–20; Dauer, *The Adams Federalists*, 27–8; Shade, "Pennsylvania Politics," 313–29; *WCA*, 31 Jan. 1840; Jordan, *William Salter*, 106–7; Brinkerhoff, *Recollections*, 1–19; Bernard C. Steiner, *Life of Henry Winter Davis* (Baltimore, 1916), 9, 40; J.H. Hopkins to E. Curtis, 13 March 1840, DU; Leonard W. Bacon, *A History of American Christianity* (New York, 1900), 305; Theodore T. Bacon, *Leonard Bacon: A Statesman in the Church* (New Haven, Conn., 1931), 386; Douglas T. Miller, *Jacksonian Aristocracy: Class and Democracy in New York, 1830–1860* (New York, 1967), 76, 166–7; *New York Evangelist*, 6 June 1844; *New York Freeman's Journal*, 14 Sept. 1844.

[77] Gienapp, "Politics Seem to Enter," 53–60; Goodman, "Social Basis," 25, 30–1.

[78] Crane, *Autobiography*, 86; Hibben, *James Havens*, 182–3. See also Fletcher, *Diary*, III, 80, IV, 96; James Roger Sharp, "The Political Culture of Middle-Period United States," *Canadian Review of American Studies*, 15 (Spring 1984), 61.

[79] Hague, *Life Notes*, 148; Brown, *Recollections of Itinerant Life*, 269–70; Murray, *Wayland*, 273; Dumond, *Letters of Birney*, I, 531–2, 535–8; Johnson, *Shopkeeper's Millennium*, 182, 198; Harold L. Lunger, *The Political Ethics of Alexander Campbell* (St Louis, Mo., 1954), 129–47. Thomas Stringfield, Methodist itinerant and controversialist in the Tennessee Conference, edited a pro-Jackson paper in 1828; by the 1840s he was a committed Whig. "Thomas Stringfield. Anecdotes and Glimpses of Early Life …," unpaginated manuscript, n.d., Stringfield Papers, SHC; *Tennessee Whig*, 19 Sept. 1839.

[80] *DAB* (for Hughes); J. Power to J.C. Spencer, 25 Feb. 1843, 2 June 1843, DU; Benson, *Concept*, 171, 187–91; *Cincinnati Telegraph*, 8, 22 June, 27 July 1844, 19, 26 Nov., 3 Dec. 1842, 9 Nov. 1844, 21 Aug. 1845; *CAJ*, 16 Feb., 8 June 1842; *WCA*, 12 March, 12 Nov. 1841; Spring, *Danger and Hope*, 26–31; Ellis, "Yankee-Dutch Confrontation," 269; Geary, *Third Parties in Pennsylvania*, 55–6; Bacon, *History of American Christianity*, 321; *New York Freeman's Journal*, 3 Aug. 1844, 5 April 1845; *Coon Dissector*, 31 May 1844; *New York Evangelist*, 27 June, 11 July 1844; Kelley, *Cultural Pattern*, 173; Scisco, *Political Nativism in New York*, 46; Feldberg, *Philadelphia Riots*, 31; Amy Beth Bridges, *A City in the Republic: Antebellum New York and the Origins of Machine Politics* (Cambridge, UK, 1984), 84. For Catholic political resurgence in Ireland itself and the simmering resentments that emigrant Protestants carried with them to America, especially after 1835, see Miller, *Emigrants and Exiles*, 233ff. Daniel Webster Fisher recollected the anti-Catholic, anti-Irish and (as his name suggests) the intensely Whig outlook of his Dutch-German-Presbyterian family in the 1840s and 1850s on their farm in Sinking Valley, Pennsylvania; Scotch-Irish and German culture tended to fuse in this part of the state. Daniel W. Fisher, *An Autobiography with Excursuses* (New York, c.1909), 17–22, 26–7, 31, 42–5, 62–3.

[81] *CAJ*, 14 Dec. 1842, 27 Nov. 1844, 12 March, 13 Aug., 17, 31 Dec. 1845, 18 Feb., 4 Nov. 1846, 24 Feb., 26 May 1847; *New York Observer*, 17 Oct. 1840; *WCA*, 21 Feb., 6, 27 March, 4 Sept. 1840, 12 Feb., 27 March, 4 June, 9 July 1841; Dixon, *Personal Narrative*, 74; George Coles, *My First Seven Years in America*, ed. D.P. Kidder (New York, 1852). For continuing evidence of interdenominational strain, however, see *SCA*, 5 March 1847; *CAJ*, 15 Oct. 1845.

[82] Howe, *American Whigs*, 13; McLoughlin, *New England Dissent*, II, 1107–27; Watson, *Jacksonian Politics and Community Conflict*, 238–40. For the connection between upwardly mobile, prospering New School Presbyterianism

and Whiggish outlook, see Divie B. Duffield, *Discourse Commemorative of Rev. George Duffield* ... (Detroit, 1883), 12–13; Doherty, "Social Basis," 69–76; Johnson, *Shopkeeper's Millennium*, 116–34.

[83] Stocking, "Brief Historical Sketch of the Life of the Rev. Selah Stocking," 9–10, *NEC*; R. Emory to J. Nichols, 8 July 1833: R. Emory to F. Emory, 19 March 1840: W. Thacher to I. Gilbert, 27 Feb. 1822, DU; *CAJ*, 25 Dec. 1844, 20 Oct. 1847, 1 Aug. 1901; A.G. Porter to M. Simpson, 26 Oct. 1844: J. Harlan to M. Simpson, 27 April 1847: E. Wentworth to M. Simpson, 30 April 1847: J. Drummond to M. Simpson, 20 April 1850, M. Simpson Papers, LC; Roche, *Durbin*, 63–4; *WCA*, 9 Sept. 1842, 21 Dec. 1853, 3 Jan. 1854, 2 Sept. 1857; Elsmere, *Beecher*, 9. Methodists made much of prestigious accessions to membership; they were delighted when ex-President Polk joined them and underwent baptism shortly before his death. *SCA*, 10 Aug. 1849. The pattern of Methodist progress was not an even one, and by no means all Calvinists accepted Methodists' new standing: in the 1850s in Galesburg, Illinois, Milton Haney experienced "persistent and bitter" opposition from a colony of transplanted New England Congregationalists. Milton L. Haney, *The Story of My Life* (Normal, Ill., 1904), 115–16.

[84] England, *Works*, IV, 85–6, 90–1; *Cincinnati Telegraph*, 4 Dec. 1841; Gunderson, *Log-Cabin Campaign*, 61; *New York Freeman's Journal*, 20 Dec. 1856.

[85] *Jonesborough Whig*, 22 Nov. 1848.

Chapter 5 *Evangelicals, Slavery, and Sectionalism in the 1840s*

[1] For the importance of religious and cultural politics, see especially Silbey, *The Partisan Imperative*; Kleppner, *Third Electoral System*; Formisano, *Birth of Mass Political Parties*. Richard H. Sewell, *Ballots for Freedom: Antislavery Politics in the United States* (New York, 1976) and Maizlish, *Triumph of Sectionalism* particularly stress antislavery considerations in

the realignment of the 1850s. Three outstanding works, David Potter, *The Impending Crisis 1848–1861* (New York, 1976), Michael Holt, *The Political Crisis of the 1850s* (New York, 1978) and, especially, Gienapp, *Origins of the Republican Party*, illustrate the complex political and ideological interconnectedness of antislavery and nativism. Gienapp's sophisticated and persuasive analysis implicitly demonstrates the unnecessary polarization of the earlier debate.

[2] Robert H. Brown, "The Missouri Crisis, Slavery and the Politics of Jacksonianism," *South Atlantic Quarterly*, 65 (Winter 1966), 55–72.

[3] For the evangelical Protestant contribution to abolitionism, see especially Gilbert Hobbes Barnes, *The Anti-Slavery Impulse 1830–1844* (New York, 1933); David Brion Davis, *The Problem of Slavery in Western Culture, 1770–1823* (Ithaca, NY, 1973); James Brewer Stewart, *Holy Warriors: The Abolitionists and American Slavery* (New York, 1976); Ronald G. Walters, *The Antislavery Appeal: American Abolitionism after 1830* (Baltimore, 1976), 37–69; David Brion Davis, "The Emergence of Immediatism in British and American Antislavery Thought," *MVHR*, 49 (Sept. 1962), 209–30; Anne C. Loveland, "Evangelicalism and Immediate Emancipation in American Antislavery Thought," *JSH*, 32 (May 1966), 172–88; Gerald Sorin, *The New York Abolitionists: A Case Study of Political Radicalism* (Westport, Conn., 1971); Scott, *From Office to Profession*, 76–94; James Essig, "The Lord's Free Man: Charles G. Finney and His Abolitionism," *CWH*, 24 (March 1978), 25–45; Edward Magdol, *The Antislavery Rank and File: A Social Profile of the Abolitionists' Constituency* (Westport, Conn., 1986).

[4] Beriah Green, *Things for Northern Men To Do: A Discourse* ... (New York, 1836), 18–19; *The Ballot Box a Remedy*, 4–5; *Oberlin Evangelist*, 11 March 1840; S. Luckey to D.P. Kidder, 10 Dec. 1838, Kidder Papers, GTS.

[5] Perry, *Radical Abolitionism, passim*;

William L. Van Deburg, "William Lloyd Garrison and the 'Pro-Slavery Priesthood': The Changing Beliefs of an Evangelical Reformer, 1830–1840," *Journal of the American Academy of Religion*, 43 (June 1975), 224–37; Louis Filler, "Parker Pillsbury: An Anti-Slavery Apostle," *New England Quarterly*, 19 (Oct. 1946), 315–37; Russel B. Nye, "Marius Robinson, A Forgotten Abolitionist Leader," *Ohio State Archaeological and Historical Quarterly*, 55 (April–June 1946), 138–54. Garrisonians did, however, as Lydia Maria Child explained, seek to exercise *moral* influence in politics, working *"through* parties, not *with* them." Douglas A. Gamble, "Joshua Giddings and the Ohio Abolitionists: a Study in Radical Politics," *Ohio History*, 88 (Winter 1979), 39. See also Stewart, *Holy Warriors*, 107.

⁶ *The True Wesleyan*, 3 Feb. 1844, quoted in McKivigan, "Abolitionism and the American Churches," 179. For a shrewd discussion of Garrison's developing attitudes to political action, see Kraditor, *Means and Ends in American Abolitionism*, 118–234. The circle of Quakers and Unitarians, antinomians and perfectionists centering on Garrison is described and analysed by Lawrence J. Friedman, *Gregarious Saints: Self and Community in American Abolition 1830–1870* (Cambridge, UK, 1982), 43–67. Perry, *Radical Abolitionism*, 158–87, stresses the far from tidy division between anarchists and political abolitionists. For the harsh criticism from orthodox evangelical abolitionists of Garrison's perception of voting as "a sin for me," see, for example, William N. Rice and Charles F. Rice, *William Rice, A Memorial* (Cambridge, Mass., 1898), 6–7; Lee, *Autobiography*, 216–22; Magoun, *Asa Turner*, 289; Davis, "Joshua Leavitt," 173–6; Allen, *Reminiscences*, 90.

⁷ Sewell, *Ballots for Freedom*, 10–20; Lewis, *Samuel Lewis*, 301–2, 324–8. Though Whigs manifested a greater natural sympathy for the cause of the slave, and enjoyed the support of a much larger number of abolitionists

than did the Democrats, McFaul rightly cautions against oversimplifying the party positions into proslavery Democracy facing proto-abolitionist Whiggery. McFaul, "Expediency vs. Morality," 25–39. See also Leonard L. Richards, "The Jacksonians and Slavery," in Lewis Perry and Michael Fellman (eds) *Antislavery Reconsidered: New Perspectives on the Abolitionists* (Baton Rouge, La., 1979), 99–118.

⁸ Lewis, *Samuel Lewis*, 287, 296–9, 335; Magoun, *Asa Turner*, 282–3; *Pittsburgh Christian Advocate*, 20 Oct. 1841. Truman Post, Illinois Congregationalist minister, abandoned the Whig party when it appeared to condone Elijah Lovejoy's murder at Alton in 1837. Post, *Truman Marcellus Post*, 94.

⁹ *Oberlin Evangelist*, 29 July 1840. See also J.G. Birney to M. Holley, J. Leavitt and E. Wright, 11 May 1840, in Dumond (ed.) *Letters of Birney*, I, 562–74.

¹⁰ *Massachusetts Abolitionist*, 17 Oct. 1839, in Sewell, *Ballots for Freedom*, 59; *The Independent*, 28 Sept. 1871. The new organization formally took the name Liberty party in 1841. For Leavitt's importance, and his attack on antislavery Whigs for practising "Abolition made Agreeable," see Davis, "Joshua Leavitt," 197, 216–19, 237–8. For Tappan's role, first opposing the Liberty enterprise and renouncing his close colleague Joshua Leavitt, but voting for Birney, and later becoming sufficiently reconciled to "Christian politics" to tour New York state on his behalf in the 1844 campaign, see Bertram Wyatt-Brown, *Lewis Tappan and the Evangelical War against Slavery* (Cleveland, Ohio, 1969), 198–9, 269–76; Friedman, *Gregarious Saints*, 89–94.

¹¹ For reflections on the relative strengths of pragmatism and moralism within the party, see especially Alan M. Kraut, "Partisanship and Principles: The Liberty Party in Antebellum Political Culture," in Alan M. Kraut (ed.) *Essays on the Relationship of the Antislavery Struggle to the Antebellum Party System* (Westport, Conn., 1983), 71–99. See also Walters, *Antislavery Appeal*, 15–16; Sewell, *Ballots*

for Freedom, 81–3, 90–2; Stanley Harrold, *Gamaliel Bailey and Antislavery Union* (Kent, Ohio, 1986), 32–3, 226.

[12] Sewell, *Ballots for Freedom*, 50–1, 94–5; *Oberlin Evangelist*, 28 Oct. 1846; Lewis, *Samuel Lewis*, 286, 302, 308–11, 336–41, 347–9; Davis "Joshua Leavitt," 186–94. For Liberty party efforts to make opposition to slavery more "a matter of money policy" (Birney) than "a matter of religious duty," by stressing slavery's detrimental effects on northern industry and agriculture, see Julian P. Bretz, "The Economic Background of the Liberty Party," *AHR*, 24 (Jan. 1929), 250–64.

[13] Lee, *Autobiography*, 281. Finney developed the theme of the relationship of moral suasion to political action in his "Letters on Revivals," arguing against a sharp dichotomy: to remove slavery or any other "legalized abomination" the Christian had to use "law, rewards, and punishments" since in its proper sense "[m]oral suasion includes whatever is designed and adapted to influence the will of a moral agent" (*Oberlin Evangelist*, 21 Jan. 1846).

[14] Lewis, *Samuel Lewis*, 325; Austin Willey, *The History of the Antislavery Cause in State and Nation* (Portland, Me., 1886), 236–9, 260; Reinhard O. Johnson, "The Liberty Party in Vermont, 1840–1848: the Forgotten Abolitionists," *Vermont History*, 47 (1979), 268–9; *The Oberlin News*, 30 Jan. 1903; John Morgan in *Oberlin Evangelist*, 9 Oct. 1844 (also 20 Nov. 1844); Colton, *Political Abolition*, 13–14. See also Crane, *Autobiography*, 86; Judah L. Richmond, Diary, 10 Aug. 1844, T. Richmond Papers, SHC.

[15] Alan M. Kraut, "The Forgotten Reformers: A Profile of Third Party Abolitionists in Antebellum New York," in Perry and Fellman, *Antislavery Reconsidered*, 132–3, 142–3; Brown, *Memoir of Rev. Abel Brown*, 98–102, 191–201; John Graham, *Autobiography and Reminiscences* ... (Philadelphia, 1870); William Goodell, *One More Appeal to Professors of Religion, Ministers, and Churches, Who Are Not Enlisted in the Struggle against Slavery* (New York, n.d.); Gerrit Smith, *Letters*

... *on Preaching Anti-Slavery Politics on Sunday* (n.p., 1843); Gerrit Smith, *To Those Ministers in the County of Madison, Who Refuse To Preach Politics* (n.p. [1845]). Reinhard O. Johnson offers evidence for the religious outlook of the Liberty party in New England, especially in its earlier phases: "Liberty Party in Vermont," 258–75; "The Liberty Party in New Hampshire, 1840–1848: Antislavery Politics in the Granite State," *Historical New Hampshire*, 33 (Summer 1978), 123–66; "The Liberty Party in Maine, 1840–1848: The Politics of Antislavery Reform," *Maine Historical Society Quarterly*, 19 (Winter 1980), 135–76; "The Liberty Party in Massachusetts, 1840–1848: Antislavery Third Party Politics in the Bay State," *CWH*, 28 (Sept. 1982), 236–65. John L. Hammond, "Revival Religion and Antislavery Politics," *American Sociological Review*, 39 (April 1974), 175–86, finds a strong correlation between Presbyterianism and Liberty strength in Ohio in 1844. For the strong connections throughout much of the Old Northwest between antislavery, evangelical "come-outers" (especially Freewill Baptists and Wesleyan Methodists) and the political come-outerism of the Liberty party, see Vernon L. Volpe, *Forlorn Hope of Freedom: The Liberty Party in the Old Northwest, 1838–1848* (Kent, Ohio, 1990), xi–xv and passim.

[16] T. Foster to J.G. Birney, 30 March 1846, in Dumond (ed.) *Letters of Birney*, II, 622–3; Theodore Clark Smith, *Liberty and Free Soil Parties in the Northwest* (New York, 1897), 59; Johnson, "Liberty Party in Maine," 146, 155. See also Ira V. Brown, "Miller McKim and Pennsylvania Abolitionism," *Pennsylvania History*, 30 (Jan. 1963), 64.

[17] J. Blanchard to M. Blanchard, 3 June 1840, 26 Oct. 1882, M. Blanchard to J. Blanchard, 9 June 1840, J. Blanchard to H. Cowles, 4 Aug. 1840, Blanchard Papers, WC; Lewis, *Samuel Lewis*, 286; G. Bailey to J.G. Birney, 21 Feb. 1840, in Dumond (ed.) *Letters of Birney*, I, 531–2. Bailey eventually supported Birney, but not before he had fought to advance

Harrison's cause. G. Bailey to G. Smith, 21 July 1840 (photocopy), Blanchard Papers, WC; Harrold, *Gamaliel Bailey*, 33–7.

[18] J. Rankin to T.E. Thomas, 31 July 1840, in Alfred A. Thomas, *Correspondence of Thomas Ebenezer Thomas: Mainly Relating to the Antislavery Conflict in Ohio . . .* (Dayton, Ohio, 1909), 18–19; H.B. Stanton to J.G. Birney, 21 March 1840, in Dumond (ed.) *Letters of Birney*, I, 541–3. See also J. Blanchard to G. Smith, 5 Aug. 1840, Blanchard Papers, WC.

[19] William H. Brisbane, *An Eulogium on the Life and Character of the late Hon. Thomas Morris . . .* (Cincinnati, 1845), 12ff. See also Johnson, "Liberty Party in Vermont," 261; Crane, *Autobiography*, 86; Daniels, *Gilbert Haven*, 34; Kraut, "Forgotten Reformers," 127, 141.

[20] Lewis, *Samuel Lewis*, 286–95, 304–7; Clyde S. Kilby, *Minority of One: A Biography of Jonathan Blanchard*, (Grand Rapids, Mich., 1959), 89, 106–9; Grim, "The Reverend John Rankin," 254; Wyatt-Brown, *Lewis Tappan*, 276; Formisano, *Mass Political Parties*, 120. See also Smith, *Liberty and Free Soil Parties in the Northwest*, 39, 50, 179.

[21] John R. McKivigan, *The War Against Proslavery Religion: Abolitionism and the Northern Churches, 1830–1865* (Ithaca, NY, 1984) indicates the nuanced complexity of abolitionist–church relationships in the North. The abolitionist/anti-abolitionist tensions within evangelicalism are shrewdly treated in Scott, *From Office to Profession*, 95–111.

[22] Leonard L. Richards, *"Gentlemen of Property and Standing": Anti-Abolition Mobs in Jacksonian America* (New York, 1970), 94, 145–58; C.L. Blanchard to J. Blanchard, 17 May 1841, Blanchard Papers, WC; *CAJ*, 25 Aug. 1841.

[23] This was of course what many of Garrison's evangelical antislavery critics had themselves feared. For the "Pastoral Letter of the General Association of Massachusetts to the Orthodox Congregational churches" in 1837 and the subsequent "Clerical Appeals," see Walter M. Merrill and Louis Ruchames (eds) *The Letters of William Lloyd Garrison*

(6 vols, Cambridge, Mass., 1971–1981), II, *A House Dividing Against Itself 1836–1840*, 199–200, 275, 300–2.

[24] Cozzens, *Prominent Sins of the Times*, 15. See also Charles Porter, *Sermon delivered in the First Presbyterian Church*, 9–10; Hunt, *Life and Thoughts*, 251–3; *WCA*, 2 Sept. 1842. That churches should declare slavery a sin and end all fellowship with slaveholders was an early demand of the AASS. See Davis, "Joshua Leavitt," 159; McKivigan, *War Against Proslavery Religion*, 41.

[25] J. McClintock to S. Olin, 31 Dec. 1846, DU; A. Kent to G. Peck, 23 Oct. 1846, Peck Papers, Syracuse University. See also John McClintock, "Slavery," in *CAJ*, 24 March 1847; Peck, *George Peck*, 219–27; M. Simpson to M. Simpson, 9 March 1838, M. Simpson Papers, LC; Brown, *Recollections of Itinerant Life*, 286–96; S. Seager to D.P. Kidder, 5 April 1838, 6 July 1839, Kidder Papers, GTS; R.M. Burt to Mr Cox, 20 June 1848, NEC; Nathan L. Rice, *Lectures on Slavery: Delivered in the North Presbyterian Church, Chicago* (Chicago, 1860), 62–3; *WCA*, 23 April 1841; *CAJ*, 21 April 1847.

[26] *Pittsburgh Christian Advocate*, 24 April 1844. See also Porter, *Sermon delivered in the First Presbyterian Church*, 9–10 ("insurrectionary" abolitionists aim "to subvert and destroy government").

[27] *WCA*, 23 April 1841; George Duffield, *A Sermon on American Slavery: Its Nature and the Duties of Christians in Relation to It* (Detroit, 1840), 31; Rice, *Lectures on Slavery*, 63. See also Cozzens, *Prominent Sins of the Times*, 15.

[28] M. Simpson to M. Simpson, 9 March 1838, Simpson Papers, LC; J. McClintock in *CAJ*, 24 March 1847; *WCA*, 20 Nov. 1840, 23 April 1841; S. Luckey to D.P. Kidder, 10 Dec. 1838, Kidder Papers, GTS; Rice, *Lectures on Slavery*, 59–61; Cozzens, *Prominent Sins of the Times*, 13–14; Duffield, *Sermon on American Slavery*, 8; *New York Evangelist*, 7 March, 23 May, 20 June 1844.

[29] A. Stevens to C.K. True, 1 Oct. 1840, NEC. See also Sprague, *Voice of the Rod*, 25.

[30] Leonard Bacon, *Slavery Discussed in*

Occasional Essays, from 1833 to 1846 (New York, 1846; repr. Miami, 1969); Cozzens, *Prominent Sins of the Times*, 7–9; Vander Velde, "Diary of George Duffield," 31; *WCA*, 20 Nov. 1840; Porter, *Sermon delivered in the First Presbyterian Church*, 9; Rice, *Lectures on Slavery*, passim; Clark, *Matthew Simpson*, 53–6, 67–70; M. Simpson to M. Simpson, 9 March 1838, M. Simpson Papers, LC.

[31] Hall (ed.) *Forty Years' Familiar Letters*, I, 52; Labaree, *Harrison*, 20–1; Duffield, *Sermon on American Slavery*, 27–8; *New York Evangelist*, 13 June 1844; Cozzens, *Prominent Sins of the Times*, 8. See also Mitchell, *Sermon on the Late Fast*, 4–5; Edwards, *God's Voice to the Nation*, 11; White, *National Fast*, 35; Abbott, *Sermon on the National Fast*, 16; Wilson, *Harrison*, 11–12; Peck, *National Evils*, 15; McKeen, *God Our Only Hope*, 12–17.

[32] *CAJ*, 19 March 1845; *WCA*, 29 May 1840, 26 March 1841, 28 Aug., 30 Oct. 1850; A.E. Murray, "Bright Delusion: Presbyterians and African Colonization," *Journal of Presbyterian History*, 58 (Fall 1980), 231.

[33] See especially Barnes, *Anti-Slavery Impulse*; Dwight Lowell Dumond, *Anti-Slavery Origins of the Civil War in the United States* (Ann Arbor, Mich., 1939).

[34] Bushnell, *Politics under the Law of God*, 12–13.

[35] J. McClintock to S. Olin, 31 Dec. 1846, DU; *CAJ*, 24 March 1847. Brock, *Parties and Political Conscience*, considers the forces that shaped "conscience" as it operated politically in the 1840s.

[36] *CAJ*, 6 April 1842; Stewart, *Giddings*, 62–83. See also Bacon, *Commercial Distress*, 14; Russell B. Nye, *Fettered Freedom: Civil Liberties and the Slavery Controversy* (Michigan State University Press, 1963), 45–53; *New York Evangelist*, 11, 18 Jan., 15 Feb. 1844.

[37] George Allen, *The Complaint of Mexico, and Conspiracy against Liberty* (Boston, 1843), 3, 22–3; *New York Evangelist*, 29 Feb., 21 March 1844; Donald K. Gorrell, "American Churches and American Territorial Expansion, 1830–1850" (PhD diss., Western Reserve, 1960), 104–26, locating north-eastern

opposition especially amongst Congregationalists, Quakers, and Unitarians; *Oberlin Evangelist*, 10 April, 18 Dec. 1844; Bushnell, *Politics under the Law of God*, 19; Hall (ed.) *Forty Years' Familiar Letters*, II, 18.

[38] Brock, *Parties and Political Conscience*, 139–43, pursues this theme. Gorrell, "American Churches," 101–2, identifies Methodists and Baptists as the two denominations whose northern wings were most sympathetic to American expansion into Texas.

[39] *SCA*, 21 March 1845. The most hesitant approach to annexation amongst southern evangelicals can be found amongst Clayite Whigs who feared it might "fuel the flame" of sectional bitterness. Valentine, *Diary*, 13 Jan., 11 Feb., 26 Oct. 1845, SHC.

[40] Gorrell, "American Churches," 9–10, quoting *Zion's Herald*; Caleb A. Malmsbury, *The Life, Labors and Sermons of Rev. Charles Pitman, D.D., of the New Jersey Conference* (Philadelphia, 1887), 131–2; *WCA*, 15 July 1842.

[41] Brock, *Parties and Political Conscience*, 170–2; *SCA*, 12 June, 28 Aug. 1846; Gorrell, "American Churches," 72–5; *CAJ*, 19 Nov. 1847; C.S. Ellsworth, "The American Churches and the Mexican War," *AHR*, 45 (Jan. 1940), 305. Had William Brownlow fought, as briefly it seemed he might, it would have been as a member of the "Protestant Invincibles." Coulter, *Brownlow*, 44.

[42] Griffis, *John Chambers*, 112; Gorrell, "American Churches," 83–4. For the minority of Protestant editors in the Northwest who were lyrical over "manifest destiny" and the possibilities presented by the war, see Norton, *Religious Newspapers*, 108.

[43] Gorrell, "American Churches," 74–7, 89–90; Ellsworth, "American Churches and the Mexican War," 303–8; Parker Pillsbury, *Acts of the Anti-Slavery Apostles* (Concord, NH, 1883), 381–5; Stephen M. Vail, *The Signs of the Times: A Thanksgiving Sermon . . .* (Poughkeepsie, NY, 1846), 9–10; *CAJ*, 11 Nov. 1846. For committed opponents of the war who nonetheless hoped it would further the

advance of Protestantism, see for example Hall (ed.) *Forty Years' Familiar Letters*, II, 80–1; McDonald and Searles, *Inskip*, 67.

[44] Joel H. Schroeder, *Mr. Polk's War: American Opposition and Dissent, 1846–1848* (Madison, Wisc., 1973), 107–15; Gorrell, "American Churches," 86–98, 104–26; Ellsworth, "American Churches and the Mexican War," 313–17; Victor B. Howard, "The Doves of 1847: the Religious Response in Ohio to the Mexican War," *The Old Northwest*, 5 (Fall 1979), 239–61. For antiwar sentiment amongst evangelicals of the Northwest, see Norton, *Religious Newspapers*, 119–20. For tensions in Iowa between the anti-war spirit of recently arrived New School Calvinists from New England and the war fever of indigenous Congregationalism, see Philip D. Jordan, "William Salter and the Slavery Controversy," *Iowa Journal of History and Politics*, 33 (April 1935), 104–6. James Dixon's exploration of northern Methodism led him to conclude over-optimistically that most MEC ministers disapproved of the war (Dixon, *Personal Narrative*, 62–3). For opposition amongst a minority of English-speaking, reform-minded, evangelical Lutherans in the Franckean Synod of upstate New York, led by Samuel S. Schmucker, see Robert Fortenbaugh, "American Lutheran Synods and Slavery, 1830–60," *Journal of Religion*, 13 (Jan. 1933), 72–92; Schmucker, *The Christian Pulpit, the Rightful Guardian of Morals, in the Political No Less than in Private Life* (Gettysburg, 1846), 30–2.

[45] Gorrell, "American Churches," 76; James M. Pendleton, *Reminiscences of a Long Life* (Louisville, Ky., 1891), 88–91; *Knoxville Whig*, 27 May 1846; Robert L. Stanton, *Two Discourses on War and Peace: preached July 5th, 1846, and July 11th, 1847*...(New Orleans, 1847); Holder, *Winans*, 180.

[46] Anderson, *The Republic and the Duties of the Citizen*, 15; W.P. Hill, Diary, 4 March 1847, SHC; David H. Riddle, *The Means of Peace: A Sermon Delivered in the Third Presbyterian Church, Pittsburgh*... (Pittsburgh, 1846), 8–9; "The War with

Mexico," *New Englander*, 5 (Oct. 1847), 604–13; Robert H. Beattie, *Sermon Delivered in the Presbyterian Church, West-Milton, Nov. 25, 1847*...(Saratoga Springs, NY, 1848), 13–14; Burchard, *Causes of National Solicitude*, 15–16; Milton P. Braman, *The Mexican War: A Discourse Delivered on the Annual Fast, 1847* (Danvers, Mass., 1847), 27–8, 32; Samuel Harris, *The Mexican War: A Sermon Delivered on the Annual Thanksgiving, at Conway, Mass.* ... (Greenfield, Mass., 1847), 16, 19. See also R.H. Morrison to J. Morrison, 13 April 1847, R.H. Morrison Papers, SHC; Leonard E. Lathrop, *A Discourse on the Obligations of a Christian People, in View of the Divine Beneficence*... (Auburn, NY, 1847), 14–19; J.T. Tuttle, "Our Late Conquests," *New Englander*, 6 (Oct. 1848), 534.

[47] Richard Tolman, *Evil Tendencies of the Present Crisis: A Discourse, Delivered July 4, 1847* (Danvers, Mass., 1847), 7–8; *Oberlin Evangelist*, 27 May 1846; Horace Bushnell, "Barbarism the First Danger," *American National Preacher*, 21 (Sept. 1847), 208–10, 215; F. Wayland and H.L. Wayland, *A Memoir of the Life and Labors of Francis Wayland, D.D.* (2 vols, Boston, 1867), II, 55; Daniel Curry, *The Judgments of God, Confessed and Deprecated: a Sermon, Preached*... *Aug. 3d. 1849*...(n.p. [1849]), 5–7; Hall (ed.) *Forty Years' Familiar Letters*, II, 70 ("I loathe and fear this war. We shall be readier for another"), 74; "Rumours of War" (editorial) in *CAJ*, 21 Jan. 1846; Burdett Hart, *The Mexican War: A Discourse Delivered at the Congregational Church in Fair Haven, on the Annual Fast of 1847* (New Haven, Conn., 1847), 3; Stanton, *Two Discourses on War and Peace*, 25–9; Burchard, *Causes of National Solicitude*, 19–20; Harris, *Mexican War*, 6; McDonald and Searles, *Inskip*, 66; T.M. Eddy, ms sermon "God's Righteous Government," 14 Jan. 1850, GTS; "The War with Mexico," 605; Fletcher, *Diary*, IV, 96 (5 March 1849); R.P. Dubois, ms Autobiography, PHS; Valentine, Diary, 11, 13, 16 June 1846, SHC; Hilliard, *Speeches and Addresses* (New York, 1855), 111–13; Holder, *Winans*, 179–80. Brownlow's attacks on Polk's "wicked"

and "unprovoked" war also included the persistent complaint that he had appointed Roman Catholic chaplains to an army of 30,000 largely Protestant volunteers for mainly party political reasons. *Knoxville Whig*, 27 May, 10, 17 June, 23 Dec. 1846, 14 July 1847.

[48] J. McClintock to R. Emory, 23 Jan. 1848, DU; Burchard, *Causes of National Solicitude*, 21; Hall (ed.) *Forty Years' Familiar Letters*, II, 51; Riddle, *Means of Peace*, 15.

[49] Burchard, *Causes of National Solicitude*, 20; Tolman, *Evil Tendencies of the Present Crisis*, 7–8. For the linkage of war with slave-power expansionism see, for example, Horace James, *Our Duties to the Slave: A Sermon, Preached before the Original Congregational Church and Society, in Wrentham, Mass. . . .* (Boston, 1847), 4–12; Thomas E. Thomas, *Covenant Breaking, and its Consequences: or the Present Posture of Our National Affairs, in Connection with the Mexican War . . .* (Rossville, Ohio, 1847); Bushnell, "Barbarism the First Danger," 208–10, 215; Braman, *Mexican War*, 25–6; Harris, *Mexican War*, 21; Jordan, *William Salter*, 150–2; Lewis, *Samuel Lewis*, 37–72; Ted C. Hinckley, "American Anti-Catholicism during the Mexican War," *Pacific Historical Review*, 31 (May 1962), 133–4.

[50] Braman, *Mexican War*, 11–19; Harris, *Mexican War*, 19; Gorrell, "American Churches," 94, citing Nathan L. Rice; Morris, *Our Country*, 51–2; Bushnell, "Barbarism the First Danger," 210; Hart, *Mexican War*, 14. See also *Brownson's Quarterly Review*, 1 (new series; July 1847), 366–7.

[51] C. White in *American Biblical Repository* (Oct. 1846), 630–2; Harris, *Mexican War*, 8–9; *Oberlin Evangelist*, 10, 24 June 1846; "The War with Mexico," 604–5; Hart, *Mexican War*, 15; Perrin, *Nation in Perplexity*, 7–8; Riddle, *Means of Peace*, 18. Upshur and Gilmer were killed in February 1844 when the new naval gun, "Peacemaker," exploded aboard the USS *Princeton*.

[52] *Brownson's Quarterly Review*, 1 (new series; July 1847), 335–6; *CAJ*, 30 Aug. 1848.

[53] James, *Our Duties to the Slave*, 9; Hart, *Mexican War*, 15. See also Braman, *Mexican War*, 24–5; Harris, *Mexican War*, 23–4; Beattie, *Sermon Delivered the Day of the Annual Thanksgiving*, 16.

[54] George Allen, *Resistance to Slavery Every Man's Duty: A Report of American Slavery Read to the Worcester Central Association, March 2, 1847* (Boston, 1847), 37. Allen had a reputation for sitting loosely to party. On the eve of the annexation of Texas he sought a people's convention led by Massachusetts clergy to create a new political alignment against the slave power. George Allen, *An Appeal to the People of Massachusetts, on the Texas Question* (Boston, 1844).

[55] [South Middlesex Conference of Churches,] *Political Duties*, 7–8, 31–2 (for Giddings); James, *Our Duties to the Slave*, 21; Morris, *Our Country*, 26–9. See also Tolman, *Evil Tendencies of the Present Crisis*, 9.

[56] Howard, "Doves of 1847," 247–8, 253–6.

[57] *Ohio State Journal*, 3 Oct. 1848; *CAJ*, 15 Nov. 1848; Hall (ed.) *Forty Years' Familiar Letters*, II, 73; Carlos Martyn, *William E. Dodge: The Christian Merchant* (New York, 1890), 178. Many of Samuel Lewis's evangelical friends in Hamilton County, Ohio, supported his bid to become Free Soil congressman, yet voted for Taylor in the presidential race. Lewis, *Samuel Lewis*, 380–1.

[58] *Watchman of the Prairies*, cited in Norton, *Religious Newspapers*, 119. See also Josiah B. Grinnell, *Men and Events of Forty Years: Autobiographical Reminiscences of an Active Career from 1850 to 1890* (Boston, 1891), 47; *WCA*, 15 Nov. 1848. For evangelicals' unease over Van Buren's nomination, and criticism of those who sustained him, see for example, Davis, "Joshua Leavitt," 321; *Oberlin Evangelist*, 13 Sept. 1848. For a defense of the Free Soilers' nominee, see Allen, *Reminiscences*, 60; and Asa Mahan's warm endorsement in Oliver Dyer, *Phonographic Reports of the Proceedings of the National Free Soil Convention* (Buffalo, NY, 1848), 24.

[59] *Oberlin Evangelist*, 8 June, 6 July

1848. For campaign literature presenting Taylor and Cass as barely distinguishable enemies of free-soil principles, see William I. Bowditch, *Cass and Taylor on the Slavery Question* (Boston, 1848), 23 and *passim*; *The General Taylor Shorter Catechism* (Rochester, NY, 1848); *General Taylor: a Buyer of Men and Women!* (Boston, 1848). For the Free Soil Convention of August 1848, see Frederick J. Blue, *The Free Soilers: Third Party Politics 1848–1854* (Urbana, Ill., 1973), 70–80; Rayback, *Free Soil*, 218–29.

[60] Bugbee, "Henry Lillie Pierce," 389.

[61] *Oberlin Evangelist*, 30 Aug. 1848; *New York Tribune*, 27 Oct. 1848; Johnson, "Liberty Party in Maine," 152–68; Emeline B. Cheney, *The Story of the Life and Work of Oren B. Cheney, Founder and First President of Bates College* (Boston, 1907), 55–8, 63–4; Davis, "Joshua Leavitt," 311–24. Lewis Tappan *"felt stabbed in the vitals"* by Van Buren's nomination, as did others of his circle; with Julius LeMoyne, James Birney, and 2,500 other abolitionists who regarded the Free Soil movement as a snare and a delusion he supported Gerrit Smith's Liberty League. Wyatt-Brown, *Lewis Tappan*, 280–2; Friedman, *Gregarious Saints*, 93–4.

[62] Thompson, *Christian Citizen*, 15. Thompson's editorial colleagues on the soon to be established New York *Independent*, the Congregationalist ministers Leonard Bacon and R.S. Storrs, would give the paper a free-soil (though not necessarily Free Soil) stance. Bacon, *Leonard Bacon*, 304–10.

[63] Fletcher, *Diary*, IV, 61–2 (12 Aug. 1848). Fletcher resisted attempts to get him to stand as a Free Soil candidate for presidential elector, but he served as a member of the state committee and, in Jan. 1849, as chairman of the State Free Soil Convention in Indianapolis (*ibid.*, xii–xiii, 66–7). For Francis Wayland's course from Whiggery to Free Soil, see Murray, *Wayland*, 273; Wayland and Wayland, *Wayland*, II, 58.

[64] Dumond (ed.) *Letters of Birney*, II,

1002–3; Howe, *American Whigs*, 167–9, 176–7. For Giddings's increasing religious heterodoxy and his defection from Whiggery, see Stewart, *Giddings*, 141–60, 208–11, 252–3; Howe, *American Whigs*, 177–8.

[65] *Ohio State Journal*, 14 Aug. 1848; Dyer, *National Free Soil Convention*, 4, 7, 13, 24–5; Sherlock Bristol, *The Pioneer Preacher: Incidents of Interest, and Experiences in the Author's Life* (New York [1887]), 125. Evangelicals who spoke or sent messages to be read included Joshua Giddings, Asa Mahan (then president of Oberlin College), Joshua Leavitt, William Slade, and Hiram Wilson. Blue, *Free Soilers*, 70–2, stresses the discrepancy between the political maneuvering behind the scenes and the high idealism of the public meetings. Frank O. Gatell, "'Conscience and Judgement': The Bolt of the Massachusetts Conscience Whigs," *The Historian*, 21 (Nov. 1958), 18–45, shows that evangelicals were not alone in contributing to the crusading mode of Free Soil: "Conscience" Whiggery's earnest concern for principle in public policy also drew on non-evangelical groups, including Unitarians.

[66] *New York Tribune*, 7 Sept. 1848. The convention's revivalist character was underscored by the absence of evident drunkenness. *Oberlin Evangelist*, 16 Aug. 1848.

[67] *Oberlin Evangelist*, 16 Aug., 27 Sept., 25 Oct. 1848; *Albany Argus*, 25 Sept. 1848; J. Blanchard to S. Williston, 28 Sept. 1848, 7 May 1849, Blanchard Papers, WC; *Ohio State Journal*, 2 Oct. 1848; *New York Tribune*, 3 Nov. 1848; Jonathan Blanchard, *Sermons and Addresses* (Chicago, 1892), 72–82, 103–17; Norman A. Graebner, "Thomas Corwin and the Election of 1848: A Study in Conservative Politics," *JSH*, 17 (May 1951), 165, 176–7.

[68] *Watchman of the Prairies*, cited in Norton, *Religious Newspapers*, 119. Gerrit Smith and other Liberty Leaguers who refused to vote for Van Buren still welcomed his campaign as a means of

"breaking up the great political parties."
Oberlin Evangelist, 30 Aug. 1848.

[69] *Oberlin Evangelist*, 16 Aug. 1848; Bristol, *Pioneer Preacher*, 127–32; S.T. Glover to A. Bullard, 24 Sept., 12 Nov. 1848, Bullard Papers, PHS; Blue, *The Free Soilers*, 133–51; *WCA*, 15 Nov. 1848. See also D.S. Jones (chairman of the Free Soil County Committee, Greenfield, Mass.), printed circular letter to county Free Soilers, 8 Nov. 1848, J. Leavitt Papers.

[70] Augustus B. Longstreet, *A Voice from the South: Comprising Letters from Georgia to Massachusetts, and to the Southern States . . .* (Baltimore, 1847), 55, 59–60; Valentine, Diary, 14 Sept. 1848, SHC; *Knoxville Whig*, 30 Aug., 4 Oct. 1848. "It seems like sheer madness for Southern men to vote for Cass whose principles are openly against us, rather than for Taylor, of whom they can only say 'they don't know'. If he were to turn out an Abolitionist & make his slaves free the day he was inaugurated, he would *only then* be just equal to Cass" (S. King to M. King, 29 Sept. 1848, King Papers, SHC).

[71] I.L. Brookes to Mssrs Greene and Orme, 20 March 1849, I.L. Brookes Papers, SHC. Evangelicals amongst the frustrated emancipationists of the border states constituted a further group whose party loyalties were severely strained in the later 1840s. The Reverend Robert J. Breckinridge, Presbyterian and Clay Whig, returned to politics to help move Kentucky in 1849 towards gradual emancipation. Having failed (along with others of the emancipation party) to be elected to the constitutional convention of 1849, he denounced both Whigs and Democrats for putting "party aggrandisement" before principle. Victor B. Howard, "Robert J. Breckinridge and the Slavery Controversy in Kentucky in 1849," *Filson Club History Quarterly*, 53 (Oct. 1979), 328–43; Breckinridge, *Speech . . . in Reply to Wickliffe*, 6–7, 20–1. Benjamin Mills came to a similarly dispiriting conclusion (B. Mills to C. Hall, 6 July 1849, AHMS Papers).

[72] My interpretation of the significance of the church conflicts over slavery is much closer to that of Donald G. Mathews, "Methodist Schism of 1844 and the Popularization of Antislavery Sentiment," *Mid-America*, 51 (Jan. 1969), 3–23, and Goen, *Broken Churches, Broken Nation*, than to Wiebe, *The Opening of American Society*, 305, who claims that following the church schisms of 1837–45 "rancor almost always ceased." Mathews rightly maintains that the Methodist schism "was one of the most important events leading to the Civil War. . . . This is not to say that the schism destroyed a 'bond of union', for the churches possessed no positive power to create unity where the will for it did not exist. But . . . [it did destroy] the 'common world of experience' that the second Great Awakening had tried to establish" (Mathews, "Methodist Schism of 1844," 16–18).

[73] King, *Reminiscences*, 63; David Reed of Kanawha Salines, in *WCA*, 7 April 1848.

[74] My understanding of the roots and emphases of southern evangelicals' proslavery thought is especially indebted to Mathews, *Religion in the Old South*, 136–84. Larry E. Tise, *Proslavery: A History of the Defense of Slavery in America, 1701–1840* (Athens, Ga., 1987) locates the intellectual roots of southern proslavery doctrine in northern Federalist thought. See also William S. Jenkins, *Pro-Slavery Thought in the Old South* (Chapel Hill, NC, 1935), 200–41; H. Shelton Smith, *In His Image, But . . . Racism in Southern Religion, 1790–1910* (Durham, NC, 1972), 129–65; Donald G. Mathews, "Religion and Slavery: The Case of the American South," in Christine Bolt and Seymour Drescher (eds) *Anti-Slavery, Religion, and Reform: Essays in Memory of Roger Anstey* (Folkestone, UK, 1980), 207–32; Bertram Wyatt-Brown, *Yankee Saints and Southern Sinners*, 155–68. For an elaboration of the view that "The distinctive religious character of antebellum southern society was directly related to slavery as a social system" and that the intellectuals who

defended slavery through religion reached and influenced both slaveholding and non-slaveholding southerners, see Eugene D. Genovese and Elizabeth Fox-Genovese, "The Religious Ideals of Southern Slave Society," *Georgia Historical Quarterly*, 70 (Spring 1986), 1–16 (quotation p. 2).

[75] J.B. Adger to R.L. Dabney, 20 Jan. 1840, cited in Thompson, *Presbyterians in the South*, I, 535. But for an early statement (at the MEC General Conference of 1800) that slavery was *not* a moral evil, see Alexander McCaine, *Slavery Defended from Scripture, against the Attacks of the Abolitionists* . . . (Baltimore, 1842), 5.

[76] I.L. Brookes to "Bro Slade," 20 March 1849, I.L. Brookes Papers, SHC; Jeremiah B. Jeter, *Recollections of a Long Life* (Richmond, Va., 1891), 67–71. For Stringfellow, see Drew Gilpin Faust, "Evangelicalism and the Meaning of the Proslavery Argument: The Reverend Thornton Stringfellow of Virginia," *Virginia Magazine of History and Biography*, 85 (Jan. 1977), 3–17.

[77] Harold Wilson, "Basil Manly: Apologist for Slaveocracy," *Alabama Review*, 15 (Jan. 1962), 40; Theodore Rosengarten, *Tombee: Portrait of a Cotton Planter, with the Journal of Thomas B. Chaplin (1822–1890)* (New York, 1986), 144. Jack P. Maddex, "Proslavery Millennialism: Social Eschatology in Antebellum Southern Religion," *AQ*, 31 (Spring 1979), 46–62, offers a shrewd analysis of this development amongst southern Calvinist thought, particularly of Old School Presbyterians.

[78] J.B. Adger to R.L. Dabney, 20 Jan. 1840, cited in Thompson, *Presbyterians in the South*, I, 535; W. Winans to W. Fisk, 5 Oct. 1837, in Ray Holder, "On Slavery: Selected Letters of Parson Winans, 1820–1844," *Journal of Mississippi History*, 46 (Nov. 1984), 341–2; Bertram Wyatt-Brown, *Southern Honor: Ethics and Behavior in the Old South* (New York, 1982), xvii–xviii, 168–9, 186, 189–90, 197; J. Bauskett to I.L. Brookes, 19 April 1851, I.L. Brookes Papers, SHC; Valentine, Diary, 13 Aug., 12 Dec. 1851, SHC;

Knoxville Whig, 27 Jan. 1847; *Christian Index* 26 Jan. 1844. For a brief discussion of how southern evangelical clergy dealt with the problem of "pride in a proud culture," by managing it and taming it in an appeal to the larger value system of honor, which would suppress sensual gratification and ego fulfillment, see Robert M. Calhoon, *Evangelicals and Conservatives in the Early South, 1740–1861* (Columbia, SC, 1988), 144–6.

[79] Patrick H. Mell, *Slavery. A Treatise, Showing that Slavery is neither a Moral, Political, nor Social Evil. By a Baptist Minister* (Penfield, Ga., 1844), 10–19; I.L. Brookes, *A Defence of Southern Slavery: Against the Attacks of Henry Clay and Alex'r. Campbell* (Hamburg, SC, 1851), 5–6. See also I.L. Brookes, *A Defence of the South against the Reproaches and Incroachments of the North* (Hamburg, SC, 1850), 45. Leviticus 25. 45 and Genesis 9. 24 were customary supportive texts.

[80] McCaine, *Slavery Defended from Scripture*, 7, 14; Jacobs, *The Committing of Our Cause to God*, 10; Jeter, *Recollections of a Long Life*, 70, paraphrasing Stringfellow; Mell, *Slavery. A Treatise*, 19; Ferdinand Jacobs, *The Committing of Our Cause to God: A Sermon Preached in the Second Presbyterian Church, Charleston, S.C.* . . . (Charleston, SC, 1850), 9. For elaboration of the themes of this paragraph, see also Wilson, "Basil Manly," 41–3; Frank W. Ryan, Jr, "The Southern Quarterly Review, 1842–1857: A Study in Thought and Opinion in the Old South" (PhD diss., University of North Carolina at Chapel Hill, 1956), 337–40, 419–20; *Biblical Recorder*, 20 July, 21 Sept. 1844; Lewis M. Purifoy, "The Southern Methodist Church and the Pro-Slavery Argument," *JSH*, 32 (Aug. 1966), 327–9; Thompson, *Presbyterians in the South*, I, 535; *Christian Index*, 17 May 1844. While evangelicals used the Bible as their principal weapon in sanctifying slavery, they also drew on two other intellectual sources: moral philosophy (in the Scottish Common Sense tradition), which stressed the slave's humanity, his inviolable moral nature, and

the mutual relations and responsibilities of master and slave; and natural law, which in its conservative southern version sustained patriarchy, regarded inequality and submission as natural in society, and rejected Jeffersonian natural rights philosophy. See Mitchell Snay, "American Thought and Southern Distinctiveness: The Southern Clergy and the Sanctification of Slavery," *CWH*, 35 (Dec. 1989), 311–28.

81 *Knoxville Whig*, 11 Aug. 1849 (citing a Kentucky Presbyterian); McCaine, *Slavery Defended from Scripture*, 19; Whiteford Smith, *National Sins: A Call to Repentance. A Sermon Preached on the National Fast, August 3, 1849*... (Charleston, SC, 1849), 18–19; Jacobs, *Committing of Our Cause to God*, 7–8. For southern (and northern) evangelicals' use of Federalist thought as a means of squaring republican values with hierarchical social theory, see Tise, *Proslavery*, 124–79, 261–307, 323–46 and *passim*.

82 Overy, "Dabney," 48–51; Maddex, "Proslavery Millennialism," 53; William M. Green, *Life and Papers of A.L.P. Green, D.D.*, ed. T.O. Summers (Nashville, Tenn., 1877), 167. Alabama Baptists had established a committee to secure an essay on the duties of masters to servants. Drawn from several denominations, it included the state's governor, Henry W. Collier, an active Methodist. *Christian Index*, 23 May 1850. Thomas Smyth believed the brotherhood of men underlay slavery, "the first law of slavery being that of kindness to the slave" (Thomas Smyth, *Autobiographical Notes*, Charleston, SC, 1914, 228). For the common origin of southern efforts to Christianize the slaves and of northern antislavery, see Donald G. Mathews, "Religion in the Old South: Speculation on Methodology," *South Atlantic Quarterly*, 73 (Winter 1974), 41–2.

83 Luther P. Jackson, "Religious Instruction of Negroes, 1830–1860, with Special Reference to South Carolina," *Journal of Negro History*, 15 (Jan. 1930), 101–2, 107; Donald G. Mathews,

"Charles Colcock Jones and the Southern Evangelical Crusade to Form a Biracial Community," *JSH*, 40 (Aug. 1975), 299–320. For planters' obstruction and indifference towards evangelical missionaries see, for example, Drury, *Scott*, 120; O.W. Taylor, "Baptists and Slavery in Arkansas: Relationships and Attitudes," *Arkansas Historical Quarterly*, 38 (Autumn 1979), 213; Rosengarten, *Tombee*, 146–7.

84 John B. Adger, *My Life and Times 1810–1899* (Richmond, Va. [1899]), 54, 147, 164–5, 178; Whiteford Smith, *God, The Refuge of His People: A Sermon, Delivered before the General Assembly of South Carolina, on Friday, December 6, 1850*... (Columbia, SC, 1850), 10–11; Brookes, *Defence of Southern Slavery*, 6–9. For an assessment of missions to slaves as "an assertion of Evangelical power and prestige," see Mathews, *Religion in the Old South*, 136–50.

85 I.L. Brookes to W. Heath, 20 March 1849, I.L. Brookes Papers, SHC; Brookes, *Defence of the South*, 45–7. See also Henry Bascom *et al.*, *Brief Appeal to Public Opinion, in a Series of Exceptions to the Course and Action of the Methodist Episcopal Church, from 1844 to 1848*... (Louisville, Ky., 1848), 28–9; Mell, *Slavery. A Treatise*, 28–40. Southern evangelicals' faith in their section's model republicanism drew strength from the perception that God had positively chosen slave-holders to win America's freedom from British rule and to lay the foundations of the new nation. *Christian Index*, 15 March 1844.

86 For the efforts of Joshua Soule and other ministers of the lower South to remove the antislavery sections of the original Methodist Discipline still operative in the MECS, see *CAJ*, 17 Oct. 1850; *WCA*, 22 May 1850; *SCA*, 28 Feb., 16 May, 6 June 1851.

87 Charles Grier Sellers, Jr, "The Travail of Slavery," in Charles Grier Sellers, Jr (ed.) *The Southerner as American* (Chapel Hill, NC, 1960), 48. Sellers's essay is a classic statement of the thesis that antebellum white southerners were ideologically confused and torn by guilt,

and that the religious defense of slavery was driven by an implicitly antislavery logic. See also James Oakes, *The Ruling Race: A History of American Slaveholders* (New York, 1982), 108–9. Maddex, "Proslavery Millennialism," 53–5, indicates some of the limits of the "positive good" argument.

[88] J.B. Logan to D.B. Coe, 25 March 1853; B. Mills to AHMS "Brethren," 1 April 1849, AHMS Papers. Mills's correspondence with the AHMS secretariat in New York provides a rich source for examining New School emancipationists in the border states in the later 1840s and 1850s. See also Hannah Bent to M. and J. Blanchard, 20 Sept. 1840, Blanchard Papers, WC; Richard D. Sears, *The Day of Small Things: Abolitionism in the Midst of Slavery: Berea, Kentucky, 1854–1864* (Lanham, Md., 1986), 1–97. For antislavery Baptists in the 1849 campaign for emancipation in Kentucky, see Pendleton, *Reminiscences*, 92–5.

[89] *Biblical Recorder*, 2 March 1844; *Christian Index*, 9 Aug. 1844. Bailey, *Shadow on the Church*, 16, 23–4, 48–9 takes issue with Donald Mathews's view that southern evangelicals avoided determining slavery as a sin, and posits a distinctively regional south-western religious culture where at least in the early nineteenth century men like David Rice of Kentucky did regard slavery as a moral evil and a sin. Mathews, *Religion in the Old South*, esp. 74, 151–2, deals shrewdly with the distinction between slavery as sin/moral evil on the one hand and as burden/curse on the other.

[90] William Winans regarded slavery as sinful in its "origination," but no longer so when sustained to protect blacks from a ruinous emancipation. Holder, "On Slavery," 335, 347. For Brownlow see, for example, *Knoxville Whig*, 17 Aug. 1850, 17 May 1851. For Hoge, Presbyterian minister of Richmond, Va., who freed the slaves he received from his wife's estate, but believed universal emancipation fraught with evil, see Hoge, *Moses Drury Hoge*, 135–7. The conception of slavery as evil but not personal sin underlay colonization senti-ment in the border South. Leroy J. Halsey, *Memoir of the Life and Character of Rev. Lewis Warner Green, D.D.* (New York, 1871), 26; Breckinridge, *Speech in Reply to Wickliffe*, 7–32; Howard, "Breckinridge and the Slavery Controversy in Kentucky," 328–43.

[91] Valentine, Diary, 18 Dec. 1844, 17 Dec. 1845, 8, 12 Feb. 1850, 1 Jan., 29 April, 17 Oct. 1851, SHC; J. Witherspoon to S.W. McDowell, 23 May 1837, Witherspoon–McDowell Papers, SHC; Flournoy, *Benjamin Mosby Smith*, 57–9, 74 (quoting from Smith's Diary, 21 Dec. 1858); Fitzgerald, *John B. McFerrin*, 269–70; Thornwell, *Christian Doctrine of Slavery*, quoted in Marilyn J. Westerkamp, "James Henley Thornwell, Pro-Slavery Spokesman within a Calvinist Faith," *South Carolina Historical Magazine*, 87 (Jan. 1986), 55, 57.

[92] Thomas Smyth, "Unity of the Races," in *Autobiographical Notes*, 228 (every man is made in the image of God); Smith, *In His Image But . . .* , 154–65; Bascom *et al.*, *Brief Appeal*, 28–9.

[93] Thompson, *Presbyterians in the South*, I, 339, 348, 535; *WCA*, 12 April 1848; *SCA*, 2 May 1845; I.L. Brookes to Messrs Greene and Orme, 20 March 1849, I.L. Brookes Papers, SHC; Howard, "Breckinridge and the Slavery Controversy in Kentucky," 328–43. See also *Oberlin Evangelist*, 20 June 1849. The churches' "hands-off" doctrine was well established. Bailey, *Shadow on the Church*, 99, 128.

[94] See, for example, Clark, *Alarm to Christian Patriots*, 22–3.

[95] For Methodist abolitionism see DeVinne, *Recollections*, 33, 40–7; David Christy, *Pulpit Politics: or, Ecclesiastical Legislation on Slavery, in its Disturbing Influences on the American Union* (3rd edn, Cincinnati, 1862), 388–9; Lee, *Autobiography*, 134–57; Crane, *Autobiography*, 80, 89; LaRoy Sunderland to R.H. Howard, 22 April 1872, NEC.

[96] J.A. Merrill to S.W. Hammond, 9 May 1840, NEC; Peck, *George Peck*, 220; Lee, *Autobiography*, 251–2. For Wesleyan Methodism, see Lucius C. Matlack, *The Life of Rev. Orange Scott . . .* (New York,

1847–48), 209–22; Lucius C. Matlack, *The History of American Slavery and Methodism, from 1780 to 1849; and History of the Wesleyan Methodist Connection of America* (New York, 1849), 301–53. For Methodist conservatives, see Donald G. Mathews, *Slavery and Methodism: A Chapter in American Morality 1780–1845* (Princeton, NJ, 1965), 212–45; McKivigan, *War against Proslavery Religion*, 46–7.

[97] William D. Cass wrote from the General Conference in 1844: "There is not much abolitionism here.... [I]f there had been no fear of secession Bishop Andrew would have had but little disturbance" (Locke, "An Abolitionist at the General Conference," *Methodist History*, 17, July 1979, 236). For premonitions of schism, see M. Caldwell to T.E. Bond, 3 April 1843, DU.

[98] The Baltimore Conference had removed Harding from the ministry until he freed the slaves he had acquired through marriage. To the fury of hardline southerners the General Conference sustained the Baltimore authorities. For the conference proceedings, see Mathews, *Slavery and Methodism*, 246–68.

[99] Mathews, *Slavery and Methodism*, 264; T. Stringfield to his wife, 1 June 1844, Stringfield Papers, SHC; Mathews, "Methodist Schism of 1844," 15.

[100] *New York Evangelist*, 15 Aug. 1844 (resolutions of Charlotte station, SC); Valentine, Diary, 25 June 1844, SHC; *SCA*, 28 June (Chesterfield circuit, SC Conference), 2, 23 Aug. ("Peace rather than Union") 1844; *CAJ*, 11, 25 Sept., 23 Oct. 1844.

[101] *SCA*, 12 July 1844; L. Waugh, *Autobiography of Lorenzo Waugh*, 149–50, 156.

[102] *CAJ*, 20 Nov. 1844; *SCA*, 18 April 1845; Bascom *et al.*, *Brief Appeal*, 44; Stewart, *Highways and Hedges*, 245–50; Mathews, *Slavery and Methodism*, 276. See also John N. Norwood, *The Schism in the American Methodist Church, 1844: A Study in Slavery and Ecclesiastical Politics* (New York, 1923).

[103] J. McClintock to R. Emory, 14 Oct. 1844, DU; *SCA*, 24 Jan., 7 Feb. 1845.

Mathews, *Slavery and Methodism*, 269–74, considers northern reaction to the General Conference proceedings.

[104] R. Emory to D. Sellers, 14 Aug. 1844, DU; *CAJ*, 20 Nov. 1844. See *DAB* for Olin and Durbin. The developing bad feeling between the sections can be followed especially in the editorial columns of Thomas Bond's *Christian Advocate and Journal* and William Wightman's *Southern Christian Advocate*.

[105] David R. McAnally, *Life and Times of Rev. William Patton and Annals of the Missouri Conference* (St Louis, 1858), 228–31; Bascom *et al.*, *Brief Appeal*, 92; *CAJ*, 18 July 1850; *SCA*, 18 Aug. 1848; Holder, *Winans*, 191–2; Arthur E. Jones, "The Years of Disagreement, 1844–61," in *History of American Methodism*, ed Emory Stevens Bucke *et al.* (3 vols, Nashville, Tenn., 1964), II, 168–76; *WCA*, 31 May 1848; *CAJ*, 12 Jan., 24 May, 19 July, 30 Aug. 1848.

[106] For the precise terms of the Plan of Separation, see Norman W. Spellman, "The Church Divides, 1844," in *History of American Methodism*, ed E.S. Bucke *et al.*, II, 62–3. Jones, "The Years of Disagreement, 1844–61," 159–67, offers a lucid analysis of the Plan's operations along the border before 1848.

[107] Fee, *Bringing the Sheaves*, 242–3; *Pittsburgh Christian Advocate*, 9 Oct. 1844; *CAJ*, 26 April, 10 May, 19 July 1848; Waugh, *Autobiography*, 156–8, 166–7. The *Western Christian Advocate*, 18 Oct. 1848, contended that some 3,000 members of the MEC, scattered through the Missouri Conference in pockets too small to sustain a minister, provided important nuclei for future growth.

[108] Bascom *et al.*, *Brief Appeal*, 93–106, 127–34; *CAJ*, 12 Jan., 24 May 1848.

[109] *SCA*, 4 Dec. 1846; *WCA*, 26 July 1848, 9 Oct. 1850; T.J. Thompson to T.E. Bond, 30 Oct. 1846, T.E. Bond Papers, Dickinson College; Jones, "The Years of Disagreement, 1844–61," 164–5, drawing on Norwood, *Schism in the American Methodist Church*, 138–40; Freeborn Garretson Hibbard, *Biography of Rev. Leonidas L. Hamline, D.D., Late One of the Bishops of the Methodist Episcopal Church* (Cincinnati,

1880), 192–3; Holder, *Winans*, 191–3.

[110] *CAJ*, 3 Nov. 1847, 24 May 1848; *WCA*, 27 Sept., 25 Oct. 1848, 9 Oct. 1850; *SCA*, 9 June 1848; Holder, *Winans*, 193–4; Hibbard, *Hamline*, 216; *Knoxville Whig*, 22 July 1846.

[111] Waugh, *Autobiography*, 164–6; Lorenzo Waugh, *A Candid Statement of the Course Pursued by the Preachers of the Methodist Church South, in Trying to Establish their New Organization in Missouri*... (Cincinnati, 1848), 60–1; Phineas L. Windsor, "A Central Illinois Methodist Minister, 1857–1891" (unpublished paper read before a Women's Study Group of Trinity Methodist Church of Urbana, Illinois, March 1944), 1; *Knoxville Whig*, 25 Aug. 1849; Hibbard, *Leonidas Hamline*, 211–13.

[112] *WCA*, 7 April 1848; Hibbard, *Hamline*, 196–8; Stewart, *Highways and Hedges*, 245–60. Fee, *Bringing the Sheaves*, 213–14, describes popular sentiment in western Virginia, including the alliance of "white trash" and "the politicians" in defense of the slave oligarchy and the MECS. For persisting antislavery in that section, see Kenneth M. Stampp, "Fate of the Southern Antislavery Movement," *Journal of Negro History*, 28 (Jan. 1943), 20–2.

[113] Hibbard, *Hamline*, 211–15; T.J. Thompson to T.E. Bond, 30 Oct. 1846; O.P. Twiford to T.E. Bond, 24 Nov. 1846, T.E. Bond Papers; *CAJ*, 5, 12 Oct., 11, 18, 25 Nov. 1846, 20, 27 Jan., 3, 10, 24 Feb. 1847.

[114] *WCA*, 11 Feb., 17, 24, 31 March, 7, 28 April 1848; *CAJ*, 19 July 1848, 13 June 1850; *SCA*, 28 March 1845, 2, 16 June 1848; Winans, *Holder*, 192; *Knoxville Whig*, 24 Jan., 6 April 1849; Bascom *et al.*, *Brief Appeal*, 5; Hamline, *Hibbard*, 218–22; Edwin H. Myers, *The Disruption of the Methodist Episcopal Church, 1844–46: Comprising a Thirty Years' History of the Relations of the Two Methodisms* (Nashville, Tenn., 1875), 151; Jones, "The Years of Disagreement, 1844–61," 177–81.

[115] W.H. Wills to editor of the *Western Methodist Protestant*, 1 June 1855, W.H. Wills Papers, SHC; Douglas R.

Chandler, "The Formation of the Methodist Protestant Church," in Bucke *et al.* (eds) *History of American Methodism*, II, 677–80. For the experience of the antislavery missionaries Adam Crooks, Jarvis C. Bacon, and Jesse McBride see Claude R. Rickman, "Wesleyan Methodism in North Carolina, 1847–1902" (MA diss., University of North Carolina at Chapel Hill, 1952), 21.

[116] The case is advanced most influentially in C. Bruce Staiger, "Abolitionism and the Presbyterian Schism of 1837–1838," *MVHR*, 36 (Dec. 1949), 391–414. Marsden, *Evangelical Mind*, 66–103, offers a judicious, balanced interpretation. See also Thompson, *Presbyterians in the South*, I, 384–98; Walter B. Posey, "The Slavery Question in the Presbyterian Church in the Old Southwest," *JSH*, 15 (Aug. 1949), 311–24; McKivigan, *War against Proslavery Religion*, 82–4; Petersen, *Divine Discontent*, 117–30.

[117] Breckinridge, *Speech in Reply to Wickliffe*, 28–9. Elwyn Allen Smith, "The Role of the South in the Presbyterian Schism of 1837–1838," *Church History*, 29 (March 1960), 44–63, cautions against overemphasizing the slavery issue.

[118] Rice, *Lectures on Slavery*, 30–1; *Oberlin Evangelist*, 20 June 1849; *New York Evangelist*, 13 June 1844; Thompson, *Presbyterians in the South*, I, 530–3; Christy, *Pulpit Politics*, 346–9. Rice, *Lectures on Slavery*, 6–9, 52–4 and *passim*, denied that 1845 represented any retreat from the historic antislavery position. For the secession of some Old School members to join the antislavery presbytery of Ripley, Ohio, in forming the Free Presbyterian Church in 1847 see Thompson, *History of the Presbyterian Churches*, 133–7.

[119] Thompson, *Presbyterians in the South*, I, 403–12, 540–2; *Oberlin Evangelist*, 24 June 1846, 8 May, 19 June 1850.

[120] *Oberlin Evangelist*, 30 Aug. 1848; Kuykendall, *Southern Enterprize*, 74–80; B. Mills to M. Badger, 6 July, 2 Oct. 1850, 20 Jan., 25 Oct. 1851, 2 Oct. 1852, 8 Feb., 1 March 1853; B. Mills to C. Hall, 4 July

1851; J.G. Fee to M. Badger and C. Hall, 29 July, 13 Sept. 1848, AHMS Papers; W.M. Blanchard to J. Blanchard, 7 Sept. 1852, Blanchard Papers, WC. See also J. Blanchard to S. Williston, 9 Dec. 1848; J. Blanchard to M. Badger and J. Hall, 16 Dec. 1850; J. Blanchard to L. Tappan, 7 Oct. 1851, photocopy from American Missionary Association Archives, Blanchard Papers, WC. For other (especially evangelical abolitionist) critics of the AHMS, and the setting up of the American Missionary Association by Lewis Tappan, Simeon Jocelyn, and George Whipple in 1846, see McKivigan, *War against Proslavery Religion*, 112–17; Colin Brummitt Goodykoontz, *Home Missions on the American Frontier: with particular reference to the American Home Missionary Society* (Caldwell, Idaho, 1939), 289–94; Clifford S. Griffin, "The Abolitionists and the Benevolent Societies, 1831–1861," *Journal of Negro History*, 44 (July 1959), 201–10.

[121] For a summary of the events of 1844–45 see William Wright Barnes, *The Southern Baptist Convention 1845–1953* (Nashville, Tenn., 1954), 12–23; McKivigan, *War against Proslavery Religion*, 87–9; Goen, *Broken Churches, Broken Nation*, 90–8; *Baptist Home Missions in North America*, 393–5.

[122] *Christian Index*, 1 Nov. 1844; *Biblical Recorder*, 23, 30 Nov. 1844; Goen, *Broken Churches, Broken Nation*, 96–7. Most southern Baptist papers, including the *Christian Index*, *Tennessee Baptist*, *Religious Herald*, and *Alabama Baptist*, warmly supported the idea of separation. Only a minority in each section, represented by the *Christian Watchman and Reflector* in Boston, the *Philadelphia Record*, the *Banner and Pioneer* of Louisville, and the *Biblical Recorder* in North Carolina were opposed. *Biblical Recorder*, 12, 19 April 1845; Henry S. Stroupe, *The Religious Press in the South Atlantic States, 1802–1865* (Durham, NC, 1956), 19–22.

[123] *Christian Index*, 1 Nov. 1844; Roger D. Bridges (ed.) "John Mason Peck on Illinois Slavery," *Journal of the Illinois State Historical Society*, 75 (Fall 1982), 187.

For Thomas Meredith's call for prudence and caution in 1844–45 see the columns of the *Biblical Recorder*. For other conservatives in 1844–45 see, for example, Jeter, *Recollections of a Long Life*, 229–31.

[124] Meredith was convinced that editorial jousting aggravated rather than soothed sectional frictions. *Biblical Recorder*, 1 Feb., 1 March 1845. His lengthy debates with the *Christian Secretary* of Connecticut, his efforts to publicize the correspondence between Fuller and Wayland, and his altercations with W.H. Brisbane's *Christian Politician*, led him to conclude that Baptists in free states deliberately misrepresented what he intended as emollient remarks. The published controversy between Richard Fuller (Baptist minister of Beaufort, SC) and Francis Wayland did little or nothing to heal sectional wounds. See, for example, Cyrus Pitt Grosvenor, *A Review of the "Correspondence" of Messrs. Fuller & Wayland, on the Subject of American Slavery* (Utica, NY, 1847).

[125] Robert R. Witten, *Pioneer Methodism; or, Itinerant Life in Missouri* (n.p., 1881), 17; Brownlow, *Americanism Contrasted with Foreignism*, 61.

[126] *Pittsburgh Christian Advocate*, 30 April 1840; Christy, *Pulpit Politics*, 389–91; *CAJ*, 14 May 1845; Locke, "An Abolitionist at the General Conference," 229, quoting Henry Slicer; *Biblical Recorder*, 4 Jan. 1845. See also Richard Fuller in *Christian Index*, 17 May 1844.

[127] Quoted in Thompson, *Presbyterians in the South*, I, 393–4. For Presbyterians of similar mind, see Christy, *Pulpit Politics*, 349. For like concern amongst Methodist Protestants, see G. Whitaker to G. Whitaker, 1 Sept. 1845, W.H. Wills Papers, SHC; G.A.T. Whitaker to J.F. Speight, 27 May 1842, J.F. Speight Papers, SHC.

[128] *SCA*, 4 Oct. 1844 (J. Evans of Augusta, Ga.), 30 May 1845 (William Winans); *Christian Index*, 17 May 1844 (N. Colver).

[129] Fitzgerald, *John B. McFerrin*, 186; Barnes, *Southern Baptist Convention*, 25; *SCA*, 7 March 1845. See also Jeter, *Recol-*

lections, 232–3; *Christian Index*, 8 Feb. 1845.

[130] *CAJ*, 30 Oct. 1844; *Christian Index*, 11 Oct. 1844.

[131] *WCA*, 17 Sept. 1851; Wightman, *William Capers*, 514; Peck, *George Peck*, 247; J.P. Durbin to M. Simpson, Aug. 1844, Simpson Papers, LC; *CAJ*, 13 Nov., 2, 25 Dec. 1844; *SCA*, 13 Dec. 1844. For a discussion of the Calhoun–Capers affair, see Goen, *Broken Churches, Broken Nation*, 110–11; Norwood, *Schism in the American Methodist Church*, 187–94.

[132] Smith, *George Foster Pierce*, 126–7; *Biblical Recorder*, 2 March, 25 May, 15, 22 June, 6 July, 12 Oct. 1844; *Primitive Baptist*, V, 363–4, VI, 91–3; *SCA*, 16 Aug., 18 Oct. (attacking the once-trusted Charles Elliott) 1844, 21 March, 2 May 1845, 23 June, 3 Nov. 1848, 31 Aug., 21 Sept. 1849, 18 Jan., 17 May 1850, 20 June 1851; Longstreet, *Voice from the South*, 60; Holder, "On Slavery," 336, 348; *WCA*, 9 Oct. 1850; Bascom *et al.*, *Brief Appeal*, 10, 28, 83; *CAJ*, 14 March 1850; Myers, *Disruption of the Methodist Episcopal Church*, 139–40; Smith, *James Osgood Andrew*, 397; Adger, *My Life and Times*, 179–80; Smith, *God, The Refuge of His People*, 7. Evangelical southerners' paranoia and isolation revealed itself in their view of the Evangelical Alliance as an ecclesiastical alliance intending "to unite the public opinion of Protestant Christendom against the churches and professors of religion in the Southern States" (*SCA*, 12 June 1846).

[133] *CAJ*, 6 Oct. 1847; Bascom *et al.*, *Brief Appeal*, 60, 165–9.

[134] Waugh, *Candid Statement*, 70; Waugh, *Autobiography*, 149–71; *CAJ*, 5 Jan., 15 March, 24 May, 19 July 1848, 17 Oct. 1850; Hibbard, *Hamline*, 205; *SCA*, 6 June, 28 Nov. 1851; Fee, *Bringing the Sheaves*, 239–40; *WCA*, 27 Sept. 1848; Stewart, *Highways and Hedges*, 260; Edward Thomson, *Life of Edward Thomson, Late Bishop of the Methodist Episcopal Church* (Cincinnati, 1885), 87–8.

[135] *CAJ*, 5 Jan. 1848.

[136] For the examples of the Presbyterian editor Benjamin Gilder-sleeve and his Baptist counterpart Thomas Meredith, see Kuykendall, *Southern Enterprize*, 87–8, 102–7; *Baptist Recorder* for 1844 and 1845. See also *CAJ*, 23 Oct. 1844, 29 Dec. 1847.

[137] As David Potter remarks (*Impending Crisis*, 48, n. 36), we lack a study of the growth of a popular dislike of slavery in the United States, as opposed to out-and-out abolitionism: northern evangelical Protestants' role in that process was extremely important.

[138] Mathews, "Methodist Schism of 1844," 19; E. Mudge to B. Putnam, 22 Oct. 1844, NEC; *CAJ*, 30 Aug. 1848.

Chapter 6 *Evangelicals and the Resolution of Political Crisis, 1850–52*

[1] Potter, *Impending Crisis*, 90–120; Holman Hamilton, *Prologue to Conflict: The Crisis and Compromise of 1850* (Lexington, Ky., 1964); Cooper, *The South and the Politics of Slavery*, 301–17.

[2] *WCA*, 10, 17, 24 April, 22 May, 28 Aug., 16 Oct. 1850; *Oberlin Evangelist*, 13 Feb. 1850; J.L. Smith to M. Simpson, 23 May 1850, M. Simpson Papers, LC; Daniel Curry, *Life-Story of Rev. Davis Wasgatt Clark . . .* (New York, 1874), 112; Daniel Foster, *Our Nation's Sins and the Christian's Duty: A Fast Day Discourse . . .* (Boston, 1851), 6, 8–9; Bugbee, "Henry Lillie Pierce," 392. See also, S.P. Chase to M. Simpson, 26 April 1850, M. Simpson Papers, DU; William C. Wisner, *A Review of Rev. Doctor Lord's Sermon on the Higher Law, in its Application to the Fugitive Slave Bill* (Buffalo, 1851), 4; Fairbank, *Rev. Calvin Fairbank*, 70–2; Hague, *Life Notes*, 246–7.

[3] *Oberlin Evangelist*, 23 Oct. 1850; Samuel T. Spear, *The Law-abiding Conscience, and the Higher Law Conscience; with Remarks on the Fugitive Slave Question: A Sermon . . .* (New York), 33–5. See also J.A. Bolles, "The Extension of Slavery," *Christian Review*, 14 (Jan. 1849), 92–3; Wisner, *Review of Lord's Sermon*, 4, 7; *WCA*, 6 March, 1 May 1850; *CAJ*, 30 May, 18 July 1850.

[4] *WCA*, 17, 24 July 1850; *Oberlin Evangelist*, 13 Feb., 17 July 1850; Isaac J.P. Collyer, *Review of Rev. W.W. Eell[s]'s Thanksgiving Sermon, . . . Delivered in the Methodist Episcopal Church, Newburyport, Dec. 29, 1850* (Newburyport, Mass., 1851), 16; Foster, *Our Nation's Sins*, 9; *New Englander*, 8 (Aug. 1850), 379–80. See also Ely, *Eulogy on Zachary Taylor*, 42.

[5] Fairbank, *Rev. Calvin Fairbank*, 76; *WCA*, 10 April 1850 (quoting *New York Evangelist*). Brock, *Parties and Political Conscience*, 304–10, shows the senator's subtlety: Seward's higher law "did not override the Constitution, but provided the rule for interpretation when it was silent or ambiguous."

[6] Wisner, *Review of Lord's Sermon*, 23; William de Loss Love, *Obedience to Rulers – The Duty and Its Limitations: A Discourse* . . . (New Haven, Conn., 1851), 3; Nathaniel Colver, *The Fugitive Slave Bill; or God's Laws Paramount to the Laws of Men: A Sermon* . . . (Boston, 1850), 8–9; Leonard Bacon, *The Higher Law: A Sermon Preached on Thanksgiving Day, November 27, 1851* (New Haven, Conn., 1851), 7–11; Wooster Parker, *The Role of Duty: A Sermon, Delivered in Dover, on Fast Day, April 10, 1851* (Bangor, Me., 1851), 10. For representative expression of the views outlined in this paragraph see Gilbert Haven, *National Sermons: Sermons, Speeches and Letters on Slavery and Its War: From the Passage of the Fugitive Slave Bill to the Election of President Grant* (Boston, 1869), 1–32 ("The Higher Law," delivered Nov. 1850); L. Smith, *The Higher Law; or, Christ and His Law Supreme* (Ravenna, Ohio, 1852), 3–16; Spear, *Law-abiding Conscience*, 6–18; William Carter, *A Reply to Hon. William Thomas' Exposition and Defence of the Fugitive Slave Law* (Winchester, Ill., 1851), 3; T. Eddy, "God's Righteous Government," ms sermon, 14 Jan. 1851 (misdated 1850), GTS; Thomson, *Edward Thomson*, 90–1; Horace T. Love, *Slavery in its Relation to God: A Review of Reverend Dr. Lord's Thanksgiving Sermon in Favor of Slavery* (Buffalo, NY, 1851), 8–24; James M. Willson, "An Essay on Submission to Civil Government," in Wylie, *Two Sons of Oil*, 103–20; "The Supremacy of God's Law – Mr. Seward's Speech," in *New Englander*, 8 (Aug. 1850), 378–88; "Doctrine of the Higher Law," *ibid.*, 11 (May 1853), 161–71; Bacon, *Leonard Bacon*, 346–7. A decade earlier, in 1839, Charles Finney had proffered his own version of the higher-law argument. Essig, "The Lord's Free Man," 25–45, persuasively argues for greater radicalism in the influential revivalist's antislavery thought than is often recognized. See also Russell D. Parker, "The Philosophy of Charles G. Finney: Higher Law and Revivalism," *Ohio History*, 82 (Summer–Fall 1973), 142–53.

[7] *Oberlin Evangelist*, 17 Dec. 1851; Colver, *Fugitive Slave Bill*, 8–9; Love, *Obedience to Rulers*, 16.

[8] *SCA*, 13 Dec. 1850; Curry, *Davis Wasgatt Clark*, 105–6; R.M. Hall, ts "Life," 85, PHS; *WCA*, 9 Oct., 20 Nov. 1850; J. Drummond to M. Simpson, 8 May 1850, Simpson Papers, LC; Eddy "God's Righteous Government," 57–8; Wisner, *Review of Lord's Sermon*, 30–1; *Oberlin Evangelist*, 9 Oct. 1850; Essig, "The Lord's Free Man," 40–2; Charles C. Cole, "Horace Bushnell and the Slavery Question," *New England Quarterly*, 23 (March 1950), 26–7. Stanley W. Campbell, *The Slave Catchers: Enforcement of the Fugitive Slave Law, 1850–1860* (Chapel Hill, NC, 1968), 66–71, underestimates the extent of hostility to the Fugitive Slave Law amongst northern clergy, tending to categorize as advocates of enforcement those like Samuel Thayer Spear whose position was much more ambiguous. Even those who called for enforcement very largely disliked the law. For a balanced assessment, see Keller "Methodist Newspapers and the Fugitive Slave Law," 322. See also Nye, *Fettered Freedom*, 266.

[9] Many recognized that the Constitution guaranteed the South some form of Fugitive Slave Law, but not one that endangered freedoms explicitly protected by that same document. Wisner, *Review of Lord's Sermon*, 30–1.

[10] *WCA*, 22 May 1850; Carter, *Reply to Hon. William Thomas' Exposition*, 5; Colver, *Fugitive Slave Bill*, 2; Lee, *Autobiography*, 321, 331–6. See also Wooster Parker, *Role of Duty*, 2.

[11] *WCA*, 4 June 1851; Daniels, *Gilbert Haven*, 41, 320–2; Foster, *Our Nation's Sins*, 27; William L. Roberts, *The Higher Law; or, The Law of the Most High; A Discourse* ... (Auburn, NY, 1851), 29–31; Arthur Dearing's essay on the Fugitive Slave Law, in John W. Lewis, *The Life, Labors and Travels of Elder Charles Bowles, of the Free Will Baptist Denomination* (Watertown, NY, 1851), 269–85. For Joshua Giddings's call for a resort to arms, see Jane H. Pease and William H. Pease, *Bound with them in Chains: A Biographical History of the Antislavery Movement* (Westport, Conn., 1972), 264–5.

[12] *WCA*, 13 Nov. 1850. The New York *Independent's* call for northerners peacefully to obstruct the law and for runaways to engage in self-defense to prevent recapture lost the paper 3,000 subscribers but won it 5,000 new, more radical readers. Bacon, *Leonard Bacon*, 341–3. The distinction between peaceable disobedience and violent resistance was commonly drawn. See, for example, the New School Presbyterian *Central Christian Herald*, reported in Norton, *Religious Newspapers*, 118–19; Vander Velde, "Diary of George Duffield," 31.

[13] *Oberlin Evangelist*, 23 Oct. 1850; Spear, *Law-abiding Conscience*, 20–6, 31–3; Love, *Slavery in its Relation to God*, 56; Collyer, *Review of Eell[s]'s Thanksgiving Sermon*, 13–14. See also Colver, *Fugitive Slave Bill*, 2; Proctor S. Campbell and other Old School Presbyterians, quoted in *WCA*, 6 Nov. 1850.

[14] *WCA*, 1 May 1850. Imprisonment for assisting fugitives was not an empty threat, as illustrated by the experience of Calvin Fairbank, a fearless Methodist elder whose underground railroad work along the Ohio river earned him two spells in jail, lasting over seventeen years in all. *Rev. Calvin Fairbank, passim*.

[15] For free-soil responses to the provisions for California, New Mexico, and Utah see, for example, *Oberlin Evangelist*, 13 Feb. 1850; J. Drummond to M. Simpson, 8 May 1850, Simpson Papers, LC; *WCA*, 6 March, 3 April, 1 May, 31 July, 11, 25 Sept. 1850; *CAJ*, 30 May 1850.

[16] *Oberlin Evangelist*, 4 June 1851, quoting from the annual report of the American and Foreign Anti-Slavery Society; *WCA*, 1, 22 May, 23 Oct., 6 Nov. 1850; Collyer, *Review of Eell[s]'s Thanksgiving Sermon*, 20.

[17] John Mason Peck, *The Duties of American Citizens: A Discourse, Preached in the State-House, Springfield, Illinois* ... (St Louis, Mo., 1851), 21–3; John C. Lord, *"The Higher Law" in its Application to the Fugitive Slave Bill: A Sermon on the Duties Men Owe to God and to Governments* ... (Buffalo, NY, 1851), 10–11; Grant, *Peter Cartwright*, 155–65; McKivigan, "Abolitionism and the American Churches," 354; *SCA*, 3 Jan. 1851; Henry A. Boardman, *The American Union: A Discourse Delivered on Thursday, December 12, 1859* ... (Philadelphia, 1851), 3–4. Most of the New School Presbyterian pastors in New York City were at this time conservatives on the slavery question, including the sometime abolitionist Samuel Hanson Cox, who feared agitation would split the church and – by extension – the Union. Dwyn Mecklin Mounger, "Samuel Hanson Cox: Anti-Catholic, Anti-Anglican, Anti-Congregational Ecumenist," *Journal of Presbyterian History*, 55 (Winter 1977), 353, 357.

[18] Boardman, *American Union*, 8–10, 15–19; George Duffield, *Our Federal Union; a Cause for Gratitude to God: A Thanksgiving Discourse* ... (Detroit, 1850), 9–11. For further paeans to the unique and inestimable blessings of a God-given Union, see, for example, George L. Prentiss, *The Obligations of American Patriotism: A Discourse Delivered in the Second Presbyterian Church, Newark, N.J.* ... (Newark, NJ, 1851), 21; William W. Eells, *Gratitude for Individual and National Blessings: A Discourse, Preached in the Second Presbyterian Church, Newburyport* ... (Newburyport, Mass., 1850), 5–18.

[19] Boardman, *American Union*, 8–10, 48–54; Lord, *"The Higher Law"*, 15. See also Charles Hodge, *Civil Government:*

reprinted from the *Princeton Review*, for January, *1851* (Princeton, NJ), 6.

[20] Duffield, *Our Federal Union*, 12–13; Boardman, *American Union*, 39–41; George F. Kettell, *A Sermon on the Duty of Citizens, with Respect to the Fugitive Slave Law* (White Plains, NY, 1851), 19.

[21] Prentiss, *Obligations of American Patriotism*, 25; Eells, *Gratitude for Individual and National Blessings*, 18–21; Lord, *"The Higher Law"*, 12–13; Hall, *Forty Years' Familiar Letters*, II, 111, 127; *CAJ*, 26 Dec. 1850 (George Peck, editorial); Boardman, *Daniel Webster*, 35.

[22] William P. Breed, *Discourse Mainly upon the Importance of the American Union: Delivered Thanksgiving Day, November 28, 1850* (Steubenville, Ohio, 1850), 7–10; Lord, *"The Higher Law"*, 14–15. See also Kettell, *Duty of Citizens*, 19; McKinney, *The Union Preserved; or, The Law-abiding Christian: A Discourse* (Philadelphia, 1851), 24.

[23] Spear, *Politico-Social Foundations*, 15–16; Ichabod S. Spencer, *Sermons... With a Sketch of his Life, by Rev. J.M. Sherwood* (2 vols, New York, 1855), 111; *CAJ*, 26 Dec. 1850; Peck, *Duties of American Citizens*, 20.

[24] Boardman, *American Union*, 36; Lord, *"The Higher Law"*, 6–9; John M. Krebs, *An American Citizen; a Discourse on the Nature and Extent of our Religious Subjection to the Government under which We Live...* (New York, 1851), 11, 13, 27–8; Peck, *Duties of American Citizens*, 8, 13; Prentiss, *Obligations of American Patriotism*, 14–17; McKinney, *The Union Preserved*, 5, 27–9; Bouton, *The Good Land*, 11–26; Hodge, *Civil Government*, 46. See also Kettell, *Duty of Citizens*, 5.

[25] Krebs, *An American Citizen*, 35–9; McKinney, *The Union Preserved*, 12–13, 19; Rev. John O. Fiske (Congregationalist of Bath, Maine), "The Duty of Obedience to the Laws," quoted in Calvin M. Clark, *American Slavery and Maine Congregationalists: A Chapter in the Development of Anti-Slavery Sentiment in the Protestant Churches of the North* (Bangor, Me., 1940), 156–7; Abel McEwen, *A Sermon Preached in the First Congregational Church, New London, Conn., on the Day of Thanksgiving, November 28, 1850* (New London, Conn., 1851), 6–7; Moses Stuart, *Conscience and the Constitution...* (Boston, 1850), 30–3. See also Hodge, *Civil Government*, 8; Peck, *Duties of American Citizens*, 18.

[26] John M. Krebs, *A Discourse on the Death of Zachary Taylor, Twelfth President of the United States...* (New York, 1850), 21; Magie, *God's Voice*, 8, 14; Adams, *Daniel Webster*, *passim*; William W. Eells, *A Discourse, Occasioned by the Death of Hon. Daniel Webster, Preached at Newburyport, Sunday, October 31, 1852* (Newburyport, Mass., 1852), *passim*. See also Boardman, *Daniel Webster*; Hitchcock, *Daniel Webster*; *Presbyterian Quarterly Review*, I (Dec. 1852), 363; Stuart, *Conscience and the Constitution*, 3–22.

[27] Peck, *The Duties of American Citizens*, 3–5 and *passim*; Boardman, *American Union*, 3; Krebs, *An American Citizen*, 3; Spencer, *Sermons*, 111–12; *WCA*, 29 Jan. 1851; "The Conspiracy of Fanaticism," *US Magazine and Democratic Review*, 26 (May 1850), 388–93; Stephen A. Douglas, *Speech... on the "Measures of Adjustment," Delivered in the City Hall Chicago, October 23, 1850*, 14–15.

[28] Spencer, *Sermons*, 111–12; Hall, *Forty Years' Familiar Letters*, II, 131; Bouton, *The Good Land*, 2–3; *SCA*, 3 Jan. 1851; *CAJ*, 19 Dec. 1850.

[29] Antislavery evangelicals sharply criticized what they regarded as a cosy alliance between conservative politicians and churchmen to keep "politics" out of the churches. See, for example, Matthew Simpson in *WCA*, 29 Jan. 1851; Grinnell, *Men and Events*, 51; George L. Prentiss, *A Discourse in Memory of Thomas Harvey Skinner* (New York [1871]), 66–7.

[30] *WCA*, 22 May 1850, 11 June, 13 Aug., 24 Sept., 5 Nov. 1851 (for Peck's speech at the Michigan Annual Conference).

[31] *CAJ*, 12, 26 Dec. 1850. See also Keller, "Methodist Newspapers and the Fugitive Slave Law," 331–6.

[32] McKinney, *The Union Preserved*, 25–7.

[33] J.E. Broome to I.L. Brookes, 2 July 1850, I.L. Brookes Papers, SHC; Brookes, *Defence of the South*, 48; *WCA*, 4

Sept., 27 Nov. 1850; *Knoxville Whig,* 5 Oct., 9 Nov. 1850.

[34] Brookes, *Defence of the South,* 36–7.

[35] *Ibid.,* 3–4, 36–7; W.I. Brookes to I.L. Brookes, 13 June 1850, I.L. Brookes Papers, SHC; J.C. Coit, *Eulogy on the Life, Character and Public Services of the Hon. John C. Calhoun, Pronounced by Appointment before the Citizens of Cheraw and Its Vicinity . . .* (Columbia, SC, 1850), 28.

[36] Coit, *Eulogy on Calhoun,* 26–8, 37–8; John C. Coit, *Discourse upon Governments, Divine and Human, Prepared by Appointment of the Presbytery of Harmony . . .* (Columbia, SC, 1853), 18–21; Brookes, *Defence of Southern Slavery,* 3–4.

[37] Coit, *Eulogy on Calhoun,* 28; Drury, *Scott,* 122; Coit, *Discourse upon Governments,* 36–7; Brookes, *Defence of the South,* 41. Even more conservative ministers who did not expressly advocate separation recognized that God might sanction the severing of political bonds. See, for example, Whitefoord Smith, *God, the Refuge of his People,* 14–15.

[38] Loveland, *Southern Evangelicals and the Social Order,* 257–8; John T. Hendrick, *Union and Slavery: A Thanksgiving Sermon, Delivered in the Presbyterian Church, Clarksville, Tennessee . . .* (Clarksville, Tenn., 1851); *Biblical Recorder,* 16 Nov. 1850; Hoge, *Moses Drury Hoge,* 138; Adger, *My Life and Times,* 201–2; Palmer, *Life of Thornwell,* 470, 477–8; B.M. Palmer to J. Thornwell, 10 Sept. 1850, Anderson–Thornwell Papers, SHC; James H. Thornwell, *Thoughts Suited to the Present Crisis: A Sermon, on Occasion of the Death of Hon. John C. Calhoun . . .* (Columbia, SC, 1850), 8, 25–6; Jacobs, *Committing of Our Cause to God,* 3–4; *WCA,* 5 March 1851; *Knoxville Whig,* 2 Nov. 1850, 15 Feb. 1851; *SCA,* 27 Sept. 1850; Holder, *Winans,* 184–90; Winans, *Henry Clay,* 9–15. Purifoy, "Southern Methodist Church and the Proslavery Argument," sees Andrew's article on "Southern Independence" as hostile to sectional peace, but in the context of South Carolinian politics his attack on

"ruthless demagogues" and call for peaceful remedies made him a force for the Union.

[39] Hendrick, *Union and Slavery,* 8–12; *Knoxville Whig,* 4 May, 17 Aug. 1850; *Dr. Breckinridge and the "Commonwealth",* 6; Valentine, Diary, 12 Feb. 1850, 8 Feb. 1851, 2 June 1852, SHC; Hilliard, *Speeches and Addresses,* 226–7; Thornwell, *Thoughts Suited to the Present Crisis,* 5, 7; J. Thornwell to J. Adger, 8 March 1850, quoted in Adger, *My Life and Times,* 202; Palmer, *Life of Thornwell,* 477–8; Jacobs, *Committing of Our Cause to God,* 4–5.

[40] Hendrick, *Union and Slavery,* 8, 10, 25–6; R.H. Morrison to J. Morrison, 29 April 1850, 1 Sept., 31 Oct. 1851, R.H. Morrison Papers, SHC; Palmer, *Life of Thornwell,* 470, 476–7; Valentine, Diary, 8, 12, 25 April, 26 June 1850, 11, 22 Jan., 25 April, 9 May, 2 Dec. 1851, SHC; *Biblical Recorder,* 26 Jan., 23 March 1850; *Knoxville Whig,* 2, 30 March, 4 May, 17, 24 Aug., 19 Oct., 30 Nov. 1850, 29 March, 10 May ("Civis"), 7 June 1851; Van Zandt, *God's Voice to the Nation,* 11–19; Henry W. Miller, *Eulogy on the Life and Character of Gen. Zachary Taylor, Delivered at the Request of the Citizens of Raleigh . . .* (Raleigh, NC, 1850), 14–16; Hilliard, *Speeches and Addresses,* 276–80, 411–44. Achitophel, David's traitorous counselor, was a synonym for treachery (2 Samuel 15).

[41] *Knoxville Whig,* 7 June 1851 ("Civis"); *SCA,* 13, 20 Dec. 1850; Curry, *Davis Wasgatt Clark,* 105–10; R.H. Morrison to J. Morison, 17 March 1851, R.H. Morrison Papers, SHC; Shields, *Discourse on Christian Politics,* 30. One antislavery minister complained that of the 30,000 ministers in the United States, fewer than one in a hundred publicly criticized the Fugitive Slave Law. Potter, *Impending Crisis,* 138.

[42] See, for example, *SCA,* 21 March, 11 April 1851; Valentine, Diary, 12 Feb. 1850, 4, 10 Jan., 11 March, 25 April 1851, SHC.

[43] *Oberlin Evangelist,* 18 June 1851; *WCA,* 12 Feb., 12, 19 March, 30 April

1851, 9 June, 25 Aug. 1852; *SCA*, 10 Dec. 1852. Northern Baptists and other Protestants made graphic use of the ghastly physical assault on Edward Mathews, agent of the American Baptist Free Mission Society in Kentucky and Virginia, and his expulsion by a lynch mob, to draw attention to the persecuting spirit of the slave power both inside and outside the churches. Foster, *Our Nation's Sins*, 15–20.

44 *Oberlin Evangelist*, 13 Aug. 1851, quoting *Zion's Herald*; *SCA*, 16 May, 6 June 1851. Most southern Methodists were by no means convinced at this stage of the wisdom of South Carolina's action, but the General Conference of the MECS was to expunge the antislavery Ninth Section (but not the General Rule on slavery) from the Discipline in 1854. *SCA*, 28 Feb. 1851; Jones, "The Years of Disagreement, 1844–61," 191.

45 Jones, "The Years of Disagreement, 1844–61," 177–80; *SCA*, 28 Nov. 1851, 5, 19 Nov. 1852; J.H. Davis to A.T.B. Davis, 17 Nov. 1851, Beale–Davis Papers, SHC; *WCA*, 24 Dec. 1851; Moody, *Life's Retrospect*, 227; Wesson G. Miller, *Thirty Years in the Itinerancy* (Milwaukee, 1875), 181.

46 The election of 1852 is discussed lucidly in Gienapp, *Origins of the Republican Party*, 13–35; Blue, *Free Soilers*, 232–68; Holt, *Political Crisis of the 1850s*, 96–8, 119–30; Sewell, *Ballots for Freedom*, 242–51; Cooper, *The South and the Politics of Slavery*, 322–41.

47 *Albany Evening Journal*, quoted in *Albany Argus*, 28 June 1852; *Scott and Graham Melodies*, 34.

48 *Albany Argus*, 2, 28, 30 June, 1 July, 18 Aug. 1852; *The Life and Public Services of Gen. Franklin Pierce, the Democratic Candidate for the Presidency of 1852. Also the Life and Public Services of the Hon. William R. King* ([Boston], 1852), 11, 13, 26–9; *The Democratic Text Book, Containing the Life of Franklin Pierce and a Biographical Sketch of Hon. William R. King . . .* (Philadelphia [1852]), 22–3; Nathaniel Hawthorne, *Life of Franklin Pierce* (Boston, 1852), 110–19.

49 *"Franklin Pierce and His Abolition Allies"* (n.p., 1852), 1–5; *The Contrast; The Whig and Democratic Platforms – the Whig and Democratic Candidates for the Presidency* (n.p. [1852]), 6, 26–7. Southern Whigs noted the "unholy coalition" of Democrats and Free Soilers in Massachusetts in 1851. *Knoxville Whig*, 17 May 1851; Valentine, Diary, 2 Dec. 1851, SHC.

50 Aaron V. Brown, *Speech of Governor A.V. Brown on the Issues of the Presidential Canvass . . . 6 August 1852* (Nashville, Tenn., 1852), 7; *The Whig-Abolitionist Attack! Whigs and Abolitionists against General Pierce* (n.p. [1852]), 1–2; *Democratic Text Book*, 43; Robert Toombs, *Speech . . . Touching the Approaching Presidential Election . . .* (Washington, DC, 1852); Meredith Gentry, *Speech . . . Vindicating His Course in the Late Presidential Election . . .* (Washington, DC, 1853); E.C. Cabell, *Speech . . . on Political Parties – Whig Congressional Caucus – the Presidency . . . June 12, 1852* (Washington [1852]); C.J. Faulkner, *Speech . . . on the Compromise – the Presidency – Political Parties . . .* (Washington, 1852), 15; *Letter from T.L. Clingman* (Raleigh, NC, 1852); James R. Morrill, "The Presidential Election of 1852: Death Knell of the Whig Party of North Carolina," *North Carolina Historical Review*, 44 (Oct. 1967), 348, 355; Valentine, Diary, 1 Nov. 1851, 26 June, 15/16 July, 11 Oct., 11 Nov. 1852, SHC; *The Contrast*, 17–18; B.F. Moore, "Speech . . . before the Young Mens' [*sic*] Scott and Graham Club, Raleigh, July 13th, 1852" (broadside).

51 Lewis, *Samuel Lewis*, 385–6, 398, 402–4; L. Tappan Journals, 27 Aug. 1852, Tappan Papers, LC; *Congregationalist*, quoted in *Oberlin Evangelist*, 4 Aug. 1852. For the conflict between Chase and Lewis within Ohio Free Soil see Blue, *Free Soilers*, 185–6; Stewart, *Giddings*, 202–3.

52 A. Willey to J.P. Hale, 19 Aug. 1852, quoted in Sewell, *Ballots for Freedom*, 246; Donald Bruce Johnson and Kirk H. Porter, *National Party Platforms*

1840–1972, (5th edn, Urbana, Ill., 1975), 18; Blue, *Free Soilers*, 242–3.

[53] *Religious Telescope*, quoted in Norton, *Religious Newspapers*, 120; *Oberlin Evangelist*, 18 Aug., 13, 27 Oct. 1852; Cheney, *Oren B. Cheney*, 73–5; Daniels, *Gilbert Haven*, 52.

[54] Sermons and addresses marking the deaths of Clay and Webster offer some measure of the broad acceptance – and even celebration – of the Compromise within evangelicalism at the time of the presidential campaign. See, for example, John C. Lord, *"Our Strong Rods Broken and Withered." A Discourse upon the Recent Decease of Calhoun, Clay and Webster*... (Buffalo, NY, 1852), 15, 18, 26; Richard H. Richardson, *National Bereavements: A Discourse*... (Chicago, 1852), 17–19; George W. Samson, *The Providence of God in Raising up under Republican Institutions, Great and Good Men as Our Rulers: A Discourse*... (Boston, 1853), 8–12; J.F. Stearns, *A Sermon Occasioned by the Death of Daniel Webster*... (Newark, NJ, 1852), 25–6; William A. Stearns, *The Great Lamentation: A Sermon in Commemoration of Daniel Webster, Delivered in Cambridge* (Boston, 1852), 24–7; Abraham B. Van Zandt, *The Voice of Years: A Sermon Occasioned by the Death of Henry Clay* (Petersburg, Va., 1852), 11–14; Thomas Williams, *A Discourse on the Conduct of God, in the Death of Great Men; Occasioned by the Death of Daniel Webster* (Providence, RI, 1858). For generous but ambivalent judgments, see George Duffield, *The American Patriot: An Eulogy Delivered on Occasion of the Funeral Obsequies of Hon. Henry Clay*... (Detroit, 1852), 31–2; Joseph Haven, *An Address Delivered before the Students of Amherst College, and the Citizens of the Town*... *Nov. 17, 1852* (Amherst, Mass., 1853), 25–7. For the acerbic comments of Joseph Gordon, editor of the *Free Presbyterian*, see Joseph Gordon, *Life and Writings of Rev. Joseph Gordon; Written and Compiled by a Committee of the Free Presbyterian Synod* (Cincinnati, 1860), 93–6.

[55] Blue, *Free Soilers*, 254–5 (citing the *National Era*); Sewell, *Ballots for Freedom*, 249; Fletcher, *Diary*, IV, 502–3 (I, 3 Nov. 1852); Howard, *Henry Clay Trumbull*, 81–100, 137–8. In Illinois and Maine, however, large numbers of Whig free soilers abstained. Gienapp, *Origins of the Republican Party*, 28.

[56] J.A. Bent to J. Blanchard, 19 Nov. 1852, Blanchard Papers, WC; Lewis, *Samuel Lewis*, 404; *Oberlin Evangelist*, 8 Dec. 1852; Blue, *Free Soilers*, 264; Benjamin W. Bacon, *Theodore Thornton Munger: New England Minister* (New Haven, Conn., 1913), 103–4; Mickey, *Huntington*, 37–8.

[57] Free Democrats treated Scott and the Whigs with more delicacy than Democrats, whom they regarded as primarily responsible for the Compromise. Blue, *Free Soilers*, 249–50.

[58] Sewell, *Ballots for Freedom*, 251. Immediately after the election Francis Wayland told a friend, "I think you may safely look on the Whig party as defunct" (Wayland and Wayland, *Francis Wayland*, I, 404).

[59] Price, *Holston Methodism*, III, 328–9; Coulter, *Brownlow*, 119; W.G. Brownlow to E.H. Foster, 28 Aug. 1852, Brownlow Papers, DU; *Knoxville Whig*, 7 Aug. 1850, 26 April, 9 Aug. 1851, 17 Jan., 14 Feb., 26 June, 3, 24 July, 7, 14, 28 Aug., 11 Sept., 30 Oct. 1852.

[60] *Knoxville Whig*, 16 Oct. 1852. See also A. Mangum to W.W. Mangum, 7 Nov. 1852, Mangum Family Papers, SHC.

[61] *Knoxville Whig*, 10 May 1851, 31 July 1852; *Oberlin Evangelist*, 8 Dec. 1852, quoting the *New York Tribune*; Valentine, *Diary*, 10 April 1852, SHC; Cooper, *The South and the Politics of Slavery*, 341–4.

Chapter 7 *The Collapse of the Second Party System: Protestant Insurgents and Know Nothing Millenialism*

[1] For immigration figures, see Potter, *Impending Crisis*, 241. Maldwyn A. Jones, *American Immigration* (Chicago, 1960), 92–176, discusses the character and impact of this first wave of mass im-

migration. See also *WCA*, 10 Nov. 1852; Gienapp, "Nebraska, Nativism, and Rum: The Failure of Fusion in Pennsylvania, 1854," *Pennsylvania Magazine of History and Biography*, 109 (Oct. 1985), 441; William G. Bean, "Puritan versus Celt, 1850–1860," *New England Quarterly*, 7 (1934), 70–1.

² F. Hemenway, "Oration," 4 July 1851, GTS; Alfred B. Ely, *American Liberty: Its Sources, Its Dangers, and Means of Preservation: An Oration . . .* (New York, 1850), 23–4; E.V. Levert to F.J. Levert, 24 March 1852, Levert Papers, SHC; *WCA*, 10 April 1850, 7 May 1851, 18 April 1855; Davis W. Clark, *Evils and Remedies of Intemperance: An Address* (New York, 1847), 6, 9, 14. See also *SCA*, 14 May 1847, 17 Jan. 1851; Joshua T. Tucker, *The Maine Law; or, Extermination the Only Cure for the Liquor Traffic: A Tract for the Times* (Holliston, Mass., 1852), 9–10; Harvey D. Kitchel, *An Appeal to the People for the Suppression of the Liquor Traffic* (New York, 1848), 30; William C. Hosmer, "The Prohibitory Liquor Law," *Methodist Quarterly Review*, 14 (April 1854), 248–50.

³ For concern over freethinking revolutionaries see, for example, Billington, *Protestant Crusade*, 328–30; *WCA*, 25 July 1855.

⁴ By the mid-1850s there were more Catholics than Protestants in St Louis (*WCA*, 27 June 1855). See also *SCA*, 17 May 1850.

⁵ G. Coles, Diary, 10 Feb. 1846, DU; Henry A. Boardman, *The Christian Ministry Not a Priesthood: A Sermon Preached at the Opening of the Sessions of the General Assembly of the Presbyterian Church . . .* (Philadelphia, 1855), 4–7, 14–49 and *passim*; *WCA*, 23 Jan., 18 Aug. 1850, 5 Feb. 1851; Rufus W. Clark, *Popery and the United States, Embracing an Account of Papal Operations in Our Country, with a View of the Dangers Which Threaten Our Institutions* (Boston, 1847), 14–15; T.M. Eddy, "The Claims of Romanism," *Methodist Quarterly Review*, 14 (Oct. 1854), 537–9; Nicholas Murray, *American Principles on National Prosperity: A Thanks-giving Sermon . . .* (New York, 1854), 25; Abraham B. Van Zandt, *A Sermon on the Romish Controversy, Its Present Aspect, and the Duty of the Church with Reference to It* (Columbia, SC, 1854), 13–14.

⁶ *Christian Watchman and Reflector*, 24 April, 15 May 1856; *WCA*, 9 Jan., 6 March 1850, 9 April, 5 Nov. 1851, 31 March 1852, 30 Nov., 28 Dec. 1853, 4, 11 Jan. 1854, 21 Feb., 23 May, 12 Dec. 1855; Daniel C. Eddy, *The Commonwealth. Political Rights of Ministers; A Sermon, Preached on Fast Day, April 6, 1854. The Times, and the Men for the Times; Sermons Preached on Sabbath Days, June 11 & 13, 1854* (Boston, 1854), 45; *CAJ*, 3 Jan. 1856; *New York Freeman's Journal*, 27 March, 10 April, 18 Sept. 1852, 29 Oct. 1853, 14 Oct. 1854; Tyrrell, *Sobering Up*, 299–300; Marsh, *Temperance Recollections*, 75; Valentine, Diary, 17 March 1851, SHC; *Independent*, 9 March 1854; Charles B. Boynton, *Address Before the Citizens of Cincinnati Delivered on the Fourth Day of July, 1855* (Cincinnati, 1855), 17–18.

⁷ Hughes's precise role is unclear, but Billington, *Protestant Crusade*, 292–3, sees his hand behind the renewed campaign in the fall of 1852.

⁸ Henry Clay Fish, *The School Question: Romanism and the Common Schools: A Discourse . . .* (New York, 1853), 4, 8–9, 13; Horace Bushnell, *Common Schools: A Discourse on the Modifications Demanded by the Roman Catholics . . .* (Hartford, Conn., 1853), 9; *WCA*, 10 Nov. 1852. See also Ely, *American Liberty*, 3, 7, 16; *Biblical Recorder*, 3, 17 Feb. 1854; *Memorial of Samuel Barstow*, 43–78; Boardman, *Daniel Webster*, 35–6; Boynton, *Address before the Citizens of Cincinnati*, 17–18; Anna E. Carroll, *The Great American Battle; or, The Contest between Christianity and Political Romanism* (New York, 1856), 104; Eddy, "Claims of Romanism," 550–1; Jean H. Baker, *Ambivalent Americans: The Know-Nothing Party in Maryland* (Baltimore, 1977), 18–19; Kaestle, *Pillars of the Republic*, 156–71.

⁹ *WCA*, 23 March 1853; *Christian Watchman and Reflector*, 17 April, 15 May 1856, 3 Sept. 1857. See also *WCA*, 8 Oct.

1851, 6, 27 Oct. 1852; *CAJ*, 21 June, 18 Oct. 1848; Boynton, *Oration before the Native Americans*, 24.

[10] Rufus W. Clark, *Popery and the United States*, 16–17; Nicholas Murray, *Special Causes of Gratitude: A Thanksgiving Sermon* ... (Elizabethtown, NJ, 1848), 11–12; *WCA*, 12 June 1850, 7 May 1851, 2 Feb. 1853.

[11] The Madiai case drew 3,000 outraged ministers and laity to a protest meeting in New York City's Metropolitan Hall. *WCA*, 19 Jan., 30 March 1853; Peterson, *Divine Discontent*, 180; *Letter of the Most Rev. Archbishop Hughes on the Madiai. Speech of Hon. Lewis Cass, on Religious Freedom Abroad. Letter of Archbishop Hughes, in Reply to General Cass, and in Self-Vindication* (Baltimore, 1854), 4–18.

[12] *WCA*, 16 Feb., 16 March 1853; W. Davis to R.B. Davis, 23 Oct. 1855, Beale–Davis Papers, SHC. For a broader contextualizing of American Protestants' struggle against Romanist despotism, see Baird, *The Noblest Freedom; or, The Influence of Christianity upon Civil Liberty: A Discourse* ... (New York, 1846), 11–30; Ely, *American Liberty*, 6–18; Boynton, *Oration before the Native Americans*, 3–18.

[13] Eddy, *The Commonwealth*, 40–1; *WCA*, 6 March 1850, 13 April 1853. For John Hughes's defense of the Pope's political course in 1848–49, see Henry J. Browne (ed.) "The Archdiocese of New York a Century Ago: A Memoir of Archbishop Hughes, 1838–1858," *United States Catholic Historical Society, Records and Studies*, 39–40 (1952), 171–2.

[14] Catholic hostility to Kossuth is evident in *New York Freeman's Journal*, 25 Oct., 1 Nov., 27 Dec. 1851, 31 Jan. 1852; N.M. Gaylord, *Kossuth and the American Jesuits: A Lecture Delivered in Lowell, Jan. 4, 1852* (Lowell, Mass., 1852). For evangelicals' "fever" over Kossuth and their turning him into a messianic figure, see J. McClintock to G.R. Crooks, 6 Dec. 1851, DU; W. Daily to M. Simpson, March 1852, M. Simpson Papers, LC; B.F. Tefft to D.P. Kidder, 15 Dec. 1851, Kidder Papers, GTS; Nathaniel West, *The*

Overturning of Tyrannical and Wicked Governments: A Sermon ... (Pittsburgh, 1852), 2 and *passim*; George Preston Mains, *James Monroe Buckley* (New York, 1917), 41; Lewis, *Elder Charles Bowles*, 269–85; William Henry Brisbane, *Lecture on the Character and Mission of Kossuth, Delivered before the Allentown Lyceum, January 29, 1852* (n.p. [1852]), 6–7; Hall (ed.) *Forty Years' Familiar Letters*, II, 166–7; Moody, *Life's Retrospect*, 227; *Oberlin Evangelist*, 4 Feb. 1852; *WCA*, 28 Jan., 18, 25 Feb. 1852. Fearing America's embroilment in overseas adventures, some evangelicals distanced themselves from the "presumptuous," "enthusiastic," wine-drinking Hungarian. See R.H. Morrison to J. Morrison, 1 Jan. 1852, R.H. Morrison Papers, SHC; *Knoxville Whig*, 24, 31 Jan. 1852; Valentine, Diary, 8, 12 Nov., 22, 31 Dec. 1851, 5 March 1852, SHC. The ex-priest Alessandro Gavazzi was similarly lionized on his turbulent American lecture tour (under the auspices of the American and Foreign Christian Union). See Billington, *Protestant Crusade*, 301–4; *WCA*, 12, 26 Oct. 1853, 11 Jan. 1854.

[15] Billington, *Protestant Crusade*, 295–300; *WCA*, 6 March 1850, 17 Dec. 1851, 7 April 1852, 21 Sept., 28 Dec. 1853, 25 Jan., 1 Feb., 26 April 1854, 20 June 1855; Henry M. Baird, *Life of the Rev. Robert Baird* (New York, 1866), 283–4; *Independent*, 9 Feb. 1854; *Biblical Recorder*, 17 Feb. 1854; Stritch, "Political Nativism in Cincinnati," 268–9. Billington, *Protestant Crusade*, 302–3, describes the ugly scenes that accompanied Bedini's visit.

[16] Brunson, *Western Pioneer*, II, 228–29; Clark, *Popery and the United States*, 12, 19; Eddy, *The Commonwealth*, 40–2; William P. Strickland, *The Life of Jacob Gruber* (New York, 1860), 347; *WCA*, 30 April 1851, 26 April, 15 Nov. 1854, 31 Jan. 1855; Murray, *American Principles on National Prosperity*, 42. See also Marlatt (ed.) *Stuart Letters*, I, 481–2.

[17] Clark, *Popery and the United States*, 3. Catholics claimed a population of 4 million in 1850, compared with a total Protestant church membership of 3.5

million. *New York Freeman's Journal*, 25 Dec. 1850.

[18] For Brownson's approach, see *Brownson's Quarterly Review*, 7 (April 1850), 267–8; 9 (Oct. 1852), 519–22; 11 (July 1854), 329–54; 11 (Oct. 1854), 447–87; 12 (Jan. 1855), 114–35; Thomas T. McAvoy, "The Formation of the Catholic Minority in the United States 1820–1860," *Review of Politics*, 10 (Jan. 1948), 25–30. Billington, *Protestant Crusade*, 289ff., believes Hughes and the Catholic hierarchy made a strategic blunder in adopting such an aggressive stance.

[19] John Hughes, *The Decline of Protestantism and its Cause: A Lecture Delivered . . . Nov 10th, 1850* (New York, 1851), 9, 14, 16–23, 25–6. During the 1850s a number of Catholic orders, including the Jesuits, Redemptorists, and Paulists, pursued missionary efforts and evangelical outreach into Protestantism, with enough success to inspire considerable optimism. Jay P. Dolan, *Catholic Revivalism: The American Experience, 1830–1900*, (Notre Dame, Ind., 1977), 1–112.

[20] *WCA*, 26 March, 2 April 1851, 5 April 1854; *CAJ*, 23 March 1854; Fish, *The School Question*, 20–6; Eddy, *The Commonwealth*, 45, 64; Fletcher, *Diary*, V, 29.

[21] *WCA*, 27 March, 3 April 1850, 5 Feb., 12, 19 March, 8 Oct. 1851, 31 March 1852, 9 Feb., 16 March, 6 April, 11 May 1853; Marlatt (ed.) *Stuart Letters*, I, 323–4, 451, 494; Coles, *My First Seven Years in America*, 37; Alexander T. McGill, *Popery the Punishment of Unbelief: A Sermon before the General Assembly of the Presbyterian Church . . .* (Philadelphia, 1848), 26; "Romanism and Protestantism," *Christian Review*, 44 (April 1851), 161–99. See also J. Rowland, *The Glorious Mission*, 15–21; James P. Stuart, *America and the Americans versus the Papacy and the Catholics: A Lecture . . .* (Cincinnati, 1853), 7; *Independent*, 5 Jan., 23 March, 20, 27 April 1854.

[22] Boynton, *Our Country*, 13; Hemenway, "Oration," 4 July 1851,

GTS; Nathan S.S. Beman, *Characteristics of the Age: A Discourse Delivered in the First Presbyterian Church, Troy, N.Y. . . .* (Troy, NY, 1851), 23–30; Thomas De Witt *et al.*, "Circular," July 1855, A. Bullard Papers, PHS; *WCA*, 4 Jan. 1854. See also Stuart, *America and the Americans*, 20.

[23] A. Barnes to A.H. Foote, 1 May 1851, DU.

[24] Support for temperance and hostility to immigrants (both Protestant and Catholic) were closely related; the anti-Catholic element in the movement grew increasingly evident once Catholic spokesmen excoriated the Maine Law and prohibitionism generally. Jed Dannenbaum, *Drink and Disorder: Temperance Reform in Cincinnati from the Washingtonian Revival to the WCTU* (Urbana, Ill., 1984), 106–55; Gienapp, *Origins of the Republican Party*, 44–5. But prohibitionists' targets also embraced native-born Protestants, including not only tipplers but those connected commercially with brewing and distilling, and often in full church membership.

[25] Nathan S.S. Beman, *The Crisis and the Triumph; or, The History and Present Attitude of the Temperance Cause: A Discourse . . .* (Troy, NY, 1846), 6–7, 29; *Independent*, 18 May 1854; Marsh, *Temperance Recollections*, 177–8; *CAJ*, 14 June, 23 Aug. 1848; *WCA*, 17 Sept., 8 Oct. 1851, 7 Jan., 11 Feb. 1852. See also, *The Law of Maine and the Law of God. Also a Review of Lovejoy's Lecture on Prohibitory Laws in Regard to the Use of Intoxicating Drinks . . .* (Boston, 1852), 20; Samuel T. Spear, *Law and Temperance: A Sermon* (New York, 1852), 23.

[26] Loveland, *Southern Evangelicals and the Social Order*, 153; C.W. Dabney to R.L. Dabney, 1 March 1842, Dabney Papers, SHC; Marsh, *Temperance Recollections*, 195; Ian Tyrrell, "Drink and Temperance in the Antebellum South: An Overview and Interpretation," *JSH*, 48 (Nov. 1982), 485–510; W.J. Rorabaugh, "The Sons of Temperance in Antebellum Jasper County," *Georgia Historical Quarterly*, 64 (Fall 1980), 266–9,

272; Charles C. Pearson and J. Edwin Hendricks, *Liquor and Anti-Liquor in Virginia, 1619–1919* (Durham, NC, 1967), 97–100; William A. Shaw, *The Firebell! Or an Apology for the Order of the Sons of Temperance* ... (Raleigh, NC, 1851), 5, 19–20, 42; *Biblical Recorder*, 27 Jan. 1854. For ambivalence and caution about teetotalism within southern evangelicalism see, for example, *SCA*, 19 April 1850, 22 July 1853; Pearson and Hendricks, *loc. cit.*, 103–9, 117–20, 144–50. For the uneasy relationship between many temperate evangelicals (north and south) and the various fraternal temperance orders, with their secrecy, regalia, and echoes of Freemasonry and Catholicism, see Valentine, Diary, 27 Oct. 1847, 17 Nov. 1852, SHC; *Biblical Recorder*, 6 Jan., 24 March 1854; *Knoxville Whig*, 15 June 1850, 15 March, 14 June, 25 Oct. 1851, 21 Feb., 29 May, 27 Nov. 1852; Marsh, *Temperance Recollections*, 230–2; Tyrrell, *Sobering Up*, 211–14; A. Barnes to A.H. Foote, 1 May 1851, DU; Joseph Schafer, "Prohibition in Early Wisconsin," *Wisconsin Magazine of History*, 8 (March 1925), 293; Dannenbaum, "The Crusader: Samuel Cary and Cincinnati Temperance," *Cincinnati Historical Society Bulletin*, 33 (1975), 142.

[27] *CAJ*, 5 June 1829; "The Origin, Nature, Principles and Prospects of the Temperance Reform," *American Quarterly Observer*, 3 (July 1834), 46; Tyrrell, *Sobering Up*, 196–9, 208–10; Loveland, *Southern Evangelicals and the Social Order*, 153–7; James B. Sellers, *The Prohibition Movement in Alabama, 1701 to 1943* (Chapel Hill, NC, 1943), 36; Blanchard, *Sermons and Addresses*, 15–23; Lee, *Autobiography*, 233. See also Luther Lee, *A Sermon for the Times: Prohibitory Laws* (New York, 1852). For other early evangelical calls to political action see *Christian Examiner*, 18 (March 1835), 30–50; Thomas P. Hunt, *Address ... on the Duty of Temperance Men at the Ballot Box* (Philadelphia, 1838); *A Review of Mr Lovejoy's "Lecture on the Subject of Prohibitory Laws, in Regard to the Use of Intoxicating Drinks": by a Citizen of Maine*

(Boston, 1852), 9–10 (for E.N. Kirk); Tyrrell, "Drink and Temperance," 488 (for Josiah Flournoy); Enoch Pond, *Autobiography of Rev. Enoch Pond, D.D. for Fifty Years Professor at Bangor Theological Seminary* (Boston, 1883), 106–8; *Proceedings of the Mass. State Temperance Convention, held in Boston, February 12, 1840* (Boston, 1840), 3–27; Pilcher, *Elijah H. Pilcher*, 115–20; Sellers, *Prohibition Movement in Alabama*, 32.

[28] Marsh, *Temperance Recollections*, 84, 98, 119, 136; *New York Evangelist*, 11 July 1844; *CAJ*, 6 Dec. 1848, 11 Jan. 1849; Tyrrell, *Sobering Up*, 214–15; Pearson and Hendricks, *Liquor and Anti-Liquor in Virginia*, 122–40; T.M. Eddy, undated cutting from *Madison Courier*, T.M. Eddy Papers, GTS; *WCA*, 10 April, 9 Oct. (quotation) 1850; Alexander T. McGill, *A Sermon for the Times: Preached in the Second Presbyterian Church, Pittsburgh, September 18th, 1853* (Pittsburgh, 1853), 16–17; Clark, *Evils and Remedies of Intemperance*, 11, 13–15; Thomas A. Goodwin, *Seventy-Six Years' Tussle with the Traffic; Being a Condensation of the Laws Relating to the Liquor Traffic in Indiana from 1807 to 1883* ... (Indianapolis, 1883), 8–9; Mark Hopkins et al., *Address to the People of Massachusetts, on the Present Condition and Claims of the Temperance Reformation* (Boston, 1846), 11–12; *The Law of Maine and the Law of God*, 13.

[29] Beman, *The Crisis and the Triumph*, 23; *CAJ*, 21, 28 June 1848; *The Law of Maine and the Law of God*, 6, 11. See also Clark, *Evils and Remedies of Intemperance*, 14; Lee, *Sermon for the Times*, 6.

[30] W.J. Rorabaugh, "Prohibition as Progress: New York State's License Elections, 1846," *Journal of Social History*, 14 (Spring 1981), 427, 431; Marsh, *Temperance Recollections*, 135–40, 242–3; *WCA*, 28 May, 22 Oct. 1851. For similar complaints against new laws in Michigan and Vermont, see *WCA*, 30 July, 3 Sept. 1851.

[31] Cheney, *Oren B. Cheney*, 64–5; Stephen Allen, *The Life of Rev. John Allen, Better Known as "Camp Meeting John"* (Boston, 1888), 97–8; *WCA*, 16 July, 20

Aug. 1851, 14 April 1852; S.W.S. Dutton, "The Maine Temperance Law," *New Englander*, 10 (1852), 76; J. Spencer Kennard, *Joseph H. Kennard, D.D: A Memorial* (Philadelphia, 1867), 162–4. See Frank L. Byrne, *Prophet of Prohibition: Neal Dow and His Crusade* (Madison, Wisc., 1961), 27–46, for the genesis and passage of the Maine Law.

[32] Spear, *Law and Temperance*, 12, 15, 16; Hosmer, "Prohibitory Liquor Law," 247–58; Kitchel, *Appeal to the People*, 24–31; Henry M. Dexter, *Temperance Duties of the Temperate: A Discourse Delivered before the Boston Young Men's Total Abstinence Society . . .* (Boston, 1850), 17; *WCA*, 22 Oct., 10 Dec. 1851; *The Law of Maine and the Law of God*, 4; *CAJ*, 13 Oct. 1852; Tucker, *The Maine Law*. For a sharp scriptural critique of the law, see Hall (ed.) *Forty Years' Familiar Letters*, II, 170.

[33] Valentine, Diary, 17 Nov. 1852, SHC; *WCA*, 24 Dec. 1841, 4 Sept., 9 Oct. 1850, 19 March, 16, 23 April 21 May, 11, 18 June 1851, 21 April, 8 Dec. 1852; *Pittsburgh Christian Advocate*, 28 May 1840; *CAJ*, 31 Dec. 1845, 15 July 1846, 12 June 1849; *Oberlin Evangelist*, 19 Dec. 1849, 21 May 1851; *Samuel Aaron, His Life, Sermons, Correspondence, etc.* (Norristown, Pa., 1890), 120–21; Dannenbaum, *Drink and Disorder*, 97–8. Gienapp, *Origins of the Republican Party*, 52, suggests the extraordinary capacity of the temperance issue to mobilize those who hitherto had voted infrequently or not at all.

[34] *SCA*, 16 Aug. 1850; Dan E. Clark, "The History of Liquor Legislation in Iowa, 1846–1861," *Iowa Journal of History and Politics*, 6 (Jan. 1908), 68–9; *WCA*, 9 July, 22 Oct., 19, 26 Nov. 1851, 29 Sept. 1852; *CAJ*, 12 July 1849. Dannenbaum, *Drink and Disorder*, 98–99, indicates the divisions amongst Cincinnati's temperance activists on independent political action in 1851.

[35] Holt, *Political Crisis*, 101–38; Gienapp, *Origins of the Republican Party*, 37–67. Gienapp, while essentially accepting Holt's argument regarding the "loss" of issues and the parties' failure to find new ones, asks more searchingly why Whigs suffered greater damage than Democrats from the growth of new ethnocultural issues. As the likelier repository of extreme nativism and of Yankee moral uplift, Whigs were much more vulnerable to voter disaffection over these questions.

[36] Gienapp, *Origins of the Republican Party*, 44–60; Paul Kleppner, *Third Electoral System*, 67–70.

[37] Rorabaugh, "Prohibition as Progress," 431–32, 442; *Knoxville Whig*, 2 July 1853.

[38] "The Maine Liquor Law," *Democratic Review*, 30 (March 1852), 273, 541; *Knoxville Whig*, 21 May 1853. Virginia Democrats denounced temperance societies as "damnableness." Pearson and Hendricks, *Liquor and Anti-Liquor*, 140.

[39] Gienapp, *Origins of the Republican Party*, 47–52; Byrne, *Prophet of Prohibition*, 42–46. See Kevin Sweeney, "Rum, Romanism, Representation and Reform: Coalition Parties in Massachusetts, 1847–1853," 116–37, for Democratic disunity in Massachusetts.

[40] Formisano, *Mass Political Parties*, 116–17, 230; Pearson and Hendricks, *Liquor and Anti-Liquor*, 137–8; John F. Reynolds, "Piety and Politics: Evangelism in the Michigan Legislature, 1837–1860," *Michigan History*, 61 (Winter 1977), 328–32; Sweeney, "Rum, Romanism, Representation and Reform," 129–32 (for "wet" Whiggery in Massachusetts); Rorabaugh, "Prohibition as Progress," 433; Gienapp, "Nebraska, Nativism, and Rum," 426; *Knoxville Whig*, 21 May 1853, quoting *Nashville True Whig*, 11 May 1853; Daniel Jay Whitener, "History of the Temperance Movement in North Carolina 1715 to 1908" (PhD diss., University of North Carolina at Chapel Hill, 1932), 97–8.

[41] Seward, *The True Greatness of Our Country*; Van Deusen, *William Henry Seward*, 67–71; Vincent Peter Lannie, "William Seward and Common School Education," *History of Education Quarterly*, 4 (Sept. 1964), 181–92; Richard Hildreth,

Native-Americanism Detected and Exposed (Boston, 1845); Bean, "Puritan Versus Celt 1850–1860," 71–9; Purcell and Poole, "Political Nativism in Brooklyn," 35; Gienapp, *Origins of the Republican Party*, 60–4; Formisano, *Mass Political Parites*, 223–9.

[42] D.W. Bartlett, *The Life of Gen. Franklin Pierce, of New Hampshire, the Democratic Candidate for President of the United States* (Auburn, NY, 1852), 24–5, 86, 127–34, 241–3; Hawthorne, *Franklin Pierce*, 11, 15, 46, 132; *Sketches of the Lives of Franklin Pierce and W.R. King . . .* (Boston [1852]), 7, 28; *The Life of Gen. Frank Pierce, the Granite Statesman . . . By Hermitage* (New York, 1852), 21, 39; *Life of Gen. Franklin Pierce, the Democratic Candidate for President* (Trenton, NJ, 1852), 4, 7–8; *Life and Public Services of Gen. Franklin Pierce*, 10, 18, 30; *Democratic Text Book*, 10; William J. Cotter, *My Autobiography*, (Nashville, Tenn., 1971), 133; *SCA*, 1 April 1853; Fuller and Green, *God in the White House*, 92–5. See also Stephen M. Vail, *Life in Earnest; or, Memoirs and Remains of Rev. Zenas Caldwell, A.B., First Principal of the Maine Wesleyan Seminary* (Boston, 1855), 56–61. Democrats called Scott a hypocrite for fighting a duel, declining another (against Andrew Jackson) on religious grounds, and then challenging Governor Clinton, between 1809 and 1820. *Albany Argus*, 9, 20 July 1852.

[43] Hawthorne, *Franklin Pierce*, 119–26; *Life and Public Services of Gen. Franklin Pierce*, 25; *Democratic Text Book*, 21, 40–1; *Life of Gen. Franklin Pierce*, 14–16; Bartlett, *Life of Gen. Franklin Pierce*, 191–207; *Albany Argus*, 2, 9, 10, 24, 25 June, 3, 5, 12, 16, 20, 29 July, 7, 11 Aug., 22, 23 Oct. 1852; *Papers for the People: To Be Issued Weekly during the Campaign, under the Patronage of the Entire Democratic Delegation in Congress* (New York [1852]), 78; *Life of Gen. Frank Pierce*, 55–6, 64; *Memoir of General Scott, from Records Contemporaneous with the Events* (Washington, 1852), 16–18.

[44] *Life of General Scott* (New York [1852]), 16–19, 20–31; *Scott and Graham*

Melodies, 34, 38, 47; Edward D. Mansfield, *The Life of General Winfield Scott, Embracing His Campaign in Mexico* (New York, 1848), 414; *Life and Public Services of Winfield Scott, General-in-Chief of the Army of the United States* (Philadelphia, 1852), 22–3; *Albany Argus*, 12, 15, 17 June, 1 Nov. 1852; *New York Freeman's Journal*, 3 July 1852. See also *Life of Gen. Franklin Pierce*, 8, 45; *Democratic Text Book*, 35–6.

[45] *Albany Argus*, 27 Sept., 6, 21, 22, 26 Oct. 1852 1852; J.T. Headley, *The Lives of Winfield Scott and Andrew Jackson* (New York, 1852), 27–9; *Life of General Scott*, 2–7, 9–14, 30; *Life and Public Services of Scott*, 28–30; *The Contrast*, 6–7, 28; *Democratic Text Book*, 38–9. See also Heale, *Presidential Quest*, 127–9, 183, 203. For a Whig appeal to Catholic conservatism and respectability, see Charles O. Gorman, *An Irish Catholic Whig to his Fellow Countrymen in the United States* (Providence, RI, 1852), 2.

[46] William E. Robinson, *Franklin Pierce and Catholic Persecution in New Hampshire . . .* (n.p. [1852]), 10; *Albany Argus*, 14 (quotation), 30 Aug., 11 Sept. 1852; *New York Freeman's Journal*, 2 Oct. 1852. For Whig attempts to exploit Irish-Americans' anti-British feeling by likening the New Hampshire religious test to English penal enactments, see Gorman, *An Irish Catholic Whig*, 3–4. Gienapp, *Origins of the Republican Party*, 24, indicates that Hughes privately supported Scott.

[47] *WCA*, 23 April 1852; *Albany Argus*, 9, 10, 17 June, 1 July, 3, 6, 7, 12, 14, 16, 24, 30 Aug., 1, 2, 12 Oct. 1852; *The Whig Charge of Religious Intolerance against the New Hampshire Democracy and General Franklin Pierce* (Boston [1852]), 9, 21–3; *Democratic Text Book*, 40–1; Stephen A. Douglas, *Speech . . . Delivered in Richmond, Virginia, July 9, 1852* (n.p. [1852]), 4–5.

[48] *Knoxville Whig*, 28 Feb. (quotation), 3, 17 July, 21, 28 Aug., 4 Sept., 25 Oct., 20 Nov. (quotation) 1852; I. Newton to M. Fillmore, 13 Nov. 1852, M.N. Everly to M. Fillmore, 1 Feb. 1853, M. Fillmore Papers [WEGT]; Gienapp, *Origins of the Republican Party*, 25–6, 30;

Holt, *Forging a Majority*, 106, 108; Fletcher, *Diary*, IV, 470–1, 494 (19 Aug., 13 Oct. 1852).

[49] Van Zandt, *The Romish Controversy*, 26; *CAJ*, 19 Jan., 6, 27 Sept. 1848; Colwell, *Politics for American Citizens*, 51–71; Elisha Lord Cleaveland, *A Discourse Occasioned by the Death of Hon. Daniel Webster* . . . (New Haven, Conn., 1852), 10–12; Eddy, *The Commonwealth*, 49, 63; *WCA*, 4 May, 21 Dec. 1853, 1 Feb. 1854; Gienapp, "Nebraska, Nativism, and Rum," 442–3; McClure, *Old Time Notes*, I, 205; *Knoxville Whig*, 9 Dec. 1854; *Baltimore Clipper* and *Pennsylvania Telegraph*, quoted in *Biblical Recorder*, 21 Sept. 1854. See also Eddy, "Claims of Romanism," 551; Burchard, *Causes of National Solicitude*, 10–12, 22; James S. Smart, *Political Duties of Christian Men and Ministers: A Sermon for the Times* . . . (Detroit, 1854), 2 ("An attempt has been made entirely to expel God and Conscience from our political affairs").

[50] *WCA*, 17 Aug. 1853. For the Free Soilers' near-universal support for prohibition and the Maine Law, see Gienapp, *Origins of the Republican Party*, 47, 50, 52–4, 56; Floyd B. Streeter, "History of Prohibition Legislation in Michigan," *Michigan History*, 2 (April 1918), 296–7; Sweeney, "Rum, Romanism, Representation and Reform," 128–9.

[51] *WCA*, 31 Aug. 1853.

[52] For the themes of this paragraph, see Smith, *Liberty and Free Soil Parties in the Northwest*, 269–77; Gienapp, *Origins of the Republican Party*, 56–60; Dannenbaum, "The Crusader: Samuel Cary," 146–9; *WCA*, 15, 29 June, 24 Aug., 7, 14 Sept., 19 Oct., 2, 9 Nov.; Lewis, *Samuel Lewis*, 65–7, 405–16; Dannenbaum, *Drink and Disorder*, 122–48.

[53] Quoted in *Independent*, 19 Jan. 1854.

[54] Formisano, *Mass Political Parties*, 237–8; Frank L. Byrne, "Maine Law versus Lager Beer: The Dilemma of Wisconsin's Young Republican Party," *Wisconsin Magazine of History*, 42 (Winter 1958–59), 115. Schafer, "Prohibition in Early Wisconsin," 296–7, discusses the continuing animus of Wisconsin prohibitionists towards old-line politicians.

[55] *WCA*, 29 Dec. 1852, 12 Jan., 15 June 1853, 5 April, 21 June 1854; Goodwin, *Seventy-Six Years' Tussle with the Traffic*, 9–14; Fletcher, *Diary*, IV, 383–410; V, xviii, 47–52, 210–13. For similar prohibitionist threats to the major political parties in Minnesota, see *WCA*, 7 April 1852.

[56] W.E. Caldwell to AHMS secretaries, 1 March 1853, 28 Feb. 1855, AHMS Papers; Fitzgerald, *John B. McFerrin*, 239–52; *Knoxville Whig*, 8, 15 Jan., 26 Feb., 5 March, 23 April, 16 July, 6, 13, 20 Aug., 3 Sept. (quotation), 24 Sept., 26 Nov., 31 Dec. (quotation) 1853, 7, 14 Jan., 28 Oct., 4 Nov. 1854; *Dr Breckinridge and the "Commonwealth"*, *passim*; B. Mills to D.B. Coe, 10 Jan., 14 Oct. 1853, 1 Jan. 1854, B. Mills to M. Badger, 1 March 1853, G.W. Nicholls to D.B. Coe, 3 Feb. 1854, AHMS Papers; *WCA*, 15 March, 20 Dec. 1854; Douglas Bowers, "Ideology and Political Parties in Maryland 1851–1856," *Maryland Historical Magazine*, 64 (Fall 1969), 205–9; *Independent*, 23 Feb. 1854; H.A. Scomp, *King Alcohol in the Realm of King Cotton* (n.p., 1888), 495–516; Rorabaugh, "Sons of Temperance in Antebellum Jasper County," 275; *SCA*, 9 March 1855.

[57] Gienapp, *Origins of the Republican Party*, 147–58; G. Coles, Diary, 5, 8 Nov. 1853, DU; Marsh, *Temperance Recollections*, 278; P.H. Fowler, *Historical Sketch of Presbyterianism within the Bounds of the Synod of Central New York* (Utica, NY, 1877), 649–50; Alonzo C. Morehouse, *Autobiography of A.C. Morehouse, an Itinerant Minister of the New York and New York East Conferences of the Methodist Episcopal Church* (New York, 1895), 43–4; *WCA*, 8 Nov. 1854.

[58] Marsh, *Temperance Recollections*, 280–3; Gienapp, *Origins of the Republican Party*, 158–60; William J. Rorabaugh, "Rising Democratic Spirits: Immigrants, Temperance, and Tammany Hall, 1854–1860," *CWH*, 22 (June, 1976), 149–51; John A. Krout, "The Maine Law in New

York Politics," *New York History*, 17 (July, 1936), 260–72. During 1855 New York, Indiana, Delaware, Iowa, New Hampshire, and the territory of Nebraska joined the list of northern and western states that had already passed prohibition laws: Maine itself (in 1851); Massachusetts, Minnesota, Rhode Island, and Vermont (all 1852); Michigan (1853); and Connecticut (1854). Tyrrell, *Sobering Up*, 260; August F. Fehlandt, *A Century of Drink Reform in the United States* (New York, 1904), 125–30.

[59] Formisano, *Mass Political Parties*, 222–9; E.E. Stuart to her son, 26 Feb., 12 March 1853, in Marlatt (ed.) *Stuart Letters*, I, 481, 491; *WCA*, 18 May, 27 July 1853; *SCA*, 25 Nov, 1853; Bowers, "Ideology and Political Parties in Maryland," 202–5.

[60] Gienapp, *Origins of the Republican Party*, 62–4; Dannenbaum, *Drink and Disorder*, 117–22; *WCA*, 9, 23 March, 13 April 1853; Fish, *The School Question*, 19–20.

[61] *WCA*, 12 March 1841, 8 April, 18 Nov. (quotation) 1842; *Baptist Banner and Western Pioneer*, quoted in *Catholic Telegraph*, 30 Nov. 1844; Boynton, *Oration Before the Native Americans*, 24; Holt, *Forging a Majority*, 110–13.

[62] Sisco, *Political Nativism*, 62–83, 97–8; Gienapp, *Origins of the Republican Party*, 100–1; Gienapp, "Nebraska, Nativism, and Rum," 450–1, 455; Larry Anthony Rand, "The Know-Nothing Party in Rhode Island: Religious Bigotry and Political Success," *Rhode Island History*, 23 (Oct. 1964), 102–16; Mulkern, "Know-Nothing Party in Massachusetts," 75–115; Constance Mary Gay, "The Campaign of 1855 in Virginia and the Fall of the Know-Nothing Party," *Richmond College Historical Papers*, 1 (June 1916), 323; *Knoxville Whig*, 2 June 1855; Philip Morison Rice, "The Know-Nothing Party in Virginia 1854–1856," *Virginia Historical Magazine*, 55 (1947), 61–75, 159–67. For an overview see Holt, "Antimasonic and Know Nothing Parties," 593–620, and Holt, *Political Crisis of the 1850s*, 156–70. For Know

Nothings in the South see W. Darrell Overdyke, *The Know Nothing Party in the South* (Baton Rouge, La., 1950).

[63] "Massachusetts Journal of the House," Massachusetts State House, 1730 (21 May 1855); Hall (ed.) *Forty Years' Familiar Letters*, II, 208; *SCA*, 12 Jan. 1855; *WCA*, 2 Aug., 22 Nov. 1854.

[64] *Knoxville Whig*, 7 Oct. 1854. See Valentine, Diary, 11 Nov., 15 Dec. 1854, 26, 27 Jan. 1855, SHC, for a similarly enthusiastic response from another ex-Whig.

[65] E.R. Ames to M. Simpson, 24 June 1854, M. Simpson Papers, LC; *WCA*, 26 July 1854; Samuel D. Baldwin, *Armageddon; or the Overthrow of Romanism and Monarchy: the Existence of the United States Foretold in the Bible*... (Cincinnati, 1845). By the mid-1850s this and subsequent printings had sold over 10,000 copies.

[66] For economic emphases in the interpretation of Know Nothingism, see Holt, "Antimasonic and Know Nothing Parties," 598–600. Robert William Fogel, *Without Consent or Contract: The Rise and Fall of American Slavery* (New York, 1989), 354–69, points to the influence of hidden economic depression on nativist developments in the 1850s. See also Bridges, *A City in the Republic*, 90–8; Robert Ernst, "Economic Nativism in New York City during the 1840s," *New York History*, 29 (April 1948), 170–86.

[67] Ely, *American Liberty* (repr. 1854), 27–8, 30; George Robertson, *The American Party: Its Principles, Its Objects and Its Hopes* (Lexington, Ky., 1855), 4, 10–12; J. Morrison to R.L. Dabney, 28 June 1855, Dabney Papers, SHC; Harry J. Carman and Reinhard H. Luthin, "Some Aspects of the Know-Nothing Movement Reconsidered," *South Atlantic Quarterly*, 39 (April 1940), 221–2; Rice, "Know-Nothing Party in Virginia," 62–5; Ralph A. Wooster, "An Analysis of the Texas Know Nothings," *Southwestern Historical Quarterly*, 70 (Jan. 1947), 417–18. See also Palmer, *Life of Thornwell*, 479; Franklin [pseud.], *Know Nothingism; or, The American Party* (Boston, 1855), 15.

[68] Gienapp, *Origins of the Republican Party*, 93–100, though not ignoring the element of class protest in Know Nothingism, adopts this emphasis. See also Mulkern, "Know-Nothing Party in Massachusetts"; Virginia C. Purdy, "Portrait of a Know-Nothing Legislature: The Massachusetts General Court of 1855" (PhD diss., George Washington University, 1970), 103–4; Bean, "Puritan versus Celt." California forms an important exception to the rule of anti-Catholic animation. Peyton Hurt, "The Rise and Fall of the 'Know Nothings' in California," *California Historical Society Quarterly*, 9 (1930), 16–49, 99–128; Leonard Pitt, "The Beginnings of Nativism in California," *Pacific Historical Review*, 30 (1961), 23–38; R.A. Burchell, *The San Francisco Irish 1848–1880* (Manchester, UK, 1979), 4, 125–33, 181–3.

[69] *New York Freeman's Journal*, 18 Aug. 1855, quoting the Montgomery *Advertiser*. Josiah Grinnell recollected Independence Day celebrations in Iowa in 1854 when in a roll of the states and foreign nations silence fell at the naming of Ireland; an American explained "There is not an Irishman within ten miles of here," whereupon an ardent Methodist politician "jumped up and clapped his hands shouting 'Bless the Lord! Bless the Lord!'" (Grinnell, *Men and Events*, 105–6).

[70] Franklin, *Know Nothingism*, 9–12; Anna E. Carroll, *The Romish Church Opposed to the Liberties of the American People, with a Biographical Sketch of the Hon. Erastus Brooks* ... (Boston, 1856), 3–4; Boynton, *Address before the Citizens of Cincinnati*, 5–6 and *passim*; *Knoxville Whig*, 17 Feb., 27 Oct. 1855; Warren F. Hewitt, "The Know Nothing Party in Pennsylvania," *Pennsylvania History*, 2 (April 1935), 73; Milwaukee *Daily American*, 4 Oct. 1855, quoted in Joseph Schafer, "Know-Nothingism in Wisconsin," *Wisconsin Magazine of History*, 8 (Sept. 1924), 14; Nicholas Murray, *American Principles on National Prosperity*, 22; *WCA*, 25 Oct., 27 Dec. 1854. For proposals to exclude all but native-born Protestants from public office, see Robert D. Parmet, "Connecticut's Know-Nothings: A Profile," *Connecticut Historical Society Bulletin*, 31 (July 1966), 84.

[71] For an emphasis on the limits to southern anti-Catholicism see, for example, Arthur W. Thompson, "Political Nativism in Florida, 1848–1860: A Phase of Anti-Secessionism," *JSH*, 15 (Feb. 1949), 49–53; Gay, "The Campaign of 1855 in Virginia," 328; James H. Broussard, "Some Determinants of Know-Nothing Electoral Strength in the South, 1856," *Louisiana History*, 7 (Winter 1966), 5. For the contention that there was no significant anti-Catholicism amongst Know Nothings in Louisiana, where Catholics were received into the Order, see Arthur C. Cole, "Nativism in the Lower Mississippi Valley," *Mississippi Valley Historical Association Proceedings*, 6 (June 1912–13), 272; Overdyke, *Know Nothing Party in the South*, 218–33. But it is more likely that party members distinguished between upper-class Creoles, whom they accepted, and more recent Irish and German Catholic immigrants, whom they did not: see Robert Reinders, "The Louisiana American Party and the Catholic Church," *Mid-America*, 40 (Oct. 1958), 218–28.

[72] D.J. Baldwin to S.J. Baird, April 1853, S.J. Baird Papers, LC; *SCA*, 10 Nov. 1854, quoting the *Boston Traveller*; *Biblical Recorder*, 24 Feb. 1854. For appeals to anti-Romanism in Florida, Tennessee, Virginia and North Carolina, see J.B. Cottrell, Diary, 20 Feb., 9 Nov. 1855, SHC; Robertson, *The American Party*, 2–3 and *passim*; Gay, "The Campaign of 1855 in Virginia," 328–9; Jeffrey, "National Issues, Local Interests," 67; Kenneth Rayner, *Reply of Hon. Kenneth Rayner, to the Manifesto of Hon. Henry A. Wise* (Washington, DC, 1855), *passim*; J.L. Chapman, *Americanism versus Romanism: or, The Cis-Atlantic Battle between Sam and the Pope* (Nashville, Tenn., 1856), *passim*.

[73] *Thoughts for the People of Virginia, in the Present Conflict between the Ancient*

Principles of Virginia Republican Politics, and the New Ism and Secret System of Tactics which Northern Know Nothings and Abolitionists are Foisting upon Them . . . (?Richmond, Va. [1855]), 23–31; J. Morrison to R.L. Dabney, 28 June 1855, Dabney Papers, SHC. Morrison's son-in-law, Benjamin Mosby Smith, shared his perception of Rome as the Antichrist. Flournoy, Benjamin Mosby Smith, 56. See also Valentine, Diary, 26, 27 Jan. 1855, SHC.

74 Knoxville Whig, 3 March 1855; Louisville Daily Courier, quoted in New York Freeman's Journal, 4 Aug. 1855. See also Fletcher, Diary, V, 251, 253; J. Morrison to R.L. Dabney, Dabney Papers, SHC; Henry Winter Davis, The Origin, Principles and Purposes of the American Party (n.p., 1855), 5–15; Frederick R. Anspach, The Sons of the Sires: A History of the Rise, Progress, and Destiny of the American Party . . . (Philadelphia, 1855), 29, 46–7, 89–92.

75 E.R. Ames to M. Simpson, 24 June 1854, M. Simpson Papers, LC; WCA, 25 Oct. 1854; Franklin, Know Nothingism, 14; Eddy, The Commonwealth, 51–2; Ely, American Liberty, 35, 38; The Know Nothing Almanac; or, True Americans' Manual, for 1855 (n.p., n.d.), 30; Robertson, The American Party, 3. Cold reality did not match up to Know Nothings' exuberant hopes. Marius Carriere, "Political Leadership of the Louisiana Know-Nothing Party," Louisiana History, 21 (Spring 1980), 183–95, emphasizes the role of the party in acting as a refuge for beached Whig politicians, not a new breed of idealist.

76 Tyrrell, Sobering Up, 266, argues against equating temperance and nativism. Even some socially respectable, churchgoing nativists (principally Episcopalians and Lutherans) adopted a very cool attitude to prohibition.

77 Knoxville Whig, 30 Dec. 1854 (quotation), 19 May 1855.

78 Gienapp, Origins of the Republican Party, 99; Gienapp, "Nebraska, Nativism, and Rum," 443–4. Allen Trimble, American candidate for governor of

Ohio in 1855, was a strict prohibitionist. Trimble, Autobiography, 220–2, 224. For the strong affinities between the two causes in a wide variety of settings, see George H. Haynes, "A Chapter from the Local History of Knownothingism," New England Magazine, 15 (Sept. 1896), 90; G. Coles, Diary, 20 Sept., 6 Nov. 1855, DU; Purdy, "Massachusetts General Court of 1855," 37; Thomas A. Goodwin's "Introduction" to Joseph Tarkington, Autobiography of Rev. Joseph Tarkington, One of the Pioneer Methodist Preachers of Indiana (Cincinnati, 1899), 62; SCA, 1 Sept. 1854; Fletcher, Diary, V, 234 (10 June 1854); Rand, "Know-Nothing Party in Rhode Island," 114–16; Sellers, Prohibition Movement in Alabama, 35–6.

79 Baker, Ambivalent Americans, 33–4, discusses the manichean world view of nativists and emphasizes its debt to Protestant revivalism.

80 New York Freeman's Journal, 9 June (quotation), 18 Aug. 1855; Mulkern, "Know-Nothing Party in Massachusetts," 110, 122; McClure, Old Time Notes, I, 240. Gienapp, Origins of the Republican Party, 162, quotes a Pennsylvania Democrat's complaint to Governor Bigler in 1854: "We owe our defeat more to the Protestant Ministry, and the professed religious press, than to any other Cause."

81 Tennessee Baptist, quoted in William G. Brownlow, The Great Iron Wheel Examined (Nashville, Tenn., 1856), 288–90; Trafton, Scenes in My Life, 228–30; Mulkern, "Know-Nothing Party in Massachusetts," 124; Purdy, "Massachusetts General Court of 1855," 84; McClure, Old Time Notes, I, 238–41; WCA, 25 Oct. 1854. In Maryland some Protestant vestries, especially those of Presbyterian and Methodist churches, produced an unusually large number of Know Nothing leaders. Baker, Ambivalent Americans, 69–71.

82 Benjamin F. Butler, Butler's Book: Autobiography and Personal Reminiscences of Major-General Benj. F. Butler (Boston, 1892), 121; Haynes, "A Know Nothing Legislature," in Annual Report of the

American Historical Association for the Year *1896* (Washington, DC, 1897), I, 178. The 24 included 7 Unitarians, 6 Congregationalists, 4 Methodists, and 3 Baptists. *Poole's Annual Register . . . of Massachusetts* for 1855, 6–15.

[83] Parmet, "Connecticut Know-Nothings," 85–6; Trafton, *Scenes in My Life,* 238–9; Purdy, "Massachusetts General Court of 1855," 162–9.

[84] *Sons of the Sires,* 54; *WCA,* 18 April 1855. "Kirwan" (the Presbyterian minister Nicholas Murray) told the General Conference of the MECS in 1850 he hoped Presbyterian and Methodist churches would "coalesce more and more" in common protection of Protestantism against Catholic encroachments. *Knoxville Whig,* 15 June 1850.

[85] Gienapp, *Origins of the Republican Party,* 132, 136–7; George H. Haynes, "A Chapter from the Local History of Knownothingism," 90. For some examples of youthful enthusiasm for the Americans, see A.W. Mangum Notebook (unpaginated), Mangum Family Papers, SHC; G.G. Smith, Diary (typescript), 19–20, 66–8, G.G. Smith Books, SHC.

[86] L.W. Berry to M. Simpson, 9 June, 22 July, 5 Aug., 23 Nov. 1854, M. Simpson Papers, LC; *WCA,* 7 Dec. 1853, 17 May, 28 June, 30 Aug., 18 Oct. (indicating that Elliott, though not a member of the Order, probably voted for the Know Nothings); *New York Freeman's Journal,* 3 May 1856; Coulter, *Brownlow,* 125–6; J. Morrison to R.L. Dabney, 28 June 1855, Dabney Papers, SHC; Valentine, Diary, SHC, esp. 11 Nov., 15 Dec. 1854, 26, 27 Jan., 19 April, 24 May, 6 Aug., 13 Oct. 1855; Gienapp, *Origins of the Republican Party,* 158; Gienapp, "Nebraska, Nativism, and Rum," 469.

[87] Mulkern, "Know-Nothing Party in Massachusetts," 123; Amy B. Bridges, "Another Look at Plutocracy and Politics in Antebellum New York City," *Political Science Quarterly,* 97 (Spring 1982), 62–3; *DAB* (for Phelps); *WCA,* 14 Feb. 1855; C.W. Dabney to R.L. Dabney, 11 April, 15 June 1855, Dabney Papers, SHC; Gienapp, *Origins of the Republican Party,*

100–1, 137, 145; Baker, *Ambivalent Americans,* 147–9. William Valentine believed that in his own region of eastern North Carolina the American party was composed mostly of ex-Whigs. Valentine, Diary, 6 Aug., 13 Oct. 1855, SHC.

[88] *Knoxville Whig,* 18 Aug. (quotation), 22 Sept. 1855. See also Anspach, *Sons of the Sires,* 25–6, 30.

[89] Fitzgerald, *Judge Longstreet,* 119, 125; *Knoxville Whig,* 17 March 1855; A.V. Brown, *Letter to the Bishops, Elders, and other Ministers, Itinerant and Local, of the Methodist Episcopal Church, South,* in Brownlow, *Americanism Contrasted with Foreignism,* 42; R. Beale to A. Davis, 7 Jan. 1858, Beale–Davis Papers, SHC; *Knoxville Whig,* 24 March (quotation), 12 May 1855.

[90] J.A. Wright to M. Simpson, 23 Oct. 1854, M. Simpson Papers, LC; R.S. Staunton to J.G. Davis, 21 Oct. 1854, J.G. Davis Papers [WEGT] (spelling corrected); Gienapp, *Origins of the Republican Party,* 111, 147, 162, 508. Some three-quarters of Indiana's Methodist preachers subscribed to Thomas Goodwin's prohibition and Know Nothing paper, the *Indiana American.* Goodwin, "Introduction," 62.

[91] *WCA,* 20 Sept., 25 Oct. 1854; 18 April, 30 May, 22 Aug. 1855; 6 Aug. 1856; George Prentice, *The Life of Gilbert Haven, Bishop of the Methodist Episcopal Church* (New York, 1883), 148; *BDAC,* 1726. For further evidence of Methodists' deep involvement, see Spottswood, *Brief Annals,* 135–6; Mulkern, "Know-Nothing Party in Massachusetts," 122; Fletcher, *Diary,* V, 253; J.C. Harper, Diary, 14 July 1855, SHC; Baker, *Ambivalent Americans,* 137–9.

[92] *WCA,* 7 Feb., 3 Oct. 1855; Malmsbury, *Charles Pitman,* 219; Bacon, *History of American Christianity,* 321; *Democratic Review,* 37 (1856), 495; *Brownson's Quarterly Review,* (Oct. 1854), 447; Browne, "A Memoir of Archbishop Hughes," 180; Purcell and Poole, "Political Nativism in Brooklyn," 49; *New York Freeman's Journal,* 15 Oct 1853,

10 June 1854. See also J.B. Cottrell, Diary, 9 Nov. 1855, SHC; Chapman, *Americanism versus Romanism*, 134–5, 217–19.

[93] *Catholic Vindicator*, quoted in *Catholic Telegraph*, 29 March 1856; McClure, *Old Time Notes*, I, 233; Felicity O'Driscoll, "Political Nativism in Buffalo, 1830–1860," *Records of the American Catholic Historical Society*, 48 (Sept. 1937), 298, 306–8; Gienapp, *Origins of the Republican Party*, 162–3, 507–8; *Knoxville Whig*, 12 May 1855; R.H. Morrison to J. Morrison, 9 Aug. 1855, Morrison Papers, SHC; Baker, *Ambivalent Americans*, 137–9.

[94] Gienapp, *Origins of the Republican Party*, 162–3, 508; J.W. Forney, *Address on Religious Intolerance and Political Proscription . . .* (Washington, DC, 1855), 27–8. That a Baptist church member presided over the National Council of the American party in 1855 was an aid in recruitment. *Knoxville Whig*, 23 June, 21 July 1855; Brownlow, *Great Iron Wheel Examined*, 288–90.

[95] *WCA*, 25 April, 9 May 1855 (for Jonathan Blanchard); *Independent*, 9 March 1854; Ely, *American Liberty*, 2; Parmet, "Connecticut's Know-Nothings," 84, 86–7; Grinnell, *Men and Events*, 105–6.

[96] For German Methodists see, for example, *WCA*, 11 April 1855. For free-thinking, anti-Catholic Germans' readiness to side with native-born Protestants in Cincinnati in the early 1850s, indicating the primacy of anti-Romanism over anti-foreignism, see William A. Baughin, "Development of Nativism in Cincinnati," 253–5. See also McClure, *Old Time Notes*, I, 203. Holt, *Forging a Majority*, 135, 147–8, 151, shows the anti-papal sentiment amongst Pittsburgh's naturalized German Protestants, who voted Know Nothing in 1854. Gienapp, *Origins of the Republican Party*, 145, 159, 162–3, 508, reaches a similar conclusion for Protestant Germans in the state as a whole, except perhaps in Philadelphia, and indicates that some Lutherans supported the

Know Nothings in Pennsylvania and New York, though more remained loyal to the Democrats.

[97] Baker, *Ambivalent Americans*, 138–9.

[98] Gienapp, *Origins of the Republican Party*, 507–8; *Knoxville Whig*, 21 Oct. 1854, 12 May, 7 July, 18, 25 Aug., 22 Sept. 1855; Longstreet, *Letter from President Longstreet to the Public*; *Biblical Recorder*, 27 Sept. 1855; *New York Freeman's Journal*, 9 June 1855; *Primitive Baptist*, 29 Sept. 1860; Overdyke, *Know Nothing Party in the South*, 237–8; Davis, "Joshua Leavitt," 343; *WCA*, 25 Oct. 1854; Gienapp, "Nebraska, Nativism, and Rum," 462; McClure, *Old Time Notes*, I, 235. See also Bugbee, "Henry Lillie Pierce," 393; L.M. Wilson to A.W. Mangum, 18 Oct. 1854, Mangum Family Papers, SHC.

[99] Brownlow, *Americanism Contrasted with Foreignism*, 6. See also Chapman, *Americanism versus Romanism*, 228.

[100] *Knoxville Whig*, 7 Oct. 1854. See also *New York Freeman's Journal*, 4 Aug. 1855. There was a considerable turnover in Know Nothing support. Many early supporters in Massachusetts and New York later backed off. See Holt, "Anti-masonic and Know Nothing Parties," 608.

[101] Richardson, *From Sunrise to Sunset*, 104–5.

[102] *Knoxville Whig*, 2, 23 June, 28 July (quoting *Nashville Union*, 15 May 1855), 22 Sept. (quoting *Tennessee Baptist*) 1855. See also Queener, "Brownlow as an Editor," 75. Johnson was just one of many Democrats countrywide who presented 'their party as the safest defender of religious freedom and toleration against Know Nothing bigotry. See, for example, J.W. Forney, *Address on Religious Intolerance; A Few Words to the Thinking and Judicious Voters of Pennsylvania* (n.p. [1854]); *Letters of A.H. Stephens and Rev. H.H. Tucker, on Religious Liberty . . .* (Atlanta, Ga., 1855); *Facts for the People of the South: Abolition Intolerance and Religious Intolerance United: Know-nothingism Exposed* (Washington, DC,

1855); *Letter of an Adopted Catholic, Addressed to the President of the Kentucky Democratic Association of Washington City, on Temporal Allegiance to the Pope . . .* (Washington, DC, 1856).

103 For the impact of Graves's book throughout the South, and the climate of bitterness between the two denominations see, for example, *Biblical Recorder*, 28 June, 12, 19, 26 July, 2, 9 Aug. 1855; *North Carolina Christian Advocate*, 29 Feb., 7 March, 25 April, 9 May, 6, 13 June, 4, 11 July 1856. Graves also exercised considerable influence as editor of the *Tennessee Baptist*, which had a circulation of about 10,000. J.J. Burnett, *Sketches of Tennessee's Pioneer Baptist Preachers* (Nashville, Tenn., 1919), 184–200. For a similar debate in northern states, where the Baptist protagonists included the editor of the Cincinnati *Journal and Messenger* and the Reverend John Quincy Adams, minister of lower New Jersey, see *WCA*, 31 Jan., 21 March, 21 Nov. 1855.

104 *Biblical Recorder*, 12 July, 2 Aug., 11 Oct. 1855; *South Western Baptist*, quoted in *Biblical Recorder*, 19, 26 July 1855. For the themes of this paragraph see, for example, *Christian Index*, 3 April 1856; *Primitive Baptist*, 29 Sept. 1860; *Biblical Recorder*, 14 June 1855, 21 Feb., 18 Sept. 1856, 15, 22 Jan., 5, 12, 26 Feb., 5 March 1857.

105 See the anti-Baptist fusillades of Leroy M. Lee, pugnacious editor of the *Richmond Christian Advocate*, William A. Smith, and Peter Doub and other Methodist spokesmen in *Biblical Recorder*, 19 April, 31 May, 2, 9, 23 Aug., 20 Sept., 11, 18, 25 Oct., 1, 8 Nov., 6 Dec. 1855. See also Daniel Wise, *Popular Objections to Methodism Considered and Answered . . .* (Boston, 1856); *WCA*, 21 March 1855.

106 *Biblical Recorder*, 15 May 1856. All 5,000 copies of the first printing of Brownlow's polemic had sold within a few days. *North Carolina Christian Advocate*, 2 May 1856.

107 "Many of our best brethren are Democrats," Graves explained, "but they do not think Democracy and Catholicism identical." However, should the party actively promote Catholicism, "there is not a Baptist in the land, worthy of the name, who would not abandon it in disgust" (*Tennessee Baptist*, quoted in *Knoxville Whig*, 22 Sept. 1855).

108 *SCA*, 16 March 1855.

109 For concern even amongst friendly Baptists about the "Romish" practices and doctrines of the Methodists, see Valentine, Diary, 13, 18, 19 Oct. 1853, SHC.

110 *Biblical Recorder*, 28 June, 27 Sept., 18 Oct. 1855. The hostility between John Q. Adams (Baptist and Democrat) and John Inskip (Methodist and American) in New Jersey took on the same religio-political coloring. *Biblical Recorder*, 15 Jan. 1857.

111 Disputes between Baptists and Methodists over their republican credentials were widely understood to have implications for electoral politics. *Biblical Recorder*, 21 June 1855, quoting the *Western Watchman*.

112 Rhys Isaac, *The Transformation of Virginia, 1740–1790* (Chapel Hill, 1982), 163–72; Goodman, *Towards a Christian Republic*, 38 and *passim*; Cross, *Burned-Over District*, 116–24; Cole, *Jacksonian Democracy in New Hampshire*, 174–75; Holt, "The Antimasonic and Know Nothing Parties," 577–88; Howe, *American Whigs*, 57–8.

113 Valentine, Diary, 22 Oct. 1849, SHC; *Knoxville Whig*, 7 June 1851, 12 May, 30 June 1855; Scouller, *Manual of the United Presbyterian Church*, 182; *WCA*, 6 Aug. 1856; William H. Brackney, "The Fruits of a Crusade: Wesleyan Opposition to Secret Societies," *Methodist History*, 17 (July 1979), 239–52; Lee, *Autobiography*, 248–9, 272–3; *Christian Index*, 13 March 1856. Some sense of the fracturing potential of the issue in the various branches of Methodism, for example, can be gleaned from *CAJ*, 15 Sept. 1847, 23 Aug. 1848, 23 Oct. 1850; *SCA*, 16 April 1847; Burgess, *Pleasant Recollections*, 211–13; *WCA*, 2 June 1852; Palmer, *Leonidas L. Hamline*, 323–4; *Albany Argus*, 21 May 1852; Elias Bowen,

History of the Origins of the Free Methodist Church (Rochester, NY, 1871), 42–3; Charles N. Sims, *The Life of T.M. Eddy, D.D.* (New York, 1879), 109–10; Manship, *Thirteen Years Experience*, 174; Haney, *Story of My Life*, 87–90; John Scott, *Recollections of Fifty Years in the Ministry: with Numerous Character Sketches* (Pittsburgh, 1898), 124–5; Prentice, *Wilbur Fisk*, 229; T.J. Brown to M. Simpson, 13 April 1850, M. Simpson Papers, LC. For tensions in other denominations see, for example, Vandervelde, "Notes on the Diary of Duffield," 61; Justin A. Smith, *Memoir of Rev. Nathaniel Colver, D.D.* (Boston, 1873), 67–84; Allen, *Reminiscences*, 14–15.

114 Blanchard, *Sermons and Addresses*, 11; Jonathan Blanchard, *Secret Societies: a Discourse* (Cincinnati, 1845); *idem, Secret Societies: an Argument . . .* (Chicago, 1851), 5, 7, 9, 23–4; P. Godwin, "Secret Societies – The Know Nothings," *Putnam's Monthly Magazine*, 5 (New York, 1855), 85; Thomas Smyth, "The Principle of Secrecy and Secret Societies: Two Discourses . . ." in Thomas Smyth, *Complete Works*, ed. J. William Flinn (10 vols, Columbia, SC, 1908–12), V, 379–404 (quotation 402–3); *Oberlin Evangelist*, 17 July 1850, 3 March 1852, 3 Jan. 1855; J.A. Wright to M. Simpson, 23 Oct. 1854, M. Simpson Papers, LC.

115 Reverend W. Easton, whose views were set out in William R. Dewitt, *A Discussion of the Order of the Sons of Temperance . . .* (Philadelphia, 1847), iii–viii, 9–10, 34–5, 62–3, 178–9, 209, 213.

116 See, for example, *WCA*, 25 Oct. 1854; Zebedee Warner, *The Life and Labors of Rev. Jacob Bachtel, of the Parkersburg Annual Conference, United Brethren in Christ* (Dayton, Ohio, 1868), 72–5, 110–17; *Knoxville Whig*, 17 Feb. 1855; Brownlow, *Americanism Contrasted with Foreignism*, 34–6.

117 Haynes, "A Chapter from the Local History of Knownothingism," 89; J.B. Cottrell, Diary, 19 Feb. 1855, SHC; Baker, *Ambivalent Americans*, 70–1.

118 Holt, *Forging a Majority*, 150; Gienapp, "Nebraska, Nativism, and

Rum," 448. But for the suggestion that some former Antimasons were drawn into Know Nothingism, see J.W. Forney, *Address on Religious Intolerance*, 48; O'Driscoll, "Political Nativism in Buffalo," 307.

119 Fitzgerald, *Judge Longstreet*, 123–7; *WCA*, 21 Feb.,14 March, 20 June 1855; *Oberlin Evangelist*, 3 Jan. 1855; Spottswood, *Brief Annals*, 135; R. Beale to A. Davis, Beale–Davis Papers, 7 Jan. 1858, SHC. See also Billington, *Protestant Crusade*, 417; *The Know Nothings: An Exposé of the Secret Order of Know Nothings; the Most Ludicrous and Startling Yankee "Notion" Ever Conceived. By a Know Something* (New York, 1854), 3.

120 William H. Ryder (ed.) *Our Country: or, The American Parlor Keepsake* (Boston, 1854), vi; Ely, *American Liberty*, 17; Boynton, *Oration Before the Native Americans*, 16; *Oberlin Evangelist*, 3 Jan. 1855. See also Van Nest, *Bethune*, 313; Brainerd, *Thomas Brainerd*, 315.

121 *Biblical Recorder*, 21 Sept. 1854; *Oberlin Evangelist*, 3 Jan. 1855; Ninde, *William Xavier Ninde*, 52–3; Charles Wadsworth, *America's Mission: A Sermon Preached in the Arch Street Presbyterian Church, Philadelphia* (Philadelphia [1855]), 27–8; *New York Freeman's Journal*, 20 Jan. 1855.

122 See, for example, *WCA*, 16 June 1852; *Independent*, 9 Feb. 1854; *CAJ*, 15 May, 2 Oct. 1856; Norton, *Religious Newspapers*, 15.

123 *Annual Report of the American Baptist Home Missionary Society* (1855), 88.

124 W. Barrows, "Immigration: Its Evils and Their Remedies," *New Englander*, 13 (1855), 269–70; *Biblical Recorder*, 18 Oct. 1855; A.B. Van Zandt, *The Romish Controversy*, 29–30; Van Nest, *Bethune*, 292–8; *WCA*, 18 Oct., 22 Nov. 1854, 7 Feb., 28 March, 11 July, 22 Aug. 1855; Anspach, *Sons of the Sires*, 57, 102–5; Brownlow, *Americanism Contrasted with Foreignism*, 116–17; John C. Pitrat, *Review of the Speech of Hon. J.R. Chandler, of Pennsylvania, on the Political Power of the Pope . . .* (Boston, 1855), 59–72.

[125] *WCA*, 7 May 1851. See also Lewis, *Samuel Lewis*, 373; *Christian Lawyer*, 262–3; Prentice, *Gilbert Haven*, 147–8. These critics of Know Nothingism were at the same time unsentimental about Rome, dismissing as misguided (if sincere) those like Joseph R. Chandler who denied that the Pope had political ambitions outside Italy. George R. Crooks, *Life and Letters of the Rev. John M'Clintock, D.D.,LL.D., Late President of Drew Theological Seminary* (New York, 1876), 256; *WCA*, 17 Jan. 1855.

[126] Longstreet, *Letter from President Longstreet to the Public*, 11; "A Calm Discussion of the Know-Nothing Question," *Southern Literary Messenger*, 20 (Sept. 1854), 542; Fitzgerald, *Judge Longstreet*, 120–6; "Know Nothingism," *Democratic Review*, 37 (1856), 492.

[127] Mulkern, "Know-Nothing Party in Massachusetts," 121–61; Haynes, "A Know Nothing Legislature," 182; Baker, *Ambivalent Americans*, 80–107; Holt, "Antimasonic and Know Nothing Parties," 606.

[128] See, for example, *History of the Rise, Progress and Downfall of Know-Nothingism in Lancaster County. By Two Expelled Members* (Lancaster, Pa., 1856).

[129] Mulkern, "Know-Nothing Party in Massachusetts," 162–95; *Christian Watchman and Reflector*, 8 May 1856.

[130] Billington, *Protestant Crusade*, 420–2; *Knoxville Whig*, 14 April 1855; Stritch, "Political Nativism in Cincinnati," 270–6; William A. Baughin, "Bullets and Ballots: The Election Day Riots of 1855," *Historical and Philosophical Society of Ohio Bulletin*, 21 (Oct. 1963), 267–72; Chapman, *Americanism versus Romanism*, 17; *New York Freeman's Journal*, 31 March, 1 Sept. (quoting *Albany Patriot*), 13 Oct. 1855; *WCA*, 19 July, 13 Sept. 1854, 2 May, 15 Aug., 12 Sept. 1855; J.D. Proctor to A.W. Mangum, 2 March 1855, Mangum Family Papers, SHC; Purcell and Poole, "Political Nativism in Brooklyn," 41–9, 51; J.T. Crane, "Party Politics," *Methodist Quarterly Review*, 20 (Oct. 1860), 580; Barrows, "Immigration," 263–5, 273.

See also *Christian Watchman and Reflector*, 10 April 1856; *WCA*, 27 Sept. 1854, quoting *Watchman and Evangelist* (Presbyterian; Louisville, Ky.). David A. Gerber, "Ambivalent Anti-Catholicism: Buffalo's American Protestant Elite Faces the Challenge of the Catholic Church, 1850–1860," *CWH*, 30 (June 1984), 120–44, thoughtfully explores the dissonance and tensions within evangelical responses to Catholicism: Protestants concerned for social order included those who saw the Roman church as an ally in the control of immigrant and lower-class lawlessness and immorality.

[131] *Christian Watchman and Reflector*, 10 April 1856; Bushnell, *Barbarism the First Danger*, 217. For similar pleas, see *WCA*, 11 Nov. 1842 (quoting Bela B. Edwards), 4 May 1853 (quoting *New York Observer*); Jonathan Blanchard, "Christianizing Papists," in his *Sermons and Addresses*, 25–34; *Oberlin Evangelist*, 18 Dec. 1844; *SCA*, 26 May 1854; Clifford S. Griffin, "Converting the Catholics: American Benevolent Societies and the Ante-Bellum Crusade against the Church," *Catholic Historical Review*, 47 (1961), 334–41.

[132] Barrows, "Immigration," 275–6; *Biblical Recorder*, 24 Feb. 1854; *WCA*, 16 June 1852; *Christian Watchman and Reflector*, 10 April, 1 May 1856; McGill, *Popery, the Punishment of Unbelief*, 42.

[133] *WCA*, 27 Sept. 1854, 2 May 1855.

[134] See, for example, Binns, *Recollections*, 325–35; *Oberlin Evangelist*, 3 Jan. 1855; Longstreet, *Letter from President Longstreet to the Public*, 3–9; *Knoxville Whig*, 17 March 1855; *Thoughts for the People*, 13–17; *Facts for the People of the South*, 17–18; Rice, "Know-Nothing Party in Virginia," 65.

[135] James L. Huston, "The Demise of the Pennsylvania American Party, 1854–58," *Pennsylvania Magazine of History and Biography*, 109 (Oct. 1985), 473–97 and Gienapp, *Origins of the Republican Party*, *passim*, stress the potency of anti-Catholicism and nativism as politically destructive forces, but also see that their proponents lacked the political

coherence and unity needed to construct a new political order, especially once the slavery issue had launched an irreconcilable conflict between many of the Know Nothings' state organizations and the national body.

Chapter 8 *The Emergence of the Third Party System: Evangelicals and Sectional Antagonism, 1854–56*

[1] *WCA*, 25 Jan. 1854. For the introduction and passage of the Kansas–Nebraska bill, and the propaganda masterstroke of the Appeal of the Independent Democrats see, in particular, Potter, *Impending Crisis*, 145–67; Eric Foner, *Free Soil, Free Labor, Free Men: The Ideology of the Republican Party before the Civil War* (New York, 1970), 93–5; Gienapp, *Origins of the Republican Party*, 70–8; Holt, *Political Crisis of the 1850s*, 144–9; Sewell, *Ballots for Freedom*, 254–65. Chase and another of his co-authors, Charles Sumner, sought to distribute copies of the Appeal to every Congregational, Baptist, Presbyterian, and Methodist minister in the North. Edward E. Lacy, "Protestant Newspaper Reaction to the Kansas–Nebraska Bill of 1854," *The Rocky Mountain Social Science Journal*, 7 (Oct. 1970), 66.

[2] *Presbyterian of the West*, quoted in *WCA*, 12 April 1854.

[3] See, for example, *Proceedings of a Public Meeting of the Citizens of Providence, held in the Beneficent Congregational Church, March 7, 1854, to Protest against Slavery in Nebraska* (Providence, RI, 1854), *passim*; William Salter, *Sixty Years, and Other Discourses, with Reminiscences...* (Boston, 1907), 239–40; Foster, *Four Pastorates*, 71; Magoun, *Asa Turner*, 285–6; *Independent*, 16, 23 Feb., 2, 23 March 1854; *WCA*, 15 March 1854; *CAJ*, 16 Feb. 1854; Victor B. Howard, "The 1856 Election in Ohio: Moral Issues in Politics," *Ohio History*, 80 (Winter 1971), 26. Magdol, *The Antislavery Rank and File*, 121–8, describes the involvement of lay members of New York and Mass-

achusetts churches in anti-Nebraska petitioning.

[4] Johnson, *Chaplains of the General Government*, 5; Norton, *Religious Newspapers*, 122–3; Bacon, *History of American Christianity*, 284; *WCA*, 5 April 1854; *Independent*, 18 May 1854. Following Everett's resignation of his Senate seat Sumner happily took on the job of receiving late signatures and defending the anti-Nebraska clergy from attack. Donald, *Charles Sumner and the Coming of the Civil War* (New York, 1961), 259–60; Charles Sumner, *Final Protest for Himself and the Clergy of New England against Slavery in Kansas and Nebraska: Speech... on the Night of the Passage of the Kansas and Nebraska Bill...* (Washington, DC, 1854), 4. For clerical criticism of Everett for being "a most perfect lady" compared to the manly Sumner, see Charles M. Bower, *Discourse on the Nebraska Bill, Preached in the Baptist Meeting House, Clinton, June 4th, 1854* (n.p. [1854]), 14; Eddy, *The Commonwealth*, 52–3.

[5] James Meacham, *Defense of the Clergy: Speech... in the House of Representatives, May 17, 1854* (Washington, DC, 1854), 2. See also *WCA*, 5 April 1854 (quoting the *Indiana State Journal*), 24 May 1854 (quoting S.S. Cox, editor of the *Ohio Statesman*); Lucy F. Bittinger, *Memorials of the Rev. Joseph Baugher Bittinger, D.D.* (Woodsville, NH, 1891), 58–9. Congressional debates can be followed in *Right of Petition: New England Clergymen: Remarks on the Memorial from Some 3,050 Clergymen...* (Washington, DC, 1854). For speeches in support of the clergy, see Meacham, *Defense of the Clergy*; Sumner, *Final Protest*. Defenders included Sam Houston, one of the few southerners to oppose the bill. *Right of Petition*, 4–7, 7–9, 12–13. John Pettit of Indiana and other confirmed clergy-haters took advantage of this climate of hostility to propose the dismissal of all chaplains employed by the federal government. Johnson, *Chaplains of the General Government*, 6–7.

[6] *Right of Petition*, 3–6, 10–12; Johnson, *Chaplains of the General Govern-*

ment, 58–9; Stephen A. Douglas, *Letter of Senator Douglas, Vindicating His Character and His Position on the Nebraska Bill against . . . Twenty-five Clergymen of Chicago* (Washington, 1854), 11; "Abolition and Sectarian Mobs," *Democratic Review*, 34 (Aug. 1854), 92–120.

7 Leonard Bacon, "The Morality of the Nebraska Bill," *New Englander*, 12 (May 1854), 305–6; R.H. Richardson, *Wickedness in High Places: A Discourse Occasioned by the Bill for the Government of Kansas and Nebraska . . .* (Chicago, 1854), 17, 20, 23–4; *Right of Petition*, 3; *WCA*, 1 March, 5 April, 28 June, 22 Nov. 1854; *CAJ*, 16 Feb. 1854; Francis Wayland, *Dr. Wayland on the Moral and Religious Aspects of the Nebraska Bill: Speech at Providence, R.I.* (Rochester, NY, 1854), 5–6; Bowers, *Discourse on the Nebraska Bill*, 6–7; Joseph Bittinger, *A Plea for Humanity: A Sermon Preached in the Euclid Street Church, Cleveland, Ohio* (Cleveland, Ohio, 1854), 27–8; Charles Beecher, *A Sermon on the Nebraska Bill* (New York, 1854), 5–8.

8 Richardson, *Wickedness in High Places*, 26–7, 30–2; Heman Humphrey, *The Missouri Compromise: An Address Delivered Before the Citizens of Pittsfield . . .* (Pittsfield, Mass., 1854), 16–19; George F. Magoun, "A Conservative View of the Nebraska Bill," *New Englander*, 12 (Nov. 1854), 539; Bowers, *Discourse on the Nebraska Bill*, 8–10; Horace Bushnell, *The Northern Iron* (Hartford, Conn., 1854), 9.

9 *WCA*, 1, 29 March, 12 April (quoting *Presbyterian of the West*), 10 May 1854; Moody, *Life's Retrospect*, 226; Bacon, "Morality of the Nebraska Bill," 325; Beecher, *Nebraska Bill*, 3–4; Humphrey, *Missouri Compromise*, 8, 28; Bittinger, *Plea for Humanity*, 17; Bowers, *Discourse on the Nebraska Bill*, 4.

10 Wisner, *Review of Lord's Sermon*, 32; Duffield, *Our Federal Union*, 13; Bouton, *The Good Land*, 10. See also Beman, *Characteristics of the Age*, 13; Breed, *American Union*, 10.

11 *Congregational Herald*, quoted in *Independent*, 12 Jan. 1854; C.H.A. Bulkley, *Removal of Ancient Landmarks: or the Causes and Consequences of Slavery*

Extension: A Discourse . . . (Hartford, Conn., 1854), 4–6, 8; Magoun, "Conservative View," 536, 543–8. See also Mears, *Kirk*, 249. Even staunch conservatives like Nehemiah Adams and George Blagden publicly attacked the bill. *Independent*, 27 April 1854; Clark, *American Slavery and Maine Congregationalists*, 169–70.

12 Beecher, *Nebraska Bill*, 11; Wayland, *Nebraska Bill*, 6; Humphrey, *Missouri Compromise*, 28–30; *WCA*, 29 March 1854; Bacon, "Morality of the Nebraska Bill," 326; Lewis, *Samuel Lewis*, 420; Humphrey, *Missouri Compromise*, 29–30; Alexander C. Twining, "The Nebraska Bill and Its Results," *New Englander*, 12 (May 1854), 217; Bowers, *Discourse on the Nebraska Bill*, 1; *Independent*, 23 March 1854.

13 Bittinger, *Plea for Humanity*, 14; Twining, "Nebraska Bill," 230–1; Wayland, *Nebraska Bill*, 4–5; Humphrey, *Missouri Compromise*, 12–13; *WCA*, 29 March 1854; Charles B. Boynton and Timothy B. Mason, *A Journey through Kansas; with Sketches of Nebraska: . . . The Results of a Tour Made in the Autumn of 1854* (Cincinnati, 1855), 135–6, 199–200; *WCA*, 8 Feb. 1854; Moody, *Life's Retrospect*, 226–7; Beecher, *Nebraska Bill*, 12–14. See also Bushnell, *Northern Iron*, 3–5, 14–15, 19–23; Bulkley, *Ancient Landmarks*, 13, 18–19.

14 John Nelson, *A Discourse on the Proposed Repeal of the Missouri Compromise; Delivered on Fast Day, April 6th, 1854 . . .* (Worcester, Mass., 1854), 11; *Independent*, 9 Feb., 30 March, 18 May 1854; Mears, *Edward Norris Kirk*, 250; Humphrey, *Missouri Compromise*, 20–6; Edwin Leonard, *A Discourse Delivered in the Second Evangelical Congregational Church, Milton, 4 June 1854* (Boston, 1854), 6–13; Bittinger, *Plea for Humanity*, 4; Edward Thomson, *The Pulpit and Politics: A Discourse Preached in the College Chapel of the Ohio Wesleyan University, April 23, 1854* (Columbus, Ohio, 1854), 16; *Zion's Herald*, 12 April 1854, quoted in Lacy, "Protestant Newspaper Reaction," 70; Bacon, "Morality of the Nebraska Bill,"

317, 321. Bacon, *Leonard Bacon*, 385–95, discusses Bacon's influential open letter to Toucey (of Connecticut) in the *Independent*, and his subsequent forceful rejection of Douglas's attack on the clergy (written and published at Joshua Giddings's request).

[15] Moody, *Life's Retrospect*, 225; Bowers, *Discourse on the Nebraska Bill*, 5; Bushnell, *Northern Iron*, 25–6; *WCA*, 13 Sept., 25 Oct. 1854; William Warren Sweet, "Some Religious Aspects of the Kansas Struggle," *Journal of Religion*, 7 (Oct. 1927), 583; Clark E. Carr. *The Illini: A Story of the Prairies* (Chicago, 1904), 163–8; Twining, "Nebraska Bill," 235–6.

[16] Richardson, *Wickedness in High Places*, 33; Humphrey, *Missouri Compromise*, 14–16; Eden B. Foster, *The Rights of the Pulpit, and Perils of Freedom: Two Discourses Preached in Lowell, Sunday, June 25th, 1854* (Lowell, Mass., 1854), 46–8; Beecher, *Nebraska Bill*, 13.

[17] Bushnell, *Northern Iron*, 18, 28; Wayland, *Nebraska Bill*, 1, 5; Bacon, "Morality of the Nebraska Bill," 305; Richardson, *Wickedness in High Places*, 32; *Right of Petition*, 3. For a readiness in some quarters to contemplate disunion as a means of preventing the greater evil of slavery expansion, see Bulkley, *Removal of Ancient Landmarks*, 12–15.

[18] Bushnell, *Northern Iron*, 27; *Independent*, 13 April 1854; Nelson, *Proposed Repeal of the Missouri Compromise*, 8–10; Bulkley, *Removal of Ancient Landmarks*, 13–14; *WCA*, 22 Feb., 1 March 1854; Bittinger, *Plea for Humanity*, 24–5; Richardson, *Wickedness in High Places*, 40–1.

[19] For the resurgence of protests against the Fugitive Slave Law, and the enactment of personal liberty laws, following the passage of the Kansas-Nebraska Act, see Campbell, *Slave Catchers*, 83–95.

[20] See, for example, Bulkley, *Removal of Ancient Landmarks*, 17; *WCA*, 5 April, 28 June 1854; Keller, "Methodist Newspapers and the Fugitive Slave Law," 336–7.

[21] Moody, *Life's Retrospect*, 229;

Independent, 23 March 1854; Bowers, *Discourse on the Nebraska Bill*, 16–17; C.M. Ellis to C.L. McCurdy, 7 June 1854, NEC; Leonard, *Discourse Delivered in the Second Evangelical Congregational Church, Milton*, 16–19; J.W. Dadmun, Diary, 2 June 1854, NEC. See also Eddy, *The Commonwealth*, 37–9.

[22] *WCA*, 6 Sept. 1854; *Oberlin Evangelist*, 28 Feb. 1855; Moody, *Life's Retrospect*, 230; Boynton and Mason, *Journey through Kansas*, 28, 50, 76, 130–7; Silas McKeen, *Rev. S. McKeen's Review of "A Letter of Inquiry to Ministers of the Gospel of All Denominations, on Slavery . . ."* (n.p. [NH], 1855), 20; *Christian Watchman and Reflector*, 22 May 1856.

[23] Bushnell, *Northern Iron*, 19–20; *Oberlin Evangelist*, 14 Feb. 1856; *WCA*, 21 March, 5 Sept. 1855; *Christian Watchman and Reflector*, 22 May 1856.

[24] Henry Ward Beecher, *Defence of Kansas* (Washington, 1856), 5; Boynton and Mason, *Journey through Kansas*, 139; *WCA*, 21 March, 13 June 1855; Eli Thayer, *A History of the Kansas Crusade: Its Friends and Its Foes* (New York, 1889), 123–36.

[25] Eugene H. Berwanger, *The Frontier against Slavery: Western Anti-Negro Prejudice and the Slavery Extension Controversy* (paper edn, Urbana, Ill., 1971), 97–118.

[26] *Independent*, 7 Dec. 1854; Emory Lindquist (ed.) "Letters of the Rev. Samuel Young Lum, Pioneer Kansas Missionary, 1854–1858," *Kansas Historical Quarterly*, 25 (Spring and Summer 1959), 50; Bernard A. Weisberger, "The Newspaper Reporter and the Kansas Imbroglio," *MVHR*, 36 (1949–50), 649–51; Potter, *Impending Crisis*, 218–20; *WCA*, 13, 20 Feb. 1856.

[27] *WCA*, 27 Aug., 10 Sept. 1856; *Oberlin Evangelist*, 21 May, 18 June 1856.

[28] Albert T. Swing, *James Harris Fairchild, or Sixty-Eight Years with a Christian College* (New York, 1907), 163; G. Frederick Wright, *Story of My Life and Work* (Oberlin, Ohio, 1916), 90; Howard, "The 1856 Election in Ohio," 30; *New*

York Observer, 31 Jan. 1856; *WCA*, 13 Feb. 1856; *CAJ*, 5 June 1856; Crane, *Autobiography*, 127–8; *Christian Watchman and Reflector*, 17 April 1856; Bacon, *History of American Christianity*, 341. See James Connor, "The Antislavery Movement in Iowa," *Annals of Iowa*, 40 (Fall 1970), 460–2, for the role of Iowa's Congregational clergy; Essig, "The Lord's Free Man," 42–3, for Charles Finney's role in recruiting men and supplies for Kansas. For the debate within antislavery circles about the moral legitimacy of physical force and concern amongst the older generation over the trend towards violence, see for example Wyatt-Brown, *Lewis Tappan*, 328–34; Stewart, *Joshua Giddings*, 238–9; Gamble, "Joshua Giddings and the Ohio Abolitionists," 50–1.

[29] J. Harlan to M. Simpson, 11 Feb. 1856, M. Simpson Papers, LC; *Christian Watchman and Reflector*, 22 May 1856; Lindquist (ed.) "Letters of Samuel Young Lum," 175–7; Edward Norris Kirk, *"Our Duty in Perilous Times": A Sermon, Delivered in Mount Vernon Church, Boston, Sunday, June 1, 1856* (Boston, 1856), 8; Beecher, *Defence of Kansas*, 7; Hodge, *Charles Hodge*, 394; W.P. Hargrave, *Personal Recollections* (n.p., n.d.), 192–3; *WCA*, 8 Oct., 12 Nov. 1856. Few northern evangelicals raised their voices in defense of the South's cause in Kansas. The conservative *New York Observer*, however, offered a conciliatory plan involving the division of Kansas diagonally into two equal parts, one for each of the warring parties. *WCA*, 2 July 1856.

[30] Foster, *Four Pastorates*, 71–2; Kirk, *"Our Duty in Perilous Times"*, 8–9; Abbott, *Reminiscences*, 96. By endorsing Brooks and deluging him with trophies of appreciation southerners only reinforced evangelicals' perception of an unbridgable moral divide between the sections. *WCA*, 10 Sept. 1856. The South's sympathetic response to Brooks, rather than the original act of caning, was what particularly infuriated northern conservative evangelical opinion, including

the *New York Observer*. See, for example, *Oberlin Evangelist*, 30 July 1856. For a discussion of the South's double standards, see *WCA*, 25 June 1856: "had General Pierce, for certain of his acts, been cow-hided by any northern man, all Washington would have been up in arms." For a full discussion of the caning and its impact, see David Donald, *Charles Sumner*, 278–311.

[31] Sermon of W.D. Haley 6 July 1856, reprinted in *New York Tribune*, 5 Aug. 1856; Noah Porter, *Civil Liberty: A Sermon* (New York, 1856), 20; George W. Perkins, *Facts and Duties of the Times: A Sermon, Delivered before the First Congregational Church, Chicago, Illinois* (New York, 1856), 9; Daniels, *Gilbert Haven*, 323. For Haven's radical political and social outlook in the 1850s, see William B. Gravely, *Gilbert Haven: Methodist Abolitionist: A Study in Race, Religion, and Reform, 1850–1880* (Nashville, Tenn., 1973), 61–77.

[32] Henry Clay Fish, *Freedom or Despotism: The Voice of Our Brother's Blood: Its Source and Its Summons: A Discourse Occasioned by the Sumner and Kansas Outrages…* (Newark, NJ, 1856), 5–6; *Oberlin Evangelist*, 18 June, 30 July 1856; Perkins, *Facts and Duties of the Times*, 9; *New York Examiner*, quoted in Richard H. Watkins, Jr, "The Baptists of the North and Slavery, 1856–1860," *Foundations*, 13 (1970), 319; *Christian Watchman and Reflector*, 29 May 1856; Kirk, *"Our Duty in Perilous Times"*, 12; S. Caldwell to J. Blanchard, 29 May 1856, Blanchard Papers, WC; Fletcher, *Diary*, V, 529 (5, 6 June 1856). See also William E. Gienapp, "The Crime against Sumner: The Caning of Charles Sumner and the Rise of the Republican Party," *CWH*, 25 (Sept. 1979), 218–45.

[33] S.Y. Lum to M. Badger, June 1856, in Lindquist (ed.) "Letters of Samuel Young Lum," 175–7; Goodykoontz, *Home Missions on the American Frontier*, 295–7; Weisberger, "The Newspaper Reporter and the Kansas Imbroglio," 643; *WCA*, 9 July, 17 Sept., 1 Oct. 1856; Harrell, *Quest for Christian*

America, 115–19. See also L.B. Dennis to M. Simpson, 22 Jan. 1856, M. Simpson Papers, LC; *Twenty-Fourth Report of the American Baptist Home Missionary Society* ... (New York, 1856), 22–3; *Oberlin Evangelist*, 18 June 1856.

34 S.Y. Lum to the *Home Missionary*, Dec. 1855, in Lindquist (ed.) "Letters of Samuel Young Lum," 65–7; *St Louis Christian Advocate*, 19 April 1855; *WCA*, 14 June 1854, 2, 16 May, 6 June, 18 July 1855; Sweet, "Religious Aspects of the Kansas Struggle," 592–3; William Phillips, *The Conquest of Kansas by Missouri and Her Allies* (Boston, 1856; repr. NY, 1971), 17.

35 F. Starr to A. Bullard, 25 Aug. 1854, T.S. Reeve to A. Bullard, 19 April 1855, Bullard Papers, PHS; *WCA*, 2, 23 May, 25 July, 15, 22 (quoting *Central Christian Advocate*), 29 Aug., 5, 26 Sept., 10 Oct., 7 Nov. 1855; *Northwestern Christian Advocate*, 25 May, 29 Oct. 1856, transcript in Allen H. Godbey Papers, SHC; *CAJ*, 10 July, 7 Aug. 1856.

36 *WCA*, 28 Feb., 23 May, 6 June, 11 July 1855, 30 July 1856. See also Smith, *James Osgood Andrew*, 422.

37 Wesley Smith, *A Defence of the Methodist Episcopal Church against the Charges of Rev. S. Kelly and Others, of the M.E. Church, South* (Fairmont, Va., 1855), 21, 42, 45 and *passim*.

38 Brown, *Recollections of Itinerant Life*, 364–6; W.H. Wills to A. Wills, 11 May 1854, W.H. Wills to the editor of the *Western Protestant*, 1 June 1855, Wills Papers, SHC; *WCA*, 31 Jan., 18 July, 8 Aug. 1855, 17 Sept. 1856.

39 Lewis, *Samuel Lewis*, 421–4; Nicholas Vansant, *Sunset Memories* (New York, 1896), 90; G.R. Crooks to his wife, 26 May 1856, Crooks Papers, DU; Crooks, *John M'Clintock*, 259–60; Henry B. Ridgaway, *The Life of Edmund S. Janes, D.D., LL.D.* (New York, 1882), 196–9; Peck, *George Peck*, 353–5; *CAJ*, 5, 19 June 1856; *WCA*, 11 June 1856; M. Simpson to E. Simpson, 14 May 1856, M. Simpson Papers, LC. While there was no neat correspondence between Methodists' party political loyalties and

their stand on the General Rule, conservative delegates were often firm Democrats. See, for example, Henry Slicer, *Speech . . . Delivered in the General Conference at Indianapolis, 28th May, 1856, on the Subject of the Proposed Change in the Methodist Discipline* . . . (Washington [1856]).

40 Mitchell Snay, "American Thought and Southern Distinctiveness," 328; *New York Examiner*, quoted in *Biblical Recorder*, 6 Nov. 1856.

41 *Oberlin Evangelist*, 31 Jan., 11 April, 6 June, 12 Sept., 10 Oct. 1855, 20 June 1856; *New York Observer*, 5, 19 June, 3 July 1856, 11 June 1857; *Minutes of the General Assembly of the Presbyterian Church in the United States of America . . . 1856* (New York, 1856), 197–216; Thompson, *Presbyterians in the South*, I, 543–4; *Independent*, 26 Jan. 1854; William W. Patton *et al.*, *The Unanimous Remonstrance of the Fourth Congregational Church of Hartford, Conn., against the Policies of the American Tract Society* . . . (Hartford, Conn., 1855), 9–16 and *passim*; Gaylord, *Gaylord*, 164. For sectional acrimony in Campbellite and Dutch Reformed churches, see *WCA*, 6 Dec. 1854, 31 Oct., 7 Nov. 1855; David Christiano, "Synod and Slavery, 1855," *New Jersey History*, 90 (1972), 27–42.

42 Fish, *Freedom or Despotism*, 17; Boynton, *Address before the Citizens of Cincinnati*, 26; Kirk, *"Our Duty in Perilous Times"*, 7.

43 George W. Perkins, *Facts and Duties of the Times*, 8–9; Fish, *Freedom or Despotism*, 21–2. See also Thomas Williams, *Considerations on Slavery in the United States* (Providence, RI, 1856), 20; Nathaniel P. Bailey, *Our Duty as Taught by the Aggressive Nature of Slavery: A Discourse Preached in the Baptist Chapel, Akron* . . . (Akron, Ohio, 1855), 5–18.

44 For evangelicals' apprehensions about the Ostend Manifesto and the Pierce administration's response to William Walker's filibustering expeditions in central America, see for example *WCA*, 21 June 1854; *Oberlin Evangelist*, 28 Feb. 1855; *Christian Watchman and Re-*

flector, 1 May 1856; *Northwestern Christian Advocate*, 29 Oct. 1856; *CAJ*, 6 Nov. 1856; A.D. Field, Diary, 4 Nov. 1856, GTS; Brinkerhoff, *Recollections*, 30–66.

[45] *Oberlin Evangelist*, 18 June 1856; Humphrey, *Missouri Compromise*, 24; Lewis, *Samuel Lewis*, 422; Daniels, *Gilbert Haven*, 323; Fish, *Freedom or Despotism*, 17–18; Bailey, *Our Duty*, 21; Bittinger, *Plea for Humanity*, 25; Moody, *Life's Retrospect*, 229, 283–4; Foster, *Rights of the Pulpit, and Perils of Freedom*, 68, 72; Bushnell, *Northern Iron*, 28–9; Bulkley, *Removal of Ancient Landmarks*, 13–18; Beecher, *Nebraska Bill*, 15; *CAJ*, 16 Feb. 1854 (Thomas Bond); Bowers, *Discourse on the Nebraska Bill*, 14; Twining, "Nebraska Bill," 232–5; Leonard, *Discourse Delivered in the Second Evangelical Congregational Church*, 26–8.

[46] See, for example, *WCA*, 7, 21, 28 June, 18 Oct., 1854; Fletcher, *Diary*, V, 225; Davis, "Joshua Leavitt," 344–5; *Oberlin Evangelist*, 24 Oct. 1855; Norton, *Religious Newspapers*, 125. For persisting wariness of political parties see, for example, the warning of Boynton and Mason, *Journey through Kansas*, 205–6: "Political parties have hitherto used the anti-slavery feeling of the country very much as a vessel uses a steam-tug . . . to get it well out of the harbor, and then it spreads its sails and commits itself to other influences. The political party which is now likely to become the dominant one, has quite other purposes lying nearer to its heart than the abolition, or even repression of slavery."

[47] For the early history of the Republican party and an elucidation of the complexities of party political realignment between 1854 and 1856, see Gienapp, *Origins of the Republican Party*, *passim*; Potter, *Impending Crisis*, 247–65; Holt, *Political Crisis of the 1850s*, 139–81; Sewell, *Ballots for Freedom*, 254–91; Maizlish, *Triumph of Sectionalism*, 188–93, 197–203.

[48] Trafton, *Scenes in My Life*, 30, 240–4; "Massachusetts Journal of the House" (1855), 1675, 1732, 1738, Massachusetts State House. For antislavery sentiment in

Massachusetts Know Nothingism, and the Order's success in attracting most former Free Soilers, see Mulkern, "Know-Nothing Party in Massachusetts," v, 75–107; Dale Baum, *The Civil War Party System: The Case of Massachusetts, 1848–1876* (Chapel Hill, NC, 1984), 32–3. For an overview of the role of Know Nothings in the anti-Nebraska movement, see Gienapp, "Nativism and the Creation of a Republican Majority," esp. 531–3.

[49] *WCA*, 7 June 1854; 9 May 1855. For the interconnectedness of these causes, see Billington, *Protestant Crusade*, 425–7; Gienapp, "Nativism and the Creation of a Republican Majority," 531–5; Ronald P. Formisano, "To the Editor," *CWH*, 21 (June 1975), 188; Potter, *Impending Crisis*, 252; Gilbert Osofsky, "Abolitionists, Irish Immigrants, and the Dilemmas of Romantic Nationalism," *AHR*, 80 (Oct. 1975), 889–912; Stephen E. Maizlish, "The Meaning of Nativism and the Crisis of the Union: The Know-Nothing Movement in the Antebellum North," in Maizlish and Kushma (eds) *Essays on Antebellum Politics*, 173–9.

[50] *WCA*, 29 March, 19 April, 28 June 1854; Cuthbert E. Allen, "The Slavery Question in Catholic Newspapers, 1850–1865," *United States Catholic Historical Society Records and Studies*, 26 (1936), 99–169; Walter G. Sharrow, "John Hughes and a Catholic Response to Slavery in Antebellum America," *Journal of Negro History*, 57 (July 1972), 254–69; *New York Freeman's Journal*, 9 Dec. 1850, 21 June 1851, 18, 25 Jan., 22 Feb. 1851, 18 March 1854, 24, 31 May, 14 June, 4 Oct. 1856; *Catholic Telegraph*, 14 June, 23 Aug. 1856.

[51] Foster, *Rights of the Pulpit, and Perils of Freedom*, 44; William W. Patton, *Slavery and Infidelity; or Slavery in the Church Ensures Infidelity in the World* (Cincinnati, 1856), 10; *WCA*, 1 March 1854, 12 Dec. 1855; Gordon, *Life and Writings*, 302; Fish, *Freedom or Despotism*, 15; *Independent*, 13 April 1855; Ebenezer P. Rogers, *The Repeal of the Missouri Compromise Considered* (Newark, NJ, 1856), 8; George W. Perkins, *Facts and Duties of the*

Times, 7–8; Bowers, *Discourse on the Nebraska Bill*, 14. See also Boynton, *Oration before the Native Americans*, 18; Peterson, *Divine Discontent*, 180; Smith, *Defence of the Methodist Episcopal Church*, 17.

⁵² D.G. Parker, *A Compilation of Startling Facts; or, Romanism against Republicanism* (Chicago, 1856), 62–8; Calvin Arnold, "Memoirs," 8–9, 11, DU; Clark, *Evils and Remedy of Intemperance*, 9; Kitchel, *Appeal to the People*, 5, 15–16, 31 and *passim*; *Independent*, 18 May 1854; Mark Hopkins *et al.*, *Address to the People of Massachusetts*, 10–11.

⁵³ The theme of this paragraph and the next draws especially on various works by William E. Gienapp: *Origins of the Republican Party*; "Salmon P. Chase, Nativism, and the Formation of the Republican Party in Ohio," *Ohio History*, 93 (Winter–Spring, 1984), 5–39; and "Nativism and the Creation of a Republican Majority," 529–59. Dale Baum, *Civil War Party System*, 31–5, rightly identifies the unease many early Republicans felt about exploiting nativism politically. However, these were not only a minority of the party but, as former Know Nothings moved in considerable numbers into the Republican coalition, an ever smaller minority. Gienapp, *Origins of the Republican Party*, 419–20, 470. For the Germans' anti-Nebraskaism and anti-Catholicism, and the opportunities thus open to the Republicans, see also Don E. Fehrenbacher, *Prelude to Greatness: Lincoln in the 1850s* (Stanford, Calif., 1962), 12–13; George M. Stephenson, "Nativism in the Forties and Fifties with Special Reference to the Mississippi Valley," *MVHR*, 9 (Dec. 1922), 201; Kelley, *Cultural Pattern*, 174–5; Fletcher, *Diary*, V, 533 (17 June 1856); Schafer, "Know Nothingism in Wisconsin," 15–20; Kathleen Neils Conzen, "Precocious Reformers: Immigrants and Party Politics in Ante-Bellum Milwaukee," *Historical Messenger of the Milwaukee County Historical Society*, 33 (Summer 1977), 49.

⁵⁴ *WCA*, 25 July 1855; *Oberlin*

Evangelist, 19 Dec. 1855; John B. Weaver, "Ohio Republican Attitudes towards Nativism, 1854–1855," *Old Northwest*, 9 (1983–84), 289–305. In fact Chase seems to have secured only about 10 percent of German voters, many of whom abstained in protest at the presence of nativist associates on the Republican ticket. Gienapp, "Chase", 36–7.

⁵⁵ *WCA*, 12, 26 July, 30 Aug. 1854; *Oberlin Evangelist*, 7 May 1856; Marsh, *Temperance Recollections*, 285–7; Tyrrell, *Sobering Up*, 282–309. For the stunning effect on Indiana evangelical activists of the state Supreme Court's annulment of the 1855 Prohibition Law see Goodwin, *Seventy Six Years' Tussle with the Traffic*, 19–23: "the sadness of a funeral" hung over the annual temperance convention of 1856.

⁵⁶ *WCA*, 14, 21 Nov., 5 Dec. 1855, 22 Oct. 1856; Wheelock Craig, *Legislation as an Implement of Moral Reform: A Sermon Preached in the Trinitarian Church, New Bedford, Oct. 4, 1857* (New Bedford, Mass., 1858), 5–15. In New York by the fall of 1856 antislaveryites had seized the political initiative from prohibitionists. Marsh, *Temperance Recollections*, 294–7; *New York Tribune*, 1 Oct. 1856.

⁵⁷ Gienapp, *Origins of the Republican Party*, 190, 206–8, 235, 292–5; Byrne, "Maine Law Versus Lager Beer," 117–20; Goodwin, *Seventy Six Years' Tussle with the Traffic*, 22.

⁵⁸ Foner, "Causes of the American Civil War," 19; Gienapp, *Origins of the Republican Party*, *passim*. See also Hendrik Booraem, V, *The Formation of the Republican Party in New York: Politics and Conscience in the Antebellum North* (New York, 1983), 222–7 and *passim*.

⁵⁹ McKivigan, "Abolitionism and the American Churches," 367–8; Robert J. Cook, *Baptism of Fire: The Republican Party in Iowa, 1838–1878* (forthcoming, 1993).

⁶⁰ See, for example, John C. Clyde, *Life of James H. Coffin, LL.D. . . . .* (Easton, Pa., 1881), 71–7.

⁶¹ *DAB* (for Lovejoy); Edward Magdol, *Owen Lovejoy: Abolitionist in Congress* (New Brunswick, NJ, 1967),

127–48; Victor B. Howard, *Conscience and Slavery: The Evangelistic Calvinist Domestic Missions, 1837–1861* (Kent, Ohio, 1991), 177; J. Jones to L. Trumbull, March 1856, L. Trumbull Papers [WEGT]; *BDAC*, 594, 1177; *WCA*, 27 Sept. 1854, 27 May 1857; Holbrook, *Recollections*, 165; Grinnell, *Men and Events*, 117–19; Magoun, *Asa Turner*, 190–2, 279–89; *Independent*, 16 Feb., 6 April 1854; Cook, *The Republican Party in Iowa*; *Galesburg Free Democrat*, 8 May 1856: transcript in Blanchard Papers, WC. Grinnell, a New Englander, was a moving spirit behind the party's formation in Iowa and the author of its address to voters in 1856; Waters withdrew as Free Soil candidate for governor in 1854 to give the prohibitionist Whig, James W. Grimes, a clear run for the office; Turner's role in securing Grimes's victory led to the governor's dubbing him his "foster-father."

62 *New York Freeman's Journal*, 22 Dec. 1855; *WCA*, 20 Feb. 1856; E. Everett, Diary, 25 Oct. 1856, E. Everett Papers [WEGT]; Hall (ed.) *Forty Years' Familiar Letters*, II, 217–18, 225, 227. See also Henry C. Alexander, *The Life of Joseph Addison Alexander* (2 vols, New York, 1870), II, 805; *New York Observer*, 28 Feb., 6, 27 March 1856.

63 *A Statement of the Congregation of the Church of the Epiphany, Philadelphia, of Facts Bearing on the Action of the Vestry in Requesting the Resignation of the Rector* ... (Philadelphia, 1856), *passim*. See also W.H. Lewis, "Political Preaching," *American Church Review*, 9 (Oct. 1856), 348–57.

64 Foster, *Rights of the Pulpit, and Perils of Freedom*, 8–36; Thomson, *Pulpit and Politics*, 12; Moody, *Life's Retrospect*, 229; C.W. Clapp, "The Sphere of the Pulpit," *New Englander*, 15 (Feb. 1857), 145. For the text see Matthew 22. 21.

65 William T. Dwight, *The Pulpit in its Relation to Politics: A Discourse, Delivered in the Third Congregational Church of Portland* ... (Portland, Ohio, 1857), 18. For similar arguments see, for example, John Maltby, *Government: A Sermon* (Bangor, Me., 1856), 7 and *passim*; David D. Demarest, *Religion in Politics: A Sermon Preached in the Reformed Dutch Church of Hudson, N.Y.* ... (Hudson, NY, 1856), 4 and *passim*; Samuel Harris, "Politics and the Pulpit," *New Englander*, 12 (May 1854), 254–75.

66 Nathaniel Bailey, *Our Duty*, 22–4; *WCA*, 8 Oct., 19 Nov. 1856; Eddy, *The Commonwealth*, 13–14, 25; Richardson, *Wickedness in High Places*, 11; Bowers, *Discourse on the Nebraska Bill*, 2; Humphrey, *Missouri Crisis*, 4–6.

67 George D. Armstrong, *Politics and the Pulpit: A Discourse* (Norfolk, Va., 1856), 9–34; *SCA*, 24 March 1854.

68 *Biblical Recorder*, 10 Feb., 24, 31 March 1854; *New Orleans Christian Advocate* and *Western Recorder*, quoted in *WCA*, 22 March 1854; Lacy, "Protestant Newspaper Reaction," 68–9; *Knoxville Whig*, 11 Nov. 1854; T.S. Reeve to A. Bullard, 23 Dec. 1854, Bullard Papers, PHS; Overton Bernard, Diary, 5 Nov. 1860, SHC; *SCA*, 24 March 1854; *St Louis Christian Advocate*, 10 Aug. 1854.

69 *Biblical Recorder*, 31 March, 21 April, 4, 25 May 1854; Thomas Smyth, *Autobiographical Notes*, 445.

70 See, for example, *Knoxville Whig*, 19 April, 14 Oct. 1856; *Biblical Recorder*, 28 April 1854; Valentine, Diary, 10 May 1855, SHC; *St Louis Christian Advocate*, quoted in *WCA*, 12 March 1856.

71 Smith, *George Foster Pierce*, 278–93. See also *SCA*, 22 Dec. 1854, 2, 26 July 1855; *Texas Christian Advocate*, quoted in *WCA*, 11 July 1855; *North Carolina Christian Advocate*, 15 Feb., 28 March, 4 April, 20 June, 15 Aug. 1856.

72 *Biblical Recorder*, 5 June 1856. See also *ibid.*, 3 May, 13 Dec. 1855, 10 July, 7 Aug. 1856; *Christian Index*, 10 April, 21 Aug. 1856.

73 *Knoxville Whig*, 31 May 1856; Overy, "Dabney," 81, 95; *Biblical Recorder*, 12 June 1856. See also S. Colton, Diary, 4 June 1856, SHC.

74 *Baptist Examiner* (New York), quoted in *WCA*, 8 Oct. 1856. See also *Biblical Recorder*, 26 June 1856; *South Western Baptist*, quoted in *Columbus Enquirer*, 17 June 1856; *North Carolina*

Christian Advocate, 13, 20 June 1856.

[75] *SCA*, 13 May, 5 Aug. 1853, 21 April 1854, 12 July 1855, 22 May, 5 June, 31 July 1856; *Charleston Mercury*, 2 July 1856; *Richmond Christian Advocate*, 27 April, 7 Sept., 5 Oct. 1854, 11 Oct. 1855, 5 June 1856, *WCA*, 30 July 1856; *Knoxville Whig*, 10 May 1856; *Biblical Recorder*, 7 June 1855, 20 March, 6 Nov. 1856; *Christian Index*, 4 Sept., 16 Oct. 1856. The term "Black Republican" was intended, of course, to suggest the party pursued abolition, racial equality and miscegenation.

[76] Stroupe, *Religious Press in the South Atlantic States*, 28–9, 40, 53–4; Overy, "Dabney," 73–5; *Biblical Recorder*, 24 July 1856.

[77] *WCA*, 8, 15, 22 March 1854; *New Englander*, 14 (Nov. 1856), 528; *Biblical Recorder*, 25 May 1854; *Christian Index*, 3 July 1856. See also Loveland, *Southern Evangelicals and the Social Order*, 262–4.

[78] *SCA*, 17 April, 18 Sept. 1856; *Nashville Christian Advocate*, 2 Oct. 1856; *WCA*, 15 Oct. 1856.

[79] For the significance of the 1856 election in the wider context of party realignment see especially Gienapp, *Origins of the Republican Party*, 413–48 and Kleppner, *Third Electoral System*, 16–74. See also Roy F. Nichols and Philip S. Klein, "Election of 1856," in Schlesinger and Israel, *American Presidential Elections*, III, 1007–94.

[80] *CAJ*, 2 Oct., 13 Nov. 1856; *New York Observer*, 23, 30 Oct. 1856; Cole, *Social Ideas*, 137; Fletcher, *Diary*, V, 571 (19 Sept. 1856).

[81] Holt, *Political Crisis of the 1850s*, 198; Gienapp, *Origins of the Republican Party*, 526.

[82] For Democratic ideology in the 1850s, see Bruce Collins, "The Ideology of the Ante-bellum Northern Democrats," *Journal of American Studies*, 11 (April 1977), 103–22, and Baker, *Affairs of Party*, *passim*.

[83] *Official Proceedings of the Democratic Convention, Held in Cincinnati, June 2–6, 1856* (Cincinnati, 1856), 25, 76. See also *Words of Counsel to Men of Business. By a Man of Business* (n.p., 1856), 16–18;

"Know-Nothingism," *Democratic Review*, 37 (June 1856), 495–6.

[84] Josiah Randall, *Speech of Josiah Randall, Esq., of Philadelphia, Delivered at Chambersburg, August 6, 1856, at the Request of the Democratic State Convention, of Pennsylvania* (n.p. [1856]), 2–3; *Infidelity and Abolitionism: An Open Letter to the Friends of Religion, Morality, and the American Union* (n.p. [1856]), 1–6; *Catholic Telegraph*, 18 Oct. 1856.

[85] R. McMurdy to J. Buchanan, 15 Oct. 1856, J. Buchanan Papers, Hist. Soc. of Pennsylvania [WEGT]; J. Williams to L. Summers, 3 Sept. 1856, L. Summers Papers, Iowa State Dept of History [WEGT]; A.M. Roberts to S. Cary, 1 Aug. 1856, S. Cary Papers, Maine Hist. Soc. [WEGT]; *Conspiracy Disclosed!! Kansas Affairs. Read! Read!! Read!!!* (Washington, DC, 1856), 16–17; M.W. Cluskey, comp., *Buchanan and Breckinridge: The Democratic Handbook . . .* (Washington, 1856), 16–19; *Review of a Political Sermon delivered in Dubuque, Iowa . . . July 16, 1856, by Rev. John C. Holbrook, Pastor of the Congregational Church. By a Layman* (Dubuque, Iowa, 1856), 3, 5; *New York Tribune*, 15, 16 Aug., 10 Sept. 1856. For the strenuous efforts of the Democratic press in Ohio to discredit "political clergy," see Howard, "The 1856 Election in Ohio," 40–2.

[86] Jeremiah S. Black, "*Religious Liberty*": *An Address to the Phrenakosmian Society of Pennsylvania College . . . September 17th, 1856* (Chambersburg, Pa., 1856); John L. Dawson, *Speech . . . before the Great Democratic Mass Meeting at Waynesburg, Greene County, Pennsylvania, August 21, 1856* (Washington, 1867), 34; *CAJ*, 8 May 1856; Johannsen, *Douglas*, 149–50, 457, 470, 478.

[87] *New York Observer*, 12 June 1856; *WCA*, 26 Nov. 1856; Fuller and Green, *God in the White House*, 96–100; William U. Hensel, *The Religious Convictions and Character of James Buchanan* (Lancaster, Pa., n.d.), 5–16, 28–9; *Infidelity and Abolitionism*, 6–7.

[88] Millard Fillmore, *Speeches . . . at New York . . .* (New York, 1856), 10; Johnson and Porter, *National Party Platforms*, 22; *Life of Millard Fillmore* (New

York, 1856), 28; *The Romish Intrigue: Fremont a Catholic!!* (New York [1856]), 16; Rayback, *Millard Fillmore*, 407–8.

[89] W.L. Barre, *The Life and Public Services of Millard Fillmore* (Buffalo, NY, 1856), 289–97; *The American Textbook for the Campaign of 1856* (Baltimore, 1856), 23; *Life of Millard Fillmore*, 10–12, 26–7.

[90] Holt, *Political Crisis of the 1850s*, 185.

[91] *The Duty of Native Americans in the Present Crisis* (n.p., 1856), 5.

[92] J.C. *Fremont's Record: Proof of His Romanism: Proof of His Pro-Slavery Acts . . .* (n.p. [1856]), 3, 6, 8–14; New York *Daily Times*, quoted in *New Orleans Bee*, 29 Sept. 1856; *New York Tribune*, 9 July 1856; Fillmore, *Speeches*, 23; *Fremont: Only 17 Working Days in the U.S. Senate . . .* (n.p. [1856]), 2–20; *Duty of Native Americans*, 4; J.C. *Fremont: "Is He Honest? Is He Capable?"* ([Boston] 1856), 1–8. See also Allan Nevins, *Frémont: Pathmarker of the West* (New York, 1955), 305–42, 391, 444–7.

[93] Quoted in Erastus Brooks, *Speech . . . at Hartford, Conn., July 8, 1856 . . .* (New York, 1856), 5. Gienapp, *Origins of the Republican Party*, 367–72, discusses the origins and political effects of these allegations, which were not invented by the American party and were circulating before Frémont's nomination.

[94] J.C. *Fremont's Record*, 3–5; *Col. Fremont's Religious History: The Authentic Account: Papist or Protestant, Which?* (n.p. [1856]), 5, 8–11; *The Romish Intrigue*, 6, 9; *New York Tribune*, 9 July, 22 Aug. 1856; *New York Express*, quoted in *Albany Evening Journal*, 14 Oct. 1856.

[95] *New York Tribune*, 9 Aug. 1856; *The Romish Intrigue*, 1–5, 15–16.

[96] McDonald and Searles, *Inskip*, 58, 127–8; Hiram Ketchum, *Connecticut Aroused! Great Demonstration at New Haven. Speech of Hon. Hiram Ketchum* (New York, 1856), 5.

[97] Fuller and Green, *God in the White House*, 89–91; Barre, *Fillmore*, 81, 370–4; Ketchum, *Connecticut Aroused!*, 11; Carroll, *Great American Battle*, 355, 360–1; Barre, *Fillmore*, 13–14, 19–20, 94–5, 132, 140–4, 152–60, 389, 406–7; *Duty of Native*

Americans, 1; Johnson and Porter, *National Party Platforms*, 22; *Life of Millard Fillmore*, 28; Brooks, *Speech at Hartford*, 2–3.

[98] *Proceedings of the First Three Republican National Conventions of 1856, 1860, and 1864 . . .* (Minneapolis, Minn. [1893]), 21. For an analysis of the convention, the somewhat surprising radicalism of the platform and the selection of the unknown and unproven Frémont over the Methodist John McLean, see Gienapp, *Origins of the Republican Party*, 334–45.

[99] Gienapp, *Origins of the Republican Party*, 334; Russell E. Francis, "The Religious Revival of 1858 in Philadelphia," *Pennsylvania Magazine of History*, 70 (Jan. 1946), 57; Magdol, *Lovejoy*, 150–1; *Oberlin Evangelist*, 18 June 1856; Stewart, *Joshua Giddings*, 239–40; *Proceedings of the Republican National Conventions*, 29–31, 72–4; *The Fremont Songster . . .* (New York, 1856), 38. See also *Fremont & Dayton*, 13.

[100] *James Buchanan, His Doctrines and Policy*, 5–14. See also *Facts and Figures for Fremont and Freedom*, 4–6, 17–22.

[101] *The Republican Scrap Book . . .* (Boston, 1856), 22; Edwin B. Morgan, *Mr. Fillmore's Political History and Position . . .* (New York, 1856), 5–7; Ephraim Marsh, *Reasons for Going for Fremont: Letter from Ephraim Marsh . . .* (New York (?), [1856]), 4. The American party's schism over the Nebraska Act in June 1855 was followed by further antislavery defections over the territorial issue in February 1856. See Holt, *Political Crisis of the 1850s*, 171.

[102] *The Romish Intrigue*, 5; *New York Tribune*, 29 Aug. 1856, quoting the *Congregationalist*.

[103] *Albany Evening Journal*, 1, 6, 12, 30 July, 8, 28 Aug., 3, 11, 30 Sept., 14, 19, 30 Oct. 1856; *New York Tribune*, 1, 16 Sept., 13, 25 Oct. 1856; Chauncey Shaffer, *Chauncey Shaffer's Reasons for Voting for John C. Fremont* (New York, 1856), 2–3.

[104] Fred H. Harrington, "Frémont and the North Americans," *AHR*, 44 (July 1939), 842–8; Potter, *Impending*

Crisis, 256–7; Holt, *Political Crisis of the 1850s,* 177–8.

[105] Gienapp, *Origins of the Republican Party,* 336, 366–7; Purcell and Poole, "Political Nativism in Brooklyn," 55–6; Bean, "Puritan versus Celt," 79–85 (for the strong nativist element within Massachusetts's Republicanism throughout the mid-1850s).

[106] *Boston Atlas,* quoted in *New York Tribune,* 13 Sept. 1856; *Read and Ponder. Letter from Rev. Allen Steele of the Methodist Episcopal Church,* (n.p. [1856]), 3. For Republican appeals to antislavery, foreign-born Protestants, see for example *Albany Evening Journal,* 3, 6 Sept., 3, 9 Oct. 1856; *New York Tribune,* 3, 8, 31 July, 2 Aug. 1856. In fact, Republicans did not give up all hope of winning Catholic votes and sought to address the economic interests of "free laboring men" whom they claimed Democrats and planters would shut out of the rich western territories. *The Pope's Bull and the Words of Daniel O'Connell . . .* (New York, 1856), 4–7. Holt, *Political Crisis of the 1850s,* 176–80, and Gienapp, "Nativism and the Creation of a Republican Majority," 541–6, draw a distinction between Republicans' sensitivity towards Protestant immigrants on the one hand and their more assertive anti-Catholicism on the other. By contrast, Foner, *Free Soil, Free Labor. Free Men,* 226–60, and Sewell, *Ballots for Freedom,* 265–77, are more impressed by the anti-nativist elements of Republican propaganda.

[107] *New York Tribune,* 9, 21 July, 17 Sept., 11 Oct. 1856; *Col. Fremont's Religion: The Calumnies against Him Exposed by Indisputable Proofs* (n.p. [1856]); *Fremont a Protestant! . . . Proofs of His Membership of the Protestant Episcopal Church* (n.p. [1856]); Roswell Marsh, "Col. Fremont and His Slanderers," undated cutting from *New York Herald,* British Library; *Col. Fremont Not a Roman Catholic* (n.p., 1856); Gienapp, *Origins of the Republican Party,* 368–72.

[108] Frémont's visitors included the secretary of the American Home Missionary Society and an editor of the *New York Evangelist,* David B. Coe; Professors Henry B. Smith and R. D. Hitchcock of Union Theological Seminary, Thomas De Witt of the Dutch Reformed church and the Episcopalian C.S. Henry. *New York Evangelist,* 18 Sept. 1856; *New York Tribune,* 9 Oct. 1856; *Facts and Figures for Fremont and Freedom* (Providence, RI, 1856), 13–15.

[109] *Boston Pilot,* quoted in *WCA,* 25 June, 23 July, 1, 29 Oct. 1856; *New York Freeman's Journal,* 14, 21 June, 6 Sept. 1856; Allen, "Slavery Question in Catholic Newspapers," 157; *Catholic Telegraph,* 9, 23 Aug., 6 Sept. 1856; *New York Tribune,* 21 July 1856. See also Jasper W. Cross, "The St. Louis Catholic Press and Political Issues, 1845–1861," *American Catholic Historical Society Records,* 80 (Dec. 1969), 216–17.

[110] *Fremont a Protestant!,* 6. For the claim that Fillmore's religious heterodoxy made him a friend of Mormons, see *New York Tribune,* 11 Aug. 1856.

[111] *New York Tribune,* 11 July, 27 Aug. 1856; *Newark Advertiser,* repr. in *Albany Evening Journal,* 23 Sept. 1856; *Fremont a Protestant!,* 6; *Chauncey Shaffer's Reasons for Voting for Fremont,* 3–4; *Col. Fremont's Religion,* 8; *Albany Evening Journal,* 30 Sept. 1856.

[112] Gienapp, *Origins of the Republican Party,* 372; Steele, *Read and Ponder,* 2–3; *Albany Evening Journal,* 1, 2 Nov. 1856.

[113] *Albany Evening Journal,* 1, 8, 13 Aug., 4 Oct. 1856; *New York Tribune,* 31 Oct. 1856; Mains, *Buckley,* 55; Abbott, *Reminiscences,* 110–12. For Calvin Fletcher's organizing of Republican poll watchers in Indianapolis, see Fletcher, *Diary,* V, xx.

[114] Wayland and Wayland, *Francis Wayland,* I, 155. For Lyman Abbott's quite contrary advice to ministers not to remain silent, whatever their fears of offending elements in their congregations, see Ira V. Brown, *Lyman Abbott, Christian Evolutionist* (Cambridge, Mass., 1953), 19–20, quoting *Maine Evangelist,* 2 Aug. 1856. Finley was physically attacked in Lewisburg, Ohio for his efforts on behalf of the Republicans. *WCA,* 24 Sept. 1856; *SCA,* 15 Jan. 1857.

[115] C.F. Adams, Diary, 8 Nov. 1856,

Adams Family Papers, Massachusetts Historical Society [WEGT]; *Oberlin Evangelist*, 30 July 1856; *Albany Evening Journal*, 17 Sept., 6 Oct. 1856. Republicans implied that Democratic clerics were doughfaces and placemen whose loyalty had been bought. *New York Tribune*, 10 Oct. 1856. For other examples of active evangelical support for Frémont, clerical and lay, see Crooks, *John M'Clintock*, 262; William E. Barton, *Joseph Edwin Roy 1827–1908: A Faithful Servant of God and of His Own Generation* (Oak Park, Ill.), 15; Alphonso A. Hopkins, *The Life of Clinton Bowen Fisk* (New York, 1890), 50–2; Bridges, "Peck on Illinois Slavery," 182; Lewis Tappan, Journal, 4, 5 Nov. 1856, L. Tappan Papers, LC; Frank H. Swan, *Woodbury Kidder Dana: A Biographical Sketch* (Providence, RI), 34–8.

[116] *Albany Evening Journal*, 1, 28 Aug. (Methodist church at Olean, NY; Old Dutch church, Brooklyn; Wesleyan Methodist church in Seneca Falls), 17 Sept. (Galesburg, Ill.; Waterville, Me.; Montrose, Pa.; Syracuse, NY), 27 Sept. 1856 (Salem, Washington County, NY); Lewis, *Samuel Lewis*, 305 (Methodist church in Cincinnati); *Galesburg Free Democrat*, 2 Oct. 1856; *New York Tribune*, 19 Aug., 23 Sept., 13 Oct. 1856; J. Graham to J. Buchanan, 17 Oct. 1856, J. Buchanan Papers, Historical Society of Pennsylvania [WEGT].

[117] *Galesburg Free Democrat*, 17 July 1856, transcript in Blanchard Papers, WC; W. Patton to J. Buchanan, 7 Nov. 1856, quoted in Gienapp, *Origins of the Republican Party*, 432; B. Adams, Diary, 12 May 1854, 22, 29 Aug., 29, 30 Sept., 17 Oct., 4 Nov. 1856, DU; Cole, *Social Ideas*, 137; *Albany Evening Journal*, 13, 17 Sept., 23 Oct. 1856; *New York Tribune*, 22 Sept, 10, 17 Oct. 1856. See David H. Moore, *John Morgan Walden, Thirty-Fifth Bishop of the Methodist Episcopal Church* (New York, 1915), 38, for Methodists working the stump for Frémont in Kentucky and the West.

[118] *New York Tribune*, 21, 28, 31 Oct., 3, 4 Nov. 1856 (Cheever's "The Crime of Extending Slavery" and "God against Slavery"; Thompson's "Responsibilities of Men in the Exercise of Suffrages"); George I. Rockwood, "George Barrell Cheever, Protagonist of Abolition: Religious Emotionalism the Underlying Factor in the Causes of the Civil War," *American Antiquarian Society Proceedings*, 46 (April 1936), 105–6; *Albany Evening Journal*, 10 Oct. 1856. See also Perkins, *Facts and Duties of the Times*; C.M. Damon, *Sketches and Incidents: or, Reminiscences of Interest in the Life of the Author* (Chicago, 1900), 25–6, recalling Gilbert De La Matyr's pulpit appeals for Frémont; Alfred Cookman to M. Simpson, 13 Oct. 1856, M. Simpson Papers, LC, indicating Cookman's alignment with the Republicans' "union" ticket against the Democrats.

[119] Howard, *Henry Clay Trumbull*, 142–3; Rollo Ogden (ed.) *Life and Letters of Edwin Lawrence Godkin* (2 vols, New York, 1907), I, 117–18; *New York Tribune*, 22 July, 29 Aug., 16, 18, 24 Oct. 1856 (Long Island Consociation of Congregational Churches; New York and New Jersey State Conventions of Baptists; New School Presbyterian Synods of New York and New Jersey); *Albany Evening Journal*, 3 Nov. 1856 (Massachusetts Baptist Convention); *WCA*, 20 Aug., 3, 10 Sept., 8, 15, 22, 29 Oct. 1856 (Michigan Annual Conference, South-East Indiana Annual Conference of the MEC); *New York Observer*, 4 Sept. 1856; *Oberlin Evangelist*, 4 June, 2 July, 27 Aug. 1856; Richard H. Watkins, "Baptists of the North and Slavery, 1856–1860," *Foundations*, 13 (Oct., Dec. 1970), 322–3; *Northwestern Christian Advocate*, 29 Oct. 1856; Howard, *Conscience and Slavery*, 142–55. Such influential sheets as the *New York Evangelist*, *Western Christian Advocate*, *Christian Watchman and Reflector*, *New York Baptist Examiner* and *Northwestern Christian Advocate* made little secret of their hostility towards the Democrats.

[120] *WCA*, 13 Feb. 1856 (Boynton); G. Cheever to H. Cheever, 27 Sept. 1856, G.B. Cheever Papers, American Antiquarian Society [WEGT]; Abbott, *Reminiscences*, 98–100; B. Adams, Diary, 12 May 1854, 22, 29 Aug., 29, 30 Sept., 17

Oct., 4 Nov. 1856, DU; "HCJ" in the *Oberlin Evangelist*, 10 Sept. 1856; *New York Tribune*, 17 Sept. 1856, quoting Henry Ward Beecher at the Broadway Tabernacle; *New York Observer*, 30 Oct. 1856; *New York Daily News*, quoted in *New York Freeman's Journal*, 20 Dec. 1856.

121 See, for example, Carriere, "Slavery, Consensus, and the Louisiana Know-Nothing Party," *Mid-America*, 66 (April–July 1984), 51–63.

122 See Overdyke, *Know Nothing Party in the South*, 127–55, for the American party's southern campaign in 1856.

123 Brownlow, *Americanism Contrasted with Foreignism*, 3–4, 7–8, 80–5, 97–8; Carroll, *Great American Battle*, 108–9, 328–9; *Knoxville Whig*, 5, 26 April, 24 May, 7 June, 30 Aug., 15 Nov. 1856; *New Orleans Bee*, 3 Oct. 1856.

124 Brownlow, *Americanism Contrasted with Foreignism*, 17–23, 147, 155–8, 181; *New Orleans Bee*, 24 Oct. 1856; *Knoxville Whig*, 5 Jan., 9 Feb., 11 Oct. 1856; Chapman, *Americanism versus Romanism*, 303–4; Fitzgerald, *Judge Longstreet*, 114–16; *New Orleans Bee*, 29 Aug. 1856. The fear that immigrants (particularly Germans, but also the Irish) would abolitionize the territories had been especially potent in the advance of Know Nothingism in the South through 1854 and 1855. William G. Bean, "An Aspect of Know Nothingism – The Immigrant and Slavery," *South Atlantic Quarterly*, 23 (1924), 324–34. Carriere, "Slavery, Consensus, and the Louisiana Know-Nothing Party," 59, suggests that in 1856 Louisiana Know Nothings, in contrast to earlier campaigns, made relatively half-hearted attempts to link foreigners to abolition. But the state's peculiar chemistry of Whiggism and Catholicism did not make it typical.

125 *North Carolina Whig*, 10 June 1856; Carroll, *Great American Battle*, 276. For the alleged antislavery impulses of the papacy, see also Chapman, *Americanism versus Romanism*, 121–5.

126 For Republican support amongst antislavery evangelicals in the border

South, see for example S. Sawyer (ed. of the *Presbyterian Witness*) to D.B. Coe (secretary of the AHMS), 23 July 1856; B. Mills to D.B. Coe, 2 Feb. 1857, AHMS Papers.

127 Brownlow, *Americanism Contrasted with Foreignism*, 100, 178–83; *North Carolina Whig*, 27 Aug. 1856; *Knoxville Whig*, 20 Sept 1856; *Columbus Enquirer*, 23 Sept. 1856.

128 Brownlow, *Americanism Contrasted with Foreignism*, 197–201; *New Orleans Bee*, 16, 17 Sept. 1856. For the claim that the "blasphemous" 3,000 clergy who signed the Nebraska protest included a dozen seducers and sexual perverts, see *Columbus Enquirer*, 16 Sept. 1856, citing the *New Haven Register*.

129 *Columbus Enquirer*, 21 Oct. 1856; *New Orleans Bee*, 19 Sept. 1856.

130 *New Orleans Bee*, 16, 17 Sept., 2 Oct. 1856; A.E. Carroll, *Which? Fillmore or Buchanan*, (Boston, 1856), 19–20; *North Carolina Whig*, 24 June, 19 Aug. 1856; Brownlow, *Americanism Contrasted with Foreignism*, 134–5; *Knoxville Whig*, 25 Aug. 1855, 15 March, 26 April, 2, 16 Aug., 15 Nov. 1856; *Columbus Enquirer*, 23 Sept. 1856.

131 Biennial Message of Governor David Reid of North Carolina, Nov. 1854, cited in Paul A. Reid, "Gubernatorial Campaigns and Administrations of David S. Reid, 1848–1854," (MA diss., University of North Carolina at Chapel Hill, 1938), 146, 169; Aaron V. Brown, *An Address on the Parties and Issues of the Presidential Election . . .* (Nashville, Tenn., 1856), 16–35; *Richmond Enquirer*, quoted in *Albany Evening Journal*, 21 July 1856; *North Carolina Standard*, 12 April, 16, 19 July, 17 Sept. 1856; *New Orleans Bee*, 1 Oct. 1856; Andrew Johnson, *Speech . . . on the Political Issues of the Day, Delivered before the Citizens of Nashville, on the 15th of July, 1856* (Nashville, Tenn., 1856), 4–24.

132 Augustus Baldwin Longstreet, *Letter from President Longstreet* [to the Know Nothing Preachers of the MECS] (New Orleans, 1855), 6–9. Longstreet's appeal was published by the Democratic

State Central Committee of Louisiana and was widely circulated. See also Longstreet, *Know Nothingism Unveiled*, in Fitzgerald, *Judge Longstreet*, 119. For Know Nothing responses see Brownlow, *Americanism Contrasted with Foreignism*, 25–36; Fitzgerald, *Judge Longstreet*, 112 (for William Winans).

133 C.W. Dabney to R.L. Dabney, 18 March 1856, 5 April 1856, Dabney Papers, SHC; *New York Freeman's Journal*, 26 May 1855.

134 *Nashville Union*, cited in *Knoxville Whig*, 26 April, 17 May, 15 Nov. 1856; *Montgomery Advertiser*, 2 Sept. 1856, cited in *Columbus Enquirer*, 16 Sept. 1856. See also *North Carolina Standard*, 19 April, 3 May 1856; Johnson, *Speech on the Political Issues of the Day*, 24–8; Aaron V. Brown, *Address of Ex-Gov. Aaron V. Brown, before the Democratic Association of Nashville, June 24, 1856* (Nashville, Tenn., 1856), 4–7.

135 *New Orleans Bee*, 25, 27 Aug., 18 Sept. 1856; *North Carolina Standard*, 28 June 1856; *Knoxville Whig*, 12 Jan., 30 Aug., 6, 27 Sept., 15 Nov. 1856; *Columbus Enquirer*, 16 Sept. 1856.

136 John Hall, Journals, 4 Nov. 1856, PHS; Palmer, *Leonidas L. Hamline*, 88, 461.

137 "Puritanism and Abolitionism," *Democratic Review*, 36 (July 1855), 82; Edward A. Lawrence, *The Life of Rev. Joel Hawes, D.D., Tenth Pastor of the First Church, Hartford, Conn.* (Hartford, Conn., 1871), 220–1; J. Drummond to M. Simpson, 20 April 1850, M. Simpson Papers, LC. See also Richard Wheatley, *The Life and Letters of Mrs. Phoebe Palmer* (New York, 1876), 305; *WCA*, 3 April 1850, 9 Aug. 1854; W. Gordon, "Autobiography," NEC.

138 See, for example, *WCA*, 9 June 1852, discussing the relations between the MEC and the American and Foreign Christian Union; *CAJ*, 27 March 1856. Ellis, "Yankee Dutch Confrontation," 269, argues that Catholic immigration was the decisive element in ameliorating Dutch–New Englander conflicts in this period.

139 See, for example, Tefft, *Methodism Successful*, 194–5; M. Simpson, "Reasons for Building," 4–7, Simpson Papers, DU; Manship, *Thirteen Years' Experience*, 228–9; Schaff, *America*, 137; Jobson, *America, and American Methodism*, 33, 378–80; Stephen Parks, *Troy Conference Miscellany, Containing a Historical Sketch of Methodism within the Bounds of the Troy Conference . . .* (Albany, NY, 1854), 67. For persisting abrasiveness between northern evangelical denominations, however, see for example Haney, *Story of My Life*, 115–16; *WCA*, 31 Jan., 21 March, 14 Nov. 1855; *Christian Watchman and Reflector*, 24 April 1856; Wise, *Popular Objections to Methodism*, passim.

140 Crane, *Autobiography*, 88–9; Bacon, *Munger*, 103–4; Rice and Rice, *William Rice*, 6–7; Grim, "The Reverend John Rankin," 254; Burlingame-Cheney, *Oren B. Cheney*, 103. See also Daniels, *Gilbert Haven*, 52; R.M. Hall, "Life," 79–89, PHS. Lewis Tappan voted as reluctantly for Frémont as he had earlier done for John P. Hale, believing the Republicans to be "a white man's party united for selfish purposes." He felt guilty about not voting for Gerrit Smith, whom he had nominated as the Radical Abolitionist candidate. Wyatt-Brown, *Lewis Tappan*, 333–4.

141 *CAJ*, 14 Aug. 1856 [Shaffer]; Hodge, *Charles Hodge*, 393; Jordan, *William Salter*, 112; James, "Colin Dew James," 464. For other examples, see R.C. Colmery, *Memoir of the Life and Character of Josiah Scott* (Columbus, Ohio, 1881), 36–37; Ellis, "Assimilation of the Welsh," 326–7; Hammond, "Alfred Ely," 146. For ex-Whigs within Republicanism in 1856, see Gienapp, *Origins of the Republican Party*, 416–18.

142 For ex-Democrats in Republican ranks in 1856, see Gienapp, *Origins of the Republican Party*, 417–19. Many Democrats, of course, had already entered the Repubican party via the staging-post of the Know Nothing order; others returned to their former home after rebelling over the Nebraska bill (*ibid.*, 423, 446). Paul Goodman, "The Politics of Industrialism: Massachusetts,

1830–1870," in Richard L. Bushman, *et al.* (eds) *Uprooted Americans: Essays to Honor Oscar Handlin* (Boston, 1979), 181, 184, 194–6, shows how in Massachusetts the political revolution of the 1850s reduced the Democrats to a "hopeless minority." Republicans inherited from Whiggery the near-solid support of Congregationalists. At the same time, "pure" dissenting towns with mostly Baptist, Methodist, and Universalist churches, which had previously contributed to the Democrats' occasional majorities, also moved into the Republican camp. Dale Baum and Dale T. Knobel, "Anatomy of a Realignment: New York Presidential Politics, 1848–1860," *New York History*, 65 (Jan. 1984), 72, argue that over half the Republican voters in New York state in 1856 had Democratic antecedents.

[143] Gienapp, *Origins of the Republican Party*, 433–4; Kelley, *Cultural Pattern*, 200, 217–20, 328; McCulloch, *Men and Measures*, 74–5; Formisano, *Mass Political Parties*, 261–2, 312–15.

[144] Anson R. Graves, *The Farmer Boy Who Became a Bishop: The Autobiography of the Right Reverend Anson Rogers Graves, S.T.D., LL.D.* (Akron, Ohio, 1911), 34; Brinkerhoff, *Recollections*, 92–6, 123–7; Norton, *Religious Newspapers*, 126–7. For the defection of Jeremiah Hall, president of Baptist Denison University, from the Democrats to Frémont, see Howard, "The 1856 Election in Ohio," 29.

[145] "Red letter days in the life of Sheldon Jackson," PHS; Mains, *Buckley*, 54–5; A.D. Field, Diary, 4 Nov. 1856, GTS. The movement of northern evangelicals into Republicanism was the most marked element in the northern political realignment, but it was by no means the only direction of evangelical traffic. For the desertion to the Democracy of immigrant Dutch Protestant Whigs in the mid-1850s, see Swierenga, "The Ethnic Voter and the First Lincoln Election," 99–115.

[146] *Ohio State Journal*, quoted in Gienapp, *Origins of the Republican Party*, 434; *New York Tribune*, 1, 13, 18, 25 Oct., 4 Nov. 1856; Fairbank, *Rev. Calvin Fairbank*, 81–3; Lewis, *Samuel Lewis*, 318; *Albany Evening Journal*, 1, 8 Aug., 13 Sept. 1856.

[147] McKivigan, *War against Proslavery Religion*, 156–60. Nordquist, "The Ecology of Organized Religion," 43, indicates overwhelming anti-Democratic voting where Quakers were predominant.

[148] *Catholic Telegraph*, 25 July 1856; William L. Fisk, "The Associate Reformed Church in the Old Northwest: A Chapter in the Acculturation of the Immigrant," *Journal of Presbyterian History*, 46 (June 1968), 167; Chapman, *Memoirs of an Itinerant*, 132–4; Fehrenbacher, *Prelude to Greatness*, 12.

[149] Mulkern, "Know-Nothing Party in Massachusetts," 243, 254; Smith, *Pillars in the Temple*, 242–7; *New York Tribune*, 13 Oct. 1856; Ketchum, *Connecticut Aroused!*, 2, 5; Dodge, *Wm. E. Dodge*, 201–2; Hall (ed.) *Forty Years' Familar Letters*, II, 225, 227, 230, 232; Hodge, *Charles Hodge*, 393; Howard, "The 1856 Election in Ohio," 33–4; Howard, "Presbyterians and the Election of 1856," 137–50; Howard, *Conscience and Slavery*, 151; Gienapp, *Origins of the Republican Party*, 433, 540–2.

[150] Nathan L. Rice, *Ten Letters on the Subject of Slavery: Addressed to the Delegates from the Congregational Associations of the Last General Assembly of the Presbyterian Church* (St Louis, Mo., 1855), 29; L. Cass to W.A. Scott, 6 Oct. 1856, Scott Papers, Bancroft Library [WEGT]; Hutchinson, *Cyrus Hall McCormick*, I, 26, 463–4; Howard, "Presbyterians and the Election of 1856," 151–3; Bethune, *Sermon on Thanksgiving Day*, 29–33; Van Nest, *Bethune*, 352–3; Gienapp, *Origins of the Republican Party*, 540. Swierenga notes how "political inertia" kept Dutch evangelicals in Iowa within the Democratic party. "The Ethnic Voter and the First Lincoln Election," 113.

[151] M. Simpson to E.V. Simpson, 15 May 1856, M. Simpson Papers, DU. See also Grant, *Peter Cartwright*, 155–64; WCA, 2 April 1856 (letter from Peter Cartwright).

[152] Howard, "The 1856 Election in Ohio," 29; Daniels, *Gilbert Haven*, 55–7;

Prentice, *Gilbert Haven*, 147. Baum, *Civil War Party System*, 95—6, suggests that Republicanism was much stronger in late antebellum Massachusetts amongst the Methodist clergy than within their congregations. For Democratic Methodists in Pennsylvania, see Spottswood, *Brief Annals*, 151—2; C.V. Arnold, "Memoir," 8—11, DU. Formisano, *Mass Political Parties*, 312—15, suggests a significant persistence of Democratic loyalty amongst rank-and-file Methodists in Michigan. He also identifies a shift towards the Democrats amongst Episcopalians. See also Howard, "The 1856 Election in Ohio," 35—6; Mullin, *Episcopal Vision*, 200.

[153] Gienapp, *Origins of the Republican Party*, 434—5, concludes that in Pennsylvania, Iowa, and Illinois Republicans were more successful than Fillmorites in winning the support of temperance men; the American party did better in Ohio. Streeter, "Prohibition Legislation in Michigan," 297, suggests that Michigan Republicans secured the support of the state's prohibitionists; Byrne, "Maine Law versus Lager Beer," 115, takes a similar view of Republicans in Wisconsin. For the view that Indiana Republicans lost the votes of previous temperance Democrats, see Goodwin, *Seventy Six Years' Tussle with the Traffic*, 23.

[154] Gienapp, *Origins of the Republican Party*, 428—31; Richard Lyle Power, *Planting Corn Belt Culture: The Impress of the Upland Southerner and the Yankee in the Old Northwest* (Indianapolis, 1953), 5—25, 81—6, 115—20 and *passim*; Cook, *The Republican Party in Iowa*; Flinn, "Continuity and Change in Ohio Politics," 542; John L. Hammond, *The Politics of Benevolence: Revival Religion and American Voting Behavior* (Norwood, NJ, 1979), 130; Nordquist, "The Ecology of Organized Religion," 42, 61. For a modest exception to this rule of southern settlers' antipathy to "Yankee reformers," see Howard, "The 1856 Election in Ohio," 27, 42—3, discussing the Virginia Military District of Ohio, which was settled by antislavery southerners, at least some of whom shifted from Whiggery to Republicanism in 1856.

[155] Cooper, *The South and the Politics of Slavery*, 362—9; Holder, *Winans*, 213—14; Warner, *Jacob Bachtel*, 97—8; Mann, *Haygood*, 1—12; *Knoxville Whig*, 5 April, 16 Aug., 22 Nov. 1856; Mathews, *Peeps into Life*, 48—50; Kallenbach, II, 591; D. Barkalow to A. Hagaman, 7 Oct. 1856, Hagaman Papers, PHS; *New York Freeman's Journal*, 3 May 1856. For political divisions within families, see R.B. Davis to W.F. Davis, 16, 21 Oct. 1856, Beale—Davis Papers, SHC.

[156] *SCA*, 13 Nov. 1856; W.F. Davis to R.B. Davis, 11 Nov. 1856; R.B. Davis to W.F. Davis, 15 Nov. 1856, Beale—Davis Papers, SHC; R.H. Morrison to J. Morrison, 17 Nov. 1856, Morrison Papers, SHC. For Henry Hilliard's post-election "desertion" to the Democrats, see Cozart, "Hilliard," 288—9.

[157] R.H. Morrison to J. Morrison, 17 Nov. 1856, Morrison Papers, SHC; R.B. Davis to W.F. Davis, 1, 8 Dec. 1856, Beale—Davis Papers, SHC; Van Nest, *Bethune*, 352—3.

[158] Haven, "The National Midnight," in *National Sermons*, 92, 100—6. See also H. Maloy to T. and J.A. Richmond, 23 Nov. 1856, T. Richmond Papers, SHC.

[159] *Oberlin Evangelist*, 19 Nov. 1856; Fletcher, *Diary*, V, 579—84, 595—6; Haven, "The National Midnight," 92, 107—11. See also William Goodell, *The Kansas Struggle, of 1856, in Congress & in the Presidential Campaign* (New York, 1857), 78—80; G. Bent to M. Blanchard, 23 Dec. 1856, Blanchard Papers, WC.

[160] Haven, "The National Midnight," 120—1; *Oberlin Evangelist*, 19 Nov. 1856; Fletcher, *Diary*, V. 595—6.

Chapter 9 Houses Divided: Evangelical Churches and the Sundering of the Union, 1857—61

[1] C.W. Dabney to R.L. Dabney, 6 Feb. 1860, C.W. Dabney Papers, SHC. Loveland, *Southern Evangelicals and the Social Order*, esp. 263—5, places southern evangelicals' theory of Providence in the context of their views on the

omnipotence of God. I believe she takes their declared position too literally: in practice many southern clergy assumed an active role in the unfolding political drama.

2 John Dixon Long, *Pictures of Slavery in Church and State* (Philadelphia, 1857), 282, 302; *WCA*, 27 May 1857. For the Dred Scott case see, especially, Don E. Fehrenbacher, *The Dred Scott Case: Its Significance in American Law and Politics* (New York, 1978); Potter, *Impending Crisis*, 267–96.

3 See, for example, Cyrus W. Wallace, *A Sermon on the Duty of Ministers to Oppose the Extension of American Slavery* . . . (Manchester, NH, 1857), 5–6, 13–20; Nathan S.S. Beman, *Antagonisms in the Moral and Political World: A Discourse* . . . (Troy, NY, 1858), 31–5; Barton, *Joseph Edwin Roy*, 26; *New Englander*, 59 (Aug. 1857), 345–65, 462–529; "Josiah Bushnell Grinnell," in *DAB*; *WCA*, 26 Aug. 1857 (for a variety of resolutions of Methodist annual conferences). For the unanimity of the Methodist press in the free states, see *WCA*, 27 May 1857. For northern Baptist reactions, see Watkins, "The Baptists of the North and Slavery," 323–35. If there were any element of anti-Romanism in the attacks on Taney, a member of an old Catholic family, it was not pronounced.

4 *WCA*, 18 March, 8 April 1857; Long, *Pictures of Slavery*, 302–4; *Christian Watchman and Reflector*, 8 May, 19 Nov. 1856, 10 Dec. 1857; *CAJ*, 2 April 1857.

5 Sims, *Thomas M. Eddy*, 265. See also *WCA*, 29 April 1857.

6 *New York Observer*, 12 March, 2, 9 April 1857; *WCA*, 26 Aug. 1857; *A Narrative of the Recent Occurrences in the Church of the Puritans, New York* . . . (New York, 1857), 33 and *passim*; *Reply of the Church of the Puritans to the Protest of Their Late Deacons* . . . (New York, 1857). Bennett filled the whole front page of the *Herald* on 9 April 1857 with the text of Cheever's sermon on the Dred Scott decision, under the heading "Incitement to Revolution." Rockwood, "George Barrell Cheever," 105–8.

7 Brownlow, *Ought American Slavery To Be Perpetuated? A Debate between Rev. W.G. Brownlow and Rev. A. Pryne* . . . (Philadelphia [1858]), 226–7; *CAJ*, 19, 26 March, 2 April 1857.

8 *WCA*, 1, 15 April, 12 Aug. 1857. See also *WCA*, 3 Dec. 1856, 26 March, 15 April, 19 Aug. 1857; *CAJ*, 26 March, 2 April 1857; *New York Observer*, 22 Jan., 26 March, 9 April, 9, 30 July 1857; J. Harlan to M. Simpson, 17 Nov. 1856, M. Simpson Papers, LC. For the politics of the Lecompton crisis, in Kansas and Washington, see Potter, *Impending Crisis*, 297–327.

9 *WCA*, 19 July, 4, 25 Nov., 2, 16, 23 Dec. 1857; *Christian Watchman and Reflector*, 26 Nov., 24 Dec. 1857, 8 Jan., 1858. See also, Moore, *John Morgan Walden*, 47–9.

10 G.F. Fort to J.P. Fort, 10 Dec. 1857, in J.P. Fort, "Reminiscences," DU.

11 J. Blanchard to S.A. Douglas, 1 May 1858, photocopy in Blanchard Papers, WC. But within a few months Blanchard's enthusiasm had cooled, quite probably in consequence of Lincoln's onslaught on Douglas's "don't care" attitude to the spread of slavery. Blanchard to *Knox Republican*, 18 Aug. 1858, transcript in Blanchard Papers, WC.

12 *Christian Watchman and Reflector*, 5, 26 Nov. 1857, 28 Jan. 1858.

13 Ronald T. Takaki, *A Pro-Slavery Crusade: The Agitation to Reopen the African Slave Trade* (New York, 1971), esp. 146–59; Harvey Wish, "The Revival of the African Slave Trade in the United States, 1856–1860," *MVHR*, 27 (March 1941), 569–88; Barton J. Bernstein, "Southern Politics and Attempts to Reopen the African Slave Trade," *Journal of Negro History*, 51 (Jan. 1966), 16–35.

14 *Biblical Recorder*, 1 Jan., 5 March 1857; *North Carolina Presbyterian*, 18 June, 9 July, 5 Nov., 17 Dec. 1859; *Southern Baptist* (Charleston, SC) and *Southern Presbyterian*, quoted in *Christian Watchman and Reflector*, 1 Jan. 1857; Palmer, *Life of Thornwell*, 422–3; Long, *Pictures of Slavery*, 203; *SCA*, 8 July 1858, quot-

ing *CAJ*; William De Loss Love, "The Reopening of the African Slave Trade," *New Englander*, 18 (Feb. 1860), 90–100. See also *CAJ*, 6 Nov. 1856, 17 Feb. 1859; *Christian Watchman and Reflector*, 1 Oct. 1857.

[15] *New Orleans Christian Advocate* and *Texas Christian Advocate*, cited in *WCA*, 8 April 1857; *SCA*, 19, 26 Feb., 5, 12 March, 14 May 1857; Fitzgerald, *Judge Longstreet*, 100; *North Carolina Presbyterian*, 13 Oct. 1860. For a discussion of events in Harper's Ferry and their wider significance, see Potter, *Impending Crisis*, 356–84; Stephen B. Oates *To Purge This Land with Blood: A Biography of John Brown* (New York, 1970), 229–358.

[16] A.T. Davis to R. Davis, 5 Dec. 1859, Beale-Davis Papers, SHC; *North Carolina Presbyterian*, 31 March 1860; *Biblical Recorder*, 8 Dec. 1859.

[17] Crane, *Autobiography*, 132; Van Nest, *Bethune*, 353–9, 368–9; *North Carolina Presbyterian*, 31 Dec. 1859; "Sermon by Henry Ward Beecher," in James Redpath, *Echoes of Harper's Ferry* (Boston, 1860), 261; Foster, *Four Pastorates*, 72–4. See also Adin Ballou, *Autobiography of Adin Ballou 1803–1890* (Lowell, Mass., 1896), 416–22.

[18] For Brown's relationships with Thomas Wentworth Higginson, Theodore Parker, Erastus O. Haven, Josiah B. Grinnell, Joseph Bittinger and other ministers (some of whom were deeply implicated in his schemes), see Tilden G. Edelstein, *Strange Enthusiasm: A Life of Thomas Wentworth Higginson* (New Haven, Conn., 1968; New York paper edn, 1970), 197–236; Henry Steele Commager, *Theodore Parker: Yankee Crusader* (Boston, 1936), 250–4; Haven, *Autobiography*, 135; Charles E. Payne, *Josiah Bushnell Grinnell* (Iowa, 1938), 106–15, 121–3; Bittinger, *Bittinger*, 71; Oates, *To Purge This Land with Blood*, 184–91, 232–8, 265.

[19] Smith, *Nathaniel Colver*, 236–7; George B. Cheever, *The Curse of God against Political Atheism: with Some of the Lessons of the Tragedy at Harper's Ferry: A Discourse . . . (Boston, 1859), 23; Haven,

Autobiography, 135; W.W. Patton, *The Execution of John Brown: A Discourse Delivered at Chicago, December 4th, 1859 . . .* (Chicago [1859]), 9–12; R.W. Landis, "Journal," 2 Dec. 1859, PHS; Bacon, *Munger*, 104–5; William Salter, *Slavery, and the Lessons of Recent Events: A Sermon . . .* (n.p. [1859]), 6. See also Albert H. Currier, *The Life of Constans L. Goodell, D.D.* (New York, 1887), 120; Wayland and Wayland, *Francis Wayland*, II, 236. The *Independent* condemned the raid but acknowledged Brown's high purpose and self-sacrifice; one of its editors, Leonard Bacon, had met Brown – an old schoolmate – and considered his mind "diseased and unbalanced." Bacon, *Leonard Bacon*, 424, 456–60.

[20] Barton, *Joseph Edwin Roy*, 29; "The Beginning of the End" and "The Martyr," in Haven, *National Sermons*, 152–76. For a similar celebratory tone, see Redpath, *Echoes of Harper's Ferry*, 141–235 (for Edwin M. Wheelock); Fales Henry Newhall, *The Conflict in America: A Funeral Discourse Occasioned by the Death of John Brown of Ossawattomie . . .* (Boston, 1859).

[21] For conservative Unionist evangelicals' criticisms of Governor Wise for over-reacting and playing to the political gallery, see O. Bernard, Diary, 1 March 1860, SHC; R.H. Morrison to J. Morrison, 28 Nov. 1859, R.H. Morrison Papers, SHC.

[22] Nathan Lord, *A Letter to J.M. Conrad, Esq., on Slavery . . .* (Hanover, NH, 1860); "Nathan Lord," in *DAB*; *North Carolina Presbyterian*, 19 Nov., 3, 10 Dec. 1859 (citing *New York Observer*, Philadelphia *Presbyterian*, *Presbyterian Expositor*, and Samuel H. Cox's address to the Southern Aid Society). See also *Biblical Recorder*, 8 Dec. 1859, citing Philadelphia *Christian Observer*.

[23] *North Carolina Presbyterian*, 31 Dec. 1859, 7 Jan. 1860; *Knoxville Whig*, 3 Dec. 1859; *SCA*, 15 Dec. 1859; Fitzgerald, *Judge Longstreet*, 103–4.

[24] *Biblical Recorder*, 9 Feb. 1860. The *North Carolina Presbyterian*, 3 Dec. 1859, linked Brown with the theological

radicalism of Oberlin. While his father, Owen, was closely associated with the college and its liberal, perfectionist doctrine in the 1830s, Brown himself fashioned his own unique antinomian creed, part Old Testament based, part New, and lacking the faith in human progress so typical of "modern" Calvinism. See Bertram Wyatt-Brown's perspicacious essay, "John Brown's Antinomian War," in Wyatt-Brown, *Yankee Saints and Southern Sinners*, 97–127.

[25] Bacon, *Munger*, 104–5; *North Carolina Presbyterian*, 21 Jan. 1860.

[26] *Christian Intelligencer*, quoted in *North Carolina Presbyterian*, 17 March 1860; *Biblical Recorder*, 22 March 1860; Fitzgerald, *Judge Longstreet*, 97–8, 104; A.T. Davis to R. Davis, 5 Dec. 1859, Beale-Davis Papers, SHC; *Texas Christian Advocate*, quoted in *SCA*, 8 Oct. 1860.

[27] John B. Adger in *Southern Quarterly Review* (Feb. 1857), 292, quoted in Ryan, "Southern Quarterly Review," 337; *North Carolina Presbyterian*, 14 Jan., 24 March 1860; *SCA*, 2 Aug. 1860. See also "Recollections of William Kennedy Blake," 69–70, ts, SHC; Calvin H. Wiley, "The Duties of Christian Masters," in Weaver, "Calvin Henderson Wiley," 17–37; George D. Armstrong, *The Christian Doctrine of Slavery* (New York, 1857); idem, *A Discussion on Slaveholding: Three Letters to a Conservative . . . And Three Conservative Replies . . .* (Philadelphia, 1858).

[28] A.T. Davis to R. Davis, 5 Dec. 1859, Beale–Davis Papers, SHC. A Scottish Presbyterian planter of North Carolina privately judged that "we have among us a great many who would not have been distressed if Jno. Brown had succeeded" (J. Anderson to R.B. Anderson, c.21 Dec. 1859, Anderson–Thornwell Papers, SHC). See also Brantley York, *The Autobiography of Brantley York* (Durham, NC, 1910), 80.

[29] Enoch M. Marvin, *The Life of Rev. William Goff Caples, of the Missouri Conference of the Methodist Episcopal Church, South* (St Louis, Mo., 1871), 258; *Richmond Christian Advocate*, quoted in *WCA*, 9 Dec.

1857; *CAJ*, 6 Dec. 1860. Bailey, *Shadow on the Church*, 248ff., describes the polishing of a full-blown proslavery argument within Alabama and Mississippi churches during the 1850s. William A. Smith's influential lectures in defense of slavery, delivered to several generations of Methodist students at Randolph-Macon College, were published by the MECS Publishing House in Nashville in 1856 as *Lectures on the Philosophy and Practice of Slavery* (ed. T.O. Summers). See also Elizabeth Fox-Genovese and Eugene D. Genovese, "The Divine Sanction of Social Order: Religious Foundations of the Southern Slaveholders' World View," *Journal of the American Academy of Religion*, 55 (Summer 1987), 211–33; Taylor, "Baptists and Slavery in Arkansas," 221–6.

[30] Marvin, *William Goff Caples*, 258; J. Tyler, Jr, quoted in Ryan, "Southern Quarterly Review," 359–60; *Primitive Baptist*, 25 Aug. 1860; *SCA*, 5 Aug. 1853; Brownlow, *Ought American Slavery To Be Perpetuated?*, 161–2. See also Loveland, *Southern Evangelicals and the Social Order*, 258–60; Kuykendall, *Southern Enterprize*, 160–3.

[31] *North Carolina Presbyterian*, 21 May 1859. See also Brownlow, *Ought American Slavery To Be Perpetuated?*, 168; *SCA*, 21, 28 May 1857; "Slavery – The Bible, and the 'Three Thousand Parsons'," *De Bow's Commercial Review*, 26 (1858), 43–51. For southern nationalists' growing concern during the 1850s (and earlier) to defend right thinking in schools and churches against northern heterodoxy, see John McCardell, *The Idea of a Southern Nation: Southern Nationalists and Southern Nationalism, 1830–1860* (New York, 1979), 177–226.

[32] W.H. Wills, ms essays, 6 Dec. 1856, 2 July 1857, to editor of the *Western Protestant Methodist*; W.H. Wills to A. Wills, 11 May 1858, Wills Papers, SHC; Douglas R. Chandler, "The Formation of the Methodist Protestant Church," in Bucke *et al.*, *The History of American Methodism*, I, 677–82.

[33] *Richmond Christian Advocate*, 13 Jan. 1859; *SCA*, 11 Feb. 1858, 16 June, 21

July, 11 Aug. 1859; *Knoxville Whig*, 15 May 1858, 8 Oct. 1859; Ridgaway, *Edmund S. Janes*, 224–9.

³⁴ *Knoxville Whig*, 21 Jan., 18 Feb., 29 Sept. 1860; *Richmond Christian Advocate*, quoted in *CAJ*, 13 Dec. 1860; *CAJ*, 19 April, 27 Sept., 22 Nov. 1860; *North Carolina Christian Advocate*, 6 Nov. 1860.

³⁵ *CAJ*, 28 April, 18 Aug. 1859. For an indication of the conflicts within New York Methodism over responses to slaveholding in the MEC, especially between radicals centered on William Hosmer and Hiram Mattison, and moderates like Freeborn Garrettson Hibbard, see F.G. Hibbard to D.P. Kidder, 19 April, 25 Oct. 1859, Kidder Papers, GTS; *CAJ*, 9 Oct. 1856, 30 July, 12 Nov. 1857, 8 April 1858, 24 March, 26 May, 2 June 1859; N. Vansant, *Work Here, Rest Hereafter; or The Life and Character of Rev. Hiram Mattison* (New York, 1870), 57–8; Hiram Mattison, *The Impending Crisis of 1860: or the Present Connection of the Methodist Episcopal Church with Slavery...* (New York, 1858). Much of the conflict between Hibbard and Hosmer had to do with personality rather than principle. F.G. Hibbard to D.P. Kidder, 10 April 1857, Kidder Papers, GTS. The expulsion of the antislavery perfectionist Benjamin T. Roberts from the Genesee Annual Conference in 1858 led ultimately to the setting up of the Free Methodist church in 1860. "Benjamin Titus Roberts," in *DAB*.

³⁶ See, for example, *CAJ*, 16 July 1857, 8 April 1858, 6 Jan., 5 May 1859; *WCA*, 27 May 1857; Long, *Pictures of Slavery*, 46–57, 281–7; G.C.M. Roberts to G.R. Crooks, 28 Oct. 1858, Crooks Papers, DU; S. Register to M. Simpson, M. Simpson Papers, LC; Curry, *Davis Wasgatt Clark*, 169.

³⁷ For the 1860 General Conference, see in particular *CAJ*, 10–31 May, 7–28 June, 5 July 1860; Brunson, *Western Pioneer*, II, 277–85; Ridgaway, *Edmund S. Janes*, 237; Wesson G. Miller, *Thirty Years in the Itinerancy*, 179–84; Christy, *Pulpit Politics*, 401–18.

³⁸ William McDonald, *Life Sketches of Rev. Alfred Cookman* (Cincinnati [1900]),

91–5; E.F. Busey to J.S. Martin, 21 May 1860, J.S. Martin Papers, SHC; *Knoxville Whig*, 30 June 1860; *SCA*, 2 Aug. 1860; *Texas Christian Advocate*, 31 May 1860, quoted in Norton, *Religious Newspapers*, 122.

³⁹ Christy, *Pulpit Politics*, 352–3; *Biblical Recorder*, 18 June 1857; *SCA*, 18 June 1857; Thompson, *Presbyterians in the South*, I, 543–50. See also R.E. Thompson, *History of the Presbyterian Churches*, 135; McKivigan, *War against Proslavery Religion*, 169; Marsden, *Evangelical Mind*, 188 (who puts the figure of seceders at 10,000). The Synod of Missouri formed itself into an independent synod, rather than join the new United Synod. *CAJ*, 19 Nov. 1857.

⁴⁰ *Biblical Recorder*, 14 June 1860; *North Carolina Presbyterian*, 18 June, 10, 24 Dec. 1859, 9 June 1860. For southern Old School Presbyterians' sense that their church, holding together a *"heterogeneous* mass" through its Scotch-Irish ties and widely circulating newspapers, was the Union's best hope, see for example Overy, "Dabney," 77–80; *North Carolina Presbyterian*, 11 June, 19 Nov. 1859; J. Morrison to R.L. Dabney, 9 May 1859, C.W. Dabney Papers, SHC.

⁴¹ Drury, *Scott*, 199–202; Nathan Rice, *Lectures on Slavery*, 23–82; *North Carolina Presbyterian*, 18, 25 Feb., 24 March 1860. The Harper's Ferry raid revived fears that "cut-throats and assassins" might use the cover of religious organizations to circulate incendiary literature. For the heated debates within the ATS, and southern reactions to them, see *Richmond Christian Advocate*, 21 May 1857; *SCA*, 28 May, 18 June, 2 July 1857, 24 June 1858; *New York Observer*, 2 July 1857; *Christian Watchman and Reflector*, 17 Dec. 1857; *Biblical Recorder*, 3 Sept. 1857; *North Carolina Presbyterian*, 26 Nov., 17 Dec. 1859; Bacon, *Leonard Bacon*, 435–55; Griffin, "The Abolitionists and the Benevolent Societies," 201–16. For conflict within the Disciples of Christ, and the secession of radical antislavery members from its only national body, the American

Christian Missionary Society, see David
Edwin Harrell, "The Sectional Origins of
the Churches of Christ," *JSH*, 30 (Aug.
1964), 264–6.

[42] Harrell, *Quest for Christian America*,
109, 121–38.

[43] See, for example, *Christian Watchman and Reflector*, 8 Jan., 3 Sept., 29 Oct.
1857; *CAJ*, 3, 10 Sept. 1857, 22 April 1858,
3 May 1860.

[44] *Christian Watchman and Reflector*, 1,
8 Oct. (quoting the *Presbyterian*), 5 Nov.
1857; *CAJ*, 2 July 1857; L. Hamline to B.
Isbell, 10 Nov. 1856, in Palmer, *Leonidas
L. Hamline*, 402; Abel Stevens, "Slavery –
The Times," *Methodist Quarterly Review*,
17 (April 1857), 260–80; Currier, *Constans
L. Goodell*, 120. See also "Who is
Responsible for the Present Slavery
Agitation?," *Presbyterian Quarterly Review*,
31 (April 1860), 532–3.

[45] *Christian Watchman and Reflector*,
24 Sept., 1 Oct. 1857; *New York Observer*,
3, 10 Sept. 1857; *WCA*, 30 Sept. 1857;
Charles Rockland Tyng, comp., *Record
of the Life and Work of the Rev. Stephen
Higginson Tyng, D.D. . . .* (New York, 1890),
306–11.

[46] *North Carolina Presbyterian*, 13
Aug., 3 Sept. 1859, 18 Feb., 24 March, 18
Aug. 1860, quoting the *Cincinnati Presbyter*,
the *Presbyterian Banner and Advocate*
(Pittsburgh), Cortlandt Van Rensselaer
and Charles Hodge in the *Presbyterian
Magazine* (Philadelphia), the *New York
Evangelist*, and the *Presbyterian Expositor*
(Chicago). Thornwell argued at the Old
School General Assembly in 1859 (and
was later sustained by Benjamin M.
Palmer and others in tune with the
theology of the Columbia, SC, seminary)
that the church should not pass judg-
ment on the American Colonization
Society or the revival of the African slave
trade: its concern lay exclusively with
agencies directly teaching Christ as
Redeemer, not with those which combined the philanthropic and the political.
North Carolina Presbyterian, 18 June, 29
Oct. 1859. See also Farmer, *The Metaphysical Confederacy*, 258–60.

[47] The MECS General Conference of
1858, by 140 to 8, voted to remove the
General Rule forbidding the buying and
selling of men, women, and children
with the intention of enslaving them.
Previous attempts to remove the rule
had foundered on the opposition of the
border conferences, within which there
had been a clear shift in opinion in the
mid-1850s. *SCA*, 24 June, 8 July, 23 Sept.,
7, 28 Oct., 18, 25 Nov., 30 Dec. 1858;
Knoxville Whig, 15 May 1858.

[48] J. Mayland McCarter, *Border
Methodism and Border Slavery . . .*
(Philadelphia, 1858); Long, *Pictures of
Slavery*. For a more sympathetic reading
in northern Methodism of events on the
border, see Abel Stevens, *An Appeal to the
Methodist Episcopal Church, Concerning
What Its Next General Conference Should
Do on the Question of Slavery* (New York,
1859), 19–26, 43–8.

[49] W.H. Wills, ms essays, 6 Dec.
1856, 2 July 1857, to editor of the *Western
Protestant Methodist*, Wills Papers, SHC;
Brown, *Recollections of Itinerant Life*, 398;
Ridgaway, *Edmund S. Janes*, 224–9; *CAJ*,
1 March, 5 April 1860. In 1860 the
Missouri legislature refused to charter a
new Methodist (MEC) university in the
state capital.

[50] M.D. Vaughan to M. Simpson, 14
April 1857, M. Simpson Papers, LC;
McCarter, *Border Methodism and Border
Slavery*, 85; T. Sewall to M. Simpson, 28
Dec. 1859, M. Simpson Papers, LC; *CAJ*,
27 Sept. 1860. For the forced exile of the
Reverend John G. Fee (of the American
Missionary Association) and other
abolitionists from Berea, Kentucky, in
the aftermath of John Brown's raid, and
for their subsequent impact on northern
opinion, see Sears, *The Day of Small
Things*, 265–412.

[51] Wyatt-Brown, *Yankee Saints and
Southern Sinners*, 199–200.

[52] *Christian Watchman and Reflector*, 1
Oct. 1857; *New York Observer*, 27 May
1857; Mears, *Edward Norris Kirk*, 271.

[53] Fletcher M. Green, "Northern
Missionary Activities in the South, 1846–
61," *JSH*, 21 (May 1955), 161–72;
Victor B. Howard, "The Southern Aid

Society and the Slavery Controversy," *Church History*, 41 (June 1972), 208–24; McKivigan, *War against Proslavery Religion*, 119; Kuykendall, *Southern Enterprize*, 142–5. For the strenuous appeals of apprehensive and conservative ministers on behalf of the Union, see John Chambers, *Thanksgiving Sermon . . . November 24, 1859 . . .* (Philadelphia [1859]); David H. Riddle, "*Such a Time as This!" A Sermon Preached in the First Presbyterian Church, Jersey City, Thanksgiving Day, Nov. 24, 1859* (Jersey City, 1860); Samuel Nott, *The Present Crisis: with a Reply and Appeal to European Advisers . . .* (Boston, 1860).

⁵⁴ Magoun, *Asa Turner*, 289–90; *Christian Watchman and Reflector*, 3 Sept., 1 Oct. 1857; Pryne, in Brownlow, *Ought American Slavery To Be Perpetuated?*, 230–1; Daniel Eastman, *On the Agencies Which Affect the Stability of the Union* (Chicago, 1860), 31 and *passim*; *CAJ*, 3 May, 16 Aug. 1860. See also Crane, "Party Politics," 577.

⁵⁵ For the course of the revival and a discussion of its wider significance, see Smith, *Revivalism and Social Reform*, 63–79 and *passim*; Carwardine, *Transatlantic Revivalism*, 159–69; McLoughlin, *Modern Revivalism*, 163–4; Marion L. Bell, *Crusade in the City: Revivalism in Nineteenth-Century Philadelphia* (Lewisburg, Pa., 1977), 169–99; Russell E. Francis, "Pentecost, 1858: A Study in Religious Revivalism" (PhD diss., University of Pennsylvania, 1948); Carl L. Spicer, "The Great Awakening of 1857 and 1858" (PhD diss., Ohio State University, 1935).

⁵⁶ E.E. Stuart to her son, 6 April 1858, in Marlatt, *Stuart Letters*, II, 862; Anna R. Eaton, *Triumph in Christ: A Memorial of Rev. Horace Eaton, D.D.* (3rd edn, Boston, 1892), 63.

⁵⁷ See, for example, Roy F. Nichols, *The Disruption of the American Democracy* (New York, 1948), 135–6; Miller, *Life of the Mind*, 88–95. For some shrewd thoughts on the revival both as a pursuit of harmony and as source of social criticism and sectional divisiveness, see William G. McLoughlin, *Revivals, Awaken-*ings, and Reform: An Essay on Religion and Social Change in America, 1607–1977 (Chicago, 1978), 143; Kenneth M. Stampp, *America in 1857: A Nation on the Brink* (New York, 1990), 237–8; James H. Moorhead, *American Apocalypse: Yankee Protestants and the Civil War 1860–1869* (New Haven, Conn., 1978), 21.

⁵⁸ Abbott, *Reminiscences*, 128; Graves, *The Farmer Boy Who Became a Bishop*, 32–3; Moorhead, *American Apocalypse*, 21.

⁵⁹ Talbot W. Chambers, *The Noon Prayer Meeting of the North Dutch Church, Fulton St., New York: Its Origin, Character and Progress* (New York, 1858), 52, 247; *New York Observer*, 5 Aug. 1858; *Christian Watchman and Reflector*, 12 Nov. 1857.

⁶⁰ See, for example, *CAJ*, 5 Nov., 3 Dec. 1857; Charles Elliott, "Introduction," to Maxwell P. Gaddis, *Brief Recollections of the Late Rev. George W. Walker* (Cincinnati, 1857), 11; *New York Observer*, 1 April, 23 Sept. 1858; *SCA*, 15 July 1858.

⁶¹ *Christian Watchman and Reflector*, 5 Nov., 17 Dec. 1857; Chambers, *Noon Prayer Meeting*, 70–1; *New York Observer*, 18 March, 25 Feb., 27 May, 29 July 1858; *SCA*, 22 April, 17 June, 15, 22 July, 28 Oct. 1858; William C. Conant, *Narratives of Remarkable Conversions and Revival Incidents: Including . . . an Account of the Rise and Progress of the Great Awakening of 1857–8* (New York, 1858), 357; *New York Observer*, 5 Aug. 1858.

⁶² Fish, *Primitive Piety*, 242–3; Bethune, *Sermon on Thanksgiving Day*, 9–20; *CAJ*, 24 April, 11 Dec. 1856; *New York Observer*, 25 June, 2 July 1857. See also *Christian Watchman and Reflector*, 3 Sept. 1857. Political and ecclesiastical conflicts by no means ceased through the winter of 1857–58 but the decline in diversionary excitement from its earlier high peak certainly assisted the harmonizers' efforts. *CAJ*, 7 Jan., 11 March 1858 (for the MEC); *SCA*, 13 May 1858 (for the MECS); *New York Observer*, 12, 26 Nov. 1857, 3, 24 June 1858 (for New and Old School Presbyterians, and Dutch Reformed).

⁶³ *Philadelphia Press*, 6 March 1858, quoted in Francis, "Religious Revival of

1858 in Philadelphia," 64. See also, J.O. Lindsay, "The Religious Awakening of 1858," *Southern Presbyterian Review*, 11 (July 1858), 256–63.

64 Conant, *Narratives of Remarkable Conversions*, 380–1; Amy Bridges, "Another Look at Plutocracy and Politics," 59–61.

65 *New York Observer*, 15 April 1858. One politician not sidelined was the President himself. Buchanan attended the daily revival meetings in Bedford Springs, Pa., in the summer of 1858. *Ibid.*, 26 Aug., 2 Sept. 1858.

66 Chambers, *Noon Prayer Meeting*, 88–9, 130–3, 239–40; Van Deburg, "William Lloyd Garrison and the 'Pro-Slavery Priesthood'," 235n.

67 Bacon, *History of American Christianity*, 345; Abbott, *Reminiscences*, 16–21, 117–40. For the antislavery and temperance aspects of Beecher's services, see *Memorial of the Revival in Plymouth Church, Brooklyn, during the Early Part of the Year 1858*... (New York, 1859), 46, 139–40. For consideration of the revival as a call to social action and as a motor behind antislavery effort see, for example, Irem W. Smith, *The Sins of the Nation: A Sermon, Preached on Thanksgiving Day, November 19th, 1857*... (Ellsworth, Me., 1857); Solon W. Bush, *The Revival: A Sermon Preached at the First Congregational Church, Medfield on the 28th March, 1858* (Dedham, Mass., 1858), 11–14; "The Revival of 1858," *Freewill Baptist Quarterly*, 7 (Jan. 1859), 65–7; William McKinley, *A Story of Minnesota Methodism* (Cincinnati, 1911), 76–80; George B. Cheever, *The Fire and Hammer of God's Word against the Sin of Slavery: Speech*... *May, 1858* (New York, 1858), 9 and *passim*; Gerrit Smith, "The Religion of Reason: A Discourse... Feb. 21st, 1858," in *idem, Three Discourses on the Religion of Reason* (New York, 1859), 16–17.

68 Carwardine, *Translatlantic Revivalism*, 160, 162; *CAJ*, 30 Dec. 1858; *New York Observer*, 3 June 1858; James W. Alexander, *The American Sunday School and Its Adjuncts* (Philadelphia, 1856), 327; *CAJ*, 17 Jan. 1856; *Independent*, 12 Jan. 1854.

69 J. Dempster to W. and M. Dempster, Dempster Papers, GTS. Conant, *Narratives of Remarkable Conversions*, 435, published during 1858, listed reports of revivals in the border slave states but noted that elsewhere in the South "very sparse instances of revival are mentioned." See also *New York Tribune*, 24 April 1858; *New York Observer*, 1, 8 April 1858; Chambers, *Noon Prayer Meeting*, 134–5.

70 *Congregational Journal* (Portsmouth, NH), quoted in *SCA*, 15 Jan. 1857; Long, *Pictures of Slavery*, 95, 103–6, 155–6, 163–5, 227–9, 261–4, 314–15. See also Gordon, *Life and Writings*, 113–21; *Slavery and the Church: Two Letters Addressed to Rev. N.L. Rice... Also a Letter to Rev. Nehemiah Adams... by Smectynmuus* (Boston, 1856), 13–14, 27–8.

71 *Christian Watchman and Reflector*, 17 Dec. 1857; Brownlow, *Ought American Slavery To Be Perpetuated?*, 223–4; Garth M. Rosell and Richard A.G. Dupuis (eds) *The Memoirs of Charles G. Finney: The Complete Restored Text* (Grand Rapids, Mich., 1989), 565. See also "William Kennedy Blake Recollections," 69–70, ts, SHC.

72 *SCA*, 8 April 1858. For calls to emulate the northern churches see, for example, *SCA*, 11, 18, 25 March 1858; *North Carolina Presbyterian*, 5 Feb., 12 March 1858; *Biblical Recorder*, 11 March 1858.

73 Lindsay, "Religious Awakening of 1858," 252. For some indication of the geographical range and character of southern revivals in 1858, see Conant, *Narratives of Remarkable Conversions*, 374–5, 434–5; Smyth, *Autobiographical Notes*, 195–7; Thornwell Jacobs, *Diary of William Plumer Jacobs* (Oglethorpe University, Ga., 1937), 21; William B. McCash, *Thomas R.R. Cobb: The Making of a Southern Nationalist* (Macon, Ga., 1983), 77–83; *Richmond Christian Advocate*, 20 Sept. 1858; S. Colton, Diary, 31 Jan. 1858, SHC; *North Carolina Presbyterian*, 26 March, 9, 23 April, 14 May 1858; *New York Observer*, 13, 27 May, 10 June, 1, 8 July 1858; *SCA*, 18, 25 March, 1, 8, 15, 22,

29 April, 6 May 1858; *Biblical Recorder*, 6 May, 24 June, 15 July, 12 Aug., 23 Sept. 1858.

74 *SCA*, 27 May, 26 Aug., 16 Sept. 1858; *North Carolina Presbyterian*, 11, 18 June, 23, 30 Oct. 1858, 10 March 1860. See also Snay, "American Thought and Southern Distinctiveness," 327.

75 For the campaign of 1860 see Reinhard H. Luthin, *The First Lincoln Campaign* (Cambridge, Mass., 1944); Elting Morison, "Election of 1860," in Schlesinger and Israel, *History of American Presidential Elections*, III, 1097–152; Potter, *Impending Crisis*, 405–47; Norman A. Graebner (ed.) *Politics and the Crisis of 1860* (Urbana, Ill., 1961); Allan Nevins, *The Emergence of Lincoln* (2 vols, New York, 1950), II, 203–317; George H. Knoles (ed.) *The Crisis of the Union 1860–1861* (Baton Rouge, La., 1965), 3–59.

76 *CAJ*, 20 Dec. 1860; *New York Tribune*, 3, 17 May 1860; *Albany Evening Journal*, 15 May 1860; *Ohio State Journal*, 19 May 1860; *Albany Argus*, 4, 19 Oct. 1860; Potter, *Impending Crisis*, 422–3.

77 *CAJ*, 1 Nov. 1860; Johnson and Porter, *National Party Platforms*, 31–3. For the public drama surrounding Joshua Giddings's securing a mention of the Declaration of Independence in the platform, see Stewart, *Giddings*, 271–2.

78 *Albany Argus*, 26 Sept. 1860; *New York Tribune*, 12 June 1860; *Albany Evening Journal*, 22 Sept. 1860; *Ohio State Journal*, 25 June 1860.

79 *New York Tribune*, 9 May, 18 Aug. 1860; *Albany Evening Journal*, 30 Oct. 1860; *Ohio State Journal*, 20 Sept. 1860.

80 Joseph C. Sitterson, "The Secession Movement in North Carolina, 1847–1861" (PhD diss., University of North Carolina at Chapel Hill, 1937), 129–30; Green, "Northern Missionary Activities," 160–1; *New York Tribune*, 8 May 1860; *Albany Evening Journal*, 1, 7 May 1860; J.G. de Roulhac Hamilton (ed.) *The Correspondence of Jonathan Worth* (2 vols, Raleigh, NC, 1909), I, 110–13. Worth, a native of North Carolina, had served in the Indiana state legislature and had been president of the Indiana Con-ference of the Wesleyan Methodist church. Rickman, "Wesleyan Methodism in North Carolina," 21–32.

81 *Ohio State Journal*, 19 Oct. 1860; *Albany Evening Journal*, 4, 6 Sept., 23 Oct. 1860; Simms, *Thomas M. Eddy*, 266; *Albany Evening Journal*, 19 Sept. 1860.

82 *Albany Argus*, 18 Sept., 16 Oct. 1860; John L. Dawson, *Speech . . . Delivered at a Democratic Mass Meeting in New Geneva, Fayette County, Pennsylvania, September 1, 1860* (Washington, DC, 1867 [*sic*]), 8.

83 *Albany Argus*, 2, 16 July, 4 Oct. 1860; Dawson, *Speech . . . at a Democratic Mass Meeting, passim*. Hilliard addressed a number of Union gatherings in New York and New Jersey. *Albany Evening Journal*, 20 Sept. 1860; *North Carolina Christian Advocate*, 18, 25 Sept. 1860; Cozart, "Hilliard," 292–4.

84 By 1860 only in Maryland, Louisiana, and California did Know Nothings remain relatively strong. Baker, *Ambivalent Americans*, 3. See also John B. Weaver, "The Decline of the Ohio Know-Nothings, 1856–1860," *Cincinnati Historical Society Bulletin*, 40 (Winter 1982), 235–46; John R. Mulkern, *The Know-Nothing Party in Massachusetts: The Rise and Fall of a People's Movement* (Boston, 1990), 155–73.

85 Pella (Iowa) *Gazette*, 25 Jan. 1860, quoted in Swierenga, "The Ethnic Voter and the First Lincoln Election," 113; Robert B. Warden, *A Voter's Version of the Life and Character of Stephen A. Douglas* (Columbus, Ohio, 1860), 75–6, 116, 129; *Albany Argus*, 4 July 1860. See also Dawson, *Speech . . . at a Democratic Mass Meeting*, 9–10.

86 *New York Freeman's Journal*, 6 Oct. 1860; *Albany Argus*, 24 Oct. 1860; *Sunday Mercury*, quoted in *New York Tribune*, 12 June 1860.

87 *New York Tribune*, 7, 8 May, 3 Oct. 1860. Greeley defended legislation to protect the Sabbath against rum-sellers, and insisted it found support in all parties. *Ibid.*, 12 June 1860. For German "Wide-Awakes," see *ibid.*, 11 Sept. 1860.

88 Johnson and Porter, *National Party Platforms*, 33; *Albany Evening Journal*, 4, 8

Oct. 1860; *New York Tribune*, 27 Sept. 1860.

[89] For an emphasis on the nativist and anti-Catholic aspects of the Republican appeal in the later 1850s, see Gienapp, "Nativism and the Creation of a Republican Majority," 548–59; Carman and Luthin, "Some Aspects of the Know-Nothing Movement," 229–34; Bean, "Puritan Versus Celt," 85–8; Formisano, *Mass Political Parties*, 271–2. Those who treat these elements as incidental and temporary features of the party include Foner, *Free Soil, Free Labor, Free Men*, 250–60; Baum, "Know-Nothingism and the Republican Majority in Massachusetts," 959–86; Sewell, *Ballots for Freedom*, 275–6, 348ff. Joel Silbey, "The Undisguised Connection: Know Nothings into Republicans: New York as a Test Case," in Joel Silbey, *The Partisan Imperative: The Dynamics of American Politics before the Civil War* (New York, 1985), 127–65, argues persuasively that, while Republicans did not offer the Americans everything they wanted in the way of a registry law and other nativist concessions, they moved far enough to win a decisive proportion of the 1856 Fillmore vote.

[90] James O. Putnam, anti-Romanist framer of New York's church property bill, headed the Republicans' electoral ticket in that state. Democrats did not exaggerate when they called him "the great high priest of Know-nothingism." *Albany Argus*, 15 Sept. 1860.

[91] McClure, *Old Time Notes*, 245.

[92] *New York Freeman's Journal*, 14, 28 March, 4 April, 29 Aug. 1857, 3 Sept., 24 Dec. 1859, 26 May, 14 July, 4, 18 Aug., 6, 13 Oct. 1860; *New York Tribune*, 31 July 1860. See also Allen, "Slavery Question in Catholic Newspapers," 120, 155–9; Cross, "St. Louis Catholic Press and Political Issues," 219–20.

[93] *New York Freeman's Journal*, 1 Sept. 1860; *New York Tribune*, 31 July 1860; *Utica Herald*, quoted in *Albany Argus*, 15 Sept. 1860; Knox County, Illinois, *Republican*, quoted in *Albany Argus*, 1 Nov. 1860. Hughes had previously supported Buchanan against Douglas

over the Lecompton issue. Sharrow, "Hughes and a Catholic Response," 268. For Republicans' (though not Lincoln's) exploiting of anti-Catholic sentiment against Douglas in the Illinois senatorial campaign of 1858, see Fehrenbacher, *Prelude to Greatness*, 13–14; Gienapp, "Nativism and the Creation of a Republican Majority," 548.

[94] David E. Meerse, "Buchanan, Corruption, and the Election of 1860," *CWH*, 12 (June 1966), 116–31; Mark W. Summers, *The Plundering Generation: Corruption and the Crisis of the Union, 1849–1861* (New York, 1987), 239–60; Collins, "Ideology of the Ante-bellum Northern Democrats," 120. See also Hall, "Life of Robert McCutcheon Hall," 97, PHS.

[95] See, for example, *Christian Watchman and Reflector*, 26 Nov., 10, 17 Nov. 1857, and *WCA*, 23 Dec. 1857, both celebrating the defeat of Fernando Wood's corrupt administration in New York City by the People's candidate, and son of a German Methodist, Daniel Tiemann. See also Daniel C. Knowles, *A Life That Speaketh: A Biography of Rev. George P. Wilson* (New York, 1874), 92–5.

[96] *Cincinnati Gazette*, 26 March 1858; *New York Tribune*, 16 May, 25 June 1860.

[97] *New York Tribune*, 26 May, 2, 21 Aug., 8, 27 Sept. 1860; *Ohio State Journal*, 17 May, 13, 17 July 1860; *The Hartford Press*, quoted in *New York Tribune*, 21 May 1860; *Chicago Tribune*, quoted in *New York Tribune*, 28 May 1860; New York *Independent*, quoted in *New York Tribune*, 15 June 1860; *Albany Evening Journal*, 16 Aug. 1860; Nathaniel Banks, quoted in *North Carolina Presbyterian*, 27 Oct. 1860; *New York Evening Post*, quoted in *New York Tribune*, 24 May 1860; *Utica Herald*, quoted in *Albany Argus*, 15 Sept. 1860. For a discussion of Lincoln's beliefs in the context of Whig views on the moral order see, for example, Kelley, *Cultural Pattern*, 214; Howe, *American Whigs*, 263–98. See also Noll, *One Nation under God?*, 90–104.

[98] *Ohio State Journal*, 24 July, 8, 14 Aug. 1860. The allusion was to King Jeroboam, "who made Israel to sin" (I

Kings 11. 28, 14. 16). See also Windsor, *A Central Illinois Methodist Minister*, 7–8.

[99] *Albany Evening Journal*, 2 Oct. 1860; *Albany Argus*, 2, 25 July, 13 Sept., 3, 9, 17 Oct., 5, 6 Nov. 1860; Warden, *A Voter's Life of Douglas*, 25–6, 60.

[100] *Albany Evening Journal*, 27 Sept. 1860; *Albany Argus*, 5 Sept. 1860; B. Adams, Diary, 4 Nov. 1858, 6 Dec. 1859, 14 Aug., 8, 28, 29 Sept., 16 Oct. 1860, DU; *Oberlin Evangelist*, 12 Sept. 1860.

[101] Simms, *Thomas M. Eddy*, 230–1; *CAJ*, 1 Nov. 1860; Goodwin, "Introduction" to Tarkington, *Autobiography*, 61–3; Norton, *Religious Newspapers*, 125–6; *New York Tribune*, 27 Oct. 1856; *North Carolina Presbyterian*, 23 June 1860; King, *Reminiscences*, 154; *DAB* (for Grinnell); *Ohio State Journal*, 9 Aug. 1860 (for J.J. Ferre); *New York Tribune*, 23 June 1860 (B.W. Gorham); *Albany Evening Journal*, 1 Sept. 1860 (E. Puffer); Howard, *Conscience and Slavery*, 177–9. Even when antislavery sermons did not mention the Republican party by name, their partisan sympathies were often very clear. See, for example, N.S. Dickinson, *Slavery: The Nation's Crime and Danger: A Sermon, Preached in the Congregational Church, Foxborough, Mass. Sept. 30, 1860* (Boston, 1860). For Democrats' attacks on Republican clergy through the later 1850s and 1860, see Griffis, *John Chambers*, 111–15; *Cincinnati Enquirer*, 18 Dec. 1857, quoted in *WCA*, 23 Dec. 1857; *Albany Argus*, 20, 22 Sept., 24 Oct. 1860.

[102] L.A. McCorkle, Diary, 30 Sept. 1860, SHC; O. Bernard, Diary, 3 Nov. 1860, SHC; *North Carolina Presbyterian*, 20 Oct. 1860.

[103] *New Orleans Christian Advocate*, 11 Aug. 1858, quoted in Purifoy, "Southern Methodist Church and the Proslavery Argument," 335–6; *Christian Intelligencer*, quoted in *North Carolina Presbyterian*, 17 March 1860. See also Kelley, *Cultural Pattern*, 220–3; Silbey, *Partisan Imperative*, 166–89 ("The Surge of Republican Power: Partisan Antipathy, American Social Conflict, and the Coming of the Civil War").

[104] *North Carolina Presbyterian*, 29 Sept. 1860. The Wide-Awakes were made up very largely of young men, many of them too young to vote. William E. Gienapp, "Who Voted for Lincoln?," 61–2, in John L. Thomas (ed.) *Abraham Lincoln and the American Political Tradition* (Amherst, Mass., 1986).

[105] *North Carolina Presbyterian*, 12 May 1860.

[106] *North Carolina Christian Advocate*, 18 Sept. 1860; R.L. Dabney to M. Hoge, 4 Jan. 1861 in Hoge, *Moses Drury Hoge*, 140; *Important Political Pamphlet, for the Campaign of 1860* . . . (Montgomery, Ala. [1860]), 59; *Knoxville Whig*, 21 July, 17, 22 Sept. 1860.

[107] See, for example, *Columbus Enquirer*, 6 Nov. 1860; *New Orleans Bee*, 14 Sept. 1860. See also Thompson, "Political Nativism in Florida, 1848–1860," 61–5.

[108] O. Bernard, Diary, August [no date], 24 Oct., 1, 5 Nov. 1860, SHC; *North Carolina Presbyterian*, 21 Jan., 2 June, 20 Oct. 1860; Robert J. Breckinridge, "An Appeal . . . to Hon. John C. Breckinridge Vice President of the United States. January 9, 1860," *Cincinnati Commercial*, 19 Jan. 1860; Overy, "Dabney," 82, 94–5; Warner, *Jacob Bachtel*, 127–8; Smith, *James Osgood Andrew*, 435–6; William G. Brownlow, *Sketches of the Rise, Progress and Decline of Secession* . . . (Philadelphia, 1862), 52–5, 76–7; *Knoxville Whig*, 28 July, 25 Aug., 8, 22 Sept., 13 Oct. 1860; Coulter, *Brownlow*, 128–9; Fitzgerald, *Judge Longstreet*, 104–7.

[109] *Knoxville Whig*, 13 Oct. 1860, quoted in Brownlow, *Sketches*, 75–8. See also Smith, *In His Image But*, 177 (for the Reverend Thomas W. Caskey, of the Disciples of Christ, who canvassed for Breckinridge in Mississippi).

[110] *Knoxville Whig*, 3 Sept. 1859, 10 March, 21, 28 July 1860.

[111] *North Carolina Whig*, 29 May, 10 July 1860; *Knoxville Whig*, 26 Nov. 1859, 21 July 1860. For the attacks of the southern Bell–Everett forces on the corruption of the Buchanan administration, see also Brownlow, *Sketches*, 192–3; *Knoxville Whig*, 14 April, 5, 26 May, 23 June, 8 Sept., 20 Oct. 1860. For Constitutional Unionists' criticisms of

Breckinridge's history of dueling and their sarcastic references to Democratic piety, see *Knoxville Whig*, 21 July 1860.

[112] Constitutional Unionists argued that, since Breckinridge was a crypto-Know Nothing "of the *old Blue Stocking Presbyterian stripe*," Archbishop Hughes had no choice but to go for Douglas. *Knoxville Whig*, 21 July 1860; *New York Freeman's Journal*, 1 Sept. 1860. Breckinridge had offered a hostage to fortune by saying in 1855 that although he deprecated Know Nothingism, he would vote for a native and a man of his own religion "all other things being equal." *New Orleans Bee*, 10 Aug. 1856. Robert C. Reinders, "The Louisiana American Party and the Catholic Church," *Mid-America*, 40 (Oct. 1958), 226–7, detects a diminution in anti-Catholicism in Louisiana in the later 1850s, and suggests it had to do with the perceived soundness of that church on the slavery question, and its loyalty to the South, at a time when the issue was dwarfing all others.

[113] *Knoxville Whig*, 29 Nov. 1860; Temple, *Notable Men of Tennessee*, 118, 200–1; Smith, *James Osgood Andrew*, 435–6; Smith, *George Foster Pierce*, 437; Mann, *Haygood*, 11, 35; *North Carolina Presbyterian*, 24 Nov. 1860; Junkin, *Rev. George Junkin*, 512; Warner, *Jacob Bachtel*, 127–8; David Coulter, *Memoir, with Reminiscences, Letters, Lectures and Sermons* (St Louis, Mo., n.d.), 88–9. See also, Smyth, *Autobiographical Notes*, 557–8, for the "Union" (Bell–Everett) loyalties of Smyth's Tennessee kinfolk, including his sister, Isabella Fauntleroy.

[114] S.Y. McMasters to ?, 26 Jan. 1861, DU; *North Carolina Christian Advocate*, 18, 25 Sept. 1860; J.K. Stringfield, Diary, 4 July, 27 Sept., 5, 6 Nov. 1860, SHC; O. Bernard, Diary, 1, 12, 16, 19 May, 5 Nov. 1860, SHC.

[115] *Primitive Baptist*, 25 Feb. 1861, 59–62; *North Carolina Christian Advocate*, 27 Nov. 1860; *Columbus Enquirer*, 6 Nov. 1860; Overy, "Dabney," 95; *Knoxville Whig*, 6 Oct. 1860. Smyth had offered the opening prayer at the Democratic national convention in Charleston in April. Smyth, *Autobiographical Notes*, 554–6. See also D. Barkalow to A. Hagaman, 16 Nov. 1860, Hagaman Papers, PHS.

[116] *Knoxville Whig*, 24 March 1860; G.D. Camden to R.M.T. Hunter, 14 Feb., 2 March 1859, in *Annual Report of the American Historical Association for the Year 1916* (2 vols, Washington, 1918), II, *Correspondence of Robert M.T. Hunter 1826–1876*, ed. Charles Henry Ambler, 297. See also Warner, *Jacob Bachtel*, 127–8; J. Lanahan to M. Simpson, 5 Oct. 1860, M. Simpson Papers, LC, for Methodist Democrats in Virginia. For a shift in loyalty from Fillmore to Breckinridge, see W. Davis to J.W.C. Davis, 3 May 1860; W. Davis to R. Davis, 14 June 1860, Beale–Davis Papers, SHC.

[117] Formisano, *Mass Political Parties*, 310–24; Kleppner, *Third Electoral System*, 73–4; Gienapp, "Who Voted for Lincoln?" 75, 87.

[118] See, for example, Mears, *Edward Norris Kirk*, 257; *Albany Argus*, 11 Sept. 1860 (for T.L. Cuyler); *Ohio State Journal*, 8 Aug. 1860 (for Jedediah Burchard); Barton, *Joseph Edwin Roy*, 26, 28–9; Salter, *Sixty Years*, 279; Davis, "Joshua Leavitt," 347. Baum, *Civil War Party System*, 91, 97, concludes that three out of every four voting Congregationalists in Massachusetts in 1860 were Lincoln men.

[119] *Ohio State Journal*, 19 Oct. 1860. For Methodist support for Lincoln see, for example, B. Adams, Diary, 6 Nov. 1860, DU; D.P. Kidder, Diary, 6 Dec. 1860, DU; Baum, *Civil War Party System*, 91, 95–6. Baum's figures for Massachusetts suggest that amongst voting Methodists two in every three supported Lincoln, as did three in every four voting Baptists. Compared with their more patrician Whig predecessors, Republicans evidently drew less well amongst Episcopalian voters. Formisano, *Mass Political Parties*, 316–17; Gienapp, "Who Voted for Lincoln?" 75; Holt, *Forging a Majority*, 296–7, 326, 354, 365–6; Baum, *Civil War Party System*, 91; Mullin, *Episcopal Vision*, 198–200.

[120] Frederick C. Luebke (ed.) *Ethnic*

Voters and the Election of Lincoln (Lincoln, Neb., 1971) usefully draws together some of the landmark historiography on the extent of German and other immigrant support for Lincoln in 1860. Paul Kleppner, "Lincoln and the Immigrant Vote: A Case of Religious Polarization," *Mid-America*, 48 (July 1960), 176–95, and Thomas W. Kremm, "Cleveland and the First Lincoln Election: The Ethnic Response to Nativism," *Journal of Interdisciplinary History*, 8 (Summer 1977), 69–86, establish that in Pittsburgh and Cleveland respectively the political cleavage was not rooted in ethnic conflict between German and non-German, but in religion: Catholic Germans voted Democrat, Protestant Germans generally Republican. The picture was even more complex than this: in Michigan and elsewhere many German Lutheran communities remained strongly Democrat, while anti-Catholic and antislavery Reformed and rationalist groups moved into the Republican column. See Ronald P. Formisano, "Ethnicity and Party in Michigan, 1854–1860," in Luebke (ed.) *Ethnic Voters*, 178–86; Gienapp, "Who Voted for Lincoln?" 72–3. See also Alexander C. Graw, *Forty-Six Years in the Ministry: Life of Rev. J.B. Graw, D.D. 1832–1901* (Camden, NJ, 1901), 376–7.

[121] Gienapp, "Who Voted for Lincoln?" 53–4, 63, 65–7. Baum and Knobel, "Anatomy of a Realignment," 76–81, conclude that in New York in 1860 the anti-Republican fusion ticket won a similar share of the 1856 American vote as Lincoln. See also Hammond, *Politics of Benevolence*, 133–4. In Massachusetts Fillmore's support went disproportionately to Bell; the minority who voted for Lincoln were not critical to his victory. Baum, *Civil War Party System*, 47–54.

[122] *New York Tribune*, 9 Aug., 19 Sept., 3, 26 Oct., 6 Nov. 1860; *Albany Evening Journal*, 26 Sept. 1860; Smith, *Pillars in the Temple*, 245; Martyn, *William E. Dodge*, 178–9; Herbert A. Gibbons, *John Wanamaker* (2 vols, New York, 1926), I, 30–9; Griffis, *John Chambers*,

16–17. For the importance of young, new voters to Lincoln's victory, see Gienapp, "Who Voted for Lincoln?" 75–6. For Republicans' *losses* amongst radical abolitionist evangelicals in 1860 (including Lewis Tappan and George B. Cheever), see McKivigan, *War against Proslavery Religion*, 160; Wyatt-Brown, *Lewis Tappan*, 336–7.

[123] Gienapp, "Who Voted for Lincoln?"; Baum, *Civil War Party System*, 90–9; Thompson, *History of the Presbyterian Churches*, 151; Herbert N. Casson, *Cyrus Hall McCormick, His Life and Work* (Chicago, 1909), 166; Hutchinson, *Cyrus Hall McCormick*, II, 37–47; G. Fort to J.P. Fort, in J.P. Fort, "Reminiscences," 125–6, DU; W. Hamilton to M. Simpson, 23 Feb. 1861, M. Simpson Papers, DU; W. Nast to M. Simpson, 23 Feb., 4 March 1861, R. Ricketts to M. Simpson, 17 April 1861, M. Simpson Papers, LC. See also Smith, *Pillars in the Temple*, 284–7 (for George T. Cobb, Methodist member of Congress from New Jersey).

[124] Grant, *Peter Cartwright*, 164; W. Daily to M. Simpson, 4 May 1860, M. Simpson Papers, LC; *New York Tribune*, 26 July 1860; Norton, *Religious Newspapers*, 126; Allen, *John Allen*, 41; Abbott, *Reminiscences*, 202–3. See also *Albany Argus*, 9 July 1860, and Samuel R. Harshman, *Memoirs of Samuel Rufus Harshman, Comprising His Autobiography, Recollections of Men and Events, Camp-meetings . . .* (Akron, Ohio, 1914), 36, 39, for Douglas's continuing support within western Methodism.

[125] Christy, *Pulpit Politics*, 613; *New York Tribune*, 11 Sept. 1860; Abbott, *Reminiscences*, 180–1.

[126] Haven, *National Sermons*, 179; Norton, *Religious Newspapers*, 13; *Presbyterian*, 8 Dec. 1860; *CAJ*, 15 Nov. 1860.

[127] *North Carolina Presbyterian*, 17, 24 Nov., 29 Dec. 1860; E.V. Levert to J.V. Levert, 1 Dec. 1860, Levert Papers, SHC. See also *North Carolina Christian Advocate*, 13 Nov. 1860.

[128] *North Carolina Presbyterian*, 1 Dec. 1860. See also S. Colton, Diary, 27 Jan. 1861, SHC; *Knoxville Whig*, 2 March 1861.

However, for evidence of some southern revivals during the winter see *Richmond Christian Advocate*, 14 Feb. 1861; *Biblical Recorder*, 6, 20 March 1861.

[129] S. Colton, Diary, 27 Jan. 1861, SHC; James S. Smart, *National Fast: A Fast Day Sermon, Delivered in the City of Flint. January 4, 1861* (Flint, Mich., 1861), 8; C.H. Read, *National Fast: A Discourse Delivered on the Day of Fasting, Humiliation and Prayer* ... (Richmond, Va., 1861), 18–23; J.H. Thornwell, "Our National Sins," in *Fast Day Sermons: or The Pulpit on the State of the Country* (New York, 1861), 45–53. See also George Duffield, *Our National Sins to be Repented of, and the Grounds of Hope for the Preservation of Our Federal Union: A Discourse* ... (Detroit, 1861), 23–35, for a jeremiad on the United States' treatment of the Cherokees and other Indian tribes, for him a source of even greater guilt than Negro slavery. For the text of Buchanan's Proclamation of 14 December, see Smart, *National Fast*, 3–4. Buchanan's call drew many scornful responses. "He is no more qualified to lead a Nation in prayer, than the Devil is to administer the Lord's Supper," sneered William G. Brownlow. *Knoxville Whig*, 5 Jan. 1861.

[130] Loveland, *Southern Evangelicals and the Social Order*, 264–5; A.S. Hunt, Diary, 5 Jan., 3 March 1861, DU; B.J. Lossing to J.B. Wakeley, 4 Feb. 1861, DU; *North Carolina Presbyterian*, 24 Nov., 15 Dec. 1860. See also *CAJ*, 6, 20 Dec. 1860; *North Carolina Christian Advocate*, 4 Feb. 1861. For fears over congregational splintering, see "CHW" (probably Calvin H. Wiley) in *North Carolina Presbyterian*, 15 Dec. 1860.

[131] Maryland Baptist Union Association address "To the Baptists of these United States of America," 15 Nov. 1860, in *Biblical Recorder*, 29 Nov. 1860.

[132] Hoge, *Moses Drury Hoge*, 139; *North Carolina Presbyterian*, 1, 8 Dec. 1860, 5 Jan. 1861; *CAJ*, 20 Dec. 1860. Lyman Abbott (by temperament not, of course, averse to engaging in politics) broke his self-censorship in the pulpit following Buchanan's call on churches to work for the Union. Abbott, *Reminiscences*, 204.

[133] Moorhead, *American Apocalypse*, 23–35, offers a fine analysis of northern evangelical responses during the winter crisis.

[134] For examples of pro-southern feeling in northern churches, see Haney, *Story of My Life*, 134–5; *North Carolina Presbyterian*, 8 Dec. 1860 (quoting the *New York Observer*, at this stage ambivalent in its attitudes to the perpetuity of the Union and strongly critical of northern "fanaticism"); J. Chambers to T. Smyth, 10 Dec. 1860, in Smyth, *Autobiographical Notes*, 561–2; Griffis, *John Chambers*, 115–17 (discussing Chambers's First Presbyterian church in Philadelphia, which became known as the "copperhead church" during the war for its identification with pro-Confederate Democrats).

[135] *WCA*, quoted in *CAJ*, 8 Nov. 1860; J. McClintock to G.R. Crooks, 6 Dec. 1860, DU; *CAJ*, 20 Dec. 1860. See also E.B. Sherwood, "Journal," n.d., PHS; Norton, *Religious Newspapers*, 127–30. Salmon P. Chase was ready to forsake the Constitution to prevent the break-up of the Union, even to the extent of crushing the secession movement immediately with force. For this, and a discussion of the psychological and spiritual springs of Chase's abolitionism, see Peter F. Walker, *Moral Choices: Memory, Desire, and Imagination in Nineteenth-Century America* (Baton Rouge, La., 1978), 305–29.

[136] W. Hamilton to M. Simpson, 23 Feb. 1861, M. Simpson Papers, DU; Bangs, *Autobiography and Journal*, 316; Charles Hodge, "The State of the Country," *Princeton Review*, 33 (Jan. 1861), 3, 6–9, 26–33; *CAJ*, 6, 20 Dec. 1860; *Memoir of John C. Lord*, 32. See also Henry A. Boardman, *What Christianity Demands of Us at the Present Crisis: A Sermon Preached on Thanksgiving Day, Nov. 29, 1860* (Philadelphia, 1860), 27. For further examples of the unyielding Unionism of politically conservative evangelicals, see Jedidiah H. Adams, *History of the Life of D. Hayes Agnew, M.D., LL.D.* (Philadelphia, 1892), 128–30; "Gardiner Spring," in *DAB*; Samuel I.

Prime, *Autobiography and Memorials*, ed. Wendell Prime (New York, 1888), 269–70; Van Nest, *Bethune*, 361; Baird, *Robert Baird*, 311.

[137] Boardman, *What Christianity Demands*, 4; Brainerd, *Thomas Brainerd*, 252–3. For conservatives' criticisms of abolitionists as libelers and mischief-makers, see for example, Moorhead, *American Apocalypse*, 25. See also Duffield *Our National Sins*, 17, 20; Hodge, "The State of the Country," 10. Old School Presbyterian ministers, acutely conscious of their position as representatives of one of the few remaining national bodies, felt a peculiarly strong sense of responsibility for finding a *modus vivendi* between North and South. See, for example, Alexander T. McGill, *Sinful But Not Forsaken: A Sermon . . . on the Day of National Fasting, January 4, 1861* (New York, 1861), 15–16.

[138] Horace Bushnell, *The Census and Slavery: A Thanksgiving Discourse Delivered in the Chapel at Clifton Springs, NY, November, 1860* (Hartford, Conn., 1860), 7, 16 and *passim*; S.J. Baird to W.L. Baird, 2 Jan. 1861, S.J. Baird to J.T. Nixon, 8 Jan. 1861 (*"Private and confidential"*), S.J. Baird Papers, LC. See also Baird's public appeal to conservative Unionist sentiment, *Southern Rights and Northern Duties in the Present Crisis: A Letter to Hon. William Pennington* (Philadelphia, 1861); G. Oliet to S.J. Baird, 14 March 1861, S.J. Baird Papers, LC.

[139] Unionist Democrats and conciliatory Republicans welcomed Hodge's efforts. Hodge, "The State of the Country," 17–18, 22, 35–6; Hodge, *Charles Hodge*, 462–6; Van Nest, *Bethune*, 363. See David M. Potter, *Lincoln and His Party in the Secession Crisis* (New Haven, Conn., 1942), 105–10, 145, 171–2, 181–4, 191–207, for the Crittenden compromise plan and its reception. For northern conservatives' desire to conciliate the slave states within an unbroken (or reconstructed) Union, while regarding secession itself as unconstitutional "coercion" by the South, see, for example, M. Jacobus to T. Smyth, 18 Jan. 1861, D. McKinney to T. Smyth, 21 Jan. 1861, H. Van Dyke to T. Smyth, 7 Feb. 1861, in Smyth, *Autobiography*, 573–5, 578–9, 587–9.

[140] *CAJ*, 20 Dec. 1860; Smart, *National Fast*, 14, 18; Ezra S. Ely, *The Crisis: The Duty of Citizens in Regard to It: A Lecture . . . Dec. 28, 1860* (n.p., n.d), 7–8; Bittinger, *Bittinger*, 86; Bacon, *Leonard Bacon*, 462–4; Moorhead, *American Apocalypse*, 34; J. McClintock to G.R. Crooks, 9 Feb. 1861, DU; *New York Chronicle*, quoted in *Biblical Recorder*, 6 March 1861. See also Goen, *Broken Churches, Broken Nation*, 115–22.

[141] Moorhead, *American Apocalypse*, 35–41; M. Simpson (uncle) to M. Simpson, 28 April 1861, M. Simpson Papers, DU (my punctuation).

[142] For southern churches during the secession crisis, see James W. Silver, *Confederate Morale and Church Propaganda* (Tuscaloosa, Ala., 1957; repr. New York, 1967), 16–24; Smith, *In His Image, But*, 171–88; Thompson, *Presbyterians in the South*, I, 553–63; Haskell Monroe, "Southern Presbyterians and the Secession Crisis," *CWH*, 6 (Dec. 1960), 351–6; W. Harrison Daniel, "1861 and After," *CWH*, 5 (Sept. 1959), 276–82; W. Harrison Daniel, "The Southern Baptists in the Confederacy," *CWH*, 6 (Dec. 1860), 389–93; W. Harrison Daniel, "Southern Protestantism and Secession," *Historian*, 29 (May 1967), 391–408.

[143] Peterson, *Divine Discontent*, 97–8, 204; Howell Cobb, *Letter of Hon. Howell Cobb to the People of Georgia, on the Present Condition of the Country* (Washington, DC, 1860) repr. in *Annual Report of the American Historical Association for the Year 1911* (2 vols, Washington, DC, 1913), II, *The Correspondence of Robert Toombs, Alexander H. Stephens, and Howell Cobb*, ed. Ulrich B. Phillips, 513; Burwell Temple in *Primitive Baptist*, 12 Jan. 1861 (XXV, 12–15); Greenberg, *Masters and Statesmen*, 135–7, quoting James H. Thornwell's comment on the South Carolina Convention; *Biblical Recorder*, 20 Feb. 1861. See also Summers, *The Plundering Generation*, 261–80.

[144] C.W. Dabney to R.L. Dabney, 14 March 1861, Dabney Papers, SHC. For political pressure on the Alabama Con-

ference of the MECS, see Smith, *James Osgood Andrew*, 473. For attempts to co-opt Methodists and Baptists in Tennessee, see *Knoxville Whig*, 2, 23 Feb., 30 March 1861.

[145] Benjamin M. Palmer, "Thanksgiving Sermon Delivered in the First Presbyterian Church, New Orleans, on Thursday, November 29, 1860," in B.M. Palmer and W.T. Leacock, *The Rights of the South Defended in the Pulpits* (Mobile, Ala., 1860), 8–9; Adger, *My Life and Times*, 327–8; N.W. Chevalier, Diary, 22 Jan. 1861, PHS. See also *SCA*, 2 Aug. 1860; Marvin, *William Goff Caples*, 259–61; Overy, "Dabney," 96–7 (for Moses Hoge); McCash, *Thomas R.R. Cobb*, 183–201.

[146] Smith, *In His Image, But*, 179, 181; D. Barkalow to A. Hagaman, 16 Nov. 1860, Hagaman Papers, PHS; E.V. Levert to J.V. Levert, 1 Dec. 1860, Levert Papers, SHC; *North Carolina Christian Advocate*, quoted in *CAJ*, 13 Dec. 1860; Griffith, *John G. Landrum*, 159–60; T. Smyth to D. Magie, 24 Dec. 1860 in Smyth, *Autobiographical Notes*, 565; J.H. Thornwell to R.L. Dabney, 24 Nov. 1860, in Thomas C. Johnson, *The Life and Letters of Robert Lewis Dabney* (Richmond, Va., 1903), 223–4; Harvey T. Cook, *The Life Work of James Clement Furman* (Greenville, SC, 1926), 197. For a stimulating discussion of the relationship between honor and secession, see Wyatt-Brown, *Yankee Saints and Southern Sinners*, 183–213.

[147] Palmer, "Thanksgiving Sermon," 4–7. See also Maddex, "Proslavery Millennialism," 56–7; C.W. Dabney to R.L. Dabney, 14 March 1861, C.W. Dabney Papers, SHC; Palmer, *Life of Thornwell*, 486–87; Farmer, *The Metaphysical Confederacy*, 265–70.

[148] *North Carolina Christian Advocate*, 11 Dec. 1860; 4 Feb. 1861; Farmer, *The Metaphysical Confederacy*, 239–45; Smith, *In His Image, But*, 171–80; Goen, *Broken Churches, Broken Nation*, 170–1 and *passim*; Wilson, "Basil Manly," 52; Silver, *Confederate Morale and Church Propaganda*, 16–19, 23–4; Potter, *Impending Crisis*, 501.

[149] Thompson, *Presbyterians in the South*, I, 558; *North Carolina Christian Advocate*, 15 Dec. 1860; *North Carolina Presbyterian*, 8 Jan. 1861; Rivers, *Robert Paine*, 142–5; Thomas Smyth, *The Sin and the Curse; or, The Union, The True Source of Disunion, and Our Duty in the Present Crisis: A Discourse...* (Charleston, SC, 1860), in Smyth, *Complete Works*, VII, 538–53; Thornwell, "Our National Sins," in *Fast Day Sermons*, esp. 55–6; Lewis G. Vander Velde, *The Presbyterian Churches and the Federal Union, 1861–1869* (London, 1932), 30–1. For Smyth's private justification of his stance, see Smyth, *Autobiographical Notes*, 564–9. For Thornwell's abandoning of his earlier Unionism, and his active secessionism in 1860–61, see Farmer, *The Metaphysical Confederacy*, 246–72; for a similar political and intellectual journeying, see McCash, *Thomas R.R. Cobb*, 88–90, 138–48, 154–5. South Carolina's religious journals, including the *Southern Christian Advocate* and the *Southern Presbyterian*, along with much of the church press throughout the lower South showed considerable enthusiasm for independence. *SCA*, quoted in *CAJ*, 22 Nov. 1860; *Texas Christian Advocate*, quoted in *CAJ*, 13 Dec. 1860; *Knoxville Whig*, 30 March 1861; Smith, *In His Image, But*, 177–8. For a more guarded judgment, see Stroupe, *Religious Press in the South Atlantic States*, 31–2.

[150] *Biblical Recorder*, 29 Nov. 1860; Benjamin F. Riley, *History of the Baptists of Alabama: from the Time of Their First Occupation of Alabama in 1808, until 1894* (Birmingham, Ala., 1895), 279–80. The New Orleans fire-eating daily, the *True Delta*, had Palmer's sermon set in type before it was delivered, and published it in full three times in successive issues. Fisher, *Daniel W. Fisher*, 119–22; Thomas C. Johnson, *The Life and Letters of Benjamin Morgan Palmer* (Richmond, Va., c.1906), 219–23.

[151] Hoole (ed.) "Diary of Dr. Basil Manly," 142, 147; *Knoxville Whig*, 2 March 1861; Smith, *In His Image, But*, 173, 177, 180; Cook, *James Clement Furman*, 201–2. See also T.S. Dunaway, *Personal Memories, Sermons and Addresses*

(Lynchburg, Va., 1900), 43; Griffith, *John G. Landrum*, 159–60, 198–9. For the clergy's active involvement in the secession conventions of South Carolina, Alabama, Mississippi, Georgia, and Texas, more or less equally divided over the issue of immediate secession, see Ralph A. Wooster, *The Secession Conventions of the South* (Princeton, NJ, 1962), 18, 32, 53–4, 94, 127, 258.

[152] *North Carolina Presbyterian*, 24 Nov. 1860. See also Jacobs, *Diary of William Plumer Jacobs*, 65–79; J.W.C. Davis to W. Davis, 25 Nov., 9 Dec. 1860, R. Davis to J.W.C. Davis, 2, 18 Dec. 1860, W.F. Davis to J.W.C. Davis, 1 Dec. 1860, Beale–Davis Papers, SHC; T.G. Pollock to A.D. and E. Pollock, 20 Nov. 1860, A.D. Pollock Papers, SHC. For exceptions to this generalization, see Edwin Holt Hughes, *I Was Made a Minister: An Autobiography* (New York, 1943), 14–15, 17 (for the ardent Unionist, Thomas Bayless Hughes), and Monroe, "Southern Presbyterians and the Secession Crisis," 359. For evidence of the relative youth of the immediate secessionists in Alabama and Mississippi, when compared with the "co-operationists" and Unionists, see William L. Barney, *The Secessionist Impulse: Alabama and Mississippi in 1860* (Princeton, NJ, 1974), 277–85, 290–6.

[153] G.G. Smith, Diary (transcription), 62–5, SHC. For Augustus B. Longstreet's initial jubilation at South Carolina's secession, his mounting alarm as war loomed, and his efforts to pull his admirers back from the precipice by publishing the pamphlet *Shall South Carolina Begin the War?*, see Wade, *Longstreet*, 339–40. Robin E. Baker and Dale Baum, "The Texas Voter and the Crisis of the Union, 1859–1861," *JSH*, 53 (Aug. 1987), 395–420, explain the patterns of Unionism and secessionism in the Lone Star state primarily along socioeconomic lines: eastern slaveholding areas were most vigorously secessionist, while the northern and west-central yeomanry tended towards the Union. But they also establish correlations between denominationalism and voting in the secession referendum, and argue that Baptists, Presbyterians, and Methodists were more likely to vote for secession than were Texas voters at large.

[154] Overy, "Dabney," 95–8; Hoole, "Diary of Dr. Basil Manly," 144; *Biblical Recorder*, 29 Nov. 1860; *North Carolina Presbyterian*, 1 Dec. 1860. For Dabney's "Pacific Appeal to Christians," signed by leading Presbyterians of Virginia and North Carolina, see Johnson, *Robert Lewis Dabney*, 215–18. For the suggestion that, in Alabama, Whigs tended to be Unionists and "cooperative secessionists" in the secession elections and had a greater awareness than immediate secessionists of the wider national interest, see Alexander *et al.*, "The Basis of Alabama's Two Party System," 267–76; see also Barney, *Secessionist Impulse*, 279–80. Peyton McCrary, Clark Miller, and Dale Baum, "Class and Party in the Secession Crisis: Voting Behavior in the Deep South, 1856–1861," *Journal of Interdisciplinary History*, 8 (Winter, 1978), 429–57, cast doubt on Alexander's conclusions, but suggest that in Mississippi, Louisiana, and Texas Bell voters did indeed go against secession in larger numbers than for.

[155] S. Colton, Diary, 20 April 1860, SHC; A.W. Plyler, *The Iron Duke of the Methodist Itinerancy: An Account of the Life and Labors of Reverend John Tillett of North Carolina* (Nashville, Tenn., 1925), 181; York, *Autobiography*, 80; Edwin H. Hughes, *I Was Made a Minister* (New York, 1943), 14–15; J. Lanahan to M. Simpson, Dec. 1860, M. Simpson Papers, LC. See also William S. White, *Rev. William S. White D.D. and His Times (1800–1873): An Autobiography*, ed. H.M. White (Richmond, Va., 1891), 169; J.D. Hufham, *Memoir of Rev. John L. Prichard, Late Pastor of the First Baptist Church, Wilmington, N.C.* (Raleigh, NC, 1867), 119–20. For the religious press see, for example, *Biblical Recorder* (Baptist, NC), 13 Dec. 1860, 9, 16 Jan. 1861; *North Carolina Christian Advocate*, 8 Jan. 1861; *Richmond Christian Advocate*, quoted in *North Carolina Christian Advocate*, 27 Nov. 1860; *Central Presbyterian* (Va.) quoted in *North Carolina Presbyterian*, 8 Dec. 1860.

For the caution of the *North Carolina Presbyterian* in neither advocating nor yet firmly rejecting secession, see the issues for 29 Dec. 1860, 19 Jan., 2 Feb. 1861.

[156] *Knoxville Whig,* 19 Jan., 9 Feb. 1861; J.K. Stringfield, Diary, 24 Dec. 1860, 4 Jan., 1 Feb. 1861, SHC; Richardson, *From Sunrise to Sunset,* 122–5; Vander Velde, *The Presbyterian Churches and the Federal Union,* 36–8. For other Tennessee Unionists see Pendleton, *Reminiscences,* 119–22.

[157] Smith, *James Osgood Andrew,* 435–6; I.W. Avery, *The History of the State of Georgia from 1850 to 1881* ... (New York, 1881), 137; Cook, *James Clement Furman,* 194–5; Moore, "Religion in Mississippi," 236–7. For James A. Lyon and other anti-secession Presbyterians in northeastern Mississippi, see Monroe, "Southern Presbyterians and the Secession Crisis," 355–6. McCrary, Miller, and Baum, "Class and Party in the Secession Crisis," 452, show some correlation in Alabama between co-operationism and counties where Baptists were strong. Baker and Baum, "The Texas Voter and the Crisis of the Union, 1859–1861," 410–18, point to strong support for the Union in counties with high levels of Lutherans and Disciples of Christ.

[158] *North Carolina Christian Advocate,* 8 Jan. 1861; *Biblical Recorder,* 29 Nov. 1860; Overy, "Dabney," 95–8; Johnson, *Robert Lewis Dabney,* 215; S. Colton, Diary, 20 April 1861, SHC. See also, *Richmond Christian Advocate,* quoted in *North Carolina Christian Advocate,* 27 Nov. 1860; *Biblical Recorder,* 13 Dec. 1860; *Knoxville Whig,* 24 Nov. 1860; Breckinridge, "The Union to be Preserved," in *Fast Day Sermons,* 104–14.

[159] S. Colton, Diary, 20 April 1860, SHC; *Knoxville Whig,* 24 Nov. 1860 (Lovick Pierce), 30 March 1861; R.L. Dabney to M. Hoge, 4 Jan. 1861, in Hoge, *Moses Drury Hoge,* 140; *North Carolina Presbyterian,* 1 Dec. 1860, 5, 12 Jan. 1861; York, *Autobiography,* 80; Smith, *James Osgood Andrew,* 472–3; J. Lanahan to M. Simpson, Dec. 1860, M. Simpson Papers, LC. See also, James W. Hunnicutt's

Freewill Baptist *Christian Banner* (Fredericksburg, Va.), quoted in Stroupe, *Religious Press in the South Atlantic States,* 57; *North Carolina Christian Advocate,* 8 Jan. 1861; "Henry W. Hilliard," in *DAB.*

[160] *North Carolina Christian Advocate,* 11 Feb. 1861.

[161] For agitation within the border conferences of the MEC through the fall and winter following the Buffalo General Conference, see James W. May, "The War Years," in Bucke *et al., The History of American Methodism,* II, 210–11; Clark, *Matthew Simpson,* 213–15. Some 100 ministers and 12,000 laymen withdrew from the Baltimore Conference after the majority voted in March 1861 to stay within the "old church."

[162] J. Lanahan to G.R. Crooks, 24 Jan., 5, 15, 28 Feb., 6 March, 4 April 1861; B.H. Nadal to G.R. Crooks, 16 March 1861, DU; J. Lanahan to M. Simpson, (no day) March 1861; L. Scott to M. Simpson, 14, 27 March, M. Simpson Papers, LC.

[163] S. Colton, Diary, 20 April 1861, SHC. Colton was a New Englander and a graduate of Yale who had taught and preached in North Carolina for almost forty years.

[164] *Knoxville Whig,* 9 March 1861; Brownlow, *Sketches,* 7. For other staunch Unionists amongst Tennessee evangelicals, see Smyth, *Autobiographical Notes,* 582–3 (for his sister Isabella Fauntleroy); Temple, *Notable Men of Tennessee,* 89–90 (for William Blount Carter, Presbyterian), 118–19 (for John M. Fleming, Methodist), 201–2 (for Nathaniel G. Taylor, Methodist).

[165] Price, *Holston Methodism,* III, 324; Richardson, *From Sunrise to Sunset,* 123; *North Carolina Christian Advocate,* 20 Nov. 1860; *North Carolina Presbyterian,* 12 Jan. 1861; Overy, "Dabney," 99; *Primitive Baptist,* 12 Jan. 1861; D. Siler to R.S. Siler, 7 Dec. 1860, Siler Papers, SHC.

[166] *North Carolina Christian Advocate,* 8 Jan. 1861; R. Paine to A.W. Mangum, 16 March 1861, Mangum Family Papers, SHC; Smith, *James Osgood Andrew,* 472–3; Weaver, "Calvin Henderson Wiley," 39–43; Hodge, "The State of the

Country," 1–36; Hodge, *Charles Hodge*, 461–7; *North Carolina Presbyterian*, 24 Nov. 1860, 5, 19 Jan. 1861; Goen, *Broken Churches, Broken Nation*, 136–7. For some sense of the depth of anger within southern Presbyterianism against Hodge (who was genuinely surprised by the response), see Robert Manson Myers, *The Children of Pride: A True Story of Georgia and the Civil War* (New Haven, Conn., 1972), 645, 649–52.

[167] *North Carolina Presbyterian*, 24 Nov. 1861; *North Carolina Christian Advocate*, 4 Feb. 1861. See also *Biblical Recorder*, 13 Dec. 1860, 13 March 1861; *Richmond Christian Advocate*, 4 April 1861.

[168] O. Bernard, Diary, 25 Feb., 6 March, 12 April 1861, SHC; Johnson, *Robert Lewis Dabney*, 225–31; Robert L. Dabney, *Letter of the Rev. R.L. Dabney, D.D., of Union Theological Seminary, Virginia, to the Rev. S.J.[sic] Prime . . . on the State of the Country* (Richmond, Va., 1861), 5 and *passim*; White, *William S. White*, 171; J.K. Stringfield, Diary, 19 April, 18 June 1861, SHC.

[169] Johnson, *Robert Lewis Dabney*, 232.

Conclusion: "God Prosper the Right"

[1] For a shrewd analysis of the historiography of Civil War causation, see Kenneth M. Stampp, "The Irrepressible Conflict," in *The Imperiled Union: Essays on the Background of the Civil War* (New York, 1980), 191–245.

[2] *New York Freeman's Journal*, 1 Dec. 1860; G. Moody to S.P. Chase, 30 April 1860, quoted in Kenneth M. Stampp, *And the War Came: The North and the Secession Crisis, 1860–61* (Baton Rouge, La., 1950), 294.

[3] The divisive historiographical issue of how far the United States enjoyed a cultural unity, and how far the sectional conflict represented serious ideological divisions is addressed, for example, in Eric Foner, *Politics and Ideology in the Age of the Civil War* (New York, 1980), 15–53; Edward Pessen, "How Different from Each Other Were the Antebellum North and South?" *AHR*, 85 (Dec. 1980), 1119–49; James M. McPherson, "Antebellum Southern Exceptionalism: A New Look at an Old Question," *CWH*, 29 (Sept. 1983), 230–44.

[4] *CAJ*, 16 Aug. 1860.

[5] For the ways in which evangelical religion gave meaning to the war for both Confederates and Unionists, see especially Drew Gilpin Faust, "Christian Soldiers: The Meaning of Revivalism in the Confederate Army," *JSH*, 53 (Feb. 1987), 63–90; Moorhead, *American Apocalypse*, 42–172.

Select Bibliography

The bibliography that follows is not a comprehensive listing of the works cited in the notes. It rather indicates the types of source I have used and identifies those works which I have found most valuable.

Primary Sources

Manuscripts

Evangelicals' private reflections on political issues largely echoed their public statements. But occasionally their unpublished letters, journals, and diaries do elicit confidences about voting, partisanship, and the tensions and congruences between the church and the world. I drew especially on the following:

Benjamin Adams Diary, Drew University

American Home Missionary Society Papers (Microfilming Corporation of America, 1975)

Anderson–Thornwell Papers, Southern Historical Collection, University of North Carolina at Chapel Hill

Samuel J. Baird Papers, Library of Congress

Jesse Bernard Diary, Southern Historical Collection, Chapel Hill

Overton Bernard Diary, Southern Historical Collection, Chapel Hill

William Kennedy Blake Recollections, Southern Historical Collection, Chapel Hill

Jonathan Blanchard Papers, Wheaton College, Illinois

Thomas E. Bond Papers, Dickinson College

Iveson L. Brookes Papers, Southern Historical Collection, Chapel Hill

Thomas J. Bryant Autobiography, Drew University

Artemas Bullard Papers, Presbyterian Historical Society, Philadelphia

Nicholas W. Chevalier Diary, Presbyterian Historical Society, Philadelphia

George Coles Journal and Letterbook, Drew University

Simeon Colton Diary and Papers, Southern Historical Collection, Chapel Hill

Joseph B. Cottrell Diary, Southern Historical Collection, Chapel Hill

George R. Crooks Papers, Drew University

Charles W. Dabney Papers, Southern Historical Collection, Chapel Hill

Dromgoole Family Papers, Southern Historical Collection, Chapel Hill

Thomas M. Eddy Papers, Garrett-Evangelical Theological Seminary, Evanston

Robert Emory Papers, Drew University

Alvaro D. Field Diary and Papers, Garrett-Evangelical Theological Seminary, Evanston

Charles G. Finney Papers, Oberlin College Library (microfilm)

Jacob P. Fort Reminiscences, Drew University

William Gordon Autobiography, New England Conference Archives, Boston University

Abraham Hagaman Papers, Presbyterian Historical Society, Philadelphia

John Hall Journals, Presbyterian Historical Society, Philadelphia

Robert M. Hall Autobiography, Presbyterian Historical Society, Philadelphia

Joseph Hartwell Diary, Drew University

F.D. Hemenway Diary and Papers, Garrett-Evangelical Theological Seminary, Evanston

William P. Hill Diary, Southern Historical Collection, Chapel Hill

John Hughes Papers, Catholic University, Washington, DC

Albert S. Hunt Journal, Drew University

Edmund S. Janes Papers, Garrett-Evangelical Theological Seminary, Evanston

Daniel P. Kidder Papers, Garrett-Evangelical Theological Seminary, Evanston

Mitchell King Papers, Southern Historical Collection, Chapel Hill

John Lanahan Papers, Drew University

Robert W. Landis Journal, Presbyterian Historical Society, Philadelphia

Select Bibliography

Joshua Leavitt Papers, Library of Congress

John McClintock Papers, Drew University

Lucilla A. McCorkle Papers, Southern Historical Collection, Chapel Hill

Adolphus W. Mangum Diary and Mangum Family Papers, Southern Historical Collection, Chapel Hill

Robert H. Morrison Papers, Southern Historical Collection, Chapel Hill

George Peck Papers, Syracuse University Library

Abram D. Pollock Papers, Southern Historical Collection, Chapel Hill

Judah L. Richmond Diary, Southern Historical Collection, Chapel Hill

Theodore Richmond Papers, Southern Historical Collection, Chapel Hill

Henry B. Ridgaway Papers, Garrett-Evangelical Theological Seminary, Evanston

Mary and Stephen Riggs Papers, Presbyterian Historical Society, Philadelphia

Matthew Simpson Papers, Library of Congress

Matthew Simpson Papers, Drew University

George Gilman Smith Diary and Autobiography, Southern Historical Collection, Chapel Hill

Stocking Family Papers, New England Conference Archives, Boston University

William D. Valentine Diary, Southern Historical Collection, Chapel Hill

James E. Welch Diary, Presbyterian Historical Society, Philadelphia

Wills Papers, Southern Historical Collection, Chapel Hill

Witherspoon-McDowell Papers, Southern Historical Collection, Chapel Hill

Newspapers

The weekly religious press was rarely openly partisan. It is nonetheless a rich source for evangelical perspectives on social and political issues. The historian's problem is one of selection, for there were prodigious numbers of religious weeklies. The task is lightened by antebellum editors' habit of using the newspaper-exchange system to quote extensively from their competitors. I aimed for a representative choice of denominational and regional titles. The matriarch of Methodist newspapers was the New York *Christian Advocate and Journal*. I used this extensively, as I did the *Western Christian Advocate* (Cincinnati) and *Southern Christian Advocate* (Charleston, SC); I also consulted runs of the *North Carolina Christian Advocate* (Raleigh), *Richmond Christian Advocate*, *Pittsburgh Christian Advocate*, and *Northwestern Christian Advocate* (Chicago). Amongst Baptist papers, I relied particularly on the *Christian Watchman and Reflector* (Boston), *Biblical Recorder* (Raleigh, NC), *Christian Index* (Penfield, Ga.) and the twice-monthly *Primitive Baptist* (Tarborough, NC). The most valuable Congregational-

Presbyterian titles included the *Oberlin Evangelist*, New York *Independent*, *New York Evangelist*, *New York Observer* and *North Carolina Presbyterian* (Fayetteville). I used the *Catholic Telegraph* (Cincinnati) and *New York Freeman's Journal* for Catholic perspectives. Particularly helpful guides to the religious newspaper press are Wesley Norton, *Religious Newspapers in the Old Northwest to 1861: A History, Bibliography and Record of Opinion* (Athens, Ohio, 1977), and Henry S. Stroupe, *The Religious Press in the South Atlantic States, 1802–1865* (Durham, NC, 1956).

In the main I consulted political newspapers for presidential election years only. I leant particularly on the *Albany Argus*, *Albany Evening Journal*, *Ohio State Journal* (Columbus), *Ohio Statesman* (Columbus), *New York Tribune*, *North Carolina Whig* (Charlotte), *North Carolina Standard* (Raleigh), *New Orleans Bee*, *Columbus Enquirer* (Ga.), and *Charleston Mercury*. Because it powerfully mixes political partisanship and sectarian combativeness the *Knoxville Whig* warranted close attention. An even more obvious blend of denominational and partisan chauvinism can be found in the *Highland Messenger* (Asheville, NC). John E. Haynes, "Politics in 1844: being a choice selection of the most important points contended for throughout the campaign," dated 1 May 1845 (North Carolina Collection, Wilson Library, University of North Carolina at Chapel Hill), is a valuable collection of cuttings relating to the Clay–Polk campaign, drawn from scores of newspapers across the nation.

Periodical Press

The denominational monthlies and quarterlies had a more limited circulation than the weeklies and were aimed at a higher-brow audience. As well as dealing with issues of theology, ecclesiology, and church history, they also published articles on social and political affairs and on the churches' relationship to the state and the world. I made particular use of the *New Englander* (Congregationalist; New Haven); *Methodist Quarterly Review* (New York), *Christian Review* (Baptist; Boston, New York, and Baltimore), *Biblical Repertory and Theological Review* (Presbyterian; Princeton), *American Biblical Repository* (Presbyterian; New York); *Presbyterian Quarterly Review* (Philadelphia); *Southern Presbyterian Review* (Columbia, SC); *Brownson's Quarterly Review* (Catholic; Boston).

Published Diaries, Journals and Correspondence

Evangelicals reflected on a variety of political and social matters in their diaries, journals, and correspondence. Amongst the most valuable published editions are James W. Alexander, *Forty Years' Familiar Letters*, ed. John Hall (2 vols, New York, 1860); Gayle Thornbrough, Dorothy L. Riker and Paula Corpuz (eds) *The Diary of Calvin Fletcher* (9 vols, Indianapolis, 1972–83); Helen S.M. Marlatt (ed.) *Stuart Letters of Robert and Elizabeth Sullivan Stuart, 1819–1864* (2 vols, New York, 1961); and the letters of Charles Colcock Jones and his extended family in Robert Manson Myers (ed.) *The Children of Pride: A True Story of Georgia and the Civil War* (New Haven, Conn., 1972). Other collections and selections include Dwight L. Dumond (ed.) *Letters of James Gillespie Birney* (2 vols, New York, 1938);

Select Bibliography

Gilbert H. Barnes and Dwight L. Dumond (eds) *Letters of Theodore Dwight Weld, Angelina Grimké Weld and Sarah Grimké 1822–1844* (2 vols, 1934; repr. Gloucester, Mass., 1965); Ray Holder, "On Slavery: Selected Letters of Parson Winans, 1820–1844," *Journal of Mississippi History*, 46 (Nov. 1984), 323–54; W. Stanley Hoole, "The Diary of Dr. Basil Manly, 1858–1867," *Alabama Review*, 4 (April 1951), 127–49; Thornwell Jacobs (ed.) *Diary of William Plumer Jacobs* (Oglethorpe University, Ga., 1937); Emory Lindquist (ed.) "The Letters of the Rev. Samuel Young Lum, Pioneer Kansas Missionary, 1854–1858," *Kansas Historical Quarterly* (Spring and Summer 1959), 39–67, 172–96; Alfred A. Thomas (ed.) *Correspondence of Thomas Ebenezer Thomas* (Dayton, Ohio, 1909); and Lewis G. Vander Velde (ed.) "The Diary of George Duffield," *MVHR*, 24 (June 1937), 21–34.

Autobiographies, Memoirs, and Reminiscences

Antebellum evangelicals' autobiographies are variable in their quality, scope, and degree of objectivity. Some of these offer no reflections on political developments or issues. But most proffer some judgment on politics and secular matters, if only obliquely or in passing; and a sizeable number are – by the standards of the genre – well focused and sometimes helpfully indiscreet when they come to discuss political questions.

The theme of "Calvinist" political engagement is especially evident in the memoirs of Congregationalists. Amongst the more valuable of these are Lyman Abbott, *Reminiscences* (Boston, 1915); George Allen, *Reminiscences* (Worcester, Mass., 1883); Lyman Beecher, *The Autobiography of Lyman Beecher*, ed. Barbara Cross (2 vols, Cambridge, Mass., 1961); Sherlock Bristol, *The Pioneer Preacher* (New York [1887]); Adison P. Foster (ed.) *Four Pastorates: Glimpses of the Life and Thoughts of Eden B. Foster, D.D.* (Boston, 1883); Josiah B. Grinnell, *Men and Events of Forty Years: Autobiographical Reminiscences of an Active Career from 1850 to 1890* (Boston, 1891); John C. Holbrook, *Recollections of a Nonagenarian Life in New England, the Middle West, and New York* (Boston, 1897); John Marsh, *Temperance Recollections: Labors, Defeats, Triumphs: An Autobiography* (New York, 1866); Garth M. Rosell and Richard A.G. Dupuis (eds) *The Memoirs of Charles G. Finney: The Complete Restored Text* (Grand Rapids, Mich., 1989); William Salter, *Sixty Years, and Other Discourses, with Reminiscences* (Boston, 1907); and James Barr Walker, *Experiences of Pioneer Life in the Early Settlements and Cities of the West* (Chicago, 1881).

Presbyterians' reminiscences remind us what a large, diverse, and fissiparous family Presbyterianism was, but they also show the ubiquity of "Calvinist" approaches to political responsibility. The most politically assertive Presbyterians inhabited staunchly antislavery branches of the family, like the Free Presbyterians, and gave a special tone to the New School. Yet Old School men, too, even in the South, were concerned to cultivate proper standards of citizenship and sustain a moral political order. Representative of the range of approaches are John B. Adger, *My Life and Times 1810–1890* (Richmond, Va. [1899]); Joseph Badger, *A Memoir* (Hudson, Ohio, 1851); David Coulter, *Memoir, with Reminiscences, Letters, Lectures and Sermons* (St Louis, Mo., n.d.); *The Life and Writings of Rev. Joseph Gordon: Written and Compiled by a Committee of the Free*

Presbyterian Synod (Cincinnati, 1860); John Graham, *Autobiography and Reminiscences* (Philadelphia, 1870); Ashbel Green, *The Life of Ashbel Green* (New York, 1849); Thomas P. Hunt, *Life and Thoughts of Rev. Thomas P. Hunt: An Autobiography* (Wilkes-Barre, Pa., 1901); Wendell Prime, *Samuel Irenaeus Prime: Autobiography and Memorials* (New York, 1888); Thomas Smyth, *Autobiographical Notes* (Charleston, SC, 1914); and H.M. White (ed.) *Rev. William S. White, D.D. and His Times (1800–1873): An Autobiography* (Richmond, Va. 1891). Roeliff Brinkerhoff, *Recollections of a Lifetime* (Cincinnati, 1900), traces a fascinating personal religious odyssey from the Dutch Reformed to the Presbyterian church via Congregationalism.

Methodist autobiographies are legion. Many are preoccupied with conversion, the experience of itinerancy, and revivals of religion. But this politically quietist strain is far from universal. Most authors offer some perspective on "worldly" issues; collectively they shed light on the political implications of denominational and cultural conflict, on Methodists' burgeoning social and political status, and on the process of sectional alienation. Amongst the most illuminating works are George Brown, *Recollections of Itinerant Life* (3rd edn, Cincinnati, 1866); Alfred Brunson, *A Western Pioneer* (2 vols, Cincinnati, 1880); John Burgess, *Pleasant Recollections of Characters and Works of Noble Men* (Cincinnati, 1887); William W. Crane, *Autobiography and Miscellaneous Writings* (Syracuse, NY, 1891); Calvin Fairbank, *Rev. Calvin Fairbank during Slavery Times* (Chicago, 1890); William I. Fee, *Bringing the Sheaves: Gleanings from the Harvest Fields in Ohio, Kentucky and West Virginia* (Cincinnati, 1896); Thomas A. Goodwin, *Seventy-six Years' Tussle with the Traffic* (Indianapolis, 1883); Milton L. Haney, *The Story of My Life* (Normal, Ill., 1904); C.C. Stratton (ed.) *Autobiography of Erastus O. Haven, D.D., One of the Bishops of the Methodist Episcopal Church* (New York, 1883); Chauncey Hobart, *Recollections of My Life: Fifty Years of Itinerancy in the Northwest* (Redwing, Minn., 1885); William F. King, *Reminiscences* (New York, 1915); Luther Lee, *Autobiography of the Rev. Luther Lee, D.D.* (New York, 1882); Andrew Manship, *Thirteen Years' Experience in the Itinerancy* (Philadelphia, 1872); John Mathews, *Peeps into Life: Autobiography of Rev. John Mathews, D.D.* (n.p. [1904]); Wesson G. Miller, *Thirty Years in the Itinerancy* (Milwaukee, 1875); Sylvester Weeks (ed.) *A Life's Retrospect: Autobiography of Rev. Granville Moody* (Cincinnati, 1890); George Peck, *The Life and Times of George Peck, D.D.* (New York, 1874); Frank Richardson, *From Sunrise to Sunset: Reminiscence* (Bristol, Tenn., 1910); Wilson L. Spottswood, *Brief Annals* (Harrisburg, Pa., 1888); Mark Trafton, *Scenes in My Life* (New York, 1878); Allen Trimble, *Autobiography and Correspondence of Allen Trimble, Governor of Ohio* (n.p., 1909); Lorenzo Waugh, *Autobiography of Lorenzo Waugh* (Oakland, Calif., 1883); and W.P. Strickland (ed.) *Autobiography of Dan Young* (New York, 1860).

Baptists' reminiscences, too, are often exclusively devoted to issues of conversion and spiritual development. But the following offer insights into the political postures and concerns of some of the church's clerical leaders and laymen: Samuel Aaron, *His Life, Sermons, Correspondence, Etc.* (Norristown, Pa., 1890); Emerson Andrews, *Living Life* (Boston, 1872); George W. Clark, *Struggles and Triumphs of a Long Life: Personal Sketches and Autobiography* (Philadelphia, 1914); T.S. Dunaway, *Personal Memoirs, Sermons and Addresses* (Lynchburg, Va., 1900); William Hague, *Life Notes* (Boston, 1888); Jeremiah B. Jeter, *The Recollec-*

tions of a Long Life (Richmond, Va., 1891); F.M. Jordan, *Life and Labors of Elder F.M. Jordan, for Fifty Years a Preacher of the Gospel among North Carolina Baptists* (Raleigh, NC, 1899); James M. Pendleton, *Reminiscences of a Long Life* (Louisville, Ky., 1891); and Thomas S. Sheardown, *Half a Century's Labors in the Gospel, including Thirty-five Years of Back-woods Mission Work and Evangelizing, in New York and Pennsylvania: An Autobiography* ([Lewisburg, Pa.], 1865).

Contemporary and Near-contemporary Biographies

Many contemporary biographies of nineteenth-century evangelicals are as hagiographical as the era's autobiographies are self-serving. However, biographers frequently quoted at length from their subjects' private papers. I drew particularly from the treasure-house of Methodist biographies. The following deserve special attention: *The Christian Lawyer: Being a Portraiture of the Life and Character of William George Baker* (New York, 1859); George R. Crooks, *Life and Letters of Rev. John M'Clintock, D.D., LL.D.* (New York, 1876); Daniel Curry, *Life Story of Rev. Davis Wasgatt Clark* (New York, 1874); W.H. Daniels (ed.) *Memorials of Gilbert Haven, Bishop of the Methodist Episcopal Church* (Boston, 1882); Oscar P. Fitzgerald, *John B. McFerrin: A Biography* (Nashville, Tenn., 1888); Oscar P. Fitzgerald, *Judge Longstreet: A Life Sketch* (Nashville, Tenn., 1891); J.T. Fleharty, *Glimpses of the Life of Rev. A.E. Phelps and his Co-Laborers* (Cincinnati, 1878); Moses M. Henkle, *The Life of Henry Bidleman Bascom* (Nashville, Tenn., 1856); William G. Lewis, *Biography of Samuel Lewis, First Superintendent for Common Schools for the State of Ohio* (Cincinnati, 1857); David R. McAnally, *Life and Times of Rev. S. Patton, D.D. and Annals of the Holston Conference* (St Louis, 1859); David R. McAnally, *Life and Times of Rev. William Patton, and Annals of the Missouri Conference* (St Louis, 1858); William McDonald and John E. Searles, *The Life of Rev. John S. Inskip, President of the National Association for the Promotion of Holiness* (Chicago, 1885); Enoch M. Marvin, *The Life of Rev. William Goff Caples, of the Missouri Conference of the Methodist Episcopal Church, South* (St Louis, 1871); David H. Moore, *John Morgan Walden, Thirty-Fifth Bishop of the Methodist Episcopal Church* (New York, 1915); Walter C. Palmer, *Life and Letters of Leonidas L. Hamline* (New York, 1866); James E. Pilcher, *Life and Labors of Elijah H. Pilcher* (New York, 1892); George Prentice, *The Life of Gilbert Haven, Bishop of the Methodist Episcopal Church* (New York, 1883); Henry B. Ridgaway, *The Life of Edmund S. Janes, D.D., LL.D.* (New York, 1882); Richard H. Rivers, *The Life of Robert Paine, D.D., Bishop of the Methodist Episcopal Church, South* (Nashville, Tenn., 1916); John A. Roche, *The Life of J.P. Durbin* (New York, 1889); Charles N. Sims, *The Life of Thomas M. Eddy* (New York, 1879); George G. Smith, *The Life and Times of George Foster Pierce* (Sparta, Ga., 1888); George G. Smith, *The Life and Times of James Osgood Andrew, Bishop of the Methodist Episcopal Church, South* (Nashville, Tenn., 1883); Edward Thomson, *Life of Edward Thomson, Late Bishop of the Methodist Episcopal Church* (Cincinnati, 1885); and N. Vansant, *Work Here, Rest Hereafter; or, The Life and Character of Rev. Hiram Mattison, D.D.* (New York, 1870).

Amongst Baptist lives I found the following especially useful: Emeline Burlingame-Cheney, *The Story of the Life and Work of Oren B. Cheney* (Boston, Mass., 1907); H.P. Griffith, *The Life and Times of Rev. John G. Landrum*

(Philadelphia, 1885); H. Harvey, *Memoir of Alfred Bennett, First Pastor of the Baptist Church, Homer, N.Y., and Senior Agent of the American Baptist Missionary Union* (3rd edn, New York, 1852); J.D. Hufham, *Memoir of Rev. John L. Prichard, Late Pastor of the First Baptist Church, Wilmington, N.C.* (Raleigh, NC, 1867); J. Spencer Kennard, *Joseph H. Kennard, D.D.* (Philadelphia, 1867); John W. Lewis, *The Life, Labors and Travels of Elder Charles Bowles, of the Free Will Baptist Denomination* (Watertown, NY, 1852); James O. Murray, *Francis Wayland* (Boston, 1891); Archibald T. Robertson, *Life and Letters of John Albert Broadus* (Philadelphia, 1901); *Sketch of the Life and Character of George N. Briggs, Late Governor of Massachusetts* (Boston, 186–?); Justin A. Smith, *Memoir of Rev. Nathaniel Colver, D.D.* (Boston, 1873); and F. Wayland and H.L. Wayland, *A Memoir of the Life and Labors of Francis Wayland, D.D.* (2 vols, Boston, 1867).

Representative of the range of Congregationalist and Presbyterian postures on public issues are Henry C. Alexander, *The Life of Joseph Addison Alexander* (New York, 1870); T.C. Anderson, *Life of Rev. George Donnell, First Pastor of the Church in Lebanon* (Nashville, Tenn., 1859); Henry M. Baird, *Life of the Rev. Robert Baird* (New York, 1866); William E. Barton, *Joseph Edwin Roy 1827–1908: A Faithful Servant of God and of His Own Generation* (Oak Park, Ill., 1908); Lucy F. Bittinger, *Memorials of the Rev. Joseph Baugher Bittinger, D.D.* (Woodsville, NH, 1891); Mary Brainerd, *Life of Rev. Thomas Brainerd* (Philadelphia, 1870); Talbot W. Chambers, *Memoir of the Life and Character of the Late Hon. Theo. Frelinghuysen, LL.D.* (New York, 1863); D. Stuart Dodge (ed.) *Memorials of Wm. E. Dodge* (New York, 1887); William E. Griffis, *John Chambers: Servant of Christ and Master of Hearts and His Ministry in Philadelphia* (Ithaca, NY, 1903); Archibald A. Hodge, *The Life of Charles Hodge* (New York, 1880); Peyton H. Hoge, *Moses Drury Hoge: Life and Letters* (Richmond, Va. [1899]); Philip E. Howard, *The Life Story of Henry Clay Trumbull: Missionary, Army Chaplain, Editor, and Author* (New York, 1906); Thomas C. Johnson, *The Life and Letters of Robert Lewis Dabney* (Richmond, Va., 1903); Thomas C. Johnson, *The Life and Letters of Benjamin Morgan Palmer* (Richmond, Va. [1906]); David X. Junkin, *Rev. George Junkin, D.D., LL.D: A Historical Biography* (Philadelphia, 1871); George F. Magoun, *Asa Turner: A Home Missionary Patriarch* (Boston, 1889); Carlos Martyn, *William E. Dodge: The Christian Merchant* (New York, 1890); David O. Mears, *Life of Edward Norris Kirk, D.D.* (Boston, 1877); *Memoir of John C. Lord, D.D., Pastor of the Central Presbyterian Church for Thirty-Eight Years* (Buffalo, NY, 1878); Theodore T. Munger, *Horace Bushnell, Preacher and Theologian* (Boston, 1899); Benjamin M. Palmer, *The Life and Letters of James Henley Thornwell, D.D., LL.D., Ex-President of the South Carolina College* (Richmond, Va., 1875); and Truman A. Post, *Truman Marcellus Post, D.D: A Biography, Personal and Literary* (Boston, 1891).

Also of value are Abraham R. Van Nest, *Memoir of Rev. Geo. W. Bethune, D.D.* (New York, 1867), a life of the scholarly, influential Dutch Reformed minister and Democrat; Charles R. Tyng (comp.) *Record of the Life and Work of Stephen Higginson Tyng, D.D.* (New York, 1890), for the autocratic low-church Episcopalian and his brother, Dudley A. Tyng; and Zebedee Warner, *The Life and Labors of Rev. Jacob Bachtel, of the Parkersburg Annual Conference, United Brethren in Christ* (Dayton, Ohio, 1868). Useful biographical essays are to be found in William C. Smith, *Pillars in the Temple; or, Sketches of Deceased Laymen of the Methodist Episcopal Church* (New York, 1872), and in William B. Sprague's compendious *Annals of the*

Select Bibliography

American Pulpit; or, Commemorative Notices of Distinguished American Clergymen of Various Denominations (9 vols, New York, 1857–69).

Sermons, Tracts and Religious Polemics

I made extensive use of the prodigious outpourings of the pulpit. Many sermons were published in denominational newspapers and journals. Thousands more were independently distributed, their publication commonly encouraged by the minister's congregation. Some sermons made a lasting impact. Students at Iowa College actually memorized Truman M. Post's attack on the Missouri Compromise. Many sermons circulated widely, beyond the limits of denomination and locality. A few achieved national fame or notoriety and were reprinted in thousands: such was the case, for example, with John C. Lord's pro-Union sermon of 1850, *"The Higher Law" in Its Application to the Fugitive Slave Bill* (Buffalo, NY, 1851) and Benjamin M. Palmer's encouragement to secession, "Thanksgiving Sermon Delivered in the First Presbyterian Church, New Orleans, on Thursday, November 29, 1860," in B.M. Palmer and W.T. Leacock, *The Rights of the South Defended in the Pulpits* (Mobile, Ala., 1860). But even discourses which enjoyed a more limited readership are valuable, for collectively they help identify the points of philosophical disagreement and of common political understanding within the churches.

Amongst the more interesting collections of sermons by particular ministers are Jonathan Blanchard, *Sermons and Addresses* (Chicago, 1892); Cornelius C. Cuyler, *The Signs of the Times* (Philadelphia, 1839); Gilbert Haven, *National Sermons: Sermons, Speeches and Letters on Slavery and Its War* (Boston, 1869); Ichabod S. Spencer, *Sermons . . . With a Sketch of His Life, by Rev. J.M. Sherwood* (2 vols, New York, 1855); and J. William Flynn (ed.) *The Complete Works of Rev. Thomas Smyth* (10 vols, Columbia, SC, 1908–12).

Many discourses were composed for formal public occasions. The tradition in Massachusetts of the annual election sermon carried on into the antebellum period. State and national days for fasting and prayer (in particular those called in May 1841, following President Harrison's death, and in January 1861, when James Buchanan found political events moving beyond his control) elicited an abundance of ruminations on the moral condition of the country: Silas McKeen, *God Our Only Hope* (Belfast, Me., 1837); Nathaniel Gage, *Sins and Dangers of the Times* (Haverhill, Mass., 1838); John Maltby, *Characteristics of the Times* (Bangor, Me., 1838); William L. Breckinridge, *Submission to the Will of God* (Louisville, Ky., 1841); George Peck, *National Evils and Their Remedy* (New York, 1841); William B. Sprague, *Voice of the Rod* (Albany, NY, 1841); William Wisner, *Nations Amenable to God* (Ithaca, NY, 1841); Whitefoord Smith, *National Sins: A Call to Repentance* (Charleston, SC, 1849); Daniel Curry, *The Judgments of God, Confessed and Deprecated* (n.p. [1849]); Daniel Foster, *Our Nation's Sins and the Christian's Duty* (Boston, 1851); and Thomas Smyth, *The Sin and the Curse* (Charleston, SC, 1860) offer quintessential examples of the genre.

Thanksgiving sermons, too, were frequently published. These might strike a celebratory note, but preachers commonly used the occasions for warning and even lamentation. Distinguished examples include John M. Krebs, *Righteousness the Foundation of National Prosperity* (New York, 1835); George Duffield, *A Thanksgiving Sermon: The Religious Character of a People the True Element of Their Prosperity* (Detroit, 1839); Mark Tucker, *A Discourse Preached on Thanksgiving Day* (Providence, RI, 1842); Davis W. Clark, *An Alarm to Christian Patriots* (Hartford, Conn., 1843); James Rowland, *The Glorious Mission of the American People* (Circleville, Ohio, 1850); Nicholas Murray, *American Principles on National Prosperity* (New York, 1854); Charles Wadsworth, *America's Mission* (Philadelphia, 1855); Irem W. Smith, *The Sins of the Nation* (Ellsworth, Me., 1857); and John Chambers, *Thanksgiving Sermon . . . November 24, 1859* (Philadelphia [1859]).

The other set-piece occasion was the funeral sermon for public figures, when ministers and lay officers seized the opportunity to reflect on the progress of the republic and the deeper meaning of the life and death of the recently departed. Quite apart from the scores of sermons published after Harrison's death – unique in the attention it received from the pulpit – dozens of discourses commemorated the other presidents and ex-presidents who died during the period. Examples include George W. Bethune, *Truth the Strength of Freedom* (Philadelphia, 1845); Leonard E. Lathrop, *A Discourse on the Death of John Quincy Adams* (Auburn, NY, 1848); James M. Porter, *Eulogium upon James Knox Polk* (Easton, Pa., 1849); and Abraham B. Van Zandt, *God's Voice to the Nation* (Petersburg, Va., 1850). The deaths of Calhoun, Clay, and Webster in the early 1850s also occasioned a series of clerical responses, which included J.C. Coit, *Eulogy on the Life, Character and Public Services of the Hon. John C. Calhoun* (Columbia, SC, 1850); George Duffield, *The American Patriot* (Detroit, 1852); John C. Lord, *"Our Strong Rods Broken and Withered"* (Buffalo, NY, 1852); Richard H. Richardson, *National Bereavements* (Chicago, 1852); William A. Stearns, *The Great Lamentation: A Sermon in Commemoration of Daniel Webster* (2nd edn, Boston 1852); James H. Thornwell, *Thoughts Suited to the Present Crisis* (Columbia, SC, 1850); Abraham B. Van Zandt, *The Voice of Years* (Petersburg, Va., 1852); and William Winans, *A Funeral Discourse on the Occasion of the Death of Hon. Henry Clay* (Woodville, Miss., 1852).

At some time or another most ministers were drawn to reflect on the relationship between political and religious liberty. What were the scriptural duties of the devout Christian and of the politician under a Constitution which formally separated church and state? Should ministers preach politics? What responsibility did the pulpit bear for educating citizens to defend the republic? These and similar concerns were the burden, for example, of George D. Armstrong, *Politics and the Pulpit* (Norfolk, Va., 1856); Robert Baird, *The Noblest Freedom: or, the Influence of Christianity upon Civil Liberty* (New York, 1846); Horace Bushnell, *Politics under the Law of God* (Hartford, Conn., 1844); J.C. Coit, *Discourse upon Government, Divine and Human* (Columbia, SC, 1853); David D. Demarest, *Religion in Politics* (Hudson, NY, 1856); William T. Dwight, *The Pulpit, in its Relations to Politics* (Portland, Me., 1857); John Maltby, *Government: A Sermon* (Bangor, Me., 1856); John M. Peck, *The Principles and Tendencies of Democracy* (Belville, Ill., 1839); William A. Scott, *The Duty of Praying for Our Rulers* (New Orleans, 1843); Charles W. Shields, *A Discourse on Christian Politics* (Philadelphia, 1851); Thomas H. Skinner, *Religion and Liberty* (New York, 1841); James S. Smart, *The Political Duties of Christian Men and Ministers* (Detroit, 1854); Benjamin F. Tefft, *The Republican Influence of Christianity* (Bangor, Me., 1841); Joseph P.

Thompson, *Duties of the Christian Citizen* (New York, 1848); Edward Thomson, *The Pulpit and Politics* (Columbus, Ohio, 1854); and Nathaniel West, *The Overturning of Tyrannical and Wicked Governments* (Pittsburgh, 1852). Valuable book-length treatments of these same themes include Stephen Colwell, *Politics for American Christians* (Philadelphia, 1852); Theodore Frelinghuysen, *An Inquiry into the Moral and Religious Character of the American Government* (New York, 1838); and Samuel B. Wylie, *The Two Sons of Oil* (3rd edn, Philadelphia, 1850).

A torrent of sermons warned of the dangers to the republic from Romanists and drunkards. Powerful examples include Nathan S.S. Beman, *The Crisis and the Triumph* (Troy, NY, 1846); Henry A. Boardman, *The Intolerance of the Church of Rome* (Philadelphia, 1844); Charles B. Boynton, *Our Country, the Herald of a New Era* (Cincinnati, 1847) and *Address before the Citizens of Cincinnati* (Cincinnati, 1855); Horace Bushnell, *Common Schools: A Discourse on the Modifications Demanded by the Roman Catholics* (Hartford, Conn., 1853); Davis W. Clark, *Evils and Remedy of Intemperance* (New York, 1847); Rufus W. Clark, *Popery and the United States* (Boston, 1847); Henry M. Dexter, *Temperance Duties of the Temperate* (Boston, 1850); Henry C. Fish, *The School Question: Romanism and the Common Schools* (New York, 1853); Harvey D. Kitchel, *An Appeal to the People for the Suppression of the Liquor Traffic* (New York, 1848); Luther Lee, *A Sermon for the Times: Prohibitory Laws* (New York, 1852); Alexander T. McGill, *Popery, the Punishment of Unbelief* (Philadelphia, 1848); Samuel T. Spear, *Law and Temperance* (New York, 1852); James P. Stuart, *America and the Americans versus the Papacy and the Catholics* (Cincinnati, 1853); Joshua T. Tucker, *The Maine Law; or Extermination the Only Cure of the Liquor Traffic* (Holliston, Me., 1852); and Abraham B. Van Zandt, *The Romish Controversy* (Columbia, SC, 1854).

As time passed few ministers could avoid reflecting on the moral and scriptural basis of slavery. The sermonic and other literature on the subject is daunting. Southern ministers' often aggressive apologies for slavery include Alexander McCaine, *Slavery Defended from Scripture* (Baltimore, 1842); Patrick H. Mell, *Slavery: A Treatise Showing that Slavery Is Neither a Moral, Political Nor Social Evil* (Penfield, Ga., 1844); Iveson L. Brookes, *A Defence of Southern Slavery* (Hamburg, SC, 1851); William A. Smith, *Lectures on the Philosophy and Practice of Slavery*, ed. T.O. Summers (Nashville, Tenn., 1856); and George D. Armstrong, *The Christian Doctrine of Slavery* (New York, 1857). Northern critiques range from harsh indictments like George B. Cheever's address *The Fire and Hammer of God's Word against the Sin of Slavery* (New York, 1858) to the more cautious and moderate tone of Nathan L. Rice, *Lectures on Slavery* (Chicago, 1860). Cyrus P. Grosvenor, *A Review of the "Correspondence" of Messrs. Fuller and Wayland, on the Subject of American Slavery* (Utica, NY, 1847), offers some sense of the breakdown of understanding between moderates on both sides.

Ministers' approaches to slavery and related questions can be traced through their public responses at moments of political drama or crisis. The annexation of Texas and the Mexican war provoked animated responses from both pulpit and public platform, especially in the Northeast. These included George Allen, *An Appeal to the People of Massachusetts, on the Texas Question* (Boston, 1844); Milton Braman, *The Mexican War* (Danvers, Mass., 1847); Samuel D. Burchard, *Causes of National Solicitude* (New York, 1848); Samuel Harris, *The Mexican War* (Greenfield, Mass., 1847); Burdett Hart, *The Mexican War* (New Haven, Conn., 1847); Horace

James, *Our Duties to the Slave* (Boston, 1847); Thomas E. Thomas, *Covenant Breaking and Its Consequences* (Rossville, Ohio, 1847); and Stephen M. Vail, *The Signs of the Times* (Poughkeepsie, NY, 1846). Robert L. Stanton, *Two Discourses on War and Peace* (New Orleans, 1847) offers a southern perspective.

Representative of free-soil and "higher-law" voices in response to the political crisis and settlement of 1850 were Leonard Bacon, *The Higher Law* (New Haven, Conn., 1851); William Carter, *A Reply to Hon. William Thomas' Exposition and Defence of the Fugitive Slave Law* (Winchester, Ill., 1851); Nathaniel Colver, *The Fugitive Slave Bill; or God's Laws Paramount to the Laws of Men* (Boston, 1850); Horace T. Love, *Slavery in its Relation to God* (Buffalo, NY, 1851); Wooster Parker, *The Role of Duty* (Bangor, Me., 1851); L. Smith, *The Higher Law; or, Christ and His Law Supreme* (Ravenna, Ohio, 1852); and Samuel T. Spear, *The Law-abiding Conscience, and the Higher Law Conscience* (New York, 1850). The spectrum of conservative Unionist sentiment in response to the same events can be identified in Henry A. Boardman, *The American Union* (Philadelphia, 1851); William P. Breed, *Discourse Mainly upon the Importance of the American Union* (Steubenville, Ohio, 1850); George Duffield, *Our Federal Union; a Cause for Gratitude to God* (Detroit, 1850); William W. Eells, *Gratitude for Individual and National Blessings* (Newburyport, Mass., 1850); John T. Hendrick, *Union and Slavery* (Clarksville, Tenn., 1851); Charles Hodge, *Civil Government* (Princeton, NJ, 1851); George F. Kettell, *A Sermon on the Duty of Citizens, with Respect to the Fugitive Slave Law* (White Plains, NY, 1851); John C. Lord, *"The Higher Law"* (cited earlier, p. 448); McKinney, *The Union Preserved; or, The Law-abiding Christian* (Philadelphia, 1851); John Mason Peck, *The Duties of American Citizens* (St Louis, 1851); and George L. Prentiss, *The Obligations of American Patriotism* (Newark, NJ, 1851), 5–18. A sense of the varying degrees of insistence with which southern rights were asserted emerges from Iveson L. Brookes, *A Defence of the South against the Reproaches and Incroachments of the North* (Hamburg, SC, 1850); J.C. Coit, *Eulogy on Calhoun* (cited earlier, p. 449); Ferdinand Jacobs, *The Committing of Our Cause to God* (Charleston, SC, 1850); Whitefoord Smith, *God the Refuge of His People* (Columbia, SC, 1850); and James H. Thornwell, *Thoughts Suited to the Present Crisis* (cited earlier, p. 449).

Northern evangelicals who attacked the Kansas–Nebraska Act and identified the slave power as the culprit behind the subsequent violence in Kansas and in the Senate chamber included Leonard Bacon, *The Morality of the Nebraska Bill* (New Haven, Conn., 1854); Charles Beecher, *A Sermon on the Nebraska Bill* (Newark, NJ, 1854); Joseph B. Bittinger, *A Plea for Humanity* (Cleveland, Ohio, 1854); C.H.A. Bulkley, *Removal of Ancient Landmarks: or, the Causes and Consequences of Slavery Extension* (Hartford, Conn., 1854); Henry C. Fish, *Freedom or Despotism: The Voice of Our Brother's Blood* (Newark, NJ, 1856); Heman Humphrey, *The Missouri Compromise* (Pittsfield, Mass., 1854); Edward N. Kirk, *"Our Duty in Perilous Times"* (Boston, 1856); George W. Perkins, *Facts and Duties of the Times* (New York, 1856); Noah Porter, *Civil Liberty* (New York, 1856); R.H. Richardson, *Wickedness in High Places* (Chicago, 1854); and Francis Wayland, *Francis Wayland on the Moral and Religious Aspects of the Nebraska Bill* (Rochester, NY, 1854).

John Brown's raid at Harper's Ferry prompted widespread comment in the northern pulpit, much of it distinguishing between the means employed and the ends pursued. Of importance are George B. Cheever, *The Curse of God against Political Atheism* (Boston, 1859); Fales H. Newhall, *The Conflict in America* (Boston, 1859); William W. Patton, *The Execution of John Brown* (Chicago [1859]); David H. Riddle, *"Such a Time as This"* (Jersey City, NJ, 1860); and William Salter, *Slavery, and the Lessons of Recent Events* (n.p. [1859]). A number of sermons delivered from an antislavery perspective are collected together in James Redpath (ed.) *Echoes of Harper's Ferry* (Boston, 1860). Nathan Lord, abolitionist turned slavery apologist, in *A Letter to J.M. Conrad, Esq, on Slavery* (Hanover, NH, 1860), provides the most forceful of northern indictments of John Brown's actions.

Some responses to the winter crisis of 1860–61 were collected in *Fast Day Sermons: or The Pulpit on the State of the Country* (New York, 1861). Amongst the more luminous contributions to public debate in the North were Samuel J. Baird, *Southern Rights and Northern Duties in the Present Crisis* (Philadelphia, 1861); Henry A. Boardman, *What Christianity Demands of Us at the Present Crisis* (Philadelphia, 1860); George Duffield, *Our National Sins To Be Repented Of* (Detroit, 1861); Ezra S. Ely, *The Crisis: The Duty of Citizens in Regard to It* (n.p. [1861]); Charles Hodge, "The State of the Country," *Princeton Review*, 33 (1861), 1–36; Alexander T. McGill, *Sinful but Not Forsaken* (New York, 1861); and James S. Smart, *National Fast* (Flint, Mich., 1861). Important southern voices and pens included Robert L. Dabney, *Letter . . . to S.J. Prime* (Richmond, Va., 1861; Benjamin M. Palmer, "Thanksgiving Sermon Delivered in the First Presbyterian Church, New Orleans" (cited earlier, p. 448); C.H. Read, *National Fast* (Richmond, Va., 1861); Thomas Smyth, *The Sin and the Curse; or, The Union, the True Source of Disunion, and Our Duty in the Present Crisis* (Charleston, SC, 1860); and James H. Thornwell, "Our National Sins," in *Fast Day Sermons* (cited above).

Publications dealing with church and benevolent society abrasions over slavery are legion. Those which show most clearly the breakdown of consensus and the cultivation of sectional demonologies include Henry B. Bascom *et al.*, *Brief Appeal to Public Opinion, in a Series of Exceptions to the Course and Action of the Methodist Episcopal Church* (Louisville, Ky., 1848); Charles Elliott, *History of the Great Secession from the Methodist Episcopal Church* (Cincinnati, 1855); John D. Long, *Pictures of Slavery in Church and State* (Philadelphia, 1857); J. Mayland McCarter, *Border Methodism and Border Slavery* (Philadelphia, 1858); Hiram Mattison, *The Impending Crisis of 1860; or, the Present Connection of the Methodist Episcopal Church with Slavery* (New York, 1858); Edward H. Myers, *The Disruption of the Methodist Episcopal Church, 1844–46: Comprising a Thirty Years' History of the Relations of the Two Methodisms* (Nashville, Tenn., 1875); William W. Patton *et al.*, *The Unanimous Remonstrance of the Fourth Congregational Church of Hartford, Conn., against the Policies of the American Tract Society on the Subject of Slavery* (Hartford, Conn., 1855); Nathan L. Rice, *Ten Letters on the Subject of Slavery: Addressed to the Delegates from the Congregational Associations to the Last General Assembly of the Presbyterian Church* (St Louis, 1855); Wesley Smith, *A Defence of the Methodist Episcopal Church against the Charges of Rev. S. Kelley and Others, of the Methodist Episcopal Church, South* (Fairmont, Va., 1855); and Lorenzo Waugh, *A Candid Statement of the Course Pursued by the Preachers of the Methodist Episcopal Church South* (Cincinnati, 1848).

Political Tracts and Campaign Material

A cascade of political literature matched in volume and polemics the torrent of religious titles that poured from antebellum steam presses. No candidate for the presidency or vice-presidency lacked his hagiographer, and few of these omitted to trace their subject's religious pedigree and laud his moral stature. A listing of these titles would require a bibliography in itself, but representative and instructive are Richard Hildreth, *The People's Presidential Candidate; or, The Life of William Henry Harrison of Ohio* (Boston, 1839); Cortlandt Parker, *A Sketch of the Life and Public Services of Theodore Frelinghuysen* (n.p., 1844); Nathan Sargent, *Brief Outline of the Life of Henry Clay* (Washington, 1844); *The Life and Public Services of. . . J.K. Polk* (Baltimore, 1844); Joseph Gales, *A Sketch of the Personal Character and Qualities of General Zachary Taylor* (Washington [1848]); Henry R. Schoolcraft, *Outlines of the Life and Character of Gen. Lewis Cass* (Albany, NY, 1848); *Life of General Scott* (New York, 1852); Nathaniel Hawthorne, *Life of Franklin Pierce* (Boston, 1852); W.L. Barre, *The Life and Public Services of Millard Fillmore* (Buffalo, NY, 1856); and Robert B. Warden, *A Voter's Version of the Life and Character of Stephen A. Douglas* (Columbus, Ohio, 1860).

Campaign songs often incorporated the music, language, and millennialist outlook of evangelicalism. Amongst the songbooks produced for particular campaigns were *The Harrison Medal Minstrel* (Philadelphia, 1840); John S. Stockton, *The Clay Minstrel; or, National Songster* (Philadelphia, 1844); *Scott and Graham Melodies* (New York [1852]); *Fremont & Dayton: Campaign Songs for 1856* (Cleveland, Ohio, 1856); and *The Wide-Awake Vocalist; or, Railsplitters' Song Book* (New York, 1860).

Partisan literature openly exploited religious and sectarian questions in order to tap evangelical support. Such issues as Martin Van Buren's "subservience" to the papacy, Henry Clay's dueling, Pierce's stand on the religious test for office in New Hampshire, and Frémont's alleged Roman Catholicism engaged the talents of polemicists on all sides. Representative of this literature are William G. Brownlow, *A Political Register, Setting Forth the Principles of the Whig and Locofoco Parties in the United States* (Jonesborough, Tenn., 1844); *Henry Clay's Duels: Campaign of 1844* ([Washington, DC, 1844]); Joshua Leavitt, *The Great Duellist* (Boston [1844]); Charles O. Gorman, *An Irish Catholic Whig to His Fellow Countrymen in the United States* (Providence, RI, 1852); William E. Robinson, *Franklin Pierce and Catholic Persecution in New Hampshire* (n.p. [1852]); *The Whig Charge of Intolerance against the New Hampshire Democracy and Gen. Franklin Pierce* (Boston [1852]); *J.C. Fremont's Record* (n.p. [1856]); *The Romish Intrigue: Fremont a Catholic!!* (New York [1856]); *Col. Fremont's Religion* (n.p. [1856]); and *Col. Fremont Not a Roman Catholic* (n.p. [1856]). The nativism and anti-Catholicism addressed in much of this literature achieved most dramatic political expression in the Know Nothing party, of course, whose publicists included deeply committed evangelicals. Important in this context are William G. Brownlow, *Americanism Contrasted with Foreignism, Romanism, and Bogus Democracy* (Nashville, Tenn., 1856) and J.L. Chapman, *Americanism versus Romanism: or, The Cis-Atlantic Battle between Sam and the Pope* (Nashville, Tenn., 1856). The response of anti-Know Nothing, pro-Democrat evangelicals was firmly articulated in such publications as *Facts for the People of the South: Abolition Intolerance and Religious*

Intolerance United: Know-Nothingism Exposed (Washington, 1855) and Augustus B. Longstreet, *Letters from President Longstreet* (New Orleans, 1855), published by the Democratic State Central Committee of Louisiana.

The impropriety of evangelicals "meddling" in political affairs was a common theme of political literature, principally of the Democrats. Illustrative of the genre are John Wentworth, *Speech of Mr. Wentworth of Illinois* [US House of Representatives, April 1844] (n.p. [1844]); Stephen A. Douglas, *Speech . . . on the "Measures of Adjustment" Delivered in the City Hall, Chicago, October 23, 1850* (Washington, 1851); *Right of Petition. New England Clergymen. Remarks on the Memorial from some 3,050 Clergymen . . . Remonstrating against the Passage of the Nebraska Bill* (Washington, 1854); Stephen A. Douglas, *Letter of Senator Douglas, Vindicating His Character and Position on the Nebraska Bill* (Washington, 1854); *Letters of A.H. Stephens and Rev. H.H. Tucker, on Religious Liberty* (Atlanta, Ga., 1855); John W. Forney, *Address on Religious Intolerance and Political Proscription* (Washington, 1855); and Jeremiah S. Black, *"Religious Liberty"* (Chambersburg, Pa., 1856).

Secondary Sources

There are countless studies of the role of religion in American politics and public life. Amongst the broadest in scope and implications are Robert Bellah's classic essay, "Civil Religion in America," *Daedalus*, 96 (Winter 1967), 1–21; Sacvan Bercovitch, *The American Jeremiad* (Madison, Wisc., 1978), which considers the pulpit's persisting historical role as a moral and political exhorter; Furio Colombo, *God in America: Religion and Politics in the United States*, trans. Kristin Jarratt (New York, 1984), which focuses principally on religious warfare in politics in 1980; Samuel P. Huntington, *American Politics: The Promise of Disharmony* (Cambridge, Mass., 1981); Robert L. Kelley's bravura studies, *The Cultural Pattern in American Politics: The First Century* (New York, 1979) and "Ideology and Political Culture from Jefferson to Nixon," *AHR*, 82 (June 1977), 531–62; Gerhard Lenski's influential *The Religious Factor: A Sociological Study of Religion's Impact on Politics, Economics and Family Life* (New York, 1961); Mark A. Noll, *One Nation Under God? Christian Faith and Political Action in America* (New York, 1988), a thoughtful Christian statement; and Anson Phelps Stokes and Leo Pfeffer (eds) *Church and State in the United States* (3 vols, 1950). Two recent works of particular importance are: Mark A. Noll (ed.) *Religion and American Politics: From the Colonial Period to the 1980s* (New York, 1990) and Garry Wills, *Under God: Religion and American Politics* (New York, 1990).

Works which have especially shaped my understanding of American religious life in the mid-nineteenth century include Nathan O. Hatch, *The Democratization of American Christianity* (New Haven, Conn., 1989); Fred J. Hood, *Reformed America: The Middle and Southern States, 1783–1837* (University of Alabama, 1980); William G. McLoughlin, *Modern Revivalism: Charles Grandison Finney to Billy Graham* (New York, 1959) and *Revivals, Awakenings and Reform* (Chicago, 1978); George Marsden, *The Evangelical Mind and the New School Presbyterian Experience*

(New Haven, Conn., 1970); Donald G. Mathews, "The Second Great Awakening as an Organizing Process, 1780–1830: An Hypothesis," *AQ*, 21 (Spring 1969), 23–43; James L. Moorhead, "Between Progress and Apocalypse: A Reassessment of Millennialism in American Religious Thought, 1800–1880," *JAH*, 71 (Dec. 1984), 524–42; Donald M. Scott, *From Office to Profession: The New England Ministry* (Philadelphia, 1978); Gordon Wood, "Evangelical America and Early Mormonism," *New York History*, 61 (Oct. 1980), 359–86. Essential for an understanding of the South are Donald G. Mathews, *Religion in the Old South* (Chicago, 1977); E. Brooks Holifield, *The Gentlemen Theologians: American Theology in Southern Culture, 1795–1860* (Durham, NC, 1978); and Bertram Wyatt-Brown, "The Antimission Movement in the Jacksonian South and West: A Study in Regional Folk Culture," *JSH*, 36 (Nov. 1970), 501–29. Important local studies include Whitney R. Cross, *The Burned-Over District: The Social and Intellectual History of Enthusiastic Religion in Western New York, 1800–1850* (Ithaca, NY, 1950); Robert Doherty, "Social Bases for the Presbyterian Schism of 1837–1838: The Philadelphia Case," *Journal of Social History*, 2 (Fall 1968), 69–79; Randolph A. Roth, *The Democratic Dilemma: Religion, Reform, and the Social Order in the Connecticut River Valley of Vermont, 1791–1850* (Cambridge, UK, 1987); and Mary Ryan, *Cradle of the Middle Class: The Family in Oneida County, New York, 1790–1865* (Cambridge, UK, 1981). Denominational histories vary enormously in quality and value. Especially worthy of mention here are Emory S. Bucke *et al.*, *The History of American Methodism* (3 vols, Nashville, Tenn., 1964); David E. Harrell, *Quest for Christian America: The Disciples of Christ and American Society to 1866* (Nashville, Tenn., 1966); Byron C. Lambert, *The Rise of the Anti-Mission Baptists: Sources and Leaders, 1800–1840* (New York, 1980); and Ernest Trice Thompson, *Presbyterians in the South* (3 vols, Richmond, Va., c.1963–73).

Outstanding amongst the biographies of evangelicals are Theodore T. Bacon, *Leonard Bacon: A Statesman in the Church* (New Haven, Conn., 1931); E. Merton Coulter, *William G. Brownlow, Fighting Parson of the Southern Highlands* (Chapel Hill, NC, 1937); Hugh Davis, *Joshua Leavitt: Evangelical Abolitionist* (Baton Rouge, La., 1990); James O. Farmer, *The Metaphysical Confederacy: James Henley Thornwell and the Synthesis of Southern Values* (Macon, Ga., 1986); Ray Holder, *William Winans: Methodist Leader in Antebellum Mississippi* (Jackson, Miss., 1977); William T. Hutchinson, *Cyrus Hall McCormick* (2 vols, New York, 1930–35); James B. Stewart, *Joshua Giddings and the Tactics of Radical Politics* (Cleveland, Ohio, 1970); and Bertram Wyatt-Brown, *Lewis Tappan and the Evangelical War against Slavery* (Cleveland, Ohio, 1969).

Other valuable biographies which place evangelicals in a public context are Benjamin W. Bacon, *Theodore Thornton Munger: New England Minister* (New Haven, Conn., 1913); Robert D. Clark, *The Life of Matthew Simpson* (New York, 1956); Clifford Merrill Drury, *William Anderson Scott: "No Ordinary Man"* (Glendale, Calif., 1967); Jane S. Elsmere, *Henry Ward Beecher: The Indiana Years, 1837–1847* (Indianapolis, 1973); Francis R. Flournoy, *Benjamin Mosby Smith, 1811–1893* (Richmond, Va., 1947); Helen H. Grant, *Peter Cartwright: Pioneer* (New York, 1931); William B. Gravely, *Gilbert Haven: Methodist Abolitionist: A Study in Race, Religion, and Reform, 1850–1880* (Nashville, Tenn., 1973); Frances M.B. Hilliard, *Stepping Stones to Glory: From Circuit Rider to Editor and the Years in Between: Life of David Rice McAnally, D.D. 1810–95* (Baltimore, 1975); Philip D. Jordan, *William*

Salter, *Western Torchbearer* (Oxford, Ohio, 1939); Clyde S. Kilby, *Minority of One: The Biography of Jonathan Blanchard* (Grand Rapids, Mich., 1959); Edward Magdol, *Owen Lovejoy: Abolitionist in Congress* (New Brunswick, NJ, 1967); H.W. Mann, *Atticus Greene Haygood* (University of Georgia, 1965); David H. Overy, "Robert Lewis Dabney: Apostle of the Old South" (PhD diss., University of Wisconsin, 1967); Owen Peterson, *A Divine Discontent: A Life of Nathan S.S. Beman* (Macon, Ga., 1986); and John D. Wade, *Augustus Baldwin Longstreet: A Study of the Development of the Culture of the South* (Athens, Ga., 1969).

The stance of antebellum evangelical churches on the broad range of public issues is explored in John R. Bodo, *The Protestant Clergy and Public Issues, 1812–1848* (Princeton, NJ, 1954); Charles C. Cole, *The Social Ideas of the Northern Evangelists 1826–1860* (New York, 1954); Clifford S. Griffin, *Their Brothers' Keepers: Moral Stewardship in the United States, 1800–1865* (New Brunswick, NJ, 1960); Anne C. Loveland, *Southern Evangelicals and the Social Order, 1800–1860* (Baton Rouge, La., 1980); and Timothy L. Smith, *Revivalism and Social Reform in Mid-Nineteenth-Century America* (New York, 1965). A helpful point of contrast is provided by Robert B. Mullin's elegant *Episcopal Vision/American Reality: High Church Theology and Social Thought in Evangelical America* (New Haven, Conn., 1986). Jack P. Maddex, "From Theocracy to Spirituality: The Southern Presbyterian Reversal on Church and State," *Journal of Presbyterian History*, 54 (Winter 1976), 438–57, and James O. Farmer, "Southern Presbyterians and Southern Nationalism: A Study in Ambivalence," *Georgia Historical Quarterly*, 75 (Summer 1991), 275–94, offer important reflections on the degree of southern exceptionalism from a national norm of social and political engagement.

Protestants' deliberations on drink and other matters thrown up by the spread of Catholicism have generated a substantial secondary literature. Evangelicals' role in the temperance movement is traceable through the pages of Frank Byrne, *Prophet of Prohibition: Neal Dow and His Crusade* (Madison, Wisc., 1961); Jed Dannenbaum, *Drink and Disorder: Temperance Reform in Cincinnati from the Washingtonian Revival to the WCTU* (Urbana, Ill., 1984); John A. Krout, *The Origins of Prohibition* (New York, 1925); W.J. Rorabaugh, *The Alcoholic Republic: America 1790–1840* (New York, 1979); and Ian Tyrrell, *Sobering Up: From Temperance to Prohibition in Antebellum America, 1800–1860* (Westport, Conn., 1979) and "Drink and Temperance in the Antebellum South: An Overview and Interpretation," *JSH*, 48 (Nov. 1982), 485–510. The starting-point for evangelicals' anti-Catholicism remains Ray Allen Billington, *The Protestant Crusade: A Study of the Origins of American Nativism* (New York, 1938), though this is much more valuable for disentangling the threads of the anti-Catholic argument than for understanding the emergence and contours of political nativism. Also important are David Gerber, "Ambivalent Anti-Catholicism: Buffalo's American Protestant Elite Faces the Challenge of the Catholic Church, 1850–1860," *CWH*, 30 (June 1984), 120–43; Carl F. Kaestle, *Pillars of the Republic: Common Schools and American Society, 1780–1860* (New York, 1983); Vincent Lannie and Bernard C. Diethorn, "For the Honor and Glory of God: The Philadelphia Bible Riots of 1844," *History of Education Quarterly*, 8 (Spring 1968), 44–106; and Gilbert Osofsky, "Abolitionists, Irish Immigrants, and the Dilemmas of Romantic Nationalism," *AHR*, 80 (Oct. 1975), 889–912.

Writings on northern churches' responses to slavery have focused illuminatingly if disproportionately on the abolitionist minority and on the relationship between Protestantism and radical antislavery sentiment. Here the starting-point is Gilbert H. Barnes, *The Antislavery Impulse 1830–1844* (New York, 1933). Also important are the able studies of Lawrence J. Friedman, *Gregarious Saints: Self and Community in American Abolitionism 1830–1870* (Cambridge, UK, 1982); John R. McKivigan, *The War against Proslavery Religion: Abolitionism and the Northern Churches 1830–1865* (Ithaca, NY, 1984); Lewis Perry, *Radical Abolitionism: Anarchy and the Government of God in Antislavery Thought* (Ithaca, NY, 1973); Gerald Sorin, *The New York Abolitionists: A Case Study of Political Radicalism* (Westport, Conn., 1971); James B. Stewart, *Holy Warriors: The Abolitionists and American Slavery* (New York, 1976); and Anne C. Loveland's influential article, "Evangelicalism and Immediate Emancipation in American Antislavery Thought," *JSH*, 32 (May 1966), 172–88.

Southern churches' cultivation of a proslavery ethic has been increasingly discussed in recent years. Larry E. Tise, *Proslavery: A History of the Defense of Slavery in America, 1701–1840* (Athens, Ga., 1987) is essential and controversial reading. Also important are Drew Gilpin Faust, "Evangelicalism and the Meaning of the Proslavery Argument: The Reverend Thornton Stringfellow," *Virginia Magazine of History and Biography*, 85 (Jan. 1977), 3–17; Elizabeth Fox-Genovese and Eugene Genovese, "The Religious Ideals of Southern Slave Society," *Georgia Historical Quarterly*, 70 (Spring 1986), 1–16, and "The Divine Sanction of Social Order: Religious Foundations of the Southern Slaveholders' World View," *Journal of the American Academy of Religion*, 55 (Summer 1987), 211–33; Jack P. Maddex, "Proslavery Millennialism: Social Eschatology and Antebellum Southern Calvinism," *AQ*, 31 (Spring 1979), 46–62; Donald G. Mathews, "Charles Colcock Jones and the Southern Evangelical Crusade to Form a Biracial Community," *JSH*, 40 (Aug. 1975), 299–320; and Lewis M. Purifoy, "The Southern Methodist Church and the Proslavery Argument," *JSH*, 32 (Aug. 1966), 325–41. Some sense of a holding back within evangelicalism from wholehearted commitment to the proslavery argument and even an indication of limited public dissent is provided by D.T. Bailey, *Shadow on the Church: Southwestern Evangelical Religion and the Issue of Slavery 1783–1860* (Ithaca, NY, 1985); H. Shelton Smith, *In His Image, But . . . Racism in Southern Religion, 1790–1910* (Durham, NC, 1972); Fletcher M. Green, "Northern Missionary Activities in the South, 1846–1861," *JSH*, 21 (May 1955), 147–72; Victor B. Howard, "Robert J. Breckinridge and the Slavery Controversy in Kentucky in 1849," *Filson Club History Quarterly*, 53 (Oct. 1979), 328–43; and James B. Stewart, "Radicalism and the Evangelical Strain in Southern Antislavery Thought during the 1820s," *JSH*, 39 (Aug. 1973), 379–96. Mitchell Snay, "American Thought and Southern Distinctiveness: The Southern Clergy and the Sanctification of Slavery," *CWH*, 35 (Dec. 1989), 311–28, examines the intellectual components of proslavery Christianity and identifies unresolved tensions in the southern argument. Bertram Wyatt-Brown, *Yankee Saints and Southern Sinners* (Baton Rouge, La., 1982) offers some reflections on the congruences between the evangelical ethic and the South's code of honor, and their significance for that section's defense of its way of life.

The consequences for inter-sectional antagonism of schism and aggravation within the major evangelical churches are explored in C.C. Goen, *Broken*

Churches, Broken Nation: Denominational Schisms and the Coming of the American Civil War (Macon, Ga., 1985). This should be supplemented by C.S. Griffin, "The Abolitionists and the Benevolent Societies, 1831–1861," *Journal of Negro History*, 44 (July 1959), 195–216; Victor B, Howard, *Conscience and Slavery: The Evangelistic Calvinist Domestic Missions, 1837–1861* (Kent, Ohio, 1991); John W. Kuykendall, *Southern Enterprize: The Work of National Evangelical Societies in the Antebellum South* (Westport, Conn., 1982); Donald G. Mathews, *Slavery and Methodism: A Chapter in American Morality, 1780–1845* (Princeton, NJ, 1965) and the same author's shrewd article, "The Methodist Schism of 1844 and the Popularization of Antislavery Sentiment," *Mid-America*, 51 (Jan. 1969), 3–23; Elwyn Allen Smith, "The Role of the South in the Presbyterian Schism of 1837–1838," *Church History*, 29 (March 1960), 44–63; Bruce Staiger, "Abolitionism and the Presbyterian Schism of 1837–1838," *MVHR*, 36 (Dec. 1949), 391–414; and Lewis G. Vander Velde, *The Presbyterian Churches and the Federal Union, 1861–1869* (London, 1932).

Historians have variously assessed the impact of evangelical culture on party politics in the Jacksonian era. Studies which make much of the religious roots of party conflict and ideology include five landmark titles: Lee Benson, *The Concept of Jacksonian Democracy: New York as a Test Case* (Princeton, NJ, 1961); Ronald P. Formisano, *The Birth of Mass Political Parties: Michigan, 1827–1861* (Princeton, NJ, 1971); William R. Brock, *Parties and Political Conscience: American Dilemmas 1840–1850* (New York, 1979); Daniel W. Howe, *The Political Culture of the American Whigs* (Chicago, 1980); and Paul Goodman, *Towards a Christian Republic: Antimasonry and the Great Tradition in New England, 1826–1836* (New York, 1988). Amongst important articles and essays on the same theme are Paul Goodman, "The Social Basis of New England Politics in Jacksonian America," *JER*, 6 (Spring 1986), 23–58; Daniel W. Howe, "The Evangelical Movement and Political Culture in the North during the Second Party System," *JAH*, 77 (March 1991), 1216–39; Richard R. John, "Taking Sabbatarianism Seriously: The Postal System, the Sabbath, and the Transformation of American Political Culture," *JER*, 10 (Winter 1990), 517–67; R. Lawrence Moore, "The End of Religious Establishment and the Beginning of Religious Politics: Church and State in the United States," in Thomas Kselman (ed.) *Belief in History: Innovative Approaches to European and American Religion* (Notre Dame, Ind., 1991); William G. Shade, "Society and Politics in Antebellum Virginia's Southside," *JSH*, 53 (May 1987), 163–93; and Bertram Wyatt-Brown, "Prelude to Abolitionism: Sabbatarian Politics and the Rise of the Second Party System," *JAH*, 58 (June 1971), 316–41. Even those who believe that partisanship fed primarily on economic questions do not discount the vitamin supplement that party divisions received from religious conflict: see in particular John Ashworth, *"Agrarians & Aristocrats": Party Political Ideology in the United States, 1837–1846* (London, 1983); and Donald J. Ratcliffe, "The Role of Voters in Party Formation: Ohio, 1824," *JAH*, 59 (March 1973), 847–70, and "Politics in Jacksonian Ohio: Reflections on the Ethnocultural Interpretation," *Ohio History*, 88 (1979), 5–36. Though Harry L. Watson in *Jacksonian Politics and Community Conflict: The Emergence of the Second American Party System in Cumberland County, North Carolina* (Baton Rouge, La., 1981) sees little connection between religious attachment and party preference in that part of the South, his broader study, *Liberty and Power: The Politics of*

Jacksonian America (New York, 1990), offers an impressive synthesis of economic and cultural interpretations. Other syntheses include William G. Shade, *Banks and No Banks: The Money Issue in Western Politics 1832–1865* (Detroit, 1972) and Daniel Feller, "Politics and Society: Toward a Jacksonian Synthesis," *JER*, 10 (Summer 1990), 135–62. M.J. Heale, *The Presidential Quest: Candidates and Images in American Political Culture, 1787–1852* (London, 1982) suggests ways in which party managers sought to exploit religious sensibilities.

My understanding of politics from the later 1840s to the Civil War has been especially influenced by two magisterial works, David M. Potter, *The Impending Crisis, 1848–1861* (New York, 1976) and William E. Gienapp, *The Origins of the Republican Party 1852–1856* (New York, 1987): their interpretations share many points of similarity, though Gienapp is unpersuaded by Potter's placing the moral issue of slavery at the heart of sectional conflict and stresses the primacy of the Republicans' appeal to northern whites' hatred of the slave power. The evangelical constituency with which I am preoccupied was explicitly attentive to both issues and it is a nice judgment, perhaps beyond Solomon himself, as to which predominated within it. An emphasis on the moral dimensions of antislavery third parties' and Republicans' opposition to slavery is also evident in Richard H. Sewell, *Ballots for Freedom: Antislavery Politics in the United States, 1837–1860* (New York, 1976): while this does not single out Protestant evangelicals for special focus it provides a helpful context in which to interpret their political actions.

Evangelicals' contributions to the sectionalizing of politics in the 1840s and 1850s can be assessed through a variety of sources. Helpful on the Liberty party are Vernon L. Volpe, *Forlorn Hope of Freedom: The Liberty Party in the Old Northwest, 1838–1848* (Kent, Ohio, 1990); Alan M. Kraut, "Partisanship and Principles: The Liberty Party in Antebellum Political Culture," in Alan M. Kraut (ed.) *Essays on the Relationship of the Antislavery Struggle to the Antebellum Party System* (Westport, Conn., 1983); and a number of articles by Reinhard O. Johnson, including "The Liberty Party in Maine, 1840–1848: The Politics of Antislavery Reform," *Maine History Society Quarterly*, 19 (Winter 1980), 135–76, and "The Liberty Party in Massachusetts, 1840–1848: Antislavery Third Party Politics in the Bay State," *Civil War History*, 28 (Sept. 1982), 237–65. Free Soilers are examined in Frederick J. Blue, *The Free Soilers: Third Party Politics 1848–54* (Urbana, Ill., 1973). Protestant reactions to the Mexican war, which helped fuse together many of the elements of free soil (and, indeed, of southern rights) are explored in Clayton S. Ellsworth, "American Churches and the Mexican War," *AHR*, 45 (Jan. 1940), 301–26; Donald K. Gorrell, "American Churches and American Territorial Expansion, 1830–1850" (PhD diss., Western Reserve University, 1960); Victor B. Howard, "The Doves of 1847: The Religious Response in Ohio to the Mexican War," *The Old Northwest*, 5 (Fall 1979), 237–67; and John H. Schroeder, *Mr. Polk's War: American Opposition and Dissent, 1846–1848* (Madison, Wisc., 1973). Useful for churches, the Compromise of 1850, and the Fugitive Slave Law are R.A. Keller, "Methodist Newspapers and the Fugitive Slave Law: A New Perspective for the Slavery Crisis in the North," *Church History*, 43 (Sept. 1974), 319–39, and Stanley W. Campbell, *The Slave Catchers: Enforcement of the Fugitive Slave Law, 1850–1860* (Chapel Hill, NC, 1968). Two articles by Victor Howard give an insight into Protestants' responses to the

Kansas–Nebraska Act and evangelicals' involvement in the election of 1856: "Presbyterians, the Kansas-Nebraska Act, and the Election of 1856," *Journal of Presbyterian History*, 49 (Summer 1971), 133–56, and "The 1856 Election in Ohio: Moral Issues in Politics," *Ohio History*, 80 (Winter 1971), 24–44. The churches' role in the immediate pre-war crisis is discussed in James H. Moorhead, *American Apocalypse: Yankee Protestants and the Civil War 1860–69* (New Haven, Conn., 1978); W. Harrison Daniel, "Southern Protestantism and Secession," *Historian*, 29 (May 1967), 391–408; Haskell Monroe, "Southern Presbyterians and the Secession Crisis," *CWH*, 6 (Dec. 1960), 351–60; and James W. Silver, *Confederate Morale and Church Propaganda* (Tuscaloosa, Ala., 1957).

The historiography of American politics in the immediate antebellum decade reveals disagreements over the relative importance of slavery-related issues and "ethnocultural" questions in the break-up and realignment of parties. It is widely recognized that anti-Catholicism and nativism in their various guises played a powerful role in the collapse of the second party system. This is the particular thrust of Formisano, *The Birth of Mass Political Parties*, Gienapp, *Origins of the Republican Party* and Potter, *The Impending Crisis*, all cited earlier, pp. 458–9; and of Michael F. Holt, *Forging a Majority: The Formation of the Republican Party in Pittsburgh, 1848–1860* (New Haven, Conn., 1969) and *The Political Crisis of the 1850s* (New York, 1978); Paul Kleppner, *The Third Electoral System: Parties, Voters, and Political Cultures* (Chapel Hill, NC, 1979); and Joel Silbey, *The Partisan Imperative: The Dynamics of American Politics Before the Civil War* (New York, 1985). Know Nothingism is most authoritatively analyzed in various works by Michael Holt: as well as the two books just cited he has published "The Antimasonic and Know-Nothing Parties," in Arthur M. Schlesinger, Jr (ed.) *History of U.S. Political Parties* (4 vols, New York, 1973) and "The Politics of Impatience: The Origins of Know Nothingism," *JAH*, 55 (Sept. 1973), 309–31. Holt's strong emphasis on economic dislocation as a cause of the movement is echoed in Robert W. Fogel, *Without Consent or Contract: The Rise and Fall of American Slavery* (New York, 1989) and John R. Mulkern, *The Know-Nothing Party in Massachusetts: The Rise and Fall of a People's Movement* (Boston, 1990). It will be evident that my own interpretation of Know Nothingism attaches particular importance to the movement's cultural antipathies to Catholicism: it was, after all, the Romanist immigrant, not immigrants in general, who attracted the most venomous attack. The American party in the South can be approached through W. Darrell Overdyke, *The Know Nothing Party in the South* (Baton Rouge, La., 1950); Jean H. Baker, *Ambivalent Americans: The Know-Nothing Party in Maryland* (Baltimore, 1977); and James H. Broussard, "Some Determinants of Know-Nothing Electoral Strength in the South, 1856," *Louisiana History*, 7 (Winter 1966), 5–20.

A number of historians have insisted on the subordinate role of nativism and ethnocultural issues in shaping antebellum politics. That nativism played only a minor role in the early Republican party is the interpretation followed by Eric Foner in *Free Soil, Free Labor, Free Men: The Ideology of the Republican Party before the Civil War* (New York, 1970); Sewell, *Ballots for Freedom* (cited earlier, p. 459); Stephen Maizlish, *The Triumph of Sectionalism: The Transformation of Ohio Politics, 1844–1856* (Kent, Ohio, 1983); and Dale Baum, *The Civil War Party System: The Case of Massachusetts, 1846–1876* (Chapel Hill, NC, 1984). More convincing is William E. Gienapp's argument that anti-Catholicism was a primary ingredient in the Republicans' appeal: he pursues this theme in *Origins of the Republican Party*, cited earlier, p. 459, and in a number of important articles, including "Salmon P. Chase, Nativism, and the Formation of the Republican Party in Ohio," *Ohio History*, 93 (Winter–Spring 1984), 5–39, and "Nativism and the Creation of a Republican Majority in the North before the Civil War," *JAH*, 72 (Dec. 1985), 529–59. Victor Howard, *Conscience and Slavery*, cited earlier, p. 458, though excellent in demonstrating the element of moral fervor that evangelistic New School Calvinists brought to the early Republican movement, is far too dismissive of the best of ethnocultural historiography, and is blind to what antebellum northern evangelicals and Republican organizers saw only too well: the ideological congruence of antislavery, anti-Catholicism, and temperance issues.

Other works which address the relationship between religion and voting behavior in the immediate antebellum years are John L. Hammond, *The Politics of Benevolence: Revival Religion and American Voting Behaviour* (Norwood, NJ, 1979) and two collections of essays: Frederick C. Luebke (ed.) *Ethnic Voters and the Election of Lincoln* (Lincoln, Nebraska, 1971) and Robert P. Swierenga (ed.) *Beyond the Civil War Synthesis: Political Essays of the Civil War Era* (Westport, Conn., 1975). Also instructive are Robin E. Baker and Dale Baum, "The Texas Voter and the Crisis of the Union 1859–1861," *JSH*, 53 (Aug. 1987), 395–420; David M. Ellis, "Yankee–Dutch Confrontation in the Albany Area," *New England Quarterly*, 45 (Sept. 1972), 262–70; William E. Gienapp, "Who Voted for Lincoln?" in John L. Thomas (ed.) *Abraham Lincoln and the American Political Tradition* (Amherst, Mass., 1986), 50–97; Paul Goodman, "The Politics of Industrialism: Massachusetts, 1830–1870," in Richard L. Bushman *et al.* (eds) *Uprooted Americans: Essays to Honor Oscar Handlin* (Boston, 1979), 161–207; Paul Kleppner, "Lincoln and the Immigrant Vote: A Case of Religious Polarization," *Mid-America*, 48 (July 1966), 176–95; Thomas W. Kremm, "Cleveland and the First Lincoln Election: The Ethnic Response to Nativism," *Journal of Interdisciplinary History*, 8 (Summer 1977), 69–86; and Peyton McCrary, Clark Miller, and Dale Baum, "Class and Party in the Secession Crisis: Voting Behavior in the Deep South, 1856–1861," *Journal of Interdisciplinary History*, 8 (Winter 1978), 429–57. Jean H. Baker, *Affairs of Party: The Political Culture of Northern Democrats in the Mid-Nineteenth Century* (Ithaca, NY, 1983), though otherwise impressive, largely ignores religion and leaves unexplored the significance of Democrats' "secularist" stance.

Amongst the most thoughtful reflections on the "new political history" are Don E. Fehrenbacher, "The New Political History and the Coming of the Civil War," *Pacific Historical Review*, 54 (May 1985), 117–42; Eric Foner, "The Causes of the American Civil War: Recent Interpretations and New Directions," *CWH*, 20 (Sept. 1974), 197–214; and Richard L. McCormick, "Ethno-Cultural Inter-pretations of Nineteenth-Century American Voting Behavior," *Political Science Quarterly*, 89 (June 1974), 351–77. Especially perceptive in seeing the wider potential of ethnocultural history is Daniel W. Howe's synthesis, "The Evan-gelical Movement and Popular Culture in the North during the Second Party System," cited earlier, p. 458.

Index